Mobile Peer–to–Peer Computing for Next Generation Distributed Environments:
Advancing Conceptual and Algorithmic Applications

Boon–Chong Seet
Auckland University of Technology, New Zealand

INFORMATION SCIENCE REFERENCE

Hershey · New York

Director of Editorial Content: Kristin Klinger
Senior Managing Editor: Jamie Snavely
Managing Editor: Jeff Ash
Assistant Managing Editor: Carole Coulson
Typesetter: Chris Hrobak
Cover Design: Lisa Tosheff
Printed at: Yurchak Printing Inc.

Published in the United States of America by
Information Science Reference (an imprint of IGI Global)
701 E. Chocolate Avenue,
Hershey PA 17033
Tel: 717-533-8845
Fax: 717-533-8661
E-mail: cust@igi-global.com
Web site: http://www.igi-global.com/reference

and in the United Kingdom by
Information Science Reference (an imprint of IGI Global)
3 Henrietta Street
Covent Garden
London WC2E 8LU
Tel: 44 20 7240 0856
Fax: 44 20 7379 0609
Web site: http://www.eurospanbookstore.com

Library of Congress Cataloging-in-Publication Data

Mobile peer-to-peer computing for next generation distributed environments: advancing conceptual and algorithmic applications / Boon-Chong Seet, editor.   p. cm.

Includes bibliographical references and index.

Summary: "This book is dedicated to the coverage of research issues, findings, and approaches to Mobile P2P computing from both conceptual and algorithmic perspectives"--Provided by publisher.

ISBN 978-1-60566-715-7 (hbk.) -- ISBN 978-1-60566-716-4 (ebook) 1. Peer-to-peer architecture (Computer networks) 2. Mobile communication systems. I. Seet, Boon-Chong, 1973-

TK5105.525.M63 2009

004.6'52--dc22

                              2009001030

British Cataloguing in Publication Data
A Cataloguing in Publication record for this book is available from the British Library.

Table of Contents

Section I
Information Retrieval and Dissemination

Chapter I
P2P Information Lookup, Collection, and Distribution in Mobile Ad-Hoc Networks 1
Raphaël Kummer, University of Neuchâtel, Switzerland
Peter Kropf, University of Neuchâtel, Switzerland
Pascal Felber, University of Neuchâtel, Switzerland

Chapter II
Data Dissemination and Query Routing in Mobile Peer-to-Peer Networks 26
Thomas Repantis, University of California, Riverside, USA
Vana Kalogeraki, University of California, Riverside, USA

Section II
Overlay and Mobility Management

Chapter III
Overlay Construction in Mobile Peer-to-Peer Networks 51
Jie Feng, University of Nebraska-Lincoln, USA
Lisong Xu, University of Nebraska-Lincoln, USA
Byrav Ramamurthy, University of Nebraska-Lincoln, USA

Detailed Table of Contents

Section I
Information Retrieval and Dissemination

This section includes two chapters that look at the issue of information retrieval and dissemination, each exploring a different approach to addressing the issue.

Chapter I

Raphaël Kummer, University of Neuchâtel, Switzerland
Peter Kropf, University of Neuchâtel, Switzerland
Pascal Felber, University of Neuchâtel, Switzerland

This chapter presents an enhanced Distributed Hash Table (DHT) to facilitate information retrieval (or lookup), and a new multicast tree construction algorithm built on top of the proposed DHT to construct a multicast tree distribution infrastructure for efficient information dissemination in mobile ad hoc networks.

Chapter II

Thomas Repantis, University of California, Riverside, USA
Vana Kalogeraki, University of California, Riverside, USA

This chapter proposes to adaptively disseminate special information called content synopses and presents a content-driven routing protocol that utilizes this information to efficiently guide the queries for actual content or information retrieval.

Section II
Overlay and Mobility Management

This section includes three chapters covering overlay construction, mobility support in overlay networks in the context of publish/subscribe systems, and performance study of P2P overlay and MANET routing protocols.

Chapter III

Jie Feng, University of Nebraska-Lincoln, USA
Lisong Xu, University of Nebraska-Lincoln, USA
Byrav Ramamurthy, University of Nebraska-Lincoln, USA

This chapter reviews P2P overlay construction techniques for mobile networks, including tree- and mesh-based mobile P2P streaming networks. The authors also discuss advanced design issues, such as session mobility, robustness to high churn, incentive mechanism and content integrity, with relation to managing mobility in P2P overlays.

Chapter IV

Thomas Kunz, System and Computer Engineering, Carleton University, Canada
Abdulbaset Gaddah, System and Computer Engineering, Carleton University, Canada
Li Li, Communications Research Centre, Canada

This chapter examines the issue of subscriber mobility in publish/subscribe systems and presents a new mobility support solution through proactive context distribution, which is shown to perform better in terms of message loss/duplication, processing overhead and handoff latency than the conventional reactive approach.

Chapter V

Leonardo B. Oliveira, University of Campinas (UNICAMP), Brazil
Isabela G. Siqueira, Federal University of Minas Gerais (UFMG), Brazil
Daniel F. Macedo, Université Pierre et Marie Curie-Paris VI, France
José M. Nogueira, Federal University of Minas Gerais (UFMG), Brazil
Antonio A. F. Loureiro, Federal University of Minas Gerais (UFMG), Brazil

This chapter investigates the performance of three MANET routing protocols: AODV, DSR, and DSDV under a Gnutella P2P network, and two P2P overlay protocols: Gnutella and Chord, over MANET with AODV as the underlying routing protocol through extensive computer simulations.

Section III
Cooperative Mechanisms

This section includes four chapters devoted to discussing the different mechanisms and applications of peer-to-peer cooperation in mobile networks.

This chapter outlines the current methods for cooperation in standard and MANET-based P2P networks. The authors also describe a number of use cases to illustrate the potential of peer-to-peer cooperation technology for mobile networks, including for such applications as knowledge sharing and social networking.

This chapter identifies selfish peers as a factor that degrades performance of P2P content distribution systems in cellular mobile networks and studies several cooperation strategies, including a new strategy CyPriM proposed by the authors to improve performance in the presence of selfish peers and heterogeneous peer resources.

This chapter extends the discussion in the preceding chapter to consider the impact of mobility and vertical handover in a B3G network. The authors evaluate solutions such as mobile IP in the context of P2P content distribution, and present new strategies to manage mobility and improve utilization of scarce resources in such heterogeneous networks.

This chapter reviews the problem of cooperative cache management in mobile environments that support data broadcast, and presents two peer-to-peer based schemes: CPIX and ACP for caching and pre-fetching information, respectively, to improve the data availability and access latency in mobile environments.

Section IV
Resource Management

This section includes two chapters on methods to foster resource sharing among peers: one in the context of P2P media streaming in hybrid wireless networks; the other on general resource sharing in ad-hoc networks.

Chapter X

This chapter focuses on energy cost sharing in wireless P2P media streaming, and presents two energy efficient protocols based on game-theoretic concepts to improve collaboration and streaming performance of peers in hybrid wireless networks.

Chapter XI

This chapter presents the case for social incentives to be used to foster resource sharing in ad hoc networks, and proposes a new *cross-layer* concept that considers both social and economic solutions in application layer and network layer, respectively, in the design of incentive mechanisms.

Section V
Security

This section includes two chapters that concern security: one relates to the design of group key management schemes for mobile ad hoc networks; the other looks at the development of secure mobile P2P applications.

Chapter XII

This chapter provides a comprehensive coverage of conventional group key management schemes for dynamic peer groups, and discusses their design challenges and potential for MANET through an analysis of their communication and computation costs.

This chapter presents a development tool that considers the user's security, mobility, and P2P technology requirements, and proposes a suitable system architecture and sub-system designs for developing secure mobile P2P applications.

Section VI
Standards and Protocols

This section includes two chapters that cover current standards and protocols of interest to the research and development of mobile P2P systems.

This chapter discusses the relevance of ITU standard architecture for next generation networks, and presents an overlay architecture for integrating P2P systems in interoperable fixed-mobile environments based on the IP Multimedia Sub-system (IMS) technology.

This chapter reviews the current IETF standard for P2P-SIP (Session Initiation Protocol), which is designed to serve as a lightweight P2P based protocol for communication, session management, and service provisioning in infrastructured mobile networks such as wireless LAN and 3G cellular networks.

Section VII
Architectures and Platforms

This section includes three chapters on new architectures and platforms, including a new content-distribution architecture for cellular networks, a P2P networking platform for mobile phones, and a platform for emulation of P2P algorithms for MANET.

Chapter XVI

Kurt Tutschku, University of Vienna, Austria
Andreas Berl, University of Passau, Germany
Tobias Hossfeld, University of Würzburg, Germany
Hermann de Meer, University of Passau, Germany

This chapter first discusses the current incompatibilities between cellular mobile and P2P networks, and then presents a new P2P architecture for cellular mobile networks using content-distribution as an example application. The authors also investigate extensively the proposed architecture using analytical and simulation-based evaluation.

Chapter XVII

Norihiro Ishikawa, NTT DOCOMO, Japan
Hiromitsu Sumino, NTT DOCOMO, Japan
Takeshi Kato, NTT DOCOMO, Japan
Johan Hjelm, Ericsson Research, Japan
Shingo Murakami, Ericsson Research, Japan
Kazuhiro Kitagawa, Keio University, Japan
Nobuo Saito, Komazawa University, Japan

This chapter describes the architecture and protocols of a new P2P networking platform for mobile phones, and discusses the experimentation of the platform using three classes of mobile phone applications namely, multimedia content search, instant messaging over Bluetooth, and remote access to networked home appliances.

Chapter XVIII

Raphaël Kummer, University of Neuchâtel, Switzerland
Peter Kropf, University of Neuchâtel, Switzerland
Jean-Frédéric Wagen, TIC Institute, University of Applied Sciences of Fribourg, Switzerland
Timothée Maret, TIC Institute, University of Applied Sciences of Fribourg, Switzerland

This chapter presents Freemote, a Java-based emulation platform that could integrate emulated and real nodes such as the Berkeley motes to enable large-scale emulation of P2P algorithms for MANET with a high level of realism.

Section VIII
Applications and Services

This section includes three chapters that look at the development of collaborative applications, service discovery, and context-awareness in mobile P2P services.

This chapter describes the Peer2Me software framework for developing P2P applications that support collaboration on mobile phones with JavaME and Bluetooth. The authors also illustrate the potential use of the framework through a portfolio of developed applications that demonstrate a wide spectrum of collaborative functions.

This chapter presents a comprehensive coverage and comparative analysis of the current service discovery approaches in P2P systems for a variety of mobile networks, including infrastructured wireless networks, single-hop and multi-hop ad hoc networks.

This chapter discusses the use of context to enhance distributed services in opportunistic networks, and describes two context management architectures and their use in a context-aware opportunistic file sharing application that considers not only the social context of user, but also the utility of data objects for the context the user is in.

Foreword

We are witnessing an explosive growth in the number of mobile computing devices, including smart phones, personal assistant devices, and sensors, and in wireless communication technologies and capabilities. Despite such growth, systems in which the devices collaborate directly to process information, namely mobile P2P systems, are in their infancy.

This does not mean that research on the subject has not been done, but that the problem is very difficult. An example of an MP2P application that has been worked on for more than twenty years is routing, which is important in the digital battlefield, vehicular networks, and others. The problem is to route messages between a sender and a receiver that are out of each other's transmission range, using the mobile devices as intermediaries. Despite the extensive amount of work on this problem, it is not solved yet.

Furthermore, not all reasons for the slow start on mobile P2P systems are technological. For example, data broadcasting is a well understood mechanism that is technologically easy to implement and can facilitate mobile P2P systems development and deployment. Some of the chapters in this book discuss broadcasting. Yet it is not implemented by existing cellular service providers.

Nevertheless, technology is a major stumbling block. The technological challenges include resource constraints on the mobile device, security and privacy, variable and/or disconnected network topology, and heterogeneity of devices. More specifically, it is hard to build systems when energy, memory, CPU power, and bandwidth resources are constrained on each one of the devices participating in the P2P system. Furthermore, the wireless medium is easier to tap into, and the devices are harder to protect physically. Thus, serious security and privacy concerns arise. Additionally, many mobile P2P systems cannot rely on an infrastructure for wireless communication among the devices. For example, an infrastructure often does not exist in a battlefield. Thus, such systems depend on direct collaboration among the mobile devices via short-range wireless networks, which is difficult when mobility and failures continuously change the set of neighbors with which a node can directly communicate.

This book addresses the technological challenges. It describes the problems, some existing solutions, and proposes new ones. The first section deals with the problem of finding information in a network lacking an infrastructure. Observe that this is different than the routing problem. It is harder in the sense that even the identity of the receiver, that is the location of information, is unknown; but easier in the sense that the information may be replicated and therefore routing to a single receiver is often not strictly necessary. The proposed solutions combine query and information dissemination in an intelligent way. P2P methods have been quite successful in the fixed world, and the second section explores adaptation of the successful methods (e.g. overlays) to the mobile world. Section III continues this exploration, with a distinction between mobile P2P systems that use an infrastructure, the ones that do not do so, and the ones that use a hybrid strategy. Section IV proposes that cooperation is a useful approach to deal with the resource constraints, and it discusses incentives and mechanisms for cooperation. Section V discusses the critical topic of security, and sections VI, VII, and VIII discuss strategies that facilitate the development of mobile P2P systems. These strategies include standards, software tools, platforms, programming paradigms, service provision and discovery, and protocols.

Overall, the book is an invaluable resource for both researchers and practitioners. It addresses the most important issues in mobile P2P systems, it is well organized, very readable, comprehensive, and presented at the right level of depth. It strikes a good balance between presentation of novel ideas, and survey of the state of the art.

Ouri Wolfson
University of Illinois, USA

Ouri Wolfson's main research interests are in database systems, distributed systems, and mobile/pervasive computing. He received his PhD degree in Computer Science from Courant Institute of Mathematical Sciences, New York University. He is currently the Richard and Loan Hill professor of Computer Science at the University of Illinois at Chicago, where he directs the Mobile Information Systems Research Center. He is also an affiliate professor in the Department of Computer Science at the University of Illinois at Urbana Champaign. Ouri Wolfson is the founder of Mobitrac, a high-tech startup company that had about forty employees before being acquired. Most recently he founded Pirouette Software Inc., and currently serves as its President. Before joining the University of Illinois he has been on the Computer Science faculty at the Technion and Columbia University, and he has been a Member of Technical Staff at Bell Laboratories. Ouri Wolfson authored over 150 publications, and holds six patents. He is a fellow of the Association of Computing Machinery, and serves on the editorial boards of the IEEE Transactions on Mobile Computing and the Springer's Wireless Networks Journal. He received the best paper award for "Opportunistic Resource Exchange in Inter-vehicle Ad Hoc Networks," at the 2004 Mobile Data Management Conference.

Preface

Computing systems are playing an essential role as an indispensable nervous system of modern society. The ubiquitous use of computing systems for the operation of our society, such as in our banking, public transportation, and healthcare systems, and in our daily lives for meeting our personal learning, entertainment and productivity needs, has resulted in them being of fundamental importance to keeping our modern society alive and thriving. The subsequent trend of integrating computing systems with communication networks such as the Internet further extended the reach of computing systems beyond geographical boundaries, ushering in an era of networked computing systems.

Computer-mediated communication for distant human-to-human interaction, that is computer telephony systems, has become a cost-effective alternative to traditional telephone networks (Yarberry, 2002). Distant human-to-machine interaction has also benefited from the advent of networked computing, such as by enabling remote access to computing resources such as shared printers and databases. More recently, machine-to-machine (M2M) interaction has been a subject of interest in networked computing where machines leverage on their network (wired or wireless) connectivity to directly interact with each other and in some cases make their own decisions without human intervention (Lawton, 2004).

Networked computing systems have traditionally been based on the client-server model (Goodyear et al., 1999). In this architecture, the network consists of a server, typically a high-performance computer, and a group of clients. The server is the only provider of resources or services in the network, while the clients only request for resources or the execution of services from the server. It is apparent that each addition of a new client to the network is a new load added to the server. As the number of clients grows, the server capacity must increase to avoid becoming a bottleneck in the system. It is also apparent that in this model, the server represents a single point of failure in the network, and thus can be a major cause of downtime and a vulnerable target for security attacks.

In recent years, the development of networked computing has evolved from the centralized and hierarchical model of client-server computing to encompass a more decentralized and distributed model of peer-to-peer (P2P) computing (Subramanian & Goodman, 2005). Using the widely-accepted definition by Schollmeier (2001), P2P is a network where the participants share a part of their own resources, which can be hardware resources such as processing power, storage capacity, network link capacity, printers, and so forth, or software resources such as media content, (e.g., pictures, videos and music files, and other digital content) information stored on databases, necessary to provide the service or content offered by the network. These resources on independent peers are in turn accessible by other peers directly without going through intermediate central control entities (i.e. the servers). The participants of such a network are thus serving as resource (service and content) providers as well as resource (service and content) consumers.

Due to its promising potential to resolve the above issues of scalability and fault-tolerance in client-server computing, this radical and contrasting approach to computing has gained significant attention from both industry and academic research communities, and is suited for applications that have a mass of users in complex open distributed environments such as the Internet. Today, P2P technologies have been widely embraced by Internet users, and are best exemplified by popular file sharing systems such as eMule or BitTorrent, and Voice-over-P2P (VoP2P) applications such as Skype. Other emerging applications based on P2P that are gaining popularity include live or on-demand media (TV and video) streaming applications, for example, Joost, Zattoo, and PPLive (Krieger & Schwessinger, 2008; Mushtaq, & Ahmed, 2008; Akkanen, Karonen, & Porio, 2008), and large-scale distributed online storage systems such as Wuala (Caleido AG, 2008), which provides its users with free online storage service for private or shared data by exploiting the unused disk space of participating computers on the Internet.

In a parallel development with Internet P2P computing from late 1990s, the landscape of telecommunications also experienced profound changes with the rapid proliferation of a plethora of wireless technologies ranging from technologies for wide area networks (e.g., UMTS, HSDPA, HSPA+), metropolitan area networks (e.g., Mobile WiMAX [802.16e], Mobile-Fi [802.20]), local area networks (e.g., 802.11a/g/n/p/s), personal area networks (e.g., Bluetooth, ZigBee, WiMedia), to more recently regional area networks based on emerging cognitive radios (802.22). Today, wireless-enabled laptops and PDAs, and cellular handsets with Internet access have become widely available and increasingly affordable. It is also not uncommon to find *multi-mode* terminals where computing devices or handsets have multiple modes of wireless connectivity such as 3G UMTS, WiFi (802.11) and Bluetooth. These technological advances are believed to have fueled the uptake of a *mobile lifestyle* where the daily lives of people are increasingly empowered by and dependent on wireless technologies. For instance, the increasing need of people to stay connected to the Internet at anytime from anywhere for work or for play. This brings forth a prediction that a significant portion of future users of P2P systems will be mobile, which calls for a need to investigate the suitability of developed P2P technologies for mobile and wireless networks, such as mobile cellular networks, infrastructured wireless local area networks (WLAN), and the infrastructureless mobile ad hoc networks (MANET).

Early investigations along this direction (such as Klemm, Lindemann, & Waldhorst, 2004; Ding & Bhargava, 2004) for MANET, and (such as Eberspächer, Schollmeier, Zöls, Kunzmann, & Für, 2004) for a heterogeneous mobile and fixed environment, have shown that contemporary P2P technologies performed neither well nor efficiently as they were designed for a relatively stable and resource-rich environment where hosts are stationary, *well-endowed* (i.e., in terms of processing power, memory, and energy) and connected by high bandwidth links. Thus, research is needed to innovate new approaches to P2P computing in a mobile environment. Specifically, the design of the mobile P2P systems should address the new challenges of dynamic changes in connectivity and resource availability, the new constraints in mobile devices as well as wireless capacity, and respond to these constraints and changes in an intelligent, timely, and adaptive manner. However, the research possibilities of Mobile P2P computing are not limited to extending conventional P2P systems to perform effectively and efficiently under mobile conditions, but include, for instance, turning the new constraints into strengths by finding new usages of unique characteristics of mobile P2P, or creating new patterns of collaboration and sharing that can potentially move mobile applications and services into a new dimension for next generation distributed environments.

This book is dedicated to the coverage of research issues, findings, and approaches to mobile P2P computing from both conceptual and algorithmic perspectives. Authored by some of the most leading experts in the field, and guided by an Editorial Advisory Board of prominent international researchers, the overall aim of this book is to serve as a valuable resource that captures the present state of the field, and to inspire ideas for future challenges through presenting the latest insights and thoughts of expert researchers on major topics of this emerging discipline.

The key contribution of this book is in providing a much needed body of knowledge on mobile P2P computing in a single reference source, which to the best of our knowledge, is still largely missing from currently available book titles. Through a careful selection of topics that address some of the most important and essential issues in the field, including topics of both theoretical (e.g., models, algorithms, architectures) and practical interests (e.g., tools, platforms, applications), this book seeks to fill the gap in available titles with its dedicated and comprehensive coverage on mobile P2P computing. Readers would also benefit from the scholarly value of the book through its balanced and quality coverage of theoretical ideas and practical research. This book therefore comes as a timely contribution to the growing and flourishing research community in mobile P2P computing.

The book is intended to provide an up-to-date advanced reading of important topics for academic researchers, graduate students, and senior undergraduate students in computer science, electrical and electronic engineering, and telecommunications, to enhance their research or studies. It is also intended for industry professionals such as R&D engineers, application developers, and technology business managers who wish to keep abreast of the recent developments in the field, and who are interested or involved in the research, use, design, development, and deployment of mobile P2P technologies.

This book is organized into eight sections comprising a total of 21 chapters. Each section addresses a specific topic area or relates to works of a specific nature. Under each section, the chapters are generally self-contained, thus readers are not required to read in the order in which they are listed, but could focus directly on those chapters that interest them. The following is a summary of contents covered in each section, including a brief description of each chapter listed under the section.

Section I: Information Retrieval and Dissemination

This section includes two chapters that look at the issue of information retrieval and dissemination, each exploring a different approach to addressing the issue.

Chapter I presents an enhanced Distributed Hash Table (DHT) to facilitate information retrieval (or lookup), and a new multicast tree construction algorithm built on top of the proposed DHT to construct a multicast tree distribution infrastructure for efficient information dissemination in mobile ad hoc networks.

Chapter II proposes to adaptively disseminate special information called content synopses and presents a content-driven routing protocol that utilizes this information to efficiently guide the queries for actual content or information retrieval.

Section II: Overlay and Mobility Management

This section includes three chapters covering overlay construction, mobility support in overlay networks in the context of publish/subscribe systems, and performance study of P2P overlay and MANET routing protocols. Specifically:

Chapter III reviews P2P overlay construction techniques for mobile networks, including tree- and mesh-based mobile P2P streaming networks. The authors also discuss advanced design issues, such as session mobility, robustness to high churn, incentive mechanism and content integrity, with relation to managing mobility in P2P overlays.

Chapter IV examines the issue of subscriber mobility in publish/subscribe systems and presents a new mobility support solution through proactive context distribution, which is shown to perform better in terms of message loss/duplication, processing overhead and handoff latency than the conventional reactive approach.

Chapter V investigates the performance of three MANET routing protocols: AODV, DSR, and DSDV under a Gnutella P2P network, and two P2P overlay protocols: Gnutella and Chord, over MANET with AODV as the underlying routing protocol through extensive computer simulations.

Section III: Cooperative Mechanisms

This section includes four chapters devoted to discussing the different mechanisms and applications of peer-to-peer cooperation in mobile networks.

Chapter VI outlines the current methods for cooperation in standard and MANET-based P2P networks. The authors also describe a number of use cases to illustrate the potential of peer-to-peer cooperation technology for mobile networks, including for such applications as knowledge sharing and social networking.

Chapter VII identifies selfish peers as a factor that degrades performance of P2P content distribution systems in cellular mobile networks and studies several cooperation strategies, including a new strategy CyPriM proposed by the authors to improve performance in the presence of selfish peers and heterogeneous peer resources.

Chapter VIII extends the discussion in the preceding chapter to consider the impact of mobility and vertical handover in a B3G network. The authors evaluate solutions such as mobile IP in the context of P2P content distribution, and present new strategies to manage mobility and improve utilization of scarce resources in such heterogeneous networks.

Chapter IX reviews the problem of cooperative cache management in mobile environments that support data broadcast, and presents two peer-to-peer based schemes: CPIX and ACP for caching and pre-fetching information, respectively, to improve the data availability and access latency in mobile environments.

Section IV: Resource Management

This section includes two chapters on methods to foster resource sharing among peers: one in the context of P2P media streaming in hybrid wireless networks; the other on general resource sharing in ad-hoc networks.

Chapter X focuses on energy cost sharing in wireless P2P media streaming, and presents two energy efficient protocols based on game-theoretic concepts to improve collaboration and streaming performance of peers in hybrid wireless networks.

Chapter XI present the case for social incentives to be used to foster resource sharing in ad hoc networks, and proposes a new *cross-layer* concept that considers both social and economic solutions in application layer and network layer, respectively, in the design of incentive mechanisms.

Section V: Security

This section includes two chapters that concern security: one relates to the design of group key management schemes for mobile ad hoc networks; the other looks at the development of secure mobile P2P applications.

Chapter XII provides a comprehensive coverage of conventional group key management schemes for dynamic peer groups, and discusses their design challenges and potential for MANET through an analysis of their communication and computation costs.

Chapter XIII presents a development tool that considers the user's security, mobility, and P2P technology requirements, and proposes a suitable system architecture and sub-system designs for developing secure mobile P2P applications.

Section VI: Standards and Protocols

This section includes two chapters that cover current standards and protocols of interest to the research and development of mobile P2P systems. Specifically:

Chapter XIV discusses the relevance of ITU standard architecture for next generation networks, and presents an overlay architecture for integrating P2P systems in interoperable fixed-mobile environments based on the IP Multimedia Sub-system (IMS) technology.

Chapter XV reviews the current IETF standard for P2P-SIP (Session Initiation Protocol), which is designed to serve as a lightweight P2P based protocol for communication, session management, and service provisioning in infrastructured mobile networks such as wireless LAN and 3G cellular networks.

Section VII: Architectures and Platforms

This section includes three chapters on new architectures and platforms, including a new content-distribution architecture for cellular networks, a P2P networking platform for mobile phones, and a platform for emulation of P2P algorithms for MANET.

Chapter XVI first discusses the current incompatibilities between cellular mobile and P2P networks, and then presents a new P2P architecture for cellular mobile networks using content-distribution as an example application. The authors also investigate extensively the proposed architecture using analytical and simulation-based evaluation.

Chapter XVII describes the architecture and protocols of a new P2P networking platform for mobile phones, and discusses the experimentation of the platform using three classes of mobile phone applications namely, multimedia content search, instant messaging over Bluetooth, and remote access to networked home appliances.

Chapter XVIII presents Freemote, a Java-based emulation platform that could integrate emulated and real nodes such as the Berkeley motes to enable large-scale emulation of P2P algorithms for MANET with a high level of realism.

Section VIII: Applications and Services

This section includes three chapters that look at the development of collaborative applications, service discovery, and context-awareness in mobile P2P services. Specifically:

Chapter XIX describes the Peer2Me software framework for developing P2P applications that support collaboration on mobile phones with JavaME and Bluetooth. The authors also illustrate the potential use of the framework through a portfolio of developed applications that demonstrate a wide spectrum of collaborative functions.

Chapter XX presents a comprehensive coverage and comparative analysis of the current service discovery approaches in P2P systems for a variety of mobile networks, including infrastructured wireless networks, single-hop and multi-hop ad hoc networks.

Chapter XXI discusses the use of context to enhance distributed services in opportunistic networks, and describes two context management architectures and their use in a context-aware opportunistic file sharing application that considers not only the social context of user, but also the utility of data objects for the context the user is in.

REFERENCES

Akkanen, J., Karonen, O., & Porio, J. (2008). Peer-to-peer video streaming on mobile phones, In *Proceedings of the IEEE Consumer Communications and Networking Conference.*

Caleido AG (2008). *Wuala – The social online storage*, Retrieved December 28, 2008, from http://wuala.com/en/

Ding, G., & Bhargava, B. (2004). Peer-to-peer file-sharing over mobile ad hoc networks. In *Proceedings of the Second IEEE Annual Conference on Pervasive Computing and Communications Workshops.*

Eberspächer, J., Schollmeier, R., Zöls, S., Kunzmann, G., & Für, L. (2004). Structured P2P networks in mobile and fixed environments, In *Proceedings of the International Working Conference on Performance Modeling and Evaluation of Heterogeneous Networks.*

Goodyear, M. et al., (1999).Netcentric *and client/server computing: A practical guide.* USA: Auerbach Publications.

Klemm, A., Lindemann, C., & Waldhorst, O. P. (2004). Peer-to-peer computing in mobile ad hoc networks. In *Proceedings of the 11th IEEE/ACM International Symposium on Modeling, Analysis and Simulation of Computer and Telecommunication Systems.*

Krieger, U. R., & Schwessinger, R. (2008). Analysis and quality assessment of peer-to-peer IPTV systems. In *Proceedings of the IEEE International Symposium on Consumer Electronics (ISCE).*

Lawton, G. (2004). Machine-to-machine technology gears up for growth. *Computer, 37*(9), 12-15.

Mushtaq, M., & Ahmed, T. (2008). P2P-based mobile IPTV: Challenges and opportunities. In *Proceedings of the IEEE/ACS International Conference on Computer Systems and Applications.*

Schollmeier, R. (2001). A definition of peer-to-peer networking for the classification of peer-to-peer architecture and applications. In *Proceedings of the First International Conference on Peer-to-Peer Computing.*

Subramanian, R., & Goodman, B. D. (Eds.). (2005). *Peer-to-peer computing: The evolution of a disruptive technology.* Hershey, PA: Idea Group Publishing.

Yarberry, W. A. (2002). *Computer telephony integration.* Boca Raton, Florida: CRC Press.

Acknowledgment

The editor would like to express his sincere appreciation and gratitude to all who have rendered support in one way or another to this year-long book project, without which this book could not have been satisfactorily completed. The editor would like to first thank members of the Editorial Advisory Board for their support and help in this project, despite their demanding work schedules and commitments.

The editor would also like to thank all who are involved in the review process of the book, which includes most of the chapter authors in this book who also served as referees for chapters written by other authors. Special thanks must also go to a number of individuals who volunteered their time to serve as external referees and offered some of the most comprehensive, critical, and constructive comments in their reviews. They are: Thadpong Pongthawornkamol of University of Illinois at Urbana-Champaign; Chintada Suresh of Motorola Research Labs; Dr. Aaron Harwood of University of Melbourne; and Dr. John Buford, a Research Scientist at Avaya Labs Research.

Grateful acknowledgement must also be given to the publishing team at IGI Global for its contributions throughout the whole process from setting up a website for my initial call for chapters to the final publication of the book. In particular, the editor is most grateful to Julia Mosemann for her assistance throughout the development process of the book and her consistently quick responses to my many questions and requests via e-mail.

I am also grateful to professor Wen-Jing Hsu, whose encouragement and kind words motivated me to initially accept the challenge of taking on this project. Last but not least, I would also like to thank my parents for their moral support and encouragement over the years, which have been instrumental in getting me to where I am today.

In closing, I sincerely wish to thank all of the authors for sharing their research insights, ideas, and experiences through their excellent chapter contributions to this book.

Boon-Chong Seet
Editor, PhD
Auckland, New Zealand
December 2008

Section I
Information Retrieval and Dissemination

Chapter I
P2P Information Lookup, Collection, and Distribution in Mobile Ad-Hoc Networks

Raphaël Kummer
University of Neuchâtel, Switzerland

Peter Kropf
University of Neuchâtel, Switzerland

Pascal Felber
University of Neuchâtel, Switzerland

ABSTRACT

The most important characteristics of mobile ad-hoc networks (MANETs) such as broadcast and multi-hop communication, limited resources (particularly energy) and physical proximity are often ignored in solutions being proposed for information lookup and distribution. Thus, many lookup approaches rely on unstructured algorithms using flooding techniques, while content distribution mechanisms frequently generate inefficient multicast trees without considering the presence of nodes that are involved only as relays and are not interested in the distributed content. In this chapter, the authors present a multicast algorithm designed to build efficient multicast trees in MANETs that strive to limit the number of relay nodes and transmissions required. This distribution infrastructure relies on a lightweight distributed hash table (DHT) specifically adapted to MANETs, and exploits the physical proximity of nodes and broadcast communication. The algorithmic efficiency and scalability are evaluated by means of simulations for various network sizes and configurations.

INTRODUCTION

Wireless technologies have become ubiquitous, providing improved connectivity in urban areas and also allowing outlying areas to connect to information networks. Now almost everyone makes use of wireless technologies to surf the web using portable phones or computers. The well-known applications they rely on are spread over wide areas and the number of service access points has increased exponentially.

In addition to phone calls and web surfing, many other applications are available on wireless enabled devices. They may take the form of ad-hoc networks requiring no specific infrastructures such as access points, and where these devices produce a self-organized mesh network in which each node able to communicate directly with its closest physical neighbors.

Despite the various types of devices and communication standards on which they are based, networking infrastructures and devices are all subject to the same limitations. The main concerns are limited resources and energy, and also practicality, such as movement and deployment almost anywhere. Most often the devices are small, simple and battery powered, and make use of limited resources (i.e., memory and CPU). Related to these, communications generate non-negligible costs leading to an overall reduction in network lifetimes. At this time, communication between remote nodes requires multiple hops via relay nodes, because nodes can only communicate directly with their physical neighbors (i.e., the nodes located in its communication range), although they may listen to all the messages transiting within its physical neighborhood.

As new devices with ad-hoc networking capacities and enhanced resources become developed their use is extended well beyond original functions related to wide-area monitoring. New developments now allow information lookup and multicasting, requiring novel and efficient solutions.

The focus in this chapter is lookup and multi-casting mechanisms able to efficiently locate and distribute information in mobile ad-hoc networks (MANETs). The basic concept applied to achieve these objectives involves peer-to-peer (P2P) paradigms, which can be roughly classified as either structured or unstructured.

Unstructured approaches such as Gnutella or KaZaA (Kirk, 2003; KaZaA, 2008) typically have neither control over topology nor file placement, meaning they often rely on locating data by simply flooding the network and thus overloading it. Unstructured approaches such as these have not been adapted for MANETs because locating the desired content involves too many transmissions and too much energy. Moreover, scaling them can prove difficult (Oliveira et al., 2005).

Structured solutions on the other hand consist of specialized placement algorithms designed to assign the responsibility for each content unit (file) to a specific node and then efficiently locate the files using directed search protocols, requiring only limited communication. They are mostly based on distributed hash tables (DHTs) that locate each item and node by means of a unique key identity, producing a logical space. The nodes are thus arranged according to their logical key and are only responsible for an item located at the smallest logical distance from them. Another feature is provided so that a node responsible for a specific key can be located without flooding and without producing false negatives (i.e., a search fails only if no matching file exists in the system).

Well known solutions developed, including the Chord (Stoica, Morris, Karger, Kaashoek, & Balakrishnan, 2001), Pastry (Rowstron & Druschel, 2001) or CAN (Ratnasamy, Francis, Handley, Karp, & Schenker, 2001) are not, however, suitable for ad-hoc networks, because they do not consider a node's physical locations when creating the logical overlay network. Given this fundamental gap between logical and physical spaces, the ad-hoc network becomes overloaded because service messages need to maintain the logical neighborhood through expensive multiple hop paths, thus making simple mapping from a DHT design to ad-hoc networks unrealistic.

Similarly, solutions based on flooding will not attain acceptable performance levels when distributing content to a subset of interested nodes. Indeed in the MANET approach, all nodes are forced to participate, even when not interested in the distributed content. This leads to ineffective solutions and poor performance, with the network quickly becoming overloaded and consuming a lot of energy and bandwidth. Flooding might also be used to build a shortest-path spanning tree, except that while flooding is reduced, inefficient use of already limited resources results, given that many nodes are not interested in the content. Furthermore, some flooding is still required to build the tree, and no efficient solution for locating the multicast group is available to the content provider. Scribe (Rowstron, Kermarrec, Castro, & Druschel, 2001) for example, superimposes a structured overlay substrate on top of the physical network and is able to construct more efficient multicast trees. Here multicast trees are rooted in "rendezvous" nodes managed by an underlying Pastry DHT. The nodes interested in joining a multicast group route a request via Pastry towards the source and connect to the first member reached on their way to the rendezvous point. While it is perhaps an effective strategy in wired networks, it cannot be easily transposed to mobile ad-hoc networks where communication is multi-hop and physical proximity is an essential consideration.

In this chapter, we thus present a DHT lookup algorithm specifically designed for MANETs. It combines a minimalist overlay structure with an adaptive routing mechanism that is able to quickly locate the content. As in well-known wired approaches such as Chord or Pastry, the nodes are organized in a logical ring. Yet, no long-range links are created for the logical shortcuts, given

the prohibitive maintenance costs involved. Alternatively, the physical neighborhood of the nodes traversed by requests provides low-cost shortcuts that are able to quickly converge at their destination within the logical space. We also propose extensions that consider an extra level of visibility in the physical neighborhood (neighbors of neighbors) and memorizing previous requests to dynamically identify and exploit possible shortcuts.

We then present an algorithm for building multicast trees in mobile ad-hoc networks using this specialized lightweight DHT overlay. A tree is created by the source (i.e. the multicast group), which can be efficiently located by searching the DHT. Several techniques of connecting adjacent nodes to a physically close member are proposed, along with extensions able to reduce the number of relay nodes involved in message distribution.

We conducted simulations on both lookup and multicast algorithms to evaluate their performance in various scenarios. We did not take churns (nodes frequently joining and leaving the system) into account because we were primarily interested in evaluating their lookup efficiency and the structural properties of the multicast trees produced. Our results indicate that the DHT algorithm performs very well in MANETs and that the multicast tree-building algorithm produces well-structured trees, comprising of only a limited number of relay nodes. Moreover, both algorithms scale well to large networks.

The remainder of this chapter is organized as follows. The *Background* section discusses related approaches. The *Distributed Hash Table for Mobile Ad-hoc Networks* section presents the ad-hoc DHT algorithm in detail, including evaluation results. The *Building Multicast Trees in Mobile Ad-hoc Networks* section describes and evaluates the multicast tree-building algorithm. Finally, the chapter is summarized in the *Conclusion* section.

BACKGROUND

In this section, we provide an overview of various approaches related to the algorithms presented. We begin with the DHT paradigms and then explore the various methods of multicasting in mobile ad-hoc networks.

Existing Distributed Hash Tables for MANETs

Peer-to-peer overlays have emerged from file sharing applications placed on top of the Internet, leveraged by the IP protocol routing infrastructure and its intrinsic peer-to-peer properties. In MANETs the situation is different since the path between nodes may traverse many relay nodes not being part of the overlay. Furthermore, two nodes are directly connected only if they are physical neighbors (i.e., within communication range of each other). As discussed in the introduction, the DHT paradigm, including its regular topology (often a ring) and shortcuts (fingers) introduced at the overlay layer make direct mapping to ad-hoc networks particularly difficult. Found in literature are various approaches to carrying out these mappings.

Although GRACE (Global Replication And Consistency) (Bosneag & Brockmeyer, 2005) was not specifically designed with ad-hoc networks in mind, it does enable mobile collaboration through combining DHT properties with layered architecture. GRACE also supports mobility in wide-area networks and different layers or consistency levels are interconnected through "consistency neighbors" logically located in close proximity to each other. Requests are routed along these neighbors and the system's lookup algorithm is based on Pastry (Rowstron & Druschel, 2001). This approach still relies on the standard Internet infrastructure.

(Pucha et al., 2004b) implement Pastry on top of the routing protocol DSR (Dynamic Source Routing) used by MANETs (Johnson & Maltz, 1996). Three modifications are suggested and can be compared to implementation on the Internet: (1) the node joining procedure is modified by expanding the ring search in order to locate distinguished bootstrap nodes in charge of arrivals; (2) to reduce network load the Pastry ping metric is replaced by a distance metric; and (3) the DSR protocol is modified to inquire about the proximity used in the adapted Pastry routing.

Ekta (Pucha, Das, & Hu, 2004a) and MAD-Pastry (Zahn & Schiller, 2005) integrate the DHT paradigm with ad-hoc network routing. Both approaches introduce the functions needed at the network routing layer. The principal idea of Ekta is to move the DHT protocol from the overlay level to the MANET network layer, applying one-to-one mapping between IP addresses and logical (DHT) node IDs. MADPastry is then built on top of the AODV protocol (Ad-hoc On-demand Vector Routing) (Perkins & Belding-Royer, 1999). The purpose of this protocol is to avoid full broadcasts as much as possible, because in ad-hoc networks this becomes too costly when the entire network is targeted. MADPastry creates clusters composed of physically close nodes that also share a common overlay prefix. Given physical and logical closeness of that the nodes in a cluster, routing is based on the logical overlay node IDs.

The disadvantage of all the aforementioned approaches is the size of their routing table and the complexity involved when setting up and managing connections with all the nodes contained in them.

(Cramer et al., 2005) suggest the chord-based Proximity Neighbor Selection strategy (PNS-CHORD), in which nodes are connected to their logical successors on the ring and through logical shortcuts to further nodes, the way Chord usually does. These logical long-range neighbors are chosen according to their physical proximity in the ad-hoc network and are located either one or two steps away.

Given that routing table construction is based on physical proximity, it may happen that the logical path pursued by a request traverses the same node several times. This can only be prevented when nodes keep track of the requests that pass them and that subsequently adjust their routing tables in the event that the same request passes twice, but on different logical shortcuts.

Cell Hash Routing (CHR) (Araujo, Rodrigues, Kaiser, Liu, & Mitidieri, 2005) is a specialized ad-hoc form of DHT. To construct a DHT, CHR uses position information clusters instead of organizing individual nodes in the overlay. This approach groups nodes according to their physical location, and the routing between clusters is done by position-based routing using the GPSR (Karp & Kung, 2000) routing algorithm. A major limitation of this approach is that nodes are addressed in clusters and not individually.

Finally, (Caesar, Castro, Nightingale, O'Shea, & Rowstron, 2006) suggest Virtual Ring Routing (VRR), a DHT solution for MANETs that is quite similar to that presented in this chapter and which also targets combining ad-hoc routing and logical DHT-like addressing. However, their algorithm differs from ours in several ways. First, in their approach, they build and proactively maintain bidirectional routes between nodes, while we always try to find the best route at each node and then send the request along the selected path, making the most of local situations. Second, VRR also maintains existing routes in a proactive way. While our solution does not maintain existing routes, previous routing decisions are kept in a cache and can thus be reactivated when appropriate. Finally in an effort to improve routing, VRR nodes make use of information about the physical paths traversing the nodes. Based on our experiments however any improvement achieved is only minimal. In fact, these cached entries are only effective when a request's path goes through the node that recorded them. In the DHT shown, the nodes also capture communications from any nodes in the physical neighborhood. The information acquired thus implicitly includes routing decisions and therefore allows paths to avoid tra-

versing the same physical area twice. It should be noted that no communication overhead is needed to capture this information, given the nature of that wireless networks (i.e. radio transmissions) allow it to be captured for free.

Related MANET Multicasting Solutions

Several P2P approaches to multicasting have been suggested for ad-hoc networks, with some using a logical overlay substrate for locating sources and others relying on flooding. Here we only discuss a selection of approaches available in the literature that closely resemble the presented algorithm (see (Chen & Wu, 2003) for a good survey).

In ad-hoc networks there are various logical structures used to facilitate appropriate tree construction. To build a multicast tree, MZR (Devarapalli & Sidhu, 2001) relies on the Zone Routing Protocol (Haas, 1997). The nodes in ZRP define the area around them and proactively maintain routes to all nodes within that zone. When the destination is outside the sender's zone, a reactive route discovery protocol is used, and when a source has data to multicast, it advertises this to all the nodes in its zone, and then extends the tree to nodes located at the border of other zones. An interested node simply answers the source and then a branch is created when the message reaches a multicast group member. Although the zone structure contains the flooding needed to build the tree, it still floods the entire network zone by zone. Not only does this results in significant bandwidth and energy consumption, the protocol provides no generic lookup facilities as used in our algorithm by the DHT.

XScribe (Passarella, Delmastro, & Conti, 2006) and Georendezvous (Carvalho, Araujo, & Rodrigues, 2006) use a DHT to support the multicast tree creation. XScribe is based on CrossROAD (Delmastro, 2005), a cross layer DHT providing the same features as Pastry, but based on a proactive routing protocol needing less bandwidth. XScribe exploits the DHT's routing capacities to distribute multicast messages, wherein each source has to know all group members and then multicast messages directly to them using a unicast method. This approach thus does not scale well, nor does it make any attempt to optimize resource consumption (minimizing the number of relay nodes or the number of transmissions required).

Georendezvous relies on CHR (Araujo et al., 2005), a specialized ad-hoc DHT that groups nodes in clusters according to their physical location. The DHT is used to efficiently locate the cell responsible for a group, and the cell's nodes can manage group membership and forward the multicast messages to all the members. Membership management is centralized in a cell containing multiple nodes, which are also responsible for distributing multicast messages. The disadvantage of this approach lies in its high bandwidth and energy requirements, thus resulting in poor scalability.

Other than flooding, many solutions have been proposed to efficiently look up a key (data) in MANETs. No mention is made of transposing existing direct search algorithms to ad-hoc networks, since when creating the logical overlay no attention was given to the physical proximity of nodes. Other approaches adapted for ad-hoc networks unfortunately involve large routing tables or pathological situations, wherein a request passes repeatedly through the same node or network area.

As in the DHT algorithms, flooding is not a suitable solution to distributing content to a set of multicast group members. A large number of nodes do in fact have to participate without being interested in the distributed content, a problem that also appears in certain approaches adapted for MANETs. Given that communication is fairly expensive, it is important that the number of relays be minimized. Other solutions also suffer from centralized membership management, a technique requiring extensive memory resources and also

leading to network congestion during multicast distribution.

The following section describes DHT and multicast tree-building algorithms that target efficient information lookup and distribution in MANETs.

DISTRIBUTED HASH TABLE FOR MOBILE AD-HOC NETWORKS

In a DHT system, each node and key has a specific position within a logical identifier space, thus creating a logical overlay superimposed on the physical network. The keys are mapped to nodes according to proximity metrics in the logical space, thus allowing any node to use this DHT substrate to determine the current live node responsible for a given key. Chord (Stoica et al., 2001) for example connects each node to its closest neighbors (successor and predecessor) in the identifier space, thus organizing nodes into a logical ring. This neighborhood always allows traversing the entire ring, albeit at a very high cost. These connections are necessary however and sufficient to ensure the system's safety and reliability. Additionally, each node has a number of long-range neighbors called fingers, used to maintain liveliness properties and efficient lookups. They are located at exponentially increasing distances within the logical space, and with these links, a node can quickly reach remote locations: the expected path length of a lookup is expressed by $O(logN)$ hops, where N is the number of nodes in the system.

In the text that follows, we assume that: (1) the ad-hoc network forms a connected graph; and (2) there is an underlying ad-hoc routing protocol allowing any node to route a message towards any other node. The second assumption stems from the fact that nodes can only communicate directly with their physical neighbors (i.e., nodes within their communication range). We make no assumptions regarding the ad-hoc routing protocol, except that it always succeeds and allows a message's routing to be interrupted at intermediate nodes.

Wired network approaches such as Chord or Pastry never consider the physical position of nodes. This means that successors, predecessors and long-range links connect to remote nodes through multiple physical steps. Not only are these approaches inefficient in terms of physical path length, they are impracticable, because each node would have to maintain accurate routing information for $O(logN)$ long-range neighbors. For larger networks, and when churn and mobility are added, this becomes a major problem and leads to considerable increases in traffic, thus overloading the network. It is therefore unrealistic to directly map a wired DHT design to MANETs.

The ad-hoc DHT is thus used to maintain a minimalist overlay for safety reasons only, but without long-range links. Instead, to spontaneously discover shortcuts in the logical space, it relies on the node's physical neighborhood being traversed by a lookup request. This provides in a liveliness property, because long-range links may be encountered on a random basis. The assumption here is that lookup requests can be routed more efficiently and at much lower management costs than when deterministically maintaining $O(logN)$ long-range neighbors.

Similarly to Chord and Pastry, the nodes are organized in a logical ring (Figure 1) with each node being assigned a random identifier in the logical space, i.e., by hashing the node's IP using a cryptographic hash function such as SHA-1. As shown in Figure 1, the physical neighbors of any given nodes are thus expected to be randomly distributed within the logical space. This diversity property is important if a lookup algorithm is to be efficient. Moreover, the node responsible for a key is the closest one in the logical space.

To limit management overhead, each node n must keep track of its successors $succ(n)$ and its predecessors $pred(n)$ on the ring at all times. Additional robustness can obviously be obtained

Figure 1. Illustration of DHT model for ad-hoc networks

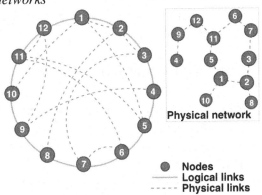

by allowing for several (logical) successors and predecessors.

Basic Algorithm

Here we describe the basic algorithm, and for improved clarity we often refer to the pseudo code presented in Algorithm 1.

To locate a key, a node creates a lookup message. This message contains the searched key (k) and the logical ID of its current destination (n_d). Upon receiving a lookup message, a node n_i first searches among its physical and logical neighbors, itself and n_d the node with the smallest logical distance toward lookup key k (line 2). If n_i is closest, it is responsible for the key and must reply to the originator of the request (line 4).

In this approach, the DHT lookup is closely integrated with the routing of messages through the ad-hoc network. If at any point there is indeed a possibility of finding a shorter logical distance to its final destination, at certain intermediate nodes the request might then diverge from its original path. In fact, if node n_j is logically closest to the key and is part of n_i's physical or logical neighborhood, it becomes the new destination. Here there are two cases to consider: if n_j is a physical neighbor of n_i then request is directly sent to that node (line 6). Otherwise, if n_j is a logical neighbor of n_i, the request will follow a multi-step path towards n_j (lines 8-9).

On the other hand, if remote node n_d is closer than any neighbors of a traversed node n_i, the request is simply forwarded to the next hop along the multi-step path to n_d (lines 11-12).

Convergence and Termination

Here we study the convergence and termination of the algorithm. For the remainder of this section, we consider the system to be in a stable state with no nodes joining or leaving.

To guarantee convergence, the algorithm always tries to reduce the logical distance from the current next logical hop n_d to key k. Thus, as node n_i receives a request for key k, it searches among its physical and logical neighbors, itself and n_d, the node n_j closest to the key, thereby always trying to reduce the logical distance to k.

We then have four cases to consider:

1. If n_i is closest to k, then it is responsible for the key and the lookup ends.
2. If a physical neighbor is closest to the key, then it receives the request directly.
3. If a logical neighbor is closest to the key, then it becomes the new next logical hop n_d for the request.
4. Finally, if n_d is closest to the key, the request's current destination does not change.

In the first three of the aforementioned cases, the logical distance decreases either because a node is located logically closer to the key than the current best ones, or the request reaches the node responsible for the searched key, hence ending the lookup. In the last case, the distance to the key

Algorithm 1. Basic DHT lookup algorithm at node n_i for key k

```
        δ(k₁, k₂): distance between keys k₁ and k₂

        id(n): logical identifier (key) of node n

        Vᵢ: physical neighbors of nᵢ

        Lᵢ = {pred(nᵢ), succ(nᵢ)}: logical neighbors of nᵢ


 1:     procedure LOOKUP(k, n_d)
        k : key to look up
        n_d: next logical hop
 2:         n_j = arg min_{n∈Vᵢ∪Lᵢ∪{nᵢ,n_d}} δ(id(n), k)
 3:         if n_j = nᵢ then                    {We are responsible for k}
 4:             return nᵢ
 5:         else if n_j ∈ Vᵢ then               {Go to physical neighbor}
 6:             send LOOKUP(k, n_j) to n_j;
 7:         else if n_j ∈ Lᵢ then
 8:             n_k ← next step on physical path to n_j;   {Go to logical neighbor}
 9:             send LOOKUP(k, n_j) to n_k;
10:         else
11:             n_k ← next step on physical path to n_d;   {Continue to n_d}
12:             send LOOKUP(k, n_d) to n_k;
13:         end if
14:     end procedure
```

does not decrease and the request is sent to n_d. When the request reaches its current destination, one of the first three cases will apply.

This last case only applies temporarily; the underlying ad-hoc routing protocol guarantees a request will be sent to a node, and eventually reach that node. It thus follows that the algorithm converges and terminates in a finite number of steps.

Increasing Visibility

In ad-hoc networks, nodes are only aware of their direct physical neighbors located within communication range, thus limiting visibility in the physical neighborhood. This visibility can be simply extended by exchanging physical neighborhood information. Hence, not only will the nodes know those that are located in their immediate communication range, but also the neighboring nodes of their neighbors. This extends the visibility to the "neighbors of neighbors" (*NoN*).

The cost of this extension is relatively limited in terms of message overhead, because the distribution of neighborhood information only requires broadcasting of a single message, in the event a change in the neighborhood takes place. Furthermore, as the number of long-range links increases, so does the probability of finding a suitable logical shortcut during the request's routing. For this reason, lookup efficiency can potentially be improved significantly.

Exploiting Request History

MANETs exhibit two major characteristics. Firstly, all nodes have to participate in the forwarding and routing of messages, and thus a node will "see" any traffic that is not targeting at itself. Secondly, as communication is broadcast, a node can listen to all messages sent by its physical neighbors.

By passively gathering information transported around the network by the requests, more long-range neighbors can now potentially be identified. A cache was introduced into the algorithm in order to achieve this, and thus for each observed request (forwarded or listened), a cache entry containing the key k and the destination of the message n_d is created.

It uses a least-recently used replacement policy and in the implementation evaluated, its size was limited to 256 entries. In the same way the lifetime of the entries was limited, being in fact the same as that of the route being maintained by the routing algorithm. Then, if cache entry was not reactivated at the end of this period (3 seconds in our implementation), it was simply discarded. Algorithm 1 can then use the cache entry (k, n_d) as a long-range neighbor. When a node receives a request for key k_r, it also considers these cache entries when searching the node with the smallest distance to that key. If k is closer to k_r, the request is redirected towards n_d.

This extension is particularly interesting because it allows all information on past requests to be passively gathered. Absolutely no extra messages are thus required and also the memory used to keep the cache entries is precisely defined and limited.

Evaluation Methodology

Here we present the experimentation methodology used to evaluate the DHT algorithm. The same simulator and methodology are used to evaluate the multicast solution presented in the following section.

We assume that the DHT algorithm runs on devices having limited resources, such as those used for professional and entertainment purposes by people in public spaces or office buildings. We assume without loss of generality that all participating devices will have 13 to 16 direct neighbors on average. The term neighbor refers to designated nodes located within communication range of each, thus enabling them to communicate with each other. Only bidirectional links are considered and thus we assume the unidirectional communication property will be handled in a hidden manner at the network layer. Through broadcasting messages all nodes within communication range of the transmitting node can listen to all transmissions. Every node in the network runs the DHT algorithm and has the ability to gather information from the relayed and listened messages, and can also influence the routing of relayed messages.

We only experimented with simple scenarios where nodes are randomly placed (according to a uniform distribution) in a rectangular area, and the results shown are issued from static and mobile configurations. In the static scenarios, nodes are placed at the beginning of the simulation, and their positions remain unchanged. For mobile configurations, on the other hand, each node can decide to stay or to move for a randomly chosen period of time t. We thus consider all participating devices (nodes) to be uniformly distributed within a Cartesian space in which they can independently decide to move during a finite period of time t with a speed of S, randomly chosen within the interval $0 < s \leq 2m/s$ in arbitrary directions, thus reflecting human displacements. If a node reaches the border of the simulation space, its direction is altered, and so it will continue its displacement inside the space. All the nodes involved in the simulations always form a connected graph.

To support the DHT, we implemented the ad-hoc on-demand distance vector (AODV). This routing protocol is able to build a multi-step path between any of the network nodes and then route messages between them. The DHT communicates with it through dedicated methods. The AODV also provides the DHT with a method for intercepting all requests traveling through the nodes.

The DHT identifiers are randomly assigned to nodes. For the algorithm's version with cache, a warm-up phase is used to populate the routing tables before evaluating the DHT. The lookup performances are obtained as a result of 2,000 lookups issued from random nodes searching for randomly chosen keys.

We then experimented with the DHT using the following simulation parameters:

- **Network sizes:** 1,000 (1K); 5,000 (5K);
- **Connectivity:** The average number of physical connections for a node (network density) varies between 13 and 16;
- **Lookup requests:** For each experiment, the paths of at least 2,000 randomly generated requests are statistically evaluated;
- **Steady state:** The variant for the ad-hoc lookup algorithm using the caching mechanism is evaluated with the simulation running a warm-up phase during 2,000 (2K) requests in order to reach a steady state before the statistical information is collected for analysis;
- **Mobility:** Randomly chosen in the interval $0 < s \leq 2m/s$ in random directions during a finite time t.

The following DHT lookup algorithm versions were evaluated:

- **Basic:** Basic DHT lookup;
- **Neighbors-of-neighbors (NoN):** Basic algorithm considering physical neighbors and also their neighbors in order to choose the next step;
- **Cache (C):** NoN algorithm using a cache to memorize previous forwarding choices;
- **Warm-up (Wup):** Simulation system executes a warm-up phase in order to reach a steady state prior to issuing analyzed requests.

In the results shown, when Cache (C) is used, it is always cumulative among the neighbors of neighbors (NoN) extension.

We evaluated the percentage of altered paths (i.e., shortcuts taken) to determine how often the shortcuts are used. To evaluate performance in terms of physical complexity and to make comparisons with other approaches, we also evaluated the average number of physical steps, the number of logical hops needed to obtain a lookup, and also the cost of a logical hop. Finally in order to determine when shortcuts were used in request paths, we evaluated the percentage of logical steps completed relative to the distance to the node responsible for the searched key.

Experimental Results

Logical Shortcuts

The algorithm evaluates the logical paths of the lookups at every physical step during its routing toward the desired key k. An intermediate node always forwards the request to the node at the shortest logical distance to the request's destination. Thus, a logical path may be altered thanks to shortcuts in the logical space provided by the physical neighbors, the neighbors of the neighbors and the cached routes. Figure 2 shows the average number of logical paths started relative to the number of logical paths terminated for different network sizes (e.g., 5K nodes and 1K nodes) and various network configurations (e.g., static and mobile configurations).

As shown, in all configurations tested more than 40% of the logical paths were not pursued because an intermediate node found a shortcut within the logical space. This can also be seen

in Table 1 showing details on the use of shortcuts during logical hops. Figure 2 allows another interesting observation wherein the basic algorithm in fact required around 30% more logical hops than all the other versions. Because a request is sent through a logical hop only if no other possibilities exist, the lookup algorithm thus makes direct use of logical shortcuts to route a request and whenever possible avoids relying on expensive logical routes. As expected this demonstrates how effective the improvements were in providing more logical shortcuts.

As the algorithm relies on close neighborhoods and cached requests to minimize the logical distance to the destination, this intuitively suggests that more and better shortcuts can be found at the beginning of a logical path. As the destination becomes closer, the probability of finding a logical shortcut decreases, and therefore the probability of the logical hops terminating without a shortcut being taken. As shown by the results in Figure 3, the percentage of terminated logical hops increased as the node responsible for the key became closer.

Cost of Requests

Figure 4 shows the average number of physical steps required to respond to a request. The DHT

Figure 2. Comparison of number of logical hops started and terminated

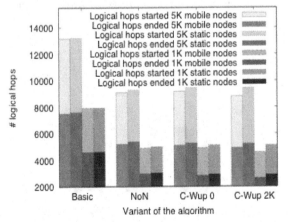

Figure 3. Percentage of terminated logical hops

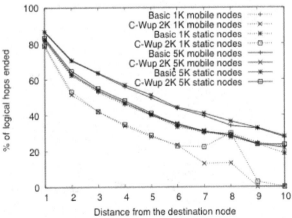

Table 1. Average use of logical shortcuts

Network size & type	Basic	NoN	C-Wup 0	C-Wup 2K
1,000 – static	41.84%	39.46%	43.07%	43.5%
1,000 – mobile	41.83%	39.76%	42.73%	42.5%
5'000 – static	42.49%	42.57%	44.39%	44.66%
5'000 – mobile	42.93%	42.78%	44.4%	44.26%

Table 2. Average cost of logical hop in terms of physical steps

Network size & type	Basic	NoN	C-Wup 0	C-Wup 2K
1,000 – static	10.72	11.17	10.93	11.06
1,000 – mobile	10.88	11.47	11.25	11.75
5'000 - static	23.01	23.49	23.01	23.14
5'000 - mobile	23.44	24.02	23.36	23.7

lookup algorithm works well with mobility, because in both configurations the average number of physical steps is almost the same. Moreover, in carrying out the request the improved algorithm requires roughly 30% fewer physical steps than does the basic version, thus confirming the efficiency of the former. This is illustrated in Figure 5 showing the average number of logical hops required to reach the node responsible for the searched key. As such, the improved algorithm needs 30% to 40% fewer logical hops than the basic algorithm. By reducing the number of logical hops the lookup algorithm reduces the total number of physical paths required to carry out a lookup. Because the cost of a logical hop in term of physical steps is almost the same for all the configurations tested as shown in Table 2, their usage needs to be reduced to decrease the total number of physical steps required.

All results listed demonstrate that the NoN improvement is the most effective method, and

that the caching effect is limited. Clearly improvements in cache efficiency are directly linked to the renewing policy. In the presented experiments, cache entries are discarded as soon as the route to the memorized destination expires. Thus, the lifetime of most cache entries was limited to 3 seconds (value chosen during implementation), because the routing algorithm discards older routes. Cache efficiency can easily be improved further through keeping entries longer.

Finally, Figure 6 shows a request's path in an ad-hoc network using the algorithm comprising all improvements made.

BUILDING MULTICAST TREES IN MOBILE AD-HOC NETWORKS

We begin our description of multicast algorithms by introducing the terminology used in this section. Table 3 lists the terms used for the nodes

Figure 4. Average number of physical steps to achieve a request

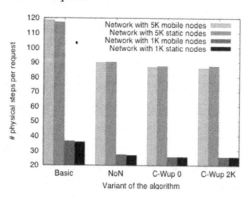

Figure 5. Average number of logical hops per lookup

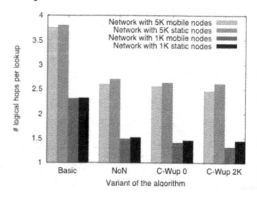

Figure 6. Path of a request routed by DHT with two extensions

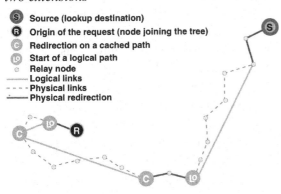

relatively to their role in running the algorithm. Figure 7 illustrates the various terms used in a sample multicast tree.

In MANETs, the information distribution to a group of nodes can essentially be achieved in two ways: flooding the network to locate the source and building a tree as done for example in MAODV (Royer & Perkins, 1999), or locating the source and building the multicast tree using directed search algorithms as done for instance by Scribe (Rowstron et al., 2001). Unfortunately, flooding methods involve all nodes in a network regardless of whether or not the distributed content concerns them. Moreover, flooding methods do not allow for easy scaling, given the number of messages sent through the entire network. By contrast, directed search based multicasting methods require less energy and bandwidth.

Unfortunately, methods such as Scribe cannot be simply transposed to a MANET context, because they do not consider specific characteristics of the underlying network such as multi-hop communication and physical awareness.

The algorithm we describe here builds a multicast tree for each group. To join a multicast group or to send a message to all its members, first a node has to lookup the data source acting as a "rendezvous" point. The algorithm then uses a DHT to efficiently locate the source (see Figure 6) without flooding the network. The multicast algorithm is supported by the previously described DHT, which provides the efficient lookup facilities needed for MANETs and which can be easily scaled to larger numbers of nodes.

Although the lookup messages do not follow the shortest path in the underlying ad-hoc

Figure 7. Sample tree describing terminology used

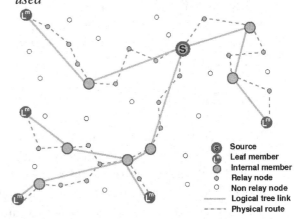

Table 3. Terminology

Term	Definition
Nodes	All nodes in system.
Members	All nodes interested in a multicast group.
Non-members	All nodes not members of a multicast group.
Internal members	Members inside a tree helping to distribute multicast messages (i.e., members with children).
Leaf members	Members at end of multicast tree branches (i.e., members without children).
Relay nodes	Non-member nodes relaying multicast messages.
Non-relay nodes	Non-member nodes not included in multicast tree activities.

network, this extra level of indirection permits better multicasting trees to be built, as it provides more connection alternatives for joining nodes. The resulting tree has less relay nodes, and the average degree remains reasonably low.

As for churns (nodes frequently joining and leaving the system), the DHT also helps the multicast algorithm in handling the unexpected departure of internal members. A member can easily find a new parent by looking up the DHT using its multicast group key.

The multicast algorithm aims at relying as much as possible on members for content distribution, thus reducing the number of relay nodes. All the network's nodes run the multicast algorithm, as in the DHT presented previously, but not all of them are necessarily members of a group. As such membership management is decentralized and a node can in fact connect to the tree simply by connecting to a member, without the source knowing it. This reduces the load on the source and also avoids bottlenecks. Best effort delivery is assumed for multicast messages but additional mechanisms could easily be implemented to ensure reliable delivery.

Basic Algorithm

To join the multicast tree, a node looks up in the DHT the identifier (key) associated with the desired multicast group (group identifier). The underlying DHT then routes the request through the network, traversing multiple nodes towards the source. When receiving a join request, a node checks whether it is a member of the searched group and whether or not the group was activated by a multicast message. If indeed it is a member and its membership has been activated, it replies and makes itself available to the requester as a potential parent, while also forwarding the request toward the source according to the DHT lookup algorithm. Otherwise, it simply forwards the request to the next hop according to the DHT lookup protocol. If a node is not in fact an active

member of the tree, it should not offer itself as a parent because this could partition the tree. As a final step the newly joined node may receive several offers from potential parents, or one at the very least, because all requests should reach the source.

To join the tree as soon as possible, the requester accepts the first connection offer it receives. Any upcoming offers from potential parents will be considered and the requester will accept one offer if and only if: (1) it has not already received a multicast from its parent; (2a) the distance to the new parent is shorter than to the previous parent, and the new distance to the root (i.e., the source) is no more than two times greater than the previous one; or (2b) the new parent is at the same distance as the previous one, but the distance to the root has shortened. At the end of the process, the requester is connected to the source of the tree or to the member it considers as being the best parent among all offers received.

This connection procedure thus allows many members to be linked to the source along direct paths including many relay nodes. Given that this situation is clearly not optimal, a number of mechanisms have been developed to improve the tree structure and to reduce the number of relay nodes involved. The first one is used during lookup and tries to provide more potential parents, while the second and third rely on information that nodes add to the multicast messages in order to reorganize the tree. Finally, the last one gathers broadcast message information in order to find potential children. These extensions take advantage of specific MANET characteristics, allowing improvements to be made to the tree structure at lower cost and always being cumulative when applied. (i.e., extension n also incorporates extensions $m<n$).

Finding More Potential Parents

The first algorithm improvement is intended to take advantage of specific MANET characteristics, its broadcast communication mode. All nodes within communication range of an emitting node can in fact listen to messages transmitted, and thus these are able to freely gather information from messages traveling next to them. This improvement basically exploits the broadcast mode characteristics so that it works just like the connection method. If a node listens to a join request for any group of which it is a member, and this group was activated through receiving at least one multicast message, it then becomes available to the requester as a potential parent.

The requester can accept connection proposals such as these as long as: (1) it has not received its first multicast message; and (2) it has no children. Indeed, as soon as it becomes a part of the tree, the risk of the tree being partitioned becomes too high, and as already stated these situations have to be avoided. Given the previous criteria, if the offer can be accepted, the node will connect to the proposed parent if: (1) the distance to the new parent is shorter than to the former parent, and the new distance to the root is not longer than twice the former one; or (2) the new parent is at the same distance as the former one, but the distance to the root has shortened.

This improvement is appealing because no extra messages are generated and listening to communication is relatively inexpensive, yet often it allows tree structure improvements. In particular, listening to messages avoids pathological situations where a multi-hop request passes by a member but do not traverse it.

Finding Better Parents

The second improvement makes use of another particular aspect of MANETs, multi-hop message routing. A multicast message being routed between a parent and a child may in fact traverse several relays. Various messages may then have common relays along their paths, as illustrated by the gray circle labeled 1 in Figure 8. In fact, if two messages follow the same physical path, their destinations are likely to be in the same area of the network.

Thus, a node can inform one of the members that the other one may possibly be a better parent or child in the multicast tree. When a relay node forwards a multicast message it memorizes the group, the message identifier and the destination address (the group and message identifiers give the message a unique identity). If a relay node receives another copy of the same multicast message (same group and message identifier), it memorizes the new destination and adds the previously memorized address to the message before forwarding it. If a message has more than one common relay, only the information added by the last one is kept in this message.

A member verifies whether an address has been added when receiving a multicast message. If so, it sends a message to the other member and suggests becoming its parent. Reconfiguration is carried out if and only if: (1) the new parent is closer than the current parent; (2) the new parent is not a descendant of the new child in the multicast tree; and (3) the node is outside of the current branch.

This validity check avoids partitioning the tree and losing connection with the source. Moreover, it is important that in such procedures that members verify last multicast identifier received is the same and the most recent one for both, thus guaranteeing they are considering the same network state.

This optimization method is effective because shortening the distance between parents and children in the tree also reduces the network's load. Moreover, the proposed solution requires no additional messages and the space overhead in the multicast message needed to transport the proposed member's address is negligible. Figure 9 shows the effect of this improvement on the tree shown in Figure 8.

Figure 8. Sample scenarios where tree is not organized optimally

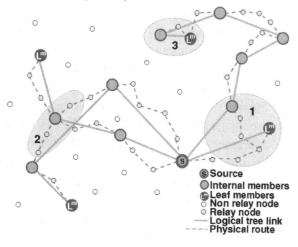

Figure 9. Scenarios of Figure 8 after applying optimizations

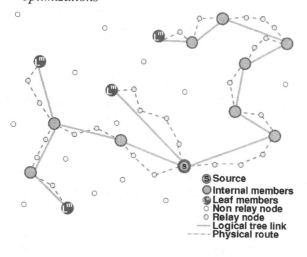

Removing Redundant Parents

As with the previous one, this extension analyses multi-hop connections between members. In particular, it tries to solve pathological problems in which a member is also a relay node or a member on a multi-hop path to its parent.

It may happen that a node is both a member and a relay on a multi-hop path between a parent and its child in the same logical tree as presented by the gray circle labeled 2 in Figure 8. Obviously,

the resulting structure is not optimal and this situation must be avoided because the affected node receives the same message twice.

Consequently, a member receiving the same multicast message from different nodes only retains the connection for the physically closest internal member (i.e., its parent) and discards other paths. It also promotes itself as the new parent of the addressee for any multicast messages only transiting through it.

If a member is on a multi-hop path to its parent, as shown by the gray circle labeled 3 in Figure 8, this member disconnects from its former parent and adds that node to its own children. It then becomes the child of its former parent's parent, thus possibly promoting itself as a new inner member of the tree along that path (if it was previously a leaf member).

In either case, one physical path is discarded or rearranged, and the number of relay nodes is reduced, as demonstrated in Figure 9 as compared relative to Figure 8. Moreover, the resulting tree provides better maps to the underlying topology and multicast efficiency is improved.

Listening to Multicast Messages

Finally, as with the first one, the last extension also aims at taking advantage of broadcast communication. During their distribution, multicast messages may in fact travel to nearby members without actually reaching them. Given that messages originating from each of its neighbors can be broadcast at all times, a node must always be aware of the various communications occurring in its neighborhood, otherwise it may miss some of its messages. Usually messages received but not intended for a node are simply discarded, but in the case shown here members may keep these messages and memorize their content for future use.

The source can then decide to intermittently allow members from a selected tree branch to use the collected information by setting a flag in the multicast message being sent to this branch. Each member of the branch then searches in the subset of valid multicast messages encountered for the one showing the largest distance to its sender in terms of physical steps. A message encountered in the neighborhood is considered valid if: (1) it has the same time stamp as the last multicast message received by the current member; (2) the current member has never considered the message's destination as the worst case and; (3a) its destination is outside the current branch or (3b) the destination is a descendant of the current member. Finally, the current member suggests to the addressee of the worst message found that it becomes its new parent.

As introduced previously, the source allows a branch to use this method only intermittently and not continuously. This method thus tends to allow the tree structure to stabilize. When improvement no longer seems possible, the algorithm tries to provide fresh enhancement opportunities by solving for the worst case known, using the gathered information. Moreover, by opting for the worst case not handled, attempting unsuitable solutions several times is avoided and only a single message to a potential child is needed, thus decreasing network load.

Given that reconnection proposals may be sent to almost all of the tree's members, the risk of breaking the tree is not negligible. The constraints described before are necessary and sufficient to avoid breaking the tree, because they always forbid a member to become the parent of a previous one. Time stamps are used to ensure that any situation being considered for reconfiguration is up to date and not an inconsistent depreciated one.

Evaluation Methodology

The multicast tree construction algorithm was evaluated by placing it on top of the experimental system that was also used to evaluate the DHT (see the *Distributed Hash Table for Mobile Ad-hoc Networks* section). Thus, this additional

layer placed on top of the existing ones (routing and DHT layers) along with the various layers communicated by means of dedicated methods. For a more detailed description of the simulation system's configuration, please refer to the evaluation methodology in the *Distributed Hash Table for Mobile Ad-hoc Networks* section.

During the system's evaluation, we again considered a set of simple scenarios. The results shown were obtained from static scenarios where the nodes are randomly and uniformly distributed in a rectangular area and throughout the entire simulation their position does not change. We also evaluated mobile situations in which nodes are distributed uniformly in a square area, similar to that used in the static scenario, except they may randomly decide to move or to stay for a randomly chosen period of time t. As a node decides to move, it picks up random speed s in the interval $0 < s \leq 2m/s$ and goes in a random direction, moving in this direction for a time t at speed s. At the end of the period t, a node follows the same procedure and decides whether to stay or to move on. If a moving node reaches the border of the simulation space, it would alter its direction in order to keep its displacement within the rectangular space.

Two nodes may be connected with each other and communicate if within communication range of each other. A given radius defines this communication range and the space construction method ensures the nodes will form a connected graph.

Similarly to the DHT experiments, DHT identifiers are randomly assigned to nodes and a multicast group identifier is randomly selected within the DHT logical space. When the simulation starts, the DHT gets warmed by performing 100 lookups to populate the DHT routing tables (for more details, please refer to the DHT in the *Distributed Hash Table for Mobile Ad-hoc Networks* section). Following the warm-up phase, one to three randomly selected nodes will issue a request to the DHT using the defined multicast group ID as a key. This process continues until the desired number of members is reached, and simultaneously the multicast message distribution starts. In every one to five simulation steps, a message is sent through the tree. For static scenarios, the simulation stops once the tree structure stabilizes (i.e., when the algorithm stops making changes to the tree structure), and for mobile situations, the simulation stops after a given time following the joining of the last node in the tree.

The multicast messages are routed by an AODV implementation that groups multicast messages having the same next hop.

We experimented with various configurations and network sizes:

- **Network sizes:** 1,000 (1K); 5,000 (5K);
- **Connectivity:** A node's average number of physical connections (network density) varies between 13 and 16;
- **Multicast group members:** Unless specified, 10% of all nodes join the tree;
- **Mobility:** Randomly chosen in the interval $0 < s \leq 2m/s$ in random directions during a finite time.

Using these configurations, we evaluated the various versions of the multicast tree construction algorithm:

- **Basic:** Construction algorithm with no extensions;
- **Ext. #1:** When joining, members listen and make themselves available as parents when applicable;
- **Ext. #2:** When sending messages, we try to identify common sub-paths and reconnect members to better parents;
- **Ext. #3:** We prevent nodes from receiving duplicate messages when acting both as a member and a relay node in a multicast tree;
- **Ext. #4:** A member listens to multicast messages to propose becoming the new parent of another member that is the farthest away from its parent.

In the results presented, these various extensions are always cumulative when applied. This multicast algorithm was then compared to the unicast message distribution (unicast) and a shortest path tree (SPT).

The unicast message distribution is executed directly by the source that controls information distribution and membership. The source sends the content directly to every interested node independently. As the source is responsible for membership management, nodes interested in the content provided, connect to the source.

In the shortest path tree, information distribution and the membership are centralized and controlled exclusively by the source. Any interested members must subscribe directly to the group by contacting it. To distribute the information, the source transmits the message along the shortest path to all registered members. The messages are then grouped if they have a common next hop, thus forming a shortest path tree closely integrated within the physical network and able to adapt efficiently to topology changes.

In the following results, we evaluated the tree structure generated by the multicast algorithm. In particular, we looked at internal members' degree, the number of relay nodes, the relative distance between two members and the total number of transmissions required to reach all members. (Jacquet & Rodolakis, 2005) also proposed normalized multicast cost evaluation, which we used to obtain measurements not dependent on the network's size in order to compare all approaches and network sizes with each other. The general multicast cost corresponds to:

$$R(n) = \frac{\text{multicast cost}}{\text{average unicast cost}}$$

where the multicast cost is expressed in number of hops (equals the number of transmissions) needed to reach all tree members, and the average unicast cost equals the average route length from the source to a random member. To compute the average unicast cost in a defined network size, we assume that members are all directly connected to the source. We then calculate the average unicast cost in terms of the number of transmissions (equals the number of hops) for use as a unicast cost reference.

We built the tree without using the DHT to support source location. A joining node contacts the source directly to connect itself to the multicast tree. We used the algorithm with all its extensions and evaluated the number of relay nodes included in the tree.

Finally, we obtained the results shown by averaging the results of 10 experiments conducted on different node distributions with various DHT key distributions and different multicast group keys.

A discussion on the validity of these experiments is presented at the end of the *Experimental results* section. We based this evaluation on the coefficient of variability (*COV*), representing the ratio of standard deviation to the mean. It is an effective measurement because it allows scale-free comparisons without any variability considerations. Basically this would not be the case if the variance were used for this purpose.

Experimental Results

In the previous section, the use of the DHT to support the multicast algorithm revealed an interesting fact. Although the DHT lookups efficiently located the source, the requests used a path longer than that provided by the underlying routing algorithm. However, as shown in Table 4, the tree built with DHT systemically included fewer relay nodes. In fact, the small indirect requests in DHT routing

Table 4. Percentage of relay nodes involved in multicast tree with direct request or DHT lookup

Network size (# nodes)	500	1,000	2,500
No-DHT	12.5%	13.82%	15.64%
DHT	10.46%	11.32%	11.69%

increased the probability of locating a better parent for connecting to the tree.

Degree of Member Nodes

Figure 10 shows the cumulative percentage of members involved in message relaying relative to their degree. The results also compare the mobile and static scenarios. For a good tree structure, the ideal case is a curve in which the *Y* value grows more quickly and stops with a small *X*. In fact, a curve such as this means that many members participate in message distribution but their degree is limited.

Clearly, in the tree produced by the basic algorithm for both static and mobile configurations, less than 30% of members participated in the message distribution and 60% are then only leaf members. Moreover, some nodes had quite a high degree (most notably the source). By contrast, when the various extensions were applied, more than 50% of members helped to distribute the content, thus acting as internal members. For all network sizes considered, the degree for the internal members did not exceed 7. The algorithm thus contributed to distribute multicast and membership management load between members. A comparison of mobile and static scenarios shows

Figure 10. Cumulative percentage of members acting as internal members as a function of their degree (static - mobile comparison)

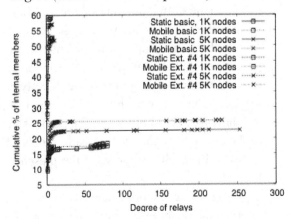

Figure 11. Percentage of relay nodes involved (static - mobile comparison)

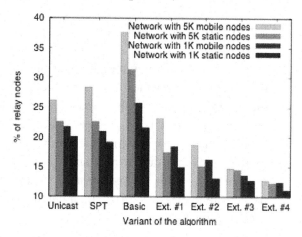

node mobility does not make the algorithm any less effective.

Relay Nodes

With the improved algorithm and due to the increased number of internal members relaying messages, the number of relay nodes should decrease. Figure 11 confirms this for all the multicast algorithm versions except the basic one. Clearly, the shortest path algorithm and unicast distribution methods used fewer relay nodes than the basic algorithm. Given that the same routes were used many times to reach the members, this limited the number of relay nodes involved. By using members to help with message distribution, the multicast algorithm created branches not connected to the source and thus included additional relay nodes. At the same time, as shown in Figure 16, the basic multicast algorithm is close to the unicast and shortest path tree method, as an important number of members are directly connected to the source. It thus uses approximately the same number of branches around the source as the unicast and the shortest path tree, but has additional branches because of the presence of internal relays.

Because the multicast algorithm uses more internal members to distribute messages, it re-

duces the load at the source. This is confirmed by the transmission costs shown in Figure 13. For the basic algorithm transmission costs are only slightly higher than those of the shortest path algorithm and noticeably lower than that of the unicast distribution method.

Although the basic algorithm required more nodes in the mobile context, the trees built with all extensions in the mobile scenarios needed roughly the same number of nodes as in the static experiments. This result is really interesting. Remember that the simulation continued after the tree was built. For the static situation, this allows the tree structure to stabilize, while for the mobile situation, as the nodes continue to move, we evaluate the tree at the end of the simulation only, thus demonstrating that the algorithm and its extensions not only build efficient multicast trees but they are able to preserve their good properties. This fact is confirmed by other measurements presented in Figure 10 and Figure 12.

Average Distance Between Member Nodes

The multicast algorithm builds a tree in which physically close members can discover each other and simply connect by passively gathering information as messages are broadcast. Thus, as shown Figure 12, the physical path length between two consecutive members is small, and in all cases is obviously smaller than that in the shortest path tree and unicast solutions. This is not surprising given that all members are leaf members directly connected to the source, and consequently the average distance between the two members (i.e., the average distance to the source) is maximal, since no connection to a physically close member is envisaged.

The tree built by the presented algorithm connects close-by members together and the tree is thus closely mapped to the topology of the underlying network. This is an advantage in MANETs because short paths reduce the probability that the

Figure 12. Average number of physical steps separating two members (static - mobile comparison)

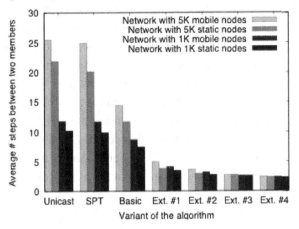

Figure 13. Average number of transmissions required to cover tree (static - mobile comparison)

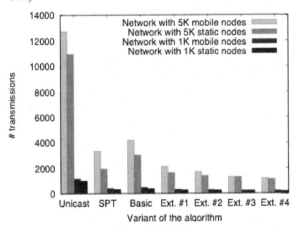

route will break, and when this happens, the time needed to rebuild it is diminished.

Number of Transmissions Needed to Reach all Members

Since this algorithm was specifically adapted for MANETs with resource limited mobile devices, the total energy consumption is an important factor. If the nodes involved use too much energy to communicate with each other, the network lifetime's is affected. It is thus crucial to avoid unnecessary energy consumption, and because wireless communication requires energy, this can be achieved by limiting the total number of transmissions required to cover the tree. As shown in Figure 13, the multicast algorithm requires fewer transmissions than the shortest path tree and the unicast distribution methods, and only the basic version requires a few more transmissions than the shortest path algorithm. As explained, both trees in fact have the same structure around the source but the basic algorithm builds more branches between members. With all its extensions, the multicast algorithm saves energy by reducing the number of transmissions required to cover the entire tree.

Multicast Cost

For the basic multicast algorithm, the cost of multicasting is less than that of the unicast distribution method, but slightly higher than that of the shortest path tree, as shown in Figure 14. As previously explained, the basic algorithm builds a tree with a structure close to the shortest path method with internal members. Some branches are created but a few additional transmissions are required to cover these branches, thus increasing the multicasting cost. The multicast algorithm is cheaper than the shortest path tree and the unicast in all other cases.

Scalability

When the four extensions are applied, the physical distance between two members, the number of involved relay nodes and the degree of internal members are nearly the same for all network sizes considered. At the same time, the experiments on mobile conditions also demonstrate that the algorithm is able to maintain the tree structure, regardless of the number of nodes in the network.

Figure 14. Average multicast cost (R(n)) (static mobile comparison)

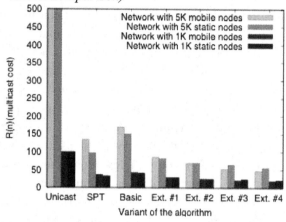

Figure 15. Multicast cost evolution in different network sizes (static configuration)

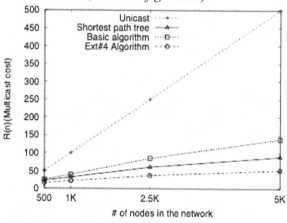

comparisons to be made while considering variability as opposed to the variance.

For all network sizes and configurations using the extended algorithm, the average number of steps between two members (Figure 12) has a maximum COV of 0.7%. This therefore means that for the experiments conducted there were no significant differences between them. Similarly, for experiments on the number of relay nodes (Figure 11) we obtained a maximum COV of 8%, increased variance only occurred for the number of transmissions. The specific routing algorithm implementation can in fact provide some opti-

Figure 16. Sample tree built by basic algorithm (static configuration)

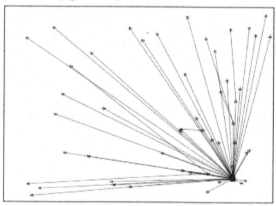

These two results support our approach's claim of scalability, which is confirmed in Figure 15, where the multicast cost of the improved algorithm is not only lower, but also increases more slowly than the multicast cost for the shortest path tree and unicast methods.

Variability of Results

In the various experiments presented here, we evaluated the coefficient of variability (COV), which represents the ratio of the standard deviation to the mean. This measurement allows scale-free

Figure 17. Sample tree built by improved algorithm (static configuration)

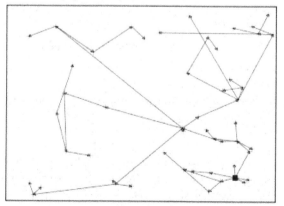

mization, such as in message grouping, whose applicability depends on the ad-hoc network's topology and member node positioning. This improvement increases variations in the number of transmissions required to cover the tree.

Tree Structure

Finally, Figure 16 shows a tree built using the basic algorithm and illustrates the effect that improvements have on tree structure. Clearly this structure is not optimal and only a few members take part in the relaying of messages. When compared to the tree in Figure 17, which corresponds exactly to the same network configuration and the same source, the effects of the improved algorithm can be seen. The structure is obviously much better adapted to the physical topology, with the load on the source being greatly reduced and also many more members participating as internal members.

CONCLUSION

Presently, the widespread use of ad-hoc networking is still limited, but this technology is steadily growing, and being supported by a great deal of research conducted to improve device and application efficiency. Most preliminary approaches to these types of networks rely on flooding, allowing the development of quick and easy solutions to information lookup and distribution in MANETs. These approaches do come with major drawbacks related to the amount of network load generated, high transmission costs, and the number of nodes involved (including those not interested in the content distributed). Moreover, flooding algorithms do not scale well, and they are easily rendered prohibitive due to the number of messages generated and the time needed to transmit them. This is especially true for lookup algorithms, due to limitations related to their lookup scope, the physical steps needed by flooding methods

and the false negatives generated (i.e., negative answers to lookup requests even if the desired element exists).

As an alternative solution, directed search protocols based on overlay substrates can greatly improve lookup efficiency and also reduce transmission costs. In this chapter, we presented a DHT algorithm that is able to efficiently lookup any data identified by its key, involving no false negatives and only a limited number of messages. Performance levels for this algorithm are quite effective in simulated scenarios and it makes efficient use of MANET characteristics, particularly when discovering logical shortcuts.

Similarly to information lookup (or retrieval), information distribution can be achieved through applying flooding-based approaches. Again these solutions force the network to generate high loads and participation by nodes not interested in the content distributed. As an alternative, we presented our multicast tree-building algorithm. As the simulations demonstrated, this method of building a multicast tree makes the most of the network's specific properties and minimizes the use of relay nodes and having to develop a proper fit with the underlying network's physical topology. This approach is also able to reduce the load on the nodes, while also successfully distributing membership management and sharing information distribution loads among the participating devices.

The satisfactory results obtained through simulation encourage further work in this direction. Certain problems such as latency in large networks have to be investigated, and efficient churn resistance and cheap recovery methods need to be explored for both the DHT overlay and multicast layers. Analytical studies are needed to confirm performances observed and to determine these approaches' limitations in confirming simulation results. Furthermore, it would be interesting to conduct experiments on larger networks populated with wireless devices.

In conclusion, the continuously growth of new devices with ad-hoc communication capabilities (i.e., PDAs, cell phones with Wi-Fi built-in) calls for more appropriate methods in application development and deployment. The approaches and solutions presented in this chapter represent a valuable contribution for filling this gap.

REFERENCES

Araujo, F., Rodrigues, L., Kaiser, J., Liu, C., & Mitidieri, C. (2005). CHR: A distributed hash table for wireless ad hoc networks. In *Proceedings of the International Conference on Distributed Computing Systems Workshops.*

Bosneag, A. M., & Brockmeyer, M. (2005). GRACE: Enabling collaborations in wide-area distributed systems. In *Proceedings of the International Workshops on Enabling Technologies: Infrastructure for Collaborative Enterprises.*

Caesar, M., Castro, M., Nightingale, E. B., O'Shea, G., & Rowstron, A. (2006). *Virtual ring routing: Network routing inspired by DHTs.* Paper presented at the Special Interest Group on Data Communications.

Carvalho, N., Araujo, F., & Rodrigues, L. (2006). Reducing latency in rendezvous-based publish-subscribe systems for wireless ad hoc networks. In *Proceedings of the International Conference on Distributed Computing Systems Workshops.*

Chen, X., & Wu, J. (2003). *Multicasting techniques in mobile ad hoc networks.* Boca Raton, FL, USA: CRC Press, Inc.

Cramer, C., & Fuhrmann, T. (2005). Proximity neighbor selection for a DHT in wireless multi-hop networks. In *Proceedings of the 5th IEEE International Conference on Peer-to-Peer Computing.*

Delmastro, F. (2005). From pastry to CrossROAD: CROSS-layer ring overlay for ad hoc networks. In *Proceedings of the IEEE International Conference on Pervasive Computing and Communications Workshops.*

Devarapalli, V., & Sidhu, D. (2001). MZR: A multicast protocol for mobile ad hoc networks. In *Proceedings of the IEEE International Conference on Communications.*

Haas, Z. (1997). A new routing protocol for the reconfigurable wireless networks. In *Proceedings of the IEEE 6th International Conference on Universal Personal Communications Record.*

Jacquet, P., & Rodolakis, G. (2005). Multicast scaling properties in massively dense ad hoc networks. In *Proceedings of the 11th International Conference on Parallel and Distributed Systems.*

Johnson, D. B., & Maltz, D. A. (1996). Dynamic source routing in ad hoc wireless networks. In T. Imielinski & H. Korth (Eds.), *Mobile Computing* (pp. 153-181). Kluwer Academic Publishers.

Karp, B., & Kung, H. T. (2000). GPSR: Greedy perimeter stateless routing for wireless networks. In *Proceedings of the 6th Annual International Conference on Mobile Computing and Networking.*

KaZaA. (2008). Music downloads now Kazaa. com: Music and ringtone downloads. Retrieved September 10, 2008, from http://www.kazaa. com

Kirk, P. (2003). Gnutella - A protocol for a revolution. Retrieved September 10, 2008, from http://rfc-gnutella.sourceforge.net/

Oliveira, L. B., Siqueria, I. G., Macedo, D. F., Loureiro, A. A. F., Wong, H. C., & Nogueira, J. M. (2005). Evaluation of peer-to-peer network content discovery techniques over mobile ad hoc networks. In *Proceedings of the Sixth IEEE International Symposium on a World of Wireless Mobile and Multimedia Networks.*

Passarella, A., Delmastro, F., & Conti, M. (2006). XScribe: A stateless, cross-layer approach to

P2P multicast in multi-hop ad hoc networks. In *Proceedings of the International Workshop on Decentralized Resource Sharing in Mobile Computing and Networking*.

Perkins, C. E., & Belding-Royer, E. M. (1999). Ad-hoc on-demand distance vector routing. In *Proceedings of the IEEE Workshop on Mobile Computing Systems and Applications*.

Pucha, H., Das, S. M., & Hu, Y. C. (2004a). EKTA: An efficient DHT substrate for distributed applications in mobile ad hoc networks. In *Proceedings of the IEEE Workshop on Mobile Computing Systems and Applications*.

Pucha, H., Das, S. M., & Hu, Y. C. (2004b). How to Implement DHTs in Mobile Ad Hoc Networks?. In *Proceedings of the 10th ACM International Conference on Mobile Computing and Networking*.

Ratnasamy, S., Francis, P., Handley, M., Karp, R., & Schenker, S. (2001). A scalable content-addressable network. In *Proceedings of the Conference on Applications, Technologies, Architectures, and Protocols for Computer Communications*.

Rowstron, A., & Druschel, P. (2001). *Pastry: Scalable, decentralized object location, and routing for large-scale peer-to-peer systems*. Paper presented at the Middleware 2001.

Rowstron, A., Kermarrec, A.-M., Castro, M., & Druschel, P. (2001). *SCRIBE: The design of a large-scale event notification infrastructure*. Paper presented at the Networked Group Communication.

Royer, E. M., & Perkins, C. E. (1999). Multicast operation of the ad-hoc on-demand distance vector routing protocol. In *Proceedings of the International Conference on Mobile Computing and Networking*.

Stoica, I., Morris, R., Karger, D., Kaashoek, M. F., & Balakrishnan, H. (2001). Chord: A scalable peer-to-peer lookup service for internet applications. In *Proceedings of the Conference on Applications, Technologies, Architectures, and Protocols for Computer Communications*.

Zahn, T., & Schiller, J. H. (2005). MADPastry: A DHT substrate for practicably sized MANETs. In *Proceedings of the Workshop on Applications Services in Wireless Networks*.

Chapter II
Data Dissemination and Query Routing in Mobile Peer-to-Peer Networks

Thomas Repantis
University of California, Riverside, USA

Vana Kalogeraki
University of California, Riverside, USA

ABSTRACT

In this chapter the authors study the problems of data dissemination and query routing in mobile peer-to-peer networks. They provide a taxonomy and discussion of existing literature, spanning overlay topologies, query routing, and data propagation. They proceed by proposing content-driven routing and adaptive data dissemination algorithms for intelligently routing search queries in a peer-to-peer network that supports mobile users. In the authors' mechanism, nodes build content synopses of their data and adaptively disseminate them to their most appropriate peers. Based on the content synopses, a routing mechanism is being built, to forward the queries to those peers that have a high probability of providing the desired results. The authors provide an experimental evaluation of different dissemination strategies, which shows that content-driven routing and adaptive data dissemination is highly scalable and significantly improves resource usage.

INTRODUCTION

Mobile ad-hoc networks composed of mobile devices such as laptops, cell phones and PDAs with limited communication power and transmission range have emerged as a widely deployable infrastructure without the need of centralized support (Cao et al., 2005; Kortuem et al., 2001; Papadopouli and Schulzrinne, 2001). The typical characteristic of these networks is that the users are interested in receiving data and services available in their vicinity, or want to be notified about local events that are pertinent to their interests. Receiving this information by forming mobile peer-to-peer networks offers several advantages in comparison to retrieving it from fixed access points or the satellites of a cell phone carrier: First, the costs for installing, maintaining, and operating an infrastructure to provide the requested data are avoided. Second, data are updated automatically as users move, without the overhead of continuously collecting updates in centralized locations. This is particularly useful for locations where users change frequently, such as busy streets or stores. Third, users find themselves in places and situations where an infrastructure may not exist, or is not accessible. Examples include trying to access traffic information while driving in isolated areas (Xu et al., 2004), or trying to retrieve emergency notifications after a natural disaster. Finally, mobile peer-to-peer networks enable users to publish data in a cost-efficient way, in addition to receiving them. This gives rise to a wealth of new applications, such as identifying nearby users with similar interests (Amir et al., 2004), or locally organized events. Thus, enabling mobile devices to dynamically self-organize in ad-hoc networks and communicate in a peer-to-peer fashion enables cost-effective data dissemination for a variety of environments and applications. Mobile nodes that are in the transmission range of each other can communicate with their peers directly. To communicate with peers outside a node's transmission range, messages are propagated across multiple hops in the network.

The goal of this chapter is to study the problems of data dissemination and query routing in mobile peer-to-peer networks. We explore the synergy of mobility and peer-to-peer, focusing on the aforementioned problems. We identify the challenges introduced by mobility. We survey existing approaches and identify their shortcomings. Finally, we explore promising data dissemination and query routing solutions and evaluate their performance and overhead experimentally.

Delivering data to interested users in an efficient manner in a mobile environment challenges existing peer-to-peer solutions for wireline networks due to several reasons: First, peers have limited bandwidth and energy, which restrains the message overhead allowed for data dissemination protocols. Second, peer connections are transient, due to the frequent movement of the mobile nodes. This makes it costly to maintain an overlay topology on top of the underlying network topology, which is the way wired peer-to-peer networks are built, and to keep up-to-date routing information. The performance of wired peer-to-peer dissemination protocols would be further exacerbated in a mobile environment due to churn and network partitioning. Churn is introduced by peers frequently joining and leaving the network, while network partitioning is caused by node mobility.

The remaining of this chapter is organized as follows: The *Survey of Existing Research* section surveys existing solutions for data dissemination and query routing in mobile peer-to-peer networks, focusing on overlay topologies, query routing for data discovery, and data propagation. The *Mobile Peer-to-Peer Data Dissemination and Query Routing* section presents mechanisms for content-driven routing and adaptive data dissemination. The *Experimental Study* section describes an experimental study of the performance of data discovery and dissemination mechanisms. Finally, we present our conclusions and discuss avenues to future work.

SURVEY OF EXISTING RESEARCH

We extend our discussion of existing research in the area into three different directions: Topologies for organizing the network to facilitate peer interaction, query routing mechanisms for data discovery, and mechanisms for data propagation. Table 1 summarizes our taxonomy of the relevant literature.

Table 1. Taxonomy of representative research in mobile peer-to-peer data dissemination and query routing

Overlay Topology	Location-Aware Structure	GHT (Ratnasamy et al., 2002) SOLONet (Patil et al., 2004)
	Location-Agnostic Structure	VRR (Caesar et al., 2006)
	Exploiting Peer Heterogeneity	Tork (Brown et al., 2007) SGDACp2p (Xue et al., 2004)
Query Routing for Data Discovery	Physical Network Routing	DSDV (Perkins and Bhagwat, 1994) DSR (Johnson et al., 2001) AODV (Perkins, 1999)
	Guided Query Routing	RBB (Wolfson et al., 2006) SBSD (Ouksel, 2006) SBSD-SP (Lundquist and Ouksel, 2007)
Data Propagation	Supporting User Mobility	Distr. DB (Pitoura and Samaras, 2001) Distr. Pub/Sub (Burcea et al., 2004)
	Epidemic Dissemination	7DS (Papadopouli and Schulzrinne, 2001) PDI (Lindemann and Waldhorst, 2004) PeopleNet (Motani et al., 2005)
	Cooperative Caching	Infrastructure-Less: (Goel et al., 2002; Sailhan and Issarny, 2003; Shen et al., 2005; Yin and Cao, 2004)
		Infrastructure-Based: (Chow et al, 2004; Hara 2002; Lim et al., 2004)

Overlay Topology

Topologies like Distributed Hash Tables (DHTs) impose structure on wired peer-to-peer networks in order to improve data lookup times. Creating similar overlay topologies for mobile peer-to-peer networks is more challenging due to the transient peer connections. A few studies of the feasibility of applying existing structures to mobile environments have been performed (Gerla et al., 2005; Hu et al., 2004; Seet et al., 2007).

Location-Aware Structure

One approach for building a topology that aids data dissemination in a mobile environment is to create an overlay structure that takes into account the topological proximity. As representative examples we discuss GHT and SOLONet.

Geographic Hash Table (GHT) (Ratnasamy et al., 2002) creates an overlay structure to support a data-centric storage model. It hashes keys into geographic coordinates, and stores a key-value pair at the node geographically nearest to the hash of its key. Hence, rather than using hashing

in the namespace, as DHTs do, GHT hashes in the geographic space. To support this functionality and route messages to the corresponding nodes, GHT requires GPS support and is built on top of the GPSR (Karp and Kung, 2000) geographic routing protocol.

SOLONet (Patil et al., 2004) builds an overlay multicast tree using location information. The goal is to have nodes that are physically close to each other be neighbors in the multicast tree, and have the logical distance of any member node from the source node be proportional to its actual distance from the source. By taking advantage of location information, the relaying of messages through other nodes is minimized and the latency of data dissemination in the tree is reduced. However, providing such a location-aware multicast tree induces the overhead of storing and broadcasting precise location information. SOLONet provides approximate location information, by dividing the physical topology into smaller cells. Only location changes that result to crossing the border of a cell are reported. Furthermore, a leader node is responsible for maintaining and providing location information for all nodes within each cell.

Location-Agnostic Structure

Another approach is to assign identifiers to nodes that are independent of the topology and allow peers to maintain paths between their overlay neighbors, while storing data objects at the nodes whose identifiers are closest to the objects' keys. As a representative example we discuss VRR.

Virtual Ring Routing (VRR) (Caesar et al., 2006) builds such a location-agnostic overlay. It is implemented directly on top of the link layer and does not rely on an underlying network routing protocol. VRR provides both traditional point-to-point network routing and DHT routing to the node closest to a key. It does not require network flooding or translation between fixed identifiers and location-dependent addresses. Nodes are organized into a virtual ring ordered by their identifiers and each node maintains a small number of routing paths to its neighbors in the ring. The nodes along a path store the next hop towards each path endpoint in a routing table. VRR uses these routing tables to route packets between any pair of nodes in the network, i.e., a packet is forwarded to the next hop towards the path endpoint whose identifier is numerically closest to the destination.

Exploiting Peer Heterogeneity

Taking advantage of the heterogeneity of the mobile environment is another approach for building a mobile peer-to-peer topology. As representative examples we discuss Tork and SGDACp2p.

Tork (Brown et al., 2007) is a variable-hop peer-to-peer overlay that adjusts hop-count according to a peer's bandwidth capabilities. Hop-count refers to the number of physical network hops required for an overlay hop. For high-bandwidth peers, Tork offers $O(1)$-hop performance, while for low-bandwidth peers, Tork has multi-hop performance. Hop-count can be decreased, and consequently communication latency can be increased, with the use of larger routing tables

on each peer. However this leads to increased network traffic to maintain these larger routing tables. Tork combines active stabilization and opportunistic updating to decrease that maintenance traffic. Since a variable-hop overlay is adaptive, peers of different bandwidth capacities can exist in the same overlay. A peer might have high bandwidth capacity in one interval and low bandwidth in another.

SGDACp2p (Xue et al., 2004) is a Stable Group Differentiated Admission Control algorithm to exploit correlated mobility patterns in mobile ad-hoc networks. Its goal is fast amplification of the total streaming capacity of a mobile peer-to-peer media streaming system. Consumer peers store media data during a streaming session and therefore become supply peers themselves. Thus, system capacity is amplified when the number of peers it serves increases. To communicate with a peer outside its transmission range, a mobile peer has to rely on one or many intermediate peers as relays, which can be disconnected very frequently. SGDACp2p tries to improve the media streaming efficiency and build more stable routes, by attempting to predict the future availability of wireless links, based on individual peer mobility models.

Query Routing for Data Discovery

Routing queries for data discovery has been studied extensively in wired peer-to-peer networks. (Zeinalipour-Yazti et al., 2004) provides an overview of relevant research.

Improving upon the efficiency of simple flooding is even more crucial for mobile peer-to-peer networks due to the energy and communication constraints.

Physical Network Routing

In wireless ad-hoc networks several protocols have been proposed to route messages on the physical network (Broustis et al., 2006) and one could utilize those to route queries in mobile peer-to-peer networks. (Oliveira et al., 2003) compares how a mobile peer-to-peer application performs under three different routing protocols, namely Destination-Sequenced Distance-Vector routing (DSDV) (Perkins and Bhagwat, 1994), Dynamic Source Routing (DSR) (Johnson et al., 2001), and Ad-Hoc On Demand Distance Vector routing (AODV) (Perkins, 1999). DSDV is pro-active in maintaining routing information, while DSR and AODV are reactive. The peer-to-peer application examined was Gnutella-like (Kirk, 2003) file sharing. The study showed that each of the analyzed routing protocols performed well in some scenarios and had drawbacks in others. Hence, the authors showed that it is important to consider characteristics of both the application and the network when choosing a routing protocol.

Guided Query Routing

To efficiently use discovery mechanisms employed in wired unstructured peer-to-peer networks in a mobile setting, disseminating information that can guide queries can be utilized. We discuss two representative algorithms that follow this approach, RBB and SBSD (and its extension SBSD-SP).

Rank-Based Broadcast (RBB) (Wolfson et al., 2006) uses a hybrid push and pull approach for resource discovery. Mobile peers broadcast both reports regarding available resources, and queries. Upon receiving a broadcast, a neighboring peer incorporates the reports and queries into its local database and subsequently broadcasts its most relevant reports and queries. RBB determines how to rank the reports and queries in terms of relevance, when to broadcast them, and how many to broadcast. The relevance of a report depends on the queries in the local database (which represent the global demand in the network), i.e, more relevant reports satisfy more queries. RBB triggers a broadcast when new information can be communicated to the neighbors, either because

enough new information was received or because the set of neighbors has changed. Finally, RBB determines how many reports and queries to broadcast using a formula. The formula computes the optimal transmission, according to the length of time between subsequent broadcasts, so that overall dissemination is maximized.

Self-Balancing Supply/Demand (SBSD) (Ouksel, 2006) extends to a mobile environment the traditional publish/subscribe paradigm. Brokers are responsible for managing subscriptions and delivering events, while subscribers register with the brokers their interest in certain events. SBSD relies on the supply and demand principle to self-balance latency and workload through local updates of utility values. The utility functions favor the replication of the most recent and highly frequent profiles and events, while taking into account the negative congestion effects of excessive replication on the whole network. The goal is to minimize the average latency to find the matching events, and maximize the percentage of answered queries, as the network scales up. Self-Balancing Supply/Demand with Subscription-based Permission (SBSD-SP) (Lundquist and Ouksel, 2007) extends SBSD to reduce redundant broadcasting. It does so without sacrificing coverage, by exploiting high density. For any given subscription, Subscription-based Permission (SP) prohibits a consistent set of brokers from accepting its replicas. This both enlarges subscription propagation areas and increases the variety of subscriptions stored by the brokers within a given area.

Data Propagation

Data dissemination in mobile peer-to-peer networks refers both to disseminating data that users are interested in and data that can guide users' queries efficiently in the network, for example by observing peer interaction patterns (Repantis and Kalogeraki, 2005). Existing solutions from the domains of distributed databases or publish/subscribe systems need to be adapted in order to be used in networks of self-organizing, frequently disconnecting, resource-constrained, highly mobile nodes.

Supporting User Mobility

Here we discuss how user mobility can be supported by extending distributed databases and publish/subscribe systems.

(Pitoura and Samaras, 2001) presents various approaches to the problem of storing, querying, and updating the location of nodes in mobile computing. Location management techniques use information concerning the location of moving nodes stored in location databases, in combination with search procedures that exploit knowledge about the nodes' previous moving behavior. Various enhancements include caching, replication, forwarding pointers, and partitioning. The databases for storing the location of mobile objects are distributed in nature and must support very high update rates since the location of objects changes as they move. The two most common architectures for distributed databases used for storing the location of moving users are a two-tier scheme, in which the current location of each moving user is saved at two network locations, and a tree-structured distributed database, in which space is hierarchically decomposed into sub-regions. Graphic-theoretic approaches that employ regional directories, as well as centralized database approaches have also been proposed.

(Burcea et al., 2004) discusses how a distributed publish/subscribe architecture can be extended to support mobility, i.e., moving users with intermittent network connectivity. Several factors affect the performance of such an architecture, such as the network (bandwidth and latency, placement of brokers, broker topology, number of brokers), the users (connection and disconnection times, mobility patterns), and the application (number of publishers and subscribers, publishing rate, specificity of subscriptions, subscriber locality, subscription (interest) locality, event (publication)

size). An analytical model for the network cost of supporting mobility is presented, as well as mobility algorithms and optimizations such as prefetching and logging. The analysis focuses on unicast traffic generated to support mobile users, as opposed to the regular multicast traffic used for event dissemination to stationary clients.

Epidemic Dissemination

Exploiting the mobility of the peers to improve data transfer throughput has led to utilizing epidemic data dissemination algorithms. We discuss three representative systems that employ epidemic data dissemination, 7DS, PDI, and PeopleNet.

Seven Degrees of Separation (7DS) (Papadopouli and Schulzrinne, 2001) is a system for data exchange between mobile or stationary peers, enabling data sharing, message relaying and network connection sharing. It tries to exploit the host mobility and the spatial locality of information and queries to provide efficient epidemic data dissemination. 7DS supports both peer-to-peer (cooperative) and server-to-client interactions. 7DS peers collaborate by data sharing, by forwarding messages, or by caching popular data objects. The performance analysis of 7DS showed that the density of the cooperative hosts, their mobility, and their transmission power have great impact on data dissemination.

Passive Distributed Indexing (PDI) (Lindemann and Waldhorst, 2004) is a distributed lookup service. PDI stores (key, value) pairs in index caches located at mobile peers. Index caches are filled by epidemic dissemination of popular index entries. By exploiting node mobility, PDI can resolve most queries without sending messages outside the radio coverage of the inquiring node. For keeping index caches coherent, PDI uses implicit invalidation (configurable timeouts), as well as explicit invalidation (lazy caching). Inconsistency in index caches due to weak connectivity or node failure is handled by value timeouts. Lazy invalidation caches reduce the fraction of stale index entries due to modified data at the origin node. Similar to index caches, invalidation caches are filled by epidemic distributions of invalidation messages.

PeopleNet (Motani et al., 2005) is a wireless virtual social network which mimics the way people seek information via social networking. This approach offers significant advantages for information that is location-, community- and time-specific. PeopleNet propagates queries of a given type to users in specific geographic locations, called bazaars. The bazaars are pre-determined geographic regions and each bazaar handles only queries of certain pre-determined types. For example, a sports related query is directed to a sports bazaar. Within each bazaar, the query is further propagated between neighboring nodes via peer-to-peer connectivity, until it finds a match. By comparing a swap and a spread model for query propagation within a bazaar, the authors of PeopleNet have shown that swapping leads to higher matches. The probability of matching is further improved if prior to swapping queries the peers exchange some limited information about their buffer contents. Based on this observation, PeopleNet uses a greedy algorithm which uses this limited information to decide which queries to swap.

Cooperative Caching

Several parameters can affect data availability when introducing replication in a mobile peer-to-peer network. (Budiarto et al., 2002) discusses replication dynamics, replication level, and replica placement. Replication can be static or dynamic, depending on whether the location and the number of replicas are decided before deployment or can change following the access patterns. Regarding the replication level, increasing the number of replicas decreases the cost of queries but increases the maintenance cost. Finally, several choices exist regarding the replica location, e.g., close to home, close to writer, or close to reader.

The comparison of different replication schemes examining the aforementioned trade-offs shows that the performance of a replication strategy depends heavily on many conditions, including network scale, mobility, access ratio and access concentration.

We now discuss replication among peers, i.e., cooperative caching, that allows the sharing and coordination of cached data among multiple peers. We divide cooperative caching approaches according to whether they target infrastructure-less or infrastructure-based environments. In the first case all peers are equal and communicate using an ad-hoc network, while in the second case an infrastructure of static stations that act as servers exists to enhance data delivery.

Infrastructure-Less Environments. (Goel et al., 2002) proposes a Street-and-Building mobility model that is suitable for a civilian environment, such as a college campus or a downtown business area. It then presents a protocol that enables efficient and reliable data dissemination in mobile ad-hoc networks by applying the technique of Tornado coding. In the protocol, supplying peers of a data file broadcast the Tornado-encoded file segments to requesting peers. A requesting peer downloads the encoded segments from different supplying peers, at different times and in different locations. When it receives sufficient segments, a peer is able to reconstruct the original file and also become a supplier. By using Tornado coding, the proposed protocol is more robust against packet losses, and highly efficient in data transmission, eliminating the need for multiple unicast downloading connections from multiple suppliers. The Street-and-Building mobility model is used to determine the Tornado coding parameters.

Proximity Regions for Caching in Cooperative MP2P Networks (PReCinCt) (Shen et al., 2005) is a cooperative caching scheme that aims to improve data accessibility in mobile environments. PReCinCt divides the network topology into geographical regions. Each region is responsible for a set of keys representing the data. Hashing is used to map keys to regions. To reach the region of a data object, queries are routed using a geographic-aided routing protocol such as GPSR (Karp and Kung, 2000). After reaching an object's region, localized flooding is used to locate the peer holding the requested object. PReCinCt cooperatively caches data among a set of peers in a region. Cache replacement is determined by considering the importance of a data object to the peer caching it, and also to other peers in the same region. A utility function is employed to evaluate the importance of each data object in a peer's cache. That function takes into account the popularity of an object in its region, the size of the object, and the region distance between the requesting and responding peers. PReCinCt also employs a hybrid push/pull mechanism to maintain data consistency among replicas in the network, and manages to reduce both access latency and energy consumption.

(Yin and Cao, 2004) compares cooperative caching techniques that can improve the query delay and message complexity of data accesses in mobile ad-hoc networks. Specifically, three techniques are compared, namely caching the actual data, caching the data path, and a hybrid approach that combines the two. Caching the data enables intermediate nodes to serve future requests, instead of fetching data from a data center. Caching the data path enables mobile nodes to use it to redirect future requests to the nearby node which has the data instead of the faraway data center. Finally, in the hybrid approach caching the data is preferred for small data sizes, while caching the data path is preferred for data that expire soon, or data that are many hops away.

(Sailhan and Issarny, 2003) focuses on Web data caching to minimize the energy cost of peer-to-peer communication. The environment in this case is a mobile ad-hoc network of peers that share their Web access. The cooperative caching protocol builds upon the Zone Routing Protocol (ZRP) (Haas, 1997). ZRP implements proactive routing with mobile nodes and reactive

routing with stationary nodes. The local cache replacement policy weighs for each cached data object its popularity, the energy cost to access it remotely, and its expiration time.

Infrastructure-Based Environments. In COoperative CAching (COCA) (Chow et al., 2004) data is replicated in low activity nodes so that the workload of high activity nodes can be reduced. The target environment includes mobile support stations that act as data servers, as well as mobile clients that can cooperatively cache data. Thus, when a client does not have a data object locally, it queries its neighboring client peers' caches, before enlisting the server for help. In COCA each mobile client and its neighboring peers residing in its transmission range work as a dynamic group that shares their cached data objects cooperatively. COCA is appropriate for an environment in which a group of mobile clients possesses a common access interest.

(Lim et al., 2004) discusses cache invalidation strategies for Internet-based mobile ad-hoc networks. In such networks, mobile nodes connect to the Internet directly through selected access points, or indirectly through message relay via other nodes. An enhanced scheme is proposed, called Global Positioning System-based Connectivity Estimation (GPSCE), for assessing the connectivity of a node to an access point. With this enhancement, a node can check whether it can access a server directly or indirectly through a multi-hop relay. Three cache invalidation schemes are compared, both push- and pull-based. The first one, called Aggregate Cache-based On Demand (ACOD), is based on a pull strategy; while the other two, namely modified timestamp (MTS) and MTS with updated invalidation report (MTS+UIR) are based on a push strategy. The comparison indicates that the pull-based ACOD strategy provides high throughput, low query latency, and low communication overhead.

(Hara, 2002) discusses caching of data items in push-based information systems. In these systems a server repeatedly broadcasts data to clients through a broadband channel. Clients in such a system can construct and ad-hoc network to cache such data. Three cooperative caching strategies are discussed. These strategies shorten the average response time for data access by replacing cached items based on their access frequencies, the network topology, and the time remaining until each item is broadcasted next. Each of the three strategies differs in the set of nodes for which the average response time is minimized. In the case of a local optimal strategy, the set consists of only a single mobile node. In the case of a global optimal strategy, the set includes all connected mobile nodes. Finally, in a stable group optimal strategy, the set is a stable group of bi-connected mobile nodes.

MOBILE PEER-TO-PEER DATA DISSEMINATION AND QUERY ROUTING

When disseminating data in a mobile peer-to-peer network, the primary goal is to reach users with the same interests while keeping the number of propagated messages small. To achieve this goal we propose adaptively disseminating content sum-

maries that are used to guide queries for data. As users move, their devices may keep establishing several short-lived connections to other peers along the way and thus become bombarded by unnecessary event notifications or advertisements about locally available services, data, and events. Even if a user is not highly mobile, the amount of forwarded queries from other mobile devices can be overwhelming, especially for devices with lower processing and communication capabilities. Guiding queries using the content summaries enables nodes to avoid this problem, by contacting only those peers that have a high probability of providing the desired results. Figure 1 illustrates our system's operation. In a mobile environment, changes to the stored data happen more often than they can be communicated to a single peer. We propose data dissemination algorithms that adaptively decide to which peers to propagate the content synopses to improve data discovery and make more efficient use of the bandwidth and processing power resources.

Overlay Model

We consider an overlay network of N nodes (peers) that store objects. We use the term "object" to

Figure 1. System operation example: Each node maintains a local content synopsis, as well as content synopses of remote peers. In this example, peer C propagated its content synopsis CS to peer B. B based on CS was able to route peer A's query Q only to C, and the result QH is routed back to A..

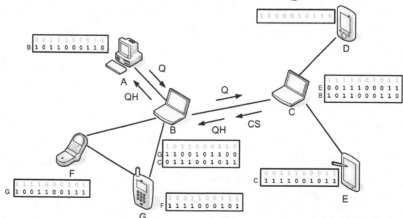

Figure 2(i). Counting Bloom filter: The counters keep track of the number of objects that are hashed in the same position

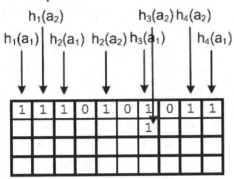

Figure 2(ii). Multi-level Bloom filter: The filter of each level is appended to that of the previous level

refer to data, services or events. Each peer has a globally unique identifier (e.g., randomly generated using SHA-1) and maintains connections with other peers. The network is unstructured, decentralized and self-organizing, meaning that peers make their own decisions as to which peers to connect to or to query for objects. The number of connections of a peer can vary and is typically restricted by the resource capabilities of the peer. Peers that are not directly connected communicate through relaying. In other words, peers not only exchange messages with their neighbors, but also route messages coming from other peers. Each object is uniquely identified by the means of intrinsic references (Eshghi, 2002) which are generated when the object is first inserted in the system. Intrinsic references are based on the hash digest of the object's actual contents rather than its name or location and therefore allow us to create persistent, state-independent, and immutable storage. Alternatively, each object can be associated with a set of keywords to allow meta-data types of searching. The mechanisms presented in this work are orthogonal to the type of search and therefore we just focus on searching by an object's intrinsic reference.

Content Synopses

Each peer uses the *Bloom filter* data structure (Bloom, 1970) to build a synopsis of its local content which is disseminated to other peers. Assume that peer p has a group of n objects given by the set $S_p = a_1, a_2, ..., a_n$. The Bloom filter that represents the set S_p is described by a bit array BF_p of length m, with all bits initially set to 0. We assume k hash functions, $h_1, h_2, ..., h_k$ with $h_i : X \rightarrow 1...m$. Each hash function maps each element of the set S to a value between 1...m in a totally random fashion. For each element $s \in S$, the bits at position $h_1(s), h_2(s), ..., h_k(s)$ are set to 1. To determine whether a certain element x is in S, we check whether all the bits given by $h_1(x), h_2(x), ..., h_k(x)$ are set to 1. If any of them is 0, then we are certain that the data item x is not in the set S. If all $h_1(x), h_2(x), ..., h_k(x)$ are set to 1, we conclude that x is in S, although there is a certain probability that we are wrong. This is the case that a Bloom filter may yield a *false positive*. There exists a trade-off between k, m, n, and the accuracy of the objects' representation using Bloom filters (Repantis, 2005). This trade-off is investigated experimentally in the *Experimental Study* section. Our system exploits the probability that a small number of false positives do not greatly affect the performance of our searching mechanism. This fact makes the Bloom filter approach highly suitable for locating objects accurately and fast.

To support the removal of members from the sets represented by the Bloom filters we use counting Bloom filters (Fan et al., 1998). In this approach, a counter is added to each bit in the filter, so that the number of objects that are hashed in the same position is counted. Removing members causes the corresponding counters to be decremented and therefore the representation accuracy is not affected. An example of a counting Bloom filter is shown in Figure 2 (i). Each peer stores two types of filters, a *local filter* for the objects available locally at the node and *remote filters* for objects stored in remote peers, indexed by their IDs. Hence, to store multiple content synopses, we use multi-level Bloom filters. Figure 2 (ii) shows an example of a multi-level Bloom filter. Notice that the Bloom filter of each level is not merged but appended to that of the previous level. That approach consumes more memory space to store the Bloom filters, but allows us to estimate the location of a larger number of objects more accurately.

Content-Driven Routing

Using content-driven query routing each peer stores the content synopses of other peers, and utilizes that information in order to route queries more efficiently. In particular, when a peer receives a query, apart from searching its local content, it also searches the stored content synopses of other peers. If there is no match in the peer's local content, the query is forwarded only to the immediate peers whose synopses indicate that they or their neighbors contain the requested object. Only if the object is not found in any content synopsis, is the query forwarded to a set of random neighbors. To provide a termination condition so that messages are not propagated indefinitely in the network when no objects are found, each message is associated with a time to live (TTL) field that represents the maximum number of times the message can be propagated in the network. Additionally, if a node receives the same message from two different peers, it detects the duplicates and discards the second message.

Adaptive Data Dissemination Strategies

We have implemented and compared three different strategies for content synopses dissemination, illustrated in Figure 3:

Figure 3. The content synopses dissemination strategies IL, AL, and ALR: In IL, node C propagates only its local synopsis to all peers one hop away. In AL, C propagates its local synopsis to selected immediate and remote peers. In ALR, C propagates both its local and stored remote synopses to selected immediate and remote peers.

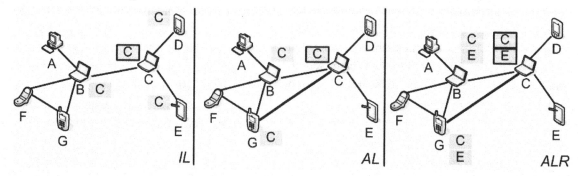

Disseminate local content synopsis to immediate peers (Immediate Local – IL). According to IL each peer sends its local content synopsis to all its immediate peers and routes queries by taking into account only the content synopses of its immediate peers. IL is simple, but of limited use: Since only a small number of content synopses is examined for the routing decision to be taken, a lot of the queries cannot be directed using the content synopses. The protocol then resorts to randomly choosing peers to further forward the query and thus generates a lot of traffic.

Disseminate local content synopsis to peers selected adaptively (Adaptive Local – AL). Using AL each peer sends its local content synopsis to a selection of peers, according to several parameters. Again the routing is done following the synopses of the local content of other peers. The recipients of the content synopsis of a peer are selected not only among its immediate neighbors, but also among remote peers whose queries have been answered successfully from local content in the past. The adaptive selection of the synopses recipients aims to make the content synopses available to the peers that have a high probability of using them again in the future and yet keep the number of synopses transfers limited. The parameters used to decide to which peers to disseminate the content synopses are described in a following section. As the number of content synopses used in routing is limited, AL is also often obliged to resort to randomly forwarding queries.

Disseminate both local and remote content synopses to peers selected adaptively (Adaptive Local Remote – ALR). ALR differs from the previous, in that the peers disseminate and use for their routing decisions not only the synopses of the local content of their immediate peers or peers they have interacted with, but also synopses of the content of remote peers. More specifically when a peer propagates its local content synopsis to other peers, it also propagates the content synopses of remote peers it has stored. Other peers store those remote content synopses together with the local synopsis of that peer and use them to route queries to it. Since each peer stores and disseminates remote content synopses of peers it is connected to, it can easily route queries for content stored in them. ALR enables the peers to examine a lot of content synopses before routing a query. Therefore a lot of the queries can be routed accurately and randomly forwarding queries is not used that often. The processing time spent in examining the content synopses is still small. The amount of information transferred between the nodes in order to disseminate the remote and the local synopses is higher than in the previous strategies, but is still restricted through the use of adaptive selection of the synopses recipients. The parameters used to decide to which peers to disseminate the content synopses are described in the next section.

Content synopses do not necessarily have to be propagated as individual messages, but can rather be piggybacked on the current usage messages (e.g. queries and replies). All of the aforementioned strategies are assuming a simple network infrastructure, where peers route queries through their immediate neighbors. In AL and ALR a more advanced overlay network is built, where peers can open direct connections to peers that provide them with good results (share similar interests with them) and routing can also be based on content synopses of peers outside a node's current horizon. Exploiting interest locality however comes at the cost of managing many –possibly short-lived– connections. Allowing "transient" content synopses to traverse the network would be the physical continuation of this approach. Yet, even though the cost of propagating a synopsis may not be too high, in a large-scale system the cost of maintaining up-to-date information throughout the path that a transient content synopsis travels, about where it came from and about how to reach its source would be prohibitive. This would be even more the case for dynamic environments, with frequent topology changes or content updates.

Adaptive Synopses Dissemination Parameters

Each node in the system is associated with a list of characteristics, which are summarized in Table 2. In order to decide which peers would benefit most from obtaining the content synopses, AL and ALR take into account the following parameters:

- The number of queries qi that a node has received by a peer, and their frequency. Peers that have sent a lot of queries to us will most probably make good use of our content synopsis in their routing decisions. A lot of forwarded queries indicate peers that route a lot of traffic. They can use our content synopsis to avoid sending us queries for content we do not have.

- The number of replies ri that a node has provided a peer with, and their frequency. This parameter identifies the popularity of our stored objects among specific peers. Peers that generated a lot of local hits and got a lot of replies by us to their requests will also most probably need our content synopsis in their routing decisions.

- The number of connections conni that other peers maintain. This parameter identifies the connectivity degree of a peer and is a factor in estimating the average number of messages per time unit this peer may route. A peer that plays the role of a hub in the network, routing many queries, will most probably need the content synopses more.

Dynamic Peer Behavior

Since the network is dynamic and self-organizing, nodes may leave or join independently. The system must be able to disseminate content synopses to reflect such changes in the connections. Moreover content synopses must be updated whenever an object is added, deleted, or its contents have changed. When the content is updated, a new content synopsis is disseminated by the peer. To minimize the traffic in the network our approach does not generate an update unless the contents of the peers have changed and groups individual Bloom filter updates into group updates to propagate them to the peers. Content synopses are disseminated due to both local and remote content changes.

As nodes in a mobile peer-to-peer network move, the peers in their vicinity change. Therefore old connections are dropped and new ones are established. We distinguish between two different modes in a peer's operation: i) When a peer is *static*, its position does hardly change and neither do the connections with its neighbors; ii) When a peer is *dynamic*, it moves frequently and its neighbors and the connections with them change constantly. A peer can alternate between static and dynamic mode. A peer is considered static by its neighbors, when it has been connected with them

Table 2. Parameters of each peer i in the system

peer_id$_i$	The peer's globally unique identifier.
connected_peers$_i$	The list of peers currently connected to this peer.
object_list$_i$	The list of objects stored locally at the peer.
queries_received$_i$	The total number of queries this peer has processed.
searh_msgs_received$_i$	The number of search messages this peer has received, indexed by the IDs of the query originators.
local_hits$_i$	The number of local hits generated by queries, indexed by the IDs of the query originators.
sent_contentSynopsis_to$_i$	The list of peers that have received a current version of the local content synopsis.

for longer than a time threshold ts. To efficiently disseminate content synopses we push them to static peers, but let dynamic peers only pull them when needed. When a dynamic peer needs to search for something or route a query, it first asks for the content synopses of its current neighbors. On the other hand, a static peer's vicinity does not change often and by pushing synopses we avoid the overhead of explicitly asking for them. The same rules apply to a newcomer's decision to disseminate its own content synopsis.

When a peer permanently disconnects from the network, neither the content synopses of other peers stored in it, nor its content synopsis stored in other peers will be useful anymore. Its immediate peers sense the dropped connection and all the relevant content synopses are removed after a time threshold tr. In addition, a DISCONNECTED message is sent to the non-immediate peers to remove their corresponding content synopses.

EXPERIMENTAL STUDY

We continue by presenting an extensive experimental evaluation of the presented mechanisms in large-scale, mobile, peer-to-peer networks. We used the Neurogrid simulator (Joseph, 2003) with the Gnutella (Kirk, 2003) P2P communication protocol. Our implementation of content-driven routing and adaptive data dissemination was done in approximately 3500 lines of Java code. The parameters used in the simulation are presented in Table 3. We chose the network size to vary up to 3000 nodes, an estimate of the number of concurrently active nodes in a university campus. In our implementation we used counting, multi-level Bloom filters. To create the hash functions used in generating the Bloom filters, similarly to (The XLattice Project, 2005), we took advantage of a cryptographic message digest algorithm (SHA-1) and of its property of pseudo randomness. More specifically, we used SHA-1 to hash strings of arbitrary length, representing the peers' content, to 160 bits. We then built the hash functions by dividing the SHA-1 output into smaller sets of bits.

In our *first* set of experiments, we investigated the tradeoff in the representation of objects through Bloom filters. Three parameters may affect the accuracy of the representation, i.e. the

Table 3. Simulation settings

Node Parameters	Number of nodes	Varying
Network Parameters	TimeToLive of query messages	7
	Initial number of connections per node	3
	Minimum number of connections per node	3
	Maximum number of connections per node	10
	Network topology	Random
Content Parameters	Size of pool of available objects	2000
	Number of objects per node	30
	Distribution of objects over nodes	Uniform
Bloom Filter Parameters	Size of filter, in bits	10
	Number of hash functions	4
	Size of counter for each position, in bits	4
Simulation Parameter	Number of averaged measurements	20
	Number of searches per experiment run	400
	Number of search targets	100

Figure 4. Bloom filter false positives for varying size of the filter (in bits)

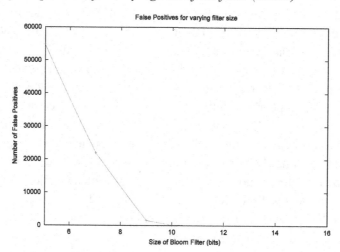

Figure 5. Bloom filter false positives for varying number of hash functions

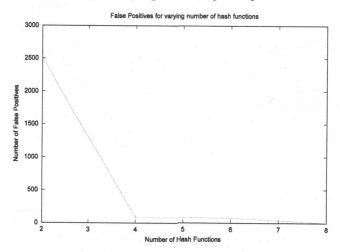

number of false positives yielded: The size of the Bloom filter in bits (memory overhead), the number of hash functions used (computation overhead), and the number of represented objects. We used counting Bloom filters with 4-bit counters, the simplest content-driven routing algorithm (IL), 4000 possible objects, and 1000 nodes and focused on the number of false positives.

Effect of filter size to the number of false positives. As Figure 4 shows, filter size can greatly affect the number of false positives. Small filter

sizes can result to thousands of false positives. However, false positives are virtually eliminated above 10 bits (when representing 30 objects per filter and using 4 hash functions).

Effect of number of hash functions to the number of false positives. As Figure 5 shows, the number of false positives greatly decreases when using 4 hash functions or more (when representing 30 objects per filter and using 10 bits for the filter size).

Effect of number of represented objects to the number of false positives. Figure 6 shows that when using 4 hash functions and Bloom filters of 10 bits size, not more than 30 objects can be represented by a filter without significant loss in accuracy.

Taking into account the aforementioned results, we decided to use Bloom filters 10 bits long, 4 hash functions, and 30 objects per node (chosen out of 2000 unique objects) for the rest of the experiments that use content synopses.

In our *second* set of experiments we compared content-driven query routing to a traditional Breadth-First Search (BFS) algorithm.

Average message transfers during a search. Figure 7 shows that content-driven routing drastically decreases the number of query messages transferred during a search. As the number of nodes increases, the number of message transfers grows dramatically in flooding-based BFS, while the content-driven routing mechanisms manage to keep the message transfers almost at a fixed level. Thus, by using the network bandwidth efficiently, content-driven routing is able to scale to thousands of nodes. ALR, by disseminating content synopses of both local and remote peers

Figure 6. Bloom filter false positives for varying number of represented objects per node

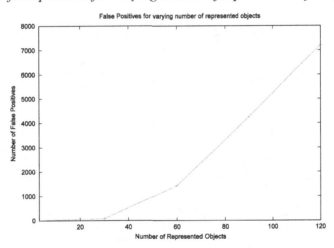

Figure 7. Average number of query messages sent during a search for different network sizes.

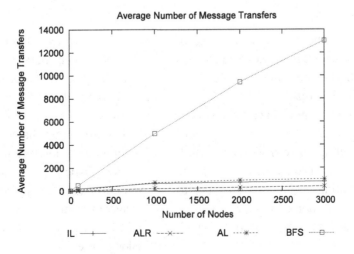

Figure 8. Average number of nodes reached during a search for different network sizes

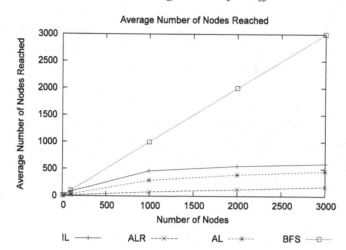

Figure 9. Average proportion of possible matches discovered over the number of queries transferred

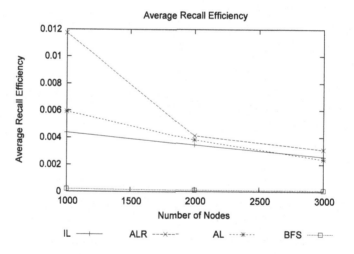

adaptively, achieves the minimum number of message transfers needed to answer a query. It is noteworthy that the decrease in query messages between ALR and BFS reaches 97%.

Average number of nodes reached during a search. Figure 8 again shows the benefits of content-driven routing in terms of bandwidth and processing power usage efficiency. All the content-driven routing techniques are able to provide query hits by contacting more than one order of magnitude less peers than BFS, which

contacts a lot of peers unnecessarily. Moreover the content-driven routing strategies keep the number of reached nodes at an almost constant level, while the nodes that are reached with BFS grow linearly as the total number of nodes increases. The figure shows that the adaptive AL and ALR techniques guide queries more efficiently than the simplistic IL, in which content synopses are disseminated blindly to all immediate peers. ALR is again the most efficient and scalable technique of all, due to the adaptive use of the multi-level Bloom filters.

Average Recall Efficiency during a search.
Figure 9 shows the value of the query messages that are disseminated during a search, in terms of their contribution to the discovery of possible matches. Even though BFS is able to discover a lot of matches, it does so by flooding, which results to its low recall efficiency. ALR again has the highest recall efficiency, followed by the other adaptive content-driven routing strategy, AL. The reason is that adaptive content synopses dissemination places the Bloom filters where they are more likely to be needed, achieving better performance than

the blind IL. As the number of nodes grows, the proportion of the total matches discovered by the content-driven routing mechanisms decreases, since the queries are guided, in order to contact a small number of nodes and to produce a small number of messages.

In our *third* set of experiments we compared the different content-driven routing protocols to each other in more detail.

Content synopses hits over misses. Figure 10 shows how much the query routing actually benefits from the use of the content synopses. We

Figure 10. Ratio of hits over misses of the content synopses for different network sizes

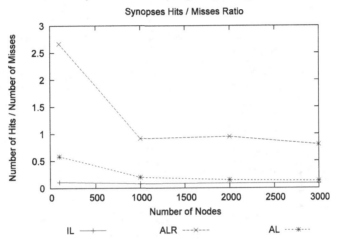

Figure 11. Ratio of Bloom filter false positives over total positives for different network sizes

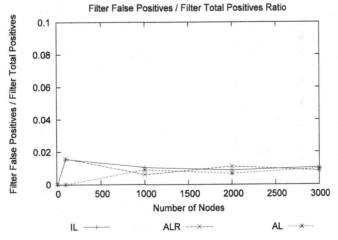

notice that simply placing content synopses of local content to immediate neighbors (IL) is useful for routing only about 10% of the queries. On the other hand, adaptively placing content synopses (AL and ALR) improves their usefulness to 20% for AL and to 90% for ALR. By disseminating local and remote content synopses, ALR manages to drastically decrease the number of Bloom filter misses and achieves a hit/miss ratio close to 1, meaning that half of the queries can be routed based on the content synopses.

False positives over total positives. Figure 11 shows that content-driven routing is extremely accurate. For all three routing strategies that use

content synopses only a very small percentage (around 1%) of the total queries that are routed based on them is falsely routed, due to Bloom filter false positives. Thus, our choice of the Bloom filter parameters allowed us to minimize the false positives.

Total content synopses messages. Figure 12 shows the relative cost of the different content-driven routing protocols, in terms of content synopses dissemination messages. By simply disseminating content synopses only to immediate peers, IL keeps the protocol overhead low. However the usefulness of the content synopses in that approach is limited, as Figure 10 indicates.

Figure 12. Total content synopses dissemination messages transferred for different network sizes.

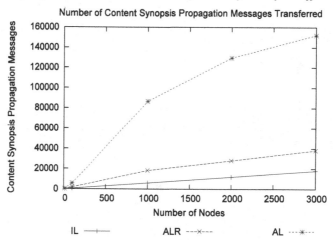

Figure 13. Total number of query messages transferred for varying network size.

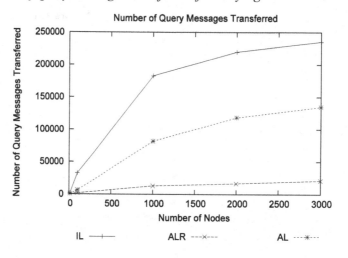

Figure 14. Bloom filter false positives over total positives for different percentages of disconnected nodes

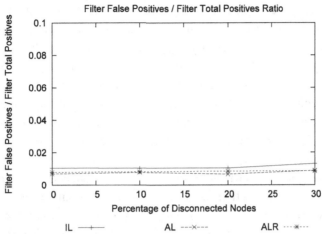

Figure 15. Content synopses hits over misses for different percentages of disconnected nodes.

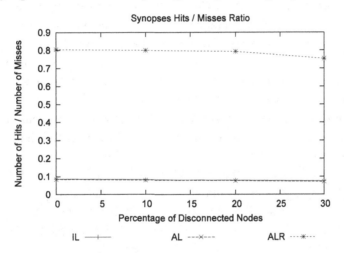

AL on the other hand has to disseminate a lot of content synopses for them to be useful in query routing. ALR, by adaptively disseminating local and remote content synopses, manages to route queries effectively and yet keep the protocol overhead at a reasonable level, even as the number of nodes increases. That overhead is acceptable, if one takes into account the drastic saving of query messages ALR achieves.

Total query messages. Figure 13 shows the query messages transferred in the overlay, regardless of the underlying physical network. The

adaptive strategies achieve significant savings in query messages. Especially ALR, by guiding queries through the use of local and remote content synopses, manages to keep the number of query messages low and easily scale to thousands of nodes. Bandwidth is thus used more efficiently in ALR than in any other of the content-driven routing protocols. ALR reduces the number of query messages by utilizing a lot of content synopses and placing them intelligently in the network. Notably, ALR decreases the number of query messages transferred by half an order of magnitude compared to AL and by one order of magnitude compared to IL.

In our **fourth** set of experiments we evaluated our protocols in a mobile environment, where peers leave the network dynamically. We gradually disconnected peers throughout the experiment run and we conducted experiments for disconnections reaching to 10, 20, and 30% of the total number of peers, which was initially 3000. We report the effects of the disconnections on the Bloom Filter behavior.

False positives over total positives. Figure 14 shows that content-driven routing remains very accurate even when a lot of peers disconnect. The neighbors of a leaving peer realize the disconnection and update their summaries, while peers further away also update their synopses when they are notified by a DISCONNECTED message they receive from the immediate peers. Hence false positives are not increased by the peer disconnections.

Content synopses hits over misses. Figure 15 shows that peer disconnections do not affect the success of the synopses in query routing either. ALR, which is the most aggressive mechanism in synopses dissemination, often routes queries successfully using the summaries. When a lot of peers disconnect, less synopses are available to help in query routing, hence a small degradation in the hit ratio.

CONCLUSIONS AND FUTURE TRENDS

In this chapter we have discussed data dissemination and query routing for mobile peer-to-peer networks. We have provided a comprehensive study of existing literature in the area, spanning overlay topologies, query routing, and data propagation. We have proceeded by presenting adaptive content-driven routing and data dissemination mechanisms. Based on content synopses, nodes forward queries intelligently only to their

peers that are able to provide replies with a high probability. By disseminating the content synopses adaptively, we have shown how they can be strategically placed where they are most probably going to be needed.

User mobility and peer-to-peer interaction introduce several challenges with regards to data dissemination and query routing. Important questions that do not have a clear answer as of yet include:

- Can peer-to-peer applications be directly used in mobile settings?
- How does network scale affect query routing and data discovery?
- How structured should an overlay topology be?
- What are realistic user mobility models to evaluate overlay topologies under?
- How can peer-to-peer incentive, security, trust, and reputation techniques be applied to mobile environments?

Data dissemination and query routing in mobile peer-to-peer networks give rise to a multitude of exciting opportunities. Existing infrastructure-based mobile applications such as content delivery and media streaming can be augmented by peer-to-peer interaction. Furthermore, novel purely peer-to-peer platforms may emerge, such as rooftop or vehicular networks, introducing new use cases. These would come to complement related research in sensor and ad-hoc networking.

REFERENCES

Amir, A., Efrat, A., Myllymaki, J., Palaniappan, L., & Wampler, K. (2004). Buddy tracking – efficient proximity detection among mobile friends. In *Proceedings of IEEE Conference on Computer Communications (INFOCOM)*.

Bloom, B. H. (1970). Space/time trade-offs in hash coding with allowable errors. *Communications of the ACM, 13*(7), 422–426.

Broustis, I., Jakllari, G., Repantis, T., & Molle, M. (2006). A comprehensive comparison of routing protocols for large-scale wireless MANETs. In *Proceedings of the 3rd International Workshop on Wireless Ad Hoc and Sensor Networks.*

Brown, A., Buford, J., & Kolberg, M. (2007). Tork: A variable-hop overlay for heterogeneous networks. In *Proceedings of the 4th IEEE International Workshop on Mobile Peer-to-Peer Computing (MP2P).*

Budiarto, Nishio, S., & Tsukamoto, M. (2002). Data management issues in mobile and peer-to-peer environments. *Elsevier Data and Knowledge Engineering, 41*(2-3), 183–204.

Burcea, I., Jacobsen, H., Lara, E., Muthusamy, V., & Petrovic, M. (2004). Disconnected operation in publish/subscribe middleware. In *Proceedings of the IEEE International Conference on Mobile Data Management.*

Caesar, M., Castro, M., Nightingale, E., O'Shea, G., & Rowstron, A. (2006). Virtual ring routing: Network routing inspired by DHTs. In *Proceedings of the ACM SIGCOMM Conference on Applications, Technologies, Architectures, and Protocols for Computer Communications.*

Cao, H.,Wolfson, O., Xu, B., & Yin, H. (2005). MOBI-DIC: MOBIle DIscovery of loCal resources in peer-to-peer wireless network. *Bulletin of the IEEE Computer Society Technical Committee on Data Engineering, 28*(3), 11–18.

Chow, C., Leong, H., & Chan, A. (2004). Peer-to-peer cooperative caching in mobile environments. In *Proceedings of the 24th International Conference on Distributed Computing Systems Workshops (ICDCSW).*

Eshghi, K. (2002). *Intrinsic references in distributed systems* (Tech. Rep. HPL-2002-32). HP Labs.

Fan, L., Cao, P., Almeida, J., & Broder, A. (2000). Summary cache: A scalable wide-area web cache sharing protocol. *IEEE/ACM Transactions on Networking, 8*(3), 281-293.

Gerla, M., Lindemann, C., & Rowstron, A. (2005). P2P MANETs - new research issues. In *Proceedings of the Perspectives Workshop: Peer-to-Peer Mobile Ad Hoc Networks - New Research Issues.*

Goel, S., Singh,M., Xu, D., & Li, B. (2002). Efficient peer-to-peer data dissemination in mobile ad-hoc networks. In *Proceedings of the International Conference on Parallel Processing Workshops.*

Haas, J. (1997). A new routing protocol for the reconfigurable wireless networks. In *Proceedings of the 6th IEEE International Conference on Universal Personal Communications.*

Hara, T. (2002). Cooperative caching by mobile clients in push-based information systems. In *Proceedings of the 11th International Conference on Information and Knowledge Management.*

Hu, Y., Das, S., & Pucha, H. (2004). Peer-to-peer overlay abstractions in MANETs. In J. Wu (Ed.), *Theoretical and algorithmic aspects of sensor, ad hoc wireless and peer-to-peer networks.* CRC Press.

Johnson, D., Maltz, D., & Broch, J. (2001). DSR: The dynamic source routing protocol for multi-hop wireless ad hoc networks. In C. E. Perkins (Ed.), *Ad hoc networking.* Addison-Wesley.

Joseph, S. (2003). An extendible open source P2P simulator. *P2P Journal,* 1–15.

Karp, B. & Kung, H. (2000). Greedy perimeter stateless routing for wireless networks. In *Proceedings of the 6th ACM/IEEE International Conference on Mobile Computing and Networking (MobiCom).*

Kirk, P. (2003). Gnutella - A protocol for a revolution. Retrieved October 7, 2008, from http://rfc-gnutella.sourceforge.net/

Kortuem, G., Schneider, J., Preuitt, D., Thompson, T., Fickas, S., & Segall, Z. (2001). When peer-to-peer comes face-to-face: Collaborative peer-to-peer computing in mobile ad-hoc networks. In *Proceedings of the International Conference on Peer-to-Peer Computing.*

Lim, S., Lee, W., Cao, G., & Das, C. (2004). Performance comparison of cache invalidation strategies for Internet-based mobile ad hoc networks. In *Proceedings of the 1ˢᵗ IEEE International Conference on Mobile Ad-hoc and Sensor Systems (MASS).*

Lindemann, C. & Waldhorst, O. P. (2004). Exploiting epidemic data dissemination for consistent lookup operations in mobile applications. *ACM Mobile Computing and Communications Review, 8*(2), 44–56.

Lundquist, D. & Ouksel, A. (2007). An efficient demand-driven and density-controlled publish/subscribe protocol for mobile environments. In *Proceedings of the International Conference on Distributed Event-Based Systems.*

Motani, M., Srinivasan, V., & Nuggehalli, P. (2005). PeopleNet: Engineering a wireless virtual social network. In *Proceedings of the ACM International Conference on Mobile Computing and Networking (MobiCom).*

Oliveira, L., Siqueira, I., & Loureiro, A. (2003). Evaluation of ad-hoc routing protocols under a peer-to-peer application. In *Proceedings of the IEEE Wireless Communications and Networking Conference (WCNC).*

Ouksel, A. (2006). Self-balancing selective information dissemination and discovery in mobile environments. In *Proceedings of the 22ⁿᵈ IEEE International Conference on Data Engineering (ICDE).*

Papadopouli, M. & Schulzrinne, H. (2001). Effects of power conservation, wireless coverage and cooperation on data dissemination among mobile devices. In *Proceedings of the 2ⁿᵈ ACM International Symposium on Mobile Ad Hoc Networking and Computing (MobiHoc).*

Patil, A., Liu, Y., Xiao, L., Esfahanian, A., & Ni, L. (2004). SOLONet: Sub-optimal location-aided overlay network for MANETs. In *Proceedings of the 1ˢᵗ IEEE International Conference on Mobile Ad-hoc and Sensor Systems (MASS).*

Perkins, C. (1999). Ad hoc on-demand distance vector routing. In *Proceedings of the 2ⁿᵈ IEEE Workshop on Mobile Computing Systems and Applications.*

Perkins, C. & Bhagwat, B. (1994). Highly dynamic destination-sequenced distance-vector routing (DSDV) for mobile computers. *ACM SIGCOMM Computer Communication Review, 24*(4), 234-244.

Pitoura, E. & Samaras, G. (2001). Locating objects in mobile computing. *IEEE Transactions on Knowledge and Data Engineering, 13*(4):571–592.

Ratnasamy, S., Karp, B., Yin, L., Yu, F., Estrin, D., Govindan, R., & Shenker, S. (2002). GHT: A geographic hash table for data-centric storage. In *Proceedings of the 1ˢᵗ ACM International Workshop on Wireless Sensor Networks and Applications (WSNA).*

Repantis, T. (2005). *Adaptive data dissemination and content-driven routing in peer-to-peer systems.* Unpublished master's thesis, University of California, Riverside, USA.

Repantis, T. & Kalogeraki, V. (2005). Data dissemination in mobile peer-to-peer networks. In *Proceedings of the 6ᵗʰ IEEE International Conference on Mobile Data Management (MDM).*

Sailhan, F. & Issarny, V. (2003). Cooperative caching in ad hoc networks. In *Proceedings of* the *4ᵗʰ International Conference on Mobile Data Management (MDM)*.

Seet, B., Lau, C., & Hsu, W. (2007). P2P models and complexity in MANETs. In D. Taniar (Ed.), *Encyclopedia of mobile computing and commerce*. Hershey, PA: Information Science Reference.

Shen, H., Joseph, M., Kumar, M., & Das, S. (2005). PReCinCt: A scheme for cooperative caching in mobile peer-to-peer systems. In *Proceedings of the 19ᵗʰ International Parallel and Distributed Computing Symposium (IPDPS)*.

The XLattice Project (2005). *XLattice*. Retrieved October 7, 2008, from http://xlattice.sourceforge. net/.

Wolfson, O., Xu, B., Yin, H., & Cao, H. (2006). Search-and-discover in mobile p2p network databases. In *Proceedings of the 26ᵗʰ IEEE International Conference on Distributed Computing Systems (ICDCS)*.

Xu, B., Ouksel, A., & Wolfson, O. (2004). Opportunistic resource exchange in inter-vehicle ad hoc networks. In *Proceedings of the IEEE International Conference on Mobile Data Management (MDM)*.

Xue, G., Li, M., Deng, Q., & You, J. (2004). Stable group model in mobile peer-to-peer media streaming system. In *Proceedings of the 1ˢᵗ IEEE International Conference on Mobile Ad-hoc and Sensor Systems (MASS)*.

Yin, L. &Cao, G. (2004). Supporting cooperative caching in ad hoc networks. In *Proceedings of IEEE International Conference on Computer Communications (INFOCOM)*.

Zeinalipour-Yazti, D., Kalogeraki, V., & Gunopulos, D. (2004). Information retrieval in peer-to-peer systems. *IEEE CiSE Magazine, Special Issue on Web Engineering*, 12–20.

Section II
Overlay and Mobility Management

Chapter III
Overlay Construction in Mobile Peer-to-Peer Networks

Jie Feng
University of Nebraska-Lincoln, USA

Lisong Xu
University of Nebraska-Lincoln, USA

Byrav Ramamurthy
University of Nebraska-Lincoln, USA

ABSTRACT

With the evolution of wireless technologies, mobile networks can provide much more interesting services and resources to users than before. Consequently storing, sharing and delivering resources efficiently have become popular topics in the field of mobile networks. Mobile Peer-to-Peer (the authors use mobile P2P for short hereinafter) networks, which are inspired by the great success of P2P networks, have been proposed to efficiently share the network resources among the peers in mobile networks. However, due to the characteristics of mobile networks and stringent constraints of applications, it is fairly difficult to construct mobile P2P networks. In this chapter, the authors present a survey of overlay construction in mobile P2P networks. First, they outline the design issues of running P2P networks on top of mobile networks. The authors then present a survey of existing overlay construction techniques for mobile P2P networks. They highlight the advantages and disadvantages of various overlay construction techniques for mobile P2P networks and further compare these methods. They also point out the open research issues in each sub-area and conclude with possible future research directions in mobile P2P overlay construction.

INTRODUCTION

With the evolution of mobile technology, we have witnessed a great improvement in the communication ability, computing power and memory size of mobile devices. Mobile networks thus can provide much more interesting services and resources to users than before. Consequently storing, sharing and delivering resources efficiently have become popular topics in the field of mobile networks. The great success of P2P (Peer-to-Peer) networks has inspired academic and industrial researchers to propose mobile P2P networks to efficiently share network resources. However, due to the unique features of mobile networks, it is difficult to construct a P2P network over mobile networks. In this chapter, we discuss the design issues and approaches for constructing overlays in mobile P2P networks.

P2P Networks

P2P networks are widely deployed in existing non-mobile networks, such as LAN, WAN, and the Internet. Peers that join the network are organized into a logical topology, which is generally called an overlay network. Such an organization facilitates the data or information exchange among peers. In general, the construction and maintenance of a logical topology do not require any underlying topology information, though some researchers have proposed location-aware overlay construction (Liu *et al.*, 2005) with the consideration of physical topology.

P2P networks can be considered as scalable and distributed application layer multicasts (Chu *et al.*, 2002). However, P2P networks are different from the traditional application-layer multicast. Peers in P2P networks act as servers as well as clients, and therefore there is no peer that only plays the role of a router in the multicast. Consequently, P2P networks are highly distributed and self-organized (Padmanabhan, *et al.*, 2003).

There are two main categories of P2P networks according to their major applications: (1) P2P File Sharing Networks, such as Gnutella (Klingberg & Manfredi, 2002) and BitTorrent (BitTorrent, 2001); (2) P2P Streaming Networks, such as CoolStreaming (Zhang *et al.*, 2005), PPLive (PPlive Inc., 2005) and PPStream (PPSteam, 2005). The key difference between these two kinds of networks is that data carried over streaming networks are time-sensitive, where every packet or block requested by the neighbors must meet the playback deadline, while in file sharing systems, there is no such time constraint. Deploying P2P streaming systems over mobile networks is more challenging than constructing mobile P2P file sharing networks, due to the low connectivity, low bandwidth and high peer mobility of mobile networks and the tight time constraints of streaming applications.

As discussed before, a P2P network constructs and maintains an overlay network, which is the basis for data delivery among peers. There are various overlay structures to support file sharing and streaming applications (Magharei *et al.*, 2007; Castro *et al.*, 2003), and all of them have two main procedures: overlay construction and overlay maintenance.

1. The overlay construction procedure consists of two parts:
   o *peer discovery,* which means finding peers who are already in the overlay as a set of potential neighbors, called *S*;
   o *peer selection,* which considers how to select neighbors from the set *S*.
2. The overlay maintenance procedure includes:
   o *peer replacement,* which replaces neighbors providing poor service (i.e. low bandwidth, high end-to-end delay and etc.) with high quality peers;
   o *overlay maintenance and recovery,* which deals with peer joining/leaving and peer failure.

In summary, P2P networks are efficient overlay structures to facilitate data sharing among peers, and they have been widely used in non-mobile networks. A comprehensive survey of P2P overlay networks can be found in (Lua *et al.*, 2004).

Mobile Networks

Mobile networks are often accompanied by wireless technologies, with which mobile users can communicate with each other via wireless channels. Consequently, mobile networks are designed to provide ubiquitous connectivity for mobile devices, such as PDAs, cell phones and laptops etc. However, because mobile networks are heterogeneous with different features, ubiquitous connectivity has yet to be achieved.

Generally, mobile networks can be classified into three categories (Chakrabarti *et al.*, 2005) based on their signal coverage range, bandwidth connectivity, data traffic support and device mobility. The representative networks of the first category are cellular networks. Cellular networks provide a wide coverage area with relatively low bandwidth connectivity, limited data traffic support and high mobility of devices. In cellular networks, there are base stations, and mobile devices connect to those base stations. The second category of mobile networks is WLAN (Wireless Local Area Network/Wi-Fi), which provides wireless broadband access and large data traffic support for low mobility devices within a limited area. In WLANs, mobile devices connect to the Internet via access points. From the perspective of device organization, Mobile Ad hoc Networks (MANET) are the third category of mobile networks. In MANETs, mobile devices directly establish network connections for a single session in a P2P mode. In MANETs, different from WLANs, there are no access points.

Even though the organization of a MANET is similar to that of a P2P network, a MANET does *not* maintain an overlay structure. A P2P network, however, constructs and maintains an overlay structure, with which it is easy to implement the multicast at the application layer instead of at the physical layer. Nevertheless, the study of MANETs sheds some insight on constructing P2P networks over mobile networks.

Overview of the Chapter

Mobile networks and P2P networks, if combined, can actualize systems which will enable mobile users to efficiently share the network resources and exploit the advantages of the two networks. However, it is very challenging to construct mobile P2P networks due to the features of mobile networks and P2P networks. In this chapter, we study the design issues first, and then provide a survey of existing approaches.

The rest of the chapter is organized as follows. We first present the design issues of running P2P networks on top of mobile networks. Next, we provide a survey of existing solutions of mobile P2P networks. Then we discuss the open problems in mobile P2P networks. Finally, the conclusions are provided.

DESIGN ISSUES IN MOBILE P2P NETWORKS

Constructing mobile P2P networks involves constructing and maintaining a P2P overlay structure on top of mobile networks. It is very challenging to construct mobile P2P networks due to the characteristics of mobile networks and P2P networks. In this section, we list some critical design issues in mobile P2P networks to spur the future research. Design issues in mobile P2P networks include technical, business and legal issues. In this chapter, we focus on the technical issues.

We discuss two groups of design issues. First, basic design issues such as peer discovery and peer selection are discussed. Second, advanced design issues including session mobility, robustness to high churn rate (Stutzbach & Rejaie, 2006), incentive mechanism, content integrity, and legal issues are discussed.

Basic Design Issues: Constructing Overlay Networks

Peer discovery is the procedure of finding the information about other existing peers in a mobile P2P network, when a peer initially joins the network. In P2P networks, the track server maintains the information about existing peers and provides a list of potential neighbors when a peer wants to join the network. Peers register to the server when they join the network and are deleted when they leave. In a mobile network, the network topology changes unpredictably because peers usually move around in the communication range; in addition, peers may also move out of the communication range or exhaust the energy. Peers, accordingly, join and leave the network frequently. The unpredictable and frequent topology change brings excessive loads to the server and may also lead to information inconsistency. Consequently, simply using P2P protocols in mobile networks is not a feasible solution.

Peer selection includes parent selection and children selection. Parent selection considers from whom a peer receives data to maximize its application quality. Children selection considers to whom a peer forwards its data in order to improve the performance of the whole network.

Peers in mobile networks have their own features such as power consumption, transmission delay and mobility. Intuitively, peers prefer those who have low power consumption, low delay and relatively stable peers as their neighbors. However, if the system only chooses those peers, the network is highly likely to be separated, which degrades the overall network performance. Thus, peer selection schemes need to keep a balance between the performance of individual peers and that of the overall network.

Advanced Design Issues: Improve the Performance of Mobile P2P Networks

Session mobility means that mobile devices have to handover P2P sessions seamlessly and transparently when devices move among different networks. As discussed in the previous section, cellular networks provide low bandwidth but wide coverage; whereas a WLAN provides high bandwidth and limited coverage. Accordingly, peers are expected to use high bandwidth data networks, such as a WLAN, whenever they are available and switch to cellular networks only when the coverage of a WLAN is not available. Thus, how to make roaming users seamlessly and transparently switch among different mobile networks with minimum quality degradation on active sessions is essentially important in mobile P2P networks.

High churn rate brings huge performance degradation in mobile P2P networks. Churn means frequent node joining and leaving. The reasons of high churn rate in the mobile P2P networks are as follows:

1. Exhaustion of the device's energy;
2. The device moves out of the transmission range;
3. Users quit from the session or the overlay.

High churn rate leads to dynamic overlay topology, and it makes the mismatching problem (Liu *et al.*, 2007) between logical topology and physical network topology much worse than usual.

Incentive mechanism is another design issue in mobile P2P networks. Free-riders, also called selfish nodes, consume network resources without contributing their data to other peers in the network. The problem of free-riders is not unique to mobile P2P networks. However, the characteristics of mobile systems impose additional challenges to design incentive schemes. Existing mobile P2P overlay constructions largely do not consider the incentive mechanism for enticing peer cooperation. In addition, existing incentive mechanisms for wired P2P networks are not feasible to mobile P2P networks because they cannot effectively manage mobile resource constraints such as energy consumption, frequent network topology and membership changes.

Content integrity issues are also important when we design a mobile P2P network. The characteristics of mobile systems such as their highly distributed nature, the lack of centralized control, and the vulnerability of the wireless link, contribute to increased probability of security violations in mobile P2P networks (Hubaux, *et al*, 2001). The content integrity of a system is violated when unauthorized peers illegally modify the information. Without a central trusted authority or a stable network topology, it is very difficult to identify a peer, and is also hard to develop a scheme to trust peers. High mobility also makes it difficult to detect a compromised or malicious peer in mobile networks. In addition, the constraints of mobile devices, such as high energy consumptions and a slow-speed CPU, make it a great challenge to design an effective solution for solving content integrity. All of the aforementioned limitations have led to non-trivial security problems in mobile P2P networks.

OVERVIEW OF EXISTING APPROACHES

In the previous section, we list some technical challenges in designing mobile P2P networks. Researchers have proposed several approaches to solve those problems. In this section, we first give the taxonomy of mobile P2P approaches based on our study, and then we discuss a non-exhaustive list of representative solutions for each class.

Taxonomy and Architecture of Existing Mobile P2P Networks

In this chapter, mobile P2P networks, similar to P2P networks, are divided into two categories: mobile P2P file sharing networks and mobile P2P media streaming networks. Mobile P2P file sharing networks can be further subdivided into structured and unstructured networks. Mobile P2P media streaming networks are also divided into tree-based, mesh-based and hybrid networks according to their overlay architectures. The taxonomy is depicted in Figure 1.

A mobile P2P network includes a set of modules (Gruber, 2004): a module which takes care of the overlay construction at the application layer, a module which finds routings among peers at IP layer and a communication module, also known as an interlayer communication channel, which

Figure 1. The taxonomy of mobile P2P approaches.

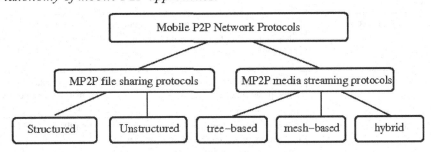

Figure 2. Basic architecture of Mobile P2P networks (Adapted from Gruber et al., 2004)

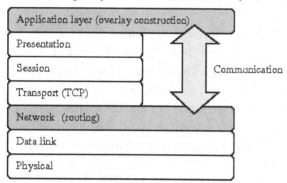

links the application layer and network layer to deal with requests and replies in between. The basic architecture described before is shown in Figure 2.

In next two subsections, we will discuss current mobile P2P file sharing and mobile P2P streaming networks respectively.

Mobile P2P File Sharing Networks

To understand the mobile P2P file sharing networks, in this section, we focus on their char-

acteristic features such as their overlay graph; lookup process; peer joining/leaving and overlay maintenance. The protocols that will be discussed in this subsection are summarized in Table 1.

Unstructured P2P File Sharing Networks

Basically, existing unstructured mobile P2P networks integrate one of the unstructured P2P networks and a mobile ad hoc routing algorithm. The unstructured overlay is constructed at the application layer, which is similar to that in P2P networks. The integral part is the routing protocol that combines unstructured overlay flooding and an ad hoc routing algorithm, with which when a peer requires a file, the request is flooded through mobile networks. On receiving a request, a node communicates with the application layer to see whether it has the matching file. If so, a reply message is sent back to the peer that requests the file. After finding the required file, peers begin to transmit the content. The content delivery process is quite similar to that in Internet-based P2P networks, except for the underlying routing protocol. The process is shown in Figure 3.

Table 1. Features of mobile P2P file sharing networks (unstructured and structured)

	Unstructured	
Example	ORION (Klemm *et al.*,2003)	MPP (Gruber *et al.*, 2004)
Corresponding P2P network	Gnutella (Klingberg, & Manfredi, 2002)	Gnutella
Underlying routing protocol	modified AODV	Extended DSR
Overlay structure	Unfixed	Unfixed
Peer discovery and peer selection	Use query flooding to find possible neighbors. The neighbors are selected within a network, and the selection considers the physical topology.	Use query flooding to find possible neighbors. Multiple neighbors are selected within a network considering the physical topology.
Security	Low, threatened by: flooding malicious content, virus spreading and etc.	Low, threatened by: flooding malicious content, virus spreading and etc.
Mobile feature	The searching algorithm sets up the overlay routes when it is required, thus the overlay routes closely match the topology change.	MPP uses HTTP over TCP to transfer files, and uses EDSR protocol to find the routes. Because they do not depend on reliable nodes, they work well in mobile P2P networks.

continued on the following page

Table 1.continued

	Structured	
Example	ISPRP (Cramer, 2005)	Ekta (Pucha *et al.*, 2004)
Corresponding P2P network	Chord (Stoica *et al.*, 2001)	Pastry (Rowstron & Druschel, 2001)
Underlying routing protocol	DSR	DSR
Overlay structure	Ring	Plaxton-style
Peer discovery and peer selection	A peer joins the overlay structure according to its overlay ID, and every peer keeps the IDs of its successor and predecessor peers.	A peer joins the overlay structure according to its overlay ID. The structure of the overlay is maintained by matching the prefix of the overlay ID
Security	Low, suffer from man-in-the-middle attacks	Low, suffer from man-in-the-middle attacks
Mobile feature	DSR protocol works well for mobile networks, thus it is supposed to work well in mobile P2P networks.	Ekta uses DSR routing protocol which works well in mobile ad hoc networks.

Figure 3. Data sharing in unstructured mobile P2P file sharing networks

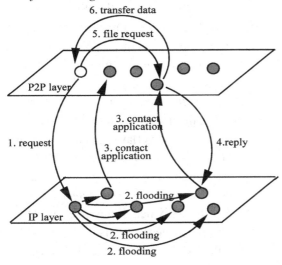

Some examples of unstructured mobile P2P file sharing networks are ORION (Optimized Routing Independent Overlay Network) (Klemm *et al.*, 2003) and MPP (Mobile Peer-to-Peer Protocol) (Gruber et al, 2004; Schollmeier *et al.*, 2003). To follow, we discuss the two systems.

1. ORION

Overlay structure: Unstructured, not a fixed topology.

Peer discovery and peer selection: Overlay connections of ORION are set up on demand and maintained only as long as necessary, and thus it closely matches the current topology of the underlying network. The discovery process combines application-layer query flooding with network-layer routing process. When a peer N wants to transfer a file, it contacts its neighbors and establishes a link between them. Peer N first issues a query and the query is flooded in the IP layer. Along its way through the network, the query sets up reverse paths to N in the routing table. The other peers respond to the query by sending a response back to N. After receiving the response message, N finds the peers who have the matching files, and then N chooses one of the peers as a neighbor, setups a link between them and downloads the files from its neighbor.

Note that, the process discussed before is very similar to the Gnutella-style flooding to send the query and AODV-like routing to locate the requested files.

Mobile feature: To deal with the mobile feature of the physical network, the searching algorithm sets up the overlay routes when it is required. Thus, the overlay routes closely match the topology change. However, this method causes a huge unnecessary overhead on topology change.

2.   MPP

Overlay structure: Unstructured, not fixed topology.

Peer discovery and Peer selection: MPP uses Gnutella-style flooding and Enhanced Dynamic Source Routing[1] (EDSR) (Gruber et al., 2004; Schollmeier et al., 2003). MPP implements a function called MPCP to communicate between the application layer and EDSR. On startup, a peer on the mobile device announces itself to the EDSR layer using MPCP, and it randomly selects its neighbors within the whole network. The logical links are setup on-demand, and the detailed steps of how to detect peers and setup links among them are as follows: When a peer, called the source, issues a query, it is forwarded to EDSR located in the network-layer. EDSR then floods the request. On receiving a request, a peer contacts the application layer to see if it has the requested file. If it has, the application sends a reply to EDSR and then reverts to the source peer by using DSR-like routing. After the source peer receives the information, it chooses several peers as its neighbors, joins the overlay network and transfers the file through those peers. Consequently, if any peer leaves while transferring the file, the source peer can still get the file trunks from other neighbors. Thus, this overlay construction can reduce the overhead and reduce the problem of topology mismatch and frequent peer joining and leaving.

Advantages: Unstructured and flooding-based mobile P2P networks are straight-forward approaches since slight changes to underlying routing protocols can meet the requirements of the construction. In a small network, unstructured and flooding-based mobile P2P networks are feasible solutions for constructing P2P networks over mobile networks.

Disadvantages: These networks are not scalable, because broadcasting messages is not a scalable method in a network of large size and with high request rate. Furthermore, the system performance depends on the choice of routing protocols.

Structured Mobile P2P File Sharing Networks

There are several relatively mature structured P2P networks (Zahn, 2006), such as Content Addressable Network (CAN), Tapestry, Chord, and Pastry. Some of them have been adapted to mobile P2P networks by integrating structured P2P networks with a mobile network routing protocol.

1.   Chord based

Chord-based mobile P2P networks maintain a Chord-like structure on top of a mobile network. The first structured mobile P2P file sharing network is ISPRP (Iterative Successor Pointer Rewiring Protocol) (Cramer, & Fuhrmann, 2005) that uses Chord structured P2P network and ad hoc routing protocols in mobile P2P networks. The ISPRP network is discussed.

Overlay structure: ISPRP constructs a Chord-like double link ring in mobile networks. Basically, each node has an overlay ID, and it stores overlay IDs of its one-hop neighbors and its successor and predecessor.

Peer discovery and Peer selection: The general idea is that when a new peer wants to join the overlay, the peer assigns itself an overlay ID. Using this ID, the new peer can find the successor peer and predecessor peers in the overlay structure and join the overlay. Specifically, when a node i intends to select node j as its successor, it sends a Successor Pointer Solicitation (SPS) message to node j, and the message has the DSR routing information between node i and node j. After receiving the SPS message, node j checks whether there is an inconsistency. If there is, say that node j already has a node y as its predecessor, then node j will choose another node z (which is the potential successor of i suggested by j) for joining node i. Node j sends a SPS to node z, and the message contains the concatenated routing information from i to z via j. The process will be repeated until a correct successor of i is found. When a peer intends to leave the network, it sends all its information to its successor, and then leaves the network.

However, ISPRP does not address how to deal with the frequent route breakup, peer joining and peer leaving. In addition, ISPRP does not describe any mechanisms to deal with a broken overlay ring.

2. Pastry based

Ekta (Pucha *et al.*, 2004) is a representative Pastry-based mobile P2P network. In Ekta, Pastry-based DHT protocol operates at the logical layer, and a modified multi-hop routing protocol DSR operates at the physical layer.

Overlay structure: Ekta has a circular identifier space and each peer maintains a standard Pastry leaf set and a routing table. Ekta leaf sets and routing tables contain the overlay ID and a DSR-style source route from the current peer to the respective entry peers. The overlay ID is obtained by hashing the IP address of a node and the ID is divided up into digits with each digit being b bits long, which provides a numbering system with base 2^b. The node at n^{th} row with ID M contains 2^b-1 nodes with the first $n-1$ digits the same as M.

Peer discovery and peer selection: When a new peer N wants to join an overlay, it assigns itself a random Pastry overlay ID, and N asks its bootstrap peer to lookup its overlay ID. Once a join request is received by a peer j, j first checks whether the new ID falls into the range of peer IDs covered by its leaf set. If not, the lookup is forwarded to the peer in the interval where the new ID belongs, that is forwarded to a peer that shares more digits than the prefix between peer j and peer N. Otherwise, j replies a message containing its leaf set to N. Peer j will also broadcast a message to all the leaf set members to inform

them about the new arrival. After N joins the network, the information of all peers in the leaf set will be updated.

When a peer wants to leave the network, it floods the LEAVE message to the leaf set, and all peers in the leaf set will delete the peer from their routing tables after receiving the message.

Advantages: By using a structured overlay, it is easy to find a peer in an overlay. The peer discovery process is faster than that in unstructured overlays.

Disadvantages: Although the structured overlay has lots of advantages, it is very expensive to maintain a fixed structure. It is also difficult to recovery from frequent peer joining and peer leaving. In addition, since there is no discussion on the routing scheme, the path returned by peer discovery may not be the desired one, which will greatly influence the performance of the network. In a large mobile network, structured networks might meet the scalable requirement due to the large control overhead.

Mobile P2P Streaming Networks

P2P streaming networks are inspired by the success of P2P file sharing networks. Mobile P2P streaming systems, thus, have attracted a lot of interests after the success of mobile P2P file sharing networks. Mobile P2P streaming systems are a fairly new research field that faces huge challenges. Following the classification of P2P streaming networks, we also divide mobile P2P streaming networks into tree-based and mesh-based networks. In this section, we study the mobile P2P streaming networks by using CHUM (Kang & Mutka 2005), COSMOS (Leung & Chan, 2007) and P2PMLS (Zhang *et al.*, 2007) as examples. Table 2 summarizes the basic information of the two systems.

In the following subsections, we will briefly introduce CHUM, COSMOS and P2PMLS to motivate further design improvements to mobile P2P streaming networks.

Table 2. Mobile P2P streaming networks.

	Tree-based	*Mesh-based*	
Sample networks	CHUM	COSMOS	P2PMLS
Overlay structure	Tree; pull-based	Mesh; pull-based	Mesh based
Puller selection	One puller, the puller will be changed according to Round Robin scheduling algorithm	Multiple pullers Pullers change to a passive receiver when all descriptions are available or time out	*Seeds:* multiple seeds, the seeds download the contents from the Internet directly
Children selection	Active server selects the rebroadcast peers	1, Rebroadcast packets until TTL becomes zero 2, First level peers broadcast packets, and other peers rebroadcast packets only when a certain criteria is satisfied	The management server and membership sever find the possible neighbors for the peer.
Routing	Broadcast	Broadcast	Transparent to any routing protocols
Communication	Primary channel	Peers pull the contents via primary channel and broadcast them via secondary channel	Not specified
Control overhead	High, since global topology information is needed	Middle, only local topology information is needed, but the rebroadcast range needs to calculate.	Middle, since the management servers find the peer information and do not need to keep the routing information
Security	Low, suffer from passive attack, such as denial of service.	Low, suffer from denial of service.	Low, no mechanism to deal with security issues is introduced in the paper.

Tree-Based Mobile P2P Streaming Networks

CHUM (cooperating ad hoc networking to support messaging) is a tree-based mobile P2P streaming network which shares media streaming data among mobile nodes in an ad hoc manner. In CHUM, one peer pulls streaming contents from the content provider and shares the contents with other peers in the same group.

Architecture: CHUM constructs a tree structure (Leung & Chan, 2007) and each peer associates a chumcast server. Among all peers, only one peer is chosen as a proxy to contact the content provider, and its corresponding chumcast server is called an active server. The proxy pulls contents from the content provider on the Internet, and broadcasts the streaming data to its neighbors. The active server also chooses a

minimum set of rebroadcasting peers, and then the rebroadcasting peers transmit the content to all peers in the CHUM network. As a result, a single tree structure is constructed.

Peer discovery: When a new peer, say *P*, joins the network, it broadcasts a JOIN message which contains a default Peer ID (PID) with a random number to its nearby peers. Peers who receive the JOIN message and have the same PID reply with an ACCEPT message. Then, peer *P* sends the information to its associated chumcast server. The corresponding chumcast server registers *P* to the active server. After that, the active server sends the Group ID and group key to the associated chumcast server. Finally, the Group ID and key are passed to the peer that is trying to join the CHUM network. The peer *P* can use the Group ID and key to communicate with the discovered peer.

Puller selection. In a CHUM network, a peer that pulls the content plays the role of a proxy, and all peers take turns to be a proxy to share data with other peers. The active server manages a circular scheduling list of all peers and uses round robin scheduling to transfer the proxy authority to other peers.

Children selection. The proxy in a CHUM network has the responsibility to pull the content from the content provider in the Internet and to broadcast contents to its neighbors. The active server collects the information of the global topology, and finds a minimum connected dominating set of the network as the set of rebroadcasting peers. The rebroadcasting peers propagate contents to other peers in the CHUM network.

Advantages: CHUM provides a mobile P2P streaming network that can reduce the communication costs. CHUM shares the contents by broadcasting. Thus, the system performance would not be influenced by the routing schemes in the ad hoc network.

Disadvantages: CHUM only considers the network as a layered topology: a proxy broadcasts the content to the first layer peers (neighbors), and then some first layer peers (rebroadcasting peers) broadcast the contents to whole network. Thus, it constructs a tree topology (Leung & Chan, 2007); however, the relationship among those peers in the same layer is not clear. Second, the tree-based structure does not fully utilize the upload capacity of the lower level peers. Third, CHUM needs the global information of the network to choose the rebroadcasting peers, and therefore it is not scalable.

Mesh-Based Mobile P2P Streaming Networks

To solve the problems of tree-based P2P networks, researchers have proposed mesh-based overlay networks. In this subsection, we study two mesh-based mobile P2P streaming networks: COSMOS and P2PMLS.

1.   COSMOS

A recently proposed network, COSMOS (Collaborative Streaming among Mobiles), builds a mesh-based physical mobile P2P networks. In this subsection, we study the construction of COSMOS.

Architecture: COSMOS establishes a mesh structure. In COSMOS, some nodes use their primary Telecommunication Interfaces to pull the contents from the content provider on the Internet, while broadcasting contents via their secondary channel to other peers.

Puller Selection: Peers with more neighbors are expected to be pullers and share their pulled data.

COSMOS uses the primary channel to connect the content provider, and uses the secondary channel to broadcast contents. If a puller pulls contents for a long time, it switches itself as a passive receiver. Then, the peer broadcasts a packet with a SWITCH flag and a RPT (residual pull time) to the others in the network. Other peers which receive the packets will generate a random number between 0 and RPT. The next puller will be the one with the earliest timer.

Children Selection: After pulling contents from the content provider on the Internet, the peer broadcasts them among a set of peers, and we call them children in this section. Two schemes are introduced by COSMOS to determine the broadcast region. The *first* one is to use TTL: the broadcast packet has a fixed TTL (Time To Live). When the packet is broadcasted to puller's neighbors, it subtracts one from TTL. The packet will be broadcasted until the TTL becomes zero. The *second* one is that pullers broadcast packets to the first level neighbors. A first level peer, say *x*, rebroadcasts packets only when certain criteria are satisfied.

Advantages: Compared with tree-based architectures, the mesh-based architectures are resilient to device mobility in mobile networks. COSMOS broadcasts contents by using secondary channels with low costs and high bandwidth.

Disadvantages: Since the broadcast may cause the duplication of the packets, which leads to low resource utilization, a broadcast tree is needed to minimize the resource duplication. The problem of choosing rebroadcast peers can be modeled as the minimum connected dominating set problem, which is proved to be an NP-hard problem. The proposed method in COSMOS is a solution with high complexity and high control overhead.

2.   P2PMLS

Broadcast-based P2P streaming networks, such as CHUM and COSMOS, have a narrow range of peer selection, and thus the network architecture cannot be applied to a large scale network. The problem is shown in Fig. 4.

As shown in Figure 4, we can see that in the physical topology, peers A, B and C can communicate with each others, but peer D is in a different range. Thus, in a broadcast-based P2P network, if peer A can pull the data from streaming server directly, then it can only broadcast its data to peer B and peer C directly. By using broadcast-based architecture, it is difficult or impossible to choose

peers that are far away from the peer A in physical topology as its neighbors.

To solve the scalability problem, P2PMLS (P2P-leveraged mobile live streaming system) (Zhang *et al.*, 2007), another mesh-based mobile P2P streaming network is proposed. In theory, the peer in the P2PMLS network can choose any peer located anywhere in the world as its neighbor. For example, peer A can choose those peers which cannot be reached directly as its neighbors such as peer D and peer E. Next, we will study the overlay construction of P2PMLS.

Architecture: P2PMLS establishes a mesh structure. In P2PMLS, some peers are selected as seed peers which receive data from the content server and transmit the data to other peers.

Seeds Selection: In P2PMLS, there are two cases where the seed peers need to be selected. The first case is when a peer wants to join an overlay, and it asks the management server for the program list and the list of possible seeds. If there is no seed peer for the required program, the peer will request the program directly from streaming server and it is chosen as a seed peer. The second case is when the management server

Figure 4. The difference between broadcast-based mobile P2P networks and other mobile P2P overlay networks. In this figure, a physical communication link means that the two mobile devices can communicate with each other without the help of any other intermediate node.

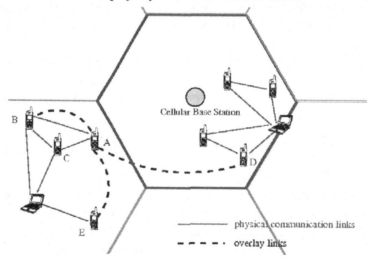

finds that a seed peer, say peer A, is leaving, and then the server selects a partner of peer A as the new seed peer.

Neighbor Selection: When a peer joins the network, it asks the management server for the program list and the list of seeds peers. If seed peers are found, the membership manager finds the possible neighbors among those who are downloading the program. Then, the partnership manager chooses some neighbors as the partner peers. Finally, the new peer joins the overlay and downloads the program from the partner peers.

Advantages: Compared with broadcast-based mobile P2P networks, the mobile P2P network has a broader search scope and less unnecessary traffic. Second, in a P2PMLS network, more peers can cooperate with each others than that in a broadcast-based P2P network, so that the upload bandwidth and other resources are utilized more efficiently.

Disadvantages: There are lots of issues that P2PMLS does not address. The first issue is that due to the high mobility, mobile peers tend to move into clusters, thus, the network is separated easily. Second, since the streaming applications have a very tight playback deadline, P2PMLS may still have a low quality because of the long transmission delay, the long adaptation time or long recovery time. Third, data security and incentive mechanism are also not addressed in the paper.

OPEN PROBLEMS

A brief review of existing approaches on mobile P2P networks is discussed in previous sections. The proposed mobile P2P file sharing networks can set up P2P networks in a mobile environment. In addition, networks can be easily implemented by slightly modifying the corresponding P2P protocol and the ad hoc routing protocol. However, several design issues are not addressed yet.

First, the existing mobile P2P file sharing approaches may cause several side effects:

a.   Peers may be clustered at some powerful neighbors and resources of other peers may not be fully utilized; one illustrative example is shown in Figure 5.

As shown in Figure 5, peers prefer to connect with powerful nodes, for example, the peer A and peer B in the figure. And thus most of the peers might be clustered at one or more powerful nodes. On the other hand, some peers which also have sufficient resources, such as peers C, D and E, may not be fully utilized. Accordingly, the overall network resources are not effectively used.

b.   Peers may not have equal opportunity to connect to the powerful nodes and therefore such peers, which do not select the powerful nodes as their neighbors, are unable to improve their playback quality with the assistance of powerful nodes; this situation is shown in Fig. 6.

In Figure 6, powerful peers, such as the peer A, can help other peers to improve their performance.

Figure 5. Cluster problem in mobile P2P file-sharing networks

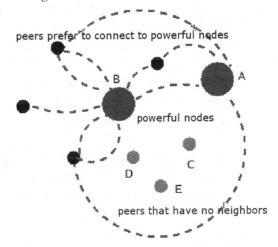

Figure 6. Fairness problem in mobile P2P file-sharing networks.

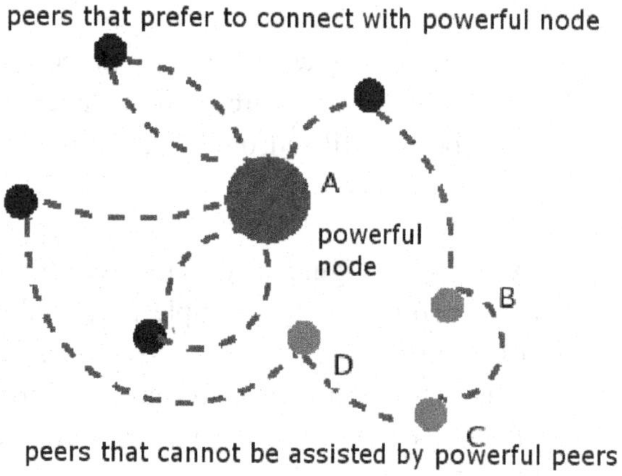

peers that prefer to connect with powerful node

peers that cannot be assisted by powerful peers

However, peers may not have equal opportunities to connect to the powerful nodes in current mobile P2P systems. For example, peers B, C and D in the Fig. 6, cannot be selected as the neighbor of the powerful peer A, and thus they are unable to improve their playback quality by receiving the assistance from the powerful peer.

c. The proactive approaches may also cause high control overhead, in that each peer has to probe the status of other peers in the network, or peers have to exchange such information and the methods may not be scalable.

Second, there is a lot of space for improving the design of mobile P2P streaming networks. The two broadcast-based P2P streaming networks are economical and feasible P2P solutions to sharing media streaming in mobile networks; however, the two approaches have their potential shortcomings comparing with other solutions.

- The two protocols broadcast their resources among the network, which limits the search scope and results in much unnecessary traffic.

- The upload bandwidth cannot be fully utilized since those passive receivers do not share their resources.
- Due to the high mobility, mobile peers tend to move into clusters, thus, the network is separated easily.

P2PMLS, does implement a P2P overlay mobile P2P network, but there are lots of important things that are not addressed, such as how to make the overlay structure more robust to the frequent peer leaving due to the high mobility, how to inspire free riders to contribute their resources to the overall network, etc.

Third, seamless handover problem (Hsieh *et al.*, 2003) is not addressed also. Seamless session handover refers to maintaining a P2P session while it is transferred to another interface or peer. There are three types of handover, and all of them need to be addressed in mobile P2P networks.

- **Peer handover:** A P2P session moves from one peer to another peer whenever a peer's neighbor is changed.
  Three main factors lead to the peer handover. First, the signal of mobile peers is too low to maintain the transmission. Second, mobile peers have to be replaced because they run out of battery or other resources. The third reason is that peers move out of the network range.
  To solve the problem of peer handover, the protocol needs to detect the power status, moving direction (away from the base station or towards the base station), moving velocity and signal strength of peers.
- **Point of attachment handover:** A P2P session moves an interface between two cellular base stations or WLAN access points.
  When a peer moves out of the transmission coverage of a base station or an access point, it has to find another base station or an access point to resume the P2P session. To solve the problem, mobile nodes need to

listen to the signal strength which is in use and the radio transmission for any other base stations or access points in a certain range. Mobile nodes, then, report the information to the protocol to make a decision.

- **Interface handover:** A P2P session moves from the cellular to WLAN interface or vice versa.

In order to obtain relatively high quality streaming, peers prefer WLAN to transfer data. Thus, peers tend to use WLAN interface whenever they can access it. Peers contact the track server to get enough information by using cellular interface when they join the network. Otherwise, peers only change to cellular interface when it moves out of any WLAN area after the data transfer begins. Consequently, seamless interface handover is very important for constructing mobile P2P networks, especially mobile P2P streaming networks.

Fourth, designing an efficient and simple mechanism is also an important issue in mobile P2P networks. Free riders consume network resources without any contribution, so it is very important to encourage free riders to cooperate with other peers so that the overall utility of the network can be maximized.

CONCLUSIONS

With the evolution of mobile technology, mobile networks can provide much more interesting services and resources to users than before. Thus, how to efficiently store, share and deliver resources becomes an appealing problem. Mobile P2P networks, expected to combine the advantages of mobile networks and P2P networks, are proposed to solve the problem. However, it is fairly difficult to construct mobile P2P networks.

In this chapter, we list two classes of design issues in mobile P2P networks: basic issues and advanced design issues. Based on these design issues, existing and proposed mobile P2P networks were discussed. By analyzing existing approaches, we find that very few application-layer mobile P2P streaming networks have been designed. In addition, only a few have focused on solving advanced design issues, such as session mobility. Thus, there are more remaining issues in the field of mobile P2P networks that need to be addressed in future research.

REFERENCES

Ahuja, R. K., Magnanti, T. L., & Orlin, J. B. (1993). *Network flows: Theory, algorithms, and applications.* Englewood Cliffs, N.J., Prentice Hall.

BitTorrent, (2001). BitTorrent. Retrieved September 9, 2008, from http://www.bittorrent.com/

Castro, M., Druschel, P., Kermarrec, A-M., Nandi, A., Rowstron A., & Singh, A. (2003). Split-stream: High-bandwidth multicast in a cooperative environment. In *Proceedings of the ACM Symposium on Operating Systems Principles.*

Cramer, C., & Fuhrmann, T. (2005). ISPRP: A message-efficient protocol for initializing structured P2P networks. In *Proceedings of the 24th IEEE International Performance, Computing, and Communications Conference (IPCCC).*

Chakrabarti, S., Vuong, S. T., Sinha, A. & Paul, R. (2005). BlueMobile-a mobile IP based handoff system for blue tooth, 802.11 and GPRS links. In *Proceedings of the IEEE Consumer Communications and Networking Conference.*

Chu, Y., Rao S., Seshan, S. & Zhang, H. (2002). A case for end system multicast. *IEEE Journal on Selected Areas in Communications, 20*(8), 1456-1471.

El-Ansary, S. & Haridi, S. (2005). An overview of structured overlay networks. In J. Wu (Ed.), *Theoretical and algorithmic aspects of sensor, ad hoc wireless and peer-to-peer networks*. USA: CRC Press.

Flick, H., Helpworth, E., Eisel, J. & Uno, S. (2004). Issues of advanced mobility management in ambient network. In *Proceedings of the 12th Wireless World Research Forum (WWRF)*.

Kirk, P. (2003) Gnutella – stable – 0.4. Retrieved September 9, 2008, from http://rfc-gnutella. sourceforge.net/developer/stable/index.html

Gruber, I., Schollmeier, R., & Kellerer, W. (2004). Performance evaluation of the mobile peer-to-peer service. In *Proceedings of the IEEE International Symposium on Cluster Computing and the Grid*.

Gupta, V., & Williams, M. G. (2007). IEEE 802.21, from http://www.ieee802.org/21

Hsieh, R. Zhou, Z.G., & Seneviratne, A. (2003). S-MIP: A seamless handoff architecture for mobile IP. In *Proceedings of the IEEE International Conference on Computer Communications (INFOCOM)*.

Hubaux, J., Buttyan, L., & Capkun, S. (2001). The quest for security in mobile ad hoc networks. In *Proceeding of the ACM Symposium on Mobile Ad Hoc Networking and Computing*.

Johnson, D., Perkins, C., & Arkko, J.(2004). *IP mobility support for IPv6* (RFC 3775).

Kang, S.-S., & Mutka, M. W. (2005). A mobile peer-to-peer approach for multimedia content sharing using 3G/WLAN dual mode channels. *Wireless Communications and Mobile Computing Journal, Special Issue on WLAN/3G Integration for Next-Generation Heterogeneous Mobile Data Networks, 5*(6), 633-645.

Klemm, A., Lindemann, C., & Waldhorst, O. (2003). A special-purpose peer-to-peer file sharing system for mobile ad hoc networks. In *Proceedings of the Workshop on Mobile Ad Hoc Networking and Computing*.

Klingberg, T. & Manfredi, R. (2002). Gnutella Protocol Development. http://rfc-gnutella.sourceforge.net/src/rfc-0_6-draft.html

Leung, M.-F., & Chan, S.-H. (2007). Broadcast-based peer-to-peer collaborative video streaming among mobiles. *IEEE Transactions on Broadcasting Special Issue on Mobile Multimedia Broadcasting, 53*(1), 350-361.

Liu, Y., Li, X., Liu, X., Ni, L. M., & Zhang, X. (2005). Location awareness in unstructured peer-to-peer systems. *IEEE Transactions on Parallel and Distributed Systems, 16*(2): 163-174.

Liu, Y., Xiao, L. & Ni, L. M. (2007). Building a Scalable Bipartite P2P Overlay Network, *IEEE Transactions on Parallel and Distributed Systems (TPDS), 18*(9), 46-56.

Lua, E. K., Crowcroft, J., Pias, M., Sharma, R., & Lim, S. (2004). A survey and comparison of peer-to-peer overlay network schemes. *IEEE Communications Survey & Tutorials, 7*(2), 72-93.

Magharei, N., Rejaie, R., & Y. Guo. (2007). Mesh or multiple-tree: A comparative study of P2P live streaming services. In *Proceedings of the IEEE International Conference on Computer Communications*.

Mondal, A., Madria, S. K., & Kitsuregawa, M. (2007). Research issues and overview of economic models in mobile-P2P networks. In *Proceedings of the 18th International Conference on Database and Expert Systems Applications*.

Padmanabhan, V. N., Wang, H. J., & Chou, P. A. (2003). Resilient peer-to-peer streaming. In *Proceedings of the 11th IEEE International Conference on Network Protocols*.

Perkins, C.(2002). *IP Mobility Support for IPv4* (RFC 3344).

PPLive Inc. (2007). PPLive. Retrieved September 9, 2008, from http://pplive.com/

PPStream. (2005). Retrieved September 9, 2008, from http://ppstream.com/

Pucha, H., Das, S. M., & Y. C. Hu, (2004). Ekta: An efficient DHT substrate for distributed applications in mobile ad hoc networks. In *Proceedings of the 6th IEEE Workshop on Mobile Computing Systems and Applications (WMCSA).*

Raivio, Y. (2005). A peer-to-peer overlay architecture for mobile networks. *T110.7190 Research Seminar on Telecom Software.*

Rowstron, A. I. T., & Druschel, P. (2001). Pastry: Scalable, decentralized object location, and routing for large-scale peer-to-peer systems. In *Proceedings of the IFIP/ACM International Conference on Distributed Systems Platforms.*

Schollmeier, R., Gruber, I., & Niethammer, F. (2003). Protocol for peer-to-peer networking in mobile environments. In *Proceedings of 12th IEEE International Conference on Computer Communications and Networks.*

Stoica, I., Morris, R., Karger, D., Kaashoek, M., & Balakrishnan. H. (2001). Chord: A scalable peer-to-peer lookup service for internet applications. In *Proceedings of the ACM SIGCOMM Conference on Applications, Technologies, Architectures, and Protocols for Computer Communications.*

Stutzbach, D., & Rejaie, R. (2006). Understanding churn in peer-to-peer networks. In *Proceedings of the Internet Measurement Conference.*

Wang, F., Xiong, Y., & Liu, J. (2007). mTreebone: A hybrid tree/mesh overlay for application-layer live video multicast. In *Proceedings of the International Conference on Distributed Computing Systems (ICDCS).*

Wu, C., & Li, B. (2007). Strategies of conflict in coexisting streaming overlays. In *Proceedings of IEEE International Conference on Computer Communications (INFOCOM).*

Wu, J. (2005). *Handbook on theoretical and algorithmic aspects of sensor, ad hoc wireless, and peer-to-peer networks.* Boston, MA, USA: AUERBACH.

Zahn, T. C. (2006). *Structured peer-to-peer services for mobile ad hoc networks.* Unpublished doctoral dissertation, Fachbereich Mathematik u. Informatik, Freie Universitat, Berlin, Germany.

Zhang, J., Niu, J., He, R., Hu, J., & Sun, L. (2007). P2P-leveraged mobile live streaming. In *Proceedings of the 21st International Conference on Advanced Information Networking and Applications Workshops.*

Zhang, X., Liu, J., Li, B., & Yum, T.-S. P. (2005). DONet/CoolStreaming: A data-driven overlay network for live media streaming. In *Proceedings of IEEE International Conference on Computer Communications (INFOCOM).*

ENDNOTE

[1] The EDSR protocol adds request and reply type on top of the DSR protocol.

Chapter IV
Mobility Support in a P2P System for Publish/Subscribe Applications

Thomas Kunz
Systems and Computer Engineering, Carleton University, Canada

Abdulbaset Gaddah
Systems and Computer Engineering, Carleton University, Canada

Li Li
Communications Research Centre, Canada

ABSTRACT

Peer-to-Peer computing is a popular, relatively new, distributed computing paradigm. It allows for a flexible set of participants to coordinate their resources with little overhead or reliance on central servers/ services and is becoming particularly relevant in mobile computing environments, where peers come and go. Communication between an (unknown) number of peers, which may or may not be online at the same time, is greatly facilitated by the publish/subscribe model. In this chapter, the authors review the state-of-the-art in publish/subscribe systems, focusing on the support for mobile peers in infrastructure-based networks. They propose a novel handoff approach that proactively distributes pub/sub-related informa-tion to brokers/superpeers ahead of a peer's movement. They show through extensive experiments in a small testbed that the new approach has significant performance benefits, compared to the more typical reactive approach, in which pub/sub context is only established after a handoff event occurred.

MOTIVATION

Peer-to-Peer (P2P) computing has gained both scientific and social importance recently due to the success of systems such as Freenet, Gnutella and Napster. Harnessing P2P technology has the potential to produce systems that combine good scalability with minimal infrastructure cost. P2P systems are designed to start out small and seamlessly evolve to very large distributed systems with thousands of participants.

To coordinate the communication between entities, the publish/subscribe model is very promising (Kangasharju, 2005). As P2P applications grow, the need for selective data dissemination increases, in particular for *many-to-many* aggregate queries, which is at the core of the publish/subscribe approach. Many publish/subscribe systems have been implemented, using either centralized or distributed matching and routing algorithms (Burcea et al., 2004), (Cugola et al., 2001), (Fiege at al., 2003), and (Muthusamy et al., 2005). More recently, a number of researchers have explored how to implement publish/subscribe over large P2P networks in a scalable fashion. This is done either using structured P2P overlays such as CHORD or CAN, or unstructured P2P overlays, see for example (Bender et al., 2007), (Chand & Felber, 2005), or (Choi & Park, 2006).

We are interested in particular in the performance of Pub/Sub approaches in a cellular/infrastructure-based wireless network. In such networks, publishers and subscribers are free to roam randomly, attaching to a fixed core network at different locations over time. Example networks are cellular networks (GSM or CDMA), WiFi-based wireless LANs, or WiMAX/Wireless Mesh Access networks. One important characteristic of such networks is the fact that they contain a fixed core, which enables these networks to scale to many users. This contrasts to the other popular form of wireless networks, Mobile Ad-Hoc Networks, or MANETs, which are completely infrastructure-less and typically rather small-scale (at most 100 users/nodes).

Efficiently supporting publish/subscribe-style applications in such infrastructure-based mobile networks raises some interesting challenges. Typically, mobile devices, connected over a wireless link, are severely resource-limited in terms of CPU power, memory size, and/or network connectivity. One option to implementing a P2P-based pub/sub middleware in such an environment is to treat the mobile devices simply as weak peers but to otherwise not distinguish further between mobile and stationary devices, as advocated in (Kellerer et al., 2005). This will, in general, not result in good overall application performance. As our own experience (Kunz & Omar, 2002) and others such as (Barr et al., 2002), (Fox et al., 1998), (Zenel & Duchamp, 1997) have shown, the key to increasing the performance of mobile applications is to partition the application. Code/application logic that requires lots of computational power and/or high communication bandwidth is offloaded to the fixed infrastructure.

A similar division of the application logic can be seen in many P2P designs. For example, the Gnutella network originally consists of a number of equal nodes, called peers or servants. These peers are connected by an application level overlay network that provides routing and forwarding of Gnutella messages. A newly participating servant can connect to Gnutella network by handshaking with the already connected node whose address is learned somehow out-of-band. Once a servant has connected successfully to the network, it communicates with the other servants by sending and receiving Gnutella protocol messages. Having random connections with the other servants results in, among other things, routing inefficiencies. To address this problem, the ultrapeer system has been introduced by organizing nodes in a hierarchical fashion with ultrapeers and leaves. A leaf keeps only a small number of connections with ultrapeers. On the other hand, an ultrapeer maintains many leaf connections as well as a small number of connections to the other ultrapeers. It acts as a proxy to the Gnutella network for the leaves connected to it and shields leaves from the majority of message traffic (Park et al., 2007). KaZaA has a similar notion called superpeers, which are well-connected, resource-rich peers, providing service to regular peers.

Publish/Subscribe applications also support this approach to application partitioning well by introducing the notion of brokers. Brokers are the entities matching publications with subscriptions, requiring potentially complex matching algorithms and high communication bandwidths to deal with the volume of publications. Once the appropriate publications are filtered, they are then forwarded to the relevant subscribers, potentially applying further transcoding operations (compression, selective filtering, reducing the fidelity of media components, etc.) to achieve additional reductions in the required bandwidth. We therefore assume an architecture in which mobile subscribers (and potentially publishers, though we focus in this chapter on the subscriber side) connect to a network of brokers, organized in a Peer-to-Peer fashion.

Given this architecture, the following question arises: How to efficiently support the mobile subscribers? This question involves two key issues. The first issue arises when a mobile peer disconnects from the network. A mobile peer can be disconnected from the fixed core due to a wireless connection failure, or when the peer moves to areas of no wireless coverage. How will the network effectively handle disconnected peers with regard to its subscriptions and any matching publications currently in the network? The second issue arises as the peer reconnects to the network. As a roaming mobile peer connects to the fixed core at different locations, it selects typically the "closest" or the "least-loaded" broker to join the P2P overlay. The mobile peer has its subscriptions for the events/files/objects of its interest. Meanwhile, publications are being routed through the network of the brokers. The mobile peer should be able to receive the publications that match its subscriptions in a timely manner without negative performance impact on the connected network. This chapter reviews the solution options and evaluates their performance using an experimental testbed.

BACKGROUND: PUBLISH/SUBSCRIBE SYSTEMS AND ARCHITECTURES

Publish/Subscribe Systems

A generic publish/subscribe system (or *Event Notification Service*) consists of a set of broker (or *dispatcher*) nodes distributed over a communication network. The clients of this system are classified based on their roles into *publishers*, which are information producers, and *subscribers*, which are information consumers. The interaction takes place by passing messages (or *events*) from publishers to interested subscribers through the brokers of the publish/subscribe system. Brokers coordinate themselves in order to route information to all interested subscriber clients. Publishers notify the outside world about the occurrence of certain events. Subscribers that are interested in receiving particular sets of messages can express their interest by means of *subscriptions*. Upon receiving a new message, the broker entity matches the message against all the subscriptions and then forwards it to all interested subscribers. Messages are forwarded to the subscribers in an asynchronous manner. Thus, the architecture of a publish/subscribe system depends basically on a mediated entity that manages subscriptions as well as the delivery of messages and acknowledgements. Figure 1 illustrates the basic components of a publish/subscribe system.

The strength of the publish/subscribe communication model lies in the full decoupling of message publishers from subscribers in time, space, and flow (Eugster et al., 2001). The communication model is decoupled in time, because simultaneous interaction between publishers and subscribers is not required; decoupled in space, because publishers and subscribers do not need to know the identity of each other; decoupled in flow, because publishers are not blocked while publishing messages and subscribers can asynchronously receive messages during performing

Figure 1. Components of a publish/subscribe system

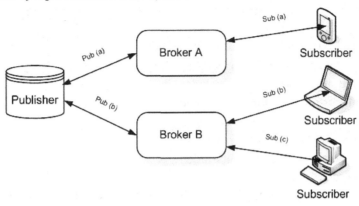

some concurrent activity. The decoupling of message publishers and subscribers makes publish/subscribe systems highly scalable and flexible by removing all explicit dependencies between the interacting participants. Indeed, it makes the resulting communication model well adapted to highly dynamic distributed environments that are asynchronous by nature, such as mobile computing environments (Huang & Garcia-Molina, 2004).

Publish/subscribe systems are based on two different subscription schemes: topic-based (or *subject-based*) and content-based (or *property-based*). In the topic-based systems, subscribers may register to one or more topics and thus receive all the messages delivered to those topics. Subscribers that share the same topic will receive a copy of each message within that topic. Although topic-based subscriptions are simple and easy to implement, they represent a static scheme that offers only limited expressiveness. The content-based systems, on the other hand, extend the notion of topics by using a subscription scheme that is based on the actual content of the desired messages. Such a scheme allows subscribers to assign certain queries on the message properties as part of their subscriptions. Hence, subscribers are able to receive selective sets of messages published on a particular topic. It should be noted that messages do not rely on an explicit destination address set by the publishers. Instead, they are routed to the end destination based on their content.

Broker Architecture

The mediator (*broker*) architecture can be either centralized or distributed. A centralized architecture consists of a single broker entity that connects several publisher and subscriber components. This central entity is potentially a performance bottleneck and a single point of failure. This affects system scalability and limits the use of centralized architectures to small-scale deployments. In a distributed architecture, a set of distributed brokers collaborate in collecting subscriptions and forwarding messages to the interested subscribers. Publishers and subscribers are not attached to a single broker entity; instead, they are distributed over several interconnected brokers. This can potentially reduce the network load and improve system scalability. The distributed brokers can be organized in several topologies that differ in terms of their strategies in routing subscriptions and messages. Two different broker topologies are presented in Figures 2 and 3. In a hierarchical (or *multicast*) topology, the brokers are organized in a forwarding tree that has a root broker and several downward brokers. Excluding the root broker, each broker is considered as a client to the broker at the upward level of the hierarchy. Subscribers may connect to any broker regardless of the location of the corresponding publishers in the hierarchy. Whenever a new subscription is received, the broker forwards it upward to the root broker. Each broker on the way from the subscriber to the root broker stores a copy of the subscription. When a message is received by a broker, it is forwarded to the broker's parent. The message is also matched against all the stored subscriptions. This includes any subscriptions from downstream brokers. The broker forwards the message to any interested children (subscriber/broker) only if the matching result is true. Thus, messages are always forwarded upward to the root broker, and downward towards any interested subscribers. In this topology, each broker node is a critical point of failure. Also, parent brokers are potentially overloaded as they perform extra work for their children.

A peer-to-peer (or *broadcast*) topology, and the one we are interested in here, consists of a set of brokers that are connected in the form of symmetrical peers. Their communication model supports a bi-directional flow of subscriptions and messages. Each broker is responsible for a subset of subscriptions. A publisher sends a message to any broker that it is connected to. That broker then becomes responsible for propagating the message to all other brokers in the topology. When a new message enters the system, each broker checks the message against its own subscriptions and forwards it as necessary. It is apparent that the matching and forwarding overhead is reduced compared to the previous topology. This is because each broker needs to match messages against a portion of subscriptions. In this topology, the

Figure 3. Peer-to-peer broker topology

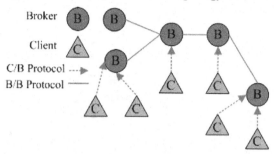

network will be flooded by the generated messages since they travel to all brokers.

There is currently a great deal of interest in publish/subscribe systems due to their high flexibility and scalability in dynamic distributed environments. As discussed earlier, the properties of publish/subscribe systems make them a good candidate for supporting mobility and weakly connected environments in a natural manner. First, the interacting parties can operate in the system without being aware of each other. Second, they can always be plugged in and out of the system without impacting each other directly. Third, the publish/subscribe paradigm is better adapted than the traditional point-to-point paradigm to cope with unannounced disconnection of interacted parties, which characterizes mobile wireless environments. However, most existing publish/subscribe systems are optimized for fixed environments and have not considered the issues imposed by mobile wireless settings. They assume (1) permanent network connectivity and that (2) information producers and consumers are stationary. Thus, this indicates a pressing need to extend publish/subscribe systems to the mobile wireless context.

Issues of Subscriber Mobility

As discussed previously, the broker topology of a publish/subscribe system can be either centralized or distributed. To reflect mobility scenario and to meet scalability aspects, the work reported

Figure 2. Hierarchical broker topology

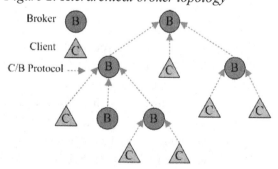

here focuses on a publish/subscribe system that is deployed as a distributed network of brokers. Figure 4 shows the architecture of such a system in a mobile wireless LAN network. A mobile client that can be either a producer or a consumer of messages (or both) connects to one of several distributed brokers through a wireless access point. The wireless access points form the boundary of the distributed communication service and maintain connections to the clients. The message brokers are run on stationary machines that are located within the fixed network infrastructure. They are interconnected through a set of routers in the form of a P2P overlay to form a distributed communication service. Here we only focus on the mobility challenges from the subscriber's prospect. Publisher mobility is beyond the scope of this chapter.

In this scenario, a subscriber is no longer connected to the same broker all the time. Mobile subscribers may disconnect from one broker and reconnect to another broker while they are roaming. Due to the *handoff* procedure, subscribers may go through a temporary blackout period. There is also a possibility for the subscribers to get frequently disconnected from the network due

to the absence of network connectivity or running out of battery. During such blackout periods, subscribers will lose their ability for receiving messages. This may result in missing some or all of their subscribed messages. Hence, mobility and temporary disconnections are the major problems that need to be managed by a publish/subscribe system. Limited bandwidth environments can be another challenging issue that may prevent or delay message delivery. Broker performance is also a major concern when extending publish/subscribe systems to the mobile wireless context. The broker may become a performance bottleneck due to the additional load imposed by dealing with the aforementioned issues.

Clearly, some support for disconnected and mobile subscribers is needed. Otherwise, if subscribers consume messages only when connected to a broker, they will loose information/messages during periods of disconnection or during a handoff. One proposal to deal with mobile clients is the use of durable subscriptions, as advocated by Publish/Subscribe systems such as the Java Messaging Service (Sun Microsystems, 2008). Durable subscriptions give the brokers the ability to track inactive subscribers and to deliver their

Figure 4. A distributed publish/subscribe system in WLAN networks

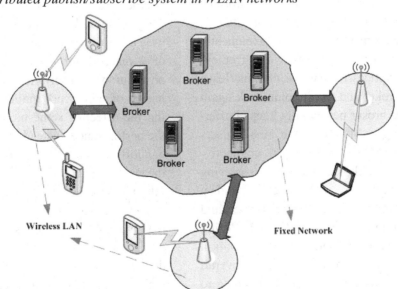

messages when they become active again. While durable subscriptions directly address the problem of spurious disconnections, they are not sufficient to deal with subscriber mobility, as discussed in more detail next.

Initially, the subscriber is connected to broker *A1* and consumes messages through *A1*. Eventually, the subscriber disconnects from broker *A1* and reconnects to broker *A2* (potentially being disconnected for some time during that handoff). Broker *A1* will keep locally buffering the messages that the subscriber would have consumed if it had been connected. As the subscriber reconnects to the broker *A2*, it needs to submit new subscriptions in order to receive messages. Once the subscriber established its subscriptions, broker *A2* starts forwarding messages to the subscriber based on its new subscriptions. Broker *A2* may not have any previous knowledge about the former subscriptions that had been attached to the old broker. Also, broker *A2* cannot retrieve the buffered messages at *A1* if it has no information about the location of the old broker. Therefore, the subscriber may end up losing all the messages that were generated during the time it was not connected to either *A1* or *A2*.

In addition, as the subscriber migration is transparent to the system, broker *A1* will have an inactive subscriber and continues to store its messages locally. This can happen quite often in the mobile environment as mobile users frequently migrate from one broker to another without removing their subscriptions. Even worse, they may leave the original broker and never come back again and hence the broker perpetually keeps buffering the messages. Moreover, the mobile users may occasionally lose their network connectivity due to poor wireless connections, triggering buffering activity. Thus, each broker may end up having a large number of inactive subscribers and has to deal with their messages. Since buffering messages for disconnected subscribers puts a substantial overhead on the broker, the overall system performance may gradually degrade to the point of failure.

Let us consider the scenario when the disconnected subscriber reconnects to the original broker (broker *A1*) after it has been connected to a different broker (broker *A2*). By default, broker *A1* will stop the buffering activity for that subscriber and start sending the buffered messages to the subscriber. Since the broker is not aware of the messages that have been delivered by the other broker, the subscriber may receive duplicated messages. Some applications cannot tolerate duplicated messages which can be a major issue for them. Moreover, such duplication will flood the wireless channel and consume a significant amount of the channel bandwidth.

STATE-OF-ART: SUBSCRIBER MOBILITY SUPPORT

Many publish/subscribe systems have been designed, implemented, and tested. The majority of them address fixed networks, not providing any support for mobile scenarios. Relatively few papers explicitly address supporting mobile subscribers. (Farooq, Majumdar, & Parsons, 2004) and (Farooq, Parsons, & Majumdar, 2004) presented their experience in evaluating the performance of a commercial JMS-based pub/sub middleware in wired and mobile cellular networks. They proposed two mobility extensions, one uses a middleware level handoff protocol based on a reactive approach and the other is based on a durable subscription-based approach. The nature of their work mainly focuses on studying the effect of some mobility parameters on the performance, instead of proposing a specific handoff approach. *Caporuscio et al.* evaluated the performance of SIENA (Caporuscio et al., 2003) in wired and GPRS-based networks. They mainly focused on measuring the behavior of a reactive mobility support service developed specifically for extending SIENA to mobile wireless domains. Their experimental results have proven the applicability of their service and investigated the number of duplicated and lost messages, but defined no other metrics to evaluate the system performance. (Podnar & Lovrek, 2004) proposed a mobility extension based on persistent messages that require the delivery of valid messages just after the activation of a new subscription in the systems. Each broker is responsible for storing the arrived messages in a persistent buffer and then forwards them to interested subscribers and neighboring brokers. The messages are deleted once their validity period expires. The broker also maintains a list of valid messages that have been delivered to subscribers and brokers. When a subscriber reconnects to the system, the broker activates its subscriptions and sends the valid buffered messages. The subscriber must provide a list of the previous consumed messages to avoid duplicate messages. This approach clearly creates extra traffic in the broker network, and increases broker memory consumption and processing time. In contrast, our approach reduces this overhead as it propagates only the subscriptions to the neighboring brokers and buffers messages only when subscribers become inactive/disconnected. The REBECA project (Zeidler & Fiege, 2003) relies on a reactive approach for supporting mobility. The last visited broker plays the role of a proxy subscriber. Whenever a subscriber reconnects to a new broker, it re-submits its subscriptions. The broker network finds the old broker by locating a broker at the junction of delivery paths to the new and old broker. It is straightforward to find a junction broker if the broker network uses simple routing, because each broker keeps entries about all active subscriptions. The notifications stored by the old broker are routed through the junction to reach the new broker, and then the subscriber. The authors do not justify why subscribers cannot maintain the information about the last visited broker. There are currently no results that evaluate the performance of the approach. The mobility extension in ELVIN (Sutton et al., 2001) is mainly based on a central caching proxy server that mediates between the original server

and mobile terminals for storing messages for disconnected subscribers. This approach creates a performance bottleneck at the proxy server as the subscribers must always reconnect to the central proxy. It also induces significant network traffic due to potential triangular routing. JEDI (Cugola et al., 2001) has added an extension to support mobility that is based on explicit *moveIn* and *moveOut* operations to relocate subscribers. The mobile subscribers are explicitly triggering these operations during the relocation process, which can be problematic if a wireless connection breaks down unexpectedly due to physical mobility or interference.

In summary, those publish/subscribe systems that support mobility typically do so with a reactive model. The reactive approach is based on a proxy component that acts on behalf of a disconnected client, storing published messages during the disconnection period in a dedicated buffer and delivering them to the client after its reconnection. As the client reconnects to a new broker, a handoff protocol is triggered, which forwards the stored messages from the old broker to the new one and then transfers them to the client. Mobility extensions based on such a state-transfer approach may result in a drastic increase in the load on a network. It is shown in (Burcea et al., 2004) that mobility can increase the average network traffic by up to 100%. This may result in a significant increase in the handoff latency as the message transfer is initiated only after the mobile user reattaches to the next broker. It may also result in degrading the system's performance due to the increased overhead on the network link.

A NEW MOBILITY SUPPORT PROPOSAL: PRO-ACTIVE MOBILITY SUPPORT

This section describes a pro-active context distribution approach that aims to cope with subscriber mobility at significantly minimized cost in terms of message loss/duplication, processing overhead, and handoff latency. Our proposed approach achieves its objectives by transparently managing active subscriptions and incoming messages, both while the subscriber is disconnected or/and during its handoff process. In the pro-active approach, subscriptions can be either in *active* or *passive* modes. A subscription is active if it is used for matching the subscriber interests against the published messages and is passive otherwise. When a subscription is active, the matched messages are either routed to the interested subscribers or stored in a local buffer for future use. A passive subscription on the other hand does not enforce any message routing or caching and simply ignores incoming messages. Initially, a subscriber submits an active subscription to a broker to consume its messages. A passive copy of this subscription is propagated to all immediate neighbor brokers. As the subscriber disconnects from the original broker, the propagated subscription becomes active, in anticipation that the subscriber may reconnect shortly in the nearly neighborhood. Whenever the subscriber reconnects to a broker, the subscription in any other neighboring broker goes back to the passive mode.

The pro-active context distribution algorithm can be decomposed into the following three phases: 1) transfer/cache subscriptions to/at the neighbor brokers; 2) activate/deactivate subscriptions and cache messages locally; 3) deliver messages and reset cache. Figure 5 contains the high-level description of the algorithm, described as a sequence of steps, which are discussed in more detail later on, and correspond to various connection, disconnection, and handoff scenarios. Although each broker in the system locally executes a copy of this algorithm, the description here assumes that the algorithm executes at some broker B_j. The following notation is used throughout the description:

- S: a subscriber who is potentially mobile.
- B_j: the initial hosted broker for subscriber S.

- B_i: one of the next-hop brokers of B_j.
- **Neighbor(B_j)**: the set of neighbor brokers of B_j.
- **Sub(S)**: the subscriptions related to subscriber S.
- **Msgs(S)**: the actual messages of subscriber S.
- **Context(S)**: the information (subscriptions/messages) of subscriber S.
- **Timeout(S)**: a chosen time $T_{timeout}$ for managing the context of a disconnected subscriber S. when $T_{timeout}$ expires, subscriber context is garbage collected. ($T_{timeout} \geq$ the average disconnection interval at all brokers).

Pro-active Context Distribution Algorithm – executed on broker (B_j) (see Figure 5).

Our algorithm makes a few assumptions about the target pub/sub middleware system. The algorithm assumes a set of brokers organized in a general graph (or *peer-to-peer*) topology to form a distributed communication service. The peer brokers, connected by a high-bandwidth (overlay) network, communicate directly with each other to exchange messages and subscriptions. Our approach is also based on the assumption that mobile subscribers will, with high probability, reconnect to a broker close to their current locations. So tracking which peers are neighbors (i.e., likely handoff candidates) will be beneficial and keep the pro-active overheads small. In the worst case, every other peer is a potential neighbor, which will not scale well as the number of subscribers and brokers increases. However, infrastructure-based wireless systems such as WLAN or cellular networks match this assumption well – special infrastructure elements (Access Points, Base Stations, etc.) are responsible for serving users in a given geographical region, collectively covering a much larger area. And many network protocols are optimized for handling handoffs between geographically adjacent infrastructure elements (location management, connection re-establishment, etc.).

Figure 5. The pro-active context distribution algorithm

```
1: Initial connection
        IF subscriber S connects to B_j THEN
                    FOR all B_i ∈ Neighbor(B_j) DO
                            Forward Sub(S) to B_i
                    ENDFOR
        ENDIF
2: Subscriber disconnects
        IF subscriber S disconnects from B_j THEN
                    FOR all B_i ∈ Neighbor(B_j) DO
                            Activate Sub(S) stored at B_i
                            Forward Msgs(S) to B_i until Sub(S) activated
                    ENDFOR
        ENDIF
3: Subscriber Reconnection
        IF subscriber S reconnects to B_j THEN
                    FOR all B_i ∈ Neighbor(B_j) DO
                            Deactivate Sub(S) stored at B_i
                            Delete Msgs(S) stored at B_i
                    ENDFOR
        ENDIF
4: Subscriber hands off to peer broker
        IF subscriber S reconnects to B_k from B_j THEN
                    FOR all B_i ∈ Neighbor(B_j) DO    /* B_i ≠ B_k */
                            Delete Context(S) stored at B_i
                    ENDFOR
        ENDIF
5: Subscriber hands off from peer broker
        IF subscriber S reconnects to B_j from B_k THEN
                    IF Sub(S) is not in B_j buffer THEN
                            Obtain Context(S) stored at B_k
                    ENDIF
                    FOR all B_i ∈ Neighbor(B_j) DO
                            Forward Sub(S) to B_i
                    ENDFOR
        ENDIF
6: Subscriber unsubscribes
        IF subscriber S unsubscribes from B_j THEN
                    FOR all B_i ∈ Neighbor(B_j) DO
                            Delete Context(S) stored at B_i
                    ENDFOR
        ENDIF
7: Subscriber times out
        IF B_j triggers Timeout(S) THEN
                    FOR all B_i ∈ Neighbor(B_j) DO
                            Delete Context(S)
                    ENDFOR
        ENDIF
```

We next give a stepwise description of the proposed algorithm. Although it is intended to serve multiple mobile subscribers that are connected to the same broker, for simplicity, we only describe the algorithm from the viewpoint of an individual subscriber. Figure 6 depicts a simplified UML sequence diagram that describes all the necessary steps.

When a subscriber S initially connects to broker B_j (step 1), this broker sends a passive copy of the subscriber's subscription $Sub(S)$ to each immediate neighbor $Neighbor(B_j)$. Each neighbor $B_i \in Neighbor(B_j)$ locally stores $Sub(S)$. In the meantime, broker B_j routes the published messages to subscriber S throughout its active subscription. The pro-active approach is based on the notion of *neighbor graph*, which will be described later in this chapter. The knowledge of the connected-neighbor graph is learned automatically over time by each broker in the system.

When subscriber S temporarily disconnects from the network due to poor network connectivity or a handoff (step 2), broker B_j detects this (for example through periodic ping messages, or the failure in delivering buffered messages to that subscriber). The broker will then send an activate request to each immediate neighbor B_i. Broker B_j also needs to forward stored messages to its neighbors until the receipt of activation request is acknowledged. This is necessary to avoid message loss that may occur due to the activation latency. Following the activation of *Sub(S)*, the brokers B_i will locally buffer all the incoming messages that match *Sub(S)*. It should be noted that the ID of the last message consumed by S (for each subscription) is enclosed with the activation request and thus only the messages with higher ID are stored. Similarly, broker B_j keeps buffering the messages for S as it may reconnect to it again.

In case the subscriber S was only temporarily disconnected from the broker B_j due to poor network connectivity, it will reconnect to the same broker (step 3). Broker B_j sends a Deactivate request to each of its neighbors B_i, informing them to deactivate *Sub(S)*, terminate the buffering process, and clean up the local buffer. In the meantime, broker B_j delivers all buffered messages to subscriber S.

If a subscriber S reconnects to a different broker B_k (step 4), broker B_k informs B_j that S reconnected to it. Thus, broker B_j requests its neighbors B_i to delete the context of S from their buffers, excluding broker B_k. Broker B_k is excluded because S is already connected to it. It should be noted that broker B_k and B_j exchange the list of their neighbor graphs to reduce the overhead of context transfer. Throughout these lists, broker B_j can decide which *Sub(S)* should be deleted and which *Sub(S)* should be deactivated for later use by broker B_k. Similarly, broker B_k can identify which *Sub(S)* should be forwarded to its neighbors.

When subscriber S reconnects to broker B_j from broker B_k (step 5), broker B_j first checks if *Context(S)* is available in its buffer. If it is not found in the buffer, then broker B_j will request the subscriber context from broker B_k. This typically indicates that broker B_j is not a neighbor of broker B_k. Thus, broker B_j has no information about the subscriber S. There are two distinct scenarios when this occurs. 1) Initially, the neighbor graph is empty, and subscriber S is the first to visit broker B_j from its neighbor B_k. 2) Even if a neighbor relation existed at some time between B_j and B_k, no mobile subscriber has handed off from B_k to B_j for some time. As explained later, the neighbor graph will time out such not-recently-used edges to control the protocol overhead. If *Context(S)* is found in the buffer of broker B_j (or successfully retrieved), similar actions to step 1 will be performed.

When subscriber S unsubscribes from broker B_j (step 6), broker B_j requests its neighbors B_i to delete *Context(S)* from their buffers. When subscriber S disconnects from broker B_j for a long interval (step 7), reaching a timeout threshold of $T_{timeout}$, broker B_j informs its neighbors B_i to delete *Context(S)* from their buffers. This is a necessary task as buffering and managing the *Context(S)* can severely affect the broker performance.

The effectiveness of our pro-active caching approach largely relies on the successful approximation of the subscriber's movement. For a better chance of success, the broker B_j can approximate a set of potential brokers that are most likely to be the next location of the mobile subscriber S. This approximation can be achieved, for instance, through observations of the mobility patterns of subscribers. We therefore define a data structure, *neighbor graph*, which provides the abstractions to achieve this goal. The neighbor graph forms the basis for our pro-active approach and is used as a means for pre-loading the subscriber context one hop ahead of its current location. It is an undirected graph with a number of edges that represent mobility paths between the vertices (or *brokers*). Hence, the neighbors of a given vertex

Figure 6. UML sequence diagram for the pro-active context distribution algorithm

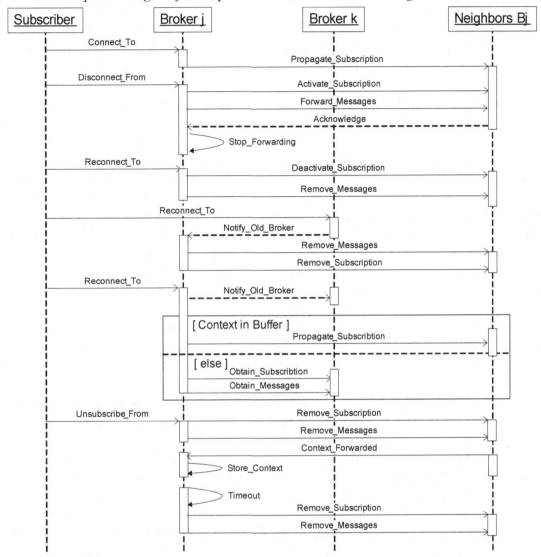

v in the graph correspond to the set of potential next brokers. It is used to identify the candidate set of future brokers in order to transfer/cache the subscriber context (*subscriptions*) before the occurrence of the handoff operation.

Definitions:

- **Neighboring relation:** Two brokers B_i and B_j can form a neighboring relation if it is possible for a subscriber S to reestablish its connection through a direct motion path between the physical locations of B_i and B_j. The neighboring relation between a set of distributed brokers forms the basis for the creation of the neighbor graph and depends on the distribution of the brokers in the network topology as discussed later.

- **Broker neighboring graph:** is an undirected graph $G = (V, E)$, where V is the vertex set of all brokers, $V = \{B_1, B_2, ..., B_k\}$, and E is a set of unordered distinct pairs of edges, e

$= \{B_i, B_j\}$ where $B_i \neq B_j$. We say that vertices B_i and $B_j \in V$ have a neighboring relation if $\{B_i, B_j\} \in E$. We thus define the set of all B_i neighbors in G as follows: *Neighbor*(B_i) $= \{B_{ik} : B_{ik} \in V, (B_i, B_{ik}) \in E\}$.

The neighbor graph can be constructed either in a static manner (i.e., manually created once and never changes over time) or in a dynamic manner (i.e., automatically generated and adaptively changes according to the mobility pattern). A static neighbor graph is problematic as it fails to adapt itself to the dynamic changes in the mobility pattern. The neighbor graph also can be maintained either in a centralized manner (i.e., a single server stores the entire neighbor graph) or in a distributed manner (i.e., each broker stores a local view of the neighbor graph). A centralized neighbor graph has a scalability limitation. Therefore, we considered a dynamic and distributed manner for generating the neighbor graph.

Two complementary methods can be applied by each broker to effectively learn the edges in the graph. The first method is to attach the address of the old broker with the reconnection request sent by the mobile subscriber to the new broker, thus establishing the neighboring relation between the two brokers. The second method is to use the request for context transfer received from another broker to establish the relationship. This request is usually received whenever the subscriber context is missed at that broker. Such a case may occur in two scenarios: 1) when the first subscriber moves through some motion path between two brokers; 2) when a subscriber disconnects (*voluntary* or *involuntary*) from the network and potentially moves to various locations to reconnect to any other broker in the coverage area. When applying these methods, some outlier edges (the ones that do not correctly model the neighboring relation) can be added to the graph. The neighbor graph may also hold some unused edges that are created through rarely used paths. The impact of the outlier and unused edges on the performance of

our pro-active approach can be significant due to the additional overhead required to cache the subscriber context over time. It is thus essential to remove such edges from the graph over time. In this regard, a timestamp-based *Least Recently Used (LRU)* method is used to ensure the correctness and freshness of the graph. It is clear that the autonomous creation of the graph makes it self-adaptive to dynamism in the neighboring relation (e.g., adding/deleting brokers, changing the network topology). Each broker independently builds and locally stores a *subgraph* of the complete graph of all broker nodes. The following pseudocode is used to build the local view of the graph at each broker in a LRU manner. Here, we refer to the broker that executes the algorithm as $B_{current}$.

- **Receive a reconnection request:** If a mobile subscriber S moves to $B_{current}$ from B_i, $B_{current}$ induces the edge $\{B_i, B_{current}\}$ in its list of neighbors with a timestamp.

- **Receive a context transfer request:** If $B_{current}$ receives a context transfer request from B_i, it will add the edge $\{B_i, B_{current}\}$ to its list neighbors with a timestamp.

- **Edge-removal:** If none of the above edge-addition operations is performed through a motion path between B_i and $B_{current}$ within a given time T, the stored edge $\{B_i, B_{current}\}$ will be removed from the list of neighbor graph. $T \geq$ the average frequency interval of edge-addition operations at all broker nodes.

Since the neighbor graph is initially an empty graph, the majority of handoff operations, based on our creation algorithm, cause edge-insertion during the early age of the neighbor graph, thereby reducing its benefit in our proposed *pro-active* approach. Each time a mobile subscriber hands off between two peer brokers that are not linked by an edge in the neighbor graph, no pro-active context can be established in the target broker. The algorithm described in step 5 in Figure 5 falls back on a *reactive* approach to retrieve subscriptions and buffered messages from the previous peer. As this handoff will then result in the insertion of an edge in the neighbor graph, subsequent handoffs between these two peers can employ (and benefit from) the *pro-active* handoff.

IMPLEMENTATION AND EXPERIMENTAL RESULTS

System Implementation

We next describe the prototype implementation of the mobility approaches. The pro-active approach is implemented within an independent layer of *proxies* between the subscribers and their messaging brokers. This layer is mainly responsible for replicating dummy subscribers at the next future brokers to buffer messages on behalf of the moving subscriber. It also dynamically captures the mobility graph of the distributed brokers' network to identify the subset of next neighboring brokers. A single proxy process runs with each broker to manage user mobility from one broker to the other. Note that the proxy layer is completely transparent to the brokers and the applications. We have integrated a monitoring component with the broker process to transparently track the subscribers' states (i.e., connect, disconnect, handoff) as well as the ID of the last message consumed by the subscriber. Also, each subscriber has to keep track of the last broker to which it was connected to.

When a subscriber connects to a broker, the proxy will be notified and receives a copy of the subscriber's subscription. The proxy locally stores the subscription and uses it to instantiate an inactive dummy subscriber. Meanwhile, it propagates a copy of the subscription to all neighbors, and instructs its peers to create the same dummy subscriber using the forwarded subscription. When the subscriber disconnects

from its current broker, all the corresponding dummy subscribers at the neighboring brokers are activated to buffer messages on behalf of the disconnected subscriber. The dummy subscribers use the ID of the last received message of the actual subscriber to prevent message duplication. Hence, only messages with higher ID are stored for the subscriber. When the subscriber reconnects to a new broker, the proxy at that broker notices this and informs the related dummy subscriber to stop storing messages and to return to inactive mode. The broker in the meanwhile starts delivering the buffered messages to the subscriber. The set of neighbor graphs located at the old and new brokers now must be inspected to ensure that new dummy subscribers are created on all neighboring nodes of the new broker and old dummy subscribers are either removed or deactivated. In this implementation, tracking the address of the broker is necessary as it is needed during the creation of the neighbor graph and when the reactive approach is applied before the building of this graph. We also use the broker address to distinguish the handoff state from the reconnect state.

The pro-active approach can be affected by the issues of race conditions that may result in message loss and duplication. However, the message loss and duplication practically can be rare. Due to the network conditions of the distributed brokers, it is possible that some messages reach certain brokers later or earlier than others. As the ID of the last received message is used whenever the mobile subscriber reconnects to a new broker, message duplication caused by race conditions can be eliminated. This can be noted in the performance evaluation results shown later. The reactive approach does not require the use of the last message ID and hence it shows higher sensitivity to the race conditions, particularly in terms of message duplication.

Although the pro-active approach significantly reduces network traffic (message transfer between the old and new brokers), it imposes additional overhead on the next neighboring brokers. This overhead is introduced by the caching procedure that is triggered whenever a mobile subscriber moves to a new broker. The storing overhead proportionally increases with an increasing number of moving subscribers. This may lead to degradation of the brokers' performance and creation of a bottleneck point at such brokers from which the subscribers are disconnected for a large interval.

The mobile subscribers practically may now end up losing some messages if they reconnect after a large interval. This is because every broker's buffer can store only a limited number of messages. Since each buffer is configured to use the Oldest Message Overwriting Policy as it gets filled, buffer contents can be overwritten due to a long disconnecting period. It is worth mentioning that the pro-active service involves only one broker in each handoff operation. Thus, message overwrite due to buffer size limitation influences the service only at its new broker. In contrast, as the reactive mobility service involves two brokers in each handoff operation, message overwrite can occur at the old and new locations of a mobile subscriber. As a result, the reactive service may under certain conditions (i.e., congested network) experience a higher impact due to the buffer content overwrite.

The implementation of the *reactive* approach shares as much code and data structures as possible with the pro-active mobility support. This provides us with a fair comparison and baseline indicator to evaluate the adequacy of our proposed approach. The main idea of the reactive approach involves uncoupling and retrieval of messages from the old broker that was previously serving the mobile subscriber. When the messages arrive at the new broker, they will be merged with the subscriber messages stored at the local buffer of the new broker, ordered, and delivered to the mobile subscriber.

The reactive approach is implemented by running a *proxy process* with each broker entity to manage subscribers' mobility. Note that the proxy process is largely independent from the target broker. Every broker maintains a single buffer that is used to buffer the messages of all disconnected subscribers. To optimize buffer space usage, the Oldest Message Overwriting Policy is applied to control which messages should be overwritten when the buffer is filled up. Each mobile subscriber uses a *mobility service library* that is attached to the subscriber application. This library mediates the subscriber requests made to the target broker and is used to interact with the proxy process during the occurrence of connect/disconnect operations. When the mobile subscriber disconnects from its current broker, the proxy process creates a *proxy object* that takes control over the subscriber subscriptions at that broker in order to manage the subscriber messages. Once the subscriber reconnects and receives the buffered messages, the proxy object is garbage collected. Note that each subscriber keeps track of the last broker to which it was connected to in a log file. This is required as the new broker needs to communicate with the old broker to fetch the subscriber messages.

Experimental Environment

For our experimental study, we have reviewed a representative set of pub/sub systems to motivate our choice of the target platform for our work activities. We have selected Java Message Service (JMS) (Sun Microsystems, 2008) as our base pub/sub platform to investigate the adequacy of the proposed extension and to compare its behavior with the reactive solution.

Figure 7 shows our experimental setup. We performed all our experiments on an overlay network of six Intel based Pentium 4 nodes running RedHat Linux 9, inter-connected by a 100 Mbps switch. Two nodes were used for running two instances of the JMS broker with default configuration values. A router node was used for running a wireless network emulator. One node was used for running a single, stationary message

Figure 7. Experimental setup

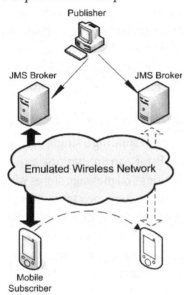

publisher. The remaining two nodes were used for running the mobile subscribers. Clients that share the same machine run in separate threads and connections, but use the same Java Virtual Machine and JMS Client library. The JVM used for running the JMS broker and the clients is Sun SDK 1.4.2 (build 1.4.2_05-b04), started with the options –Xms64m and –Xmx256m as a minimum and maximum heap size. Although this is a limited configuration, it is sufficient for our purpose: evaluating and comparing different mobility support solutions.

In our setup, a single stationary publisher is used to send messages to two instances of the JMS broker running on separate nodes. Each generated message has assigned a single selector value ranging from 0 to 99. The selector values are randomly generated with uniform distribution during the publishing runtime. Similarly, each subscriber expresses its interest in receiving messages within a specific selector range that is also randomly chosen to be 1/5th of the total selector range.

A mobile subscriber in this setup represents an application running on a mobile terminal that

transparently moves from one broker to the other. It initially registers with one of the two JMS brokers by sending a single durable subscription. Through a mobility scenario written in Java, the subscriber keeps migrating between the two brokers during the course of the experiments. In our experiments, two hundred subscriber threads were created and executed on two stationary machines. Subscribers are initially split evenly between the two JMS brokers. However, due to subscribers' mobility, this number fluctuates over time, resulting in a broker serving a lager number of subscribers at times while at other times the broker may serve only a small number of subscribers.

A Java program is implemented to emulate subscribers' mobility. Each subscriber goes through a mobility scenario that is presented in the state diagram shown in Figure 8. The *connect state* is the starting point for all subscribes in our mobility model: a subscriber is connected to one of the two JMS brokers and consumes messages. Each subscriber remains in this state for a randomly generated, exponentially distributed time with a mean β. With a probability of 0.5, a subscriber either moves to disconnect state or handoff state. The *disconnect state* reflects the case of signal breakdown due to poor network connectivity. A subscriber remains in this state for a randomly generated, exponentially distributed time with a mean δ. With a similar probability of 0.5, the

Figure 8. Mobility state diagram

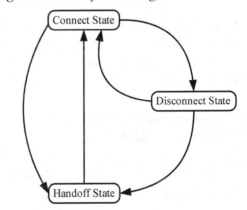

subscriber moves either back to the connect state and reconnects to the same broker or goes to the handoff state. The *handoff state* corresponds to the case where a subscriber moves out of the covered range of its previous broker. After staying in the handoff state for a randomly generated, exponentially distributed time with a mean δ, the subscriber moves back to the connect state and connects to a different broker.

All the communications between the subscribers and the brokers are tunneled via an emulated wireless channel that is created using a network emulator called NistNet (National Institute of Standards and Technology, 2005). NistNet is a popular software tool that is implemented as a kernel module extension to the Linux operating system. It can be used to emulate various network environments. We used NistNet to model the characteristics of an IEEE 802.11 wireless LAN network based on a set of configuration parameters such as packet delay, packet loss, packet duplication, and network bandwidth. All these parameters were set to the most commonly used values reported for IEEE 802.11 wireless LAN networks (Gupta & Kumar, 2003), (Yin et al., 2005).

Our testbed only allows us to experiment with handoffs between two brokers. As such, we can draw some initial conclusions about the relative strengths and weaknesses of the *pro-active* and *reactive* handoff approaches, assuming that the neighbor graph is perfect. Future work, discussed later, will explore how well the simple neighbor graph construction algorithm mentioned above allows us to capture user mobility patterns. We are also planning to explore the performance of these handoff approaches in networks with more brokers/peers.

Workload Parameters and Performance Metrics

The reported results were captured from the measurement data obtained under different workloads.

Each experiment was run for a duration that was long enough to reach a steady state. We ensured that the publisher and subscriber machines were not the bottlenecks in our experiments. We kept both CPU and memory utilizations at less than 65%, thereby preventing publisher and subscriber bottlenecks from impacting the overall system performance. Each broker machine was fully dedicated to running a single instance of the JMS broker. Prior to running any experiment, topic destinations and message stores were purged and reinitiated to start each test with a clean slate. All subscribers were consuming messages in asynchronous style. Each subscriber was using a separate connection to consume its messages. Also, network latencies for establishing subscribers' connections were not included in our results.

Workload Parameters

- *Publishing rate*: number of messages per second sent by a single publisher to the two instances of JMS broker in a synchronized manner. Publishing rates of 5, 10, 15, 20, and maximum (the rate that the system can sustain without crashing) were used to study the impact of the publishing rate on the system behavior.

- *Number of subscribers*: total number of subscribers that are served by each broker in the system. The total subscriber service demand per broker varies as subscribers keep moving between the two brokers. We have varied the number of subscribers from 10 to 200, with initially evenly assigning subscribers to the two brokers.

- *Queue size*: maximum buffer space in bytes that is used to temporarily store received messages. Queue sizes of 10, 30, 60, and 90 Kbytes were used in our experiments. The queue size is an important parameter as it has a direct impact on the system behavior. A large queue size decreases the message loss but will diminish the overall throughput. It imposes additional overhead by increasing the JVM heap size, which may repeatedly trigger the garbage collection procedure. A small queue size on the other hand may cause higher message losses but will have lower impact on the system performance.

- *Message size*: total length of a message payload, which is the sum of the lengths of the header, property fields, and the body part. Since the size of the first two parts is almost the same for all the messages, we only varied the message body size to range from 64 to 512 bytes.

- *Message selector*: defines the subscription pattern that expresses the subscriber's interest. As discussed earlier, the selectors are randomly generated to be 1/5th of the total range of message selector values.

- *Network bandwidth*: available bandwidth that can be used by the brokers to deliver messages to the subscribers. Two input values, 1Mbps and 11Mbps, were used to respectively represent low/high bandwidth environments.

- *Mean of disconnect interval* (δ): mean time interval of signal breakdown between the subscribers and their brokers. Mean values of 10 and 20 seconds were used.

- *Mean of connect interval* (β): mean time interval during which the subscriber is attached to a broker. Mean values of 60 and 120 seconds were used.

Performance Measures

- *Subscriber throughput* (*Ts*): total number of messages received per second. It is obtained by adding up the number of messages received by individual subscribers and dividing by the total duration of the experiment.

- *Percentage of message loss* (*L*): percentage of missed messages by all the subscribers. It was calculated by taking the difference between the total sent and received messages and then dividing by the total sent messages.

- *Percentage of message duplication* (*D*): percentage of duplicated messages received by all the subscribers. It is obtained by dividing the total duplicated messages by the total received messages.

- *Message processing time* (*Ls*): average processing time, in milliseconds, that it takes the broker to process messages. It is obtained by adding up the processing time of each message and then dividing the total by the total number of received messages.

- *Handoff latency (H):* time, in milliseconds, between sending the reconnect request and receiving the first message of the corresponding subscriber at its new broker.

Table 1 summarizes the workload parameters. Unless otherwise stated, experiments were conducted using the default values.

Experimental Results

We evaluate the pro-active and reactive approaches in terms of message processing overhead, handoff latency, message loss, message duplication, and overall throughput. Unless otherwise stated, the results shown next were achieved using the default input values listed in Table 1. We also compare the results of both mobility approaches.

The overhead of using the pro-active and reactive extensions is evaluated in terms of two different metrics: the average processing time of the messages and the aggregated throughput of the subscribers. These metrics provide a good indicator of the overhead incurred by both extensions. To study this overhead under different load conditions, we have varied the total number of subscribers that can be served by the brokers.

Figure 9 shows the incurred message processing time (*Ls*) and the overall throughput (*Ts*) as the number of subscribers increases. From the

Table 1. Workload Parameters

Parameters	Input Values	Default Values
Number of subscribers	10, 50, 100, 150, and 200	100 per broker
Message size	64, 128, 256, and 512 bytes	64 bytes
Publication rate	5, 10, 15, 20, and Maximum	Maximum
Network bandwidth	1Mbps and 11Mbps	11Mbps
Queue size	10K, 30K, 60K, and 90K	30Kbytes
Mean disconnect interval	10 and 20 seconds	10 seconds
Mean connect interval	60 and 120 seconds	60 seconds
Subscription pattern	1/5th of the total range	1/5th of the total range

graph, it can be noted that there is a proportional relationship between the message processing time and the number of served subscribers. This is an expected behavior of the system since increasing the number of subscribers adds extra load on the system, thereby the message processing time increases. The system throughput beyond a certain number of subscribers will hit its breakpoint and start to decrease due to the increased load of the served subscribers. This can be clearly seen in the figure when the number of subscribers reaches 200.

The figure shows that the pro-active approach experiences relatively less overhead in terms of message processing compared to the reactive ap-

proach. The reason for this lies in the semantic of the reactive approach, which remotely fetches the subscriber messages from the old broker, merges them with the locally buffered messages, and arranges all the messages before delivering them to the subscriber. The pro-active approach also shows better throughput results than the reactive approach as it prevents message duplication and eliminates the overhead of message fetching, which exists in the reactive approach.

We evaluate the handoff latency under different load conditions imposed by the number of served subscribers (10, 50, 100, 150, and 200). We define the handoff latency as the time, in milliseconds, between sending the reconnect

Figure 9. The mobility extension overhead

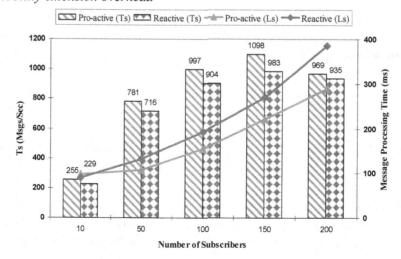

request and receiving the first message of the corresponding subscriber at its new broker. The cumulative distribution graph of the handoff time observations is shown in Figure 10.

From the figure, we observe that there is a substantial difference in the handoff time of the pro-active and reactive approaches. The pro-active approach shows that almost 80% of the handoffs are performed in less than 50 ms whereas the reactive approach shows that almost 80% of the handoffs take longer than 400 ms. This implies that the pro-active approach can provide fast handoffs since the subscriber context is always ready at its new broker before its movement. A portion of the handoff latency in the pro-active approach is a result of the switchover process involved between the actual and dummy subscriber before the buffered messages start being forwarded. While the actual subscriber takes over the dummy one should be deactivated and all neighbors should be notified about the arrival of the actual subscriber. Another portion of this latency, which also exists in the reactive approach, is attributed to the preparation time for the broker to start delivering the stored messages. This time is mainly based on the broker's load conditions. The reason for suffering higher handoff latency in

the reactive approach is that every handoff causes the entire messages for the moving subscriber to be read from the buffer, transferred to the new location, merged with the messages in the new location, arranged, and eventfully delivered to the subscriber.

We study the system performance in terms of message loss, duplication, and overall throughput with the pro-active and reactive approaches. The results of these metrics are given as a function of publication rate and queue size. This allows us to analyze conditions under which, if any, one approach can perform better than the other.

Figures 11(a) and 11(b) show the results of message loss and duplication, along the left y-axis, and the overall throughput along the right y-axis. The results are measured as the publishing rate increases up to the maximum, the rate that the system can sustain.

The publication rate has a direct impact on the percentage of message loss when we have a limited queue size. This can be seen in the graphs where the message loss increases almost linearly with the increase of publishing rate. From the graphs, we can note that the pro-active and reactive approaches achieve approximately similar results, excluding the case of maximum publication rate.

Figure 10. The cumulative distribution of handoff time

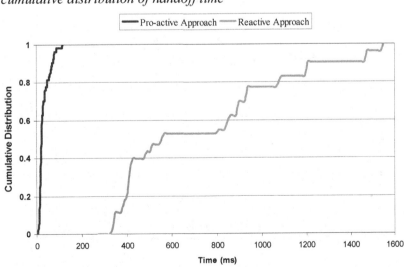

In this case, the reactive approach experiences a slightly higher percentage of message loss than the pro-active approach. With maximizing the publication rate, the old broker will discard more messages from its buffer as it gets filled up fast. As a result, only a part of the subscriber messages will be transferred to the new broker during the handoff operation. Furthermore, when the subscriber moves to the new broker, it has to wait for a while (more than 400 ms with probability of 0.8) to receive its messages from the old broker. During this waiting time, the new broker keeps storing the subscriber messages. Based on the waiting period, some of the subscriber messages

might be discarded from the buffer if it gets filled prior to the subscriber reactivation. The pro-active approach shows zero message duplication in all cases as it involves only one broker in delivering the messages of the reconnected subscribers. In this approach, the ID of the last consumed message is also used to prevent the impact of race conditions during the subscriber handoffs. In contrast, a negligible portion of duplicated messages occurs in the reactive approach due to race conditions. A larger part of duplicated messages is attributed to the semantic of reactive approach as it involves the old and new brokers to store messages for the moving subscriber. This may

Figure 11. The overall system performance at given publishing rates

(a) The Pro-active Approach

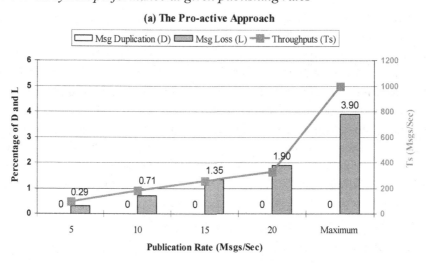

(b) The Reactive Approach

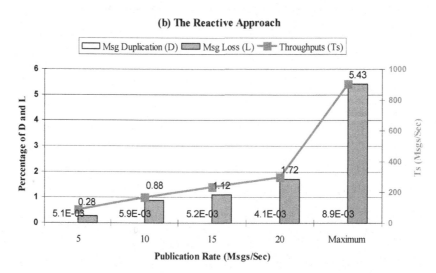

lead to storing similar messages at both brokers and hence the subscriber may receive a number of duplicated messages. From Figure 11(b), we observe that the reactive approach is sensitive to higher publication rates since it shows the highest message duplication at the maximum rate. At this rate, more messages are stored at the old and new brokers for the moving subscriber, thereby increasing the possibility of receiving larger number of duplicated messages. Also, the impact of race conditions in terms of message loss and duplication increases with higher publication rates.

The pro-active approach achieves relatively higher throughput results than the reactive approach. This is a result of preventing message duplication in the pro-active approach as well

as eliminating the overhead of message transfer adapted by the reactive approach. Message transfer can significantly increase the network load and hence decreases the publication rate.

Figures 12(a) and 12(b) respectively present the results of message loss, duplication, and overall throughput for the pro-active and reactive approaches with an increase of the queue sizes. The figures show an inversely-proportional relationship between the queue size and the percentage of message loss. As the queue size increases, more messages can be accommodated and remain longer in the queue. Thus, the percentage of message loss decreases. This implies that the queue size has a direct impact on the system behavior and should be well selected. Increasing queue size beyond

Figure 12. The overall system performance at given queue sizes

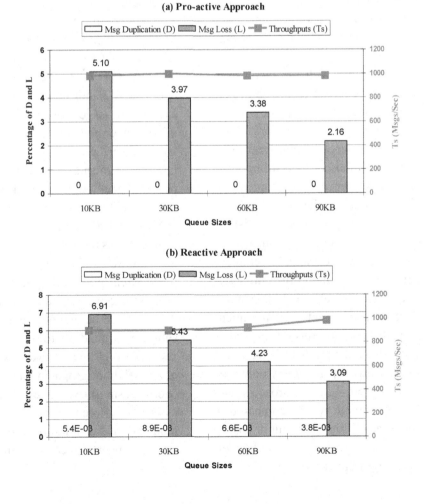

a threshold that provides zero message loss will only increase the overhead on the system without any reduction in message loss.

Both approaches show almost similar percentages of message loss. The pro-active approach however presents marginally less message loss in all queue sizes. This indicates that the reactive approach is more sensitive to the queue length than the pro-active approach. This is because the reactive approach is designed to buffer messages at the old and new brokers for every moving subscriber. Hence, a larger number of messages can be discarded from the buffers of the two brokers. In contrast, for the two-broker scenario we are exploring here, the pro-active approach involves only one broker for storing the messages of the moving subscriber.

Figure 12(a) shows that the pro-active approach has eliminated message duplication in all cases. In contrast, the reactive approach exposes negligible percentages of message duplication due to the race conditions and the dual buffering of its syntax.

The figures show that with the increase in the queue size, the achieved throughput does not change significantly. As the queue size increases, the publishing rate tends to decrease due to the overhead of the larger queue sizes. This includes the increased load of forwarding more messages to the subscribers and the frequent call to garbage collection due to the growth of heap memory size within the JVM. As the publishing rate decreases, the subscriber throughput tends to decrease as well. On the other hand, larger queue sizes reduce message loss that in turn increases the throughput. Hence, the subscriber throughput more or less remains constant until the queue size hits its threshold value. Beyond this value, the throughput will be negatively affected as the publishing rate decreases without any reduction in message loss. The pro-active approach shows slightly higher throughput results compared to the reactive approach. This is a result of having lower cost in terms of message processing, handoff latency, and message duplication.

CONCLUSION AND FUTURE WORK

In this chapter, we present a *pro-active* approach to support mobility in pub/sub middleware systems. This approach ensures that the subscriber context is always one hop ahead of its current location. We investigated the potential of our proposed approach using a simple prototype testbed, presented evaluation results that investigate system performance with the proposed solution and compared it to the solution based on the more common reactive approach. The experimental results show that the pro-active approach is superior to the reactive approach with respect to handoff latency and message duplication. The results indicate that our approach can provide fast handoff support with zero duplicated messages. It also achieves relatively higher throughput results and lower message loss compared to the reactive approach.

We recognize that the experimental environment described in this chapter does not model a truly large network. For example, in networks with many brokers, and a dense neighbor graph, the overhead of handling inactive subscriptions and caching messages for disconnected subscribers may reduce the benefits of our approach. Similarly, subscribers that are disconnected for long periods of time may negatively impact the overall performance. We are currently setting up a bigger testbed with 5-6 brokers and started collecting performance data in this environment. This bigger testbed raises interesting questions. For example, how do we model subscriber mobility and to what extent does the dynamic neighbor graph proposed above accurately model this mobility. As discussed before, our approach assumes that subscribers hand off to only a small number of "neighboring" peers/brokers, keeping the degree of the neighbor graph and therefore the protocol overhead small. We can explore this relationship using two different mobility models. In a random mobility model, all subscribers hand off to an arbitrary peer/broker, resulting in a fully connected neighbor graph. This represents the worst-case scenario for our approach, as all peers now maintain dummy subscribers for all subscribers, and actively buffer messages for all disconnected subscribers. On the other hand, we can enforce certain limitations on subscriber mobility, for example due to physical constraints. As a result, only a subset of peers will be connected in the neighbor graph, presumably resulting in a better performance of our approach. In addition, the load on individual peers/brokers may be uneven and a function of the peer's degree in the neighbor graph. These and other similar questions are currently under investigation.

Improving the neighbor graph construction and maintenance is also an interesting future research goal. We start with an initially empty neighbor graph. But in some scenarios, we may be able to employ cross-layer approaches to collect information from the routing table about the distance to various brokers. We could then investigate whether close neighbors (in network terms) constitute an initial approximation for the neighbor set that we are interested in (which is determined by physical proximity). Also, once we created the neighbor graph, we need to explore how well it reacts to changes in the set of peer broker topology, as peers are added and/or leave.

Another research avenue that is worth investigation is how to efficiently propagate subscriptions to the neighboring brokers in order to buffer incoming messages for disconnected subscribers. Unnecessary proliferation of subscriptions among the brokers results in significant overheads, particularly on network bandwidth requirements and routing time at the brokers. A key technique is required to quench the subscription propagation, thereby minimizing the propagation overhead and optimizing routing time. Subscription covering (Carzaniga et al., 2001) is a promising technique that provides abstractions to achieve this goal. Given two subscriptions $S1$ and $S2$, $S1$ covers $S2$ (denoted $S1 \supseteq S2$) if and only if any message matching $S2$ also matches $S1$. The mechanism

of subscription covering is as follows: when a newly admitted subscription X is covered by an existing subscription Y, then X is not sent to the neighboring brokers since Y can be used to store all messages matching X. Note that subscription Y cannot be removed unless it is not in use by any subscriber.

Our prototype implementation of a Pub/Sub system is based on JMS and focuses on only generic properties of a pub/sub system, i.e., the existence of publishers, subscribers, and a peer network of brokers that provide the core communication infrastructure. We have deliberately abstracted from the specifics of how the brokers interact to focus on the handoff aspects. (Bender et al., 2007) for example, distinguishes two design patterns that can be used to implement publish/subscribe applications over structured P2P networks and compares their complexity and performance. They show that no "one-fits-all" pub/sub approach exists, but that the optimal design pattern highly depends on a large number of system parameters, such as the expected ratio between subscribers and publishers or the rate at which publishers generate new content. In addition to implementing the pub/sub paradigm over structured P2P networks, others (see above) proposed implementing pub/sub using unstructured P2P overlays. In future work, we will explore how to integrate the proposed pro-active handoff approach with specific P2P architectures and determine the unique handoff opportunities and challenges for the given architecture.

REFERENCES

Barr, R., Bicket, J., Dantas, D., Du, B., Kim, T., Zhou, B., & Sirer, E. (2004), On the need for system-level support for ad hoc and sensor networks. *ACM SIGOPS Operating Systems Review, 36*(2), 1–5.

Bender, M., Michel, S., Parkitny, S., & Weikum, G. (2007). A comparative study of pub/sub methods in structured P2P networks. *Databases, Information Systems, and Peer-to-Peer Computing, Springer Lecture Notes in Computer Science, 4125*, 385-396.

Burcea, I., Jacobsen, H. -A., Lara, E. D., Muthusamy, V., & Petrovic, M. (2004). Disconnected operation in publish/subscribe middleware. In *Proceedings of the IEEE International Conference on Mobile Data Management (MDM'04)*, Berkeley, CA, USA.

Caporuscio, M., Carzaniga, A., & Wolf, A. L. (2003). Design and evaluation of a support service for mobile, wireless publish/subscribe applications. *IEEE Transactions on Software Engineering, 29*(12), 1059-1071.

Carzaniga, A., Rosenblum, A. D., & Wolf, A. L. (2001). Design and evaluation of a wide-area event notification service. *ACM Transactions on Computer Systems, 19*(3), 332–383.

Chand, R., & Felber, P. (2005). A semantic peer-to-peer overlays for publish/subscribe networks. In *Proceedings of Euro-Par 2005*, Lisbon, Portugal.

Choi, Y., & Park, D. (2006). Mirinae: A peer-to-peer overlay network for large-scale content-based publish/subscribe systems. *IEICE Transactions on Communications*, E89-B(6), 1755-1765.

Cugola, G., Di Nitto, E., & Fuggetta, A. (2001). The JEDI event-based infrastructure and its application to the development of the OPSS WFMS. *IEEE Transactions on Software Engineering, 27*(9), 827–850.

Eugster, P. T., Felber, P., Guerraoui, R., & Kermarrec, A. M. (2001). *The many faces of publish/subscribe* (Tech. Rep.DSC ID: 2000104). Lausanne, Switzerland: Swiss Federal Institute of Technology (EPFL).

Farooq, U., Majumdar, S., & Parsons, E. (2004). Engineering mobile wireless publish/subscribe systems for high performance. In *Proceedings*

of 12th *IEEE International Symposium on Modeling, Analysis, and Simulation of Computer and Telecommunications Systems*, Volendam, Netherlands.

Farooq, U., Parsons, E., & Majumdar, S. (2004). Performance of publish/subscribe middleware in mobile wireless networks. In *Proceedings of 4th International Workshop on Software and Performance*, Redwood City, CA, USA.

Fiege, L., Gartner, F. C., Kasten, O., & Zeidler, A. (2003). Supporting mobility in content-based publish/subscribe middleware. In *Proceedings of ACM/IFIP/USENIX International Middleware Conference (Middleware'03)*, Rio de Janeiro, Brazil.

Fox, A., Gribble, S. D., Chawathe, Y., & Breuer, E. (1998). Adapting to network and client variation using infrastructure proxies: Lessons and perspectives. *IEEE Personal Communications, 5*(4), 10-19.

Gupta, N., & Kumar, P. R. (2003). A performance analysis of the IEEE 802.11 wireless LAN medium access control. *Communications in Information and Systems, 3*(4), 279-304.

Huang, Y., & Garcia-Molina, H. (2004). Publish/subscribe in a mobile environment. *Wireless Networks Journal, Special Issue on Pervasive Computing and Communications, 10*(6), 643-652.

Kangasharju, J. (2005). Peer-to-peer and ubiquitous computing. In K. Wehrle & R. Steinmetz (Eds.), *Peer-to-Peer Systems and Applications, Springer Lecture Notes in Computer Science 3485*.

Kellerer, W., Schollmeier, R., & Wehrle, K. (2005). Peer-to-peer in mobile environments. In K. Wehrle & R. Steinmetz (Eds.), *Peer-to-Peer Systems and Applications, Springer Lecture Notes in Computer Science 3485*.

Kunz, T., & Omar, S. (2002). An adaptive MP3 player: Reducing power consumption and increasing application performance. In *Proceedings of the 35th Hawaii International Conference on System Sciences (HICSS-35)*, Hawaii, USA.

Muthusamy, V., Petrovic, M., & Jacobsen, H. -A. (2005). Effects of routing computations in content-based routing networks with mobile data sources. In *Proceedings of 11th International Conference on Mobile Computing and Networking*, Cologne, Germany.

National Institute of Standards and Technology (2005). NIST Net Home Page. Retrieved September 30, 2008, from http://snad.ncsl.nist.gov/itg/nistnet/index.html

Park, H. -H., Kim W., & Woo M. (2007). A Gnutella-based P2P system using cross-layer design for MANET. *International Journal of Electronics, Circuits and Systems, 1*(3), 139-144.

Podnar, I., & Lovrek, I. (2004). Supporting mobility with persistent notifications in publish/subscribe systems. In *Proceedings of 3rd International Workshop on Distributed Event-based Systems (DEBS 2004)* Edinburgh, Scotland, UK.

Sun Microsystems (2008). Java message service (JMS) API specification. Retrieved September 30, 2008, from http://java.sun.com/products/jms

Sutton, P., Arkins, R., & Segall, B. (2001). Supporting disconnectedness-transparent information delivery for mobile and invisible computing. In *Proceedings of 1st International Symposium on Cluster Computing and the Grid*, Washington, DC, USA.

Yin, J., Wang, X., & Agrawal, D. P. (2005). Modeling and optimization for wireless local area network (WLAN). *Computer Communications Journal, Special Issue on Performance Issues of Wireless LANs, PANs, and Ad Hoc Networks, 28*, 1204 -1213.

Zeidler, A., & Fiege, L. (2003). Mobility support with REBECA. In *Proceedings of 23rd International Conference on Distributed Computing Systems Workshops*. Providence, Rhode Island, USA.

Zenel, B., & Duchamp, D. (1997). A general proxy filtering mechanism applied to the mobile environment, In *Proceedings of the Third Annual ACM/IEEE Conference on Mobile Computing and Networking*, Budapest, Hungary.

Chapter V
P2P over MANETs:
Application and Network Layers' Routing Assessment

Leonardo B. Oliveira
University of Campinas (UNICAMP), Brazil

Isabela G. Siqueira
Federal University of Minas Gerais (UFMG), Brazil

Daniel F. Macedo
Université Pierre et Marie Curie-Paris VI, France

José M. Nogueira
Federal University of Minas Gerais (UFMG), Brazil

Antonio A. F. Loureiro
Federal University of Minas Gerais (UFMG), Brazil

ABSTRACT

Both Mobile Ad hoc Networks (MANETs) and Peer-to-Peer (P2P) networks are decentralized self-organizing networks with a dynamic topology, used to route queries in a distributed environment. However, whilst MANETs are composed of resource-constrained devices susceptible to faults, P2P networks are popular for their resilience and fault-tolerance. This makes P2P networks the ideal data sharing system for MANETs. This chapter focuses on the integration of these networks. More specifically, the authors evaluate routing strategies of both the network layer and the application layer. Their results indicate that the performance of the protocols depends greatly on the environment and point out the need for new approaches.

INTRODUCTION

Peer-to-Peer (P2P) networks have emerged as a solution for data sharing as well as processing in distributed environments (Borg, 2003; Talia & Trunfio, 2003; Oliveira, Siqueira, & Loureiro, 2005), and have been rapidly and widely adopted in the Internet.

At the same time, Mobile Ad hoc Networks (MANETs) have enabled a wide range of novel applications in areas such as medicine, including pre-hospital and in-hospital emergency care, rescue team communication in disaster situations, and exchange of information in battle fields (Zhou & Haas, 1999; Borg, 2003), situations where it is not possible to rely on previous infrastructure.

The P2P paradigm (Oram, 2001) is the basis for both P2P networks and MANETs. One of the most significant characteristics of the P2P paradigm is the fact that central units, which manage and meet the needs of the network, are non-existent. In this model, nodes have equivalent features and capabilities and as a consequence, are called "peers". Every peer thus is able to launch and answer requests originated from any other peer. Additionally, both MANETs and P2P networks are self-organizing networks with dynamic topology responsible for routing queries in a distributed environment.

MANETs and P2P networks are not only similar, but complement each other. Nodes in a MANET typically have low computing capacity and, therefore, are unable to play the role of servers. On the other hand, a P2P application appears to be a powerful tool to disseminate information in MANETs. In other words, since a P2P network does not possess a unique service provider at a certain time, the distribution of tasks among nodes prevents them from becoming overloaded.

Some MANET-enabled applications (e.g. rescue team communication in a disaster scenario and information exchange in battle fields) are bound to have peers cooperating continuously with other peers. For instance, a rescue team player could request the location of his nearest colleague. Although a central server could store such an information, this approach is not only more expensive (as it requires more hops and frequent location updates) but also less resilient: a single point of failure is not desirable in rescue team situations, and servers are the target of attacks in battle fields. In spite of the synergy between P2P systems and MANETs, their integration is not straightforward.

Routing in MANETs was conceived for *client-server* applications, which usually employ asymmetric flows (i.e., many-to-one). This characteristic contrasts sharply with P2P systems, which have a many-to-many traffic pattern. P2P networks, conversely, have been designed assuming the conventional Internet infrastructure, i.e., a static and fixed underlying topology. As a result, it is crucial that novel solutions, which would take into account the idiosyncrasies of both P2P and ad hoc networks, be devised for P2P systems operating over MANETs (P2P over MANETs).

In this work, we conduct a detailed routing assessment of P2P over MANETs. Specifically, we carried out the following evaluations: (i) AODV (Perkins & Royer, 1999), DSR (Johnson & Maltz, 2001), and DSDV (Perkins & Bhagwat, 1994) routing protocols under a Gnutella P2P network; and (ii) two P2P protocols Gnutella & Chord (Stoica et al., 2003) over MANET with AODV as the network routing protocol.

The remainder of this work is organized as follows. We first explain the synergy between P2P networks and MANETs. Next, we discuss related works on P2P over MANETs. This is followed by a description of the network characterization process. We then evaluate several MANET routing protocols under P2P networks and provide a discussion of the results. Finally, we conclude the chapter.

SYNERGY BETWEEN P2P NETWORKS AND MANETS

P2P networks and MANETs have several aspects in common (Schollmeier et al., 2002; Hu et al., 2003; Kortuem et al.; 2001; Borg, 2003). Both systems lack centralizing units, since the network is established as soon as the participants opt to interact with one another. The decision to connect to the network can be taken at distinct moments, so changes are constantly introduced in the environment. Another similarity is their dynamic topology, which is a result of the constant changes in connections used by peers. In MANETs, these modifications are mainly caused by node mobility. That is, as a node moves, it might leave the transmission range area of its current neighbors and as a consequence its links break. Thus, in order to reestablish contact with peer entities, the peers must set new connections. Conversely, the low availability of peers creates dynamic topologies on P2P networks. Usually, P2p networks are executed mostly over fixed networks and the main reason for link breakage is not the mobility of nodes, but the short session duration times.

Interestingly, because P2P applications are usually built over a network based on the client/ server model, their networks present some characteristics that differ from the P2P paradigm.

MANETs, on the other hand, have their own communication mechanisms and therefore are more faithful to the distributed model.

As previously mentioned, peers in the P2P architecture can communicate with one another without the intervention of any centralized access point. Paradoxically, P2P applications are, in fact, clients of services provided by external servers – such as DHCP (Dynamic Host Configuration Protocol), DNS (Domain Name Service), and Web servers. In MANETs, requests are really handled by any network participant. Another evidence that MANETs are more in conformity with the P2P paradigm than P2P application networks is the fact that in the former, peers are only a single-hop away from their neighbors, whereas in the latter, the neighbors are logic, and might be geographically apart by many hops. Typical differences between the two technologies (Schollmeier et al., 2002) are described in Table 1.

RELATED WORK

There is significant amount of research on P2P over the Internet, focused on the characterization as well as the optimization of P2P protocols. (Lv et al., 2002) studied the performance of unstructured P2P networks on the Internet for various

Table 1. Comparison between P2P networks and MANETs

Item	P2P Network	MANET
Motivation for establishing the network	create a logical infra-structure to provide a service	create a physical infrastructure to provide connectivity
Connection between two nodes	fixed medium and direct communication	wireless and indirect communication
Connection reliability	high (physical connections, many paths)	low (wireless connections)
Peer location	any place in the Internet	restricted geographic area
Structure	physical structure differs from logical structure	physical structure corresponds to the logical structure
Routing	only reactive algorithms	reactive and proactive exist
Peer mobility	none	mobile
Broadcast	virtual, multiple unicasts	physical, to all nodes in the transmission range

forwarding strategies, file popularity and query distributions. Due to the high load imposed on the network and the amount of query messages sent, the authors propose two new forwarding strategies. The first is based on random walks, where the query message wanders until a TTL expires or the content is found. The "expanded ring" technique is an iterative method, where the TTL is increased on each round until the content is found. The authors showed that both techniques reduce significantly the query overhead; however, they did not measure their response time.

Random Walks have been proposed as a solution for the scalability issues of flooding-based query dissemination (Lv et al., 2002). Random Walks have been used on the routing level (Servetto & Barrenechea, 2002; Barrett et al., 2003) as well as on the application level (Gkantsidis et al., 2004). The principle works as follows. Instead of flooding the network with queries, random walk based protocols rely on a fixed amount of messages, called *walkers*, which wander around the network at random. Whenever a node receives a walker, it checks if it has the requested information. If not, it forwards the walker to one of its neighbors, selected randomly. Walkers have a time to live (TTL), in order to purge unsuccessful queries out of the network. The key to this approach, thus, is setting the correct value for the TTL and using topology information to bias the forwarding decision towards nodes with high probability of having the information sought. Random walks solve as much queries as flooding-based strategies and are more scalable; however, the response time is higher. To our knowledge, in the context of file sharing, this method has only been evaluated over wired networks, thus lacking measurements concerning response time and energy consumption on small networks, such as in MANETs.

Only recently the research community realized the synergy between MANETs and P2P networks. (Schollmeier et al., 2002) and (Borg, 2003) discuss similarities and differences of MANETs and P2P networks. The former focuses mainly in routing

aspects, while the latter discusses content discovery, security and quality of service, among others. (Kortuem, 2002) presented Proem, a middleware for developing and deploying P2P applications tailored to PANs (Personal Area Networks), a special class of MANETs. (Hu et al., 2003) propose Dynamic P2P Source Routing (DPSR), a MANET routing protocol that integrates strategies used by DSR routing protocol and Pastry P2P protocol (Rowstron & Druschel, 2001) to improve scalability.

MANETs running P2P networks have been used in the context of virtual collaborative environments (VCE) to support military or emergency situations (Mecella et al., 2006; Boukerche et al., 2006). In the Workpad project, a hybrid MANET-infrastructured network is used to disseminate geographical data and reports, with the wired network serving as a backbone for the several deployed MANETs. Furthermore, a P2P network is created at the MANET level for local communication, while another P2P runs on the backbone. On the other hand, (Boukerche et al., 2006) built a single Gnutella network with several "channels", which act similarly as multicast groups, separating the interests of the network into groups. This organization was employed in order to reduce the amount of control information that must be exchanged and stored by each P2P peer. Those works are complementary to ours, since they apply P2P concepts to support a well-defined task.

The works cited focus on the application of P2P over MANETs, however they do not characterize the performance of the P2P application or attempt to improve it by adapting the protocols to the limitations of MANETs. Due to the characteristics of MANETs, such as frequent topology changes, high bit error rates and the presence of node failures, algorithms devised for wired networks such as the Internet must be adapted. Sometimes those protocols may not be applicable at all, and new ones must be proposed.

In order to improve existing protocols or propose new ones, it is necessary to understand the effects of the wireless medium on existing protocols to identify the weak and strong points of each design choice. This chapter is a step further into that direction, as are other works in the literature. (Oliveira, Siqueira, & Loureiro 2005; Oliveira et al., 2003) studied an unstructured P2P application running over a MANET where different ad hoc routing protocols are considered under a number of scenarios. Results show that each protocol analyzed performed well in some scenarios for some metrics yet had drawbacks in others. The same group has also looked into P2P content discovery techniques in MANETs (Oliveira, Siqueira, Macedo, Loureiro, Wong, & Nogueira, 2005). (Ding & Bhargava, 2004) performed a theoretical comparison between P2P systems over MANETs and presents important results in O-notation. Nevertheless, they did not evaluate real P2P systems and did not take into account of the practical aspects such as node mobility and channel error.

Some works proposed new P2P protocols that are more adapted to particular MANET scenarios. (Papadopouli & Schulzrinne, 2001a; Papadopouli & Schulzrinne, 2001b) and (Klemm et al., 2003) present P2P data sharing systems tailored to MANETs, namely *Seven Degrees of Separation* (7DS) and *Optimized Routing Independent Overlay Network* (ORION), respectively. 7DS focus on enabling the exchange of data among peers not directly connected to the Internet by exploring peer mobility, while ORION concentrates on file sharing applications by setting up overlay routes on demand. (Lee et al., 2006) proposed the use of network coding to adapt BitTorrent-like protocols to vehicular MANETS (VANETs). The use of network coding, combined with a gossiping-like broadcast strategy, allows nodes to cope with the high degree of mobility and bad links of VANETs. (Seet et al., 2005) studied how a fleet of city buses may be used to deploy a mobile backbone infrastructure for communication and Internet access. In their work, a P2P network runs on top of the backbone and buses play the role of super peers.

(Franciscani et al., 2005) concentrate on minimizing the impact of the highly dynamic topology obtained through the combination of P2P networks and MANETs. They proposed algorithms for the configuration of these networks. In the algorithms, three combinations of neighborhood assignment are compared: 1) *regular*, where P2P neighborhood corresponds to the physical neighborhood; 2) *random*, where authors try to achieve the small-world (Milgram, 1967; Watts & Strogatz, 1998) phenomenon by picking each neighbor at random among online peers; and 3) *hybrid*, where links are built following a hierarchy and each peer communicates through an intermediate.

(da Hora et al., 2007) considered the limitations of structured and unstructured protocols in MANETs to propose modifications to both paradigms. The authors proposed the use of more than one query message in structured protocols to cope with the low link reliability of wireless networks. For unstructured networks, the authors proposed the use of gossiping, where messages are forwarded according to a probability that varies with network load. This modification tries to cope with the high overhead incurred by the exponential number of messages sent by flooding-based P2P protocols. Results showed an improvement of up to 10% in the delivery rate as well as a significant reduction in the response time.

NETWORK CHARACTERIZATION

In order to accomplish the purposes of this work, we have conducted simulation experiments using the Network Simulator (*ns-2*) (Fall & Varadhan, 2001) and its CMU wireless and mobility extension (CMU Project, 2004). Due to the lack of actual production data, we derived our simulation model from a hypothetical search and rescue (e.g., in forests, deserts and battle fields) application. In our application, the ad hoc network is composed of Wi-Fi devices (handhelds or PDAs) where data gathered from the field is made available to a P2P network. We envision that in this scenario every member of the team will perform searches and share data with others in the P2P network.

The P2P application runs on top of the UDP protocol, since TCP does not perform well in this type of environment. Nodes are configured with typical PDA network parameters (11 Mbps IEEE 802.11b with 50 m of range). The interface queue (IFQ) length is set to 30 packets and the energy consumption is 230 mW for reception and 330 mW for transmission (Cano & Manzoni, 2000). Radio propagation follows the two-ray-ground model. Nodes are equipped with sufficient energy to allow the application to run during the entire simulation – since we focus on efficiency rather than network lifetime.

The mobility scheme employed was the random waypoint (since it is frequently used for individual movements (Broch et al., 1998)). Unless otherwise noticed, the transmission range of all nodes was set to 50 m. The radio propagation model chosen was the Shadowing Propagation Model with a rate of 95% of correct reception within the range area. The IEEE 802.11 was the protocol used in the MAC layer. The radio interface chosen was the 914 MHz Lucent WaveLAN.

The simulator does not provide P2P protocols and thus we implemented ourselves the structured and unstructured protocols. Our implementation followed the specification in Chord paper (Stoica et al., 2003) and the Gnutella protocol specification

v0.4. For a fair comparison, we chose not to use any optimization that could improve performance over ad hoc networks. We briefly describe their implementation below.

Chord: We implemented Chord's complete set of functionalities, including the protocols necessary for building and maintaining the distributed indexes. We also implemented file insertion and deletion in the network, using protocols similar to the ones used for search. Regarding Chord's simulation parameters, the *finger table* is updated every 5s and *stabilize* runs every 10 s. PING messages (used for topology control) are sent every 10 s. Packet size is fixed in 64 bytes.

Gnutella: In Gnutella, we handle the problem of indefinite query propagation by creating a time-to-live (TTL) field embedded in every query message. This field is decremented by one at each hop. Also, every node maintains a message cache. Messages arriving with zero TTL value or with an entry in the cache are discarded. A logical neighborhood composed of a fixed number of peers is assigned to each peer about to join the network. The neighbors are picked at random among the pool of peers online. This assignment is done offline, similar to a central server that functions as the P2P network entry point (this is usual in most Internet Gnutella clients). Finally, Gnutella peers periodically send PING messages to their neighbors and wait for an answer (the PONG message), in order to check if their neighbors are still online.

Table 2. Messages transmitted in P2P Application Network

Message Type	Function	Size (Bytes)
broadcast-send	Look for neighbors	23
broadcast-reply	Answer a broadcast-send	38
Ping	Check the activity of a peer	23
Pong	Answer a ping	38
query-send	Search for a file	26
query-forward	Retransmit a query originated by another peer	26
query-reply	Answer a query (a *query-hit* has occurred)	26
Push-request	Require the transfer of a file	51
pull-request	Transmit data (pieces of a file)	210 (maximum)

When no answer is received, the neighbor is substituted in the neighbors list by a new neighbor randomly chosen from the set of nodes online at the moment. The TTL for queries is set to 4 and PING messages are sent every 10 s. As for Chord, packet size is fixed at 64 bytes. Table 3 presents the Gnutella message types which we will refer to a few times throughout this chapter.

MANET ROUTING PROTOCOLS UNDER P2P NETWORKS

In this section we evaluate the performance a Gnutella P2P network running over MANETs. Three different routing protocols are considered: AODV, DSDV, and DSR. In what follows, we first describe the simulation setup and the evaluation metrics, and subsequently the results.

Simulation

We have broken down the simulation results into sections, according to the property evaluated, namely:

- Workload;
- Mobility;

- Network Density;
- Number of peers;

Besides the settings described in Section *Network Characterization*, the simulation here comprised 40 mobile nodes, 12 of which implement a single instance of the P2P application in 200×200 m² area. With respect to Gnutella parameters, a peer could have at most 3 neighbors and the initial number of files per peer was set to be 10. The choice of the initial file names as well as their sizes follows the normal distribution model. The average file size is adjusted to 10 KB. The simulation parameters are summarized in Table 3. For every scenario, we vary only one parameters at a time, while keeping the others constant.

Metrics

In what follows, we describe the main metrics used during the evaluation.

- **Routing overhead:** total number of routing messages transmitted during the simulation.
- **Latency:** the delay perceived by a user, from the time a query is sent to the time the corresponding response is received.

Table 3. Simulation parameters for the evaluation of routing algorithms

Parameter	Value
MAC protocol	IEEE 802.11b
Node placement	Uniform distribution
Node mobility	Random Waypoint, $0 \leq$ speed ≤ 1.0 m/s.
Number of files	10 files per peer, distributed using a normal distribution.
File queries	Each node will query 10% of the files in the network, with query times based on a uniform distribution.
Channel losses	5%
Number of nodes	40
Number of peers	12
Area size	200×200 m²
File size	10KB on average

- **Energy consumption:** average energy consumption per MANET node at the end of the simulation;
- **Queries not responded:** percentage of queries that have not been answered;
- **Delivery rate:** number of P2P application packets that successfully arrived at the destination;
- **Number of hops:** average number of hops for a query to discover a content;
- **Connectivity between peers:** takes into account how easy a peer fills up its neighboring list and how often its neighbors are available.

Workload

In the first scenario we evaluate the effect of the number of queries in the performance of the network. We varied the number of queries per node from 1 to 10, 100 and 1000.

The three routing protocols introduced distinguishing amounts of overhead when the number of queries by a node was varied. As shown in Figure 1(a), DSDV exhibits the highest overhead, followed by AODV and then DSR. The former, for one query, introduced ten times more control packets than DSR. Comparing DSDV to AODV and DSR on-demand protocols, the considerable

increase in overhead obtained was due to route update messages that were constantly triggered by DSDV. Although DSDV produced more overhead, it demonstrated a steady behavior with respect to the workload. The others, in contrast, did not suggest to be as scalable – the DSR overhead, specifically, doubled from one extreme of the x axis to the other.

DSDV was the protocol that consumed the highest amount of energy for low, medium, and high loads, as depicted in Figure 1(b). This is a result of the higher number of control packets sent and received by the nodes.

Figure 2(a) depicts the fraction of messages delivered to the application, as the shared file sizes were incremented. For all protocols, the curves assumed almost identical shapes. It can be noticed that while for 1 KB files the delivery rate is higher than 90%, for 1000 KB practically all packets were dropped. This is due mainly to the low bandwidth available in the ad hoc network.

The results for initiated file transfers indicate that a good cost-benefit for all protocols is achieved when the average file size is 10 KB. This metric is represented by the number of pull-data messages received in Figure 2(b), which can also be considered a result of throughput.

On the whole, DSDV performed better for extremely high loads. It obtained the lowest number

Figure 1. Number of queries variation

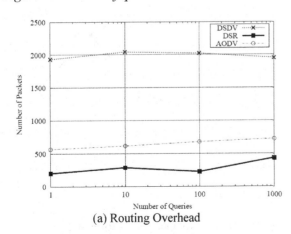

(a) Routing Overhead

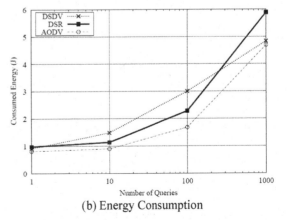

(b) Energy Consumption

Figure 2. File size variation

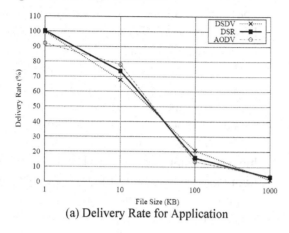

(a) Delivery Rate for Application

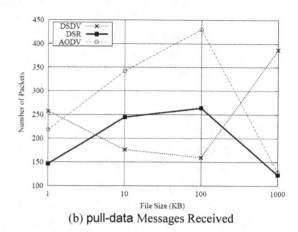

(b) **pull-data** Messages Received

of queries not responded, the highest throughput and more successfully transferred files. From Figure 2(b), it is clear that DSR and AODV did not support the application requirements, in contrast to DSDV. This is due to the huge congestion generated, which caused difficulties for them to find routes on demand.

Mobility

In order to evaluate the effects of node mobility, in this scenario we vary the pause time of the nodes. In the random waypoint model, nodes move from a point to another and then pause for a certain time, called pause time. We varied the pause duration from zero up to five minutes.

Figures 3(a) and 3(b) show the behavior of the connections among peers. It is noticed that none of the protocols had a remarkable performance compared to the others. For lower mobility, the average number of neighbors and the amount of ping messages sent were reduced, while the number of broadcast-send messages and the number of queries not responded grew for all protocols. That is, DSDV, DSR and AODV produced more information unavailability and worse P2P connectivity.

As mobility was incremented, surprisingly, the connectivity degree rose (see Figure 3(a)). This

Figure 3. Pause time variation

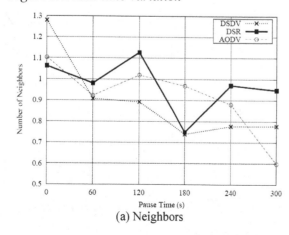

(a) Neighbors

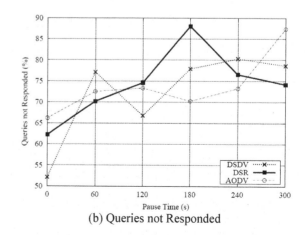

(b) Queries not Responded

is due to the partitioning of the network. When mobility is low, the network might isolate peers during the whole simulation, whereas in a higher mobility scenario these partitions are eliminated because of peer movement. As a result, for high pause-time values, i.e., for low mobility, the number of queries not responded is also high.

Paradoxically, Figure 4(a) demonstrates that the increase in speed did not have significant influence after 2.5 m/s. It is important to observe, though, that the DSDV and AODV curves stabilized earlier than the DSR curve.

Figure 4(b) shows the time elapsed for a query-hit to happen after the query-send message was sent. Both DSDV and AODV protocols had similar behaviors and shown to be insensitive to node speed, whereas DSR was very sensitive to node speed.

DSR was the protocol that presented the highest number of hops and latency when mobility was increased. The term hops refers to the average amount of hops for a query to reach an information source. Due to its source routing nature, when nodes move at high speeds, a route might become outdated, even at the time when the packet is traversing the network from the source to the destination. As a result, more time and hops are consumed with routing.

Network Density

In this scenario we evaluate the effect of the number of nodes in the performance of MANETs. We varied the number of nodes from 10 up to 80, while keeping the area size fixed. With this scenario, we evaluated the cost of the routing overhead when node density increases.

Concerning routing overhead, as shown in Figure 5(a), DSDV was badly affected by the increase in the number of nodes, as it requires periodic routing updates and broadcast of triggered beacon messages. In contrast, this scenario modification did not influence the other protocols, which scale gracefully. Interestingly, this performance decline did not occur when the transmission range was extended.

The three protocols behaved equivalently for both number of nodes and transmission range variation with respect to connectivity among application peers. The protocols had higher latency times for denser networks, as presented in Figure 5(b). Particularly, DSDV appears to be less scalable regarding this metric due to its routing overhead, as previously highlighted.

Regarding both numbers of queries not responded and network delivery rate, the performance of

Figure 4. Speed variation

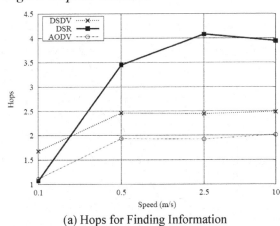

(a) Hops for Finding Information

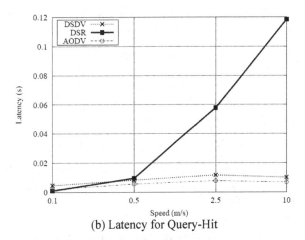

(b) Latency for Query-Hit

Figure 5. Nodes variation

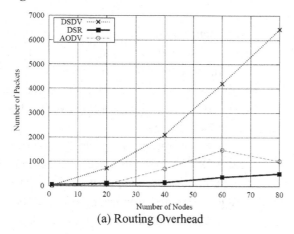

(a) Routing Overhead

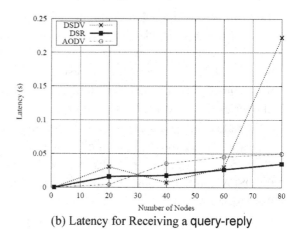

(b) Latency for Receiving a query-reply

DSDV, DSR, and AODV was similar. The former protocol, despite producing more routing overhead, managed to maintain the same delivery rate for a denser network. Figure 6(a) shows the results obtained for the delivery rate.

In regards to path length, it was observed that this metric depends on network density, as shown in Figure 6(b). The highest average number of hops and forwarded packets were recorded for DSR and DSDV protocols for denser and less dense networks, respectively. The result relative to the DSR can be easily explained, as the protocol does not take into account of the path optimality when routes are generated. DSDV's performance,

though, can be considered a positive result, since the others obtained nearly zero average hops, i.e., they did not deliver the contents. In other words, this result means that DSDV is the only protocol that really delivers packets and provides support to the P2P application layer in less dense scenarios. Regarding the curve shapes of the three protocols, a change in the behavior could be detected for ranges higher than 100m. At this point, the number of hops falls suddenly, as a consequence of the proximity of the desired information. That is, when the number of existent nodes in the network is higher, it is more likely that the required information is stored on a near or easily reachable

Figure 6. Nodes and transmission range variation

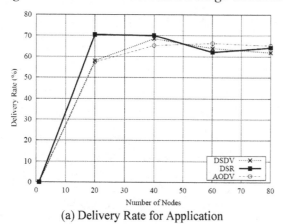

(a) Delivery Rate for Application

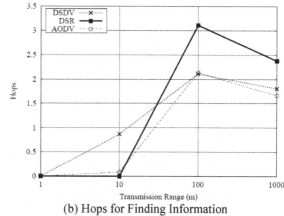

(b) Hops for Finding Information

node. Furthermore, when the transmission range is expanded, the packets predictably tend to arrive in the destination with fewer hops.

Number of Peers

In this scenario we varied the number of nodes running the P2P application. The number of P2P peers was varied from 10 to 40, with increments of 5 peers. The aim of this scenario is to evaluate the cost required to add more peers into the P2P topology.

Figure 7(a) indicates that DSR needs more hops to find the information than the others (nearly 2 times more hops than AODV, in the worst case), in agreement with the previously described results. Nevertheless, the shape of the curves is similar for the three protocols. When the network is populated with less instances of P2P applications, the desired information tends to be found in a fewer number of P2P hops. Also in this case, the amount of P2P neighbors of a peer is lower, since the number of reachable peers is lower as well. As a result, the network is likely to become partitioned, and in the rare cases in which the information is found, it will be located one or two hops apart. The growth in the number of peers, by contrast, may expand route lengths of the P2P application layer, demanding a higher amount of P2P hops, and obviously the same for network hops. After a

certain point in the increase of peers, the number of neighbors reached its maximum value and no more influences were detected.

Regarding the throughput, all protocols were affected equivalently by the number of peers. AODV was responsible for the best performance concerning routing overhead, while DSDV, generated more routing control packets, as expected. AODV also achieved better results with respect to time. DSR, in contrast, presented the highest latency not only because it does not provide an optimal path, but also due to the fact that packets to be transmitted are held in its buffer until a path to the destination is found.

Finally, Figure 7(b) presents the energy consumption. It is possible to observe that the shape of the curves for all the evaluated protocols was similar, as the number of peers increased. AODV, however, consumed less energy (0.35 J less, approximately), since it possesses the lowest overhead.

P2P CONTENT DELIVERY PROTOCOLS OVER MANETS

We also contribute to the development of efficient information sharing in MANETs by evaluating existent Internet content discovery techniques in these new distributed environments.

Figure 7. Peer variation

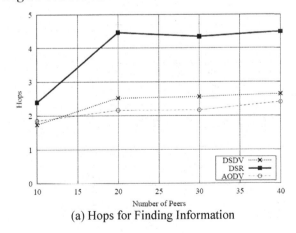

(a) Hops for Finding Information

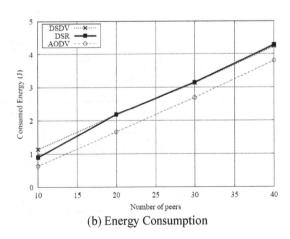

(b) Energy Consumption

Broadly speaking, there are two classes of content discovery techniques for P2P networks (Li & Wu, 2005): unstructured and structured. In the former (e.g., Freenet, Napster, and Gnutella), data can be stored in any node in the network, hence nodes must flood the network with queries to locate the desired information. In the latter (e.g., Chord, CAN, PASTRY), content discovery is optimized by the creation of a Distributed Hash Table (DHT) which determines a direct path to the desired information. We used a network simulator to instantiate a Gnutella-like protocol and a Chord-like (Stoica et al., 2003) protocol as the main representatives of unstructured and structured P2P flavors, respectively and evaluated their performance under different simulated scenarios. The chosen scenarios investigate the impact of different parameters on the performance of both protocols.

Simulation

We have broken down simulation results into sections, i.e., by property evaluated, namely:

- Network size;
- Channel error rate;

- Mobility;
- Application dynamics.

Besides the settings described in Section *Network Characterization*, we assume a network of 50 nodes scattered in a 200×200 m^2 grid area. Nodes move according to the random waypoint mobility model with a pause time of 0.1 s and an average speed uniformly selected from 0 to 1.0 m/s. At any given point of the simulation, 50% of the nodes are always online, while the remaining nodes join the network at some point and leave after a time interval. Join and leave times are chosen following an uniform distribution. Each node provides 5 different files, thus there are 250 different files in the network. Table 4 summarizes the parameters employed in the simulations. Again, we vary one parameter at a time in order to simplify the analysis of the results.

Metrics

In what follows, we describe the main metrics used during the evaluation.

- **Hit rate:** the fraction of the queries successfully resolved in the P2P network;

Table 4. Simulation parameters for the evaluation of the type of P2P protocol

Parameter	Value
MAC protocol	IEEE 802.11b
Node placement	Uniform distribution
Node mobility	Random Waypoint, $0 \leq$ speed ≤ 1.0 m/s.
Percentage of online nodes	50%
Number of files	250 different files in the network, each node has a 10% probability of having the file.
File queries	Each node will query 10% of the files in the network, with query times based on a uniform distribution.
Channel losses	0%
Number of nodes	50
Number of peers	50
Area size	200x200 km

- **Response time:** delay perceived by a user requesting some content, including the time for transmitting the query to the network, locating the desired content and returning a response back to the user;
- **Energy per hit:** energy consumed per 1% of the total hits (this metric indicates how energy efficient the content delivery technique is);
- **Energy per node:** average energy consumed per node during the simulation time;
- **Sent messages:** total number of messages sent during simulation time;
- **Dropped messages:** total number of messages dropped during simulation time.

Network Load

We analyze the effect of network load over the performance of the two P2P protocols. We varied the total number of queries from 100 up to 500 and added distinct files to the network according to the increase in the number of queries.

As seen in Figure 8(a), Gnutella presents higher hit rates (between 60% and 70%, approximately, against 10% to 20% from Chord). However, as observed in Figures. 8(b) and 8(c), Gnutella's good result comes at a higher cost in terms of response time and traffic overhead. To be specific, Gnutella incurred 200% to 1570% and 111% to 851% more overhead in response time and traffic, respectively, when compared to Chord.

Figure 8(d) shows that, even though Gnutella incurs higher overall consumption (explained by

Figure 8. Results for network load variation

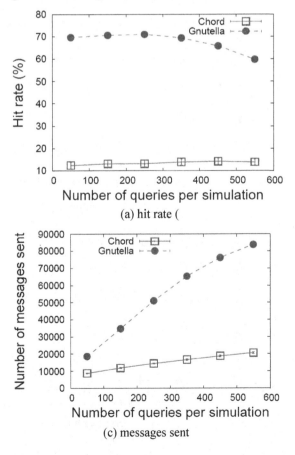

(a) hit rate (

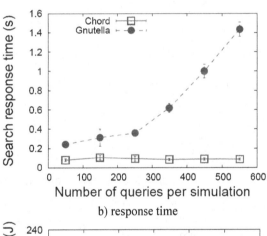

b) response time

(c) messages sent

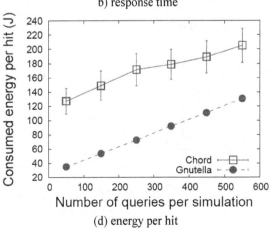

(d) energy per hit

its higher overall traffic), its energy consumption per hit is lower than Chord's. This is due to the high overhead of Chord, which has to periodically update information concerning current network state.

It is worth noting that, although Chord presents lower hit rates (i.e., somewhat larger than 10% for all scenarios), it scales gracefully and is less affected by load variations.

The difference in the hit rates between the two protocols is due to message redundancy in Gnutella. At each node, an arriving query is sent to each of its neighbors. Chord, however, relies on just one copy of a query. Given that message drops are frequent in wireless networks, redundancy in Gnutella provides better hit rates, at the expense of an increase in network traffic and querying delay.

Network Size

We also evaluate the impact that the number of nodes has on the network. The goal is to evaluate the performance of both protocols when the average hop count between two arbitrary nodes is different. The average hop count impacts search performance, as queries have to pass through more nodes before locating the desired content. To keep network density fixed (1.0 node/m²), we change the grid size in conjunction with the number of nodes. The number of queries per peer is fixed.

In Figure 9 we show the results as a function of the number of nodes in the network.

For networks having less than 100 nodes, Gnutella achieves a higher hit rate when compared to Chord, namely: 370%, 580%, and again 370% for 25, 50 and 75 nodes, respectively (Fig-

Figure 9. Results for network size variation

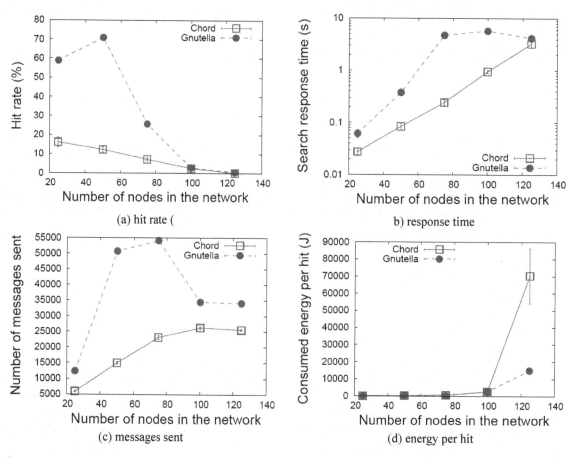

(a) hit rate (

b) response time

(c) messages sent

(d) energy per hit

ure 9(a)). When considering response time and traffic overhead, Chord outperforms Gnutella: the former is 77% faster and incurs from 25% to 70% less traffic overhead (Figure 9(b) and Figure 9(c), respectively). On the other hand, both protocols present similar energy consumption per hit (Figure 9(d)).

It is interesting to note that both protocols are very sensitive to variations in network size and have a performance peak at medium-sized networks (from 20 to 50 nodes). Neither P2P protocol seems to handle larger networks well. The larger the number of nodes, the higher the load each protocol (or the network has to carry.

Figure 10. Results for channel error variation

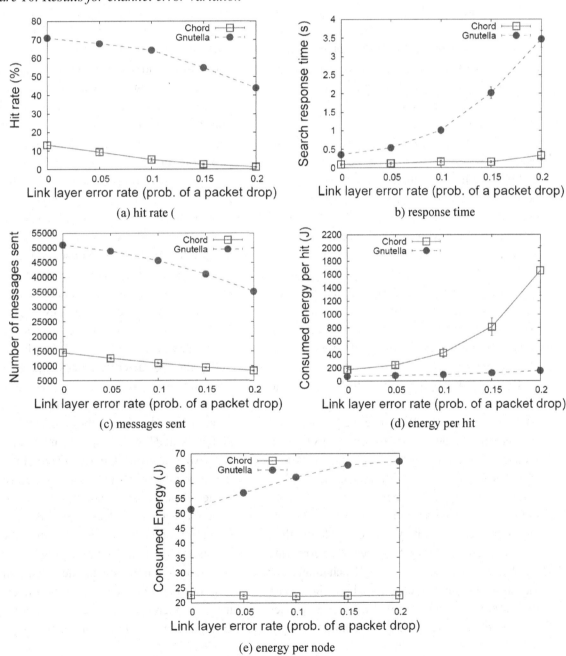

(a) hit rate (

b) response time

(c) messages sent

(d) energy per hit

(e) energy per node

In Gnutella, the probability of reaching a desired content decreases even if the content is available in the network, due to its limited TTL.

Channel Error

Wireless networks typically face much higher bit error rates (BER) when compared to wired networks, and this leads to significant packet losses. Link quality is highly dependent to the environment and node position, varying significantly from one region to another (Gaertner & Cahill, 2004; De Couto et al., 2003). As a characterization of network error rates for such environments is a daunting task and is out of the scope of our work, we varied packet loss probability of all nodes from 0% up to 20%.

As shown in Figure 10(a), Chord has hit rates below 10%. Due to its dependency on link reliability (as it has no redundant messages), Chord performs best when channel error rates are low. Gnutella, on the other hand, can perform well in environments with low and medium channel error rates.

For high channel error rates, although query message drops are mitigated by Gnutella's redundant messages, control messages such as PING, PONG and RESULT messages are not redundant. Hence, Gnutella and Chord are affected by high channel error rates.

Results for response time, traffic overhead and energy per hit are shown in Figure 10(b), 10(c), and Figure 10(d), respectively. Gnutella's response time grows almost exponentially (600%) with channel error variation. Chord, on the other hand, is more stable and varies at most 12%. Chord also sends fewer messages than Gnutella (72% less, approximately). Nevertheless, the energy consumed per hit by Gnutella is lower than Chord's (approximately, 8× lower when error rate is 20%) and is almost not affected by channel error variation. The same metric for Chord showed an undesirable exponential growth. As fewer queries are completed, the overhead for maintaining a

Chord ring dominates energy consumption, thus leading to an increase in energy consumed per hit. This is supported by Figure 10(e), which shows that Chord still consumes less energy per node when compared to Gnutella, even for scenarios where Chord spends more energy per hit.

Node Mobility

A key difference between ad hoc networks and fixed networks is mobility. Due to node mobility, routes must be constantly updated. P2P networks are tolerant to failures, as they accommodated node failure and disconnection, but current algorithms are designed to work in a wired environment, where disconnections are much less frequent than in ad hoc networks. In this subsection, we evaluate the impact of topology changes on the two protocols.

Figure 11 shows the results for the mobility factor as a function of average node speed, namely: 0, 0.25, 0.5, 1, 2, 4 and 8 m/s. Under low mobility, Gnutella transmitted more messages (Figure 11(c)) and, as a consequence, response times (Figure 11(b)) were increased. From Figure 11(b), we can conclude that some mobility is beneficial for Gnutella, since fewer packets are correctly delivered and thus less traffic is imposed on the network. However, under higher mobility, both protocols suffer from performance degradations; in particular, an increase in response time and a decrease in hit rate. Unlike in other sets of simulation, Chord was the less stable protocol and presented high variation in many metrics. As speed was increased, Chord's hit rate (Figure 11(a)) decreased from 50% to 5% at 2 m/s, and achieves values close to zero when mobility is increased. Gnutella was less affected and its hit rate was above 60% for the whole set of simulations.

Figure 11(e) shows the average energy consumption by a node during the entire simulation. It shows that energy consumption decreases as mobility increases. Concerning energy per hit, Gnutella remains stable whereas Chord increases

Figure 11. Results for mobility variation

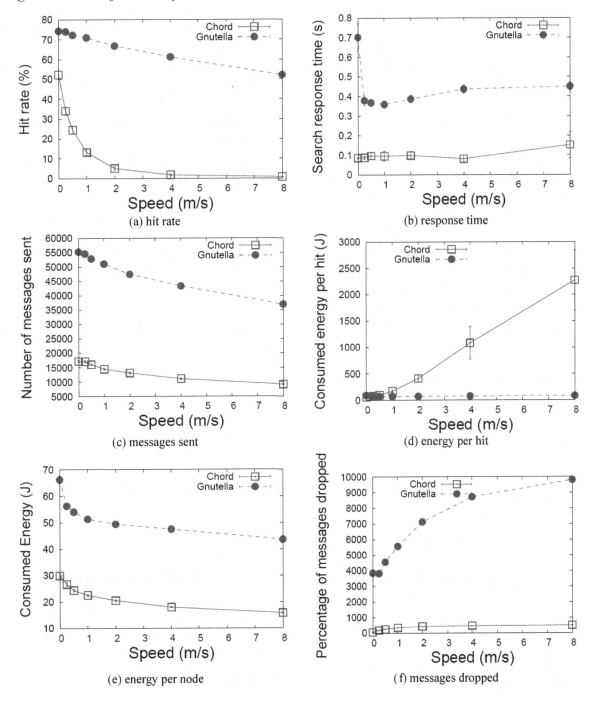

(a) hit rate

(b) response time

(c) messages sent

(d) energy per hit

(e) energy per node

(f) messages dropped

its consumption and achieves the peak of approximately 2300J for speeds of 8m/s. This difference is due to an imbalance between control packets (used for neighbor discovery and topology maintenance) and query packets.

Finally, note that the lower the mobility the smaller the number of messages dropped during the simulation (Figure 11(f), plotted in logarithmic scale in the Y axis). These drops are caused by collision and neighbors out of reach. The increase in mobility results in more broken routes and collisions in the MAC layer. For speeds over 4 m/s, however, the number of dropped messages seems to stabilize at around 500 for Chord and 10000 for Gnutella.

Application Dynamics

Next, we evaluate how the network dynamics, i.e., nodes joining and leaving the network, impacts the performance of both protocols. We varied the amount of nodes offline at any time from 0% to 50%. That is, for 0%, all the 50 nodes are active for the entire simulation time, while for 50% of dynamics 50% of the nodes will be offline for a certain period of the simulation. Network dynamics require an increased amount of control packets, in order to reconfigure the overlay network. Gnutella has fast setup, as a node's task before joining the network is to find neighbors. Chord, in contrast, requires a node to carry out a lengthy set of operations in order to join and leave the network. This influences the performance of the protocols, as nodes that are presumed to be online may be off-line.

We varied the percentage of nodes leaving the network from 0% to 50%. Initially, we varied the number of dynamic nodes, i.e., nodes that leave the network at some point in the simulation, in a mobility environment. In this situation, both protocols showed no performance variation. Inspired by the results achieved in the speed variation scenario, we decided to repeat the simulations for a stationary network. The results are presented to follow.

Figure 12 shows the results for application dynamics. Metrics are shown as a function of the

Figure 12. Results for application dynamics variation

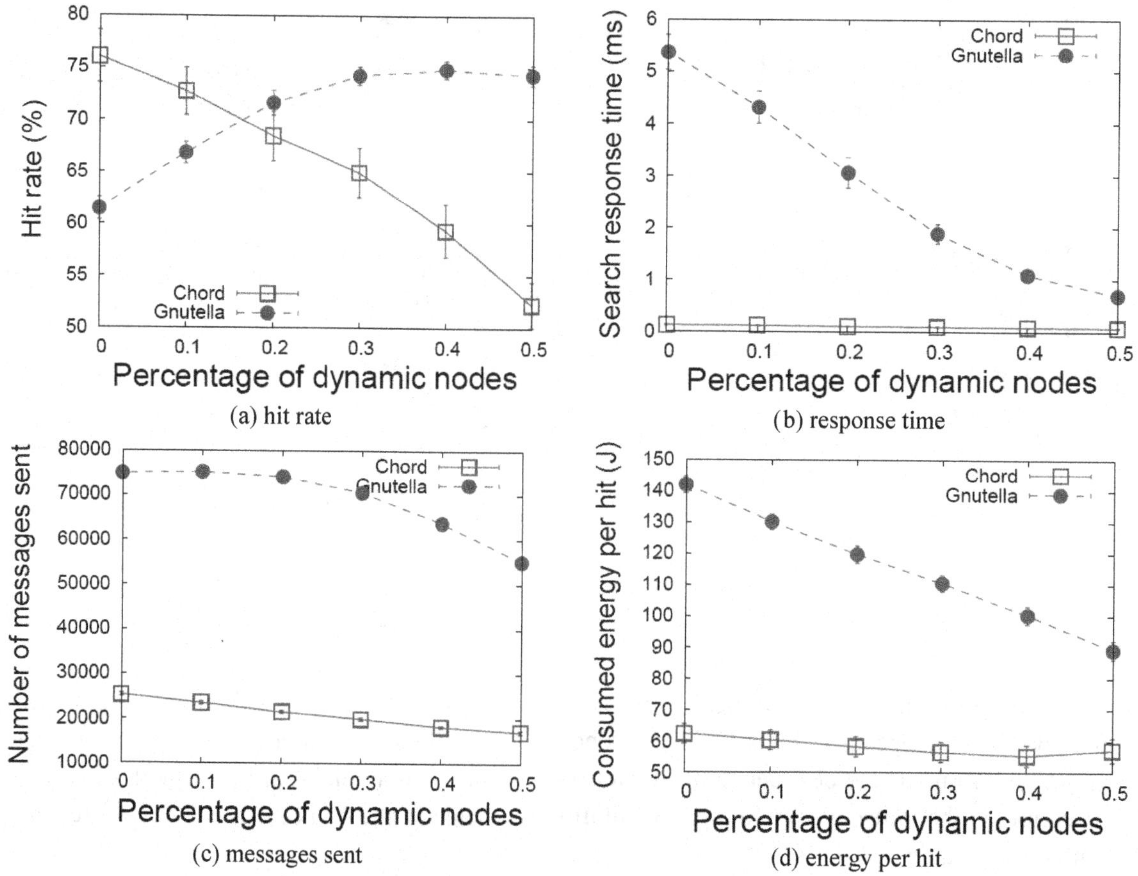

(a) hit rate

(b) response time

(c) messages sent

(d) energy per hit

percentage of dynamic nodes. Results indicate that Gnutella performs better for more dynamic scenarios. This is mostly due to the flooding of queries.

When the number of dynamic nodes decreases, Gnutella saturates the network with queries, as more nodes will forward messages. This is apparent from the response time, which becomes higher (Figure 12(b)) as fewer nodes are dynamic, together with a decrease in the number of messages sent (Figure 12(c)).

In this scenario, we show that Chord does not perform well in highly dynamic topologies. With less than 20% of dynamic nodes, in contrast, Chord achieves hit rates similar to those of Gnutella, while being faster and more energy efficient (Figure 12(b) and Figure 12(d), respectively). When the network is not saturated, the increase of traffic imposed by more Chord nodes in the network is more than compensated by the increase in the hit rate.

It is worth mentioning that some ad hoc networks (such as the ones employed in rescue situations) will exhibit a significant amount of disconnections due to harsh environmental conditions. However, there are also more "well-behaved" ad hoc networks. This scenario shows that Chord is more suitable for less dynamic networks, requiring less energy consumption and yielding lower response times when compared to Gnutella. For applications where disconnections are frequent, conversely, Gnutella is the more robust choice.

DISCUSSION

In a nutshell, the performance of the protocols was dictated by the scenario in which they were executed. We note that, for a number of times, the variation of a parameter can cause a completely different result, making protocols that performed well to start performing inefficiently. In other words, there is no single best protocol, but a protocol that is best for a particular occasion or metric.

DSDV has presented the highest routing overhead and, as a result, it has been considered the least power-efficient. Nevertheless, the protocol has performed best when the average file size was set to 1,000K; and it was the most stable when varying the number of requisitions per node.

DSR has its performance degraded in several scenarios because of its source-routing characteristic. Such a strategy under a dynamic topology appears to build long routes thus incurring more energy consumption. On the other hand, DSR performed well when the pause time and radio range have been varied, showing good connectivity and delivery rate.

AODV has outperformed other protocols in the majority of scenarios. This becomes clear when we observe its power consumption and number of pull-data messages delivered. Additionally, it has been able to find the shortest route in most of the scenarios. The evaluation of P2P content discovery techniques also revealed that the environment must be taken into account before opting for a given strategy.

Our study shows that Chord is not suitable for highly dynamic or low reliability environments. However, when the network is reasonably static and interference is low, Chord outperforms Gnutella, yielding higher hit rates with lower energy consumption. This performance is mainly due to the highly dynamic behavior of ad hoc networks, which influence packet losses.

Results show that mobility is the main cause for query misses. When nodes are static, the performance of Chord is mainly bounded by the number of nodes that are online, i.e., the availability of the network. On the whole, Gnutella presents better hit rates, however at a higher cost.

Unstructured protocols are clearly the most adequate for most scenarios, as their "flooding" of queries throughout the network increases resilience. Structured protocols, on the other hand, are more suitable for controlled scenarios, where there is little or no mobility and node disconnections are rare, such as wireless networks in indoor environments. We must note that an implementation of structured protocols using reliable transmission may enhance the performance of such protocols over ad hoc networks, despite the increase in complexity and in the number of messages sent.

CONCLUSION

P2P systems and MANETs are similar and complementary. In this work, we have focused on the integration of these networks by assessing both application and network layer routing strategies in P2P over MANETs. Our results indicate directions to be taken while designing protocols tailored to this novel scenario.

Not surprising, it looks like there is no panacea and therefore protocols for P2P over MANETs must be designed taking into consideration of both applications' and the environment's idiosyncrasies.

Ad hoc protocols must have mechanisms to cope with network dynamics. Simply put, proactive protocols should be redesigned in order to update routes more often; reactive protocols, likewise, need to adjust their route searching mechanism for that novel context. For instance, protocols should opt for hop-by-hop routing rather than source routing in highly dynamic topologies.

On the other hand, P2P content discovery techniques must take into consideration the characteristics of the wireless medium, and thus incorporate redundancy mechanisms. Note that this must be done without being lax about bandwidth constraints, though.

Finally, P2P protocols should employ cross-layering techniques. For example, a P2P protocol that is going to be used on top of a routing protocol with mechanisms that guarantee message delivery, should not send redundant queries since the routing layer would provide a reliable service. On the other hand, if the delivery is not guaranteed, the

P2P protocol could send more than one message to increase the chances of its reception.

REFERENCES

Barrett, C. L., Eidenbenz, S. J., Kroc, L., Marathe, M., & Smith, J. P. (2003). Parametric probabilistic sensor network routing. In *Proceedings of the 2nd ACM international conference on Wireless sensor networks and applications*.

Borg, J. (2003). A comparative study of ad hoc & peer to peer networks. Unpublished master's thesis, University College London, UK.

Boukerche, A., Zarrad, A., & Araújo, R. (2006). Smart gnutella overlay formation for collaborative virtual environments over mobile ad-hoc networks. In *Proceedings of the IEEE International Symposium on Distributed Simulation and Real-Time Applications (DS-RT)*.

Broch, J., Maltz, D. A., Johnson, D. B., Hu, Y.-C., & Jetcheva, J. (1998). A performance comparison of multi-hop wireless ad hoc network routing protocols. In *Proceedings of the 4th Annual ACM/IEEE International Conference on Mobile Computing and Networking*.

Cano, J.-C., & Manzoni, P. (2000). A performance comparison of energy consumption for mobile ad hoc network routing protocols. In *Proceedings of the 8th International Symposium on Modeling, Analysis and Simulation of Computer and Telecommunication Systems (MASCOTS)*.

CMU Project (2004). *The CMU Monarch projects on wireless and mobility extension to ns*.

da Hora, D. N., Macedo, D. F., Nogueira, J. M. S., & Pujolle, G. (2007). Optimizing peer-to-peer content discovery over wireless mobile ad hoc networks. In *Proceedings of the 9th IFIP/IEEE International Conference on Mobile and Wireless Communications Networks (MWCN)*.

De Couto, D. S. J., Aguayo, D., Bicket, J., & Morris, R. (2003). A high-throughput path metric for multi-hop wireless routing. In *Proceedings of the 9th Annual International Conference on Mobile Computing and Networking (MOBICOM)*.

Ding, G., & Bhargava, B. (2004). Peer-to-peer file-sharing over mobile ad hoc networks. In *Proceedings of the 2nd IEEE Annual Conference on Pervasive Computing and Communications Workshops*.

Fall, K., & Varadhan, K. (2001). *Network Simulator Notes and Documentation*. The VINT Project.

Franciscani, F. P., Vasconcelos, M. A., Couto, R. P., & Loureiro, A. A. F. (2005). (Re)configuration algorithms for peer-to-peer over ad hoc networks. *Journal of Parallel and Distributed Computing, 65*(2), 234–245.

Gaertner, G., & Cahill, V. (2004). Understanding link quality in 802.11 mobile ad hoc networks. *IEEE Internet Computing, 8*(1), 55–60.

Gkantsidis, C., Mihail, M., & Saberi, A. (2004). Random walks in peer-to-peer networks. In *Proceedings of the IEEE International Conference on Computer Communications (INFOCOM)*.

Hu, Y. C., Das, S. M., & Pucha, H. (2003). Exploiting the synergy between peer-to-peer and mobile ad hoc networks. In *Proceedings of the 9th Workshop on Hot Topics in Operating Systems*.

Johnson, D. B., & Maltz, D. A. (2001). Dynamic source routing in ad hoc wireless networks. In C. E. Perkins (Ed.), *Ad hoc networking*. USA: Addison-Wesley.

Klemm, A., Lindemann, C., & Waldhorst, O. P. (2003). A special-purpose peer-to-peer file sharing system for mobile ad hoc networks. In *Proceedings of the IEEE Semi-Annual Vehicular Technology Conference*.

Kortuem, G. (2002). Proem: A middleware platform for mobile peer-to-peer computing. *SIGMOBILE Mobile Computing and Communication Review, Special Feature on Middleware for Mobile Computing, 6*(4), 62–64.

Kortuem, G., Schneider, J., Preuitt, D., Thompson, T. G. C., Fickas, S., & Segall, Z. (2001). When peer-to-peer comes face-to-face: Collaborative peer-to-peer computing in mobile ad hoc networks. In *Proceedings of the IEEE 1st International Conference on Peer-to-Peer Computing (P2P)*.

Lee, U., Park, J.-S., Yeh, J., Pau, G., & Gerla, M. (2006). Code torrent: Content distribution using network coding in VANET. In *Proceedings of the 1st International Workshop on Decentralized resource sharing in mobile computing and networking (MobiShare)*.

Li, X., and Wu, J. (2005). Searching techniques in peer-to-peer networks. In J. Wu (Ed.), Handbook on theoretical and algorithmic aspects of sensor, ad hoc wireless, and peer-to-peer networks. Boca Raton, FL, USA: CRC Press,.

Lv, Q., Cao, P., Cohen, E., Li, K., and Shenker, S. (2002). Search and replication in unstructured peer-to-peer networks. In *Proceedings of the 16th International Conference on Supercomputing*.

Mecella, M., Angelaccio, M., Krek, A., Catarci, T., Buttarazzi, B., and Dustdar, S. (2006). Workpad: An adaptive peer-to-peer software infrastructure for supporting collaborative work of human operators in emergency/disaster scenarios. In *Proceedings of the International Symposium on Collaborative Technologies and Systems*.

Milgram, S. (1967). The small-world problem. *Psychology Today, 1*(1), 60–67.

Oliveira, L. B., Siqueira, I. G., & Loureiro, A. A. F. (2003). Evaluation of ad hoc routing protocols under a peer-to-peer application. In *Proceedings of the IEEE Wireless Communications and Networking Conference (WCNC)*.

Oliveira, L. B., Siqueira, I. G., & Loureiro, A. A. F. (2005). On the performance of ad hoc routing protocols under a peer-to-peer application. *Journal of Parallel and Distributed Computing (JPDC): Special issue on the design and performance of networks for super-, cluster-, and grid-computing, 65*(11): 1337–1347.

Oliveira, L. B., Siqueira, I. G., Macedo, D. F., Loureiro, A. A. F., Wong, H. C., & Nogueira, J. M. (2005). Evaluation of peer-to-peer network content discovery techniques over mobile ad hoc networks. In *Proceedings of the IEEE International Symposium on a World of Wireless, Mobile and Multimedia Networks*.

Oram, A. (2001). *Peer-to-peer: Harnessing the power of disruptive technologies* (first ed.). O'Reilly.

Papadopouli, M., & Schulzrinne, H. (2001a). Effects of power conservation, wireless coverage and cooperation on data dissemination among mobile devices. In *Proceedings of the 2nd ACM International Symposium on Mobile ad hoc networking and computing*.

Papadopouli, M., & Schulzrinne, H. (2001b). A performance analysis of 7ds a peer-to-peer data dissemination and prefetching tool for mobile users. In *Proceedings of the Advances in wired and wireless communications, IEEE Sarnoff Symposium*.

Perkins, C. E., & Bhagwat, P. (1994). Highly dynamic destination-sequenced distance-vector routing (DSDV) for mobile computers. In *Proceedings of the ACM Conference on Communications Architectures, Protocols and Applications*, London, UK.

Perkins, C. E., & Royer, E. M. (1999). Ad hoc on-demand distance vector routing. In *Proceedings of the 2nd IEEE Workshop on Mobile Computing System and Applications*.

Rowstron, A., & Druschel, P. (2001). Pastry: Scalable, distributed object location and routing for large-scale peer-to-peer systems. In *Proceedings of the IFIP/ACM International Conference on Distributed Systems Platforms (Middleware)*.

Schollmeier, R., Gruber, I., & Finkenzeller, M. (2002). Routing in peer-to-peer and mobile ad hoc networks: A comparison. In *Proceedings of International Workshop on Peer-to-Peer Computing*.

Seet, B.-C., Lau, C.-T., Hsu, W.-J., & Lee, B.-S. (2005). A mobile system of super-peers using city buses. In *Proceedings of the PerCom Workshops*.

Servetto, S. D., & Barrenechea, G. (2002). Constrained random walks on random graphs: Routing algorithms for large scale wireless sensor networks. In *Proceedings of 1st ACM international workshop on Wireless sensor networks and applications*.

Stoica, I., Morris, R., Liben-Nowell, D., Karger, D. R., Kaashoek, M. F., Dabek, F., & Balakrishnan, H. (2003). Chord: A scalable peer-to-peer lookup protocol for internet applications. *IEEE/ACM Transactions on Networking, 11*(1), 17–32.

Talia, D., & Trunfio, P. (2003). Toward a synergy between P2P and grids. *IEEE Internet Computing, 7*(4), 94–95.

Watts, D., & Strogatz, S. (1998). Collective dynamics of small-world' networks. *Nature, 393*(6), 440–442.

Zhou, L., & Haas, Z. J. (1999). Securing ad hoc networks. *IEEE Network, Special Issue on Network Security, 13*(6), 24–30.

Section III
Cooperative Mechanisms

Chapter VI
Enabling Cooperation in MANET–Based Peer–to–Peer Systems

Fotis Loukos
Aristotle University of Thessaloniki, Greece

Helen Karatza
Aristotle University of Thessaloniki, Greece

ABSTRACT

Mobile Peer-to-Peer networks are an emerging topic in networking. One of the major usages is the cooperation between peers. The aim of this chapter is to outline cooperation methods and architectures used in these networks. Furthermore, it provides the necessary background on Peer-to-Peer technologies and Mobile Ad Hoc networks together with a comparison that presents the similarities and differences of these two types of networks. Moreover, the major problems the authors face when implementing mobile Peer-to-Peer networks are presented and some proposed solutions are discussed. They then focus on the problem of cooperation in Mobile Peer-to-Peer networks. Furthermore, a number of examples from past research are illustrated and their experimental results are discussed and summarized. Finally, some of the future trends and remaining challenges to be addressed are presented.

INTRODUCTION

Peer-to-Peer (P2P) technology has recently become one of the most frequently mentioned technologies when it comes to file sharing or distributed computation. The term *P2P* denotes a network of equal peers composing an overlay structure over another network (Schoder et al., 2005). The most important aspect of P2P is that these peers communicate using certain protocols without the need of a central coordinator.

This type of communication has been mainly used in file sharing applications, but other uses such as distributed computation, voice over P2P and P2P television are also possible.

Most of these protocols require a hard-wired infrastructure with a standard topology such as the Internet. On the other hand, Mobile Ad Hoc Networks (MANETs) do not have such an infrastructure and their topology is constantly changing. This leads us to the challenge of finding new protocols and creating new techniques for implementing P2P networks over MANETs.

By using these protocols and techniques, we can introduce new services or improve existing ones. There are features of MANETs such as context awareness and resource availability, which do not exist in classic wired networks and can help improve P2P networks (Gold & Mascolo, 2001). New algorithms have been proposed to improve the performance of various aspects such as routing. Furthermore, new services have been introduced, e.g. collaboration frameworks (Kortuem et al., 2001), which are based on the social encounters in Mobile P2P networks.

The remainder of the chapter is organized as follows. The *Background* section presents a short introduction to P2P and MANETs and how P2P technology works over MANETs. The *Cooperation in Mobile Peer-to-Peer Networks* section describes current methods for cooperation over standard and Mobile P2P networks. Examples of such networks are also given in addition to a discussion about their potential usage. The *Future Trends* section discusses a number of open research issues and identifies some areas for future research. Finally, the chapter concludes with a summary of the materials presented.

BACKGROUND

Peer-to-Peer Networks

The most common architecture of communication over a network is the client–server model. A single computer is acting as the server which runs the server application and the rest of the nodes are acting as the clients of this computer. By using a different application, the clients can send requests to the server and wait for its response. The server is the main coordinator of the network and has the duty to execute all computations in order to present the results to the clients.

Contrary to this conventional model, P2P networks began as computer networks consisting of only equal nodes, where they run a common application that can either act as a server or a client. There is no coordinator responsible for the computations, which are instead carried out by all the peers in the network in a distributed way.

Their first use was the sharing of computer files, especially with audio and video content between peers over the Internet. Prior to P2P networks, the architecture used for such purpose required a central server with plenty of storage space and bandwidth to serve all the clients. However, with the introduction of the P2P architecture, the storage space was distributed between all peers and there was less demanding need for bandwidth. Furthermore, there was no central point of failure, i.e., even if the originator node of a certain file leaves the network, the file would still continue to exist at some other peers.

Recently, new applications in many areas, such as voice over IP telephony, media streaming and distributed computation have emerged (Androutsellis-Theotokis & Spinellis, 2004). Several large distributed computing projects, such as climateprediction.net and Folding@Home, which share common principles with P2P networks, have also been conducted. In addition, many software companies have started developing new protocols or transforming existing ones to distributed protocols over P2P networks in order to maximize the utilization of the resources belonging to the users of the network. Skype is an example of such Voice over IP application, which began with using a client–server model and later transformed into a P2P network that benefits from the resources contributed by all users (Guha et al, 2006).

The types of P2P networks have evolved through time since their first appearance. Cur-

Figure 1. A simple Peer-to-Peer network

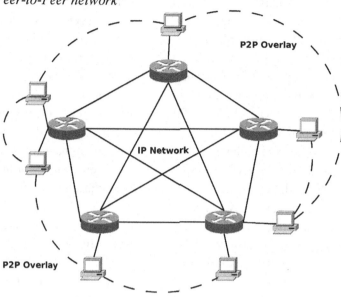

rently, there exist a number of different architectures used by various networks. These allow the distinction between first and second generation P2P networks and the hybrid ones. The two main classifications are based on whether the networks are structured or unstructured, and on how decentralized they are.

In an unstructured P2P network, all peers are allowed to connect to any peer they have discovered without any constraints. Such a discovery is possible using a static cache built in the client node or a web cache that is updated continuously in an automatic manner by special programs connected to the network. An example network that uses this architecture is Gnutella (Clip2, 2000). On the other hand, structured networks require that a peer connects only to specific peers based mainly on routing decisions. There exist a lot of algorithms for deciding where a new peer will connect to, such as the Distributed Hash Tables (DHT) (Wehrle et al, 2005) and its variants. Examples of structured networks that use these algorithms are Chord (Stoica et al, 2001) and CAN (Ratnasamy et al, 2001). All of the first generation P2P networks have used an unstructured topology. The second generation networks, however,

can be both unstructured, structured or use a hybrid of both.

Centralized networks are networks that depend on a single central node for operations such as resource discovery or the routing of specific types of messages. Although this is a characteristic of a client–server architecture, the other parts of the communications, such as file transfers, happen between peers of the network without the intervention of the central node. Most first generation P2P networks used this architecture. One of the first widely used P2P networks is Napster (Napster, 2001), which is based on a central node operated by the network creator, responsible for all the search and directory service operations. On the contrary, fully-distributed or "pure" P2P networks have no need for a central server to act as the coordinator and to which other peers must connect. Second generation P2P networks such as Gnutella are based on this type of architecture. A third category consists of the "hybrid" networks, which can act both as fully-distributed and centralized networks.

Although P2P networks can have different topologies and architectures, all of them depend on an underlying transport layer. Most work that has been done requires an IP based network above which the P2P network defines an overlay. An example of a P2P network and how it is deployed over a classic IP based network is shown in Figure 1. The links defined by the solid lines between the routers and computers are the IP based links of the network, while the P2P overlay is displayed using the links defined by the dashed arcs. All peers use the lower level transport layer for message exchange.

Even if the transport layer can route messages between peers, many P2P architectures also use their own algorithms for routing messages at the higher level overlay layer. For example, Gnutella uses a flooding algorithm to forward search messages to all nodes in order to find a file that matches a number of criteria. However, once a match is found, a direct connection is established between the two nodes in order to transfer the file. The underlying transport layer is responsible for the proper routing of all IP packets that contain the data.

Mobile Ad Hoc Networks

MANETs are wireless computer networks consisting of different nodes that communicate without the use of a special infrastructure. There is no need for a base station as in most wireless networks such as IEEE 802.11 (WiFi). When a new node

needs to connect to the network, it must find at least one neighbor within its transmission range. A simple MANET is illustrated in Figure 2.

One of the main characteristics of MANETs is that they usually consist of small devices operated by batteries that limit their transmission power, and consequently their transmission range. Almost as always, no node can directly connect to all other nodes in the network, and thus directly connected neighbors are often used to forward packets. Numerous routing algorithms have been suggested based on routing tables, dynamic route discovery and hybrid schemes. Furthermore, clustering methods have been used on previous algorithms for greater efficiency.

Another characteristic of MANETs is the mobility of all nodes. This can lead to frequent link disruption and nodes must find new neighbors to connect in order to rejoin the network. It is obvious that there is no unchanging topology and the packet transmissions between two nodes can stop any time with the need for re-routing by passing through a different path.

Peer-to-Peer Technology over Mobile Networks

Even though P2P networks share a lot of principles with MANETs, there are also substantial differences between them. A comparison of their similarities and differences with respect to various characteristics such as topology, node lifetime, network composition, and packet routing is shown in the Table 1:

It could be seen that both types of networks have a lot in common. However, they have also differences with the main one being that P2P networks focus on the overlay network layer in contrast to MANETs, which focus on the lower level wireless transport layer. This leads to problems when routing messages of the P2P network over MANET and it is the main subject of many studies (Schollmeier et al, 2002).

Figure 2. A simple Mobile Ad Hoc network (MANET)

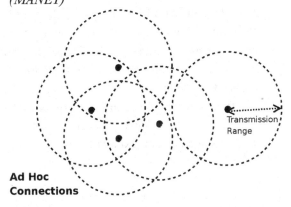

Transmission Range

Ad Hoc Connections

Table 1.

	P2P networks	MANETs
Topology	No standard topology exists for all networks. Current architectures of P2P networks, i.e. second generation or "pure" P2P, are fully decentralized with no need for a central server. However, there still exist some P2P networks that use centralized servers. For example, BitTorrent uses central trackers, while bootstrap servers are utilized by some DHTs.	No standard topology exists. All types of MANETs are created in an ad hoc manner without the need of a central infrastructure.
Node lifetime	Nodes connect and disconnect continuously. Furthermore, in 'pure' Peer-to-Peer networks, there are no standard nodes where they must connect to, but instead they use local or web caches that change dynamically over time.	Due to node mobility, the nodes disconnect continuously and may either reconnect to another node or stay out of range and become fully disconnected from the rest of the network. Furthermore, nodes in a MANET are often operated by battery power and thus their lifetime is limited.
Network composition	Peers participating in a P2P network differ in terms of both hardware and connection bandwidth. Furthermore, the computer configuration can be different, such as in terms of their operating system and the software used to connect to the network. However, all peers participate and share their resources to form the final network.	There is a high heterogeneity in the types of nodes used. MANETs can consist of mobile phones that have limited processing power, memory and storage, or they may consist of PDAs that have higher processing power, more memory and storage capacity. Still, all devices share a part of their resources with the rest of the network.
Packet routing	All P2P networks depend on a lower level transport layer to transfer packets between peers forming the P2P layout. Moreover, many P2P protocols, e.g. Gnutella, use a direct connection between nodes to transfer data and thus require the transport layer to transport the packets. In some types of P2P networks, however, content-based routing, resource-driven routing, or key based routing is used, which still depends on the lower transport layer. Currently, most works are based on an IP based network infrastructure.	There is no standard transport layer. A lot of work on MANETs focuses on a wireless transport layer. Currently, there are a lot of standards focusing on a different number of properties such as reliability, speed, security, etc. Most protocols use unlicensed ISM (Industrial, Scientific and Medical) band for wireless communications. Examples of standards include Bluetooth (IEEE 802.15.1), Zigbee (IEEE 802.15.4) and Wi-Fi (IEEE 802.11).

(Hu et al., 2003) have exploited the common features of both types of networks in order to create a new routing protocol called the Dynamic P2P Source Routing (DPSR). It is based on the Dynamic Source Routing (DSR) protocol for MANETs (Johnson & Maltz, 1996) and the Pastry P2P network protocol (Rowstron & Druschel, 2001). Here, routing of packets over the MANET is implemented in a manner analogous to the routing of messages over a Pastry P2P network overlay.

In another work, (Ding and Bhargava, 2004) proposed five different ways for file sharing using P2P networks over MANETs. They use a number of combinations of broadcasting and DHTs in order to achieve different complexity and implementation cost on the routing algorithms.

Both of these works are based on structured P2P networks. They use the DHTs in order to route all packets efficiently. Structured P2P networks allow the introduction of some routing structure to the ad-hoc nature of MANETs. On the other hand, the adoption of unstructured P2P networks over MANETs exploits the similarity of these types of networks and allows the extension of existing P2P technologies using characteristics of mobile networks such as context awareness.

COOPERATION IN MOBILE PEER-TO-PEER NETWORKS

Cooperation in Peer-to-Peer Networks

The first and main use of P2P networks is file sharing. However, a lot of work has been done on other uses such as cooperation, which in a P2P network could have many forms, such as distributed process execution and information exchange. Work has been done on all these sectors and example cases are given later in this section.

There are many factors that must be taken into consideration when implementing cooperation in a distributed environment. One of the major characteristic of P2P networks is that they consist of individual users unknown to each other and each one of them tries to maximize its own profit. Cooperation depends on the fact that all users provide resources to the network. This is in contrast to the user's personal interest and a solution must be found that maximizes both a user's profit and the network's shared resources.

The problem resembles very much to the Prisoner's Dilemma, a classic problem of game theory. (Lai et al., 2003) have studied the problem using the Evolutionary Prisoner's Dilemma (EPD), a version of the Prisoner's Dilemma problem in which continuous turns of the problem are executed and the decisions are taken through time based on a strategy and previous results. Using payoff matrices and by assigning values to cooperation and defect, they managed to create a strategy where each user must cooperate with all others in the network in order to achieve maximum interest for himself/herself.

Cooperation between nodes must also take into account the variety of platforms and architectures of the devices in the network. In a large network consisting only of computers, there can be different architectures, e.g. PC and Macintosh, which can run different operating systems, e.g. Windows, Linux and MacOSX. Since different architectures have different ways of representing data, e.g. little-endian and big-endian, a common standard must be used by all peers.

A standard that has been introduced by (World Wide Web Consortium, 2006) and used in many frameworks is the Extensible Markup Language (XML). For example, the JXTA P2P protocol specification is based upon a set of XML protocols. All messages traveling between peers are encoded using standard XML, which is independent of device architecture. Whenever a peer receives such a message, it uses a parser designed for its architecture in order to convert it to the machine's native representation.

These are two of the most common problems that we must face in P2P networks designed for cooperation between nodes. Some examples of such networks will be presented as follows.

- **Example case: Peer-to-Peer Process Execution (P³E)**
  An example of P2P cooperation is the Peer-to-Peer Process Execution (P³E). Using P³E, a decentralized execution environment can be created where many instances of one process can be executed by a service. In order to execute these instances, a number of meta-information needs to be transferred between all peers. Furthermore, a directory of all available services must exist so that a peer having to execute a process can discover the appropriate peers.

  There are a number of protocols that attempt to implement different parts of such an environment. For example, the Web Services Description Language (WSDL) (World Wide Web Consortium, 2001) is a standard language used to describe web services that can then be accessed using the Simple Object Access Protocol (SOAP) (World Wide Web Consortium, 2002). However, these protocols are only for solving one part of the problem. Recently, some frameworks have been proposed for implementing a complete environment. (Schuler et al., 2003) have described the OSIRIS infrastructure that can be used to create such a system. It is based on the concept of Hyperdatabase, which is responsible for finding the appropriate peer to route one process execution instance based on the service needed. In order to find the peer to serve each request, an internal mapping of services to real network addresses is used. To implement such a P2P network, every computer that is part of the infrastructure must be running an operating system that supports the OSIRIS Hyperdatabase Layer (HDB Layer). This layer is responsible for low level routing of all process executions to the appropriate peers. Whenever a new process is about to be invoked, the HDB layer takes over and routes it to a new peer.

Another design part of the OSIRIS architecture is the publish/subscribe mechanism. Every peer that offers a service must subscribe at a global service repository. Then when a new peer needs to access a service, it publishes its request to this service repository. The HDB layer is then responsible to route the invocation of the process to peer that

provides this service and send the required instance execution data.

A first analysis of OSIRIS has shown promising results, although it has not been fully evaluated. The authors will exploit the 128 node Xibalba cluster of ETH Zurich to get results from a real distributed system.

- **Example case: Internet Security through Peer-to-Peer cooperation**

A second example of P2P cooperation is in Internet security. One of the main threats of Internet security is botnets, which are composed of a number of infected computers running a special program called bot that performs operations without the need for user interaction. Bots are controlled by the botnet owner and can have many different payloads. Most botnets are used for initiating distributed denial of service attacks, spamming, sniffing traffic and collecting user private information and spreading malware. The first generation of botnets used a client-server architecture. An example is illustrated in the left section of Figure 3. The "Command & Control Server" is the main server where all computers running the bot connect and receive commands. This server can have

Figure 3. Botnet architectures

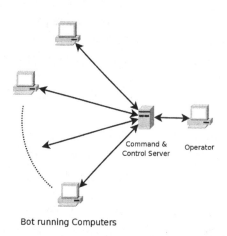
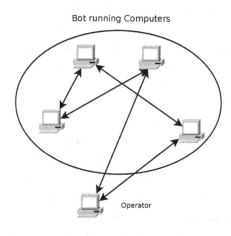

Centralized Architecture   **Peer-to-Peer Architecture**

either an IP address that is hardcoded inside the source code of the bot program or a fully qualified domain name from a free DNS lookup service so that the server can change its IP address at anytime and still the bots will be able to contact it. Once connected and authenticated by the server, the attacker can send commands, which are forwarded to the infected computers. An example of a botnet that uses this architecture is the Rustock rootkit and spam bot (Chiang & Lloyd, 2007).

Botnets that use this architecture have a number of flaws. The most important is the existence of a single point of failure which is the Command & Control Server. If the bots or the operator of the botnet cannot contact this server, then the botnet becomes unusable. The bot will replicate but will not execute any payload since it cannot get commands from the operator. This is the most common way that is used in order to bring down a botnet employing this architecture.

New generation botnets use a P2P architecture. The bot program has an integrated Command & Control Server and all infected computers create a "pure" P2P network. The operator can then connect to this network and send all commands to the rest of the nodes. In contrast to the centralized architecture described previously, this method has no single point of failure. (Grizzard et al., 2007) describe the Peacomm P2P botnet that uses the Overnet P2P protocol, an architecture based on the Kademlia algorithm (Maymounkov & Mazières, 2002). When a new computer is infected, it has a list of 146 possible peers, which makes it very difficult for the defender to ensure that they will fail in order to render the botnet unusable. These peers can then cooperate in the network to send spam mail, infect new computers or create distributed denial of service attacks.

On the other hand, P2P networks can also be used for the detection of internet threats. Apart from botnets, worms are another main threat. Worms are self-replicating malware programs with a payload that they execute automatically. In contrast to botnets, they do not communicate with each other and they do not operate based on commands given to them. Often, they use the vulnerabilities of the operating system of target computer in order to gain access and install themselves. Detection of worms is currently done mainly through antivirus programs using signature checks. All antivirus programs keep a database of signatures from all known worms. Whenever an executed program is found to have its signature in that database, it is identified as a worm and its execution stops. However, this method is inefficient for worms that have not been yet identified by the antivirus production laboratories or for computers which do not have an updated signature database.

Another method for detection of worms is using P2P cooperation. (Malan and Smith, 2005) have described such a system, which is independent of signature databases. It analyzes the system state and the similarity of system calls executed by different worms. Peers in the network compare the results of this analysis and identify abnormal behavior caused by worms. Experimental results showed that worms can be identified between 76% and 97% of the time.

These are two examples illustrating the use of cooperation over P2P networks. Their distributed architecture allows better use of resources provided by the peers of the network. This can be either processing power (as in the first case) used to reduce execution time, or the system state (as in the last part of second case) where needed information from other peers can be acquired.

Using Peer-to-Peer Cooperation Technology over Mobile Networks

Most work on P2P networking over the Internet is for networks designed for the exchange of files, such as media files containing audio or video. Works have also been done on this topic for Mobile P2P networks, such as secure file sharing based on epidemic algorithms (Mavromoustakis & Karatza, 2006), with a focus on cooperation. For some cases, the cooperation protocols and standards defined for classic P2P networks can be used for MANETs. For example, the major standard used in both cases for data exchange is XML. This is due to the fact that data representation problems are the same for all networks with heterogeneous peers. Additionally, frameworks in both cases try to implement a common application programming interface in order to be compatible with different operating systems and programming languages.

There are many platforms based on common protocols that can be easily ported to Mobile P2P networks. For example, in the previous section, a network architecture for detecting security threats was presented, which uses P2P cooperation over the Internet. A similar architecture could also be used for Mobile P2P networks to create a mobile device antivirus based on the information acquired by other peers.

However, even with common protocols, more efficient algorithms should be designed. As an example, current XML parsers use algorithms with high complexity, which are unsuitable for most mobile devices. Many programming languages designed for these devices have limited features when it comes to data parsing. Java 2 Micro edition has no support for XML, while Java 2 Standard Edition can support XML by integrating a built-in XML parser.

Furthermore, there are architectures whose usage over MANETs is impossible. For example, the network presented for the Peer-to-Peer Process Execution cannot be implemented in a Mobile P2P

network, as devices belonging to MANETs have low processing capability and a small amount of memory and storage space. The time spent in running the algorithms for remote execution and the transfer of all data for the new instance is much larger than the time that is required for local execution. Additionally, it is much more difficult to find a device offering a specific service in a network composed completely of heterogeneous devices, than in a network composed of many devices having the same architecture.

Two examples of cooperation architectures designed exclusively for Mobile P2P networks are presented as follows.

- **Example case: The Shark shared knowledge system**

  An example usage of Mobile P2P cooperation is the shared knowledge between all peers. (Schwotzer and Geihs, 2002) have described Shark, a system for management, synchronization and exchange of knowledge in Mobile P2P networks. It allows a number of users, who run a special program in their mobile devices, to exchange knowledge and synchronize it between themselves. The underlying network protocol used is Bluetooth, which is currently supported by most mobile devices and the program is written in Java 2 Micro Edition so that it can be independent of the device architecture and run under any J2ME runtime environment.

  The system is based on three components: 1) Shark Central Station; 2) Shark Mobile Station; and 3) Shark Local Station. The Central Station (CS) is a computer that plays the role of a server. Even if the system is a distributed Mobile P2P network, the CS is a special peer that holds the whole knowledge database. It also offers tools to the Shark administrator who can organize the database and approve pieces of unconfirmed knowledge coming from a peer. In order to keep the database up to date with all the knowledge in the network, it synchronizes its database using the SyncML protocol with the information held by the rest of the peers.

The Mobile Station (MS) is the software that runs in each mobile device. It contains a database that holds part of the network's stored knowledge. It acts as a peer in the Mobile P2P network and exchanges information based on topics associated with each piece of knowledge. Since MS is usually a device with limited storage space, it gathers information from the CS, the Local Station and other MSs based on some selection criteria set by the user.

Finally, the Local Station (LS) is a special kind of MS. It runs on a fixed location with the same software as the MS. However, its database does not hold knowledge coming from the users, but instead information related to its location. Thus, users coming to a new location can easily gather knowledge offered by the LS to gain information specific only to the current place.

The Shark system currently provides the framework upon which a whole infrastructure can be built. However, there are many issues that need to be solved before implementing such a solution. For example, the issue of encouraging the users to share their knowledge, which has already been discussed in the *Cooperation over Peer-to-Peer Networks* section, still exists. The creators of Shark propose that a micro payment system could be a first step in solving this problem.

- **Example case: The Proem platform**
  The Proem platform (Kortuem et al, 2001) is a platform developed by the Department of Computer Science at the University of Oregon. It has been successfully used as part of the Advanced Software Engineering topic in a P2P Computing course. Proem is a generic platform upon which different types of Mobile P2P networks can be implemented.

In contrast to other frameworks used for implementing P2P networks such as JXTA, Proem it is targeted to MANETs. It takes into consideration the fact that connections can continuously open or close as the users are constantly changing their position. Its design allows working with peer connection duration that is as low as several minutes. Moreover, it features built-in security, a very important factor for MANETs that often consist of users unknown to each other.

A number of objectives were set during the development. The interoperability and the platform independence are two of them. The platform should be able to operate under heterogeneous hardware, with different operating systems and programming languages. Additionally, it should be adaptable to any type of environment and be used for a wide range of applications. The extensibility of the platform is also a basic objective to be realized. Finally, it should provide a powerful development platform that would facilitate the implementation of user applications.

In order to achieve all these goals, web standards have been used, e.g. HTTP and XML, which were created by the World Wide Web consortium, an organization that develops most of the web standards. Since these are all non-proprietary standards that are accessible to anyone, many projects have used them to achieve interoperability.

Four network protocols are defined by the platform, one for the transport layer and the other three for higher layers. The transport protocol is a connectionless protocol based on XML to achieve interoperability between peers of different architectures. It can be implemented on top of any other lower layer protocol. The other three protocols are the Presence Protocol, Data Protocol and Community Protocol. The Presence Protocol is used for the discovery of new peers entering the network. Each node sends a presence message to the MANET in order to inform the rest of the network of its availability. The Data Protocol is used for the actual data transfers between nodes for each application. Finally, the Community Protocol is used to create communities of nodes and add or remove new peers from them.

The main components of the Proem are the Proem Runtime System and the Peerlet Development Kit. The first is an implementation of the network protocol stack together with a Peerlet Engine. Peerlets are the applications running over the Mobile P2P network. They are executed using an event-driven model in a similar way to web Servlets and mobile phone MIDlets. The Peerlet Engine is responsible for sending all events to the callback functions of the peerlets. The second component, Peerlet Development Kit, is the Java API for creating peerlets. It is a set of packages that allow creating callback functions and accessing the protocol stack for communication with other nodes.

Proem has been successfully used for implementing experimental Mobile P2P networks for the P2P computing course at University of Oregon. Further work could lead to the implementation of real world networks.

- **Example case: The SocialNet social networking platform**

SocialNet (Terry et al, 2002) is a social networking platform designed for Mobile P2P networks. Its purpose is to match users with common interests and shared friends.

Most social networking platforms require the user to enter some information about himself/herself and try to find matches based on common interests. Often, the users are put into very generic categories and inappropriate matches are created as a result. However, SocialNet uses a novel way to match users based on collocation information and common friends.

The basis of SocialNet is a portable device that is carried by the user all the time, e.g. mobile phone. Each user enters his username and a unique ID is created for each device. In addition to the username and ID, the device keeps three lists: 1) the friend list; 2) the unknown list; and 3) a list of encounter records. The friend list contains a list of all friends along with their username and ID. The device continuously broadcasts a message with its ID to declare the user's presence. Whenever a device receives such a message, it creates an encounter record. This record keeps information about the time when the two users met, the duration of their encounter and the ID of the other user. All encounter records are then used to find patterns for meetings of users through time. Infrequent encounters of long duration or frequent encounters of short duration indicate a user with common interests. Periodically, searches in the database for such users are created, and if an entry is found matching the criteria, the ID of the other user is inserted in the unknown list. Whenever two friends meet, they exchange their unknown lists. If a user has in his friend list, an ID in the unknown list he received, he receives a message to introduce his friend to the user who sent him his unknown list.

Using this method a Mobile P2P network is created. Unknown nodes do not interact with each other but only record their presence. The cooperation between friends to exchange their unknown lists and matching friends has allowed the discovery of users with common interests.

One of the main benefits of SocialNet is the privacy of users. A user never broadcasts its username or its friends. There is no way for a third peer to get unwanted information apart from the users' unknown lists. A secondary benefit is that users do not have to find the exact categories to characterize themselves, but instead their collocation information is used. Furthermore, a common friend exists, who can make the proper introduction of his two friends.

SocialNet has been tested by its creators at a major conference for three days. Ten users participated with one being the author who had a friend list with the other nine users. According to the authors, successful introduction was generated leading to promising results for future usage of the platform.

These three examples demonstrate the use of cooperation over Mobile P2P networks. Although there are similarities with cooperation methods over classic P2P networks, it is clear that due to the nature of MANETs and the users composing them, the usages are different.

FUTURE TRENDS

There are many challenges in the area of cooperation in Mobile P2P networks. In the previous section, we have presented some research that has been done, but there still exist many topics where interesting problems are yet resolved.

One of the major usages of Mobile P2P networking is in ubiquitous and pervasive computing (Kangasharju, 2005). There is a lot of work that needs to be done in order to use cooperation in these environments. Problems arise as there are unique characteristics that we must take into consideration.

As a first example, security and privacy are two major concerns in such a Mobile P2P network. Cooperation between peers gives permission to other users to access the resources of the rest of the nodes. Since nodes in pervasive computing networks have limited resources, access control is a very important research topic. Many Mobile P2P platforms have tried to address this issue but more research and careful design is needed. Every user wants to ensure his safety against malicious users who want to take advantage of his mobile devices

or the whole P2P network. Authentication allows us to establish a trust relationship with another peer and authorization helps to give appropriate privileges so that the remote peer has access to only a certain amount of information. In order to ensure privacy, we must use also other techniques, such as encryption. Encryption comes in many forms, i.e. public key encryption, symmetric key or hybrid schemes. The encryption scheme must be carefully chosen since each scheme uses different algorithms that have a different computational and memory complexity. Since most ubiquitous computing networks consist of nodes with limited processing capability, e.g. mobile phones and PDAs, the algorithms that will be used must have a low order of complexity.

Another issue is context awareness. Current research for cooperation over Mobile P2P networks focuses mainly on the distribution of data and the interoperability between architectures. However, context awareness is very important since different environmental conditions may require different actions between peers. For example, a peer could decide not to cooperate with another peer that has limited battery power since it may disconnect from the network before completing all operations.

Another challenge that we will be facing in the future is the scalability of these networks. Classic P2P networks started as small communities in the Internet, but most of them have already escalated to become overlays with thousands or even millions of peers. It has been calculated that the Gnutella alone had 1.81 million peers as of June 2005. In contrast, the development of Mobile P2P networks is still in its infancy and therefore the current networks have only a very limited number of users. Still, in the future, they will grow to also become networks consisting of thousands of users. The problems of scalability and their effects on the cooperation protocols and architectures are issues that have not been fully resolved and thus require to be further investigated.

CONCLUSION

In this chapter, we have provided an introduction to P2P networks and their implementation over MANETs. Furthermore, we discussed cooperation architectures over both classic and Mobile P2P networks. Some of the problems arising when using cooperation methods over Mobile P2P networks and their solutions were presented. We have also included a number of examples about various schemes that have been developed. In addition, remaining open issues and possible directions for future research were discussed. We have shown that cooperation over Mobile P2P networks is a promising research topic with many scientific and technological applications.

REFERENCES

Androutsellis-Theotokis, S., & Spinellis, D. (2004). A survey of peer-to-peer content distribution technologies. *ACM Computing Surveys, 36*(4), 335-371.

Bächer, P., Holz, T., Kötter, M., & Wicherski, G. (2005). Know your enemy: Tracking botnets. *The Honeynet Project & Research Alliance.*

Chiang, K., & Lloyd, L. (2007). *A case study of the rustock rootkit and spam bot.* Paper presented at the First Workshop on Hot Topics in Understanding Botnets.

Clip2. (2000). The Gnutella protocol specification v0.4. Retrieved May 13, 2008, from http://www9.limewire.com/developer/gnutella_protocol_0.4.pdf

Ding, G., & Bhargava, B. (2004). Peer-to-peer file-sharing over mobile ad hoc networks. In *Proceedings of the Second IEEE Annual Conference on Pervasive Computing and Communications Workshops (PERCOMW).*

Gold, R., & Mascolo, C. (2001). Use of context-awareness in mobile peer-to-peer networks. In *Proceedings of the Eighth IEEE Workshop on Future Trends of Distributed Computing Systems (FTDCS).*

Grizzard, J. B., Sharma, V., Nunnery, C., & Kang, B. (2007). *Peer-to-peer botnets: Overview and case study.* Paper presented at the First Workshop on Hot Topics in Understanding Botnets.

Guha, S., Daswani, N., & Jain, R. (2006). An experimental study of the Skype peer-to-peer VoIP system. In *Proceedings of the Fifth International Workshop on Peer-to-Peer Systems.*

Hu Y. C., Das S. M., & Pucha H. (2003). Exploiting the synergy between peer-to-peer and mobile ad hoc networks. In *Proceedings of the 9th Workshop on Hot Topics in Operating Systems.*

Johnson, D. B., & Maltz, D. A. (1996). Dynamic source routing in ad hoc wireless networks. In T. Imielinski & H. F. Korth (Eds.), *Mobile Computing.* U.S.: Springer.

Kangasharju, J. (2005). Peer-to-peer and ubiquitous computing. In R. Steinmetz & K. Wehrle (Eds.), *Peer-to-Peer Systems and Applications.* Springer Berlin / Heidelberg.

Kortuem, G., Schneider, J., Preuitt, D., Thompson, T. G. C., Fickas, S., & Segall, Z. (2001). When peer-to-peer comes face-to-face: Collaborative peer-to-peer computing in mobile ad hoc networks. In *Proceedings of the First International Conference on Peer-to-Peer Computing.*

Lai, K., Feldman, M., Stoica, I., & Chuang, J. (2003). Incentives for cooperation in peer-to-peer networks. In *Proceedings of the Workshop on Economics of Peer-to-Peer Systems.*

Malan, D. J., & Smith, M. D. (2005). Host-based detection of worms through peer-to-peer cooperation. In *Proceedings of the ACM Workshop on Rapid Malcode.*

Mavromoustakis, C. X., & Karatza H. D. (2006). Epidemic collaborative replication for maintaining file sharing reliability in mobile peer-to-peer devices. In *Proceedings of the International Symposium on Performance Evaluation of Computer and Telecommunication Systems (SPECTS)*.

Maymounkov, P., & Mazières, D. (2002). Kademlia: A peer-to-peer information system based on the XOR metric. In *Proceedings of the First International Workshop on Peer-to-Peer Systems*.

Ratnasamy, S., Francis, P., Handley, M., Karp, R. M., & Shenker, S. (2001). A scalable content-addressable network. In *Proceedings of the ACM SIGCOMM Conference on Applications, Technologies, Architectures, and Protocols for Computer Communications*.

Rowstron, A., & Druschel, P. (2001). Pastry: Scalable, distributed object location and routing for large-scale peer-to-peer systems. In *Proceedings of IFIP/ACM International Conference on Distributed Systems Platforms (MIDDLEWARE)*.

Schoder, D., Fischbach, K., & Schmitt, C. (2005). Core concepts in peer-to-peer networking. R. Subramanian & B. D. Goodman (Eds.), *Peer-to-Peer Computing: The Evolution of a Disruptive Technology*. Hershey, PA: Idea Group Publishing.

Schollmeier, R., Gruber, I., & Finkenzeller, M. (2002). Routing in mobile ad hoc and peer-to-peer networks. A comparison. In *Proceedings of the International Workshop on Peer-to-Peer Computing*.

Schuler, C., Weber, R., Schuldt, H., & Schek, H. (2003). Peer-to-peer process execution with OSIRIS. In *Proceedings of the First International Conference on Service-Oriented Computing (ICSOC)*.

Schwotzer, T., & Geihs, K. (2002). Shark - a system for management, synchronization and exchange of knowledge in mobile user groups. *Journal of Universal Computer Science, 8*(6), 644-651.

Stoica, I., Morris, R., Karger, D., Kaashoek, F., & Balakrishnan, H. (2001). Chord: A scalable peer-to-peer lookup service for internet applications. In *Proceedings of the ACM SIGCOMM Conference on Applications, Technologies, Architectures, and Protocols for Computer Communications*.

Terry, M., Mynatt, E. D., Ryall, K., & Leigh, D. (2002). Social net: Using patterns of physical proximity over time to infer shared interests. *CHI extended abstracts on Human Factors in Computing Systems*.

The Napster Protocol (2001). Retrieved May 13, 2008, from http://opennap.sourceforge.net/napster.txt.

Wehrle, K., Gotz, S., & Rieche, S. (2005). Distributed hash tables. In R. Steinmetz & K. Wehrle (Eds.), *Peer-to-Peer Systems and Applications*. Springer Berlin / Heidelberg.

World Wide Web Consortium. (2001). *Web services description language 1.1*. Retrieved May 13, 2008, from http://www.w3.org/TR/wsdl

World Wide Web Consortium. (2002). *SOAP version 1.2*. Retrieved May 13, 2008, from http://www.w3.org/TR/soap

World Wide Web Consortium. (2006). *Extensible markup language (XML) 1.0 (fourth edition)*. Retrieved May 13, 2008, from http://www.w3.org/TR/xml

Chapter VII
Cooperation Strategies for P2P Content Distribution in Cellular Mobile Networks:
Considering Selfishness and Heterogeneity

Tobias Hoßfeld
University of Würzburg, Germany

Daniel Schlosser
University of Würzburg, Germany

Kurt Tutschku
University of Vienna, Austria

Phuoc Tran-Gia
University of Würzburg, Germany

ABSTRACT

The performance of P2P content distribution in cellular networks depends highly on the cooperation and coordination of heterogeneous and often selfish mobile users. The major challenges are the identification of problems specifically arising in cellular mobile networks and the development of new cooperation strategies to overcome these problems. In this chapter, the authors review common cooperation strategies using multi-source downloads. They demonstrate the fundamental "last chunk" problem of typical strategies as used by eDonkey or BitTorrent. This is caused by the selfishness of users; however, an ordered chunk delivery evades this problem. In the coherent subsequent chapter "Cooperation Strategies for P2P Content Distribution in Cellular Mobile Networks: Considering Mobility and Heterogeneity", the impact of mobility and vertical handover between heterogeneous wireless access technologies is investigated.

INTRODUCTION

P2P file sharing systems contribute to the majority of traffic volume that is currently being transported in the Internet. Applications like eDonkey or BitTorrent are used to share large volume content and alleviate the problem of overloaded servers by distributing the load among all sharing peers, which makes P2P systems highly scalable and resilient content distribution systems. The performance of such P2P content distribution networks (CDN) in cellular networks depends highly on the coordination of heterogeneous and often selfish mobile users. Sophisticated cooperation strategies, such as the multi-source download and tit-for-tat principle, are the foundation of the extreme efficiency of P2P content distribution networks. Multi-source download means the simultaneous download of parts of a file, referred to as chunk, from several sources in parallel. The cooperation strategies applied in popular P2P CDN platforms such as eDonkey or BitTorrent, rely on the fundamental P2P assumption that all peers are equal. In cellular networks, however, the peers differ significantly in their characteristics, e.g. their access system and bandwidth which might change over time or their on-line behavior, thus introducing heterogeneity and even selfishness in the peer community. Hence, the P2P assumption of equal peers is not valid any more. In addition, the dynamics and heterogeneity in cellular mobile networks is further increased by the mobility of users.

Although most P2P CDNs utilize the benefits of multi-source downloads, the various platforms differ significantly in the actual implementation of the cooperation algorithms. In particular, the peer selection as well as the chunk selection mechanisms lead to different system behaviors and performance results. The detailed performance of the strategies is further determined by the actual peer characteristics and the peer behavior. The peer characteristic includes, among others the available upload and download bandwidth, as well

as the number of parallel upload and download connections. The mobility of a user makes these peer characteristics change over time. Thus, the performance depends considerably on the heterogeneity. The peer behavior is mainly described by churn, i.e. the switching of a user between offline and online state, and by the willingness of a user to participate in the CDN. A user may behave selfishly and tries to minimize the upload of data or he may redistribute the data in an altruistic way. In the context of cellular mobile networks, churn and selfish behavior appear even more distinctive, e.g. to save battery resources or scarce and expensive uplink capacities. As a result, the so-called "last chunk" problem might arise which inhibits the data dissemination process and makes individual chunks starve in the network.

Additional challenges and influence factors on the performance of the system arise in a heterogeneous, wireless cellular network. Due to the user mobility, vertical handovers (VHO) between the different wireless access technologies are required which may result in transmission delays and IP address changes of the switching peer. Mechanisms like Mobile IP allow overcoming IP address changes, nevertheless such mechanisms also introduce additional delays. Another important phenomenon occurring with vertical handovers is the abrupt change of available bandwidth, e.g., from a fast WLAN connection to a rather slow UMTS connection. This will be discussed in more detail in the coherent following chapter "Cooperation Strategies for P2P Content Distribution in Cellular Mobile Networks: Considering Mobility and Heterogeneity".

There are several possibilities to improve the performance of content distribution in cellular networks. Those are: a) particular architecture concepts introducing special entities like caches for storing contents or crawlers for locating sources, e.g. (Oberender et al., 2005); b) the optimization of parameters, like the size of chunks, as done by Hoßfeld, Tutschku & Schlosser, 2005); c) incentives to motivate the users to share files and to contribute to the system; and d) cooperation strategies for the coordination among peers. From these possibilities, we will focus on the cooperation strategies in this chapter. The goal is: i) to describe how to model a P2P content distribution system with multi-source download in a cellular wireless environment; ii) to identify the fundamental problems of typical cooperation strategies; iii) to investigate the impact of user behavior and heterogeneity, in particular selfishness; and iv) to propose solutions to overcome the derived problems.

The chapter is organized as follows. The *Background: Cooperation Strategies in CDNs* section gives comprehensive background on the multi-source download mechanism and common cooperation strategies, as used by eDonkey or Bit-Torrent. We define key metrics for evaluating the performance of such systems and review related work which addresses heterogeneity and selfishness in general. In the *Selfishness of Users and Robustness of the System* section, we discuss the fundamental last chunk problem and show how the proposed CycPriM cooperation strategy allows to overcome this. Its performance is compared with common strategies in different user behavior scenarios. Finally, the *Conclusion* section summarizes this chapter. The *Future Trends* will be outlined in the subsequent chapter "Cooperation Strategies for P2P Content Distribution in Cellular Mobile Networks: Considering Mobility and Heterogeneity" and combines the trends regarding the different aspects of heterogeneity, selfishness and mobility.

BACKGROUND: COOPERATION STRATEGIES IN CDNS

The mechanisms to control and manage content distribution in P2P networks can be distinguished in two major categories: a) resource mediation mechanisms, which are functions for searching and locating resources; and b) resource access control mechanisms, i.e. function for exchanging files or parts of it. There are several approaches focusing on resource mediation mechanisms. They vary from centralized concepts such as index servers, as in eDonkey, to highly decentralized approaches such as flooding protocols, as in the Gnutella network, or distributed hash tables, as used in the Chord protocol. Especially, the DHTs and hierarchical derivates have gained a lot of scientific interest addressing refinements to cope with reliability and efficiency in cellular environments (Zoels, Schollmeier, Kellerer & Tarlano, 2005). Special architectural entities like crawlers are used to locate files and sources of files on behalf of other users to improve the performance. This is especially important in mobile environments with scarce and expensive resources of users (Hossfeld et al., 2005a).

The resource access control mechanisms determine the coordination and cooperation among peers which means to permit, prioritize, and schedule the access to shared resources. In this context, incentive mechanisms are implemented to promote cooperative behavior. This means they try to make peers participate in the network and share their resources. Examples are credit point systems as used in eDonkey or tit-for-tat strategies like in BitTorrent. However, in this chapter, we consider a different approach, the so-called cooperation strategies, to overcome problems, like the last chunk problem caused by selfishness or inefficient usage of scarce resources in heterogeneous environments. In particular, we investigate different cooperation strategies and derive solutions for specific problems. The coordination of the peers to enable the efficient, fair and robust distribution of contents in a CDN is realized by a cooperation strategy. Its task is to decide: a) which peers requesting for blocks are served by an uploading peer using a priority function, like first-come-first-serve; and b) which is the next chunk to download by a downloading peer. These two decisions undertaken by a cooperation strategy are referred to as peer selection and chunk selection, respectively.

The question arises as to whether a cooperation strategy can leverage the effects of selfishness or heterogeneity and establish an efficient, fair and robust content distribution.

Content Distribution with Multi-Source Download

An efficient and robust way of cooperative content delivery is the multiple source download (MSD), which means that the recipient peer orders and downloads the desired data from many providing peers instead from a single one. The efficiency of MSD was demonstrated by the success of the P2P files sharing platforms eDonkey and BitTorrent and was scientifically researched for example in (Izal et al., 2004; Qiu & Srikant, 2004).

P2P content distribution mechanisms which apply MSD split files into chunks and blocks which are subparts of chunks. For the eDonkey application for example, the chunk size is typically 9.5 MB and the block size is 180 kB. A downloading peer requests blocks from serving peers, i.e. sources of that file, and might download from these sources in parallel. As soon as a peer has downloaded a complete chunk, it becomes a source for the file, i.e. it can redistribute the already received chunks. The benefit of MSD lies in the speed-up via the parallel download of data and the faster creation of additional sources for chunks. As a result, MSD does not rely on a single source and can therefore avoid bottlenecks and overcome churn.

A peer can download from an arbitrary number of sources in parallel. While the number of parallel download connections is typically not limited, the number of parallel upload connections at a peer is restricted to a maximum of n in order to guarantee a certain minimal bandwidth. Requesting peers being served simultaneously share the uploading bandwidth of the providing peer. However, if a downloading peer cannot handle the offered bandwidth due to restrictions of his own download bandwidth, the surplus id equally divides among the other peer connections.

In heterogeneous environments, this effect is emphasized, especially due to capacity changes over time due to mobility and VHOs. The resulting bandwidth sharing discipline is referred to as max-min fair share (Hoßfeld et al., 2004).

Reducing the number of parallel uploads to one, $n=1$, which means no parallel uploads at all, could possibly enhance the diffusion. This is reasonable by considering the following scenario. At time t_0, only a single initial source exists which provides a file consisting of one chunk. All peers are assumed to have the same upload bandwidth, which allows them to upload one chunk within a time T using the complete bandwidth. Thus, the number of reproduced chunks after time t is $2^{t/T}$ in the case of one upload and $k^{t/kT}$ in the case of k parallel uploads. It holds $k^{T/k} \leq 2^T$ for $k>0$, i.e., an outbound degree of one performs best in theory. However, these assumptions are not valid in practice. Selfish user behavior, churn, or heterogeneous peer capabilities will lead to other results which will be discussed later.

A user interested in a particular content sends a download request to a peer providing the desired content. If the provider already serves n peers, it pushes the request into its uplink waiting queue. As soon as an upload connection becomes available, the first peer in the uplink waiting queue is served. However, this waiting queue can be ordered according to a certain priority function. In eDonkey for example, the credit point system is used to determine a peer's position within an uplink queue. This credit point system might take into account the popularity of a file or the actual upload to download ratio of exchanged data with this peer. The simplest priority function is a first-come-first-serve (FCFS) which means the uplink waiting queue is served in FCFS manner. While being served, each peer downloads a specific amount of data in a row. In the current eMule application which is a popular client for eDonkey, these are three blocks of 180 kB, resulting in a so-called download unit (DU) of size 540 kB. After completing the download of a DU, a peer will either re-enter the waiting queue at the end or leave this peer, if it has already finished downloading the desired data. The upload queue model is demonstrated in Figure 1. It has to be noted that if a peer goes offline, the existing data connections are dropped, but the already downloaded part of a DU is stored and does not get lost.

In the studies presented in this chapter, we assume a hybrid P2P architecture. That means, the information where resources are located is offered by a central entity, which we call the index server in reference to the eDonkey network. The index server keeps track of the peers being connected to the CDN. We focus on the resource access control mechanisms and the sharing behavior of CDNs and therefore assume that global information about chunks shared in the network is available. A peer who is interested in a file, requests all available sources at an index server. Therefore, each peer knows all sources which are connected to the network at the moment of the request. New sources will be discovered by periodical source request messages of a downloading peer which are sent every ten minutes. Every time a peer receives a new source, it sends a download request containing an identifier for all required chunks. If the peer addressed by the request has none of the required chunks, the request is neglected.

Common Cooperation Strategies

(Hamra & Felber, 2005) identifies the principal design choices of content distribution that draw the behavior of the system. Among others, the structure of the P2P overlay and the cooperation strategy are emphasized. According to them, a cooperation strategy is the result of three factors coupled together, the peer selection strategy, the chunk selection strategy, and the network degree.

To define this clearly, a cooperation strategy describes the selection of the next peer being served as well as the choice which chunk should be transferred, i.e. the peer selection and the chunk selection strategy. In this section, we describe two common strategies which are used to identify problems and to compare them as benchmark test with newly proposed cooperation strategies. In particular, we introduce the random chunk strategy and the least-shared first strategy and discuss the chunk dissemination process on an example scenario. For both strategies, the peer selection is assumed to follow a FCFS approach.

As an example, the first two rounds of the distribution process of a file for the two different cooperation strategies are considered. For the sake of simplicity, we consider in this case only a single upload slot of the providing peers and a homogeneous scenario in which all peers

Figure 1. Upload queue of a providing peer(Duelli, Hoßfeld & Staehle, 2007) © 2007 IEEE

require the same amount of time for downloading any chunk.

There are three initial sources *(S1, S2, S3)* which share all chunks of a file. A peer offering all chunks of a file is referred to as a seed for this file. Table 1 shows the list of requesting peers at the seeds and the providing peers at the beginning of each round. At seed *S2*, for example, the requesting peers are *P1, P0, P3, ...* which will be served in FCFS manner order. In the beginning of round 1, only the seeds share chunks. After that round, however, the peers which were served by these peers also act as sharing peers and provide the successfully downloaded chunks to the other requesting peers.

In the example the file consists of two chunks. Furthermore there are ten peers *P0, ... , P9* who want to download the file. The first step of the download process is without loss of generality assumed to be equal for both strategies: peer *P0* downloads chunk 1 from *S1*, peer *P1* chunk 2 from *S2*, and peer *P9* chunk 1 from *S3*. After the first round of transferring chunks, the dissemination behaves different for each strategy. The strategies will be explained in the following.

Table 2 illustrated the chunk exchange for the depicted example. The columns *P0, ..., P9* shows the file requesting peers and their corresponding actions per round for both strategies. For example, in round 1, peer *P0* downloads chunk 1 from seed *S1*, indicated as *C1/S1*. Round 1 is equal for both strategies and results into five sharing peers of chunk 1 *(S1, S2, S3, P0, P9)* and four sharing peers of chunk 2 *(S1, S2, S3, P1)*, cf. #C1 and #C2 in Table 2.

Random Chunk Strategy

Applying the random chunk strategy, like the one used by eDonkey, a downloading peer issues a request to a sharing peer. The sharing peer queues this request in a first-come-first-serve (FCFS) manner. As soon as the downloading peer is served, it chooses a random chunk which it has not downloaded yet. In our example, peer *P0* selects its missing part and departures after downloading from the network. In addition, peer *P2* and peer *P4* choose chunk 1 randomly and independently and download it from *S1* and *S3*, respectively, cf. Table 2.

The random chunk strategy relies on the random selection of required chunks. The randomization avoids that all downloading peers select the same chunk. Thus, the simultaneously downloading peers get different chunks and can therefore exchange these different chunks in

Table 1. List of requesting peers at seeds and providing peers at the beginning of each round

	S1	S2	S3	P0	P1	P9
round 1	*P0, P2, P7, ...*	*P1, P0, P3, ...*	*P9, P4, P0, ...*	-	-	-
round 2	*P2, P7, ..., P0*	*P0, P3, ..., P1*	*P4, P0, ..., P9*	*P5, ...*	*P6, ...*	*P8 ,...*

Table 2. Example of chunk download for common cooperation strategies

	P0	P1	P2	P3	P4	P5	P6	P7	P8	P9	#C1	#C2
round 1	*C1/S1*	*C2/S2*								*C1/S3*	5	4
round 2: random	*C2/S2*		*C1/S1*		*C1/S3*	*C1/P0*	*C2/P1*		*C1/P9*		9	6
round 2: LSF	*C2/S2*		*C2/S1*		*C2/S3*	*C1/P0*	*C2/P1*		*C1/P9*		7	8

the further distribution process. This fosters the cooperation among peers. As will be shown in the *Selfishness of Users and Robustness of the System* section this strategy performs well as long as peers are altruistic, i.e. as long as peers are willing to share after they have completed their download.

However, if most of the peers are leeching and leave the system shortly after the download of the file or due to churn, the random selection cannot guarantee an even distribution of the chunks. This leads to the situation of one chunk being less shared than the others and the last chunk problem occurs. In our example, chunk 2 is only shared by three peers besides the initial seeds, while chunk 1 is shared by six peers. If a peer sharing chunk 2 leaves the system for any reason, this imbalance is increased further.

Least-Shared First Strategy

The least-shared-first (LSF) strategy also uses the same priority function for the peer selection like the random chunk strategy, i.e. requests are served in a first-come-first-serve manner. However, the chunk selection differs. Peers choose as next chunk to be downloaded the one which is least-shared in the P2P network. This means that this chunk has the smallest number of sharing peers, compared to the number of possible sources for other chunks. If there are several chunks fulfilling the least-shared criteria, one of these is chosen randomly. After round 1 of the example scenario, chunk 2 is the least shared one. Thus, with the same peers to be served as for the random chunk strategy, the peers *P2* and *P4* choose the least shared chunk 2 not yet being downloaded at the moment of the download. At the end of round 2, the least-shared first strategy results in a more equal chunk distribution, that are seven sharing peers of chunk 1 and eight sharing peers of chunk 2 which can also be seen in Table 2.

A peer using this strategy selects the required chunk which has the lowest number of providing

peers. This mechanism results typically in a evenly spread number of sharing peers for all chunks of the file. However, there are cases in which this is not true. As it will be shown in the *Selfishness of User and Robustness of the System* section, this strategy is very efficient as long as the chosen chunk is the least-shared one at the end of the download of this chunk. However, the decision which chunk is the currently least-shared one is done at the beginning of the download. Thus, another chunk can get the least-shared one which undermines the homogeneous chunk dissemination.

In addition, it is necessary that every peer is aware of the numbers of peers sharing a specific chunk in order to know the least-shared chunk. Although, we assume that an index server, as used by eDonkey, keeps track of the peers being connected to the CDN, the index server is not responsible for providing information about the dissemination of chunks. Thus, the evaluation presented later neglects the overhead caused by frequent status update messages or monitoring mechanisms which are necessary to maintain or predict this information. Hence, the LSF strategy might perform worse in practice, since the transmission of the overhead consumes additional resources. As a result, the download time might be longer than discussed here.

Key Performance Characteristics

The performance of a P2P CDN is determined by the implementation of the cooperation strategy, the peer characteristics, i.e. the currently available capacity resources for exchanging files (upload and download bandwidth, maximum number of inbound and outbound connections), and the user behavior. The latter one includes: a) the file request pattern taking into account flash crowd effects and popularity of contents; b) the churn behavior, i.e. the switching of an user between offline and online state which might be more frequent in mobile environments; c) mobility which mainly effects the available capacities of a peer; and d) the willingness to participate in the network, i.e. selfish or altruistic peers. As an extreme case of selfish peers we consider leechers which immediately leave the system after finishing the download of a file. In such a case, the leaving users reduce the availability of chunks. As a result, in the worst case a specific chunk may be rarely available in the system.

From the user's perspective, the key performance characteristic of a CDN is the efficiency in terms of download time which is the time from sending the request for a file until successfully receiving the entire content. Additionally, a user wants to minimize its costs in terms of the amount of uploaded data volume which consumes an expensive resource in cellular networks, the upload capacity of a peer. Beside the efficiency and the costs, in a P2P-based CDN the users are interested in a fair system, i.e., the system should ensure fairness among the peers with respect to efficiency and costs. This is especially important in the presence of selfish peers. In particular, a perfectly fair cooperation strategy makes all peers experience the same download time and upload the same amount of data, although selfish peers try to maximize only their own benefit. We choose the fairness index introduced by (Jain, Chiu & Hawe, 1984) to quantify fairness. *Jain's fairness index* is defined by

$$J = \frac{\left(\Sigma_{i \in M} x_i \right)^2}{|M| \Sigma_{i \in M} x_i^2}$$

where x_i are the values of the considered performance measures, M is the set of all measurement values, and $|M| |M|$ is the number of measurement values. It holds $J = \frac{1}{1 + c_x^2}$, where c_x^2 is the corresponding coefficient of variance. The fairness index returns values between zero and one, i.e. $0 \leq J \leq 1$. Low values of the fairness index indicate an unfair system, while a fairness index of one describe a completely fair system.

That is, all users experience deterministically the same performance with respect to the considered measure.

From a global point of view, the robustness of a CDN is of interest which is expressed by the chunk availability and the occurrence of rare chunks. More formally, we define the availability A_i of a chunk i in the time interval from t_0 to t_1 as follows

$$A_i = \frac{\int_{t_0}^{t_1} C_i(t) dt}{t_1 - t_0}$$

where $C_i(t)$ is the number of peers sharing chunk i at time t. The chunk availability A_i reflects the average number of peers sharing chunk i in the corresponding interval. The rare chunk availability A is the minimal availability of a chunk normalized by the average availability of all chunks. It is

$$A = \min_{0 \leq i < N} \left\{ \frac{A_i}{\frac{1}{N} \Sigma_{0 \leq i < N} A_i} \right\}$$

which can take values in $[0;1]$. N is the total number of chunks of a file. A low value of A indicates starving chunks, while a high value around 100% shows that all the chunks are similarly disseminated and available over time within the CDN.

According to (Birolini, 1991), robustness is a characteristic of a system, being stable under failure, misuse, and overload. For content distribution networks we see this demand fulfilled if the system is resistant against changes in the user behavior, i.e. the file transfer times and upload volumes are stable even with selfish peers in the network. Hence, a CDN which is efficient, fair and robust can provide a reliable download experience with short download times and small upload volumes. To be more detailed, a cooperation strategy is considered to be robust, if the amount of data uploaded and the time needed to finish the download of an arbitrary peer are close to the values obtained in a diffusion scenario with altruistic peers which will be explained in the *Investigated Scenarios on User Behavior* section. This implicitly requires a high chunk availability for all chunks.

Related Work on Cooperation Strategies

Cooperation Strategies define how peers interact with each other. (Penserini, Liu, Mylopoulos, Panti & Spalazzi, 2003) model peers within a special framework and research methods how to judge the cooperation strategies build up by the reasoning mechanism within the peers for a given task.

If we focus on content distribution the task is to quickly disseminate one or more files to a group of peers. Incentives help these groups to collaborate even if some of the peers behave selfish. In (Lai, Feldman, Stoica, & Chuang, 2003) the authors characterize the problem of selfish peers and have shown that solutions based on the local knowledge on a peers behavior does not scale with an increasing peer group size and other options have to be considered. But it has also been shown in (Feldman, Lai, Stoica, & Chuang, 2004) that there are possibilities to reach near optimal sharing behavior even in large groups and with high churn using incentives. A comparison between different incentive strategies is presented in (Feldman & Chuang, 2005). Many of these incentive mechanisms are based on the idea of trading upload volume against download volume by using some sort of virtual currency. However, if a new peer without any part of the file enters the system, it has to earn an amount of this currency in order to pay for its download. To encounter this problem, (Liao, Papadopoulos, & Psounis, 2006) proposes to reward peers for staying in the system instead of endowing new peers the possibility to download parts of the file. In contrast to this, (Anagnostakis & Greenwald, 2004) believe that incentives based on virtual currencies are either ineffective or much too complex. Therefore they propose a strong incentive, based

on the idea of barter trade. In their proposed architecture peers prefer to trade parts of files with other peers, which provide them with parts they currently need and vice versa. Incentives might guarantee a good cooperation between peers. But that does not necessarily mean that the exchange of data is fair for all peers, as it is demonstrated by (Veciana & Yang, 2003). However, all these approaches define incentives in order to stabilize the cooperation of peers. In our work we propose an interaction scheme without incentives and compare it to some of the architectures proposed before. Another proposal for an incentive-less architecture is (Hales, 2006). But in this work, Hales assumes that peers are able to copy the neighborhood and the behavior of other peers, which is very hard to achieve in practice and is not necessary with our approach.

(Fessant, Handurukande, Kermarrec & Massoulie, 2004) showed the measurement results of several peer-to-peer content distribution systems and concluded that these systems provide the opportunity to gain efficiency by clustering peers with the same interests and regional togetherness. The idea of selecting proper peers in order to increase the efficiency was also discussed in (Garces-Erice, Biersack, Ross, Felber & Urvoy-Keller, 2003). This contribution proposes to build hierarchical structures in order to cope with problems locally and not to affect the whole network. In the same year, (Ng, Chu, Rao, Sripanidkulchai & Zhang, 2003) discuss how measurement-based optimization may influence bandwidth demanding peer-to-peer systems. The question is discussed in (Moscibroda, Schmid & Wattenhofer, 2006) where topologies are created by peers trying to minimize their connections and optimize the response times to their overlay neighbors. The peer selection may also have an influence and can optimize the dissemination of a file in the P2P system based on random selection of parts of the file which is shown in (Norros, Prabhu & Reittu, 2006). In our contribution we do not restrict peers in their communication with other peers. A peer may interact with any other peer in the system. Thus, we focus on the timing when two peers interact and on the information they exchange, i.e. the scheduling within the resource access control and the chunk selection.

With the optimal selection of neighbors in the overlay it may be possible to structure and optimize the peer-to-peer network. However, the data exchanged between two interacting peers also influences the file dissemination. (Felber & Biersack, 2005) discuss which peer and chunk selection strategies are able to cope with flash crowd effects. A more detailed look on the behavior of the content distribution systems which we compare with our solution are presented in (Tutschku, 2004) and (Legout, Urvoy-keller & Michiardi, 2006). Whereas (Tutschku, 2004) focuses on the eDonkey network, (Legout et al., 2006) considers the BitTorrent architecture.

Beyond these performance measures it is also crucial that the content distribution system does not decay in adverse circumstances. This feature is called robustness and is discussed in (Risson & Moors, 2006) and (Triantafillou, Xiruhaki, Koubarakis & Ntarmos, 2003). While (Risson & Moors, 2006) researches the robustness of algorithms that distribute dictionaries over a group of peers, (Triantafillou et al., 2003) applies the concept of robustness to content distribution peer-to-peer networks. The resulting content distribution system is complex and uses peer clustering. In contrast to this, our proposed architecture is flat and avoids the overhead needed to stabilize a hierarchical architecture.

SELFISHNESS OF USERS AND ROBUSTNESS OF THE SYSTEM

The scope of this section is to show the impact of selfish users on the performance of the system. In particular, we will show that the selfishness of users will decrease the robustness of the system which will lead to the last chunk problem. We will further address if an appropriate cooperation strategy is able to deal with selfish user behavior and makes the system be robust again. As a result of the observation why common cooperation strategies fail to prevent chunks starving in the network, we develop the so-called CycPriM strategy. In a worst-case and a best-case scenario, we compare the performance of the CycPriM strategy with the eDonkey-like random chunk selection strategy and the BitTorrent-like least-shared first (LSF) strategy.

The Last Chunk Problem

The coordination of peers in a P2P file sharing network is no simple task. An inappropriate coordination of the peers may decrease the performance of the strategy, i.e. it may increase the overall download time of a file. A particular problem in P2P file sharing networks is the so-called "last chunk" or "starving chunk" problem (Hamra & Felber, 2005). Here, a single chunk of a file may not spread in the file sharing network as the other chunks do. Hence, a shortage of providers for this chunk may arise. As a result, the remaining providing peers may be overloaded and the file exchange is delayed.

The user behavior now decides on the willingness to participate in the network, i.e. to behave as selfish or altruistic peer. Leechers as an extreme case of selfish peers leave the system immediately after finishing the download of a file. As a leaving user sharing some or all chunks reduces the availability of the corresponding chunks, leechers cause chunks to get rare. As a result, in the worst-case a specific chunk may get rare in the system, i.e. there are only a few sources for this chunk in the CDN. As a consequence, these few sources might not be able to efficiently serve all requesting peers and the entire content distribution process is disturbed.

Figure 2 depicts two examples for such a behavior. It shows the spreading of chunks, i.e. the number of sharing peers for each chunk i of the file, over time in a leeching scenario. Most of the chunks are spreading throughout the system, cf. label 'popular chunks' in Figure 2. One of the chunks denoted as 'starving chunk' will not spread due to the leeching behavior of peers, as the downloading peer disappears from the system as soon as it has downloaded this chunk. The only remaining sources of this chunk are the initial seeds. As a result, unfinished peers which seek the final, last chunk have to wait until they receive the chunk from one of the initial sources. This leads to large download times. This problem is called the last chunk problem.

To illustrate the last chunk problem with leeching peers, we provide some simulation results in Figure 2 and Figure 3. Details on the simulation setup and scenario can be found in the *Investigated Scenarios on User Behavior* section. Figure 2(a) depicts the number of peers sharing a chunk throughout time using at most one upload connection. In this case, the random chunk strategy is applied. Each of the 17 chunks of the file is represented by one single line in Figure 2(a). It is evident that the number of peers sharing a chunk does not rise equally. At the beginning some chunks are reproduced while others are not. A chunk being shared by some more peers than

only the seeders becomes independent to churn which allows a faster reproduction of sources for these chunks. Additionally, in the beginning there are several peers that share only one chunk. Therefore, they will distribute this chunk only, as long as they do not download any other chunks. Thus these chunks will be more often downloaded than the other ones.

After the first chunk was distributed among the requesting peers, a peer downloads another chunk and this chunk spreads in the network like the first one. Later this leads to a situation in which nearly all chunks are often shared. This is the point where the leeching behavior harms the system. If a peer downloads this starving chunk there are two possible situations. In the first case, it has the other chunks already. Thus this peer has finished the download and departures from the CDN. In the second case some or all of the other chunks are still needed. Then the peer will be able to download the remaining chunks in a short time, because of the high number of peers sharing the other parts. Afterwards, it leaves the network. In any case, the time this peer provides this rare chunk as an additional source is very short. As a result, one chunk is shared only by a few peers and required by many peers which forces them to wait for this final chunk to be transferred.

Figure 2. Illustration of the last chunk problem in the leeching scenario (Schlosser, Hoßfeld & Tutschku, 2006) © 2006 IEEE

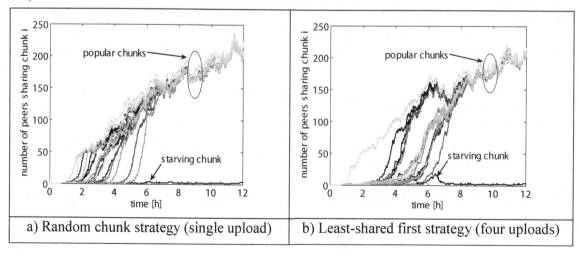

| a) Random chunk strategy (single upload) | b) Least-shared first strategy (four uploads) |

The LSF strategy tries to overcome the last chunk problem by favoring rare chunks. In order to choose the least-shared chunk, it is imperative to know the dissemination of chunks at the moment of the chunk request. Thus, this information has to be up-to-date and globally accessible, e.g., it is provided by a tracker or other more complex distributed schemes.

In Figure 2(b), we see the evolution of the number of peers sharing chunk i for the least-shared first strategy with at most four parallel uploads. In this situation, this cooperation strategy is no longer able to prevent a starving chunk. The reason is that the least-shared chunk is determined at the beginning of the download. However, this is not necessary the least-shared one when the download ends. With a rising number of parallel uploads it gets more difficult to decide the least-shared chunk at the end of the download before it starts.

The question arises whether a cooperation strategy can leverage the selfish behavior of the peers and avoids the last chunk problem. Within this chapter, different cooperation strategies are evaluated with respect to the last chunk problem by their download performance and their spreading behavior of the chunks. There are many attempts to overcome this problem like the least-shared-first chunk selection of BitTorrent (Cohen, 2003) or Avalanche network coding (Gkantsidis & Rodriguez, 2005). In this chapter we propose, however, a new cooperation strategy called CycPriM, which has efficient chunk diffusion behavior and unlike other strategies, is based only on existing local information available at the peer.

CycPriM Strategy

A sharing peer should take care of the homogeneous chunk dissemination in the network to avoid the last chunk problem. As we have seen so far, the random distribution of chunks leads to rare chunks in the presence of selfish peers or high churn rates. Although the least-shared first strategy tries to overcome this, it still cannot avoid

that chunks get rare in the system. The main problem derives from the fact that the downloading peers determine which chunk to download next. As selfish peers are only interested in their own download and not in the robustness of the CDN itself, any chunk selection undertaken by the downloading peers to their benefit cannot solve the last chunk problem if the peers are served in a first-come-first-serve manner. As the downloading peer determines which chunk is required and will be downloaded next, our idea is to modify the peer selection strategy of an uploading peer in an appropriate way. The goal of the peer selection strategy is to force the downloading peers to download chunks such that an equal dissemination of all chunk of a file prevails. Thus, the chunk selection strategy of the downloading peer is implicitly determined by the peer selection mechanism of the uploading peer.

If there is only local information available at a providing peer on the availability of chunks in the CDN, the sharing peer should deliver chunks in an ordered way. The basic idea is to distribute the entire file – instead of favoring individual chunks – in upload rounds. In each upload round the mechanisms tries to distribute a sequence of all chunks to requesting peers, as long as requests for these chunks are available. If no request is available for one of the chunks in the sequence, this chunk is skipped and the next chunk of the sequence is chosen to be distributed. After the complete sequence is processed, a new upload round starts. In order to prevent the downloading peer from selecting any other chunk, we propose the following cooperation strategy: The uploading peer offers only this one chunk. If a peer accepts this offer, or no peer wants the chunk, then the next chunk from the cycle is chosen. We call this strategy CycPriM which stands for Cyclic Priority Masking.

It has to be noted that this cooperation strategy does not require any additional information from the CDN. In contrast to the least-shared first strategy, the chunk availability has not to be monitored and signaled to providing peers and seeds. Thus, no additional signaling traffic arises. It has to be noted that each providing peer only has to decide its individual sequence of chunks. According to this sequence, the upload of chunks is determined. However, no coordination among the peers is required to define this sequence. In fact, we use a random sequence of chunk delivery for each providing peer. This sequence is locally stored at the providing peer and is kept constant while uploading chunks of this file.

We consider now the same example as in the *Common Cooperation Strategies* section. The file consists of two chunks and the chunk upload sequences for each seed are the following. Seed *S1* and *S3* first upload chunk 1 and then chunk 2, while seed *S2* first uploads chunk 2 and then chunk 1, i.e.*(C1,C2)* for *S1; (C2,C1)* for *S2;* and *(C1,C2)* for *S3.*

The first round of the download process is the same as for the random chunk strategy and the least-shared first strategy. Peer *P0* downloads chunk 1 from *S1*, peer *P1* chunk 2 from *S2*, and peer *P9* chunk 1 from *S3*. After that, however, the CycPriM strategy leads to a different system behavior. The ordered list of requesting peers at seeds and providing peers at the beginning of each round is given in Table 1.

Table 3 shows which chunk the seeds and the providing peers upload in the two rounds for the random chunk strategy (random), the least-shared first strategy (LSF), and the cyclic priority mask-

ing strategy (CycPriM). The number of sharing peers of chunk 1 and chunk 2 is denoted as #C1 and #C2, respectively. Note that Table 3 shows now the chunk dissemination process from the viewpoint of an uploading peer, in contrast to Table 2 showing the download of chunks from the viewpoint of requesting peers. This representation highlights the different peer selection of the CycPriM strategy compared to the FCFS peer selection of the random and the LSF strategy.

In Table 3 the example shows, that all seeds share the opposite chunk in the second transfer phase for the CycPriM strategy, as they did in the first. For example seed *S2* has transferred chunk 2 in step 1, thus *S2* will distribute chunk 1 in step 2. Peer *P0* would be served by seed *S2* in the second step. However, peer *P0* has been masked because it already has chunk 1. The next peer wanting to download chunk 1 (in the example: peer *P3*) is served instead.

Figure 3 shows the temporal evolution of the number of sharing peers for each chunk for a single simulation run. The considered simulation scenario is the same as described in the *Last Chunk Problem* section. Thus, we consider a leeching scenario in which the users disappear immediately after downloading a file. Figure 3(a) shows the results for the LSF strategy with a single upload per providing peer, while the results for the CycPriM strategy with a single upload is illustrated in Figure 3(b). Obviously, in both cases, the cooperation strategy avoids starving

Table 3. Example of chunk upload for CycPriM and the common cooperation strategies

	S1	*S2*	*S3*	*P0*	*P1*	*P9*	#C1	#C2
round 1	*C1/P0*	*C2/P1*	*C1/P9*				5	4
round 2: random	*C1/P2*	*C2/P0*	*C1/P4*	*C1/P5*	*C2/P6*	*C1/P8*	9	6
round 2: LSF	*C2/P2*	*C2/P0*	*C2/P4*	*C1/P5*	*C2/P6*	*C1/P8*	7	8
round 2: CycPriM	*C2/P2*	*C1/P3* (P0 masked)	*C2/P4*	*C1/P5*	*C2/P6*	*C1/P8*	8	7

chunks which is realized by an equal dissemination of chunks for LSF and the ordered delivery of chunks for CycPriM, respectively. As it will be shown later CycPriM is only a little bit slower than an optimal adjusted LSF. But it neither needs additional signaling traffic nor has the last chunk problem which appears when using several upload slots for LSF. This means the CycPriM will also lead to a robust system, if the number of upload slots differs and the peers have heterogeneous peer capabilities. Figure 3(b) shows in particular that using CycPriM the availability for the different chunks stays relatively close together in the beginning. After this, they spread in the CDN and the number of peers sharing a particular chunk is very dynamic. The most popular chunk is three times more often shared than the most unpopular one which increases slightly the download times.

Investigated Scenarios on User Behavior

The performance of the cooperation strategies is evaluated for different scenarios in which the user behavior and the peer capabilities are varied. In particular, we consider selfish and altruistic peers

and vary, the number of parallel uploads per peer. In all scenarios we assume churn which means the switching of a user between offline and online state. The duration of an ON period and an OFF period of a peer is exponentially distributed with a mean of one hour, respectively.

The selfishness of peers is investigated in a worst-case scenario, the leeching scenario, and a best-case scenario, the diffusion scenario, in which the peers are almost altruistic. In the diffusion scenario all peers finishing the file transfer will serve as uploading peers during the rest of the simulation. From the diffusion scenario it can be concluded whether a strategy uses the available resources efficiently or not. Against this, a peer finishing the download will depart from the network shortly after in the second scenario, which is called the leeching scenario. The selfishness in the leeching scenario will demonstrate if a strategy can deal with uncooperative peer behavior.

Another influence factor on the system performance are the peer capabilities. In all scenarios of this section, peers are assumed to have the same bandwidth capabilities. The impact of heterogeneous and changing bandwidths is considered afterwards in the *Content Distribution*

Figure 3. Avoidance of starving chunks by equal dissemination and ordered delivery (Schlosser, Hoßfeld & Tutschku, 2006) © 2006 IEEE

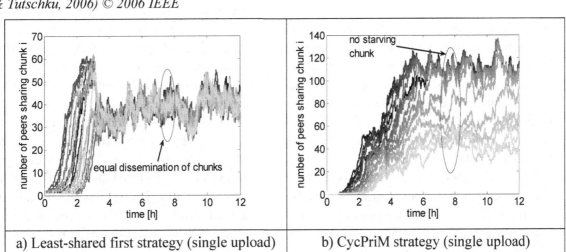

| a) Least-shared first strategy (single upload) | b) CycPriM strategy (single upload) |

in Heterogeneous Cellular Networks section. Here, the peers have GPRS access with an upload bandwidth of 12 kbps and a download bandwidth of 48 kbps. The maximum number of outbound connections, i.e. parallel uploads of a peer, might strongly impact the system and is varied between one and four connections. These settings are used in this section as a case study to see how the cooperation strategy impacts the performance and how the sophisticated CycPriM strategy improves the system. This mobile P2P CDN scenario is of particular interest to investigate the robustness of a system, due to the increased churn behavior of peers and the poor connectivity of the peers. This may increase the selfishness of peers and clearly reveals the drawbacks of the cooperation strategies.

For the numerical evaluation, we simulated ten runs for each scenario and each cooperation strategy. The considered network consists of 1,000 peers. These peers are interested in one file which is provided by three initial seeds. The file has a size of 8 MB. At the beginning one peer is chosen randomly to download the file. The interarrival time used to schedule the file requests of the other peers follows an exponential distribution with a mean of 80 seconds.

Performance Comparison of CycPriM with Common Strategies

Next, we investigate the performance of these cooperation strategies in the diffusion and the leeching scenario. The diffusion scenario represents an ideal system. The scenario is used as a reference scenario for the discussion of the leeching scenario where robustness and fairness is of major interest. The last chunk problem and the associated decrease of efficiency are assumed to be mainly caused by the selfish behavior of peers. Therefore, the robustness and availability of chunks is investigated in the leeching scenario. It has to be noted that the results for the diffusion, as well as for the leeching scenario are combined

in Figure 4 and Figure 5. Next, we start discussing the diffusion scenario.

Diffusion Scenario

Figure 4 shows the results of the simulation study from the user's point of view including the uploaded data volume as well as the download times experienced by the user. The left part of Figure 4(b) depicts the average download time in the diffusion scenario with the associated 95% and 99% quantiles. The number of parallel uploads in the scenario is varied from one to four and is labeled as "#PU" in Figure 4, as well as in Figure 5. The average download times are in the same order of magnitude for the different cooperation strategies in the diffusion scenario. They show that all cooperation strategies are very efficient and permit a short download time. However, the download time of an arbitrary peer depends highly on the actual number of available sources and their upload bandwidth. Due to the altruistic behavior a peer that starts the download late sees many sources for the file where it can choose from. Hence, a peer arriving late experiences a short download time and has to upload less data.

Figure 4(a) shows the average data volume uploaded by peers and the corresponding 95% and 99% quantiles. We see, that in the diffusion scenario the amount of uploaded data volume significantly differs among the peers which is independent of the cooperation strategy. This is also expressed by Jain's fairness index in Figure 5(b) which is around 0.5. The indices are all in the same order, independently of the observed performance measure, i.e. the upload volume or the download time, and the number of parallel uploads. The download time is closely related to the availability of chunks. The more peers provide a chunk the faster a download can be completed. The left part in Figure 5(a) shows the rare chunk availability in the diffusion scenario. It nearly reaches the optimal value of 100% for all strategies due to the altruistic user behavior.

Figure 4. Comparison of CycPriM with random chunk and least-shared-first strategy

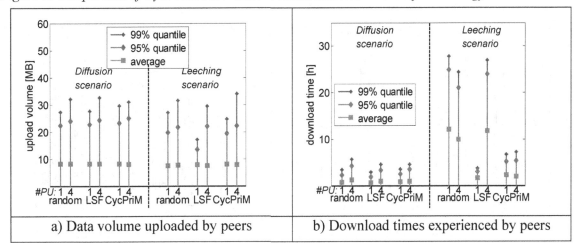

a) Data volume uploaded by peers

b) Download times experienced by peers

Leeching Scenario

We continue to investigate the leeching scenario which is depicted in the right part of Figure 4 and Figure 5. A cooperation strategy is considered to be robust, if the amount of data uploaded and the time needed to finish the download are close to the values obtained in the diffusion scenario. Figure 4(a) shows the data volume the peers have uploaded. In all scenarios, the mean value of uploaded data volume is roughly the same. The 95% quantile and the 99% quantile show how much individual peers have contributed in uploading. From this figure the high fairness index of the LSF strategy with a single upload becomes evident, cf. Figure 5(b). This variant is the only strategy that assures single peers not to upload much more data than two times of the download. All other strategy variants have much higher values for these quantiles.

The right part of Figure 4(b) shows the average download time of the peers in the leeching scenario. The LSF strategy with one parallel upload has download times which are in the same order as in the diffusion scenario, cf. left part of Figure 4(b). This feature and the low upload volume for each peer demonstrate the very good robustness

of the LSF strategy with one parallel upload against leeching behavior. The CycPriM strategy permits fast download times in the leeching scenario as well. It cannot provide always the short download times of the LSF strategy. However, the robustness of the CycPriM strategy does not depend on the peer capabilities. In contrast, the download times for the random chunk strategy and the LSF strategy with four parallel uploads are three times higher. Only the CycPriM strategy is robust against selfish behavior independent of the peer capabilities.

Figure 5(a) shows the rare chunk availability. For the leeching scenario, the last chunk problem occurs at the random chunk strategy and the LSF strategy with a high outband degree. In our simulation study, we found out that already four parallel uploads make one chunk starve in a LSF-based CDN. This is reflected by the low values presented in the right part of Figure 5. The CycPriM strategy shows a rare chunk availability of about 50% which is a result of the wide spectrum of number of sharing peers as already discussed in the *CycPriM Strategy* section. The LSF strategy with a single upload leads to the best results regarding this rare chunk availability in the leeching scenario. However, in this case,

Figure 5. Robustness and fairness of cooperation strategies

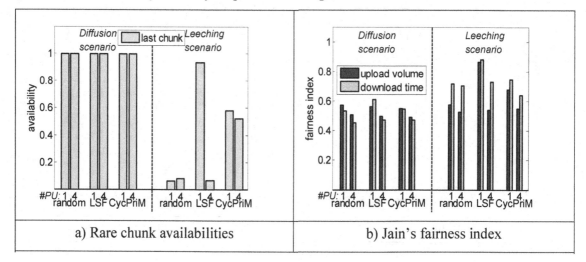

a) Rare chunk availabilities	b) Jain's fairness index

it is necessary to update or estimate the global information about the number of sharing peers for every chunk. Furthermore, the LSF strategy has to prevent changes to the peer capabilities, ie., it must not allow parallel uploads at a providing peer. The CycPriM strategy is robust against leeching as well as against changes of peer capabilities while still avoiding the last chunk problem.

Figure 5(b) visualizes Jain's fairness index for the upload volume and download times experienced by the peers. The fairness index of all cooperation strategies in the leeching scenario is mostly on the same level, see right part of Figure 5(b). Only, the LSF strategy with one parallel upload has a fairness index that is significantly higher. The fairness indices of the other strategies are more or less the same.

As a result of this performance evaluation, we have seen that in cases where most of the peers are selfish, i.e. show a leeching behavior, the performance of the CDN can be significantly improved with an appropriate cooperation strategy. The results proposed so far are also valid in a more general context of P2P-based CDNs, however, the typical features of wireless networks emphasize strongly the effects and the performance influence factors.

CONCLUSION

The performance of P2P content distribution in cellular mobile networks is determined mainly by the implemented cooperation strategy at a local peer. Major challenges which arise typically in cellular networks are the selfishness and the heterogeneity of peers. The selfishness of users leads to the last chunk problem, while the heterogeneity wastes expensive resources in the system. In this chapter, a background on common cooperation strategies which are based on the multi-source download is given. For performance evaluation purposes, the key performance characteristics are formally defined, before related work in the field of P2P content distribution is reviewed.

In this chapter, we have shown that in cases where most of the peers are selfish, i.e., show a leeching behavior, a chunk selection strategy like least-shared first is able to overcome the last chunk problem. However, it is necessary to update the global information about the number of sharing peers for every chunk. Furthermore, the LSF strategy has to prevent changes to the peer capabilities, i.e, it must not allow parallel upload at a providing peer. A more sophisticated cooperation strategy, the CycPriM strategy, has proven to be robust against leeching as well as against changes of peer capabilities. The basic idea is to modify the peer selection strategy of uploading peers which implicitly determines the chunk selection strategy of the downloading peers. This seems to be more appropriate to deal with selfish peers in a heterogeneous environment.

REFERENCES

Anagnostakis, K. G., & Greenwald, M. B. (2004). Exchange-based incentive mechanisms for peer-to-peer file sharing. In *Proceedings of the 24th International Conference on Distributed Computing Systems*, Tokyo, Japan.

Bakos, B., Farks, L., & Nurminen, J. (2006). P2P applications on smart phones using cellular communications. In *Proceedings of the 2006 IEEE Wireless Communications and Networking Conference (WCNC 2006)*, Las Vegas, USA.

Carlos, K., Djamel, S., Joseane Farias, F., Jennifer, L., & Borje, O. (2006). On the use of peer-to-peer architectures for the management of highly dynamic environments. In *Proceedings of the 4th annual IEEE international conference on Pervasive Computing and Communications Workshops*, Pisa, Italy.

de Veciana, G., & Yang, X. (2003). Fairness, incentives and performance in peer-to-peer networks. In *Proceedings of the Forty-first Annual Allerton Conference on Communication, Control and Computing*, Monticello, IL, USA.

Duelli, M., Hoßfeld, T., & Staehle, D. (2007a). Impact of vertical handovers on cooperative content distribution systems. In *Proceedings of the Seventh IEEE International Conference on Peer-to-Peer Computing (P2P2007)*, Galway, Ireland.

Duelli, M., Hoßfeld, T., & Staehle, D. (2007b). *Impact of vertical handovers on cooperative content distribution system* (Tech. Rep. No. 428). Würzburg, Germany: University of Würzburg.

Eberspaecher, J., Vogel, H.-J., & Bettstetter, C., B. (Eds.). (2001). *GSM switching, services, and protocols* (2nd ed.). Manchester: Wiley.

Felber, P., & Biersack, E. W. (2004). Self-scaling networks for content distribution. In *Proceedings of the International Workshop on Self-* Properties in Complex Information Systems*, Berinoro, Italy.

Feldman, M., & Chuang, J. (2005). Overcoming free-riding behavior in peer-to-peer systems. *SIGecom Exch., 5*(4), 41-50.

Feldman, M., Lai, K., Stoica, I., & Chuang, J. (2004). Robust incentive techniques for peer-to-peer networks. In *Proceedings of the 5th ACM conference on Electronic commerce*, New York, NY, USA.

Fenton, F. (1960). The sum of lognormal probability distributions in scatter transmission systems. *IRE Trans. Commun. Syst., CS-8*(3), 57–67.

Garces-Erice, L., Biersack, E. W., Felber, P. A., Ross, K. W., & Urvoy-Keller, G. (2003). Hierarchical peer-to-peer systems. *Parallel Processing Letters, 13*(4), 643-657.

Hales, D. (2006). Emergent group level selection in a peer-to-peer network. *ComPlexUs, 3*, 108-118.

Horozov, T., Grama, A., Vasudevan, V., & Landis, S. (2002). MOBY - A mobile peer-to-peer service and data network. In *Proceedings of the International Conference on Parallel Processing (ICPP'02)*, Vancouver, British Columbia, Canada.

Hoßfeld, T., Leibnitz, K., Pries, R., Tutschku, K., Tran-Gia, P., & Pawlikowski, K. (2004). Information diffusion in edonkey filesharing network. In *Proceedings of the Australian Telecommunication Networks and Applications Conference (ATNAC 2004)*, Sydney, Australia.

Hoßfeld, T., Mäder, A., Tutschku, K., Tran-Gia, P., Andersen, F. U., de Meer, H., & Dedinksi, I. (2005). Comparison of crawling strategies for an optimized mobile P2P architecture. In *Proceedings of the 19th International Teletraffic Congress (ITC19)*, Beijing, China.

Hoßfeld, T., Tutschku, K., & Andersen, F. U. (2005a). Mapping of file-sharing onto mobile environments: feasibility and performance of eDonkey with GPRS. In *Proceedings of the Wireless Communications and Networking Conference, 2005 IEEE*. New Orleans, LA USA.

Hoßfeld, T., Tutschku, K. & Andersen, F. U. (2005b). Mapping of file-sharing onto mobile environments: enhancement by UMTS. In *Proceedings of the Mobile Peer-to-Peer Computing MP2P, in conjunction with the 3rd IEEE International Conference on Pervasive Computing and Communications (PerCom'05)*. Kauai Island, Hawaii.

Hoßfeld, T., Tutschku. K., & Schlosser, D. (2005) Influence of the size of swapping entities in mobile P2P file-Sharing networks. In *Proceedings of the Peer-to-Peer-Systeme und -Anwendungen, GI/ITG-Workshop in conjunction with KiVS 2005*, Kaiserslautern, Germany.

Hoßfeld, T., Oechsner, S., Tutschku, K., Andersen, F. U., & Caviglione, L. (2006). Supporting vertical handover by using a pastry peer-to-peer overlay network. In *Proceedings of the 3rd IEEE International Workshop on Mobile Peer-to-Peer Computing (MP2P'06)*, Pisa, Italy.

Jain, R.K., Chiu, D.M.W., & Hawe, W.R. (1984). *A quantitative measure of fairness and discrimination for resource allocation in shared computer system* (Tech. Rep. DEC-TR-301). Hudson, MA: Eastern Research Lab, Digital Equipment Corporation.

Kempf, J. (2001). *Dormant mode host alerting ("IP paging") problem statement*. RFC Editor.

Lai, K., Feldman, M., Stoica, I., & Chuang, J. (2003). Incentives for cooperation in peer-to-peer networks. In *Proceedings of the Workshop on Economics of Peer-to-Peer Systems*, Berkeley, CA, USA.

Lee, J.K. & Hou, J.C. (2006). Modeling steady-state and transient behaviors of user mobility: Formulation, analysis, and application. In *Proceedings of the seventh ACM international symposium on Mobile ad hoc networking and computing (MobiHoc06)*, New York, NY, USA.

Le Fessant, F., Handurukande, S., Kermarrec, A. M., & Massoulie, L. (2004). Clustering in peer-to-peer file sharing workloads. In *Proceedings of the 3rd International Workshop on Peer-to-Peer Systems (IPTPS)*, San Diego, CA, USA.

Legout, A., Urvoy-Keller, G., & Michiardi, P. (2006). Rarest first and choke algorithms are enough. In *Proceedings of the 6th ACM SIGCOMM on Internet measurement*, Rio de Janeiro, Brazil.

Liao, W.-C., Papadopoulos, F., & Psounis, K. (2006). A peer-to-peer cooperation enhancement scheme and its performance analysis. *Journal of Communications (JCM), 1*(7), 24-35.

Matuszewski, M., Beijar, N., Lehtinen, J., & Hyyrylainen, T. (2006). Content sharing in mobile P2P networks: Myth or reality? *International Journal of Mobile Network Design and Innovation, 1*(3/4), 10.

Michal, F., Kevin, L., Ion, S., & John, C. (2004). Robust incentive techniques for peer-to-peer networks. In *Proceedings of the 5th ACM conference on Electronic commerce*, New York, NY, USA.

Moscibroda, T., Schmid, S., & Wattenhofer, R. (2006). On the topologies formed by selfish peers. In *Proceedings of the Twenty-fifth annual ACM symposium on Principles of distributed computing*, Denver, Colorado, USA.

Ng, T., Chu, Y., Rao, S., Sripanidkulchai, K., & Zhang, H. (2003). Measurement-based optimization techniques for bandwidth-demanding peer-to-peer systems. In *Proceedings of the 22nd Annual Joint Conference of the IEEE Computer and Communications Societies INFOCOM*, San Francisco, CA, USA.

Norros, I., Prabhu, B., & Reittu, H. (2006). Flash crowd in a file sharing system based on random encounters. In *Proceedings of the Workshop on Interdisciplinary systems approach in performance evaluation and design of computer & communications systems*, Pisa, Italy.

Oberender, J., Andersen, F.-U., Meer, H. d., Dedinski, I., Hoßfeld, T., Kappler, C., Mäder, A., & Tutschku, K. (2005). Enabling mobile peer-to-peer networking. In *Mobile and Wireless System, (LNCS, 3427)*.

Pack, S., Park, K., Kwon, T., & Choi, Y. (2006). SAMP: Scalable application-layer mobility protocol. *IEEE COMMUNICATIONS MAGAZINE, 44*, 8.

Penserini, L., Liu, L., Mylopoulos, J., Panti, M., & Spalazzi, L. (2003). Cooperation strategies for agent-based P2P systems. *Web Intelli. and Agent Sys., 1*(1), 3-21.

Risson, J., & Moors, T. (2006). Survey of research towards robust peer-to-peer networks: Search methods. *Computer Networks, 50*(17), 3485-3521.

Stoica, I., Morris, R., Karger, D., Kaashoek, M. F., & Balakrishnan, H. (2001). Chord: A scalable peer-to-peer lookup service for internet applications. In *Proceedings of the ACM SIGCOMM Conference*, San Diego, CA, USA.

Schlosser, D., Hoßfeld, T., & Tutschku, K. (2006). Comparison of robust cooperation strategies for P2P content distribution networks with multiple source download. In *Proceedings of the Sixth IEEE International Conference on Peer-to-Peer Computing (P2P2006)*, Cambridge, UK.

Sumino, H., Ishikawa, N., & Kato, T. (2006). Design and implementation of P2P protocol for mobile phones. In *Proceedings of the 4th annual IEEE international conference on Pervasive Computing and Communications Workshops*, Pisa, Italy.

Triantafillou, P., Xiruhaki, C., Koubarakis, M., & Ntarmos, N. (2003). Towards high performance peer-to-peer content and resource sharing systems. In *Proceedings of the Conference on Innovative Data Systems Research (CIDR)*, Asilomar, CA, USA.

Tutschku, K. (2004). A measurement-based traffic profile of the eDonkey filesharing service. In *Proceedings of the 5th Passive and Active Measurement Workshop (PAM2004)*, Antibes Juan-les-Pins, France.

Zoels, S., Schollmeier, R., Kellerer, W., & Tarlano, A. (2005). The hybrid chord protocol: A peer-to-peer lookup service for context-aware mobile applications. In *Proceedings of the Networking-ICN 2005, 4th International Conference on Networking*, Reunion Island, France.

Zoels, S., Schubert, S., Kellerer, W., & Despotovic, Z. (2006). Hybrid DHT design for mobile environments. In *Proceedings of the International Workshop on Agents and Peer-to-Peer Computing (AP2PC 2006)*, Hakodate, Japan.

Chapter VIII
Cooperation Strategies for P2P Content Distribution in Cellular Mobile Networks:
Considering Mobility and Heterogeneity

Tobias Hoßfeld
University of Würzburg, Germany

Michael Duelli
University of Würzburg, Germany

Dirk Staehle
University of Würzburg, Germany

Phuoc Tran-Gia
University of Würzburg, Germany

ABSTRACT

The performance of P2P content distribution in cellular networks depends highly on the cooperation and coordination of heterogeneous and often selfish mobile users. The major challenges are the identification of problems arising specifically in cellular mobile networks and the development of new cooperation strategies to overcome these problems. In the coherent previous chapter, the authors focused on the selfishness of users in such heterogeneous environments. This discussion is now extended by empha-sizing the impact of mobility and vertical handover between different wireless access technologies. An abstract mobility model is required to allow the performance evaluation in feasible computational time. As a result, the performance in today's and future cellular networks is predicted and new approaches to master heterogeneity in cellular networks are derived.

INTRODUCTION

The cooperation strategies applied in popular P2P content distribution networks (CDN) such as eDonkey or BitTorrent, rely on the fundamental P2P assumption that all peers are equal. In cellular networks, however, the peers differ significantly in their characteristics, e.g. their access system and bandwidth which might change over time or their on-line behavior, thus introducing heterogeneity and even selfishness in the peer community. In the previous chapter "Cooperation Strategies for P2P Content Distribution in Cellular Mobile Networks: Considering Selfishness and Heterogeneity", we discussed the impact of heterogeneity resulting into selfishness of users. Hence, the P2P assumption of equal peers is not valid any more. In this chapter, we concentrate on the dynamics and heterogeneity in cellular mobile networks which is further increased by the mobility of users.

Although most P2P CDNs utilize the benefits of multi-source downloads, the various platforms differ significantly in the actual implementation of the cooperation algorithms. In particular, the peer selection as well as the chunk selection mechanisms lead to different system behaviors and performance results. The detailed performance of the strategies is further determined by the actual peer characteristics and the peer behavior. The peer characteristic includes, among others the available upload and download bandwidth, as well as the number of parallel upload and download connections. The mobility of a user makes these peer characteristics change over time. Thus, the performance depends considerably on the heterogeneity. The peer behavior is mainly described by churn, i.e. the switching of a user between offline and online state, and by the willingness of a user to participate in the CDN. A user may behave selfish and tries to minimize the upload of data or he may redistribute the data in an altruistic way. In the context of cellular mobile networks, churn and selfish behavior appear even more distinctive, e.g. to save battery resources or scarce and expensive uplink capacities, resulting in the last chunk problem.

Additional challenges and influence factors on the performance of the system arise in a heterogeneous, wireless cellular network. We consider a beyond third generation (B3G) network with different infrastructure-based radio access technologies, in particular UMTS and WLAN. Due to the user mobility, vertical handovers (VHO) between the different wireless access technologies are required which may result in transmission delays and IP address changes of the switching peer. We investigate whether it is recommended to use mechanisms like Mobile IP in the context of P2P-based content distribution in cellular environments, since such mechanisms also introduce additional delays. Another important phenomenon occurring with vertical handovers is the abrupt change of available bandwidth, e.g., from a fast WLAN connection to a rather slow UMTS connection.

There are several possibilities to improve the performance of content distribution in cellular networks. Those are: a) particular architecture concepts introducing special entities like caches for storing contents or crawlers for locating sources, e.g. (Oberender et al., 2005); b) the optimization of parameters, like the size of chunks, as done by (Hoßfeld, Tutschku & Schlosser, 2005b); c) incentives to motivate the users to share files and to contribute to the system; and d) cooperation strategies for the coordination among peers. From these possibilities, we will focus on the cooperation strategies in this chapter. The goal is: i) to describe how to a model a P2P content distribution system with multi-source download in a cellular wireless environment; ii) to identify the fundamental problems of typical cooperation strategies; iii) to investigate the impact of user behavior and heterogeneity, in particular mobility and VHO; and iv) to propose solutions to overcome the derived problems.

The chapter is organized as follows. The *Related Work on Cooperation Strategies in Mobile CDNs* section reviews related work which addresses in particular P2P-based CDNs in infrastructure-based, cellular networks. A more general background on cooperation strategies in CDNs can be found in the background section of the coherent previous chapter "Cooperation Strategies for P2P Content Distribution in Cellular Mobile Networks: Considering Selfishness and Heterogeneity". There, the multi-source download mechanism and common cooperation strategies, as used by eDonkey or BitTorrent, were introduced. Key metrics for evaluating the performance of such systems were defined and related work outlined addressing heterogeneity in general and selfishness in particular. In the *Content Distribution in Heterogeneous Cellular networks* section of this chapter, the effects of user mobility in a B3G network on the traffic characteristics are revealed. This understanding makes us derive an abstract mobility model subsuming the network layout and the user mobility using a semi-Markov model. We consider the application of Mobile IP techniques and investigate the performance of common cooperation strategies in today's and future cellular networks for different load scenarios. Again, as a result of identified problems we derive a time-based cooperation strategy to master mobility and an adaptive strategy to utilize the scarce resources in such heterogeneous networks. Finally, the *Future Trends* section shows our particular viewpoint on important developments and necessary future work in this area, before the *Conclusion* section summarizes this chapter.

RELATED WORK ON COOPERATION STRATEGIES IN MOBILE CDNS

Despite the large literature on content distribution schemes, there exist only a few works on P2P CDNs in a mobile environment, especially in infrastructure-based wireless networks. Recently, mobile P2P research projects have attracted high attraction which is reflected by the popularity of the latest IEEE workshops MobiShare and MP2P. However, most the work addresses structured P2P networks based on distributed hash tables as lookup-service or considers mobile ad hoc networks. For example, (Michiardi & Urovy-Keller, 2007) proposes a cooperative P2P scheme that allows parallel download of the content based on swarming protocols in wireless ad hoc networks.

In the context of infrastructure-based, cellular networks, some investigations on P2P-based content distribution exist. (Biström & Partanen, 2004) proposes a JXTA solution to create a mobile file sharing system in 3G environment. The effect of heterogeneous, but fixed link capacities in BitTorrent-like file sharing systems was analytically evaluated with a simple fluid model (Piccolo, Neglia & Bianchi, 2004). It is shown that bandwidth heterogeneity can have a positive effect on content propagation among peers. The cooperation concept proposed by (Garbacki, Iosup, Epema & van Steen, 2006) makes peers help each other in downloading data. (Huang, Hsu & Hsu, 2007) proposes a network-aware P2P file architecture and related control schemes in cellular systems which divide a P2P file sharing network into multiple network-aware clusters. A file discovery control scheme named Mobility-Aware File Discovery Control (MAFDC) scheme is devised to obtain fresh status of shared peers and find the new resource providing peers in wireless mobile networks. Additionally, a resource provider selection algorithm is devised to enable a mobile peer to select new resource providing peers for continuous file retrieval. However, these strategies do not take into account the effects of mobility and vertical handover in a heterogeneous, cellular environment.

CONTENT DISTRIBUTION IN HETEROGENEOUS CELLULAR NETWORKS

In this section, we in-depth investigate the impact of vertical handover (VHO) in Beyond 3G (B3G) networks on cooperative content distribution systems. We consider now mobile users moving through a heterogeneous cellular network consisting of WLAN hotspots and UMTS cells. First, we clearly reveal the effects of user mobility on application layer. This allows us to model mobility and VHO for a P2P-based CDN in a cellular network appropriately. In a performance study, we analyze the impact of mobility in different load situations and emphasize the effects of mobility and VHO on the system's performance. Additionally, we consider a today's and a future network layout of the cellular network. In the future network layout, we assume a better WLAN coverage than in today's network layout. The question arises whether the increased capacity due to the higher WLAN density dominates the drawbacks of VHOs on P2P CDNs. As a result of the performance evaluation, we develop new cooperation strategies to cope with the identified problems.

Effects of Mobility

A mobile user moving through such a B3G networks needs to perform vertical handovers. This means the ongoing connection is passed from one wireless access system to another and might also include the passing from one operator to another. A VHO implies some delay Δt_{VHO} to reestablish the connections. During this period of time, no application data is transferred. Additionally, the switching between radio access technologies results in an abrupt and dramatic change of the mobile peer's uplink and downlink capacity.

Registering to a new access technology might also change the peer's IP address which leads to the loss of all TCP connections currently opened for file transfer. This concerns the peer's ongoing upload and download connections. But even worse, on application layer, when contacting a providing peer with a new IP address, the peer might not keep its old position in the providing peer's waiting queue but reenters at the end of the queue and waits to be served. In addition, a peer P performing a VHO might serve as a providing peer. The IP address change results in lost connections and the peers served by peer P need to rediscover P by asking the index server for new sources of a file. In standard eMule implementation, this is done periodically every ten minutes. In the following, we will refer to this technique as *requeueing w/o refill*.

An alternative method is called *requeueing with refill*. It introduces a minor modification of the peer's cooperation strategy to improve the system's performance and utilizes the fact that a providing peer knows all peers in its uplink waiting queue before and after the VHO. Thus, the providing peer simply re-identifies itself at the served peers with its new IP address and invites them to continue the download. Thus, it can speed up the recovery after a VHO.

Previously, we focused on the situation that a VHO implies an IP address change. However, approaches like Mobile IP preserve the peer's IP address and allow TCP connections to continue after the VHO. These mechanisms lead to an additional delay Δt_{MIP} which we assume to be static. On application layer, a peer keeps its current connections running which means that it also maintains the position in the uplink waiting queue or is still served. However, the total transmission delay during which no application data is exchanged is now $\Delta t_{VHO} + \Delta t_{MIP}$. Such a mechanism is denoted as *non-requeueing technique*. The VHO delay can be assumed to be rather small, especially compared to the additional delay caused by the non-requeueing technique, and we will use Δt_{VHO} = 100ms in the simulation studies.

Summarizing, we focus on three effects that VHO have on application layer: abrupt bandwidth change, transmission delay, and change of IP address. In particular, we investigate the impact of requeueing at a providing peer's uplink waiting queue with each VHO, as well as the use of mechanisms that preserve the IP address and connections beyond VHOs, like Mobile IP, at the cost of additional transmission delays.

Modeling Mobility and VHO in Cellular Networks

The performance evaluation of a P2P-based CDN with mobile users in a cellular network requires modeling of the mobility of the users and the aforementioned effects of mobility. In the run-up of our study, we investigated different mobility models, like the random direction mobility model (RDMM) and the Manhattan mobility model (MMM). Such a mobility model is a set of rules which determines the next point on a user's track at each decision point. We found two inadequacies for our simulation purposes. First, the effort for modeling mobility with a "classic" mobility model is not suitable with a large number of simulated users in a discrete event simulation, since it produces a lot of events and thus increases significantly simulation run time. Second, the choice of a particular mobility model is difficult and conveys a lot of following up problems, like the design of a suitable simulation plane for the users which also includes the distribution of coverage areas of the wireless cells and the choice of the corresponding technology.

Therefore, we model mobility in a more abstract way. We propose an abstract mobility model (AMM) which subsumes the network layout and the user mobility by a semi-Markov model. (Duelli, Hossfeld & Staehle, 2007a) showed that the abstract mobility model (with appropriately derived parameters) leads to the same results as the simulation of detailed mobility models like Random Direction Mobility Model or Manhattan Mobility Model, and detailed network layouts, i.e. simulation of the individual location and coverage

of any UMTS node-B and WLAN access point. The simulation of the abstract mobility model is about 50 times faster than the detailed simulation which is required in order to obtain statistically significant data and to be able to investigate a large variety of scenarios and parameters.

Semi-Markov Model

We now present an approach that releases the discrete event simulation from those events that do not affect the content distribution process at all. This is possible since the mobility of a user is only perceived on application layer when performing a VHO in the B3G network. Therefore, our approach describes a user's mobility by the user's sojourn time within a certain wireless technology and transition probabilities to other technologies. This abstract mobility model can be modeled as a semi-Markovian finite state machine as defined by (Lee & Hou, 2006) with the wireless technologies as states, general independent sojourn times, and the transition probabilities p_{ij} for switching from technology i to technology j. Note that the transition from one WLAN cell to another is also considered as a VHO, as the WLAN cells are assumed to be operated as individual hotspots.

The distribution of the technology specific sojourn times and the transition probabilities for the AMM are obtained by means of simulation using the RDMM and the MMM with different network layouts, separately. We simulated a single user moving through the simulation plane for 100 days to get statistically significant data. The technical details on the extraction process of sojourn times and probabilities can be found in (Duelli, Hoßfeld & Staehle, 2007b).

The rule set a user has to obey for the AMM still includes decision points, but these are not geographical anymore but merely time dependent. At each decision point in the AMM, a value is chose from the sojourn time distribution function of the current access technology, and then the next access technology is randomly determined according to the transition probabilities.

Simulation Scenario Description

We consider a content distribution system in a heterogeneous wireless environment. In particular, we focus again on the multi-source download mechanism which is based on the eDonkey protocol as implemented in the eMule application, as described in the *Background: Cooperation Strategies in CDNs* section of the previous chapter. As we focus on the heterogeneity instead of the user behavior in this section, the random chunk strategy is considered now with peers being served in FCFS order. The investigated radio access technologies comprise an area-wide UMTS network and WLAN hotspots which may overlap. The mobile users move in the landscape and perform VHOs between both technologies or between different WLAN cells. In this context, the switch from one WLAN cell to another is also denoted as VHO, as it might cause an additional delay and the re-assignment of IP addresses.

The UMTS users have a fixed transmission rate of 384 kbps in downlink and 64 kbps in uplink direction. For the WLAN technology, we assign a fixed symmetric bandwidth of 1 Mbps for up- and downlink each. Note, that we do not consider radio resource management mechanisms of the wireless network, like admission, power, or rate control, as we aim at the qualitatively evaluation of the effect of VHO on the P2P system. In addition, we do neither consider background traffic in the wireless network nor the case that multiple peers share the capacity of one cell. Including these effects into the simulation would on the one hand lead to unbearable simulation times and on the other hand blur the clear impact of the VHO only. A detailed description of the derived parameters for the abstract mobility model can be found in (Duelli, Hoßfeld & Staehle, 2007a).

The WLAN cells are randomly uniformly distributed within the considered area. We use the disc model with a radius of 50m to describe the coverage area of a single WLAN cell. In our simulations, we consider a typical city center which is modeled as a square of length 2400 m. According to the investigated scenario, we distinguish between a today's and a future network layout which only differ in the WLAN coverage. In today's network layout, we assume 19 WLAN cells according to the current number of public WLAN cells in Würzburg's city center of a German operator providing UMTS as well as WLAN. In the future network layout, we assume a much better WLAN coverage with 200 WLAN access points.

Impact of Mobility on Today's and Future Cellular Networks

In the investigated scenario, a single file of size 9500 kB is considered. There are 100 mobile peers that want to download this file and altruistically share this file after download. Every 120 seconds, a random peer sends a request to the sources currently available for this file until all peers have placed their request. At the beginning, the P2P network consists of a number of Internet peers with a constant uplink capacity of 768 kbps that serve as initial sources, and keep serving throughout the simulation. This ensures that the mobile peers always find equal conditions on simulation start-up. The number of these initial peers controls the load of the P2P system. Few Internet peers lead to a high load, since the first downloads may take a long time, and the file only slowly diffuses. All stochastic influences except for the mobility pattern are avoided, so, the impact of VHOs is not tampered by stochastical fluctuations not caused by mobility. For the same reason, we kept to a single set of parameters defining the network and traffic. We performed 20 repetitions with different seeds for the random number generator in every simulation run.

For our analysis, we consider four scenarios: today's network with a low load, today's network with a high load, a future network with a low load, and a future network with a high load. A high load corresponds to a single Internet peer and a low load to ten Internet peers.

In today's network, preserving the IP address outperforms loosing the IP address in a high load situation. A peer that loses its IP address is forced to reenter the uplink waiting queues of its sources and therefore has to wait much longer until it is allowed to download for the next time. There is, however, no clear impact of the non-requeueing delay even if the non-requeueing delay is extremely high around 10 seconds, since there are simply too few VHOs in today's network layout. The low load scenario in today's network nullifies the impact of the different IP address handling mechanisms, since even less VHOs occur during the shorter download time in this scenario, and the waiting queues are almost empty. Thus, the average download times are nearly the same. Detailed results and numerical values can be found in (Duelli, Hoßfeld & Staehle, 2007a).

Let us next investigate the situation in future networks with higher WLAN hotspot density. Figure 1 show CDFs for requeueing with and w/o refill as well as CDFs for non-requeueing with delays of 0 s, 1 s, 5 s, 10 s, and 100 s in the future network layout. Figure 1(a) shows the results for the high load scenario. Analogous to the results in today's network layout, non-requeueing is better than the two requeueing variants, but the differ-

ence between requeueing and non-requeueing increased from a factor of two in today's network layout to a factor of ten in the future network layout. The higher WLAN density in the future layout has two effects, a higher network capacity and more VHOs. The higher available amount of bandwidth leads to an average download time of 82.7 minutes in the future layout compared to 175.6 minutes in today's layout for the non-requeueing technique with $\Delta t_{MIP} = 1$s. However, the higher number of VHOs in the future layout increases the relative impact of the non-requeueing delay, compared to $\Delta t_{MIP} = 0$s, expressed by larger differences in download times.

Using the requeueing technique, the peer changes its IP address at every VHO. Thus, it is often losing its connections, is removed from being served, and shifted back to the end of the waiting queue. Together with frequent VHOs, this technique has to be avoided for an efficient content distribution service in a future network layout. Only for unrealistic VHO delays of 100 seconds, the requeueing and the non-requeueing technique show the same download performance in a high load scenario as can be seen in Figure 1(a).

In the following, we focus on the low load scenario in future networks for which Figure 1(b)

Figure 1. Comparison of requeueing and non-requeueing in future network layout (Duelli, Hoßfeld & Staehle, 2007) © 2007 IEEE

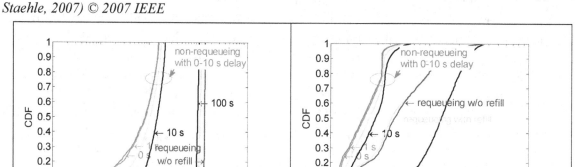

| a) High load | b) Low Load |

shows the equivalent CDFs as before. We can still see a difference in requeueing and non-requeueing as well as the non-requeueing delays even with a low load as opposed to today's network layout, since more VHOs occur even in the shorter download times. If the load in the P2P system is low, then downloads take less time which leads to less VHOs occurring during the downloading time. In general, the impact of mobility decreases with load and vice versa.

In both load scenarios, preserving the IP address with non-requeueing outperforms requeueing techniques. Nevertheless, the performance gain of non-requeueing melts in the low load scenario, since the waiting queues at the providing peers are almost empty and hence the waiting times are almost negligible. In such a scenario, a delay Δt_{MIP} exists such that the download performance is even worse than with requeueing techniques. However, this only happens for unrealistic large delays.

As a result of the performance evaluation, we see that non-requeueing techniques, like Mobile IP, are recommended in mobile P2P file sharing systems with respect to download performance, if this technique only requires a small transmission delay below a few seconds. In future network layouts, the increased uplink capacity due to the higher WLAN density leads to smaller download times. In order to foster the download from such high-capacity peers, a new cooperation strategy is proposed in the next section which tries to smoothen changes in the available uplink capacity as a consequence of the user's mobility and the resulting VHOs. This means it tries to overcome the drawbacks of heterogeneity.

Mastering Mobility with Time-Based Data Exchange

In this section, we introduce a new cooperation strategy that affects the duration a user is allowed to access the uplink capacity of a providing peer. In common P2P networks like eDonkey, the re-

source exchange is volume-based, i.e., each peer is allowed to download the same amount of data in a row, introduced as download unit (DU). We will further speak of volume-based cooperation (VBC). The problem of VBC is that a peer with a high-capacity technology, like WLAN, is thwarted by peers with smaller bandwidths, like UMTS, if these peers wait to be served by the same source. Thus, a user connected to a high capacity technology cannot finish its download quickly and serve as a new seed for other peers.

As an illustration, we imagine three peers $P0$, $P1$, $P2$ with download capacities $C0$, $C1$, $C2$. The ratio of the corresponding downlink capacities may be $C0 : C1 : C2 = 3 : 2 : 1$. If the peer with the highest capacity, i.e., $P0$, requires a download time Δt to download a DU, then it takes $2\Delta t$ for $P1$ and $3\Delta t$ for $P2$. If these three peers start downloading at the same time from the same source, then $P0$ will have to wait for $5\Delta t$, i.e., the time $P1$ and $P2$ are served until $P0$ is served next. Thus, it is thwarted by these two peers and the P2P network cannot fully profit by its higher capacities. As a consequence, the whole content distribution process is slowed down.

Our new approach avoids this thwarting due to heterogeneity by not restricting the amount of data, but the time a peer is allowed to download in a row. This approach is called time-based cooperation (TBC). Thus, peers with a higher capacity will serve earlier as new sources, since they are able to download more data in the same time. Alas, the effectiveness of this approach heavily relies on the peers' altruism to behave cooperative. The basic principle of this TBC approach is a time-out Δt which is the maximum time a user is allowed to download from a providing peer. Additionally, we still need a limitation of transferred volume, since MSD needs a reservation mechanism for the data currently downloaded to prevent downloading data twice. We set this limit to be $V = 540$ kB. As a consequence, a chunk is downloaded in blocks of size V. The providing peer stops serving the downloading peer if either the time Δt is spent or the volume V is uploaded. In particular, the downloading peer is interrupted after time $\Delta t' = \min\{\Delta t, \Delta t_V\}$ while Δt_V is the duration a peer needs to download V. Due to the time-based strategy, blocks may not be downloaded completely. Thus, when a peer gets served next, it may need to request the missing part for finishing the download of the block. Note, that Δt_V might vary due to new file requests, churn, and VHOs of the downloading or uploading peers.

For the analysis of TBC, we consider the following scenario which makes greater demands on optimization. There are 100 mobile peers which move around in the future network layout. There are a total of 20 different files, each of size 9500 kB. On average, each peer shares a single file at the beginning. The peers want to download all remaining files they not already have, i.e., 19 files on average. The interarrival time between two file requests is exponentially distributed with a mean $\mu_F = 40s$. Additionally, we consider churn here. The peers switch from online to offline with exponentially distributed lengths of the online and offline phases, each with a mean $\mu_C = 1h$.

Figure 2(a) shows the average download time and the 95% quantile (labeled 'q95%') of the download time of the VBC and TBC approach.

The latter's performance depends on the choice of the time Δt, a peer is allowed to download. The figure illustrates that the performance of TBC is always at least as good as of VBC. We see that the larger Δt the smaller is the performance gain. This results from the peers with fast technologies having to wait the longer on peers in slower technologies the larger Δt. We can see that there is an upper bound for Δt beyond which the two approaches give the same results since even a peer in the slower technology is able to finish its download before the time-limit is exceeded. Figure 2(a) suggests that there is an optimal value of the allowed download time, roughly at $\Delta t = 4s$. However, the size of the 95% confidence intervals of the average download times, indicated by error bars, is quite large. Hence, it's difficult to find an optimum. This results from the fact that we are investigating a highly dynamical and complex system. The behavior of such a system can vary largely depending on small changes in the overall situation as, e.g., a peer that stayed within WLAN for a longer time and/or became a new seed for a file faster.

A second relevant aspect of a P2P CDN is fairness, i.e., whether all peers are treated equally. Figure 2(b) shows Jain's fairness index

Figure 2. Volume-based (VBC) and time-based (TBC) cooperation strategy (Duelli, Hoßfeld & Staehle, 2007) © 2007 IEEE

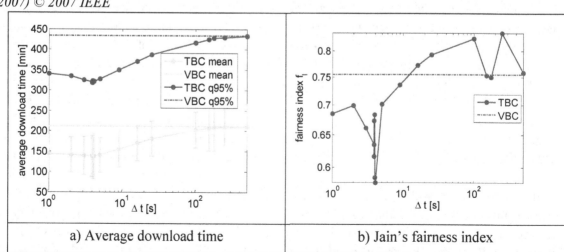

| a) Average download time | b) Jain's fairness index |

of the download time for VBC as well as TBC in dependence of Δt. The figure reveals that the fairness is lowest if the performance of TBC is best. This is due to high-capacity peers being preferred by TBC and being able to download more data in the same time. The dots in Figure 2(b) represent the average fairness index of 20 simulation runs. It has to be noted, however, that due to the highly dynamical system the fairness indices of different simulation runs of the same scenario are varying strongly. This explains, for example, the fluctuations of the fairness index of TBC for $\Delta t > 100$ s. However, a clear trend can be observed for the fairness index in dependence of the parameter Δt.

Utilization of Scarce Resources in Heterogeneous Networks

In theory, a single uplink performs best in distributing a file over a P2P file sharing network under certain assumptions. In practice, these modeling assumptions are broken. E.g. by churn which lets peers go offline, by MSD which enables peers to download files from different sources in parallel, by the fact that a peer usually downloads not only a single file in a row, and by the heterogeneity of the B3G network as well as the mobility of the peer which break the equality and constancy of down- and uplink capacities, respectively.

By the use of a single uplink, another problem emerges in our simulation scenario, the waste of uplink capacity. With a single uplink, the WLAN capacity cannot be always utilized. E.g., if a peer in WLAN lets download a peer in UMTS. With an uplink capacity of 1Mbps, this peer could almost saturate the downlinks of three peers in UMTS, with a downlink capacity of 384 kbps. Instead, it wastes almost 2/3 of its uplink capacity, when it is restricted to a single uplink. This effect is even intensified, since we investigate a P2P network that makes use of MSD. Thus, the downloading peers may not even use their total downlink capacity. This leads to an increased waste of uplink capacities.

In order to utilize the scarce resources in a heterogeneous network, we develop a simple, but effective algorithm that is trivial to implement in an existing P2P network. The main feature of this algorithm is the iterative adaption of the number N of parallel uplinks. To ensure the performance improvement by this algorithm, we also introduced an upper bound N_{max} for N, since allowing an unlimited value of N can be negative for the P2P system. This can be explained by the following scenario. A peer in WLAN is able to serve several UMTS downlinks in parallel. A sudden switch to UMTS causes that the downloading peers will be further served with a rather small bandwidth, which is only a 64 kbps / 1,024 kbps = 1/16 th part of the original WLAN uplink capacity. Hence, we ensure by setting an appropriate N_{max}, that the minimal bandwidth each connection can be assigned cannot become too small as well as that the time until N has re-adapted to a sensible value keeps short.

The actual implementation of this cooperation strategy only effects the peer selection of an uploading peer, but not the chunk selection. Therein, each peer is initialized with a single uplink, i.e. $N = 1$, whenever joining the P2P network. The peer periodically accumulates the current bandwidths of the active downloading connections. Then, it checks whether the downloading peers have left over some capacity, i.e., the uplink of this peer is not completely utilized. In that case, the number N is increased as long as N_{max} is not exceeded, or until the capacity of the uploading peer is utilized. In contrast, if the result of the capacity check shows that there is no uplink capacity left, i.e. the downloading peers use the uplink completely, then the number of uplinks is decreased by one. Thus, the remaining $N - 1$ peers can increase their bandwidth per connection, if they have downlink bandwidth left. It has to be noted that the increase or decrease of N is not applied until a peer has finished its current download volume, and a single new peer would enter the uplink. This is done in order to avoid that the uplink capacity of the peer is overbooked and download connections are cancelled. In particular, all connections are allowed to finish their current download of the DU. Thus, no connection is aborted just because a sudden overbooking situation emerges.

Figure 3 shows the average download time for the future network layout when varying the maximum number of parallel uplinks N_{max} of the proposed adaptive approach. For comparison, we also consider the random chunk strategy with a fixed number of parallel uploads. Figure 3(a) shows the means and 95%-quantiles of the average download time when using requeueing techniques, while Figure 3(b) refers to the case of using non-requeueing techniques like Mobile IP.

For $N_{max} = 1$ both approaches return the same result, since there is no possibility to adapt with a single uplink. We can also see that the download performance increases for both approaches for $N_{max} > 1$. This is due to the fact that a peer's uplink is not saturated with a single downlink connection, especially in the future network layout where peers are often connected to WLAN. Furthermore, we see that the adaptive approach shows a significantly better download performance than the fixed approach. In detail, the average download time reduced from around 150 minutes with the fixed approach to around 100 minutes with the

adaptive approach. This improvement is caused by the advantages of the adaptability, especially when switching between technologies with a big difference in the uplink capacities as it is common in the future network layout.

For $N_{max} \geq 8$, the download performance of the adaptive approach becomes invariant to further increases of N_{max}. If the uplink is already saturated by a certain number of downloading peers, the adaptive approach makes the current number N of parallel upload not exceed a certain threshold. Thus, increasing N_{max} has no more impact. In contrary, the download performance of the fixed approach decreases with increasing $N_{max} > 8$ when using requeueing techniques, as we can see in Figure 3. The reason is that with a higher number of parallel upload the download bandwidth per peer decreases, the download times for files increases, and thus sources for these files are available later. In Figure 3(b), the average download times are given when using non-requeueing techniques. For large N_{max} the adaptive and the fixed approach converge. The reason for this simple derives from the actual implementation of this approach. We do not apply an adaptation of the number N of parallel uplinks, until the download of the DU is successfully finished and another peer enters the uplink queue. Since the non-requeueing technique keeps

Figure 3. Adapting the number of parallel upload connections

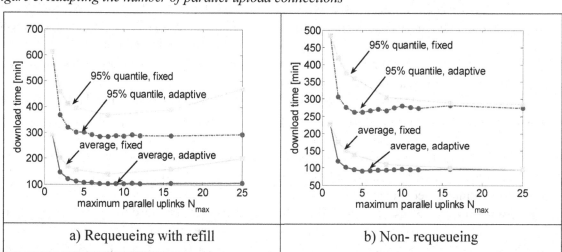

| a) Requeueing with refill | b) Non- requeueing |

the current connection although a peer conducts a VHO, N is not adapted until the DU download. Obviously, this algorithm can be further optimized to utilize efficiently the scarce resources, even in the presence of Mobile IP or other techniques. However, this is part of on-going research.

Besides the general performance improvement of the adaptive algorithm, there is another advantage. The cooperation strategy does not need to dimension an appropriate number N_{max} of parallel uplinks a priori. This is especially useful, when the CDN is established in more complex and heterogeneous environments with unknown peer characteristics.

FUTURE TRENDS

A variety of peer-to-peer content distribution systems have emerged in recent years that use logical overlays on top of the physical Internet infrastructure for distributing content among the users. In these peer-to-peer systems the available resources of the end users are utilized to help the content dissemination process: the end users assist the system by storing data locally and by uploading data to other users. Peer-to-peer file-sharing systems have been the dominant source of traffic in the Internet over the past years. The recent rise of the popularity of streaming video services, like YouTube, shows however that there is sufficient interest for video-on-demand and hence it can become a major source of Internet traffic in the future. Consequently, peer-to-peer video streaming applications, which offer either video-on-demand, live streaming or both, are expected to gain popularity. With the increasing capabilities of mobile devices in terms of computational power and graphical displays, it is expected that these applications which are quite popular in the Internet will also be implemented successfully for mobile end users.

The large amount of data exchanged in overlay applications is a significant source of costs for Internet service providers (ISPs) and also mobile operators. Overlays typically span the networks of several ISPs and operators, and due to the logical separation of the overlay and the physical network topology, content is often exchanged between end users that reside in different ISPs. Such inter-domain traffic leads to interconnection costs for the ISPs. Consequently, an ISP would like to: (i) control and manage the traffic from overlay applications in order to reduce its traffic costs; and (ii) compete with the existing applications by offering data distribution services himself instead of being just a 'bit pipe'. An ISP or operator has different options to control the overlay traffic. For example, the ISP can provide the means so that sophisticated cooperation strategies can be employed among the peers, e.g., they can take into account the network topology or any other useful information, and this cooperation might lead to a more ISP-friendly way of content distribution. The consideration of inter-domain traffic in the context of mobile P2P applications is in the focus of future investigations.

In order to meet the user's demands and requirements, the Quality of Experience, of P2P applications has to be fulfilled. Sophisticated cooperation strategies are the foundation for efficient and robust content distribution systems. In the context of mobile and heterogeneous environments, a future key topic is multi-homing for mobile P2P applications. This means that the users can utilize several access technologies at the same time. Thus, a cooperation strategy might consider several access technologies and uses the most appropriate one for specific applications. For example, a video-on-demand service requires only a low bandwidth when displayed at a mobile device, but has strict quality of service requirements in terms of delay and jitter. In this case, a UMTS connection via a dedicated channel providing a constant bandwidth might be more appropriate than a WLAN access, although the available capacity is higher for WLAN.

Furthermore, it is interesting to investigate how to realize multi-homing for P2P-based system. As incentive mechanisms of existing P2P CDNs are usually based on tit-for-tat or credit point systems and identify a user by its IP address, the simultaneous access of a user with different IP addresses per interface will lead to problems. The question arises how to implement multi-homing transparently to existing P2P protocols such that the user will achieve a performance gain.

The combination of different cooperation strategies is also a topic of future work. Cooperation strategies are often optimized to reach a particular goal. CycPriM, as introduced in the previous chapter "Cooperation Strategies for P2P Content Distribution in Cellular Mobile Networks: Considering Selfishness and Heterogeneity", tries to overcome the drawbacks of selfishness, while the time-based data exchange and the adaptive parallel upload strategy aim at mastering mobility and utilizing scarce resources. However, in an heterogeneous environment with selfish peer, the advantages of both strategies have to be integrated into a common cooperation strategy. When applying only the CycPriM strategy, the mobility of selfish peers increases the download time, as this is comparable to a higher churn rate. When applying only the time-based data exchange or the adaptive parallel upload strategy, the drawbacks of mobility are overcome and the download time is decreased. However, if the peers behave selfishly, they will leave earlier the system and do not contribute to the file dissemination anymore. As a result, the last chunk problem might occur again. The investigation of the combination of different strategies has to reveal whether they can additionally support each other and mutually improve the user's gain. For example, in further studies, we have seen that the combination of the time-based data exchange and the adaptive parallel upload strategy is fruitful and improves the download performance. However, both strategies do not address the problem of selfishness. A combination with the CycPriM strategy is feasible

in this context, as CycPriM only reorders the list of requesting peers, while the other strategies only determine the amount of uploaded data and the number of parallel upload connections. As a result, the combination of all three strategies is expected to be highly robust and efficient in mobile and heterogeneous environments with selfish peers. However, a detailed performance study and a quantification of the key characteristics when applying such a combined strategy is a topic of future work.

CONCLUSION

The performance of P2P content distribution in cellular mobile networks is determined mainly by the implemented cooperation strategy at a local peer. Major challenges which arise typically in cellular networks are the selfishness and the heterogeneity of peers. The selfishness of users leads to the last chunk problem, while the heterogeneity wastes expensive resources in the system. A basic solution is to modify the peer selection strategy of uploading peers which implicitly determines the chunk selection strategy of the downloading peers. This seems to be more appropriate to deal with selfish peers in a heterogeneous environment.

An adequate peer selection mechanism has also been shown to be efficient in a B3G network with mobile users conducting vertical handover between different wireless access technologies. In particular, the adaptation of the number of parallel upload slots of a multi-source download mechanism has shown to efficiently utilize the available resources. Common unmodified cooperation strategies as used by eDonkey or BitTorrent waste these resources, as the heterogeneity of peers is not considered.

The comparison of today's and future network layouts in different load scenarios showed that non-requeueing techniques like Mobile IP are recommended in mobile P2P CDNs if this technique only requires additional delays in the order of a few seconds. In future network layouts, the increased uplink capacity e.g. due to better WLAN coverage, will lead to smaller download times. In order to foster the download from such high-capacity peers, a time-based cooperation strategy is introduced. Although the fairness of the system is decreased, as high-capacity peers are able to download more content in the same time, this completely different approach allows for efficient exchange of files for all users. The implementation of particular cooperation strategies to overcome problems in mobile environments is an important problem and will surely constitute the basis of further studies.

REFERENCES

Biström, J., & Partanen, V. (2004). *Mobile P2P – creating a mobile file-sharing environment* (Tech, Rep. HUT T-111.590). Helsinki, Finland: Research Seminar on Digital Media, Telecommunications Software and Multimedia Laboratory, Helsinki University of Technology.

Duelli, M., Hoßfeld, T., & Staehle, D. (2007a). Impact of vertical handovers on cooperative content distribution systems. In *Proceedings of the Seventh IEEE International Conference on Peer-to-Peer Computing (P2P2007)*, Galway, Ireland.

Duelli, M., Hoßfeld, T., & Staehle, D. (2007b). *Impact of Vertical Handovers on Cooperative Content Distribution Systems* (Tech. Rep. No. 428). Würzburg, Germany: University of Würzburg.

Garbacki, P., Iosup, A., Epema, D. H. J., & van Steen, M. (2006). 2Fast: Collaborative downloads in P2P networks. In *Proceedings of the Sixth IEEE International Conference on Peer-to-Peer Computing (P2P2006)*, Cambridge, UK.

Hoßfeld, T., Tutschku. K., & Schlosser, D. (2005) Influence of the size of swapping entities in mobile P2P file-sharing networks. In *Proceedings of the Peer-to-Peer-Systeme und -Anwendungen, GI/ITG-Workshop in conjunction with KiVS 2005*, Kaiserslautern, Germany.

Huang, C.-M., Hsu, T.-H., & Hsu, M.-F. (2007). Network-aware P2P file sharing over the wireless mobile networks. *IEEE Journal on Selected Areas in Communications, 25*(1), 204-210.

Lee, J. K., & Hou, J.C. (2006). Modeling steady-state and transient behaviors of user mobility: Formulation, analysis, and application. In *Proceedings of the seventh ACM international symposium on Mobile ad hoc networking and computing (MobiHoc06)*, New York, NY, USA.

Michiardi, P., & Urovoy-Keller, G. (2007). Performance analysis of cooperative content distribution in wireless ad hoc networks. In *Proceedings of the fourth annual conference on Wireless on Demand Network Systems and Services*, Obergurgl, Austria.

Oberender, J., Andersen, F. -U., Meer, H. d., Dedinski, I., Hoßfeld, T., Kappler, C., Mäder, A., & Tutschku, K. (2005). Enabling mobile peer-to-peer networking. In *Mobile and Wireless Systems, (LNCS, 3427)*.

Piccolo, F.L., Neglia, G., & Bianchi, G. (2004). The effect of heterogeneous link capacities in BitTorrent-like file sharing systems. In *Proceedings of the 2004 International Workshop on Hot Topics in Peer-to-Peer Systems (HOT-P2P04)*, Volendarn, The Netherlands.

Chapter IX
Peer–Based Collaborative Caching and Prefetching in Mobile Broadcast

Wei Wu
Singapore-MIT Alliance, and School of Computing, National University of Singapore, Singapore

Kian-Lee Tan
Singapore-MIT Alliance, and School of Computing, National University of Singapore, Singapore

ABSTRACT

Caching and prefetching are two effective ways for mobile peers to improve access latency in mobile environments. With short-range communication such as IEEE 802.11 and Bluetooth, a mobile peer can communicate with neighboring peers and share cached or prefetched data objects. This kind of cooperation improves data availability and access latency. In this chapter the authors review several cooperative caching and prefetching schemes in a mobile environment that supports broadcasting. They present two schemes in detail: CPIX (Cooperative PIX) and ACP (Announcement-based Cooperative Prefetching). CPIX is suitable for mobile peers that have limited power and access the broadcast channel in a demand-driven fashion. ACP is designed for mobile peers that have sufficient power and prefetch from the broadcast channel. They both consider the data availability in local cache, neighbors' cache, and on the broadcast channel. Moreover, these schemes are simple enough so that they do not incur much information exchange among peers and each peer can make autonomous caching and prefetching decisions.

INTRODUCTION

Mobile broadcast is a scalable data dissemination model for mobile computing (Acharya & Alonso, 1995; Imielinski, 1997; Tan, 2000). In mobile broadcast, a server broadcasts data objects on a wireless channel and (a large number of) mobile peers get their required data objects by tuning into the broadcast channel and retrieving the data objects when they appear. Data broadcast differs from traditional point-to-point access in that the broadcast channel is open to all mobile clients and one transmission of a data object on the broadcast channel can satisfy the needs of potentially many clients. Mobile broadcast is especially suitable for data dissemination in asymmetric communication environments where the client to server ratio is large and there is a high degree of commonality among client interests. Information interesting to the majority of the clients is more suitable for broadcast. Many projects and systems are based on the data broadcast technology (Acharya & Franklin, 1995; Acharya, 1997; Acharya, 1998; Altinel, 1999; Hughes, 2008; Gifford, 1990; Imielinski, 1997; Microsoft, 2008; Zheng, 2005). They are sometimes referred to in the literature as Dissemination-Based Information Systems (DBIS) (Franklin, 1996).

Mobile peers in broadcast environments sometimes suffer from long access latency (the time elapsed from the moment a client has a query for a data object to the point when the client gets the data object), especially when the broadcast cycle is long due to large volume of data or limited broadcast channel. When the broadcast cycle is long, a mobile peer has to wait a long time before their required data objects appear on the broadcast channel.

Caching and prefetching are two effective ways to improve response time. They both store copies of data objects locally for future use. The difference is that caching happens after data access while prefetching stores data objects that are not currently under demand but believed to be useful in the future. In other words, caching is driven by data accesses, and prefetching is driven by anticipation of future accesses. In the environments of mobile broadcast, caching is the mechanism used to store a data object after it is taken from the broadcast channel to fulfill a pending request, and prefetching is to actively listen to the broadcast channel to grab objects that are anticipated to be useful. Thus in prefetching the mobile peer listens to the broadcast channel even when there is no pending request and stores interesting objects locally. A carefully designed

prefetching scheme results in better access latency than a caching scheme does, while consuming more energy (Acharya, 1996).

The fact that the mobile peers have small local storage space limits the effectiveness of caching and prefetching. Local storage constraint makes it impossible to hold all interesting data objects that may be accessed.

With short-range wireless communication technologies, such as IEEE802.11 and Bluetooth, a mobile peer is able to communicate with other mobile peers in its communication range. Figure-1 is an illustration of cooperative mobile peers in a mobile broadcast environment. A line between two mobile peers means they can communicate directly and share contents in a simple peer-to-peer fashion. This enables the mobile peers to share cached or prefetched data objects: when a mobile peer needs a data object, it can request it from its neighbors (we define a mobile peer's neighbors as the mobile peers within its communication range, i.e. one hop away). Such cooperation improves applications' response time, because a mobile peer now can probably get its required data object from its neighbors before getting it on the broadcast channel. This may even reduce energy consumption because getting a data object from a neighbor may be cheaper than getting from the broadcast channel if the mobile peer has to moni-

Figure 1. Cooperation among mobile peers. A line between two peers means they can communicate directly and share contents in a simple peer-to-peer fashion

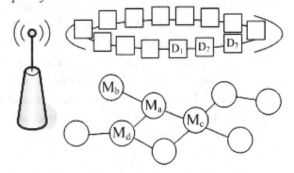

tor the broadcast channel for a long time before the data object appears.

A cooperative caching (or prefetching) strategy that takes the sharing between peers into account is more effective than an individual caching (or prefetching) scheme. For example, a simple cooperative strategy could be: a peer caches locally only the data objects that its neighbors do not have. In this way, the overall data availability among the neighborhood is improved, and then the response time is improved.

We believe that a good cooperative cache (or prefetching) management scheme for mobile peers in a broadcast environment should meet two requirements.

- First, mobile peers should retain their autonomy. By autonomy we mean that a mobile peer can make a caching (or prefetching) decision based on its own knowledge (about itself, its neighborhood, and the broadcast channel) and does not require a leader (or super-peer) to make central decisions. Because the peers are moving and their cache contents change with time, to have accurate and real-time knowledge of neighbors' cache content is very expensive. In such a highly dynamic environment leader selection and information synchronization will incur a very high communication (and battery energy) cost.

- Second, it should consider not only the data availability from the neighbors, but also the data availability on the broadcast channel. A data object can be available in three places: local cache, neighbor's cache, and the broadcast channel. In a non-uniform mobile broadcast, popular data objects are broadcast more frequently and they have a high availability on the broadcast channel. A mobile peer should consider both the availability from neighbors and from broadcast channels when making local caching decisions.

In this chapter, we discuss both cooperative caching and cooperative prefetching in a broadcast environment. For cooperative caching, we discuss in detail a scheme called CPIX (Cooperative PIX). CPIX is a modified version of GCM (Wu, 2006). CPIX extends the well-known PIX caching scheme (designed for broadcast environment) (Acharya, 1995) to the cooperative scenario. CPIX considers two important factors: local access frequency and the *global availability* of data objects. Access frequency helps to identify critical objects that should be locally cached to improve *local cache hits* (and hence reduce waiting time and energy consumption). Global data availability is used to identify the data objects that are neither widely cached by other mobile peers nor are frequently broadcast by the server. Note that here data availability not only means whether the data is available globally, but also means how long it takes for a mobile peer to get the data. For cooperative prefetching, we discuss in detail a scheme called ACP (Announcement-based Cooperative Prefetching) (Wu, 2005). The basic idea of ACP is to let a mobile peer make prefetching decisions based on its neighbors' prefetching decisions while keeping them autonomous. The objective is to help peers avoid prefetching the same data objects, and to improve data availability. Both CPIX and ACP are designed for push-based broadcast environments where the mobile peers can move freely. The schemes consider not only a mobile peer's local access pattern, but also the data availability from other mobile peers and from the broadcast channel.

In the remainder of the chapter, we give the background knowledge on mobile broadcast and individual caching and prefetching schemes, review briefly some cooperative caching and prefetching schemes, and present in detail CPIX and ACP and a performance study of their effectiveness.

BACKGROUND

Mobile Broadcast

According to the mechanism used for scheduling data objects on the broadcast channel, data broadcast can be classified into three categories: push-based, pull-based, and hybrid. In push-based broadcast (Acharya, 1995), the clients do not interact with the server: the server broadcasts data objects based on its knowledge of the mobile peers' overall data access requirements, and the mobile peers get their required data objects when they appear on the broadcast channel. In pull-based broadcast (Aksoy, 1998), which is also called on-demand broadcast, the mobile peers submit their requests through an uplink channel to the server, then the server broadcasts data objects based on the received requests (pull-based broadcast is different from point-to-point access in that the object requested by a query is delivered on a broadcast channel such that all the pending queries for that data object are answered with one transmission). Hybrid broadcast (Acharya, 1997) combines push-based broadcast and pull-based broadcast (or even point-to-point access) to complement each other: popular data objects are pushed, and infrequently accessed data objects are retrieved on demand (by pulling or point-to-point access).

Data objects are typically scheduled for broadcasting according to the overall access interests of the mobile peers in the system. The basic idea is to broadcast hot data objects more frequently than the others. Many algorithms have been proposed for scheduling the broadcast in different environments (Acharya, 1998; Guo, 2001; Hameed, 1997; Liu, 2003; Zheng, 2005).

To facilitate mobile peers saving energy, index of data objects is introduced into the broadcast. Basically, a broadcast index tells the mobile peers what data objects will be available when. The broadcast index itself is also broadcast intermittently on the broadcast channel. Once a mobile peer knows when its interested data object will

be broadcast, it can operate in sleep mode and wake up before that time. Many researches on mobile broadcast focus on designing broadcast index (Hu, 1999; Imielinski, 1994; Lee, 2003; Lo, 2000; Shivakumar, 1996; Tan, 2000).

System Model

In this chapter, we assume a broadcast environment where:

- The mobile broadcast is push-based. A server broadcasts data objects repeatedly to many mobile peers through a broadcast channel and there is no uplink for the mobile peers to send requests to the server.
- The broadcast is non-uniform. Data objects are broadcast with different frequencies. Popular data objects are broadcast more frequently than the others.
- Broadcast index is available so that mobile peers know the broadcast frequencies of data objects.
- All mobile peers are in the broadcast server's transmission range. They get their required data objects by tuning into the broadcast channel.
- All data objects are of the same size and they are not updated. This assumption lets us ignore the factor of object size and the problem of cache invalidation so that we focus on the cooperative strategies for cache management.
- The mobile peers are equipped with short range communication devices. A mobile peer can communicate with the mobile peers within its communication range.
- There is no super peer in the mobile peers. Peers have the same levels of computational ability and battery power.

Sample Applications

Many interesting applications follow the system model that we described before. In such applications, multimedia information needs to be disseminated to (potentially) a large number of audiences. Here we list two sample applications.

In an academic **conference**, people are often interested in paper abstracts, presenters' profiles, and short introduction (such as name, a small photo, university, and research interests) of each researcher who is attending the conference. Each piece of these introduction (in the form of a web page) information can be seen as a data object. These data objects can be broadcast at the conference site. Notice that paper abstracts and presenters' profiles should be broadcast more frequently than the attendees' information. Also notice that a paper abstract, a presenter's profile, and an attendee's profile are of similar sizes and they normally do not change during the conference.

In **museums**, short video clips about the items on display can be broadcast to the visitors. Each video clip is a data object. The clips are of about the same size and available throughout the exhibition. People are more interested in masterpieces; therefore clips about the masterpieces should be broadcast more frequently than the clips about other art works. Each visitor to the museum gets a mobile device that retrieves the information he/she wants (the device obtains introduction clips from the broadcast channel or a nearby device if the neighboring device happens to have cached the required clip locally).

Data Access Process

When a mobile peer wants to access a data object, it first looks for it in its own local cache. If the data object is not found in the local cache, the mobile peer requests for it from its neighbors. If none of its neighbors has the data object, the mobile peer tunes into the broadcast channel and waits for the data object to appear.

To facilitate the discussion, we define a few terms to describe the situations of cache miss and cache hit. Let M_q be a mobile peer and D_k be the data object that M_q wants to access.

Local Cache Hit: M_q's local cache has D_k.

Local Cache Miss: M_q's local cache does not contain D_k.

Neighbor Cache Hit: at least one of M_q's neighbors has D_k in its local cache.

Neighbor Cache Miss: none of M_q's neighbors has D_k in its local cache.

Broadcast Hit: M_q gets D_k from the broadcast channel.

When M_q asks for D_k from its neighbors, several types of messages are exchanged. The mobile peer first sends a **Request** message for D_k to its neighbors. M_q's neighbors having D_k in their cache send back a **Reply** message to M_q. Upon receiving the *reply* message(s), M_q sends a **Retrieve** message to the neighbor who replied first, then the target mobile peer transmits D_k to M_q.

KR: Keep Requesting

In some cooperative cache management schemes for mobile peers in broadcast systems, when a *neighbor cache miss* happens, the mobile peer simply tunes into the broadcast channel and waits for the required data object to appear. In these schemes, a *neighbor cache miss* always results in a *broadcast hit*. However, a *neighbor cache miss* only means that the **current** neighbors do not have the required data object, but not necessarily the **future** neighbors. Since a mobile peer's neighbors may be changing all the time (especially in a highly dynamic environment), a neighbor having the required data object may come by before the object appears on the broadcast channel.

In the schemes that we will discuss in detail, an enhancement called Keep Request (KR) (Wu, 2006) is used. In the KR mode, a mobile peer continues to send out *request* messages repeatedly to its neighborhood even though a *neighbor cache miss* has happened. There are two situations in which the query may be answered before the required data object is broadcast by the server. The first is after certain time the mobile peer has a new neighbor who caches the data object, because the mobile peers are moving. The second is after certain time an existing neighbor has the required data object, because it has, during the time, requested and obtained the object from its neighbors. By repeatedly sending out *request* messages, the response time will improve as some queries may be answered before *broadcast hits*. A mobile peer should control the frequency of sending out request message and avoid sending the *request* message too frequently, because broadcasting message consumes energy and increases chances of wireless signal collision. KR is independent of the cooperative cache management scheme; therefore it can be applied on any cooperative cache management scheme.

With Keep Requesting, the process of data access becomes the one shown in Figure-2. Notice that the states of *local cache miss* and *neighbor cache miss* are omitted in the figure.

Caching and Prefetching

In a broadcast system, a mobile peer's data access from broadcast channel can be demand-driven or proactive. The data access is demand-driven if the mobile peer retrieves data objects from broadcast channel only when it has local cache miss. On the contrary, if a mobile peer continuously monitors broadcast channel and stores locally the data objects that are potentially useful to it, the mobile

peer is prefetching data from the broadcast channel and its data access is proactive. Prefetching from broadcast channel improves response time, but incurs more energy consumption (Acharya, 1996; Grassi, 2000; Hu, 2003). Generally speaking, mobile peers with limited energy tend to access the broadcast channel only when there are pending requests, and mobile peers with enough energy (such as devices on vehicles) may access the broadcast channel proactively.

We assume that the mobile peers in a system are with the same type and they have the same data access fashion, i.e. they are either all demand-driven or all proactive.

In both demand-driven access and proactive access, when a mobile peer gets a data object, it faces the problem of deciding whether to store the data object locally. A caching scheme helps a mobile peer to make such decision under demand-driven access, and a prefetching scheme helps it to make such decision under proactive access.

Caching and prefetching schemes for individual mobile peer in broadcast environments have been studied extensively. Here "individual" means that the caching (or prefetching) scheme does not take the possible collaboration among the mobile peers into account. With the advance of short-range communication and mobile peer-to-peer networks, researchers have begun to study cooperative caching and cooperative prefetching for mobile peers.

Figure 2. Data access process

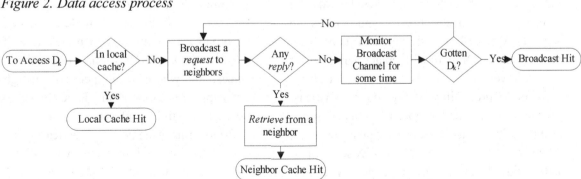

Individual Caching

We refer to the caching schemes that do not consider the collaboration among mobile peers as *individual caching* schemes.

Classic caching algorithms (like LRU) designed for client-server environments may result in poor performance in a broadcast system. In a client-server environment, accessing different data objects from the server takes similar amount of time. That being the case, caching the hottest data objects is a good idea. However, in a non-uniform broadcast environment where data objects are broadcast with different frequencies, the latencies for accessing different objects from the broadcast channel may vary greatly. This difference makes the idea of caching the most accessed data object not the best choice.

Caching strategies for mobile broadcast environments were proposed in (Acharya, 1995; Su, 1998; Xu, 2000; Xu, 2004). Here we briefly review the main idea of a scheme called PIX (Acharya, 1995). Knowing PIX will be helpful for understanding CPIX, which is the cooperative caching scheme that we will discuss in detail later.

PIX. PIX is specifically designed for non-uniform broadcast environments. The basic idea is for mobile peers to store those data objects for which the local probability of access is significantly greater than the object's frequency of broadcast. PIX (P Inverse X) uses the ratio P_i / X_i, where P_i is the probability of access to a data object D_i and X_i is the broadcast frequency of D_i, to decide whether D_i should be cached in local memory. A mobile client estimates the value of P_i using its data access history, and derives the value of X_i from broadcast index. A data object with a higher PIX score will replace a data object with a lower PIX score. For example, let object D_a's access probability be 5% and its broadcast frequency be 1%, and let object D_b's access probability be 3% and its broadcast frequency be 0.5%. The PIX score of D_a is 5, and the PIX score of D_b is 6. Object D_b may cause longer access latency,

so D_b will be cached if only one object can be cached. PIX is an optimal individual caching scheme for non-uniform broadcast because an object's PIX score is the expectation of the object's access latency.

Individual Prefetching

As in individual caching, we refer to the prefetching schemes that do not consider the collaboration among mobile peers as *individual prefetching* schemes.

Prefetching from broadcast channel is very different from prefetching from a server in traditional client-server systems or prefetching from hard disk to main memory. The most important characteristic of prefetching from broadcast channel is that the prefetching (and the related cache management scheme) is driven by broadcast program: each time a data object appears on the broadcast channel, the mobile peer needs to decide whether to prefetch the data object locally. This is also the fundamental difference between prefetching and demand-driven caching in broadcast environments. Recall that in demand-driven caching, the caching scheme is triggered only when there is an access and the needed data object is received.

The advantage of prefetching from broadcast channel is that it improves response time and does not add any extra workload and overhead to the broadcast server—the mobile peers prefetch by just listening to the broadcast channel. The disadvantage is that it incurs additional energy consumption at the mobile peer, as the mobile peer needs to be in active mode and listens to the broadcast channel when prefetching. Thus in applications where response time is the major concern and where mobile peer has enough energy supply (e.g., computing device on vehicles), prefetching will be preferable.

Prefetching schemes in broadcast environments were studied in (Acharya, 1996; Cao, 2002; Grassi, 2000; Hu, 2003). Prefetching data from broadcast channel improves response time by avoiding costly cache misses. Let us take the well-known *PT* prefetching heuristic (Acharya, 1996) as an example to show how prefetching from broadcast channel works. PT is used in ACP, the cooperative prefetching scheme that we will discuss in detail, to make an individual decision before negotiating with peers.

PT. In *PT*, *PT* values are used to make cache admission and replacement decisions. The *PT* value of a data object D_i at time t is defined as P_i*T_i, where P_i is the mobile peer's access probability to D_i, and T_i is the time that will elapse from t until D_i appears on the broadcast channel. As in PIX, the value of P_i is estimated from local access history, and T_i is derived from the broadcast index. The *PT* prefetching scheme works like this: each time when a data object is broadcast, the mobile peer finds the data object in cache with the lowest *PT* value and replaces it with the currently broadcast data object if the latter has a higher *PT* value. The rationale behind the *PT* heuristic is to prefetch data objects whose expectation of waiting time (P_i*T_i) is long. As a result, using *PT*, data objects that were just broadcast are more likely to be kept in cache and the data object that are closer to being re-broadcast, are more likely to be replaced.

Note that PT score (P_i*T_i) is not the same as the PIX score (P_i/X_i) which is used in the PIX demand-driven caching scheme, because Ti is not the same as $1/X_i$. For a data object with a fixed broadcast frequency, $1/X_i$ is fixed, but the value T_i changes with time. Remember that T_i is the time remaining from the current time to the nearest moment when the object will be broadcast. For example, if object D_a is going to be broadcast every 100 time units, T_i of D_a changes in the range from 100 to 0 when time goes on, and T_i becomes 100 after 0. If D_a's next broadcast time is t_{500}, and current time is t_{450}, then at this time $T_i = 50$.

Cooperative Caching

In recent years, cooperative data management in mobile environments are gaining more attention

(Papadopouli, 2001; Xu, 2004) and people begin to study the cooperative cache management problem for mobile peers (Chow, 2004; Chow, 2005; Hara, 2002; Lau, 2002; Shen, 2005; Wu, 2005; Wu, 2006; Yin, 2004).

(Chow et. al., 2004) proposed a cooperative caching scheme called GroCoca (GROup-based COoperative CAching) for mobile peers in a pull-based mobile environment. In GroCoca, mobile peers report their locations to a central server and access data objects from the server by sending requests to it. The central server uses a clustering algorithm to find tightly-coupled groups of mobile peers. A set of peers are said to be tightly-coupled if they have similar movement pattern and data access interest. The server informs mobile peers about the groups they are in, and then peers in the same tightly-coupled group manage data objects cooperatively. GroCoca is a centralized solution, because a central server collects mobile peers' location information and access interests and clusters the peers into groups.

(Chow et. al., 2005) further proposed a distributed solution called DGCoca (Distributed Group-based Cooperative caching) for mobile peers in push-based broadcast environments. In the DGCoca scheme, a mobile peer exchanges summary of its cached objects with its stable neighbors (a stable neighbor is defined as a neighbor who has been nearby for certain amount of time) and makes cache replacement decisions with respect to its own access frequency to the data objects and whether the data objects are available at its stable neighbors.

Cooperative Prefetching

(Hara, 2002; Wu et al., 2005) study the problem of cooperative caching management in the scenario where mobile peers prefetch from broadcast channel. As in (Wu, 2005), we call this kind of schemes *cooperative prefetching* schemes.

In (Hara, 2002), the author proposed two cooperative schemes for mobile peers in push-based broadcast systems, namely GOP (Global OPtimal) and SOP (Stable group OPtimal). The author calls them *cooperative caching* schemes. They are classified as *cooperative prefetching* schemes in this chapter because their behaviors of caching are triggered by the broadcast rather than data accesses. In GOP, the mobile peers construct an ad-hoc network and cooperate through multi-hop communication. The idea is to exchange information of access interests and cached objects among all connected mobile peers each time when a data object is broadcast, and then one of the mobile peers collects this information and decides globally which mobile peer(s) should cache the data object according to the network topology. Finally the decision is flooded to all mobile peers and every one conducts a behavior according to the decision. GOP is not practical when the number of mobile peers is large, because large amount of control information and long computational time are needed for every caching decision. In SOP (Stable group OPtimal), data objects are cooperatively cached in stable groups of mobile peers. SOP works better than GOP because limiting the cooperation in a stable group guarantees data availability and reduces communication overhead.

ISSUES, CONTROVERSIES, PROBLEMS

The aforementioned cooperative schemes have several common drawbacks. First, they all try to find stable groups of mobile peers (i.e. group of peers that are within each other's communication range for certain amount of time). Because of this, they are only suitable for environments where groups of mobile peers do exist, and cannot be applied to scenarios where the mobile peers are highly dynamic. Second, they consider the data availability from neighbors but fail to consider the data availability on the broadcast channel. Third, they require synchronization of a lot of information

in a group, such as cache summary and access interests. This will incur high communication cost (and power consumption), because the cache summary of neighbors need to be updated quite frequently.

We identify two challenges for the mobile peers to manage caching cooperatively in a broadcast environment. The first is to handle the dynamics of the neighborhoods (topology). The second is to consider data objects' multiple availabilities in the system.

The dynamics of peer's neighborhood is due to the movement of the peers. The changes of neighborhoods make it infeasible to take the cache spaces of the mobile peers in a neighborhood as a whole and manage it for the benefit of all the involved mobile peers. Managing cache space in a neighborhood as a whole imposes several requirements: 1) a clear division of peers to neighborhoods (or groups); 2) synchronization of access interests in a neighborhood; 3) agreement on which peer should cache what data objects. The movement of peers makes these requirements very difficult and expensive to achieve, because

- There is no agreement on which neighborhood(s) a mobile peer belongs to-- a mobile peer has one neighborhood but belongs to many neighborhoods at the same time. Take the mobile peers in Figure-1 as an example. M_a belongs to the neighborhoods of M_b, M_c, and M_d. Which neighborhood shall it participate in? And who shall coordinate the neighborhood?
- Even though methods are used to divide the mobile peers into neighborhoods and to select a leader, the neighborhoods are changing frequently. This may incur a lot of information exchange, because each time a neighbor leaves or a new neighbor is encountered, the overall access pattern of the neighborhood may change.

For a mobile peer that can request for data object from its neighbors and can access data from a broadcast channel, data objects can be available in three ways: local cache, neighbors' cache, and broadcast channel. A data object's availabilities in local cache and neighbors' cache are not guaranteed, while its availability on the broadcast channel is assured. The cooperative cache management scheme in fact determines which peer to cache what data objects, and as a result it determines where to access a data object. Getting data object from different places have different costs in terms of both access latency and power consumption. In this situation, when doing caching management, a mobile peer not only needs to consider its own access interest, but also needs to take into account what its neighbors have in cache and the data objects' broadcast frequencies on the broadcast channel.

We believe that an effective cooperative cache management scheme should deal with both the aforementioned challenges. In the remainder of this chapter, we discuss two such schemes. One is a cooperative caching scheme called CPIX designed for mobile peers whose access to the broadcast channel is demand-driven. The other is a cooperative prefetching scheme called ACP designed for mobile peers whose access to the broadcast channel is proactive. CPIX could be used on mobile peers with limited power, while ACP could be applied on mobile peers for whom battery is not a problem.

CPIX and ACP share several common desirable properties that distinguish them from other schemes: 1) the mobile peers using the schemes are autonomous; 2) they consider the data availability from both the neighbors and the broadcast channel; 3) they are adaptable to the broadcast program; 4) they require very few message exchanges between mobile peers.

EFFECTIVE COLLABORATIVE CACHING AND PREFETCHING SCHEMES

CPIX: Cooperative Caching

PIX (Acharya, 1995) is a well-known individual caching scheme for mobile peers in broadcast environment (refer to the Background section for a brief review of PIX). CPIX (Cooperative PIX) is an extension of the PIX scheme for the mobile peers where they can communicate with each other in a Peer-to-Peer fashion.

The approach CPIX takes is to view the data availability at other mobile peers (not only the current neighbors) together with the data availability on the broadcast channel as the *global data availability*, and every mobile peer manages its own cache space according to its own access interest and its estimate of global data availability. The following observation leads to this idea. When a local cache miss happens, a mobile peer can request the data object from its neighbors and tune into the broadcast channel to wait for the data object. These two can be done in parallel. The mobile peer is happy as long as it can get the data object in a short period of time, and there is no need to distinguish whether the data object is from a neighboring peer or it is from the broadcast channel.

It is important to point out that here data availability does not mean whether the data is available, since (in the worst case) the data object is always available from the broadcast channel. It rather means how long it takes for a mobile peer to get the data.

Intuitively (as in PIX), data objects that are frequently accessed and are not readily available should get the highest priority to be cached locally, otherwise, many *local cache miss*es will happen due to its high access frequency and these *local cache miss*es will result in long waiting time since it is not easy to get them from the neighbors or broadcast channel.

CPIX considers two important factors: local access frequency and the *global availability* of data objects. Access frequency helps to identify critical objects that should be locally cached to improve *local cache hits* (and hence reduce waiting time and energy consumption). Global data availability is used to identify the data objects that are difficult to get from outside, i.e. they are neither widely cached by other mobile peers nor frequently broadcast by the server.

Although CPIX considers local access interest rather than neighborhood's access interest, in fact it benefits the whole peer community when every mobile peer is doing this. When every mobile peer is caching the data objects that are hard to get from external sources (including neighbors and broadcast channel), the global data availability is improved.

Both the information of access frequency and the information of global data availability are estimated from local statistics. A mobile peer may estimate its access frequency to the data objects by counting historical accesses. The global data availability of its interested data objects can be estimated from the waiting time it experienced for the local cache misses. To do so, each mobile peer keeps the following statistics for every data object D_i it has accessed:

- $NumAccess_i$: number of access.
- $NumLCM_i$: number of *local cache miss*.
- $SumWaitingTime_i$: the sum of waiting time the mobile peer experienced due to the local cache misses of D_i.

Notice that the idea of global data availability (viewing the data availability at other mobile peers and the data availability on the broadcast channel as a whole) simplifies the caching scheme. In CPIX a mobile peer does not need to get the knowledge of data objects' global availability by exchanging summary of cache content with neighbors and by analyzing the broadcast index.

The CPIX scheme works as follows. Each time when a query for data object D_i arise:

1. The mobile peer increases $NumAccess_i$ by one.

2. If the query results in a *local cache miss*, the mobile peer increases $NumLCM_i$ by one, records the time point when the *local cache miss* happens, and broadcasts a *request* message to neighbors. If KR (Keep Requesting, see the Background section) is enabled, in this step the mobile peer will keep sending out request message every certain time interval if *neighbor cache miss* for D_i happens, until the mobile peer gets D_i.

3. When the mobile peer gets D_i from either a neighbor or the broadcast channel,

   a. The mobile peer records the time point and calculates the waiting time for this local cache miss of D_i, and add the waiting time to $SumWaitingTime_i$.

   b. The mobile peer decides whether to cache the data locally. If there is free cache space available, the mobile peer caches D_i using the free space. If its cache space is full, a score for D_i is calculated. If D_i's score is not the smallest among the scores of cached data objects, the mobile peer caches D_i by replacing the data object with the smallest score. The score of a data object D_i is calculated using the formula as follows.

$$Score_i = NumAccess_i * \frac{SumWaitingTime_i}{NumLCM_i}$$

The rationale behind the score formula is that $Score_i$ tells the expectation of waiting time caused by a *local cache miss* of data object D_i. We use $\frac{NumAccess_i}{\sum NumAccess}$ as the estimation of the access probability to data object D_i. Since every score has the same component $\sum NumAccess$ and we use the scores for comparison purpose only, we use $NumAccess_i$ to represent $\frac{NumAccess_i}{\sum NumAccess}$. $\frac{SumWaitingTime_i}{NumLCM_i}$ denotes the length of time it *takes on average fo*r the mobile peer to wait for each *local cache miss of Di, and gives a hint of* the global data availability of D_i.

If we consider $\frac{NumAccess_i}{\sum NumAccess}$ as P_i and $\frac{SumWaitingTime_i}{NumLCM_i}$ as $1/X_i$, CPIX can be seen as a cooperative version of the PIX scheme where P_i / X_i is used to make caching decisions. The important idea here is to use $\frac{SumWaitingTime_i}{NumLCM_i}$ to encapsulate the non-local availability, which includes both neighbors' cache and the broadcast channel.

With CPIX, the data objects that are frequently accessed (with high $NumAccess_i$ values) and difficult to get (with high $\frac{SumWaitingTime_i}{NumLCM_i}$ values) will be cached locally. Essentially, CPIX tries to reduce the number of local cache misses and to avoid costly *local cache misses*.

Note that in CPIX, $NumAccess_i$, $NumLCM_i$ and $SumWaitingTime_i$ are all cumulative. The side effect is that the estimation will be less accurate when access pattern or broadcast program changes at certain time. This problem can be resolved by using only the recent statistics.

ACP: Cooperative Prefetching

A mobile peer prefetches data objects from broadcast channel by continuously monitoring the broadcast channel and putting the data objects that are potentially useful to local cache. (Acharya, 1996) has shown that the PT prefetching scheme performs better (in terms of response time) than demand-driven caching schemes such as PIX. If the mobile peers collaborate when prefetching, then the resultant cooperative prefetching can further improve the performance. In this section, we discuss a solution called ACP, which stands for Announcement-based Cooperative Prefetching. ACP enables the mobile peers to prefetch cooperatively to improve data availability, while keeping the mobile peers autonomous.

Prefetching imposes a special challenge to cooperative caching management. The important property of prefetching is that it is driven by broadcast ticks. A consequence is that in prefetching mobile peers tend to cache the data objects that were just broadcast. For example, if the PT (refer to Background section for an introduction of PT) prefetching scheme is used, the *PT* values of objects that were just broadcast are high because their *T* values are high at this moment. As a (bad) result, the mobile peers may be caching the same set of data objects, especially when their access probabilities to the data objects are similar. In this situation, sharing cache contents with neighbors does not improve data availability much, and few queries can be answered with neighbors' cache.

The objective of ACP is to overcome the problem by avoiding prefetching multiple copies of the same data objects in a neighborhood.

The basic idea of the ACP strategy is: in deciding whether to prefetch an object D, if a mobile peer knows whether its neighbors will prefetch D, it can make a wiser prefetching decision for D. For example, if a mobile peer M_a knows that its neighbors M_b and M_c are prefetching D, then M_a may choose not to prefetch D if D is not very important to it, since it has a chance to get D from its neighbors. The benefits of this are: 1) M_a saves its cache space for another valuable data object; 2) it avoids the problem that M_a and its neighbors are prefetching the same data objects; and thus 3) the overall data availability is improved, and the mobile peer can have more queries answered by neighbors.

A simple application of this idea can be dangerous. First, a prefetched data object may be replaced by a more valuable data object soon after it was prefetched. Telling neighbors that it will prefetch data object D does not tell how long D will be kept in its cache. Accordingly, simply knowing that some neighbors will prefetch D, a mobile peer does not know the extent of reliance it can put on its neighbors. Second, if all mobile peers choose not to prefetch a data object because they think that their neighbors are prefetching it, no one prefetches the data object. They both result in a situation where some neighbors claimed to prefetch a data object but it is not available when someone wants to access the data object.

These problems are solved by enforcing the following two rules in the cooperation scheme: 1) a mobile peer informs its neighbors that it will prefetch a data object only when it will keep the data object in cache for certain time; 2) randomization is applied to let at least one of the mobile peers (that showed intention to prefetch the data object) prefetch the data object.

Considering these factors, ACP strategy is designed as follows:

- **Before** a data object D is broadcast (we assume broadcast index is available so that the mobile peers know when each data objects will be broadcast), every mobile peer decides whether to prefetch D based on the *PT* heuristic, and we call this **the first decision**.
  - If the first decision is "yes" then the mobile peer further predicts how long D will be in cache.
    - If it predicts that D will be in its cache for a long time, then the mobile peer broadcasts an **announcement** message to its neighbors.
- Each mobile peer whose first decision is "yes" counts the number of announcement messages for D it receives.

- **When** D appears on the channel, every mobile peer makes its **final decision** on whether to prefetch D according to the importance of D to it, the number of announcement messages it received, and some random factor. If the final decision is still "yes", the mobile peer prefetches D; otherwise, the mobile peer does not prefetch it.

That is, when a mobile peer decides to prefetch D and believes it will cache D for a quite long time, it sends out an announcement message to its neighbors; a mobile peer's final prefetching decision for D is based on both the importance of D and the number of neighbors who will prefetch D. The objective of the announcement is to affect the neighbors' prefetching decisions. Note that the announcement should be made *before* the broadcast of D, but the mobile peers need not make announcement at the same time. To reduce the chance that a peer makes an announcement but moves away from its neighbors, a peer should send out the announcement close to the time the associated object will be broadcast.

There are two details of ACP to be addressed: 1) How to predict the time D will be in cache and whether it deserves an announcement? 2) How should the neighbors' announcements for D, if any, affect a mobile peer's final prefetching decision for D?

Deciding Whether to Send Out Announcement

Each mobile peer makes its first decision for D with the *PT* individual prefetching scheme. If there is empty cache space, the first decision is "yes"; if the cache space is full, the mobile peer checks the cached objects and see whether there is a cached object whose *PT* value is lower than the *PT* value of D, if so, the first decision is "yes", otherwise, the first decision is "no".

In ACP, every mobile peer records how long a data object was kept in its cache the last time:

when a data object is prefetched, the mobile peer records the timestamp, and when the data object is replaced, it calculates the time the object is in cache and records it. The recorded **keeping time** of D is used to predict how long D will be in cache this time.

If the first decision is "yes", the mobile peer decides whether to send out an announcement by checking the following inequality.

$$\frac{keeping\ time}{Tinterval} \geq \delta$$

Here δ is a threshold parameter greater than zero, and *Tinterval* is the time between two consecutive broadcasts of the data object. If the inequality is satisfied, the mobile peer sends out an announcement, otherwise it does not. The intuition is: when an announcement for D is made, the neighbors know that the mobile peer may keep D longer than *Tinterval*$*\delta$, so they may have confidence to rely on the mobile peer for D.

Note that δ is a parameter that can be tuned. Also note that a mobile peer whose first decision for D is "yes" should count the number of the announcement messages for D it receives.

Making Final Decision

In ACP, a mobile peer's final prefetching decision for D is determined by the following factors:

1. PT_d, the *PT* value of D;
2. PT_c, the *PT* value of the replace candidate (the cached object with the lowest *PT* value);
3. γ, the reliance parameter;
4. n, the number of announcement messages for D the mobile peer received.

Here $\gamma(0 < \gamma \leq 1)$ is a parameter modeling the extent of reliance a mobile peer can put on a neighbor who sent out an announcement for D. In other words, γ models the probability that when the mobile peer has a query for D the neighbor

still has D and is within the mobile peer's communication range.

A mobile peer that receives more announcement messages for D means it can rely more on its neighbors for D, since the chance that all of them move beyond the mobile peer's communication range is lower and it is more possible for the mobile peer to get D from its neighbors. Thus in our scheme, the total reliance the mobile peer can put on its neighbors for D is $\gamma*n$.

When D is broadcast, each mobile peer makes its final prefetching decision for D as follows.

- If the first decision is "no", the final decision is "no".
- If the first decision is "yes" and the mobile peer did not send out announcement for D, then check whether the following inequality is satisfied.

$$PT_d(1 - \gamma*n) > PT_c$$

- If the inequality is satisfied, the final decision is "yes", otherwise it is "no".
- If the first decision is "yes" and the mobile peer has sent out an announcement for D, then if $\gamma*n$ is smaller than 1, the final decision is "no", else ($\gamma*n$ is greater than 1) the mobile peer generates a random number p between 0 and 1, if p is bigger than $1/(\gamma*n)$, the final decision is "no", else the final decision is "yes".

The intuition of the final decision process is: a) If the first decision is "no", D is not important for the mobile peer, so the mobile peer should not prefetch D. b) If the first decision is "yes" but the mobile peer did not send out an announcement, D is not very important to the mobile peer, and the mobile peer's neighbors will not rely on the mobile peer for D, so the mobile peer is free to decide whether to prefetch D based on the total reliance it can put on its neighbors. It checks whether it is still beneficial to prefetch D after considering the possibility that it can get D from its neighbors. c) If the mobile peer sent an announcement for D, D is very important for the mobile peer, and its neighbors may rely on it for D, thus the mobile peer is not free to put reliance on its neighbors and give up prefetching D. However, if it received enough announcements from neighbors ($\gamma * n > 1$), which means it is possible that the mobile peers share common access interests for D and too many mobile peers will prefetch D and the neighborhood is wasting cache space, then it is good that one or several (but not all) of them finally choose not to prefetch D. This decision is made by tossing a coin. Even though some mobile peers having made announcement may choose not to prefetch D after the coin flip, the overall availability of D is guaranteed by the process of coin flips, with a high probability.

Discussion on Relying on Neighbors

ACP and CPIX are quite different on the problem of whether to rely on current neighbors for caching some data objects. In CPIX, a peer's neighborhood does not directly participate when the peer makes a caching decision. In ACP, a peer's prefetching decision is partially based on neighbors' intensions on prefetching.

ACP's approach of relying on current neighbors may seem to be inconsistent with the analysis and arguments we made in the background section that a mobile peer should not make caching decisions based on the cache contents of its *current* neighbors, but in fact this is not a conflict because prefetching is very different from demand-driven caching. Let's use an example to show the difference.

Suppose the current time is t and data object D_l appears on the broadcast channel, and D_l will be broadcast again at time $t+t'$ (D_l is broadcast every t' time units). Mobile peer M_a gets D_l at time t. M_a has neighbors M_b, M_c and M_d. M_b and M_c will move out of M_a's communication range at time $t+t'/2$.

Suppose the mobile peers are doing demand-driven caching, and M_b and M_c have data object D_l at time t; M_a decides not to cache D_l because its neighbors M_b and M_c have it; M_a has a query for D_l at time $t + t'/2 + \Delta t$. Notice that when M_a wants to access D_l, its neighbors with D_l have moved away. The latency of the access is the time duration from time $t + t'/2 + \Delta t$ to the time when D_l is broadcast. The latency can be represented as:

$$\begin{cases} \dfrac{t'}{2} - \Delta t, & if\ \Delta t \le \dfrac{t'}{2} \\ t' - ((\Delta t - \dfrac{t'}{2})\%(t')), & if\ \Delta t > \dfrac{t'}{2} \end{cases}$$

In the expression, "%" is the *remainder* operation.

However, if the mobile peers are prefetching, and M_b and M_c will prefetch D_l, and M_a decides not to prefetch D_l because its neighbors M_b and M_c will prefetch it, then when M_a has a query for D_l at time $t + t'/2 + \Delta t$, its access latency will be:

$$\begin{cases} \dfrac{t'}{2} - \Delta t, & if\ \Delta t \le \dfrac{t'}{2} \\ 0, & if\ \Delta t > \dfrac{t'}{2} \end{cases}$$

The difference is in the second case where $\Delta t > \dfrac{t'}{2}$. In prefetching, the access latency could be 0 because at time $t+t'$ (which is before $t + t'/2 + \Delta t$), M_a will make prefetching decision for D_l again and may cache it locally if this time no neighbors will prefetch it. Recall that D_l is broadcast every t' and prefetching is driven by broadcast program.

The point is that in ACP, a peer will notice the move-away of neighbors (who prefetched an interesting object) when the data object is broadcast again. In the example, when D_l is broadcast again, M_a will make a new prefetching decision on D_l. If at this time M_b and M_c are not around, then M_a

will not receive any announcement on prefetching of D_1 so it will decide to prefetch D_1.

From this example, we see that in cooperative prefetching a mobile peer may rely on its neighbors for a data object, because the mobile peer is monitoring the broadcast channel continuously and once the data object is not available at its neighbors the mobile peer may prefetch it when it appears again, so that costly cache misses are avoided.

Nevertheless, CPIX and ACP share one important point in common: they keep the mobile peers autonomous even though each peer takes the data availability at its neighbors' into account when making caching and prefetching decisions. This ensures that small change in neighborhood will not affect CPIX and ACP. This is achieved by not relying on specific neighbors when making caching and prefetching decisions. Rather, a peer makes a decision based on its whole impression of its neighbors. In CPIX, a mobile peer makes caching decision totally based on local statistics, and it tolerates the changes of neighbors. In ACP, a mobile peer makes prefetching decision based on the number of announcements it receives. If a peer M_a makes a prefetching announcement for a data object but moves away soon, it will not have a significant effect on its neighbors because they do not rely on M_a specifically.

EVALUATION OF COLLABORATIVE CACHING AND PREFETCHING SCHEMES

To study the performance of CPIX and ACP, we conducted detailed simulation experiments. We report representative results here. The reader may find more details of the experiments and results in (Wu, 2005; Wu, 2006).

In the experiments, we compare CPIX, ACP with DGCoca (Chow, 2005), a cooperative caching scheme designed for push-based broadcast environment. We did not study the performance

of GOP and SOP because they are designed for mobile peers that form stable groups while we are interested in scenarios where each mobile peer follows its own trajectory.

Simulation Model

The simulated mobile environment is an X*Y (m²) area where there are a broadcast server and n mobile peers. The server broadcasts data objects to the mobile peers through a wireless channel. The bandwidth of the broadcast channel is bb Mbps. All mobile peers can receive data objects that the server broadcasts. A mobile peer can communicate with another peer if they are in each other's communication range. Their transmission range is *TransRange* meters. The bandwidth of the short-range communication is sb Mbps. At the beginning, the mobile peers are randomly scattered in the area. The mobile peers then move in the area following a variant of the "random waypoint" mobility model.

In the model (and experimental results), we use a time unit called *broadcast unit*. A broadcast unit is the time the server takes to broadcast one data object.

Broadcast Server

We adopt *broadcast disk*s (Acharya & Alonso, 1995) to model the server's non-uniform broadcast. The server has m broadcast disks, and they are $Disk_i$ where $1 \leq i \leq m$. $Disk_i$ stores $DiskSize_i$ data objects and spins at a speed of $DiskSpeed_i$. All data objects are read-only and of the same size which is *DataSize* KB. As in (Acharya & Alonso, 1995), we use a parameter Δ to capture the relative speeds of the disks: $DiskSpeed_i = ((m-i)*\Delta) + 1)$. For example, if the server has 3 broadcast disks and Δ is 2, then the rotation speed of the disks will be 5, 3 and 1. Δ is used to model the nonuniformity of the broadcast. When Δ is 0, the broadcast is uniform. The bigger the Δ is, the more non-uniform the broadcast is.

Mobile Peers

A variant of the "random waypoint" is used as the mobile peers' movement pattern. A mobile peer first randomly chooses a destination in the modeled area and a speed which is around *MoveSpeed* m/s. Then the mobile peer moves to the destination with that speed. After arriving at the destination, the mobile peer pauses for *PauseTime* seconds. The mobile peer repeats the aforementioned steps.

We call the set of data objects that a mobile peer is interested in as its access range. Access range consists of access regions (an access region is used to model a cluster of data objects related to one interest topic) that the mobile peer is interested in. The size of a mobile peer's access range is *AccessRange*, and the size of an access region is *RegionSize*, thus the number of access regions for each mobile peer is *AccessRange/RegionSize*. We assign a Zipf distribution with a skewness parameter θ to each mobile peer's access regions. The data objects within an access region have the same probability to be accessed. When assigning access distributions to the access regions, the access regions from faster disks get higher access probabilities.

A mobile peer's queries are generated according to its access distributions. A query is simply an access request for a data object. The time interval between a mobile peer's two consecutive queries is *ThinkTime* broadcast units. Each mobile peer generates *NumQuery* queries during the simulation.

The size of each mobile peer's cache space is *CacheSize*, which is a fraction of the size of the peer's *AccessRange*. For example, if the size of *AccessRange* is 1000 and the *CacheSize* is 20%, then the peer's cache space can hold 200 data objects.

List of Parameters

The parameters for the simulation model and their values are summarized in Table-1.

Among the parameters, δ and γ are parameters for ACP. To find the optimal values for δ and γ, we conducted detailed experiments to learn the effects of them on ACP's performance. We find that ACP performs best when δ and γ are set to values between 0.3 and 0.6. In the experiments presented as follows, we use 0.3 and 0.5 as optimal values of δ and γ. The parameters of DGCoca are not listed here. We follow (Chow, 2005) to assign values to DGCoca's parameters.

Table 1. Simulation model parameters

Parameter	Default Value	Range	Unit
System Parameters			
Area (X*Y)	1500*1500		m²
bb (broadcast bandwidth)	10		Mbps
sb (short-range bandwidth)	2		Mbps
n (num of clients)	100		
Server			
m (num of disks)	3		
DiskSizes	[500,1500,3000]		Data objects
Δ	3	[0-4]	
DataSize	10	[10-100]	KB
Mobile Peer			
TransRange	250	[0-250]	m
AccessRange	1000		Data objects
RegionSize	50		Data objects
CacheSize	20%	[1%-50%]	
MoveSpeed	2	[0-20]	m/s
PauseTime	30		s
NumQuery	3000		
θ (Zipf)	0.5	[0-1.0]	
ThinkTime	10		Broadcast Unit
ACP specific			
δ	0.3	[0-1.0]	
γ	0.5	[0-1.0]	

Experimental Results

The performance metric used in the experimental study is the average response time (access latency) measured in broadcast unit. We first study the performance of the schemes under the default parameter setting. Then we investigate the effects of some system parameters on the schemes.

Basic Performance Study

Here we investigate the performance of the schemes under the default parameter settings. The objectives are twofold: one is to compare individual schemes with cooperative schemes; the other is to study the performance differences of the cooperative schemes and to find the reasons behind the differences.

Figure-3(a) compares the response times of the five caching management schemes, namely PIX, DGCoca, CPIX, PT, and ACP. Recall that PIX is an individual caching scheme, PT is an individual prefetching scheme, DGCoca and CPIX are two cooperative caching schemes, and ACP is a cooperative prefetching scheme. From the figure, we first confirm that prefetching schemes perform better than demand-driven caching schemes: PT performs better than PIX, and ACP performs better than both DGCoca and CPIX. We also confirm that cooperative schemes perform better than individual schemes: DGCoca and CPIX perform better than PIX, and ACP performs better than PT.

Among the cooperative schemes, CPIX performs better than DGCoca, and ACP has the best performance. Figure-3(b) and Figure-3(c) reveal the underlying reasons.

Figure-3(b) shows the breakdown of query hits in each scheme. We observe that among the three cooperative cache management schemes DGCoca has the largest number of local cache hits and neighbor cache hits, and the smallest number of broadcast hits. This shows that DGCoca utilizes the local cache and neighbors' cache very well.

ACP has the largest number of broadcast hits: most of the queries are answered using the broadcast channel rather than local cache or neighbors' cache. CPIX is between them.

The interesting finding here is that the number (or the ratio) of local cache hits and neighbor cache hits is not the key factor that determines the schemes' performance (average response time). Figure-3(c) shows the key factor, the average response time of *broadcast hits*. We see that DGCoca experiences the longest average waiting time for the broadcast hits (neighbor cache misses), and ACP experiences the shortest average waiting time for the broadcast hits. This is why DGCoca has the longest average response time although it has the largest number of local cache hits and neighbor cache hits, whereas ACP has the best response time although it has the largest number of broadcast hits.

Since the response times for local cache hits and neighbor cache hits are really short, the access latency caused by *neighbor cache misses* (i.e. the requested data object is in neither local cache nor neighbors' cache) -- the product of the number of broadcast hits and the average waiting time for a broadcast hit -- determines the average waiting time of a scheme. Although DGCoca has fewer broadcast hits, it takes a longer time to get a broadcast hit if a query is not answered by local cache or neighbors' cache. On the contrary, in ACP, although more queries are answered after broadcast hits, a mobile peer waits a shorter time before the required data object appears on the broadcast channel.

Recall that DGCoca does not consider the data availability on broadcast channel, CPIX considers the data availability on broadcast channel, and ACP further exploits the dynamics of data availability on broadcast channel. The key idea we have in CPIX and ACP is that both the data availability from neighborhood and the data availability on broadcast channel are important for making caching or prefetching decisions. For data objects with similar access probability, the

Figure 3. Performance under default setting

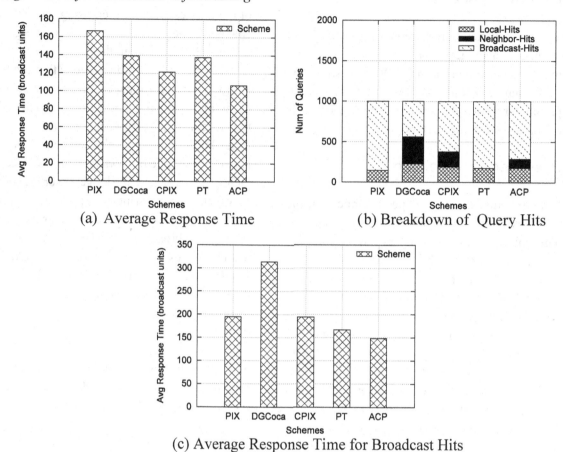

(a) Average Response Time

(b) Breakdown of Query Hits

(c) Average Response Time for Broadcast Hits

ones that are difficult to get from both neighbors and broadcast channel should be cached locally, thus long time waiting is avoided. In prefetching, the peers' cache space is refreshed with the most valuable objects at each broadcast tick.

The performance of individual cache management schemes PIX and PT are depicted in this set of experiments to show that cooperative cache management do help improve access latency. In the remainder of this section, we only compare the cooperative cache management schemes.

Adaptability to Non-Uniform Broadcast

In this set of experiments, we study their adaptability to non-uniform broadcast by varying Δ

to see the performance of the schemes under different extent of non-uniform broadcast. In the experiments the access pattern of the mobile peers does not change.

The results are depicted in Figure-4. It shows that CPIX and ACP adapt to the non-uniform broadcast better than DGCoca does: with the increase of Δ, the response times of the schemes all increase, but CPIX and ACP degrade slower than DGCoca does. The length of the broadcast cycle is $\sum(DiskSize_i * DiskSpeed_i)$ where $DiskSpeed_i = ((m-i) * \Delta) + 1$, m is the number of *broadcast disks*, and $1 \leq i \leq m$. During a broadcast circle the data objects on $Disk_i$ are broadcast $DiskSpeed_i$ times. When Δ increases, data objects on the faster disk are broadcast more frequently, and it becomes harder to get the data objects that are on the slower disks. CPIX and ACP adapt to the change of broadcast better because they both consider the data availability on the broadcast channel. DGCoca makes cache decision based on access distribution thus it is not adaptive to the broadcast program.

Effect of Moving Speed

The effect of the mobile peers' move speed on the schemes' performance is studied by varying the mobile peers' speed from 1 to 20m/s. Figure-5 shows the results.

We observe that when the mobile peers move with a faster speed: (1) the response time of DGCoca increases dramatically, (2) the response times of CPIX and ACP increase very slowly. The reason for (1) is that the mobile peer groups that DGCoca tries to form are not stable when mobile peers move fast; a mobile peer may not even be able to find stable neighbors. Recall that in DG-Coca, information about current neighbors' cache contents is used to make local caching decisions. When the mobile peers move fast, the reliance on current neighbors have negative effect. The reason for (2) is that in CPIX and ACP a mobile peer does not rely on a specific set of neighbors, but rather consider the overall availability from the external sources (include neighbors and the broadcast channel).

Effect of Transmission Range

The aim of this set of experiments is to study the effect of mobile peers' transmission range on the schemes' performance. As shown in Figure-6, all schemes' performance improves with longer transmission range. This is due to the fact that a mobile peer may contact with more neighbors with longer transmission range.

One interesting observation here is that the performance gap between the schemes decreases with the increase of transmission range. When a mobile peer can communicate with more peers, the data availability in its neighborhood improves

Figure 4. Effect of non-uniform broadcast

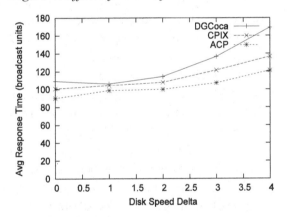

Figure 5. Effect of move Speed

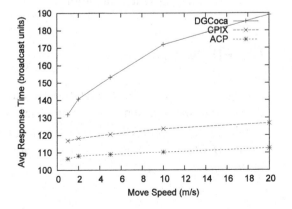

Figure 6. Effect of communication range

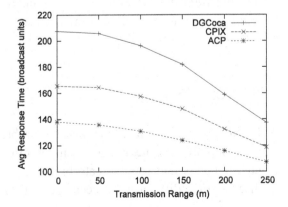

Figure 7. Effect of cache size

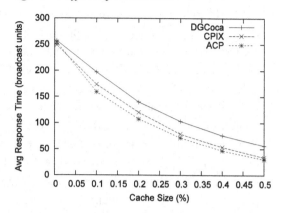

significantly. In this case, sharing of cache contents leads to performance improvement, and gain from clever cooperative cache management will be less obvious. Increasing the density of mobile peers or introducing multi-hop communication will have a similar effect.

Effect of Cache Size

The effect of cache size is studied by varying a mobile peer's cache size from 1 data object to half of its access range. Figure-7 shows that with the increase of cache size, the schemes all have better response time. This is as expected because increasing the cache size effectively improves the data availability. With larger cache space more data objects are cached locally and shared in the neighborhood. The figure also shows that even when the mobile peers have large cache size (e.g. more than 40% of its access range), CPIX and ACP still outperform DGCoca and the performance difference is fairly stable.

CONCLUSION

In this chapter, we have reviewed the problem of cooperative cache management in mobile environments that support data broadcast. We discussed the difference between access-driven caching and proactive prefetching (from the broadcast channel), and presented our view of the challenges for cooperative caching and cooperative prefetching in such environments. After reviewing some solutions based on group-based cooperative cache management, we presented two schemes in detail, namely CPIX and ACP. CPIX is a cooperative caching scheme and ACP is a cooperative prefetching scheme. They differ from other schemes mainly in two ways. First, they do not require a mobile peer to have stable neighbors. This enables a mobile peer to make caching (or prefetching) decision autonomously, and does not impose high information synchronization overhead. Second, they consider both the data availability on other peers and the data availability on the broadcast channel. While ACP is superior to CPIX in most cases, it consumes more energy. We believe that CPIX and ACP are two representative cooperative cache management schemes designed for highly dynamic mobile peers in broadcast environments.

Recently, many routing protocols have been designed to facilitate the multi-hop communication among mobile peers in the form of a MANET (Mobile Ad-Hoc Networks). Researchers are also working on P2P overlays for mobile peers. It will be interesting to investigate whether it is feasible and how to use multi-hop communication to further improve the performance of collaborative caching and prefetching in a highly dynamic environment. We believe the challenges are keeping the mobile peers autonomous and limiting the overhead (traffic) of information synchronization.

REFERENCES

Acharya, S., Alonso, R., et al. (1995). Broadcast disks: Data management for asymmetric communication environments. In *Proceedings of the ACM SIGMOD International Conference on Management of Data.*

Acharya, S., Franklin, M. J., et al. (1995). Dissemination-based data delivery using broadcast disks. IEEE *Personal Communications, 2*(6), 50-60.

Acharya, S., Franklin, M. J., et al. (1996). Prefetching from broadcast disks. In *Proceedings of the International Conference on Data Engineering.*

Acharya, S., Franklin, M. J., et al. (1997). Balancing push and pull for data broadcast. In *Proceedings of the ACM SIGMOD International Conference on Management of Data.*

Acharya, S., & Muthukrishnan, S. (1998). Scheduling on-demand broadcasts: New metrics and algorithms. In *Proceedings of the International Conference on Mobile Computing and Networking*, Dallas, Texas, USA.

Aksoy, D., & Franklin, M. J. (1998). Scheduling for large-scale on-demand data broadcasting. In *Proceedings of the IEEE Conference on Computer Communications.*

Altinel, M., Aksoy, D., et al. (1999). DBIS-toolkit: Adaptable middleware for large scale data delivery. In *Proceedings of the ACM SIGMOD International Conference on Management of Data*, Philadelphia, Pennsylvania, USA.

Cao, G. (2002). Proactive power-aware cache management for mobile computing systems. *IEEE Transactions on Computers, 51*(6), 608-621.

Chow, C.-Y., Leong, H. V., et al. (2004). Group-based cooperative cache management for mobile clients in a mobile environment. In *Proceedings of the International Conference on Parallel Processing (ICPP).*

Chow, C.-Y., Leong, H. V., et al. (2005). Distributed group-based cooperative caching in a mobile broadcast environment. In *Proceedings of the International Conference on Mobile Data Management.*

Hughes Network Systems, LLC. (2008). DIRECWAY. Retrieved May 25, 2008, from http://www.direcway.com/

Franklin, M., & Zdonik, S. (1996). Dissemination-based information systems. *IEEE Data Engineering Bulletin, 19*(3), 20-30.

Gifford, D. K. (1990). Polychannel systems for mass digital communications. *Communications of ACM, 33*(2), 141-151.

Grassi, V. (2000). Prefetching policies for energy saving and latency reduction in a wireless broadcast data delivery system. In *Proceedings of the International Workshop on Modeling Analysis and Simulation of Wireless and Mobile Systems.*

Guo, Y., Pinotti, M. C., et al. (2001). A new hybrid broadcast scheduling algorithm for asymmetric communication systems. *SIGMOBILE Mobile Computing and Communications Review, 5*(3), 39-54.

Hameed, S. & Vaidya, N. H. (1997). Log-time algorithms for scheduling single and multiple channel data broadcast. In *Proceedings of the International Conference on Mobile Computing and Networking.*

Hara, T. (2002). Cooperative caching by mobile clients in push-based information systems. In *Proceedings of the Conference on Information and Knowledge Management.*

Hu, Q., Lee, W. C., et al. (1999). Indexing techniques for wireless data broadcast under data clustering and scheduling. In *Proceedings of the Eighth International Conference on Information and Knowledge Management*, Kansas City, Missouri, USA.

Hu, H., Xu, J., et al. (2003). Adaptive power-aware prefetching schemes for mobile broadcast environments. In *Proceedings of the International Conference on Mobile Data Management.*

Imielinski, T., Viswanathan, S., et al. (1994). Energy efficient indexing on air. In *Proceedings of the ACM SIGMOD International Conference on Management of Data.*

Imielinski, T., Viswanathan, S., et al. (1997). Data on air: Organization and access. *IEEE Transactions on Knowledge and Data Engineering, 9*(3), 353-372.

Lau, W. H. O., Kumar, M., et al. (2002). A cooperative cache architecture in support of caching multimedia objects in MANETs. In *Proceedings of the International Symposium on a World of Wireless, Mobile and Multimedia Networks.*

Lee, S., Carney, D., et al. (2003). Index hint for on-demand broadcasting. In *Proceedings of the International Conference on Data Engineering.*

Liu, Y., & Knightly, E. (2003). Opportunistic fair scheduling over multiple wireless channels. In *Proceedings of the IEEE Conference on Computer Communications.*

Lo, S.-C., & Chen, A. L. P. (2000). Optimal index and data allocation in multiple broadcast channels. In *Proceedings of the 16th International Conference on Data Engineering.*

Microsoft. (2008). MSN Direct. Retrieved May 25, 2008, from http://www.msndirect.com/

Papadopouli, M., & Schulzrinne, H. (2001). Effects of power conservation, wireless coverage and cooperation on data dissemination among mobile devices. In *Proceedings of the International Symposium on Mobile Ad Hoc Networking and Computing.*

Shen, H., Joseph, M. S., et al. (2005). PReCinCt: A scheme for cooperative caching in mobile peer-to-peer systems. In *Proceedings of the International Parallel and Distributed Processing Symposium.*

Shivakumar, N., & Venkatasubramanian, S. (1996). Efficient indexing for broadcast based wireless systems. Mobile *Networks and Applications, 1*(4), 433-446.

Su, C.-J., & Tassiulas, L. (1998). Joint broadcast scheduling and user's cache management for efficient information delivery. In *Proceedings of the*

International Conference on Mobile Computing and Networking.

Tan, K.-L., & Ooi, B. C. (2000). D*ata dissemination in wireless computing environments.* Norwell, MA. USA: Kluwer Academic Publishers.

Wu, W., & Tan, K.-L. (2005). Cooperative prefetching strategies for mobile peers in a broadcast wnvironment. In *Proceedings of the International Workshop on Databases, Information Systems and Peer-to-Peer Computing.*

Wu, W., & Tan, K.-L. (2006). Global cache management in non-uniform mobile broadcast. In *Proceedings of the International Conference on Mobile Data Management*, Nara, Japan.

Xu, J., Hu, Q., et al. (2000). SAIU: An efficient cache replacement policy for wireless on-demand broadcasts. In *Proceedings of the Conference on Information and Knowledge Management.*

Xu, J., Hu, Q., et al. (2004). Performance evaluation of an optimal cache replacement policy for wireless data dissemination. IEEE *Transactions on Knowledge and Data Engineering, 16*(1), 125-139.

Xu, B., & Wolfson, O. (2004). Data management in mobile peer-to-peer networks. In *Proceedings of the International Workshop on Databases, Information Systems and Peer-to-Peer Computing.*

Yin, L., & Cao, G. (2004). Supporting cooperative caching in ad hoc networks. In *Proceedings of the IEEE Conference on Computer Communications.*

Zheng, B., & Lee, D. L. (2005). Information dissemination via wireless broadcast. *Communications of ACM, 48*(5), 105-110.

Zheng, B., Wu, X., et al. (2005). TOSA: A near-optimal scheduling algorithm for multi-channel data broadcast. In *Proceedings of the 6th International Conference on Mobile Data Management*, Ayia Napa, Cyprus.

Section IV
Resource Management

Chapter X
Wireless Peer–to–Peer Media Streaming:
Incentives and Resource Management Issues

Mark Kai-Ho Yeung
The University of Hong Kong, Hong Kong

Yu-Kwong Kwok
Colorado State University, USA

ABSTRACT

The widespread deployment of competing wireless technologies has created new research opportunities. In particular, the authors consider media streaming in hybrid wireless networks where each mobile device is equipped with two wireless network interfaces: server interface and peer interface. The server interface connects wireless clients to the server while the peer interface allows neighboring clients to communicate with one another. The two interfaces have different energy characteristics. In this chapter, the authors first give a brief account of P2P media streaming in wireless operating environments. They then survey and analyze the current state-of-the-art in tackling the security and performance issues in P2P media streaming systems. In view of the deficiencies of the existing approaches, they introduce new approaches based on game theoretic concepts. Specifically, the authors propose two collaborating relationships in which neighboring clients utilize both interfaces to share the energy cost of retrieving media content from the server. Their results show that the proposed relationships improve the streaming performance of peers without violating their energy consumption constraints. Moreover, both relationships are stable when clients neither unilaterally deviate nor voluntarily leave as a group.

INTRODUCTION

With the prevalence of wired and wireless broadband Internet connections, we are no longer bound to traditional applications such as browsing the web, checking emails, text messaging, etc. There has been a rapid growth of bandwidth-intensive applications in both wired and wireless networks (Erman et al., 2007; Henderson, Kotz & Abyzov, 2004; Khan & Ahmad, 2006; Li, 2006; Jazayeri, 2007; Sen & Wang, 2004; Wen, Longshe & Qiang, 2006). One of the most prominent examples is streaming multimedia content, or *media streaming*. Specifically, media streaming refers to the simultaneous distribution of multimedia content from a provider to a group of users. We begin with illustrating the following scenario. Consider a class of students attending a lecture on campus. The lecture is also being broadcast on the Internet so that students can watch the visual aids and listen to instructions while staying at home. At the same time, other students can subscribe to that broadcast event through their mobile devices on the way to campus.

We note that the same scenario is also applicable to a variety of contexts, such as delivery of radio programmes, TV dramas, football matches, etc. This illustrates the tremendous potentials of media streaming. In a typical media streaming application, the media provider only employs a limited number of media servers to distribute the media content, which is usually a combination of audio and video information. On the other hand, each streaming session may consist of a dramatic number of simultaneous users, ranging from tens to hundreds of thousands or more. How could the media provider achieve such scalability while still remain cost effective?

In this chapter, we first give a brief account of P2P (Peer-to-Peer) media streaming in wireless operating environments in the *Media Streaming in Hybrid Wireless Networks* section. We then survey and analyze the current state-of-the-art in tackling the security and performance issues in

P2P media streaming systems in the *State-of-the-Art Incentive Mechanisms for P2P Media Streaming* section. The *System Model of Media Streaming in Hybrid Wireless Networks* section describes the system model, and in view of the deficiencies of existing approaches, we introduce our proposed approaches to P2P media streaming based on game theoretic concepts, for which we provide some basic background in the *Game Theory - Mathematical Analysis of Conflicts* section. In the *Analysis of Proposed Collaborative Media Streaming* section, we propose and analyze two collaborating relationships in which neighboring clients utilize both interfaces to share the energy cost of retrieving media content from the server. This is followed by a detailed explanation of the proposed protocols in the *Proposed Collaborative Media Streaming Protocols* section. Our results in the *Performance Evaluation* section show that the proposed relationships improve the streaming performance of peers without violating their energy consumption constraints. Moreover, both relationships are stable when clients neither unilaterally deviate nor voluntarily leave as a group. Finally, we suggest some future research directions and conclude the chapter.

MEDIA STREAMING IN HYBRID WIRELESS NETWORKS

Traditionally, wireless networks have been dominated by voice traffic. The advancement of various wireless technologies has fostered a wide range of data-oriented applications. One of the most popular applications is on-demand wireless data access (Barbara & Imielinski, 1994; Cao, 2002; Cao, 2003; Yeung & Kwok, 2005a; 2005b; 2006a; 2006b; Yin & Cao, 2006), which enables users to query data objects kept at a remote server using their mobile devices. Another emerging wireless application is to deliver high quality media content to heterogeneous mobile devices (Andronache et al., 2006; Debnath, Cranley & Davis, 2006;

Henderson, Kotz & Abyzov, 2004; Ji et al., 2007; Korhonen & Wang, 2005; Kothari & Ganz, 2005; Hara, Mitchell & Vorbau, 2007; Sato, Katsumoto & Miki, 2006; Shida et al., 2007).

Existing P2P media streaming protocols are designed for wired environment, where peers are relatively static with abundant resources in terms of computing power, bandwidth, energy, etc. The primary objective of P2P media streaming is to support more simultaneous users using a single server, i.e., to improve scalability. There are additional constraints for media streaming in wireless environment. Specifically, wireless users do not have so abundant bandwidth resources as their wired counterparts. In particular, the outgoing bandwidth, i.e., from users to the media server, is still severely limited. Since each peer is expected to contribute its outgoing bandwidth comparable to the incoming rate of media content, existing P2P media streaming protocols cannot be directly applied to wireless environment. Furthermore, wireless users are inevitably powered by limited energy resources, which may not be easily replenished. This makes energy consumption an important concern for media streaming in wireless networks.

The widespread deployment of competing wireless technologies has created new research opportunities. In particular, we consider a special type of wireless network, called *hybrid wireless network*. In a hybrid wireless network, each mobile device is equipped with more than one wireless network interface. For example, there have been an increasing number of mobile phones equipped with both 3G and WLAN interfaces. We use *server interface* to represent the wireless interface that connects mobile devices to the media server, e.g., CDMA2000. Similarly, we use *peer interface* to represent the wireless interface that enables neighboring mobile devices to communicate with one another, e.g., IEEE 802.11g. The two interfaces are designed for different application scenarios with drastically different communication ranges. As such, they exhibit different energy consump-

tion characteristics (Cisco, 2007; GTRAN, 2007). Specifically, the peer interface offers limited coverage but consumes less energy while the server interface provides extended coverage but also expends more energy.

In a typical hybrid wireless network, the number of wireless users is often much limited, e.g., each base station typically serves only tens of mobile devices only. To the media server, this means that the requirement of its streaming capacity is much reduced. This means that scalability is a less important objective in hybrid wireless networks than in wired networks. For wireless users, energy consumption is a crucial performance metric (Feeney & Nilsson, 2001; Gurun, Nagpurkar & Zhao, 2006; He & Zeng, 2006; Ji et al., 2007; Korhonen & Wang, 2005; Pering et al., 2006; Yeung & Kwok, 2005b; Yin & Cao, 2004), and it is even more important for media streaming due to its large traffic volume. Thus, we believe that the primary research objective of media streaming in hybrid wireless networks is energy efficiency.

For media streaming in hybrid wireless networks, there are a number of new concerns that are not found in wired networks. The most critical one is that mobile devices are powered by limited energy resources. Since it is difficult to replenish batteries upon depletion, wireless users are more concerned with their energy consumption. This is especially important for media streaming which consumes much energy due to its large traffic volume. Although wireless users ultimately depend on the media server to supply media content, hybrid wireless networks have created new research opportunities. Specifically, each mobile device is equipped with two wireless network interfaces: a server interface and a peer interface. The server interface connects wireless users to the media server while the peer interface allows neighboring wireless users to communicate with one another. The two interfaces have drastically different energy consumption characteristics. When compared with the server interface, the peer interface consumes less energy per bit but the coverage is more limited. We explore the feasibility of collaboration among neighboring wireless users to share the energy cost of retrieving media content from the server. Specifically, wireless users should reduce the use of server interface to conserve energy consumed in media streaming.

STATE-OF-THE-ART INCENTIVE MECHANISMS FOR P2P MEDIA STREAMING

Most existing P2P media streaming protocols implicitly assume that peers would contribute their outgoing bandwidth to distribute media packets. Since peers are autonomous entities, they can choose to reduce their contributions to conserve resources. Thus, it is important to have an effective incentive mechanism that motivates peers to contribute (Chu, Chuang & Zhang, 2004; Sung, Bishop & Rao, 2006). We describe four existing incentive mechanisms as follows:

(Ngan, Wallach & Druschel, 2004) proposes an incentive mechanism for tree-based P2P media streaming. The objective of their proposal is to ensure that peers distribute as many media packets as they receive. Thus, peers contributing more outgoing bandwidth are expected to have better streaming performance. The incentive mechanism consists of two parts: debt maintenance; and periodic tree reconstruction. For debt maintenance, each peer is required to keep a debt counter for every other peer. The debt counter keeps track of the *net* number of media packets a peer has provided to another peer. Thus, a peer increases the debt counter of its children but decreases the debt counter of its parent. If the debt counter exceeds some threshold, a peer stops distributing media packets to the corresponding peer. This arrangement motivates peers to distribute media packets to their children. Since media packets are distributed from parent to children, the tree should be peri-

odically reconstructed so that peers are allowed to settle their debts. The reconstruction period should be carefully chosen. If it is too short, the overheads involved in tree reconstruction would be very large. If it is too long, the threshold of debt counter should be very large, which allows malicious peers to avoid paying their debts by white-washing (Feldman et al., 2004). However, reconstructing the P2P tree periodically generates significant overheads and each peer is required to keep per-peer information. Both factors limit the scalability of the incentive mechanism.

Dagster (Ooi, 2005) is a centralized incentive mechanism for DAG-based P2P media streaming. When a new peer tries to join the P2P network, the peer should indicate its intended contribution to the server. Depending on the reported contribution, the server provides a list of candidate parents to the peer. Specifically, a peer with high intended contribution would receive candidate parents that are closer to the server. On the other hand, peers with low intended contribution are given candidate parents further away from the server. Peers would experience different packet delays depending on their contributions. Furthermore, peers with higher contribution are allowed to pre-empt those with lower contribution. Effectively, increasing contribution would also decrease the chance of service interruption. This is a viable incentive mechanism to motive peers to contribute. However, the server is required to assign parents for every new peer, which introduces significant overheads. Moreover, the server relies on peers to report their intended contributions. This requires extra overheads in monitoring their actual contributions. Both factors limit the scalability of the incentive mechanism.

(Habib & Chuang, 2006) propose an incentive mechanism for unstructured P2P media streaming. The objective is to provide differentiated streaming performance to peers based on their contributions. Specifically, each peer is assigned with a score that quantifies its contribution. Based on its score, each peer is mapped to a percentile rank. A peer can only choose neighbors whose ranks are lower than its own level. As such, the higher the rank, the more number of possible neighbors the peer can select. If a peer wants to improve its rank to select better neighbors, the peer should increase its score. This requires the peer to contribute more outgoing bandwidth. Since the scores are kept locally by the peers, malicious peers may tamper their scores to improve their ranks without actual contribution. Thus, this incentive mechanism is vulnerable to such malicious behaviors.

(Keidar, Melamed & Orda, 2006) propose a game theoretic incentive mechanism for unstructured P2P media streaming, called EquiCast. Specifically, the authors model the process of distributing media packets as a non-cooperative game. The players are the set of peers. Each peer keeps a balance for each of its neighbors. The balance keeps track of the *net* number of media packets a peer has provided to one of its neighbors. Similar to (Ngan, Wallach & Druschel, 2004), the balance cannot exceed a threshold, called *H*. In the game, each player is allowed to choose any strategy from the set of protocol-obedient strategies. This means that peers can only adjust the value of *H* but should follow exactly the protocol proposed by the authors. Based on this assumption, the authors have proved that peers cooperate to distribute media packets. However, we believe that the set of protocol-obedient strategies is too restrictive because peers cannot adjust their outgoing bandwidth but follow the steps as stipulated by the protocol. Furthermore, the same value of *H* should apply to all peers. This implicitly assumes that peers have homogeneous outgoing bandwidth capacity.

We believe that existing incentive mechanisms are not satisfactory for large-scale P2P media streaming. Specifically, an effective incentive mechanism should not impose significant overheads on both the server and peers.

SYSTEM MODEL OF MEDIA STREAMING IN HYBRID WIRELESS NETWORKS

A hybrid wireless network is characterized by clients having more than one wireless network interface (Andronache, Brust & Rothkugel, 2006; He et al., 2005; Luo et al., 2003; Pering et al., 2006; Yeung & Kwok, 2006a). Figure 1 shows the system model of media streaming in hybrid wireless networks, which consists of a server and a set of mobile clients. Each mobile client is equipped with two wireless network interfaces: a server interface and a peer interface. A client uses its server interface to access the server, e.g., CDMA2000; while the peer interface allows neighboring clients to communicate with one another, e.g., IEEE 802.11g. The clients would like to obtain some media content owned by the server. We represent the rate of the media content as *r* kbps and its duration as *t* seconds. Here, the server splits the media content into *n* stripes using some multiple description coding scheme. Each stripe is then delivered as a separate stream of media packets. These *n* stripes are assumed to be independent and of equal rates. This arrangement allows heterogeneous clients to adjust their streaming quality by subscribing to different number of stripes. Specifically, the primary QoS requirement is to maintain sufficient bandwidth in order to receive those media packets from the subscribed stripes.

Table 1 shows the technical specifications of a server interface and a peer interface. We can observe that the energy consumption characteristics of the two interfaces are very different. Although the peer interface only allows neighboring clients to communicate with one another, the energy cost per bit of peer interface is lower than that of server interface. It is possible to utilize the peer interface to share the energy cost of retrieving media packets from the server. We will discuss the details of our proposed energy efficient collaborative media streaming in the *Proposed Collaborative Media*

Figure 1. System model of media streaming in hybrid wireless networks

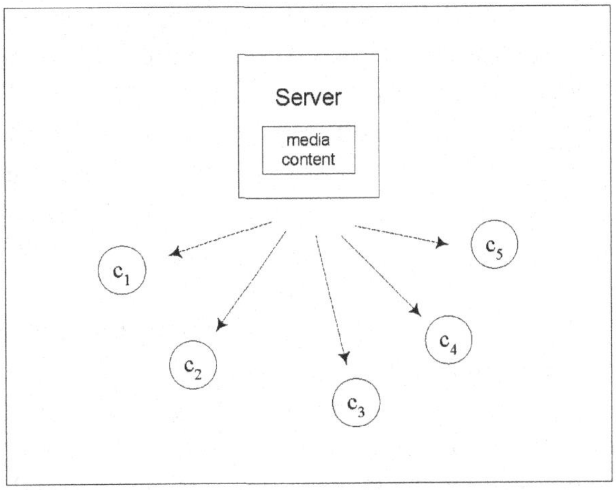

Streaming Protocols section. In particular, we would like to study how heterogeneous clients collaborate to stream the media content from the server.

GAME THEORY—MATHEMATICAL ANALYSIS OF CONFLICTS

In this section, we provide some background understanding of game theoretic techniques, based on which our proposed protocols are designed. Game theory (Myerson, 1997; Osborne & Rubinstein,

Table 1. Technical specifications of a server interface and a peer interface

GTRAN DotSurfer 6210 (GTRAN, 2007) (1xEV-DO Release 0)	
Voltage	3.3V
Receive current	150mA
Receive power	495mW
Data rate	2.4Mbps

Cisco AIR-CB21AG (Cisco, 2007) (IEEE 802.11a/b/g)	
Voltage	3.3V
Transmit current	530mA
Transmit power	1749mW
Receive current	282mA
Receive power	930.6mW
Data rate	54Mbps

1994; Osborne, 2003) has been applied to a wide range of research topics in both wired and wireless networks (Keidar, Melamed & Orda, 2006; Khan & Ahmad, 2006; Yeung & Kwok, 2005b; Yeung & Kwok, 2006a). We present a brief introduction to game theory covering both non-cooperative game and cooperative game.

Non-Cooperative Game

A non-cooperative game is characterized by a set of players denoted by, $N = \{1,...,n\}$. Each player independently chooses a particular strategy from its strategy space. The cartesian product of the strategy spaces, $S = S_1 \times ... \times S_n$, represents all possible outcomes of the game. If player i chooses the strategy, S_i, from its strategy space, S_i, we denote the outcome of the game as, $s = \{s_1,...,s_n\}$ S. The preference of a player is determined by its utility function, u_i, which maps an outcome to a numerical value, called payoff. For example, we represent player i's payoff as $u_i(s)$ when the outcome is s. Each player is modeled as a selfish but rational entity that independently optimizes its payoff. Unlike standard optimization problems, the "optimal" strategy of a player that maximizes its payoff may also depend on the strategies of other players.

In non-cooperative game theory, the most popular solution concept is called *Nash Equilib-*

rium. Specifically, a particular strategy combination, $s^* = \{s_1^*,...,s_n^*\}$, is said to achieve the state of Nash Equilibrium when no player can improve its payoff by unilaterally deviating from its chosen strategy. This requires the following conditions to be satisfied simultaneously:

$$u_i(s^*) \geq u_i(s_1^*,..., s_{i-1}, s_i, s_{i+1},...,s_n^*) \; \forall s_i \in S_i, \; i \in N \tag{1}$$

We note that players are assumed to know the utility functions of one another but there is no coordination among themselves. In other words, each player independently chooses the strategy that maximizes its own payoff. In general, a game may have any number of Nash equilibria, i.e., from zero to infinitely many. To model a specific scenario as a non-cooperative game, we should first design a utility function that generates more than one Nash equilibrium. Then, we should design a specific protocol that leads players to our desired Nash equilibrium. We use the following example as an illustration:

Consider the scenario where there are two prisoners being interrogated separately. They cannot communicate with each other and can either deny or confess the charges against them. This is called the *Prisoners' Dilemma*, which is a classical two-person non-cooperative game. The players are the two prisoners, A and B. The strategy space of each player consists of two actions: deny or confess. We represent the payoffs of the game in the payoff matrix shown in Table 2, where (x, y) represents that A's payoff is x and B's payoff is y.

We note that a, b, c and d are some constants and $a > b > c > d$. Apparently, the "optimal" outcome of the game is that both prisoners deny the charges, which results in (b, b). However, this outcome is not stable because either prisoner could improve its own payoff by switching from deny to confess $(a > b)$. If one prisoner has switched to confess, the other prisoner should also switch to confess because $c > d$. Thus, both prisoners should choose confess, which is the unique Nash Equilibrium of the game.

Cooperative Game

A cooperative game consists of a set of players denoted by, $N = \{1,...,n\}$. However, they do not act independently as in a non-cooperative game but form different coalitions with one another. As there are n players, there are 2^n possible coalitions. Each coalition, which consists of a set of players, $C \subseteq N$, is associated with a value determined by a characteristic value function, v. In other words, the value of the coalition, C, is denoted by the value, $v(C)$. By convention, it is assumed that the empty set has zero value, i.e., $v(\phi) = 0$. We note that $v(C)$ represents the utility created from the cooperation of players in C only. Since the value function is taken to be non-decreasing, $v(N)$ is the maximum utility created by the cooperation of all the players. We are interested in value functions that satisfy the following super-additive property:

$$v(C_1 \cup C_2 \cup \cdots) \geq \sum_{\forall i} v(C_i) \tag{2}$$

The solution consists of two parts. The first part is the formation of a coalition. The second part is to allocate the value of the coalition, $v(C)$, to the set of constituent players. Specifically, the value allocated to player i is denoted as v_i. Players are also modeled as selfish but rational entities. The objective of each player is to maximize its

Table 2. Payoff matrix of the Prisoner's Dilemma game.

	B chooses "deny"	B chooses "confess"
A chooses "deny"	(b,b)	(d,a)
A chooses "confess"	(a,d)	(c,c)

allocated value. As such, the question is to allocate $v(C)$ such that the constituent players of the coalition would not leave the coalition. One of the most popular solution concepts is the *core*. An allocation is said to be in the core of the game if the following two conditions are satisfied:

$$\sum\nolimits_{\forall i \in C} v_i = v(C) \tag{3}$$

$$\sum\nolimits_{\forall i \in C'} v_i \geq v(C'), \forall C' \subseteq C \tag{4}$$

The first condition ensures that the value of the coalition is completely allocated to all constituent players. This is an intuitive requirement for stability. The second condition means that a subset of constituent players cannot improve their values by forming another coalition. In other words, the best strategy is to cooperate in the original coalition. Thus, the players would neither leave the coalition alone nor as a group. This suggests that the coalition is stable. We illustrate the details with the following example:

Consider the scenario with three workers and a project. The project cannot be completed by any one of the workers alone. If all three workers take part in the project, they create one unit of payoff. If only two of them participate, the payoff is reduced to α. We can model this scenario as a cooperative game. Each worker corresponds to a player. According to the above description, the characteristic value function is shown as follows:

$$v(C) = \begin{cases} 1, & if \quad |C| = 3 \\ \alpha, & if \quad |C| = 2 \\ 0, & if \quad |C| = 1 \end{cases} \tag{5}$$

We denote the amount of payoff allocated to player i as v_i, where $i = \{1, 2, 3\}$. If the three players form a coalition, we would like to know how they should split the unit of payoff. First, we require: $v_1 + v_2 + v_3 = 1$. Second, we should have: $v_i + v_j \geq \alpha$, for any i, j. If $\alpha \leq \frac{2}{3}$, the players can always arrive at an allocation such that the coalition is stable, i.e., the core of the game.

ANALYSIS OF PROPOSED COLLABORATIVE MEDIA STREAMING

In the *System Model of Media Streaming in Hybrid Wireless Networks* section, we described the system model of media streaming in hybrid wireless networks, see Figure 1. It consists of a server and a set of mobile clients. Each mobile client is equipped with two wireless network interfaces: a server interface, and a peer interface. Each client uses its server interface to access the server, e.g., CDMA2000; while the peer interface allows neighboring clients to communicate with one another, e.g., IEEE 802.11g. The clients are interested in a piece of media content owned by the server. We denote the media rate as r kbps and its duration as t s. The server splits the media content into n stripes using some multiple description coding scheme. Each stripe is then delivered as a separate stream of media packets. These n stripes are assumed to be independent and of equal rates. We analyze the energy cost of clients in obtaining media packets in the following. Table 3 summarizes the list of symbols and their definitions used in the analysis.

Ignoring control overheads, the energy cost of receiving the complete media content, i.e., all n stripes, through the server interface is:

$$E_s^{RX} = \frac{P_s^{RX}}{R_s} \times r \times t \tag{6}$$

Correspondingly, the energy cost of receiving the complete media content through the peer interface is:

$$E_p^{RX} = \frac{P_p^{RX}}{R_p} \times r \times t \tag{7}$$

Using the values shown in Table 1, we have: $E_s^{RX} = 103.13J$ and $E_p^{RX} = 8.62J$. This suggests that it is possible to utilize the peer interface to conserve energy consumed in media streaming. In particular, we would like to study how het-

Table 3. List of symbols

Symbol D	efinition
r	rate of the media content
t	duration of the media content
n	number of stripes
P_s^{RX}	receive power of the server interface
R_s	data rate of the server interface (downlink)
P_p^{RX}	receive power of the peer interface
R_p	data rate of the peer interface (symmetric)
$E_s^{RX}(i)$	energy cost of receiving i stripes through the server interface ($i \leq n$)
$E_p^{RX}(i)$	energy cost of receiving I stripes through the peer interface ($i \leq n$)
$E_p^{TX}(i)$	energy cost of transmitting i stripes through the peer interface ($i \leq n$)
α_x	client x's type
$\alpha_1(i)$	threshold value for a client to receive i stripes from the server
$\alpha_M(i)$	threshold value for a master to receive i stripes, $i \leq n$
$\alpha_S(i)$	threshold value for a slave to receive i stripes, $i \leq n$
$\alpha_r'(i)$	threshold value for a coordinator with (r-1) helpers to receive i stripes
$\alpha_r(i)$	threshold value for a helper to receive i stripes

erogeneous clients collaborate to retrieve media content from the server.

We consider clients as heterogeneous entities with different energy consumption constraints. To quantify heterogeneity, we represent the *type* of client x as α_x, which is defined as:

$$\alpha_x = \frac{\textit{amount of energy that client x willing to consume}}{E_s^{RX}(n)} \quad (8)$$

Depending on client x's preferences, α_x may take any non-negative values. For example, $\alpha_x > 1$ means that x is willing to consume more energy than the cost of subscribing to all n stripes ($E_s^{RX}(n)$), e.g., a mobile device with plentiful energy resources. On the other hand, $\alpha_x \leq 1$ means that x is more concerned with the energy cost than the streaming quality, e.g., a mobile device with little residual energy. Specifically, the value of α_x determines the number of stripes client x would subscribe to. Since the n stripes are assumed to be of equal rates, i.e., $\frac{r}{n}$ kbps, the energy cost of streaming i stripes via the server interface is:

$$E_s^{RX}(i) = \frac{i}{n} \times \frac{P_s^{RX}}{R_s} \times r \times t \quad (9)$$

This implies that client x would stream up to i stripes from the server if $\alpha_x \geq \alpha_1(i)$, where $\alpha_1(i)$ is given by:

$$\alpha_1(i) = \frac{E_s^{RX}(i)}{E_s^{RX}} = \frac{i}{n} \quad (10)$$

The set of $\alpha_1(i)$, $i \in [0, n]$, represents the threshold values when client x independently streams from the server. Figure 2 shows the variation of the number of subscribed stripes with the type of a client for $n = 10$. For example, if $\alpha_x = 0.55$, client x would subscribe to 5 stripes from the server. This represents the performance of media streaming when clients act independently. However, neighboring clients could utilize their peer interfaces to improve streaming performance without violating their energy consumption constraints. Since clients are often under different authorities, we should also consider their incentives for collaboration. Thus, we model each client as a selfish but rational entity whose degree of selfishness is characterized by its type. Specifically, client x would only collaborate with other clients provided that the number of stripes x obtained from collaboration is no smaller than s_1, where s_1 is given by:

$$s_1 = \arg\max_{\forall i \leq n}\{\alpha \geq \alpha_1(i)\} \qquad (11)$$

This means that each client is only interested in improving its own streaming performance. We note that the type of a client defines its selfishness. For example, when $\alpha_x = 0.85$, client x would collaborate with other clients for media streaming if it can receive more stripes from collaboration. Otherwise, client x could obtain 8 stripes from the server by acting independently. We would like to study the feasibility of collaboration among selfish clients.

Two Neighboring Clients

First, we consider the scenario with two neighboring clients: $\{x, y\}$. There are two cases: x and y form a master-slave relationship, see Figure 3(a); or x and y form a peer-to-peer relationship, see Figure 3(b).

Without loss of generality, we assume that x is the master while y is the slave. As shown in Figure 3(a), x subscribes to i stripes from the server and sends them to y through the peer interface. In this case, x is an enthusiastic client, serving y at the expense of its own energy resources. This requires that the type of master x should satisfy: $\alpha_x \geq \alpha_M(i)$, where $\alpha_M(i)$ is given by:

Figure 2. Number of subscribed stripes vs. the type of a client (n = 10)

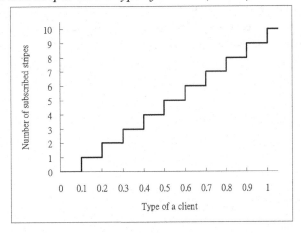

Figure 3. The scenario with two neighboring clients

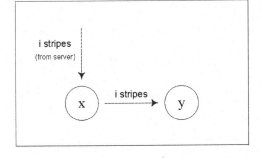

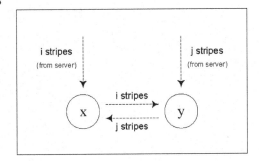

(a) Proposed master-slave relationship.

(b) Proposed peer-to-peer relationship.

$$\alpha_M(i) = \frac{E_s^{RX}(i) + E_p^{TX}(i)}{E_s^{RX}} \qquad (12)$$

On the other hand, client y may decide to free-ride because its residual energy is low. This requires that the type of slave y should satisfy: $\alpha_y \geq \alpha_S(i)$, where $\alpha_S(i)$ is given by:

$$\alpha_S(i) = \frac{E_p^{RX}(i)}{E_s^{RX}} \qquad (13)$$

From Equations (12) and (13), we plot the threshold values for the master and slave as α varies between 0 and 1.2, see Figure 4. When two neighboring clients whose types satisfy the two thresholds, they form a master-slave relationship. We can see that the type of a slave is much smaller than that of a master. This is because the slave does not contribute but depends on the master for all media packets. On the other hand, the energy cost of being a master is higher than that of acting alone, which leads to the increase in the threshold values. We illustrate the master-slave relationship with the following numerical example:

Consider two neighboring clients: x and y whose types are 1.2 and 0.25, respectively. If each of them independently streams the media from the sever, x will subscribe to 10 stripes while y will subscribe to 2 stripes. However, they may collaborate and form a master-slave relationship for media streaming, see Figure 3(a). Specifically, x becomes the master and y is the slave. Equation (12) suggests that x subscribes to 10 stripes and also sends them to y, which receives the 10 stripes via its peer interface.

The master-slave collaborating relationship allows the slave to take advantage of the generosity of the master, which provides the media content through the peer interface. The performance of the slave is improved at the expense of the master's energy resources. However, it would be more interesting if both clients contribute their resources to form a peer-to-peer relationship, see Figure 3(b). Let client x and y subscribe to i and j stripes from the server, respectively. They periodically exchange their stripes with one another using their peer interfaces. Effectively, each client obtains $(i+j)$ stripes of the media content, where $(i+j) \leq n$. This peer-to-peer collaborating relationship improves the performance of both

Figure 4. Number of subscribed stripes vs. the type of a client (n = 10)

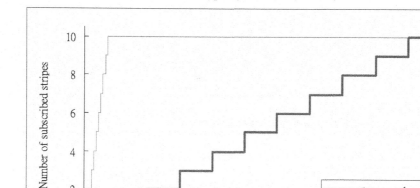

clients. However, the values of i and j depend on the type of the corresponding clients. If client x subscribes to i stripes from the server, we require: $\alpha_x \geq \alpha_2(i)$, where $\alpha_2(i)$ is given by:

$$\alpha_2(i) = \frac{E_s^{RX}(i) + E_p^{TX}(i) + E_p^{RX}(j)}{E_s^{RX}} \tag{14}$$

Similarly, we require: $\alpha_y \geq \alpha_2(j)$, where $\alpha_2(j)$ is given by:

$$\alpha_2(j) = \frac{E_s^{RX}(j) + E_p^{TX}(j) + E_p^{RX}(i)}{E_s^{RX}} \tag{15}$$

Figure 5 shows the variation of the number of subscribed stripes with the type of client x, α_x, for $j = 1, 3, 5$. This means that if $\alpha_x = 0.5$, x will obtain 7 stripes when $j = 3$, i.e., $i = 4$. We illustrate the peer-to-peer relationship with the following numerical example:

Consider two neighboring clients: x and y whose types are 0.75 and 0.55, respectively. If they independently stream the media content from the sever, x will subscribe to 7 stripes while y will subscribe to 5 stripes. However, they may

collaborate and form a peer-to-peer relationship for media streaming, see Figure 3(b). With reference to Equations (14) and (15), x subscribes to 6 stripes from the server and y subscribes to the other 4 stripes from the server. Besides that, they periodically exchange media packets via their peer interfaces. This effectively allows them to receive 10 stripes, i.e., the complete media content.

With the proposed peer-to-peer relationship, both clients increase the number of received stripes without violating their types. Thus, the collaboration between two neighboring clients would improve the performance of media streaming with the same energy consumption constraints.

Three Neighboring Clients

Next, we consider the scenario with three neighboring clients: $\{x, y, z\}$, where y and z are the neighbors of x but they may not be able to communicate with each other directly. Similar to the previous scenario, collaboration among the three clients can take two different forms: master-slave and peer-to-peer.

Without loss of generality, we assume that x is the master while y and z are the slaves. Specifically, x subscribes to i stripes from the server and

Figure 5. Number of subscribed stripes vs. the type of a client (n = 10)

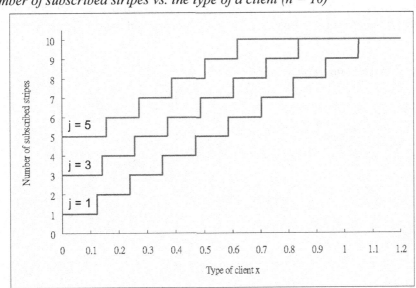

sends them to y and z through the peer interface, see Figure 6(a). Since the master can broadcast the media content to its slaves, the energy cost of being a master does not change with the number of slaves. This follows that the threshold values for both master and slave remain the same, i.e., $\alpha_x \geq \alpha_M(i)$; and α_y, $\alpha_z \geq \alpha_S(i)$.

For the peer-to-peer relationship, all the three clients contribute their resources for media streaming, where x, y, z independently subscribe to i, j and k stripes from the server, respectively, see Figure 6(b). Since y and z are generally out of communication range, x should act as the coordinator and y and z become the helpers. Specifically, y and z periodically send j and k stripes to x, respectively. Together with the media content received from the server, x broadcasts $(i+j+k)$ stripes to y and z. This collaborating relationship provides each of the three clients with $(i+j+k)$ stripes, where $(i+j+k) \leq n$. Obviously, the type of x should be higher than the others. Specifically, we have: $\alpha_x \geq \alpha_3'(i)$, where $\alpha_3'(i)$ is given by:

$$\alpha_3'(i) = \frac{E_s^{RX}(i) + E_p^{TX}(i+j+k) + E_p^{RX}(j+k)}{E_s^{RX}} \quad (16)$$

On the other hand, y and z have similar type requirements, which depend on the number of subscribed stripes. In particular, the type of y should satisfy: $\alpha_y \geq \alpha_3(j)$, where $\alpha_3(j)$ is given by:

$$\alpha_3(j) = \frac{E_s^{RX}(j) + E_p^{TX}(j) + E_p^{RX}(i+k)}{E_s^{RX}} \quad (17)$$

Similarly, the type of z should satisfy: $\alpha_z \geq \alpha_3(k)$, where $\alpha_3(k)$ is obtained by interchanging the roles of j and k in Equation (17). We illustrate the peer-to-peer relationship with the following numerical example:

Consider three neighboring clients: x, y, and z whose types are 0.65, 0.45, and 0.45, respectively. If they independently stream the media content from the sever, x will subscribe to some 6 stripes while both y and z will subscribe to some 4 stripes. However, they may collaborate and form a peer-to-peer relationship for media streaming. For y and z, each of them subscribes to 3 stripes from the server and periodically sends them to the coordinator, x. On the other hand, x subscribes to the other 4 stripes from the server and periodically broadcasts all media packets to y and z. Effectively, this peer-to-peer relationship allows the three clients to receive 10 stripes, i.e., the complete media content.

The General Scenario

Now, we generalize the analysis to the scenario with r neighboring clients. Since the master-slave relationship does not change with the number of neighboring clients, we focus our attention

Figure 6. The scenario with three neighboring clients

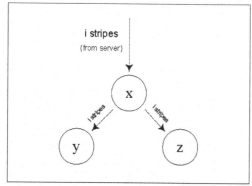

(a) Proposed master-slave relationship.

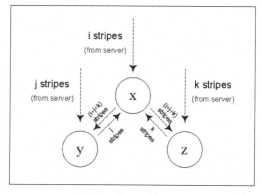

(b) Proposed peer-to-peer relationship.

on the peer-to-peer relationship. Without loss of generality, we assume that x is the coordinator, which is connected to $(r - 1)$ neighboring helpers, denoted by R_x In general, these $(r - 1)$ helpers may not be able to communicate with one another. We denote the number of stripes subscribed by y as s_y, where $y \in R_x$. On the other hand, x subscribes to s_x stripes from the server, where $\sum s \leq n$. We can obtain the threshold values for client x's type, i.e., $\alpha_r'(s_x)$ which is given by:

$$\alpha_r'(s_x) = \frac{E_s^{RX}(s_x) + E_p^{TX}(\sum s) + E_p^{RX}(\sum s - s_x)}{E_s^{RX}} \quad (18)$$

Similarly, $\alpha_r(s_y)$ represents the threshold values for helper y's type, which is given by:

$$\alpha_r(s_y) = \frac{E_s^{RX}(s_y) + E_p^{TX}(s_y) + E_p^{RX}(\sum s - s_y)}{E_s^{RX}} \quad (19)$$

This suggests that a number of neighboring clients satisfying the above thresholds can collaborate to improve the performance of media streaming by utilizing their peer interfaces. The collaborating relationship allows clients to share the higher energy cost involved in receiving media packets from the server directly. Although the coordinator requires a larger threshold, its energy cost may not be the highest because it may subscribe to fewer stripes from the server, i.e., s_x is small or even zero. Since the number of subscribed stripes depends on the client types, heterogeneous clients may form either the master-slave relationship or the peer-to-peer relationship. In the next

Algorithm 1. Proposed collaborative media streaming protocol for master-slave relationship

t_{max}: timeout in seconds;
S: maximum number of media packets cached by a master;

Master x
Upon receiving a *request* message, **do**
Calculate $s_1(\alpha_x) = \text{argmax}_{i \leq n}\{\alpha_x \geq \alpha_1(i)\}$; // see Equation (10)
Calculate $s_M(\alpha_x) = \text{argmax}_{i \leq n}\{\alpha_x \geq \alpha_M(i)\}$; // see Equation (12)
if $s_M(\alpha_x) \geq s_1(\alpha_x)$ **then**
    Send a *grant message*: grant($s_M(\alpha_x)$);
end if

Upon receiving an *acknowledgment* message, **do**
Subscribe to $s_M(\alpha_x)$ stripes from the media server;
Cache up to S media packets locally;
Broadcast S media packets to the slave(s);

Slave y
Broadcast a *request* message to its neighbors;
Calculate $s_1(\alpha_y) = \text{argmax}_{i \leq n}\{\alpha_y \geq \alpha_1(i)\}$; // see Equation (10)
Calculate $s_S(\alpha_y) = \text{argmax}_{i \leq n}\{\alpha_y \geq \alpha_S(i)\}$; // see Equation (13)
Wait for *grant* messages, grant($s_M(\alpha_x)$), for t_{max} seconds;
Set $s_M = 0$;
for each grant($s_M(\alpha_x)$) **do**
    if $s_M(\alpha_x) > s_M$ and $s_M(\alpha_x) \leq s_y$ and $s_M(\alpha_x) \geq s_1(\alpha_y)$ **then**
        $s_M = s_M(\alpha_x)$;
    end if
end for
Send an *acknowledgment* message to the chosen master;
Receive media packets periodically from the chosen master;

section, we propose two protocols to establish the two proposed collaborating relationships.

PROPOSED COLLABORATIVE MEDIA STREAMING PROTOCOLS

We discussed the principles of collaborative media streaming in the previous section. The two proposed collaborating relationships allow neighboring clients to improve streaming performance without violating their energy consumption constraints, which are modeled by different values of α. We now detail how neighboring clients establish the master-slave and peer-to-peer relationships.

We assume that each client knows its own type, i.e., x knows α_x only. Since both master-slave and peer-to-peer relationships involve neighboring clients only, we can utilize the peer interface to exchange control messages without the participation of the server. This means that the server is transparent to the proposed collaborative media streaming protocols. However, the server should split the media content into n stripes, which can be independently streamed to clients upon request.

First, we consider the process of establishing master-slave relationships. If client y wants to become a slave, it broadcasts a *request* message to its neighbors. Upon receiving the request, each client x checks if it would like to become a master or is already acting as a master. From Equation (12), x calculates the number of stripes to broadcast and replies y with a *grant* message. Upon receiving the replies, y selects the neighbor providing the largest number of stripes without violating its type (see Equation (13)). Then y sends an *acknowledgment* message to the selected neighbor, x'. This selected neighbor becomes the master, which caches media packets from the server and broadcasts them via the peer interface periodically. We note that x' should broadcast a batch of media packets. Although slaves would experience larger delay due to buffering, this

would reduce the amount of energy consumed in packetization (Feeney & Nilsson, 2001). The details of the master-slave collaborative media streaming protocol are shown in Algorithm 1.

Next, we consider the process of establishing peer-to-peer relationships. If client x wants to become the coordinator in a peer-to-peer relationship, it broadcasts a *request* message to its neighbors. Upon receiving the request, each client y specifies its type, α_y, in a *response* message. We denote C_{max} as the maximum number of helpers in a peer-to-peer relationship. Upon receiving the responses, x selects up to C_{max} neighbors with the largest types. From Equations (18) and (19), x can calculate the number of allowed stripes for each client. If the aggregate number of stripes is larger than n, x incrementally reduces the number of subscribed stripes by each client. For each selected helper y, x sends an *acknowledgment* message, specifying the stripes y should retrieve from the server. Similar to the master-slave relationship, both the coordinator and helpers cache media packets from the server. For helpers, they periodically broadcast their media packets to the coordinator via the peer interface. On the other hand, the coordinator periodically broadcasts all media packets to the helpers via the peer interface. The details of the peer-to-peer collaborative media streaming protocol are shown in Algorithms 2 and 3.

Although neighboring clients can form the proposed master-slave or peer-to-peer relationships, collaboration is on voluntary basis. To ensure that both collaborating relationships are stable, we model clients as rational entities who aim at maximizing their streaming performance, measured by the number of subscribed stripes, subject to energy consumption constraints, i.e., the values of α. We should also consider the stability of the two relationships formed by the proposed protocols. Specifically, neighboring clients form a stable relationship if neither of them would unilaterally deviate. In other words, a stable relationship achieves the state of Nash Equilibrium in which the players are the neighboring clients.

We first look at the master-slave relationship formed by Algorithm 1. What are the possible strategies of master x? First, x may reduce the number of stripes retrieved from the server. However, this is an undesirable move because its own streaming performance is reduced. The master may choose not to broadcast the cached media packets to its slaves. Since we require that $s_M(\alpha_x) \geq s_1(\alpha_x)$ in Algorithm 1, master x cannot increase its streaming performance by subscribing to more stripes without violating its type. Thus, x is indifferent with the broadcast action. On the other hand, the possible strategies of slave y are either receiving media packets from the master or from the server. Since we require that $s_M(\alpha_x) \geq s_1(\alpha_y)$ in Algorithm 1, slave y cannot subscribe to more stripes directly from the server without violating its type. As such, y would choose to

receive media packets from its chosen master. Thus, neither the master nor its slaves would unilaterally deviate. Thus, we can conclude that the proposed master-slave relationship achieves the state of Nash Equilibrium.

We then look at the peer-to-peer relationships formed by Algorithms 2 and 3. Coordinator x can receive up to $s_1(\alpha_x)$ stripes from the server, see Equation (10). Referring to Algorithm 2, x would only send acknowledgment messages to the helpers if $s > s_1(\alpha_x)$. This implies that x cannot receive more stripes from the server than from acting as a coordinator. On the other hand, if a neighbor is chosen as a helper by the coordinator, the number of stripes obtained from the peer-to-peer relationship is not smaller than what could be obtained from the server, see Algorithm 2. Thus, neither the coordinator nor its helpers would unilaterally

Algorithm 2. Proposed collaborative media streaming protocol for peer-to-peer relationship (coordinator)

Coordinator x
Broadcast a *request* message to the neighbors;
Wait for *response* messages, response(α_y), for $t_{\max}$ seconds;
Calculate $s_1(\alpha_x) = \text{argmax}_{i \leq n}\{\alpha_x \geq \alpha_1(i)\}$; // see Equation (10)
Calculate $s_r(\alpha_x) = \text{argmax}_{i \leq n}\{\alpha_x \geq \alpha'_r(i)\}$; // see Equation (18)
$H = \{s_r(\alpha_x)\}$;
Calculate $s_1(\alpha_y) = \text{argmax}_{i \leq n}\{\alpha_y \geq \alpha_1(i)\}$; // see Equation (10)
Calculate $s_r(\alpha_y) = \text{argmax}_{i \leq n}\{\alpha_y \geq \alpha_r(i)\}\forall y$; // see Equation (19)
if $(s_r(\alpha_x) + s_r(\alpha_y)) \geq s_1(\alpha_y)$ **then**
    $H = H \cup \{s_r(\alpha_y)\}$;
end if
Set $s = 0$;
for $i \in [1, n]$ **do**
    $s_z = \max\{H\}$;
    if $s_z > 0$ **then**
        $Z = Z \cup \{i\}$;
        $s_z = s_z - 1$;
        $s = s + 1$;
    end if
end for
if $s \geq s_1(\alpha_x)$ **then**
    Send each chosen helper an *acknowledgment* message: ack(Z);
end if
Subscribe to the ith stripe from the media server, $\forall i \in X$;
Cache up to S media packets locally;
Broadcast S media packets to the helpers;

Upon receiving media packets from a helper, **do**
Broadcast them to the helpers;

Algorithm 3. Proposed collaborative media streaming protocol for peer-to-peer relationship (helper)

Helper y
Upon receiving a *request* message, **do**
Send a *response message*: response(α_y);

Upon receiving an *acknowledgment* message, ack(Y), **do**
Subscribe to the ith stripe from the media server, $\forall i \in Y$;
Cache up to S media packets locally;
Broadcast S media packets to the coordinator;

deviate. Thus, we can conclude that the proposed peer-to-peer relationship achieves the state of Nash Equilibrium.

To summarize, we proposed two energy efficient protocols to establish master-slave and peer-to-peer relationships for collaborating media streaming in hybrid wireless networks. The proposed protocols allow neighboring clients to improve streaming performance by utilizing their peer interfaces. Furthermore, both relationships are stable where rational clients, with heterogeneous energy consumption constraints modeled by different types, would not unilaterally deviate. While improving streaming performance is the primary objective, we believe that stability is equally important so that clients can benefit from sustained collaboration.

PERFORMANCE EVALUATION

We evaluate the performance of the two proposed protocols in a custom simulator. The energy consumption characteristics of the server and peer interfaces are shown in Table 1. The media content has a data rate of $r = 500$ kbps and lasts for $t = 1000$s. The server divides the media content into 10 streams of equally-sized packets, i.e., $n = 10$. We assume that each of the 10 streams generates 1 packet per second. Thus, the total number of packets is 1×10^4. There are 100 clients that are evenly distributed over the 100m × 100m simulation area. The media server covers the entire area while the communication

range of the peer interface is 30m. The details of the simulation parameters are listed in Table 4. We implemented the two proposed collaborative media streaming protocols and compared them with the case of no collaboration. The results are labeled: "Independent," "Master-Slave," "Collaboration(2)," and "Collaboration(5)." In "Independent," each client independently streams the media content from the server. In "Master-Slave," clients are allowed to form master-slave relationships using Algorithm 1. In "Collaboration(2)," each peer-to-peer relationship consists of two clients. Similarly, "Collaboration(5)" means that each peer-to-peer relationship consists of up to five clients. We quantified the results with four performance metrics: (1) delivery ratio, as a measure of streaming performance; (2) number of packets received via the server interface, as a measure of reliance on the server interface; (3) number of packets sent via the peer interface, as a measure of overheads; and (4) amount of energy consumed, as a measure of consumed resources.

Table 4. Simulation parameters

Definition	Value
No. of clients	100
Media rate, r	500kbps
Session duration, t	1000s
No. of stripes, n	10
No. of packets	1×10^4
Transmission range	30m
Simulation area	100m × 100m

We also reported the percentage of lost packets in the *Effect of Link Quality* sub-section. First, we studied the homogeneous scenario, where all the clients have identical types. Second, we investigated the bimodal scenario, where clients are divided in two classes with distinct types. The third scenario focused on the impact of mobility. Finally, we investigated the effect of link quality on the performance metrics.

Effect of Homogeneous Client Distribution

We first study the effect of homogeneous client distribution where all the 100 clients have the same type, α. Figure 7 shows the performance results when the client type was varied between 0.2 and 1.2. As defined in Equation (8), the type of a client represents its energy consumption constraint in media streaming. If the type is small, clients are more conservative with regard to their energy resources. They would subscribe to fewer stripes rather than incur higher energy cost. Equivalently, the type of a client can be considered as a measure of its degree of selfishness, which determines the willingness to collaborate.

Figure 7(a) shows the delivery ratio of clients, which measures the total number of packets received from both the server and collaborating clients, if any. Of all the four schemes, the deliv-

Figure 7. Effect of homogeneous client distribution

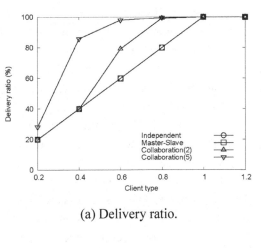

(a) Delivery ratio.

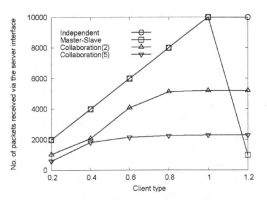

(b) Number of packets received via the server interface.

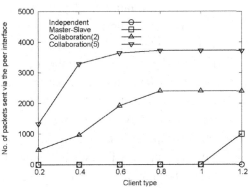

(c) Number of packets sent via the peer interface.

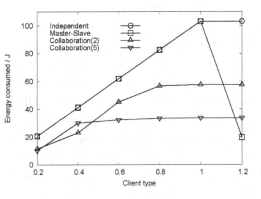

(d) Energy consumed.

ery ratio increases with the client type. This is because as the type increases, clients are allowed to consume more energy for media streaming. For "Independent," clients subscribe to all the stripes from the server. The performance peaks at 1 because the clients are already subscribing the maximum number of stripes, as suggested by Equation (10). The proposed master-slave protocol, "Master-Slave," gives the same results as "Independent." This is because of the homogeneous client distribution, which is not suitable for establishing master-slave relationships. We will see more details later. The "Collaboration(2)" scheme allows two neighboring clients form the proposed peer-to-peer relationship. In the low-end, 0.2–0.4, clients are so selfish that no one wants to collaborate. Thus, each client streams the media content from the server directly. As the type increases, clients are more willing to utilize their peer interfaces for exchanging media packets. Thus, clients with larger types would benefit more from the proposed peer-to-peer relationships. For "Collaboration(5)," each peer-to-peer relationship can have at most five clients, i.e., one coordinator and up to four helpers. Since the burden of receiving packets from the server is distributed among the clients, the threshold types become smaller, see Equations (18) and (19). This means that clients with smaller types would also collaborate. Thus, we can see that the delivery ratio is the largest throughout the simulation range.

Figure 7(b) shows the number of packets received via the server interface. This performance metric measures the traffic volume between the server and clients, which is costly in terms of energy consumption. Since clients always receive media packets from the server directly in "Independent," it is always the largest. Of the two collaboration schemes, "Collaboration(2)" and "Collaboration(5)," clients utilize their peer interfaces to exchange media packets obtained from the server. This reduces the number of packets received via the server interface. For "Collaboration(5)," the peer interface is more aggressively

utilized because each peer-to-peer relationship can have up to five clients. Thus, the number of packets received via the server interface of "Collaboration(5)" is smaller than that of "Collaboration(2)." The situation becomes more interesting in "Master-Slave." In the range between 0.2 and 1, the performance of "Master-Slave" is the same as that of "Independent." However, the number of packets received via the server interface abruptly drops when the client type is 1.2. This is because the master has a heavy burden: to receive media packets from the server, and to broadcast them to the slaves. This implies that the master should have a much larger type than any other slaves. Referring to Figure 4, the master would revert to independent streaming, i.e., without broadcasting its media packets, if its type is below 1. Given the homogeneous client distribution, no master-slave relationship can be formed for the range 0.2–1. When the client type increases to 1.2, neighboring clients could form master-slave relationships for collaborative media streaming. Since each master can support more than one slave, the number of packets received via the server interface substantially decreases.

To quantify the overheads of the two proposed protocols, we measured the number of packets via the peer interface. The results are shown in Figure 7(c). Since "Independent" does not utilize the peer interface, its results are always zero. As discussed before, no master-slave relationships are formed between 0.2 and 1. The jump at 1.2 represents the number of packets broadcast by the masters. We note that this quantity depends on the number of clients acting as masters, but does not depend on the number of slaves. This is because each master broadcasts media packets to its neighboring slaves. Since "Collaboration(5)" allows up to five clients to form a peer-to-peer relationship, their peer interfaces are more aggressively utilized for exchanging media packets. Thus, the number of packets sent via the peer interface of "Collaboration(5)" is always larger than that of "Collaboration(2)." We also note that "Collaboration(5)" peaks at 0.6 while "Collaboration(2)" peaks at 0.8. This indicates that "Collaboration(5)" is more efficient in pooling the energy resources of neighboring clients for collaborative media streaming. We can see that both "Collaboration(2)" and "Collaboration(5)" shift a large proportion of media packets to the peer interface. Although the combined traffic of the two interfaces is more than what is required without collaboration, we believe that it is justifiable to utilize the peer interface for exchanging media packets. This would reduce the reliance on the server in delivering media packets and the energy cost of receiving media packets via the server interface.

Figure 7(d) shows the average amount of energy consumed by the clients, which includes the energy cost of both server and peer interfaces. We observe that the results are very similar to those shown in Figure 7(b), which measures the number of packets received via the server interface. This indicates that the energy consumption depends largely on the amount of traffic in the server interface. We have seen that clients running "Collaboration(2)" or "Collaboration(5)" generate a large number of packets in their peer interfaces. However, both schemes consume less energy than "Independent." This suggests that receiving media packets via the server interface is the dominant source of energy consumption. It is desirable to utilize the

Figure 8. Effect of bimodal client distribution

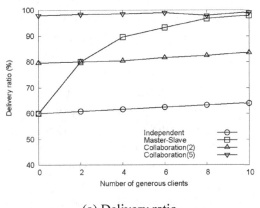

(a) Delivery ratio.

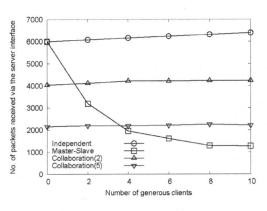

(b) Number of packets received via the server interface.

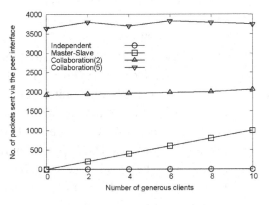

(c) Number of packets sent via the peer interface.

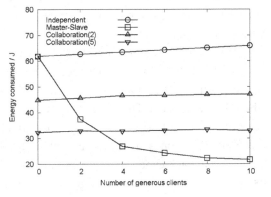

(d) Energy consumed.

energy efficient peer interface to conserve energy resources for improving streaming performance. We can conclude that the proposed protocol for establishing peer-to-peer relationships is effective in improving streaming performance in the homogeneous scenario. On the other hand, the proposed protocol for establishing master-slave relationships is only effective when the client type is high.

Effect of Bimodal Client Distribution

This set of experiments investigates the effect of bimodal client distribution. Specifically, we divided clients in two classes with different types: selfish and generous. The type of selfish clients was 0.6 while that of generous clients was 1.2. We kept the total number of clients at 100. The number of generous clients was increased up to 10. This scenario is to model the presence of heterogeneous clients in practical P2P systems. In particular, generous clients represent users who are enthusiastic to collaborate for improving performance at the expense of their energy resources. The results are shown in Figure 8.

Figure 8(a) shows the delivery ratio, which measures the total number of packets received from both the server and collaborating clients, if any. Of all the four schemes, the delivery ratio increases with the number of generous clients. This is because generous clients are allowed to consume more energy, which enables them to receive more media packets from the server. Since the majority of clients are still selfish, the improvement is not prominent, except for "Master-Slave." In the homogeneous scenario, clients cannot form master-slave relationships when the type is 0.6. However, the presence of generous clients allows neighboring selfish clients to establish the proposed master-slave relationship. We note that each generous client can support all its neighbors. As the number of generous clients gradually increases, the streaming performance improves substantially. With 4 generous clients,

"Master-Slave" outperforms "Collaboration(2)." If there are 10 generous clients, "Master-Slave" and "Collaboration(5)" show comparable performance. This suggests that a small number of generous clients are enough to form effective master-slave relationships for collaborative media streaming.

Figure 8(b) shows the number of packets received via the server interface. If we increase the number of generous clients, we observe modest increasing trends for "Independent," "Collaboration(2)," and "Collaboration(5)." For "Master-Slave," the number of packets received via the server interface substantially decreases. As explained before, generous clients would receive more packets from the server, which leads to the increasing trends. However, the decreasing trend in "Master-Slave" is affected by another factor. Since generous clients would form master-slave relationships with their neighbors, the slaves do not need to receive media packets fro the server. As there are more slaves than masters, the overall result is that clients receive fewer media packets via the server interface. Furthermore, the results decrease quickly, especially in the low-end. This also indicates that a small number of generous clients would provide substantial improvement by establishing master-slave relationships for collaborative media streaming.

We then look at the number of packets sent via the peer interface. The results are shown in Figure 8(c). Unlike the previous two metrics, the number of generous clients does not show significant impact on "Independent," "Collaboration(2)," and "Collaboration(5)." Since clients do not utilize their peer interfaces in "Independent," the results are always zero. For "Collaboration(2)," and "Collaboration(5)," the introduction of generous clients would not form new peer-to-peer relationships. Although generous clients receive more media packets from the server, they are still the minority. This results in indistinguishable changes. On the other hand, each additional generous client would form a new master-slave relationship with

Figure 9. Effect of client mobility

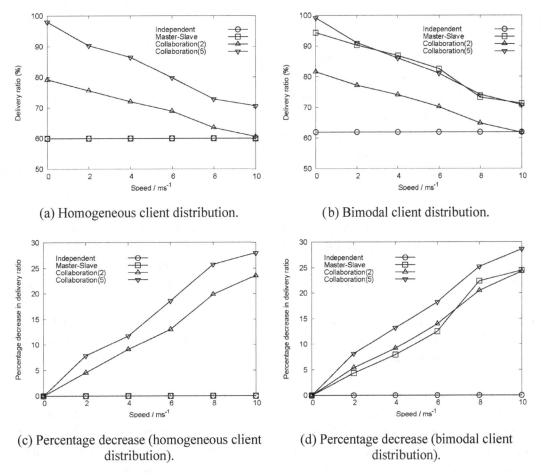

(a) Homogeneous client distribution.

(b) Bimodal client distribution.

(c) Percentage decrease (homogeneous client distribution).

(d) Percentage decrease (bimodal client distribution).

it neighbors. Thus, we observe the proportionally increasing trend for "Master-Slave." Moreover, the number of packets sent via the peer interface is maintained at a low level. This suggests that the proposed master-slave relationship is efficient in this bimodal client distribution scenario.

Figure 8(d) shows the amount of energy consumed in media streaming, which includes the energy cost of both server and peer interfaces. Similar to the homogeneous scenario, the results closely resemble those shown in Figure 8(b). This suggests that the introduction of heterogeneous clients does not have a major impact on energy consumption. In other words, receiving media

packets from the server interface is still the largest source of energy consumption. In particular, the proposed master-slave relationship allows selfish clients to receive media packets vi their peer interfaces from the masters. This substantially reduces the amount of energy consumed in media streaming. We can conclude that the proposed protocol for establishing master-slave relationships is effective in improving streaming performance in the heterogeneous scenario, where a small number of clients are generous. On the other hand, the presence of generous clients has little effect on the proposed protocol for establishing peer-to-peer relationships.

Effect of Client Mobility

In previous experiments, clients remained stationary throughout the entire streaming session. We now study the impact of client mobility on the delivery ratio of clients using the random way point model (Bettstetter, Resta & Santi, 2003; Yoon, Liu & Noble, 2003). Specifically, each client moves to a randomly chosen destination at a uniform speed of v ms $- 1$, where $v = 0, 2, 4, 6, 8, 10$. Upon arriving at the destination, the client remains stationary for 60s before moving to another destination. As discussed in the *Proposed Collaborative Media Streaming Protocols* section, both proposed relationships are stable where rational clients would not leave unilaterally. However, client mobility inevitably induces involuntary breakup of existing relationships. Figure 9 shows the effect of client mobility on the performance metrics.

Figure 9(a) shows the results for homogeneous client distribution, where the client type was kept at 0.6 and the number of clients was kept at 100. Since the server is assumed to cover the entire simulation area, client mobility has no effect on "Independent." As discussed earlier, there are no master-slave relationships when the client type is 0.6. Thus, we observe that "Master-Slave" is the same as "Independent." However, the performance of "Collaboration(2)" and "Collaboration(5)" de-

teriorates with increasing client mobility. This is because some existing relationships are broken as neighboring clients become out of range. These clients should rely on the server for all media packets before any new relationships are formed. As client mobility increases, the frequency of such involuntary breakup events becomes higher, which leads to the decreasing trend. To better visualize their performance differences, we plot the percentage decrease in Figure 9(c). We can see that "Collaboration(5)" is more severely affected by client mobility than "Collaboration(2)." This is because of the size of each relationship. If a client moves out of range, other clients in the same relationship would also be affected. Since each peer-to-peer relationship in "Collaboration(5)" consists up to five clients, client mobility affects "Collaboration(5)" more than "Collaboration(2)."

We changed to the bimodal client distribution, where clients can be selfish or generous. For generous clients, the type was set to 1.2. For selfish clients, the type was set to 0.6. There were 5 generous clients and 95 selfish clients. The results are shown in Figure 9(b). We observe that "Collaboration(2)" and "Collaboration(5)" show similar performance compared with the homogeneous scenario. On the other hand, the performance of "Master-Slave" is much different. As discussed earlier, the introduction of a small

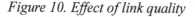

Figure 10. Effect of link quality

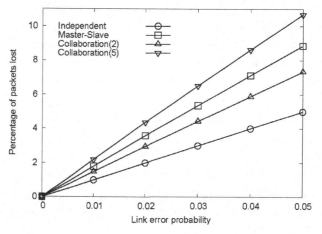

number of generous clients causes the formation of master-slave relationships. Each generous client acts as master and its neighboring clients act as slaves. With client mobility, masters and slaves may move out of range, which breaks the master-slave relationship. Thus, the performance of "Master-Slave" decreases with increasing mobility. Similarly, we plotted the percentage decrease in delivery ratio received in Figure 9(d). Although "Master-Slave" outperforms "Collaboration(2)," their rates of performance degradation are comparable. This indicates that master-slave relationships adapt well with mobile clients. We can conclude that the proposed protocols for establishing master-slave and peer-to-peer relationships maintain reasonable performance in moderate client mobility.

Effect of Link Quality

In previous experiments, the link quality was assumed to be perfect where there was packet loss. We relaxed this assumption and varied the link error probability from 0.01 to 0.05. Each wireless link, either server-to-client or client-to-client, was assigned with the same error probability. We chose the bimodal client distribution scenario with 5 generous clients and 95 selfish clients. Figure 10 shows a plot of the percentage of packets lost against the link error probability. For "Independent," clients receive all packets directly from the server. In other words, each packet traverses one server-client link only. Thus, the percentage of packets lost is the lowest. In a peer-to-peer relationship with two neighboring clients, each client receives some packets from the server and some other packets from its neighbor. Those packets received via the peer interface would suffer from higher loss because they should traverse two wireless links: server-to-client and client-to-client. Thus, we can see that the performance of "Collaboration(2)" is worse than that of "Independent." As for the master-slave relationships, the masters receive all packets from the server while the slaves receive

all packets from their masters. Since each master can support a number of slaves, we expect that the number of packets traversing two wireless links in "Master-Slave" is more than in "Collaboration(2)." Thus, "Master-Slave" suffers from higher loss. In "Collaboration(5)," each peer-to-peer relationship consists of one coordinator and up to four helpers. As discussed in the *Analysis of Proposed Collaborative Media Streaming* section, the coordinator receives packets from helpers and also delivers packets to them. As such, some packets traverse two wireless links: server-to-client; and coordinator-to-helper or helper-to-coordinator. Some other packets may traverse three wireless links: server-to-client, helper-to-coordinator, and coordinator-to-helper. Thus, the performance of "Collaboration(5)" is most affected by the link quality. In particular, when the error probability is 0.05, the percentage of packets lost exceeds 10%. To conclude, if the link quality becomes poor, clients should reduce collaboration to keep the loss at an acceptable level.

FUTURE RESEARCH DIRECTIONS

We discuss several future research directions as follows. For P2P media streaming in wireless networks, we envision that the combination of both structured and unstructured approaches would attract more attention. Existing hybrid P2P media streaming protocols focused on improving streaming performance in homogeneous environment. Each peer is considered to be identical with the same outgoing bandwidth and lifetime in the P2P network. However, we believe that it is important to consider the effect of heterogeneous peers. Specifically, peers often have different outgoing bandwidth constraints and do not stay in the P2P network for a fixed period of time. A hybrid protocol can better accommodate such heterogeneous peers. There are two major issues. First, we should provide incentives for those peers who participate in both structured and unstructured networks to contribute their outgoing bandwidth. This is because their contributions are crucial to the performance of hybrid P2P media streaming. Second, we should provide incentives for those peers who participate in both structured and unstructured networks to stay in the P2P network longer. This reduces the amount of maintenance overheads due to peer dynamics.

Most existing protocols focus on streaming of one media content only, i.e., single session. We believe that the next step is to consider the simultaneous streaming of more than one media content, i.e., multiple sessions. The reasons are two-folded. First, most media content providers are expected to deliver a variety of media content simultaneously, e.g., television broadcasting. Although each media content can be supported by an independent instance of P2P media streaming protocol, this implementation is not satisfactory. Second, some peers may not have sufficient incoming bandwidth to receive the media content at full rate. The server should provider some low-rate media content to these incapable peers. Thus, it is of great practical importance to consider the multi-session media streaming scenario. We envision that each peer can contribute outgoing bandwidth to more than one streaming session. Thus, we should devise a resource allocation algorithm to judiciously distribute the outgoing bandwidth of peers among different media streaming sessions. Specifically, peers who contribute more outgoing bandwidth can divert more resources to deliver popular media content. We believe that this could lead to the overall improvement in streaming performance.

In this chapter, we independently considered media streaming in wired and wireless networks. Another future research direction is to consider integrating media streaming in hybrid wireless networks with P2P media streaming in wired networks. The presence of wireless peers extends the reach of P2P media streaming, which creates new application scenarios. For example, the server may provide transcoding services to wireless peers with different energy consumption constraints.

Each wireless peer should pay the server for transcoding the media content. Alternatively, the server can delegate such transcoding services to some capable peers in the wired network. These peers convert the media content in a suitable format for wireless peers. Instead of paying the server, wireless peers should reward those wired peers providing the transcoded media content. This creates a market-like scenario for trading different resources between wired and wireless peers. On the other hand, wireless peers can improve the resilience of P2P media streaming because they provide different paths for distributing media packets. As such, both wired and wireless peers would benefit from the services provided by each other.

Finally, we should consider the effect of media streaming on other applications. It is assumed that the core network is not the performance bottleneck of media streaming. However, we cannot ignore its effect on other data traffic, e.g., HTTP, FTP traffic, etc. Specifically, it is desirable to have a rate control mechanism that allows routers to regulate the rate of streaming traffic. This could avoid overloading the core network, which leads to performance degradation to all traffic types. Alternatively, we can devise a novel resource reservation protocol that could accommodate media streaming traffic without excessively affecting other delay insensitive applications.

CONCLUSION

In this chapter, we first describe the advancement of wireless media streaming techniques, followed by a brief survey of state-of-the-art approaches. We observe that there are some deficiencies in existing approaches. We then propose two energy efficient protocols for collaborative media streaming in hybrid wireless networks, based on game theoretical concepts. Specifically, we consider a hybrid wireless network where each mobile client is equipped with two wireless network interfaces:

a server interface, and a peer interface. The server interface connects clients to the server while the peer interface allows communications among neighboring clients. The two interfaces exhibit different energy characteristics. We propose that neighboring clients utilize both interfaces to stream media content from the server to conserve their energy resources.

In our proposal, there are two collaborating relationships: master-slave relationship, and peer-to-peer relationship. For the master-slave relationship, the master retrieves media packets from the server and sends them to its slaves via the peer interface. On the other hand, a peer-to-peer relationship consists of one coordinator and at least one helper. Both the coordinator and helpers are responsible for retrieving media packets from the server. The coordinator gathers packets from individual helpers and subsequently delivers them to all other helpers. Our analysis shows that the relationships allow clients to share the energy cost of retrieving media content from the server. Furthermore, both relationships are stable when rational clients do not unilaterally deviate nor voluntarily leave as a group. We evaluated their performance in homogeneous and heterogeneous client distributions. Simulation results indicate that both relationships improve the streaming performance of clients without violating their energy consumption constraints.

REFERENCES

Andronache, A., Brust, M. R., & Rothkugel, S. (2006). Multimedia content distribution in hybrid wireless networks using weighted clustering. In *Proceedings of the 2nd ACM International Workshop on Wireless Multimedia Networking and Performance Modeling*.

Barbara, D., & Imielinski, T. (1994). Sleepers and workaholics: Caching strategies in mobile environments. In *Proceedings of the SIGMOD International Conference on Management of Data*.

Bettstetter, C., Resta, G., & Santi, P. (2003). The node distribution of the random waypoint mobility model for wireless ad hoc networks. *IEEE Transactions on Mobile Computing, 2*(3), 257-269.

Cao, G. (2002). Proactive power-aware cache management for mobile computing systems. *IEEE Transactions on Computers, 51*(6), 608-621.

Cao, G. (2003). A scalable low-latency cache invalidation strategy for mobile environments. *IEEE Transactions on Knowledge and Data Engineering, 15*(5), 1251-1265.

Cisco (2007). Cisco AIR-CB21AG technical specifications, from http://www.cisco.com

Chu, Y.-H., Chuang J., & Zhang, H. (2004). Considering altruism in peer-to-peer Internet streaming broadcast. In *Proceedings of the 14th International Workshop on Network and Operating Systems Support for Digital Audio and Video*.

Debnath, T., Cranley, N., & Davis, M. (2006). Experimental comparison of wired versus wireless video streaming over IEEE 802.11b WLANs. In *Proceedings of the Irish Signals and Systems Conference*.

Erman, J., Mahanti, A., Arlitt, M., & Williamson, C. (2007). Identifying and discriminating between web and peer-to-peer traffic in the network core. In *Proceedings of the 16th International Conference on World Wide Web*.

Feeney, L. M., & Nilsson, M. (2001). Investigating the energy consumption of a wireless network interface in an ad hoc networking environment. In *Proceedings of the 20th Annual Joint Conference of the IEEE Computer and Communications Societies*.

Feldman, M., Papadimitriou, C., Chuang, J., & Stoica, I. (2004). Free-riding and whitewashing in peer-to-peer systems. In *Proceedings of the ACM*

SIGCOMM Workshop on Practice and Theory of Incentives in Networked Systems.

GTRAN (2007). GTRAN DotSurfer 6210 technical specifications, from http://www.gtran.com

Gurun, S., Nagpurkar, P., & Zhao, B. Y. (2006). Energy consumption and conservation in mobile peer-to-peer systems. In *Proceedings of the 1st International Workshop on Decentralized Resource Sharing in Mobile Computing and Networking.*

Habib, A., & Chuang, J. (2004). Incentive mechanism for peer-to-peer media streaming. In *Proceedings of the 12th IEEE International Workshop on Quality of Service.*

Habib, A., & Chuang, J. (2006). Service differentiated peer selection: an incentive mechanism for peer-to-peer media streaming. *IEEE Transactions on Multimedia, 8*(3), 610-621.

He, Y., Lee, I., Gu, X., & Guan, L. (2005). Centralized peer-to-peer video streaming over hybrid wireless network. In *Proceedings of the IEEE International Conference on Multimedia and Expo.*

He, Z., & Zeng, W. (2006). Rate-distortion optimized transmission power adaptation for video streaming over wireless channels. In *Proceedings of the IEEE International Conference on Image Processing.*

Hefeeda, M., Habib, A., Botev, B., Xu, D., & Bhargava, B. (2003). PROMISE: Peer-to-peer media streaming using CollectCast. In *Proceedings of the 11th ACM International Conference on Multimedia.*

Henderson, T., Kotz, D., & Abyzov, I. (2004). The changing usage of a mature campus-wide wireless network. In *Proceedings of the 10th Annual International Conference on Mobile Computing and Networking.*

Jazayeri, M. (2007). Some trends in web application development. In *Proceedings of the International Conference on Software Engineering.*

Ji, X., Pollin, S., Lafruit, G., Moccagatta, I., Dejonghe, A., & Catthoor F. (2007). Energy-efficient bandwidth allocation for multi-user video streaming over WLAN. In *Proceedings of the IEEE International Conference on Acoustics Speech and Signal Processing.*

Keidar, I., Melamed, R., & Orda, A. (2006). EquiCast: Scalable multicast with selfish users. In *Proceedings of the 25th Annual ACM SIGACT-SIGOPS Symposium on Principles of Distributed Computing.*

Khan, S. U., & Ahmad, I. (2006). A pure Nash equilibrium guaranteeing game theoretical replica allocation method for reducing web access time. In *Proceedings of the 12th International Conference on Parallel and Distributed Systems.*

Korhonen, J., & Wang, Y. (2005). Power-efficient streaming for mobile terminals. In *Proceedings of the 15th International Workshop on Network and Operating Systems Support for Digital Audio and Video.*

Kothari, R., & Ganz, A. (2005). Archies: An end-to-end architecture for adaptive live MPEG-4 video streaming over wireless networks. In *Proceedings of the IEEE International Conference on Wireless and Mobile Computing, Networking and Communications.*

Li, J. (2006). Peer-to-peer multimedia applications. In *Proceedings of the 14th Annual ACM International Conference on Multimedia.*

Luo, H., Ramjee, R., Sinha, P., Li, L., & Lu, S. (2003). UCAN: A unified cellular and ad-hoc network architecture. In *Proceedings of the 9th Annual International Conference on Mobile Computing and Networking.*

Myerson, R. B. (1997). *Game theory: Analysis of conflict.* Harvard University Press.

Ngan, T.-W., Wallach, D. S, & Druschel, P. (2004). Incentives-compatible peer-to-peer multicast. In *Proceedings of the 2nd Workshop on the Economics of Peer-to-Peer Systems.*

Hara, K., Mitchell, A. S, & Vorbau, A. (2007). Consuming video on mobile devices. In *Proceedings of the SIGCHI Conference on Human Factors in Computing Systems.*

Ooi, W. T. (2005). Dagster: Contributor-aware end-host multicast for media streaming in heterogeneous environment. In *Proceedings of the 12th Annual Multimedia Computing and Networking.*

Osborne, M. J., & Rubinstein, A. (1994). *A course in game theory.* MIT Press.

Osborne, M. J. (2003). *An introduction to game theory.* Oxford University Press.

Pering, T., Agarwal, Y., Gupta, R., & Want, R. (2006). CoolSpots: Reducing the power consumption of wireless mobile devices with multiple radio interfaces. In *Proceedings of the 4th International Conference on Mobile Systems, Applications and Services.*

Sato, K., Katsumoto, M., & Miki, T. (2006). P2M-VOD: Peer-to-peer mobile video on-demand. In *Proceedings of the 8th International Conference on Advanced Communication Technology.*

Shida, T., Sato, T., Nakayama, H., Kosaka, H., & Sugiyama, K. (2007). Robust HD video stream transmission for wireless DTV. *IEEE Transactions on Consumer Electronics, 53*(1), 96-99.

Sen, S., & Wang, J. (2004). Analyzing peer-to-peer traffic across large networks. *IEEE/ACM Transactions on Networking, 12*(2), 219-232.

Sung, Y.-W., Bishop, M., & Rao, S. (2006). Enabling contribution awareness in an overlay broadcasting system. *ACM SIGCOMM Computer Communication Review, 36*(4), 411-422.

Yeung, M. K. H., & Kwok, Y.-K. (2005a). Wireless cache invalidation schemes with link adaptation and downlink traffic. *IEEE Transactions on Mobile Computing, 4*(1), 68-83.

Yeung, M. K. H., & Kwok, Y.-K. (2005b). A game theoretic approach to energy efficient cooperative cache maintenance in MANETs. In *Proceedings of the 16th IEEE International Symposium on Personal, Indoor and Mobile Radio Communications.*

Yeung, M. K. H., & Kwok, Y.-K. (2006a). A game theoretic approach to power aware wireless data access. *IEEE Transactions on Mobile Computing, 5*(8), 1057-1073.

Yeung, M. K. H., & Kwok, Y.-K. (2006b). On maximizing revenue for client-server based wireless data access in the presence of peer-to-peer sharing. In *Proceedings of the 17th IEEE International Symposium on Personal, Indoor and Mobile Radio Communications.*

Yin, L., & Cao, G. (2004). Adaptive power-aware prefetch in wireless networks. *IEEE Transactions on Wireless Communications, 3*(5), 1648-1658.

Yin, L., & Cao, G. (2006). Supporting cooperative caching in ad hoc networks. *IEEE Transactions on Mobile Computing, 5*(1), 77-89.

Yoon, J., Liu, M., & Noble, B. (2003). Random waypoint considered harmful. In *Proceedings of the 22nd Annual Joint Conference of the IEEE Computer and Communications Societies.*

Wen, G., Longshe, H., & Qiang, F. (2006). Recent advances in peer-to-peer media streaming systems. *China Communications, 4*(5), 52-57.

Chapter XI
Incentives for Resource Sharing in Ad Hoc Networks:
Going Beyond Rationality

Panayotis Antoniadis
Université Pierre et Marie Curie, Paris 6, France

ABSTRACT

The goal of this chapter is to analyze the incentive issues that arise in multi-hop ad hoc networks when their nodes are potentially mobile devices controlled by independent self-interested end-users. The author decomposes the problem into its economic and technological dimensions according to which he categorizes the numerous proposed solutions. He then analyzes certain drawbacks of the economics oriented approach and argues for the need to go beyond the rationality assumption. This is to exploit a variety of powerful more intrinsic, social, human motivations for encouraging participation and resource sharing in ad hoc networks. Existing successful online communities provide a good starting point for designing social software that can provide cross-layer social incentives for resource sharing. In this chapter, the author motivates this novel but challenging approach and provides some insights toward coming closer to its ambitious objective.

INTRODUCTION

For over a decade, mobile ad hoc networks (or MANETs) have been in the centre of attention of the networking research community. They have created significant anticipation for the new step in the telecommunications history: It is expected that people will be transformed to "smartmobs" that will self-organize in creating their own ad hoc communications networks to exchange all types of information, provide access to Internet gateways, socialize, and participate themselves or through their device in a large variety of peer-to-peer applications like file sharing and ubiquitous computing.

Yet until now this vision has not become a reality although significant progress has been made over the last years regarding the wireless technology (bluetooth, 802.11), the capabilities and resources of the portable devices, and the required protocols for routing, media access, and power control. Maybe a few more steps are required in order to reach the point to enable an interesting set of applications on top of a general multi-hop ad hoc network. But people are most probably the critical piece that is still missing: Users are the key component of a mobile ad hoc network because they are both the providers and the consumers of the service (and this is so at all layers of the system's architecture). In other words, MANETs are peer-to-peer (p2p) systems whose successful operation depends highly on the users' desire to participate and contribute the resources of their devices.

Participation and resource sharing are the main requirements for all p2p systems to bootstrap and survive. Significant part of ongoing research is devoted on the design of incentive mechanisms for resource sharing. However, in the case of mobile ad hoc networks this problem becomes more challenging due to the critical mass that is required for the creation of an operational ad-hoc network, the short time scales in which users might reside in the same place, and the often scarce resources that should be contributed (i.e. battery, processing power, and bandwidth). Additionally, more research is required in terms of application design to encourage participation, since the "killer application" seems to be still missing. Finally, one should take into account also psychological factors that are related to the fact that people are not used to this direct form of communication with strangers.

The most fundamental resource sharing issue in this context is packet forwarding. There is a wide variety of economic mechanisms proposed in the literature. They either assume the existence of a virtual or real currency management system or they follow a reciprocity-based approach that

adopts the notion of reputation in accounting for a user's past behavior (and provide rewards or punishment accordingly). In addition to packet forwarding, however, there are many more levels of cooperation in an ad hoc network. So, there is also work on incentive compatible topology formation and energy efficient routing, and incentives for cooperation at the lower layers of the network architecture (media access, and power control).

In general, there are two different dimensions in the problem formulation: the economic and the technological. The *economic dimension* is related to the conceptual mechanisms, the high-level rules of the system that are required to decide on certain levels of consumption and/or contribution for different users based on certain assumptions their utility, cost, and behavior (the economic model). The *technological dimension* is related to the technical means for enforcing the chosen incentive mechanism. That is, the mechanisms required to monitor and assess the behavior of users, to account for it over time, and implement the rewards and punishments prescribed by the incentive mechanisms according to each individual's behavior. Unfortunately, the constraints that are posed by technology in terms of enforcement are often the "bottleneck" in this environment, and the choices for the potential high-level incentive mechanisms become restricted.

In order to clarify the main ideas and concepts that are hidden behind these different approaches, the state of the art is presented as a function of the basic economic principles on which they are based, independently of the types of resources to be shared. Then the solutions for enforcement are analyzed separately from the corresponding economic mechanism in order to highlight their conceptual difference. However, there is criticism for the applicability of both the theoretical and practical dimension of the proposed solutions. We will support this criticism providing some additional arguments in an effort to convince the reader that a more holistic approach is required. More specifically, that the *inclusion of the applica-*

tion layer and the stimulation of intrinsic rather than extrinsic (rational) motivations of humans seem inevitable elements of the design of successful MANETs and wireless ad hoc networks in general.

The stimulation of such motivations is being studied today for encouraging participation in online communities like Flickr, Slashdot, and Wikipedia (Shirky, 2008). The term that summarizes better the tools used is the so-called *social software*. That is the user interface and feedback, the enabled user interactions, and the information management tools and rules that are put in place in order to support the activities of an online community. Current practice has shown that small details in the design of social software can have a significant impact on the success or failure (Erickson, 2005).

The main idea promoted in this chapter is to use similar social software techniques for the creation and operation of ad hoc networks. No specific solutions are proposed along these lines since integrated multidisciplinary work is required for such an approach to come to life. This chapter is a first step toward this direction. It summarizes existing research in the context of online communities, and provides insights on how this work can provide the basis for stimulating social motivations for participation and resource sharing in ad hoc networks (a cross-layer approach regarding incentives).

BASIC ECONOMIC CONCEPTS

One possible way to define an *incentive mechanism* is to consider it as a system rule, whose goal is to influence participating agents to behave in a certain manner, by rewarding or punishing their different decisions, aiming to reach a specific objective. In the presence of a benevolent social planner, the two most common objectives considered in economics are social welfare maximization (also called economic efficiency) and fairness.

Otherwise, profit maximization is also considered as an objective in commercial settings.

Social welfare is defined in economics as the sum of the utilities of the participants in a system consuming or using a certain amount of resources minus the cost for producing them. The *utility function* is an abstract construction that translates resources or services consumed to a satisfaction metric (or willingness to pay). Since it is different in principle for different people, the optimal allocation (provision) will assign a different share (requirement) for different users. The *equity* (or *fairness*) approach treats instead all agents the same in terms of utility and cost, and applies a specific fairness criterion based on observable only characteristics of agents. In the simplest case, each agent acquires or contributes exactly the same amount of resources (or if demand differs amongst agents, an agent should get more than others only if the demand of the latter is fully satisfied —see also the concept of max-min fairness in data networks, [Bertsekas & Gallager, 1992]). Notice that sometimes it is the inability to convey the true private information of agents that leaves the equity approach as the only alternative.

We could say that there are two extreme cases in resource management that are subject to an economic formulation: the *allocation* of a scarce resource and the *provision* of a public good. In the first case, one should decide whether and what percentage of a good of given predefined capacity (e.g., land) each agent should *consume*. In the second case, how much each agent should *contribute* for the provision of a pure public good, which then everybody will be able to enjoy without limitations (c.f., Figure 1). For example, in the case of resource allocation, maximizing social welfare means that agents with higher utility should acquire larger proportions of the finite resource. But in this case, people with low valuations could declare a higher value in order to get more than their "efficient" share. Alternatively, the equity approach would require that the resource be divided in equal pieces among all agents leading in general to inefficiency.

Given an incentive mechanism (or its absence) the agents participating in an economy of resource exchange, as it is an ad hoc network, have a certain set of strategies from which they can choose: the amount of resources produced and/or consumed, their participation level, and other choices depending on the problem (e.g., their mobility pattern in our case). Additionally, they might also need to decide on additional variables introduced by the corresponding incentive mechanism (e.g. a price or their cost declaration). Notably, agents' decisions will depend on their private information (utility and cost functions) and might change depending on the decisions of the other players. This is the definition of a *game* whose outcome is a *Nash equilibrium* if no agents wish to deviate from a certain state/strategy (e.g., Fundenberg & Tirole, 1992). The goal of an incentive mechanism is to enhance this game with the rules that will encourage the agents to choose strategies that will lead the system to the best possible equilibrium, according to the high-level objective and the constraints of the environment.

Before designing and evaluating such an incentive mechanism along these lines, one should first formulate the corresponding economic model, define the utility and cost functions, and describe the agents behavior in time. Obviously, the decisions taken and the assumptions made at this stage affect significantly the final outcome of the analysis and the effectiveness of the corresponding mechanism in practice. Between the two extremes presented before, there are a variety of resource allocation and provision problems for which achieving an efficient allocation is more or less difficult depending on the types of the goods (e.g., consumable vs. rivalrous), the existence of a central planner, and the assumptions and the structure of the game. In the following, we will analyze the ones related to our problem.

ECONOMIC PROBLEMS RELATED TO AD HOC NETWORKING

In a MANET, a user with her device becomes a *node* at different layers of the system architecture (physical, access, network, application, and

Figure 1. Social welfare maximization problems for the two extreme resource management problems

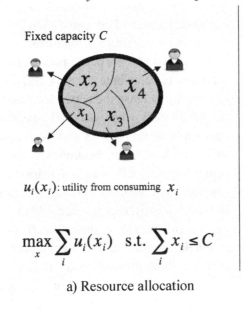

Fixed capacity C

$u_i(x_i)$: utility from consuming x_i

$$\max_x \sum_i u_i(x_i) \quad \text{s.t.} \quad \sum_i x_i \le C$$

a) Resource allocation

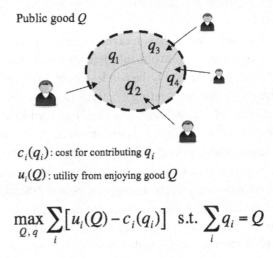

Public good Q

$c_i(q_i)$: cost for contributing q_i

$u_i(Q)$: utility from enjoying good Q

$$\max_{Q,q} \sum_i [u_i(Q) - c_i(q_i)] \quad \text{s.t.} \quad \sum_i q_i = Q$$

b) Resource provision

social). Her behavior at any layer can affect the operation of the others and the efficiency of the system in general. For example, the participation and location of these devices are subject to their owners' desire to participate (and for how much time) and their mobility, which depend on the application and social context. In the other direction, in order for the requirements of the application to be fulfilled, users should also obey the resource sharing decisions taken by the underlying protocols, although this might not be for their benefit, and contribute their possibly limited resources for supporting communications that belong to other users (e.g., battery and/or bandwidth). The latter is the main research question addressed in this chapter. Notably, the complexity of the problem and the many different layers of required cooperation have lead to numerous research papers being published the last decade on this topic (e.g., Srivastava et al., 2005; Marias et al., 2006). Most of the work is relevant for more general wireless ad hoc or mesh networks, whose nodes are not necessarily moving during the network operation, as for example in a meeting room, in a concert, or a neighborhood. So, we will use just the term ad hoc network whenever the mobility of the nodes does not play a significant role in the concept being discussed.

Resource Allocation

First, users must agree on certain levels of transmission power to avoid interferences and they should share efficiently the wireless medium. Both are problems of allocating a scarce resource. The increase of transmission power of one terminal increases the quality of its transmissions but increases also the level of interference, which has a negative effect on all transmissions. So, there is a maximum level of aggregated power that all terminals that reside in the same area can use, and if this total "power capacity" is not shared efficiently the resulting allocation could be unfair,

inefficient, or even detrimental, due to excessive interference.

Similarly, the broadcast nature of the wireless medium requires a certain level of cooperation from nodes wishing to access it. In particular, they must wait a random time before retransmitting when a collision occurs. Nodes that do not use the specified window from which this time is randomly selected, but a smaller one, could achieve higher rates at the expense of users who follow the protocol. Due to collision effects, however, this would also decrease the overall performance of the network.

Finally, when bandwidth and/or energy (battery) are limited, as is often the case, the total network capacity should be shared among competing users. But what makes this allocation problem more interesting is that the capacity of the network depends on the contributions of the potential consumers, which adds significant complexity to the economic modelling and analysis of the resulting game, as discussed in the following.

Resource Provision

At the network layer, users' available bandwidth will be reduced if they forward packets belonging to communications of other nodes. This problem becomes more prominent in MANETs where the consumable battery power (and often limited CPU) represents an additional significant constraint. This means that users participating in a MANET are asked to contribute certain (costly) resources in order to increase the network capacity.

Additionally, when users participate in peer-to-peer applications running on top of the network, such as file sharing, backup services, or grid computing, they will need to contribute additional resources (e.g., content, storage, CPU cycles, etc.). However, ideally, they would prefer to "free ride" on the contributions of their peers by consuming available resources and services without contributing anything themselves and thus avoiding the corresponding costs. This means that one should either dictate certain contribution levels (e.g., in the form of entry fees) or devise specific rewards for collaborative behavior. In economics, such rewards could be either monetary or a promised differentiated treatment at the allocation side (i.e., users that contribute more can consume more upon congestion).

The main contribution of this chapter is the categorization of such mechanisms proposed in the context of ad hoc networks. The reader is referred to Antoniadis (2006) for an overview of the work on incentives for other types of p2p systems.

Network Formation Game

The amount of resources contributed by a certain node in an ad hoc network highly depends on the specific topology and the routing decisions. But the creation of an ad hoc network is subject to the self-interested neighbor selection of the participating users. This means that an interesting network formation game is to be played among the nodes. The trade-off is that the addition of a "link" between two nodes in the network routing table is useful since it reduces the average number of hops toward all destinations but incurs a cost to one (or both) of the parties. It has been observed in the context of wired networks (Fabrikant et al., 2003; Corbo & Parkes, 2005) that in such scenarios the networks to be formed are not always efficient in terms of cost. The reason is that system-wide efficiency does not always coincide with personal objectives.

In addition to the creation of the network overlay (the topology) over which packets are forwarded, nodes can further influence the routing decisions by misreporting their private information (e.g., their available energy or achieved throughput), and thus minimize the amount of resource contributed for a given topology.

INCENTIVE MECHANISMS

Pricing

A standard approach for coordinating and regulating behavior is to use prices. When a price (a charge) is attached to the consumption of one unit of resource, the corresponding willingness to pay of an agent is considered an accepted measure of one's utility for that resource. So, the demand of a user facing a certain price for a certain resource "reveals" part of her utility function for that resource. Additionally, it brings profit to the producer.

But in an ad hoc network and in p2p systems in general, an incentive mechanism based on real currency is not always the most attractive approach for users and it is complex to implement (Jakobsson et al., 2003). Alternatively, one could consider the use of *virtual currency*, which corresponds to credits (tokens) that can be used only inside the system, thus enforcing users to contribute their own resources in order to consume (Ma et al., 2006). However, implementation issues still exist and the symmetric consumption/production required is a significant drawback in the case of ad hoc networks, where the effort required from different users for the efficient network operation depends on the topology.

In pure resource allocation problems, like the ones related to *power control* and *medium access control*, social welfare is maximized when the price for resource consumption is such that demand equals supply. Then those that value throughput more, they will be provided with a larger share, as they are willing to pay more for it. Yet, the problem is not so easy in the case of ad hoc networks. In the case of power control for example, consumption (e.g., increase of node's transmission power) is costly for the node itself due to battery constraints. Additionally, in multi-hop transmissions, the final throughput depends on the quality of the worst link in the path, and thus the gains from cheating are not obvious. The pricing schemes proposed in this context concern mainly the one-hop case: a number of mobile devices competing for access to a base station. Additionally, most of them actually treat pricing (fixed or dynamic) as a means for the system designer to coordinate devices and reach the optimal level of operation in a distributed way (e.g., Sarayadar et al., 2002; Alpcan et al., 2001; Chen & Niu, 2005; MacKenzie & Wicker, 2003; Wang & Krunz, 2006). Notice also that instead of setting a price on the parameters that affect throughput (i.e., backoff window or power) one could set a price directly on the throughput achieved in order to encourage the correct behavior at the packet forwarding level.

Prices can also be used to encourage users to reveal important information truthfully. Such information includes on the one hand their utility for a certain service in order for the resources to be allocated efficiently. A way to achieve this result is to adjust the unit price until demand equals capacity. Alternatively one could use *mechanism design* (MD). In mechanism design, prices are the outcome of a game to be played with the agents. The goal is to design the game that will encourage users to reveal their true private information (i.e. their utility or their cost depending on the specific problem). This process is necessary when price tuning is not feasible and one need to know the private information of the users in an one-shot game. So, in mechanism design users declare their information through *bidding* knowing before hand the algorithm that will decide the winner and the price to be paid. An *auction* is a standard example of such a mechanism. In a similar way, mechanism design could be also used in order to encourage the truthful declaration of their costs for providing a service (e.g. packet forwarding), in order to choose the topology and routing tables that optimize performance as discussed next.

Finally, pricing could be used for profit maximization in scenarios in which the ad hoc network can provide a service to a central entity. The most relevant scenario along these lines is

content distribution. In such cases, setting a price on the amount of content forwarded by a certain user would give her the incentive to participate and contribute her resources. The exact amount of these resources would be the ones that maximize the revenue minus the corresponding cost.

In the following, we present the different pricing approaches proposed in the context of ad hoc networks (see Table 1 for a summary including also the reciprocity-based approaches discussed next).

Free Markets

The first and second fundamental theorems of welfare economics imply that the allocation resulting from perfect competition in a free market, in which producers freely set the price of a resource unit, maximizes social welfare and no agent has an incentive to change her behavior (e.g. Varian, 1992). And this without requiring firms to know anything about the tastes of individual consumers. Neither do consumers have to know anything about the production technology of firms.

However, such an approach is rather complex to implement in a peer-to-peer system. In most cases, free markets are proposed when users are either consumers or providers of resources. For example, Neely (2007) considers users as independent from the network nodes and proposes a free market model for price setting and proves that at equilibrium all nodes will have non-negative profits.

Fixed Pricing

The simplest pricing approach is to define a fixed price for each resource unit consumed (e.g., a forwarded packet). Salem et al. (2003) and Zhong et al. (2003) propose the use of such fixed prices (per packet) that are tuned by a central point. In addition to an incentive for resource contribution prices in these works are calculated in a way to give also the correct incentives for reporting of successful or not packet forwarding resembling to mechanism design (see the following section).

Goemans et al. (2006) propose a fixed pricing approach in the case of content distribution according to which the users participating in the distribution of a content item share the corresponding profit.

Dynamic Pricing

When packet forwarding is the main resource to be charged, there are important results from Kelly et al. (1998) that extended the concept of price tuning until demand equals supply in a network setup (congestion-based pricing). They provided an important theoretical framework, which inspired numerous studies on network pricing (e.g., Courcoubetis & Weber, 2003).

In a symmetric setup, when users are both the consumers and the producers of the basic service, Marbach & Qiu (2003) generalized the work of Kelly et al. (1998) and allowed each node to decide both for the levels of production and consumption. (In the original model consumers and producers were assumed to be independent entities). Crowcroft et al. (2003) and Xue et al. (2003) have also proposed the application of Kelly's framework in the context of mobile ad hoc networks but without the aforementioned generalization. However, such dynamic prices would create uncertainty in the system that can discourage user participation.

Mechanism Design

In the context of auction design for single items, Vickrey (1961) devised the celebrated second-price sealed-bid auction, the Vickrey auction: Bidders submit simultaneously sealed bids for the item on sale; the highest bidder wins the item, but unlike standard sealed-bid auctions, the winner pays the *second-highest* bid. The bids determine only whether the corresponding bidder wins or not, and only by bidding his true value can ensure that

he will win exactly when he is willing to pay the price. So, under this mechanism it is a dominant strategy for bidders to report their values truthfully and the resulting outcomes are efficient (the item is bought by the bidder that values it the most). Since Vickrey's original contribution, his auction design has been melded with the Clarke (1971) and Groves (1973) design for public good problems and thus called Vickrey-Clarke-Groves or VCG mechanism.

Based on the principle that the final price is independent from the users' declarations, numerous variations of the VCG mechanisms are being proposed for solving a variety of problems in networking. For example, Feigenbaum et al. (2002) propose a strategyproof mechanism of the VCG family for shortest paths in BGP routing that induces truthful revelation of transit costs. But despite its very attractive and unique characteristics the VCG mechanism has some very serious weaknesses (Ausubel & Milgrom, 2005). The most important of them is that it is not *budget balanced*. That is, the system designer should "pay" the agents in order for them to reveal their private information.

Many approaches for the case of ad hoc networks are based on the VCG principle and the work of Feigenbaum et al. (2002) aiming to design incentive-compatible mechanisms for energy-efficient routing (the network formation game). That is, to design a mechanism that will encourage users to declare their true energy costs in order for the routing algorithm to choose the optimal paths (those that minimize the total energy costs). Anderegg & Eidenbenz (2003) was the first approach to propose a VCG mechanism in this context called Ad hoc VCG. Zhong et al. (2005) included in the problem formulation that the fact that users depend on others to estimate their own costs (their type). They also included the packet forwarding game proposing a solution in the spirit of Zhong et al. (2003). Ji et al. (2006) included the notion of time diversity and proposed a game with multiple stages using reverse second-price auctions where the routers bid to attract the senders. Finally, Eidenbenz et al. (2008) included in their model the option of the sender acting also strategically and simplified the price computation.

But unfortunately the drawbacks of the VCG mechanism apply in this case as well, since the main trade-off between budget balance and efficiency always exist, as demonstrated for example if one compares the two different proposals of Anderegg et al. (2003) and Eidenbenz et al. (2008) (see also arguments made by Maille & Tuffin, 2007).

Reciprocity

In the case of p2p systems resource provision and allocation problems are often modeled as evolutionary games. The incentive in this case is the individual strategy of each peer when faced with a service request: to cooperate (to provide service) or to defect. That is, the goal is to achieve a certain level of cooperation without having to trade resource units (e.g., forwarded packets). So, this approach is simpler to implement and is less strict concerning the exact levels of consumption and contribution. But it does not take into account

the possibly different utilities and costs of different peers. The goal is to encourage cooperation in a more abstract sense. In a simple cooperative two-player game known as *prisoner's dilemma* each player has two possible strategies: either to *Cooperate* or to *Defect*. The fact that in a (Cooperate, Defect) situation the cooperator loses more than if both had defected and the defector has larger payoff than if both had cooperated, makes the Nash equilibrium of the one-shot game to be that both players defect even though the benefit of both cooperating is greater.

For the repeated version of the game, Axelrod (1984) has shown that the *generous tit-for-tat* strategy, which always cooperates on the first move (it is optimistic) and reciprocates what the other player did on the previous move thereafter, outperforms all other strategies. More formally, tit-for-tat is an *evolutionary stable* strategy. Evolutionary game theory studies the equilibria of games where agents change their strategies over time, as they interact with other agents with possibly other strategies, trying to maximize their own net benefit (e.g. mutating to strategies that achieve higher benefits). Evolutionary stable are the strategies that prevail throughout this process.

There is significant work on this game-theoretic approach on cooperation in the context of ad hoc networks. One part focuses on the theoretical aspects providing formal description of the game and analyzing the corresponding equilibria under different assumptions (Srinivasan et al., 2003; Urpi et al., 2003; Félegyházi et al., 2006). More recent work by Jaramillo & Srikant (2007) addresses the problem of noise and errors in detection and analyze a 2-player game-theoretic model based on a more flexible version of the tit-for-tat mechanism showing that it can achieve full cooperation under the standard assumptions made by similar approaches (see also Ng & Seah (2008)).

On the other hand, there are many proposals focusing on the most practical aspects of detection, accounting, and punishment, which are discussed in the following section. Notice that the easier

Table 1. Summary of incentive mechanisms

Incentive Mechanism	Price Computation	Problems involved
Fixed prices	Central	Power control Medium Access Packet forwarding Content distribution
Dynamic prices	Central or Distributed	Packet forwarding Medium access Power control
Free markets	Distributed	Content distribution Packet forwarding
Mechanism design	Central or Distributed	Energy-efficient routing
Reciprocity	N/A	Packet forwarding
Barter economy	N/A	Packet forwarding

to enforce reciprocity-based approach is the one that dictates that resources should be exchanged directly between two or more involved parties, in the way it is performed for example by BitTorrent (Cohen, 2003). In economics this is called a *barter economy*, which is a special case of a fixed price economy without memory and thus no need for enforcement. However, the applicability of this approach depends largely on the context. But-tyán et al. (2007) propose a simple barter-based cooperation scheme for delay tolerant wireless networks. The application considered is content exchange between mobile users (e.g., tourist info). A similar approach is proposed by Antoniadis & Courcoubetis (2006) for a specific type of social mobile p2p applications.

ENFORCEMENT

The goal of an incentive mechanism is to improve the efficiency of the system by rewarding or punishing good or bad behavior. But the very first requirement in order to achieve this goal is to be able to characterize the behavior of a user as good or bad (monitoring). How to record this information for future use is a task of the accounting process. Then, devising the correct rewards and punishments as a function of the recorded accounting information would hopefully lead the system to the desirable equilibrium.

We could say that the goal of the economic part of an incentive mechanism is to make users declare or reveal their private information for managing resources efficiently, while the objective of the enforcement part is to reveal the history of their actions in order to implement the prescribed by the incentive mechanism's decisions.

Monitoring - Detection

The detection of possible misbehavior is a challenging problem in an ad hoc network because in many cases nodes cannot monitor the actions of

their neighbors (cannot overhear their transmissions) and identify the exact point of failure when a packet is dropped along a path. That is, there is what is called in economics *hidden action* (see Feldman et al., 2005 for a theoretical analysis of this issue in ad hoc networks). In the following, we present the main tools proposed in the literature for *locally* detecting that a node is failing to forward packets requested by its neighbors.

Watchdogs

Marti et al. (2000) introduced the term *watchdog* for the process of checking whether the next hop towards a destination actually transmitted the requested packet. This check is done by overhearing the channel when using the promiscuous mode available in many Wi-Fi implementations (passive acknowledgement). However, it assumes the wireless links are symmetric which is not always the case and is susceptible to false negatives or false positives. This is so because on the one hand the failure to overhear the requested transmission could be due to several reasons (e.g., the node moved out of range) and on the other hand even if transmitted we cannot be sure it reached the receiver (e.g., due to a collision).

Anonymous Tests

The Catch protocol (Mahajan et al., 2005) proposes the uses of anonymous broadcast packets sent by a number of *testers* to test the behavior of a *testee*. Assuming that the majority of users are following the rules, this protocol can identify misbehaving nodes and isolate them. There is no proof, however, that there are not sophisticated misbehavior strategies that can mislead this detection mechanism.

High-Level Checks

Another way to monitor the behavior of a next-hop node is to assess the performance of the flows passing through that node at a higher layer. For example, Rogers & Bhatti (2007) propose the use of unforgeable acknowledgements to verify that a packet reached the destinations (see also references therein for similar approaches). In the same spirit, for detection through observation of the consequences of misbehavior at the lower layers, statistical methods have been proposed to check whether neighboring nodes cheat, for example concerning the backoff window value (Rong et al., 2006).

Accounting

Local detection is not enough because nodes in a MANET move over time. It would be important for the effectiveness of an incentive mechanism if nodes would be accountable for their decisions after they change neighbors as well.

Trusted Hardware

The simplest accounting mechanism is the one that trusts each peer, actually her client software running on her machine, to keep a record of her own transactions. In the best case, just this information could be used to enforce the correct behavior of the corresponding peer. This could be possible under the existence of tamper-proof hardware at each node. As assumed for example in the approach of Buttyán & Hubeaux (2003), where for each packet transmitted by the source node, a credit counter is decreased by an integer amount equal to the number of intermediate hops from the source to the destination. But, of course, in most cases this mechanism is insecure since peers have the incentive to alter their records for their own benefit by altering their application, for example, or even their device – hacked versions could be made easily available in the Internet (e.g. kazaa hack, fast browsers).

Currency

Virtual currency could be seen as accounting information. Mechanisms based on virtual currency are often called *prevention* mechanisms since they dictate by construction an explicit relation between consumption and contribution and thus, if successfully enforced, they prevent misbehavior. The most important challenge is to implement the management of the payments. In this case, a trusted third party is required to ensure the reliability of the accounting information (the tokens or credits owned by each user). This and inflation/deflation issues are considered as the most important weaknesses of such approaches.

Reputation

When the issuing and management of virtual currency is not feasible or when pricing is not considered the appropriate incentive mechanism, reputation mechanisms (Resnick et al., 2000), originally introduced in distributed marketplaces, such as eBay, have been also considered as a candidate accounting mechanism. They are relevant in the context of all types of p2p applications providing a more qualitative way to represent the levels of a user's contribution in the past. More specifically, a user's reputation could be seen as a way to aggregate his past behavior into a single value. This value is in general a function of the individual users' *ratings* based on the corresponding user's observed behavior. So, reputation could be considered as a distributed counter for one's behavior computed and stored in other node's devices.

The first challenge is that information regarding the effort exerted by a user as a function of the transaction outcome is *hidden*. But the most critical challenge in the implementation of a reputation mechanism is distributed identity management. In this case it is difficult to stop misbehaving users to create new or even multiple identities and thus "whitewash" their possibly bad reputation

(Feldman et al., 2004). When the computation of reputation depends on other people's ratings then another possible attack is the creation of multiple identities for boosting one's reputation, the sybil attack (Douceur, 2002). Newsome et al. (2004) provides a nice taxonomy of possible sybil attacks in wireless ad hoc networks and possible defense mechanisms.

This is one of the reasons many approaches perform the computation of reputation only locally, using only first-hand information to estimate the reputation of a node and punish him accordingly (Bansal & Baker, 2003; Marti et al., 2000). When one aims to reach a global consensus the challenge is exactly to ensure that the reputation values are computed correctly (i.e. based on truthful ratings). Among the most cited proposals in this context are CONFIDANT (Buchegger & LeBoudec, 2002), SORI (He et al., 2004), and CORE (Michiardi & Molva, 2002) in which users are evaluated, have a reputation, both as raters and resource providers.

However, the fact that users are treated as both the selfish agents who wish to maximize their net benefit and the ones responsible for sustaining collaboration by rating and rewarding/punishing other peers creates complex theoretical games which can only be evaluated through simulations. This has led to a plethora of proposed reputation-based mechanisms for ad hoc networks and p2p systems in general (Mundinger & Le Boudec, 2006) whose comparison and formal evaluation is a challenging and open research question.

Rewards and Punishments

Differentiated Treatment

An obvious way to reward good behavior is by providing better than best effort service to well behaved users. However, the notion of reward is not considered in most existing approaches, with a few exceptions (e.g., Raghavan & Snoeren, 2003). One of the reasons is the difficulty

in providing differentiated services in a wireless ad hoc network.

Isolation (Local vs. Global)

Most research work considers punishments for encouraging collaboration. The most intuitive and simple punishment for a non-cooperative node is to be denied service. However, when a node is punished by a neighbor it does not mean that it will not have access to the ad hoc network. One needs to coordinate this punishment to completely isolate the misbehaving node, which is not a trivial task (Mahajan et al., 2005).

Jamming

Levin (2006) argues that global isolation might not be an incentive compatible punishment strategy to be followed by all users and introduces jamming as a possible means to punish misbehavior. In this work jamming corresponds to the flooding of the medium with broadcast packets that would disallow all nodes in the range of the broadcast to send any packets. Clearly, this is a much more effective punishment strategy but then noise in detection of misbehavior becomes a critical factor that should be addressed (see also the work of Jaramillo & Srikant (2007) and the more general study of noise in games by Wu & Axelrod (1995).

Cagalj et al. (2005) propose a detection and punishment scheme for MAC-level misbehavior. Personalized jamming is used to punish users that do not follow the prescribed backoff mechanism. Whenever the node to be punished transmits a packet, another node sends a packet at the same time in order for a collision to occur. It would be interesting to check whether such a "cross-layer" punishment scheme would be meaningful in order to address misbehaviors at different layers of the network architecture.

However, note that jamming could be used also by misbehaving nodes or by well-behaved nodes that got punished by mistake. This and other many more possible strategies are not considered in the simple game-theoretical models studied in the literature, which assume the existence of some very basic and often myopic types of users (e.g., always cooperate, always defect).

CRITICISM OF THE ECONOMIC APPROACH

Over the last decade there is significant progress for addressing the complexity behind the creation of a collaborative ad hoc network, both in theory and in practice. However, it seems that we are not yet close to real life implementations that will bring this vision from theory to reality. Notably, the most fundamental incentive for a user to be part in the creation of an ad hoc network is the incentive to participate. Only when there is significant value to be gained by the existence of this network a user would be "sensitive" to incentive mechanisms for encouraging resource sharing at the network layer. This is especially so, since most of the incentive mechanisms presented before introduce an additional burden for participation both practical and psychological.

Huang et al. (2004) argue that incentive mechanisms should be deployed only after the required critical mass is being built, as they can be themselves a serious disincentive for participation, especially in this specific context, where their enforcement poses significant challenges. But even when considered as candidate mechanisms for future situations, the current approaches have some important drawbacks. In the following, we analyze them distinguishing between two main types of applications of ad hoc networking: asymmetric and symmetric, where the notion of symmetry refers to the value of the network.

Asymmetric Case

In the asymmetric scenario, a MANET offers connectivity service either to a content provider or to a user wishing to have access to the Internet through a base station of a wireless Internet provider. In the first case there is a single source and in the second a single destination for all communications. Clearly, in order to agree to contribute their resources for achieving the required connectivity nodes should be somehow rewarded.

Given the clear value attached to the corresponding service, the use of real currency for rewarding nodes per number of packets forwarded is a natural choice. But although the requirements for ensuring the secure distribution of payments and accounting are well understood, the potential benefits from cheating increase also the incentives for illegal efforts to devise ways to circumvent them. Moreover, the prices should be lower than existing alternatives and there should be a minimum level of QoS offered. This is rather difficult if one takes into account the inherent unreliability of the wireless medium, the dynamic environment due to potential mobility, the large number of involved users to be rewarded, and the cost for the secure management of payments itself.

Additionally, per-usage pricing schemes are in general unattractive due to the mental burden that they require (Odlyzko, 2001). There is a clear users' preference toward simple, flat pricing policies. The fact that most telecom providers follow such policies and the failure of p2p systems with usage-based pricing mechanisms (like Mojonation) is a good indication that this is a general phenomenon that it is unlikely to be different in the case of ad hoc networks. Especially since the value of such networks becomes less and less obvious as the alternatives for cheap (or even free) communications are constantly increasing. However, simple flat policies are not suitable in this environment due to the heterogeneity of effort that is required from different nodes depending on the network topology and the demand.

Symmetric (p2p) Case

The asymmetry of required contributions is the most important challenge for symmetric, p2p, scenarios as well. In this case, users have identical roles and collaboratively build a general purpose ad hoc network which: 1) will allow them to discover content, services, or humans of interest residing in the same physical area, and/or 2) will enable them to reach specific destinations and communicate with them. Reciprocity-based reputation mechanisms or closed economies based on virtual currency are the most appropriate candidates for providing incentives. But the fact that the effort required by different users varies significantly depending on the topology, the demand and mobility patterns is an important drawback of incentive mechanisms that relate consumption with contribution in the same way for all users.

To see why, consider for example the case of a user at the edges of the network. If her position in the topology remains stable she will never be asked to forward any packet and thus will not be able to acquire any credits to satisfy her demand. Similarly, under a reputation-based mechanism, a neighboring (rational) node would not accept to forward the packets of a node at the edge of the network that cannot reciprocate. Also, a node in the centre of the network would receive a large number of packet forwarding requests and would accumulate more credit than needed to satisfy her own demand, which would be a good reason for her to stop providing service.

The only case when the assumptions made in the corresponding theoretical work to address the aforementioned issue would hold in practice is when with high probability all users will take different positions in the network topology either due to intense mobility (see Félegyházi et al., 2004) or because of repeated interactions over longer time scales. But then in both cases the reliability of the accounting becomes a very challenging task.

Additionally, existing work ignores important issues concerning the behavior of users in this setting and more specifically that their mobility pattern could be part of their strategy (Figueiredo

et al., 2004). For example, users could choose to move to the outskirts of the network to avoid being asked to forward packets and have their reputation ruined if they do not.

Finally, the lack of objective detection methods, the cost of the incentive mechanism itself, and additional psychological factors (e.g. the inconvenience of not having enough tokens when one needs them) are some additional practical constraints that raise significant criticism for the applicability and effectiveness of the proposed economic or game-theoretic approaches.

INTRINSIC MOTIVATIONS AND SOCIAL SOFTWARE

Motivation

Economic approaches assume that humans behave rationally, which is a debatable assumption of the theory of economics. Indeed, there are many cases where people seem to actually contribute without expecting any tangible reward. P2p file sharing systems, SETI@home, and wikipedia are probably the most characteristic examples of such systems whose important value is built on the voluntary contributions of highly motivated users. Clearly, there are other types of incentives that motivate such users to participate and contribute. And interestingly, in most cases it is just a small percentage of members that belong to this category but whose contributions are so high that build a critical mass that is enough to attract additional small contributions of a very large number of less motivated members (Shirky, 2008). The fact that social incentives do not limit resource provision to the levels of the required consumption is a tremendous advantage because motivated users' demand is much less than their potential contribution.

Mobile ad hoc networks are systems in which we expect a high level of heterogeneity in terms of expected contribution, because of the network topology and that certain users might have much more powerful devices than others. This heterogeneity is taken into account in game theoretic models as the one proposed by Lee et al. (2007), according to which a backbone network would be formed without incentive mechanisms just because of the waiting cost, that would force the most powerful devices to voluntarily form a backbone network over which all communication can take place. However, these approaches still follow a rational approach in terms of motivation and do not consider the potential intrinsic motivations that have proven to play a significant role in increasing participation and resource sharing in p2p systems. Additionally, the flexibility of social incentives in terms of expected contribution and optimistic nature provides a low cost for entry, which is important for less motivated users. Such users are likely to be discouraged in cases when more strict economic incentive mechanisms are in place.

Finally, the fact that one could always provide the means to users to protect their own consumption (e.g., a threshold on the battery consumption below which they will stop participating), could reduce significantly the costs of resource sharing and thus constitute social incentives more effective and economic ones unnecessarily strict and complicated.

From Economics to Social Psychology

In psychology, there are numerous theories aiming to understand the motivations based on which humans decide the amount of effort put for the accomplishment of different tasks. One of the most recognized human motivation theories, the *self-determination theory* (Ryan & Deci, 2000) distinguishes between extrinsic (external) and intrinsic (internal) motivations. On the one hand, extrinsic motivations are tangible rewards promised upon the accomplishment of a task. On the other hand, intrinsic motivations refer to an

individual's desire to perform a task for its own sake. Of course, there are also motivations that lie between these two extremes. According to the self-determination theory, people experience more self-determined (intrinsic) types of motivation when the activities they participate in make them feel that they have *autonomy* (the power to make their own choices), *competence* (the ability to effectively perform their task), and *relatedness* (authentic social connections with others).

But there is evidence (Deci et al, 1999) that extrinsic motivations could *crowd-out* the intrinsic ones as illustrated in Figure 2. Although the extent to which this is true is a traditional controversial topic between economics and psychology (see, for example, Kruglanski (1978)) it is clear, that self-determined types of motivation are desirable because they are associated with more positive experiences and persistent motivation to participate.

There is a large variety of predominantly intrinsic motivations, derived by users themselves and the community as a whole that could be exploited in our context. Self-esteem, self-efficacy, community spirit, emotional connections, social norms, interest, and fun are only some of them. Numerous theories focus on a subset of such motivations. For example, the expectancy theory (Vroom, 1964) calculates humans' motivation as a function of their belief in their success (expectancy), of the reward they expect to get from it (instrumentation), and of the value they place on this reward (valence). The *sense of community* (SOC) (McMillian & Chavis, 1986) highlights the importance of the community for encouraging people to contribute. More specifically, it identifies four important attributes that contribute toward this end: feelings of membership, feelings of influence, integration and fulfilment of needs, and shared emotional connections.

But how one could stimulate these motivations? Some possible mechanisms discussed in the social sciences literature include feedback, goal setting, social recognition, interest, social-

Figure 2. Extrinsic motivations can crowd-out intrinsic ones (© 2008, LIP6, used with permission)

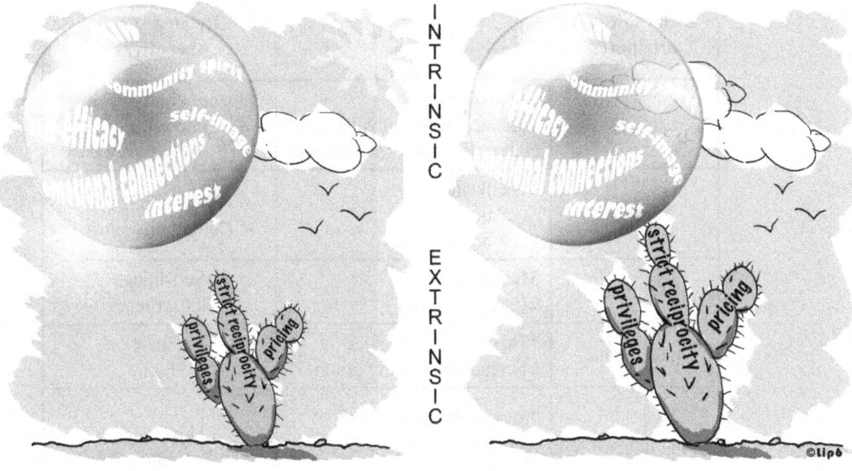

izing opportunities, community identity, personal responsibility (accountability) (see Tedjamulia et al. (2005) and references therein).

Network-Aware Social Software

In the case of online communities the means to provide this type of incentives are restricted to the interface offered by the corresponding community management software, the social software (Preece, 2000; Beenen et al., 2004). Many successful online communities owe their success to some clever details incorporated in their software to reward cooperative behavior (see Erickson, 2005 and references therein). For example, some of the functionality that can significantly affect participants' behavior and the success of the corresponding community include the following:

- The user interface (e.g., its usability and the "signals" provided for correct behavior)
- The way users can create relationships and interact with each other.
- The means they have to represent themselves.
- The feedback they receive concerning their popularity and activity on their page.
- The definition of different privileges/char-

acterizations according to their behavior.
- Content rating and filtering.

The challenge for exploiting these techniques in ad hoc networks is clearly the addition of the technological perspective. In order to achieve this goal one needs first to design the network layer in a way to provide the required information and control interface to the application, which will be now responsible for the provision of the suitable cross-layer incentives (Antoniadis et al., 2008). Second, at the application layer, a way to expose the network activity and make it part of the social activities should be devised. We propose in the following a categorization of possible cross-layer social incentives based on their architectural properties (see also Table 2).

Static. Incentives encoded in the software that do not depend on the user's behavior. For example, the wording used for the description of a community or the user interface. Such incentives would aim mainly to stimulate intrinsic motivations related to the community spirit.

Feedback. Incentives based on local accounting information with a local effect. For example, a message from the system about the importance of a user's contribution or visualization techniques could be enough to stimulate the self-efficacy motivation.

Table 2. Examples of social software techniques for encouraging network resource sharing

Social software attributes	Examples	Related social incentives
Static	Express vision Indicated expected value Highlight collaborative aspect	Community spirit Interest, fun Self-efficacy
Feedback	Visualization Statistics Personal messages	Self-efficacy Community spirit
User image	My devices My contribution	Self-image Self-efficacy
Interactions	"Thank you" messages My resource sharing group	Socialization Fun
Community rules	Top contributors Advanced roles Personal visibility	Self-image Self-efficacy

User image. The image of the user related to her contribution at the network level is crucial for building a *technologically-enhanced* social image of the user. This image will depend on her device, her behavior as a node of the ad hoc networks she participates, etc. Notably, the user image is comprised by her *home page* as seen by visitors, the representation of a user in other users' home pages, and her global image at a community level discussed to follow. How this image is affected according to her contribution at the network layer is a critical aspect of the proposed cross-layer incentive mechanisms.

User-to-user interactions. A nice example of such social incentives is the sending of "thank you" messages between users exchanging services. Additionally, one could imagine new types of relationships being introduced for users exchanging services that could form also excuses for socialization, and further stimulate user motivations for participation and resource sharing.

Community rules. This category includes the enforcement of community rules such as assignment of advanced roles to specific users, exclusion of misbehaving members, and creation of "top contributors" list. This is the most chal-

lenging category of incentives since it requires some sort of consensus between all community members.

But the most important challenge for stimulating motivations related to the user community is the fact that in the case of MANETs there is not always the time for building the required social context. However, one could think of approaches that inherit the social context created in a more static web-based online community (like Facebook) where all the above incentive mechanisms would be valid. In other words, in ad hoc networks there are two levels of community: a spontaneous short-term one, comprised by the users being part of an ad hoc network, and a long-term one including both physical and virtual interactions of the community members. How to combine the representation of these two types of communities into the corresponding social software is a very interesting research question in this context.

Note that the aforementioned are generic proposed features of network-aware social software. Additional case-specific cross-layer incentives should be incorporated in the application design. For example, one could imagine creative applications that encourage users to move toward a direction that would increase the performance of the network.

CONCLUSION

The goal of this chapter is to clarify the basic economic concepts behind the different solutions that have been proposed for encouraging resource contribution in user owned ad hoc networks, and to identify the major challenges that have to be addressed in order for this vision to become a reality. We argue in favour of departing from the economic approach to a more optimistic, and less formal, way to address the problem: investing on intrinsic, social motivations rather than rational ones, by exposing the resource sharing process to the application layer. This will both encourage resource sharing and also increase the value of the application itself creating feelings of solidarity and trust in an otherwise unknown environment.

The weakness of this approach is that candidate solutions will be difficult to be formally modelled and evaluated. The analytical tractability rather than the suitability in practice of economic approaches might be actually one of the reasons that they are so thoroughly studied and experimented with. But perhaps the time has come for the networking science to accept or even encourage methodologies and practices inspired from social sciences, and to create the required links between the applications and the networking protocols.

Existing online communities have demonstrated the power of social software in motivating users, which provides a concrete way to encode and study social motivations for network resource sharing. Moreover, a vast amount of data is available, which can be exploited to identify in more depth the most critical elements of social software and understand how they affect human behavior in terms of participation and resource sharing. Experimenting with real users on the effect of different approaches on network-aware social

software design is the problem on which research efforts should be concentrated, rather than on theoretical economic models with questionable impact and applicability.

ACKNOWLEDGMENT

This work has been partially supported by the IST European project WIP under contract 27402 and by the RNRT project Airnet under contract 01205. The author is grateful to Benedicte Le Grand and Marcelo Dias de Amorim for numerous inspiring discussions and contributions in research work related to this chapter. Thanks must also go to LIP6's graphic artist, Frédéric Delvalle, for his original drawing illustrating extrinsic and intrinsic motivations.

REFERENCES

Alpean, T., Basar, T., Srikant, R., & Altman, E. (2001). CDMA uplink power control as a noncooperative game. In *Proceedings of the 40th IEEE Conference on Decision Control.*

Anderegg, L., & Eidenbenz, S. (2003). Ad hoc VCG: A truthful and cost-efficient routing protocol for mobile ad hoc networks with selfish agents. In *Proceedings of the 9th Annual International Conference on Mobile Computing and Networking (MOBICOM).*

Antoniadis, P. (2006). Economic modelling and incentive mechanisms for efficient resource provision in peer-to-peer systems. Unpublished doctoral dissertation, Athens University of Economics and Business.

Antoniadis, P., & Courcoubetis, C. (2006). The case of multi-hop peer-to-peer implementation of mobile social applications. In *Proceedings of the International Conference on Systems and Networks Communication (ICSNC'06).*

Antoniadis, P., Le Grand, B., & Amorim, M. D. (2008). Socially-motivated wireless neighborhood communities. In *Proceedings of the 3rd International Workshop on Wireless Community Networks*.

Ausubel, L. M., & Milgrom, P. R. (2005). *The Lovely but lonely vickrey auction*. MIT Press.

Axelrod, J. 1984. *The evolution of cooperation*. New York: Basic Books.

Bansal, S., & Baker, M. (2003). Observation based cooperation enforcement in ad hoc networks. *Stanford University Technical Report*.

Beenen, G., Ling, K., Wang, X., Chang, K., Frankowski, D., Resnick, P., & Kraut, R. (2004). Using social psychology to motivate contributions to online communities. In *Proceedings of the ACM conference on Computer supported cooperative work*.

Bertsekas, D., & Gallager, R. (1992). *Data networks*. Englewood Cliffs, New Jersey: Prentice-Hall.

Buchegger, S., & LeBoudec, J.-Y. (2002). Performance analysis of the CONFIDANT protocol: cooperation of nodes — fairness in dynamic ad hoc networks. In *Proceedings of the IEEE/ACM Symposium on Mobile Ad Hoc Networking and Computing (MobiHOC)*.

Buttyán, L., & Hubaux, J.P. (2003). Stimulating cooperation in self-organizing mobile ad hoc networks. *ACM/Kluwer Mobile Networks and Applications (MONET), 8*(5).

Buttyan, L., Dora, L., Felegyhazi, M., & Vajda, I. (2007). Barter-based cooperation in delay-tolerant personal wireless networks. In *Proceedings of the IEEE International Symposium on World of Wireless, Mobile and Multimedia Networks (WoWMoM)*.

Cagalj, M., Ganeriwal, S., Aad I., & Hubaux, J-P. (2005). On selfish behavior in CSMA/CA networks. In *Proceedings of the IEEE INFOCOM*.

Chen, Q., & Niu, Z. (2005). A game-theoretical power and rate control for wireless ad hoc networks with step-up price. *IEEE Transactions on Communications, E-88B*(9).

Clarke, E. (1971). Multipart pricing of public goods. *Public Choice, 1*, 17-33.

Cohen, B. (2003). Incentives build robustness in BitTorrent. In *Proceedings of the Workshop on Economics of Peer-to-Peer Systems*.

Corbo, J., & Parkes, D. (2005). The price of selfish behavior in bilateral network formation. In *Proceedings of the ACM PODC*.

Courcoubetis, C., & Weber, R. R. (2003). *Pricing communication networks: Economics, technology and modelling*. Wiley Europe.

Crowcroft, J., Gibbens, R., Kelly, F., & Ostring, S. (2003). Modelling incentives for collaboration in mobile ad hoc networks. In *Proceedings of WiOpt'03: Modeling and Optimization in Mobile, Ad Hoc and Wireless Networks*.

Deci, E., Koestner, R., & Ryan, R. (1999). A meta-analytic review of experiments examining the effects of extrinsic rewards on intrinsic motivation. *Psychological Bulletin, 125*(6), 627-668.

Douceur, J. 2002. The sybil attack. In *Proceedings of the 1st International Workshop on Peer-to-Peer Systems*.

Eidenbenz, S., Resta G., & Santi, P. (2008). The COMMIT protocol for truthful and cost-efficient routing in ad hoc networks with selfish nodes. *IEEE Transaction on Mobile Computing*, 2008.

Erickson, T. (2005). Sustaining community: Incentive mechanisms in online systems. In *Final Report of the Group 2005 Workshop*.

Fabrikant, A., Luthra, A., Maneva, E., Papadimitriou, C., & Shenker, S. (2003). On a network creation game. In *Proceedings of the ACM PODC*.

Feigenbaum, J., Papadimitriou, C., Sami, R., & Shenker, S. (2002). A BGP-based mechanism for lowest-cost routing. In *Proceedings of the ACM PODC*.

Feldman, M., Papadimitriou, C., & Chuang, J. (2004). Free-riding and whitewashing in peer-to-peer systems. In *Proceedings of the ACM PINS*.

Feldman, M., Chuang, J., Stoica, I., & Shenker, S. (2005). Hidden-action in multihop routing. In *Proceedings of the ACM Conference on Electronic Commerce*.

Félegyházi, M., Hubaux, J.-P., & Buttyán, L. (2004). Equilibrium analysis of packet forwarding strategies in wireless ad hoc networks – the dynamic case. In *Proceedings of the WiOpt'04: Modeling and Optimization in Mobile, Ad Hoc and Wireless Networks*.

Félegyházi, M., Hubaux, J.-P., & Buttyán, L. (2006). Nash equilibria of packet forwarding strategies in wireless ad hoc networks. *IEEE Transactions on Mobile Computing, 5*(5), 463-476.

Figueiredo, D. R., Garetto, M., & Towsley, D. (2004). *Exploiting mobility in ad hoc networks with incentives* (Computer Science Tech. Rep. 04-66).

Fundenberg, D., & Tirole, J. (1992). *Game theory*. Cambridge: The MIT Press.

Goemans, M. X., Li, L., Mirrokni, V. S., & Thottan, M. (2006). Market sharing games applied to content distribution in ad hoc networks. *IEEE Journal on Selected areas in Communications, 24*(5).

Groves, T. (1973). Incentives in teams. *Econometrica, 41*, 617-663.

He, Q., Wu, D., & Khosla, P. (2004). SORI: A secure and objective reputation-based incentive scheme for ad hoc networks. In *Proceedings of the IEEE Wireless Communications and Networking Conference*.

Huang, E., Crowcroft, J., & Wassell, I. (2004). Rethinking Incentives for Mobile Ad Hoc Networks. In *Proceedings of the ACM SIGCOMM workshop on Practice and theory of incentives in networked systems*.

Jakobsson, M., Hubaux, J.-P., & Buttyan, L. (2003). A micro-payment scheme encouraging collaboration in multi-hop cellular networks. *Financial Cryptography*.

Jaramillo, J. J., & Srikant, R. (2007). DARWIN: Distributed and adaptive reputation mechanism for wireless ad hoc networks. In *Proceedings of the 13th Annual ACM International Conference on Mobile Computing and Networking*.

Ji, Z. J., Yu, W. A., & Liu, K. J. R. (2006). An optimal dynamic pricing framework for autonomous mobile ad hoc networks. In *Proceedings of the IEEE INFOCOM*.

Kelly, F., Maulloo, A., & Tan, D. (1998). Rate control for communication networks: Shadow prices, proportional fairness and stability. *Journal of Operational Research Society, 49*(3), 237-252.

Kruglanski, A. (1978). Issues in cognitive social psychology. *The hidden cost of reward: New perspectives on the psychology of human motivation*. New York: John Wiley.

Lee, S., Levin, D., Gopalakrishnan, V., & Bhattacharjee, B. (2007). Backbone construction in selfish wireless networks. In *Proceedings of the ACM Sigmetrics*.

Levin, D. (2006). Punishment in selfish wireless networks: A game theoretic analysis. In *Proceedings of the Workshop on Network Economics (NetEcon)*.

Ma, R. T.B., Chiu, D.-M. Lui, J. C.S, Misra, V., & Rubenstein, D. (2006). A budget-balanced and price-adaptive credit protocol for MANETs. *Electrical Engineering*.

MacKenzie, A.B., & Wicker, S. B. (2003). Stability of multipacket slotted aloha with selfish users and perfect information. In *Proceedings of the IEEE INFOCOM*.

Mahajan, R., Rodrig, M., Wetherall, D., & Zahorjan. J. (2005). Sustaining cooperation in multi-hop wireless networks. In *Proceedings of the Second Symposium on Networked Systems Design and Implementation (NSDI '05)*.

Maille P., & Tuffin, B. (2007). Why VCG auctions can hardly be applied to the pricing of inter-domain and ad hoc networks. In *Proceedings of the 3rd EuroNGI Conference on Next Generation Internet Networks*.

Marbach, P., & Qiu, Y. (2005). Cooperation in wireless ad hoc networks: A market-based approach. *IEEE/ACM Transactions on Networking, 13*(6), 1325-1338.

Marias, G. F., Georgiadis, P., Flitzanis, D., & Mandalas, K. (2006). Cooperation enforcement schemes for MANETs: A survey. *Wireless Communications and Mobile Computing, 6,* 319-332.

Marti, S., Giuli, T.J., Lai, K., & Baker, M. (2000). Mitigating routing misbehaviour in mobile ad hoc networks. In *Proceedings of the ACM MOBICOM*.

McMillian, D.W., & Chavis, D.M. (1986). Sense of community: A definition and theory. *Journal of Community Psychology, 14*(1), 6-23.

Michiardi, P., & Molva, R. (2002). CORE: A collaborative repudiation mechanism to enforce node cooperation in mobile ad hoc networks. In *Proceedings of the Sixth IFIP Conference on Security Communications, and Multimedia*.

Mundinger, J., & Le Boudec, J.-Y. (2006). Reputation in self-organized communication systems and beyond. In *Proceedings of the Interperf '06: Proceedings from the 2006 workshop on Interdisciplinary systems approach in performance evaluation and design of computer & communications systems*. ACM Press.

Neely, M.J. (2007). Optimal pricing in a free market wireless network. In *Proceedings of the IEEE INFOCOM*.

Newsome, J., Shi, E., Song, D., & Perrig, A. (2004). The sybil attack in sensor networks: Analysis & defenses. In *Proceedings of the 3rd International Conference on Information Processing in Sensor Networks*.

Ng, S.K., & Seah, W.K.G. (2008). Game-theoretic model for collaborative protocols in selfish, tariff-free, multihop wireless networks. In *Proceedings of the IEEE INFOCOM*.

Odlyzko, A. (2001). Internet pricing and the history of communications. *Computer Networks, 36,* 5-6, 493-517.

Preece, J. (2000). *Online communities: Designing usability supporting sociability*. John Wiley & Sons Ltd.

Raghavan, B. & Snoeren, A. C. (2003). Priority forwarding in ad hoc networks with self-interested parties. In *Proceedings of the Workshop on Economics of Peer-to-Peer Systems*.

Resnick, P., Zeckhauser, R., Friedman, E., & Kuwabara, K. (2000). Reputation systems. *Communications of the ACM, 43*,12.

Rogers, M. & Bhatti, S. (2007). A lightweight mechanism for dependable communication in untrusted networks. In *Proceedings of the 37th Annual IEEE/IFIP International Conference on Dependable Systems and Networks*.

Rong, Y., Lee, S-K., & Choi, H-A. (2006). Detecting stations cheating on backoff rules in 802.11 networks using sequential analysis. In *Proceedings of the IEEE INFOCOM*.

Ryan, R. M., & Deci, E. L. (2000). Intrinsic and extrinsic motivations: Classic definitions and new directions. *Contemporary educational psychology, 25,* 54-67.

Salem, N. B., Buttyán, L., Hubaux, J.-P., & Jakobsson, M. (2003). A charging and rewarding scheme for packet forwarding in multi-hop cellular networks. In *Proceedings of the IEEE/ACM*

Symposium on Mobile Ad Hoc Networking and Computing (MobiHOC).

Saraydar, C. U., Mandayam, N. B., & Goodman., D. J. (2002). Efficient power control via pricing in wireless data networks. *IEEE Transactions on Communications, 50*(2).

Shirky, C. (2008). *Here comes everybody: The power of organizing without organizations.* Penguin Press.

Srinivasan, V., Nuggehalli, P., Chiasserini, C., & Rao, R. (2003). Cooperation in wireless ad hoc networks. In *Proceedings of the IEEE IN-FOCOM.*

Srivastava, V., Neel, J., MacKenzie, A. B., Menon, R., DaSilva, L. A., Hicks, J. E., Reed, J. H., & Gilles, R. P. (2005). Using game theory to analyze wireless ad hoc networks. In *Proceedings of the IEEE Communications Surveys and Tutorials, 7*(2005), 46-56.

Tedjamulia, S. J. J., Dean, D. L., Olsen, D. R., & Albrecht, C. C. (2005). Motivating content contributions to online communities: Toward a more comprehensive theory. In *Proceedings of the 38th Hawaii International Conference on System Sciences.*

Urpi, A., Bonuccelli, M., & Giordano, S. (2003). Modeling cooperation in mobile ad hoc networks: A formal description of selfishness. In *Proceedings of the 1st Workshop on Modeling and Optimization in Mobile, Ad Hoc and Wireless Networks.*

Varian, H. (1992). *Microeconomic analysis.* Norton.

Vickrey, W. (1961). Counterspeculation, auctions, and competitive sealed tenders. *Journal of Finance, 16*(1), 8-37.

Vroom, V. (1964). *Work and motivation.* John Wiley and Sons.

Wang, F., & Krunz, M. (2006). GMAC: A game-theoretic MAC protocol for mobile ad hoc networks. In *Proceedings of the WiOpt '06: Modeling and Optimization in Mobile, Ad Hoc and Wireless Networks.*

Wu, J., & Axelrod R. (1995). How to cope with noise in the iterated prisoner's dilemma. *Journal of Conflict Resolution, 39*(1), 183-189.

Xue, Y., Li, B., & Nahrstedt, K. (2003). Price based resource allocation in wireless ad hoc networks. In *Proceedings of the 11th International Workshop on Quality of Service.*

Zhong, S., Chen, J., & Yang, Y.-R. (2003). Sprite: A simple, cheat-proof, credit based system for mobile ad hoc networks. In *Proceedings of the IEEE INFOCOM.*

Zhong, S., Li, L. E., Liu, Y. G., & Yang, Y. R. (2005). On designing incentive-compatible routing and forwarding protocols in wireless ad hoc networks: an integrated approach using game theoretical and cryptographic techniques. In *Proceedings of the ACM MOBICOM.*

Section V
Security

Chapter XII
Key Management for Dynamic Peer Groups in Mobile Ad Hoc Networks

Johann van der Merwe
University of KwaZulu-Natal, South Africa

Dawoud Dawoud
University of KwaZulu-Natal, South Africa

ABSTRACT

Group communication in mobile ad hoc networks (MANETs) generally occurs in the form of dynamic peer groups (DPGs). This chapter reviews the existing group key management schemes for DPGs, found in conventional networks, with respect to their suitability for MANETs. The schemes are uniquely categorized based on their underlying key establishment mechanisms and group topologies. Each group is introduced by presenting the most promising scheme belonging to the subset. The discussions reveal the strengths and weaknesses of the existing schemes and identify the challenges in designing group key management schemes compatible with the unique characteristics of generic MANETs.

INTRODUCTION

Mobile ad hoc networks (MANETs) allow users to establish communication without any fixed or pre-existing infrastructure. The network therefore has no base stations, access points or remote servers. Nodes that are within each others transmission range communicate directly, while relaying the messages for those too far apart. The

mobility of the nodes can lead to 'rapidly changing' (dynamic) network topologies. Nodes do not have any relationships prior to network formation due to the nature of the applications of MANETs (van der Merwe et al., 2007).

Generic MANETs are created solely by the end-users for a common purpose in an unplanned, i.e. ad hoc fashion. In contrast to conventional networks the users therefore cannot bootstrap the required security associations with the assistance of a priori shared information on their nodes. This unique property demands distributed collaborative protocols that enable nodes to establish security mechanisms without the assistance of a centralized online Trusted Third Party (TTP).

Many researchers have already proposed peer-to-peer key management schemes that are suitable for self-organized and authority-based MANETs (van der Merwe et al., 2007). In contrast, the available literature contains very few group key management schemes that are designed specifically for MANETs. Authors normally adapt group key management schemes for conventional networks to suite the unique characteristics of MANETs.

The military and commercial applications of MANETs incorporate many group-oriented applications (van der Merwe et al., 2007). The primary subdivision of group key management schemes emerges from the variety of different application dependent group settings that exist in practice. In Figure 1, the two main group key management settings are indicated within the dotted lines, namely:

- Group key management for centrally managed, non-collaborative groups
- Group key management for dynamic peer groups (DPGs)

Large groups, found for example in internet multicast applications, are normally non-collaborative and hard to control on a peer basis (Steiner et al., 2000). They therefore have a structured hierarchy and exhibit one-to-many broadcast communication patterns (Steiner et al., 2000; Kim et al., 2004). The control structure is maintained by a centralized TTP, chosen prior to network formation.

DPGs tend to be relatively small collaborative groups (with membership in the order of a hundred) where all group participants have a symmetric relationship and must therefore be treated equally

Figure 1. Dimensions of group key management

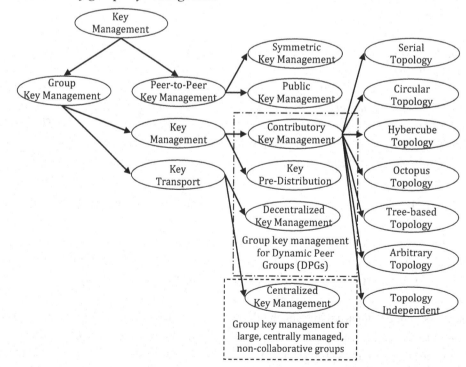

(Steiner et al., 2000). Such systems accordingly have no central point of control. This means that special roles, such as a group controller, are also not fixed prior to group formation, but allocated to any group member during and after group formation. These roles must be assigned based on group policy and must be orthogonal to the key management scheme (Steiner et al., 2000).

DPGs have many-to-many communication patterns and are dynamic in membership, i.e. members join and leave at random. Since a common cryptographic key must be shared between group members at all times, the dynamic membership makes key management protocol design complex as the computational and communication overhead on the network has to be kept to a minimum (Kim et al., 2004). Dynamic membership result in group key agreement protocol suites that accommodate initial key agreement (IKA) and auxiliary key agreement (AKA) operations (Steiner et al., 2000). IKA refers to the key agreement during the first group formation or group genesis, while AKA includes all subsequent key agreement operations. The most common AKA operations are illustrated in Figure 2 (Steiner et al., 2000).

Investigations within the available literature have shown that group communication in MA-NETs will generally occur in the form (or take on the properties) of DPGs. Considering the characteristics and applications of MANETs, as detailed in (van der Merwe et al., 2007), the dynamic nature of group communications in MANETs as nodes join or leave the network becomes apparent. Secure key management with the ability to respond to these changes in group membership is at the centre of providing network security for DPGs.

The main objective of this chapter is to analyze the existing group key management protocols for DPGs with respect to their suitability for MANETs.

A fundamental function of key management schemes is the establishment of keying material to facilitate secure communication, that is, it is

Figure 2. Common auxiliary key agreement operations

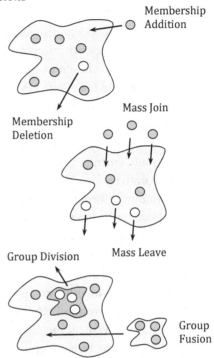

the first step towards protecting the confidentiality, integrity and availability of information. Key establishment is a process whereby a shared secret (session/symmetric key) becomes available to two or more communication entities, for subsequent cryptographic use (Menezes et al., 1996). The type of key establishment on which the group key management scheme is constructed, can be used to make a distinction between group key management schemes. As illustrated in Figure 1, group key management schemes can either use key transport or key agreement to establish shared keying material between group members:

- In a group key management scheme based on key transport, a centralized authority or TTP shares a unique secret with each group member. The TTP or designated group controller generates a session key and secretly transfer it to the other group members (Steiner et al., 2000; Menezes et al., 1996). The case where a single entity (TTP or key server) generates and distributes keys to the group members is defined as centralized group key distribution (Kim et al., 2004). The case where any group member is dynamically chosen as group controller to generate and distribute keys to the other group members is defined as decentralized group key distribution (Kim et al., 2004).

• In a group key management scheme based on key agreement, the session key is derived collaboratively by all group members as a function of information contributed by, or associated with the members, such that no member can predetermine the resulting shared key (Steiner et al., 2000; Menezes et al., 1996). If the individual contribution of each group member remains computationally secret from all other parties (even when any subset of the members collude and use their shares in an attempt to learn the individual secrets of fellow group members) then the scheme is called a contributory key agreement scheme. In (Steiner et al., 2000) contributory key agreement is defined as a protocol that gives a group key $K = H(N_1;\dots;N_n)$ as output, where $H(.)$ is a collision resistant one-way function and N_i is a secret key share randomly chosen by the ith group member.

A common offline TTP can also pre-distribute initial keying material to group members prior to network formation. These are referred to as key pre-distribution schemes. Group members can then collaborate on group formation and use the initial keying material to establish a shared group key.

The chapter focuses in particular on group key management schemes for DPGs in conventional networks due to their possible relationship to schemes that would be suitable for MANETs. It should however be clear that a group key management scheme designed for DPGs does not necessarily adhere to all the requirements of MANETs. The unique characteristics of MANETs, in particular the dynamic network topology and strong symmetric relationship between nodes, impose some additional constraints on group key management protocols that renders most of the existing schemes for conventional networks impractical.

Investigations within the available publications have shown that the current key establishment protocols for DPGs can be uniquely classified into the following subsets:

1. **Key Agreement:** Contributory Key Agreement
   a. Serial topology;
   b. Circular topology;
   c. Tree-based topology;
   d. Arbitrary topology;
   e. Hypercube topology;
   f. Octopus topology;
   g. Topology independent; and
   h. Star topology.
2. **Key Agreement:** Key Pre-distribution.
3. **Key Transport:** Decentralized Key Distribution.

The categorization of group key management schemes for DPGs is also presented in Figure 1. Subsets-1a to 1h are based on the topology formed and/or maintained by the protocol participants. The topology is forced upon the group members by the construction method used to obtain a desired group key form, i.e. the structure formed by the group members is determined by the order in which protocol participants perform operations on intermediate keying material or is determined by the order in which the participants generate intermediate keying material. The keying material is operated on or generated in such a way that when these values are combined in a predefined manner, the resulting group key will be in the desired form and will contain a unique random contribution associated with each group member.

As aforementioned, group key management protocols for MANETs share several properties with those suitable for DPGs. Besides the subsets of contributory key management, DPGs can also use group key management schemes that fall under key pre-distribution (Subset-2) as a subset of key agreement and decentralized key distribution (Subset-3) as a subset of key transport (see Figure 1).

In the subsequent sections, each of the aforementioned subsets (Subset-1a to Subset-1h, Subset-2 and Subset-3) will be introduced by presenting a prominent group key management scheme as representative of the subset. A separate discussion following the introduction of each subset is given. The discussions focus on the subsets' suitability for providing secure and efficient group key management schemes for MANETs. It is hoped that based on this work other researchers will have a view of all the subset variations and be able to propose schemes that takes the dependencies and consequent design constraints into consideration. At the end of the chapter references for further reading are provided such that the reader can apply the analysis approach advocated in this chapter to these group key management schemes.

The rest of the chapter is organized as follows: In *Contributory Key Agreement: Serial Topology* section, the Cliques protocol suite (Steiner et al., 2000) is presented to introduce group key management schemes based on a serial topology. The *Contributory Key Agreement: Circular Topology* section introduces the Ingemarsson (ING) protocol (Ingemarsson et al., 1982) to represent schemes with circular or ring topologies. The *Contributory Key Agreement: Hypercube Topology* section shows how (Becker & Wille, 1998) organize nodes in a hypercube topology to satisfy the lower bound on round complexity for contributory key agreement protocols. In *Contributory Key Agreement: Octopus Topology* section, group key agreement schemes with nodes structured in an octopus topology is considered by introducing the Octopus protocol proposed by (Becker & Wille,

1998). The *Contributory Key Agreement: Tree-based Topology* section introduces tree-based schemes by looking at the Tree-based Group Diffie-Hellman (TGDH) protocol suite (Kim et al., 2004). The *Contributory Key Agreement: Arbitrary Topology* section shows how group members in an arbitrary network topology can establish a shared key using the Arbitrary Topology Generalization of Diffie-Hellman (AT-GDH) initial key agreement protocol. In *Contributory Key Agreement: Star Topology* section, a star-based topology is considered where a group controller collects and distributes the shares of members in the group key. The *Contributory Key Agreement: Topology Independent Schemes* section presents and extends the initial key agreement protocol by (Burmester & Desmedt, 1994a) based on a broadcasting system to introduce topology independent schemes. The *Key Pre-distribution schemes* section presents key pre-distribution schemes by discussing the Distributed Key Pre-distribution Scheme (DKPS) (Chan 2004). In *Decentralized Key Distribution* section, the last subset of group key management schemes for DPGs is considered by looking at a modification of the Centralized Key Distribution (CKD) protocol suite (Amir et al., 2000). By randomly assigning the responsibility of group controller to any group member, the CKD scheme can be used as a suitable representative of decentralized key distribution schemes. The *Performance Analysis* section analyzes the efficiency of the group key management protocol suites for DPGs that consider both IKA and AKA operations. Finally, the chapter is concluded.

A good understanding of MANETS and suitable peer-to-peer key management protocols are required before considering group key management schemes (van der Merwe et al., 2007). Knowledge of 2-party and 3-party key agreement protocols is also a prerequisite (Diffie & Hellman, 1976; Dutta & Barua, 2005; Menezes et al., 1996).

CONTRIBUTORY KEY AGREEMENT: SERIAL TOPOLOGY

The first effort to extend the II-party Diffie-Hellman (DH) key exchange protocol (Diffie & Hellman, 1976) to a group setting was proposed by (Ingemarsson et al., 1982) followed by (Burmester & Desmedt, 1994a). Later (Steiner et al., 1996) proposed a natural extension of the II-party case to n-parties. These protocols evolved to become the Cliques protocol suite (Steiner et al., 2000), which was the first complete key agreement scheme that incorporated protocols for both IKA operations and the most important AKA operations (see Figure 2). The basic idea of the protocols is that the shared key is never transmitted over the network. Instead, a list of partial keys (that can be used by individual members to compute the group secret) is sent. One member of the group, normally called the group controller, is charged with the task of building and distributing this list. The controller is not fixed and has no special security privileges.

The notation that will be used in subsequent text is given as follows. For mathematical background and explanation of terms, such as "primes", the book by (Menezes et al., 1996) will provide a starting point.

n — Number of protocol participants.

i, j, k, d — Indices of group members $\in (1; n)$.

M_i — i-th group member.

M_* — All group members.

p, q — Two large primes, such that $q|(p-1)$.

G — Cyclic subgroup of Z_p with order q.

α — Generator of G.

N_i — Random secret generated by Mi ($N_i \in_R Z_q$).

S — Subsets of $\{N_1, ... N_n\}$.

$\prod(S)$ — Product of all elements is the set S.

K_n — Shared group key between n members.

K — Shared group key between n members where n is obvious.

K' — New shared group key after auxiliary key agreement.

The Cliques protocol suite includes the following protocols:

Cliques Initial Key Agreement: IKA.1

The generic n-party DH protocol (Steiner et al., 1996) is in principle almost identical to the original DH II-party protocol (Diffie & Hellman, 1976). Members agree a priori on G and a generator α of G. For key agreement each member chooses its own secret random number N_i. The generic protocol is based on a distributive computation

Figure 3. IKA.1 Algorithm – Case of a group with 4 members

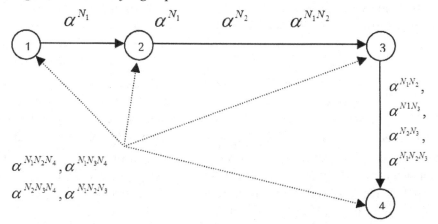

of a subset: $\{\alpha^{\prod^{(S)}} | S \subset \{N_1, N_2, ..., N_n\}\}$. From $\{\alpha^{N_1 \cdots N_{i-1} N_{i+1} \cdots N_n}\}$ member M_i can compute the group key as:

$$K = \{\alpha^{N_1, N_2 \cdots N_n}\} \tag{1}$$

The first initial key agreement protocol, IKA.1, as presented in (Steiner et al., 2000), reduces the number of rounds of the generic case by ordering the group participants in a serial topology; in the upflow stage each member M_i computes i intermediate values with i - 1 exponents and one cardinal value containing i exponents. For M_i the cardinal value will be: cardinal value = $\alpha^{N_1 \cdot N_i}$ which becomes $\alpha^{N_1 \cdot N_{n-1}}$ for M_n. M_n is thus the first member that computes $K_n = \alpha^{N_1 \cdots N_n}$ and in the final stage broadcasts all the intermediate values to the rest of the group which enable the other group members to also compute K.

In summary, IKA.1 allows group members $n \geq 2$ to establish a conference key between them over an insecure channel. The result is a group key K, secure against passive adversaries. The protocol participants agree a priori on an appropriate prime p and generator α of G.

IKA.1 consists of two stages, upflow and broadcast.

Stage–1. (Upflow): Round i; $i \in [1, n-1]$
$M_i \rightarrow M_{i+1} : \{\alpha^{\prod(N_k | k \in [1,i] \wedge k \neq j)} \big| j \in [1,i], \alpha^{\prod(N_k | k \in [1,i])}\}$

Stage–2. (Broadcast): Round n
$M_* \leftarrow M_n : \{\alpha^{\prod(N_k | k \in [1,n] \wedge k \neq j)} \big| j \in [1,n]\}$

Each member M_i can then compute the final group key as:

$$K = [\alpha^{\prod(N_k | k \in [1,n] \wedge k \neq i)}]^{N_i} = \alpha^{\prod_{i=1}^{n} N_i}$$

Figure 3 provides an example IKA.1 protocol execution between 4 group members.

Cliques Initial Key Agreement: IKA.2

The second initial key agreement protocol presented in (Steiner et al., 2000), IKA.2, reduces the number of exponentiations in comparison to IKA.1 by letting each member, M_i, factor out their exponent in the first broadcast stage. IKA.2 has an upflow stage similar to IKA.1. After processing the upflow message, M_{n-1} obtains $\alpha^{\prod(N_k | k \in [1, n-1])}$ and broadcasts this value in the second stage to all protocol participants. On reception, every M_i factors out exponent N_i or equivalently divides by N_i and forwards the result to M_n. In the third stage M_n collects all inputs from $M_1,..., M_{n-1}$ and raises every one of the n - 1 inputs to its secret value N_n. The last member in the chain (M_n) then finally broadcasts the resulting intermediate values to the rest of the group. Since all members ultimately have a value of the form $\alpha^{\prod(N_k | k \in [1,n] \wedge k \neq i)}$, they can all generate the group key K.

IKA.2 consists of four stages: upflow, broadcast, response and a final broadcast stage.

Stage–1. (Upflow): Round i, $i \in [1, n-2]$
$M_i \rightarrow M_{i+1} : \{\alpha^{\prod(N_k | k \in [1,i])}\}$
Stage–2. (Broadcast): Round n - 1
$M_* \leftarrow M_{n-1} : \{\alpha^{\prod(N_k | k \in [1,n-1])}\}$
Stage–3. (Response): Round n
$M_i \rightarrow M_n : \{\dfrac{\alpha^{\prod(N_k | k \in [1,n-1])}}{N_i}\}$
Stage–4. (Broadcast): Round n + 1
$M_* \leftarrow M_n : \{\dfrac{\alpha^{\prod(N_k | k \in [1,n])}}{N_j} \big| j \in [1,n]\}$

Cliques Auxiliary Key Agreement: Membership Addition

All AKA operations take advantage of the keying material collected during the upflow stage of the latest IKA or AKA protocol execution. Any member who cached the keying material of the most recent broadcast round can facilitate an AKA operation by taking on the responsibility of the group controller (M_C). Due to the similarity between the Cliques AKA protocols only the membership addition protocol will be considered. The reader is referred to (Steiner et al., 2000) for details on the other AKA operation protocols of Cliques.

The membership addition protocol adds a single member to the existing group. The group members, including the new member, establish a new conference key K' between them that is secure against passive adversaries. In the membership addition protocol, M_C extends the last round of the prior IKA or AKA protocol's upflow stage by one more round. The new member raises the keying material to its own new random secret before broadcasting the value to all members in the second round. Note that the group controller replaces its own secret, N_C, in the upflow message by N'_C to prevent new members from obtaining old group keys.

The Cliques membership addition protocol requires the following two stages:

Stage–1. (Upflow): Round 1
$$M_C \rightarrow M_{n+1} : \{\alpha^{N'_C \Pi(N_k|k\in[1,n]\wedge k\neq j)} \big| j \in [1,n], \alpha^{N'_C \Pi(N_k|k\in[1,n])}\}$$

Stage–2. (Broadcast): Round 2
$$M_* \leftarrow M_{n+1} : \{\alpha^{N'_C \Pi(N_k|k\in[1,n+1]\wedge k\neq j)} \big| j \in [1,n+1]\}$$

Cliques Auxiliary Key Agreement: Merge Protocol – GDH IKA.3

The merge protocol is designed to accommodate network merge, i.e. k members are added to a group of n members. The protocol, as described in (Amir et al., 2000: Amir, Kim, Nita-Rotaru, & Tsudik, 2004), works as follows. As in the case of membership addition protocol, when a merge event occurs, the current group controller M_C (which can be any member of the existing group) generates a new key token by refreshing its contribution to the group key and then passes the token to one of the new members. When the new member receives this token, it adds its own contribution and passes the token to the next new member. This continues till the token reaches the last new member. This member (the last one in the new group) becomes the new group controller. The controller broadcast the token to the group without adding its contribution. Upon receiving the broadcast token, each group member (old and new) factors out its contribution and unicasts the result (called a factor-out token) to the new group controller. The new controller collects all factor-out tokens, adds its own contribution to each of them, building the list of partial keys and broadcasts it to the group. Every member can then obtain the group key by factoring in its contribution.

The Merge-Protocol requires the following steps:

Stage 1: M_C generates a new exponent $N'_C (\in Zq)$, and sends to M_{n+1} the message:
$$M_C \rightarrow M_{n+1} : \alpha^{N'_C \Pi(N_i|i\in[1,n]\wedge i\neq C)}$$

Stage j+1 for $j\in[1, k-1]$: New merging member M_{n+j} generates an exponent N_{n+j} and forwards to member M_{n+j+1} the message:
$$M_{n+j} \rightarrow M_{n+j+1} : \{\alpha^{N'_C(N_i|i\in[1,n+j])} \big| j \in [1,k-1]\}$$

Stage k + 1: Upon receipt of the accumulated value, M_{n+k}, who is now the new group controller, broadcast it to the entire group.

Stage k + 2: Upon receipt of the broadcast, every member M_i, $\forall i \in [1,n+k-1]$ sends back to M_{n+k} the message:
$$M_{n+k} \leftarrow M_* : \{\alpha^{N'_C \Pi(N_j|j\in[1,n+k-1]\wedge j\neq i\neq C)} \big| i \in [1,n+k-1]\}$$

Stage k + 3: After collecting all responses M_{n+k} generates a new exponent N_{n+k} and broadcasts the set S to all the members of the group:
$$M_* \leftarrow M_{n+k} : S = \{\alpha^{N'_C \Pi(N_j|j\in[1,n+k]\wedge j\neq i\neq C)} \big| \forall i \in [1,n+k-1]\}$$

Stage k + 4: Upon receipt of the broadcast, every member M_i, $\forall i \in [1,n+k]$ computes the key:
$$K = (\alpha^{N'_C \Pi(N_j|j\in[1,n+k]\wedge j\neq i\neq C)})^{N_i} = \alpha^{N'_C \Pi(N_j|j\in[1,n+k]\wedge j\neq C)} = \alpha^{N_1\dots N'_C\dots N_{n+k}} \mathbf{mod}\ p$$

Cliques Auxiliary Key Agreement: Partition Protocol

GDH-partition protocol considers the case when a number of members leave a group (Amir et al., 2000; Amir, Kim, Nita-Rotaru, & Tsudik, 2004). In case of partition, L members are leaving a group of size n. The group controller who is at all time the most recent remaining group member, removes the corresponding partial products of the members leaving from the list of partial keys. It refreshes each partial key in the list and broadcasts the list to the group. Each remaining member can then compute the shared key. The protocol runs as follows:

Step 1: The group controller M_C generates a new exponent N'_d, broadcast the set S:

$$M_* \leftarrow M_C : S = \{\alpha^{N'_C \Pi(N_j | j \notin L \wedge j \neq i \neq C)}\} | \forall i \notin L$$

Step 2: Upon receipt of S, every remaining member M_i, $\forall i \notin L$ computes the key K:

$$K = (\alpha^{N'_C \Pi(N_j | j \notin L \wedge j \neq i \neq C)})^{N_i} = \alpha^{N'_C \Pi(N_j | j \notin L)} = \alpha^{N_1 \dots N'_C}$$

Discussion of the Cliques Protocol Suite

The Cliques protocol suite was designed for DPGs in conventional networks. Cliques therefore does not allow for some of the unique characteristics of MANETs. Cliques depends on a serial execution of computations in the upflow stages of its IKA protocols and thus requires nodes to form a serial topology. Considering the dynamic network topology of MANETs, caused by node mobility, this is a critical inefficiency. The serialized topology of nodes in the upflow stages of the IKA protocols is thus more suited to static networks.

The Cliques protocol suite is only secure against passive adversaries. Member authentication mechanisms, which are required to thwart active adversaries, are not specified in the Cliques protocol suite. It should be noted that incorporating such mechanisms will result in an increase in the communication and computational cost of Cliques (Ateniese et al., 1998).

Cliques fails to distribute the burden of group key management equally between all members (See Table 1 to Table 5), this in itself may be sufficient justification to declare Cliques inappropriate for MANETs. The fact that Cliques unevenly distributes the computational and communication overhead between all group members is experimentally substantiated in (Carman et al., 2000). For example, the first node in the serial upflow stage of IKA.1 (in sub-section *Cliques Initial Key Agreement: IKA.1*) performs only a single exponentiation where the last node P_n performs n exponentiations. In the case of conventional networks, which in general have sufficient communication, memory and energy resources, an uneven distribution of the overhead should cause no concern. In MANETs these resources are limited. An uneven distribution of computational overhead also makes the Cliques IKA protocols vulnerable to a selfishness attack (Buttyan & Hubaux, 2003) by legitimate group members. The highest-indexed group member P_n has to broadcast all the intermediate values to the other group members in the final round of the IKA protocols. P_n thus plays a special role and therefore it represents a bottleneck and provides adversaries with a single point of attack.

In the AKA protocols, the disadvantages of Cliques are also apparent. All the AKA protocols rely on the assumption that at least one arbitrary group member caches all the keying material broadcast during the last round of the IKA operation or previous AKA operation. This group member voluntarily takes over the functionality of group controller in the case of a subsequent AKA operation. Considering the resources required to cache the keying material and to perform the role of group controller, it should be clear that the Cliques protocol suite violates the symmetric relationship between the group members and is therefore subject to selfishness. In order to guarantee that a legitimate group member takes on the responsibility of group controller, this role will have to be assigned based on group policy. In the AKA operations for membership addition and mass join, the highest-indexed new member also plays the special role of broadcasting the intermediate values to the other group members. The highest-indexed member (and group controller) in the AKA protocols thus present a single point of vulnerability.

Lately the authenticated Cliques protocols have been shown to suffer from generic insecurities (Pereira & Quisquater, 2004).

(Amir, Kim, Nita-Rotaru, Schultz, Stanton, & Tsudik, 2004) build on the Group Diffie-Hellman proposed by (Steiner et al., 2000) to construct a robust contributory key agreement protocol resilient to a finite sequence of auxiliary key agreement operations. More specifically, the robust algorithm optimized the group change protocols (e.g. join, leave, merge etc.) and model these auxiliary operations by a state machine. The optimized algorithm is implemented using the services of the Secure Spread Library (Amir et al., 2005).

CONTRIBUTORY KEY AGREEMENT: CIRCULAR TOPOLOGY

In literature the Ingemarsson protocol, generally referred to as ING, belongs to the family of group key agreement protocols proposed in (Ingemarsson et al., 1982). It requires a synchronous startup and executes in (n - 1) rounds, where n is the total number of protocol participants. The members must be arranged in a ring or circular topology. In a given round every protocol participant raises the previously received intermediate key value to the power of its own exponent (random secret) and forwards the result to the next participant in the ring. Consequently ING also falls under the family of protocols that are a natural extension of the II-party DH protocol (Steiner et al., 2000). After (n - 1) successfully completed rounds all n participants in the ring share a group key K.

Ingemarsson Initial Key Agreement: ING

The ING protocol allows $n \geq 2$ group members, ordered in a circular topology, to establish a group key K as follows:

Round k; $k \in [1, n-1]$.
$$M_i \rightarrow M_{(i+1) \bmod n} : \{a^{\Pi(N_j | j \in [(i-k) \bmod n, i])}\}$$

Discussion of the Ingemarsson Protocol

The Ingemarsson protocol (Ingemarsson et al., 1982) is one of the earliest attempts to provide contributory key agreement by extending the DH II-party case to group settings for teleconferencing. The ING protocol requires participants to set up a logical ring or circular formation. The circular topology requirement may prohibit its use when one considers the characteristics of MANETs. As a result of forming the ring structure, the ING protocol compels group members to maintain track of the availability of their ordered neighbors at all times. It is known that MANETs are subject to error-prone wireless connectively and numerous link attacks as they may operate in hostile networking environments (Haas & Tabrizi, 1998; Zhou & Haas, 1999). The dynamic network topology and unpredictable node availability in MANETs are due to node mobility resulting in frequent network partitioning. As a consequence to these characteristics the ring structure is difficult to maintain.

The ING protocol is considered to be inefficient for the following reasons:

- At startup, synchrony is required between all members forming the group.
- A total of n - 1 simple rounds are required to establish the conference key, K_n.
- The symmetrical nature of the protocol makes dynamic membership support a costly operation.

- The n exponentiation required by each joining member is not feasible for computationally constrained devices.

The ING protocol also does not scale very well since the total exponentiation is $O(n^2)$. The computational cost thus grows exponentially with group membership.

The ING protocol is insecure allowing a passive adversary eavesdropping on the information exchanged between users to compute the conference key K (Burmester & Desmedt, 1994a). The proposal by (Ingemarsson et al., 1982) does not provide any mechanisms for authentication or AKA operations and this could be regarded as a shortcoming.

It may thus be concluded that the ING protocol is not suitable for MANETs, mainly due to the ING protocol's inefficiency, lack of support for AKA operations, inherited insecurity and underlying circular topology.

CONTRIBUTORY KEY AGREEMENT: HYPERCUBE TOPOLOGY

The Hypercube protocol by (Becker & Wille, 1998) achieves the lower efficiency bound with respect to number of rounds (as defined in (Becker & Wille, 1998)). The protocol accomplishes this by grouping members into groups of four. The four parties, A, B, C and D in each grouping can establish a secret key between them using four DH exchanges. As shown in Figure 4 (Becker & Wille, 1998), parties A and B exchange keys using the II-party DH protocol and concurrently C and D perform the same action. In the second round shown in Figure 5 (Becker & Wille, 1998), parties A and C exchange keys using the II-party DH protocol and concurrently B and D perform the same action. The resultant IV-party DH key is in the following form:

Assume there are 2^3 participants compared to 2^2, i.e. two groupings of four. The 8 participants are arranged as the vertices in a 3-dimensional hypercube topology. In the 1st and 2nd round, each group of four participants can establish a IV-party DH key value as explained before. In the 3rd and final round, each participant on a square face performs exchanges with its peer on the opposite square face using its IV-party secret key from the first two rounds as the exponent. This will result in a shared key, K_8, between the participants. This process will continue for another round for 2^4 participants and another two rounds for 2^5 etc. Thus in round i, each of the protocol participants performs a II-party DH with its peer on the ith dimension of the hypercube using the key of round i - 1 as its secret exponent. After d rounds, 2^d participants will have the same secret key K_{2^d}.

For example the shared key generated by the 8 members can be represented as:

$$K_8 = \alpha^{\{\alpha^{\{\alpha^{(r_1 \cdot r_2)}\alpha^{(r_3 \cdot r_4)}\}}\alpha^{\{\alpha^{(r_5 \cdot r_6)}\alpha^{(r_7 \cdot r_8)}\}}\}} \qquad (2)$$

Before continuing, the additional notation required in the following text is defined.

d — Cube dimension.
$GF(2^d)$ — d-Dimensional vector space.
φ — Bijection: $G \rightarrow Z_q$.
v Vector representing each participant in $GF(2^d)$.
r_v, r_i — Random secret generated by participant v or member M_i of n.

Hypercube Initial Key Agreement

The Hypercube protocol allows 2^d participants ordered in a hypercube topology to derive a conference key, K, secure against passive adversaries. All participants agree on an appropriate prime p and generator α of G. Members select their secrets r_i randomly from G. Parties are identified with linearly independent vectors spanning the d-dimensional vector space $GF(2^d)$ with basis $\vec{b}_1, \vec{b}_2, ..., \vec{b}_d$.

Hypercube protocol executes in d rounds as follows:

Round– 1.
$\vec{v}$ generates secret exponent $r_{\vec{v}}$.
$\vec{v}$ performs II-party DH exchange with $\vec{v} + \vec{b}_1$ using $r_{\vec{v}}$ as its random secret exponent.

Round–i. $(1 < i \leq d)$.
$\vec{v}$ performs II-party DH exchange with $\vec{v} + \vec{b}_i$ using the DH key generated in round i - 1 as the secret exponent.

Discussion of the Hypercube Protocol

The Hypercube protocol is only feasible for an even number of group members which may be regarded as a limiting feature. (Becker & Wille,

Figure 4. Round 1 of 2^2 Hypercube protocol

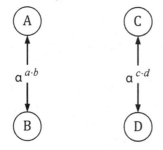

Figure 5. Round 2 of 2^2 Hypercube protocol

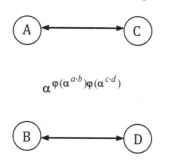

1998) use the Hypercube protocol as a foundation for the Octopus protocol as reviewed in the next section.

The reader is referred to the discussion on the Octopus Protocol (in sub-section *Discussion of the Octopus - and 2d-Octopus Protocols*) for further comments on the Hypercube protocol's suitability for MANETs, due to the close relationship between the Hypercube and Octopus protocols.

CONTRIBUTORY KEY AGREEMENT: OCTOPUS TOPOLOGY

The Octopus protocol presented in (Becker & Wille, 1998) addresses the scenario when the number of participants that form a group is not of the power 2. The Octopus protocol eliminates the limitation of the Hypercube protocol by allowing an arbitrary number of protocol participants to establish a group key as follows: In the Octopus protocol, four participants form the central control-core of the group. As illustrated in Figure 6 (Becker & Wille, 1998), the rest of the participants attach to one of the four central controllers to form an octopus topology. These attachments are also referred to as 'tentacles' or pair wise disjoint groups. All the members perform a II-party DH exchange with their respective central controller.

The four central controllers then perform a IV-party DH exchange (as defined in Section *Contributory Key Agreement: Hypercube Topology)*, using the product of the tentacle keys as secret exponents.

The following additional notation is defined as required in the subsequent text.

A, B, C,D — Controlling group members.
X — Set of central controlling nodes; $X \in \{A, B, C, D\}$.
I_X — Pair wise disjointed subgroup connected to X.

P_i —Non-controlling participants: $\{P_i | i \in I_x\}$.
r_{P_i}, r_X — Random secret generated by P_i and X respectively.
φ —Bijection: $G \rightarrow Z_q$.

Octopus Initial Key Agreement

Assume that parties P_{n-3}, P_{n-2}, P_{n-1} and P_n form the set X. The rest of the participants $P1,..., P_{n-4}$ are connected to one of $X \in \{A, B, C, D\}$.

The Octopus protocol comprises the following three steps:

Step–1.
a.   All X generate secret exponent r_x and all P_i for $i \in [1, n-4]$ generate secret exponent r_{P_i}.
b.   For all X and $i \in I_x$, X and P_i performs a II-party DH key exchange.

Step–2.
a.   The controlling nodes perform a IV-party DH exchange or 2^2 Hypercube protocol using the secret exponents a, b, c, d = $K(I_x)$, where $K(j) = \prod_{i \in j} \varphi(k_i)$ for $j \subseteq \{1,...,n-4\}$.

Step–3.
a.   Controller node A sends to all P_i, $i \in I_A$, the following values: $\alpha^{K(\frac{i}{I_B \cup I_A})}$ and $\alpha^{\varphi(\alpha^{K(I_C \cup I_D)})}$. The re-

maining controller nodes B, C and D also send their two values to P_i, $i \in \{I_B, I_C, I_D\}$ respectively.

The resulting group key is computed as:

$$K = \alpha^{\{\varphi(\alpha^{K(I_A \cup I_B)}\varphi(\alpha^{K(I_C \cup I_D)}))\}} \tag{3}$$

2d-Octopus Initial Key Agreement

An alteration to the Octopus protocol, called the 2^d-Octopus protocol is also presented in (Becker & Wille, 1998). If n is the number of participants and ($2^d < n < 2^{d+1}$), the first 2^d participants perform the functionality of the central controllers in contrast to only four in the Octopus protocol. The remaining nodes attach to one of the 2^d controller nodes. The 2^d scheme follows the same algorithm as the Octopus protocol to establish a group key known to all members.

Discussion of the Octopus - and 2d-Octopus Protocols

(Becker & Wille, 1998) propose the Octopus protocol and 2^d-Octopus protocol as an example of a DH based group key agreement protocol that satisfies the lower bound on efficiency for message

Figure 6. Network topology of Octopus protocol

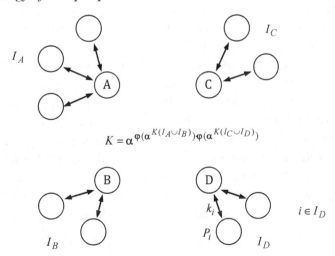

$$K = \alpha^{\varphi(\alpha^{K(I_A \cup I_B)})\varphi(\alpha^{K(I_C \cup I_D)})}$$

exchanges and round complexity respectively. In contrast to the 2^d-Hypercube protocol in the preceding section, the Octopus and 2^d-Octopus protocols can accommodate an uneven number of group members. In the case of $n \neq 2^d$ the minimal number of simple rounds is exceeded by one ($d = \log_2 n + 1$) and in the case where $n = 2^d$ the minimal number of simple rounds ($d = \log_2 n$) is equaled.

In (Becker & Wille, 1998) the authors do not consider AKA operations. Investigations on the 2^d-Hypercube, Octopus and 2^d-Octopus protocols show that membership additions may be performed efficiently, but membership exclusions fail completely. (Steiner et al., 2000) point out that splitting the group on the dth dimension into two halves seems to be the only possible exclusion procedure. Efficiently performing AKA operations in MANETs is essential since these operations are guaranteed to occur more frequently than in conventional network settings.

The hypercube and octopus topologies make the 2^d-Hypercube, Octopus and 2^d-Octopus protocols unsuitable for MANETs for reasons similar to those making the Cliques protocol suite's serial topology (sub-section *Cliques Auxiliary Key Agreement: Merge Protocol – GDH IKA.3*) and the ING protocol's circular topology (sub-section *Discussion of the Ingemarsson Protocol*) unsuitable for MANETs.

The protocols are also not fully distributed therefore violating the symmetric relationships between the members in MANETs. The members forming the control-core are a central point of vulnerability, which is not ideal in MANETs.

(Asokan & Ginzboorg, 2002) propose improvements on the 2^d-Octopus protocol. Their protocol use the password authenticated II-party DH key agreement protocol (as a specific case of the generic encrypted key exchange protocol (Bellovin & Merritt, 1992)) to defend against active adversaries. In (Asokan & Ginzboorg, 2002), the II-party DH key exchanges used in the 2^d-Octopus protocol are simply replaced by the

password authenticated II-party DH key agreement protocol given before.

The password authenticated group key agreement protocol presented by (Asokan & Ginzboorg, 2002) considers a collaborative networking scenario where small groups form an ad hoc network. The key agreement scenario in itself is fairly restrictive and the requirement for distribution of a password between members a priori limits the practicality of the protocol. Although the proposal incorporates a weak authentication mechanism into the 2^d-Octopus protocol it fails to eliminate the protocol's other shortcomings as given before.

CONTRIBUTORY KEY AGREEMENT: TREE-BASED TOPOLOGY

In tree-based group key management schemes, keys are organized into a tree hierarchy, based on different construction strategies. The motivation behind employing a tree-based topology is to reduce the rekeying cost by localizing the effects of AKA operations (see Figure 2). This provides improved scalability especially for secure communications in large dynamically changing groups.

The Tree-based Group Diffie-Hellman (TGDH) protocol suite (Kim et al., 2004) provides a solution with a full array of IKA and AKA protocols, which are very similar to the Cliques protocols (Steiner et al., 2000). The only major difference is the organization of nodes during the key agreement process. TGDH improves on the efficiency of Cliques, with respect to AKA operations, by reordering group members in a binary tree structure. The effect of group events (members joining, leaving etc.), as aforementioned, becomes localized and therefore reduces the effect of the group dynamics on the protocol efficiency. (Kim et al., 2004) do not explicitly specify any IKA protocol and therefore TGDH cannot be compared to any other IKA group protocols.

In Figure 7 (Kim et al., 2004) a TGDH key tree example is given to illustrate the TGDH key tree model. The example is used by (Kim et al., 2004) to explain the notation of TGDH key trees and the fundamental operation of the protocol.

The root of the binary tree is located at level 0 and the depth of the tree may extend to level h. In the binary tree, nodes may be either being a leaf or a parent of two other nodes. A node key is derived from the contribution of the two children via a II-party DH key agreement protocol execution. In the tree model, leaf nodes are denoted by $<l, v>$, where $0 \leq v \leq 2^l - 1$, since each level l can host at most 2^l nodes. Every node, $<l, v>$ in the tree is also associated with a key $K_{<l,v>}$ and a blinded key $BK_{<l,v>} = f(K_{<l,v>})$ where f() is a modular exponentiation in a prime order group (i.e. f(k) $= \alpha^k \bmod p$). Group members M_i ($i \in [1, n]$) are hosted by the leaf nodes, $<l, v>$ and know its random session key $K_{<l,v>}$. The member M_i located at node $<l, v>$ also knows every key along the key path from $<l, v>$ to the root node $<0, 0>$. The key path is denoted as KEY_i^*.

Before continuing it would be beneficial to take note of the following additional notation.

h — Height of binary tree.

$<l, v>$ — v^{th} node at level l in binary tree.

T_i — M_i's view of the key tree.

$\hat{T}_i$ — M_i's modified view of the key tree.

H(.) — Collision free one-way hash function.

r_i — Random secret chosen by member M_i.

In Figure 7 (Kim et al. 2004), member M_2 owns the tree T_2 and knows every key $\{K_{<3,1>}, K_{<2,0>}, K_{<1,0>}, K_{<0,0>} \}$ in the key path, $KEY_2^* = \{< 3, 1 >, < 2, 0 >, <1, 0 >, < 0, 0 >\}$ and every blinded key $BK_2^* = \{BK_{<0,0>}, BK_{<1,0>}, ..., BK_{<3,7>} \}$.

Every key is computed recursively as: $K_{<l,v>} = f(K_{<l+1,2v>}, K_{<l+1,2v+1>})$. Computing $K_{<l,v>}$ thus requires the knowledge of the keys of the two children nodes and the blinded key ($BK_{<l,v>}$) of the other child. $K_{<0,0>}$ is the shared secret by all M_i. The final group key is derived from $K_{<0,0>}$ as $K_{GROUP} = H(K_{<0,0>})$.

For example M_2 in Figure 7 can compute the group key $K_{<0,0>}$ as:

$$K_{<0,0>} = \alpha^{(\alpha^{r_3(\alpha^{r_1r_2})})(\alpha^{r_4(\alpha^{r_5r_6})})} \tag{4}$$

To simplify the protocol description, the authors of (Kim et al., 2004) introduced the term co-path, denoted as CO_i^*. CO_i^* is the set of siblings to each node in the key path on tree T_i as seen by M_i, i.e. every member M_i at leaf node $<l, v>$ can derive the group secret $K_{<0,0>}$ from all blinded keys on the CO_i^* and its own random session key $K_{<l,v>}$.

TGDH, similar to Cliques (Steiner et al., 2000), provides protocols in support of all the common AKA operations. These include the join, leave, merge, partition and key refresh operations. TGDH requires certain members to take on a special role during the AKA operations. These members, called sponsors, have the responsibility of computing blinded keys and broadcasting

Figure 7. TGDH key tree model example

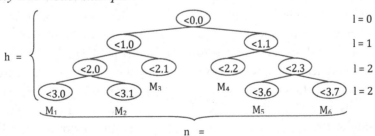

these to the other group members. Two of these operations, join and leave will be given further consideration.

TGDH Auxiliary Key Agreement: Membership Addition

The new member joining the group M_{n+1}, initiates the protocol by broadcasting a join request message that contains its own blinded key $BK_{<0,0>}$. When the current group members receive this message, they determine a new insertion node. The insertion occurs at the shallowest rightmost node that will not increase the tree depth h. The sponsor is defined as the rightmost leaf node in the subtree rooted at the insertion node. The sponsor generates a new intermediate node and a new member node, and promotes the new intermediate node to the parent of its node and the new member's node. After updating the tree, only the sponsor can compute the group key since it is the sibling of the joining node and knows all the necessary blinded keys. After computing the group key, the sponsor broadcasts the new tree $\hat{T}_i$ containing all blinded keys. All other members update their tree using the contained information, and compute the new group key K'.

The TGDH membership addition protocol executes in three steps:

Step–1. New member M_{n+1} broadcasts a request to join the group.

$$M_{n+1} \rightarrow M_* : BK_{<0,0>} = \alpha^{r_n+1}$$

Step–2. Binary tree update procedure.
  a. Each M_i does the following:
    i. Updates its key tree by adding a new member and intermediate node.
    ii. Removes all keys and blinded keys from the leaf node, related to the sponsor, up to the root node.
  b. The sponsor of the intermediate node M_s additionally:

  i. Generates a new share and computes all (K; BK) pairs on the KEY*.
  ii. Broadcasts updated tree $\hat{T}_s$ including only blinded keys.
  $$M_* \leftarrow M_s : \hat{T}_s(BK_s^*)$$
Step–3. All M_i compute K' using $\hat{T}_s$.

In Figure 8 (Kim et al., 2004), an example is shown of member M_4 joining a group, where M_3 is the sponsor, M_s and performs the following actions:

1. Renames node < 1, 1 > to < 2, 2 >.
2. Generates a new intermediate node < 1, 1 > and a new member node < 2, 3 >.
3. Promotes < 1, 1 > as the parent node of < 2, 2 > and < 2, 3 >.

All members know $BK_{<2,3>}$ and $BK_{<1,0>}$. M_3 can compute the new group key $K_{GROUP} = H(K_{<0,0>})$. Note that $K_{<0,0>}$ is never used for real communication. Members use a strong one-way hash function to compute K_{GROUP}, which improves the randomness of the group key. Every other member also performs Step 1 and 2, but cannot compute the group key in the first round. Upon receiving the broadcast blinded keys from M_s, every member can compute the new group key.

TGDH Auxiliary Key Agreement: Membership Exclusion

Assume member M_d leaves the group. In this case, the sponsor M_s is the sibling node of M_d. If the sibling is not a leaf node, the sponsor is the right-most leaf node of the subtree which has the sibling node as root of the subtree. In the leave protocol, every member updates its key tree by deleting the node of M_d and its parent node. The sponsor picks a new secret share, computes all keys on its key path up to the root and broadcasts the new blinded keys of its key path to the group. This information allows all members to recompute the group key.

The TGDH membership exclusion protocol executes in two steps:

Step–1. Binary tree update procedure.

    a.   Each M_i does the following:

        i.   Updates key tree by removing the leaving member node and relevant parent node.

        ii. Removes all keys and blinded keys from the leaf node, related to the sponsor, to the root node.

    b.   The sponsor M_s additionally:

        i.   Generates new share and computes all (K;BK) pairs on the KEY*.

        ii. Broadcasts updated tree $\hat{T}_s$ including only blinded keys.

$$M_s \rightarrow M_* : \hat{T}_s(BK_s^*)$$

Step–2. All M_i compute K' using $\hat{T}_s$.

In Figure 9 (Kim et al., 2004), an example is shown of member M_3 leaving a group, with M_5 as the sponsor. Every remaining member deletes < 1, 1 > and < 2, 2 >, i.e. updates the key tree. The sponsor, M_s, performs the following additional actions:

1. Picks a new share $K_{<2,3>}$ and recomputes $K_{<1,1>}$, $K_{<0,0>}$, $BK_{<2,3>}$ and $BK_{<1,1>}$.
2. Broadcasts the updated tree $\hat{T}_5$ with BK_5^* included.

After receiving the broadcast message from M_s, every member can compute the new group key. The excluded member M_3 does not hold a share in the group key and therefore cannot compute the new group key K'.

Discussion of the TGDH Protocol Suite

As in the case of Cliques (Section *Contributory Key Agreement: Serial Topology*), the TGDH protocols do not consider the unique characteristics of MANETs. The mobility of the nodes results in a dynamic network topology, where dynamic in this case should not be confused with dynamic group membership events. The dynamic nature of the network topology has the consequence that protocols cannot rely on any form of order or structure that is dependent on the network topology.

Figure 8. TGDH update: join example

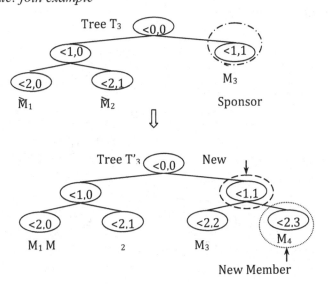

The burden of group key management in TGDH is not equally distributed to all group members. As explained in Section *Introduction*, groups in MANETs are mostly DPGs where all members have a strong symmetric relationship and should be treated equivalently. As TGDH fails to distribute the communication and computational overhead fairly between group members, it may be subject to selfishness (Buttyan & Hubaux, 2003).

Steiner et al. also point out that the special roles performed by members should be left to group policy and should be orthogonal to the key management scheme (Steiner et al., 2000). In TGDH, the majority of the work during AKA operations is performed by the sponsor nodes. The members thus rely on the sponsor to facilitate AKA operations. Assuming the sponsor to be available and always able to perform the associated tasks correctly is impractical in MANETs and introduces a single point of failure. Similar to the highest-indexed member in Cliques, M_s also plays a special role and therefore provides adversaries with a single point of attack.

In (Bresson & Manulis, 2008a; Bresson & Manulis, 2008b) tree based key agreement is revised within a strong adversarial model. The adversary (A) is considered as a Probabilistic

Polynomial-Time (PPT) algorithm with complete network control. This gives A the ability to participate on behalf of corrupted group members. The paper and the extended version propose a protocol constructed on the main mechanisms of the TGDH protocol and prove the revised protocol secure within the adversarial model.

(Desmedt et al., 2006) recall the tree-based BD protocol (BD-II) (Burmester & Desmedt, 2006). (Burmester & Desmedt, 2006) in turn extend and generalize the conference scheme presented in (Burmester & Desmedt, 1994a). The BD-II protocol is improved from O(n) computational complexity per user to O(log n). (Desmedt et al., 2006) further adjusts the compiler of (Katz & Yung, 2007) to preserve the improvement in computational complexity under a transformation from an unauthenticated to an authenticated group key agreement protocol.

CONTRIBUTORY KEY AGREEMENT: ARBITRARY TOPOLOGY

(Hietalahti, 2001) recognizes the unsuitability of topology dependent group initial key agreement

Figure 9. TGDH update: leave example

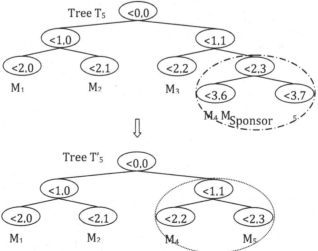

protocols for MANETs. (Hietalahti, 2001) adapts the TGDH IKA algorithm (Kim et al., 2004) to accommodate an arbitrary network topology and therefore be more suitable for MANETs. The protocol is called Arbitrary Topology Generalization of Diffie-Hellman (AT-GDH). The protocol, in contrast to TGDH, constructs an arbitrary spanning tree dependent on the physical location of the members in the network at the time of group formation.

The initial state of the protocol assumes that the group members know their neighbors and have bidirectional communication. The group formation initiator sends a message to each of its neighbors. The initiator becomes the root of the tree and the neighbors its children. The children send a similar message to their neighbors, excluding the parent. The nodes acknowledging the message become children. The process repeats until all group members have received a message. A leaf is defined as a node that does not receive any acknowledgements. Figure 10 (Hietalahti, 2001) illustrates the construction of such an arbitrary spanning with initiator or root ε.

Once the tree is constructed, the protocol gathers contributions towards the group key in the first phase. All the leaves of the spanning tree, i.e. nodes with no children, generate a secret value, compute its share and send their share to the parent nodes. The process continues until the root has collected all the contributions from all children. The root then makes the final contribution. In the second phase, the root starts to distribute the keying material down the tree towards all children that use the information to compute the group key.

The following additional notation is defined:

ε — Protocol initiator (root node of spanning tree).

k_x, e_x — Random secret generated by node x.

c_x — Number of children connected to node x.

$m_{x,i}$ — Message which member x sends to its child i.

As illustrated in Figure 10, nodes have a universal address in a rooted tree sequence. The address of the root ε is an empty sequence. The children of the root have addresses 1, 2, 3,…. respectively. When a node x in level $l \geq 1$ has children their addresses are given as x.1, x.2, x.3,…

A graph is a pair G = (V,E) where V is a finite non-empty set and $E \subseteq \{< x, y > | x \in V, y \in V, x \neq y\}$. The elements of V are called nodes and the elements of E are called edges. An undirected (minimally connected) graph is a tree if it is connected and does not contain any cycles.

AT-GDH Initial Key Agreement

The AT-GDH initial key agreement protocol as given in (Hietalahti, 2001), executes in two phases (see Figure 11 - Figure 14):

Figure 10. Constructing a spanning tree

(a) Nodes with arbitrary network topology form a spanning tree

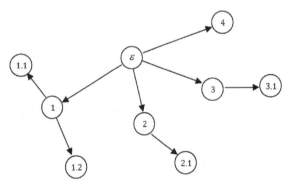

(b) Figure 10(a) rearranged for clarity

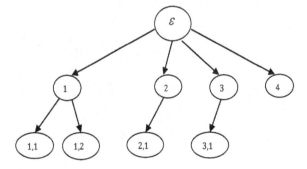

Phase–1.

Round–1. For all nodes x = y.i with $c_x = 0$
    a.   x generates a random secret $k_x \in Z_q$.
    b. $x \rightarrow y : \alpha^{k_s}$.

Round–i ($i \in [2,h]$. For all nodes x with $c_x \neq 0$;
    a.   x generates a random secret ex $\in$ Zq.
    b.   x waits to receive $\alpha^{k_{x,j}}$ for all j = 1, ..., cx.
    c.   x computes $k_x = \varphi(K(x, c_x))$ from:
        $K(x, 0) = e_x$
        $K(x, j) = \alpha^{k_{x,j}\varphi(K(x,j-1))}$ (j = 1, ..., c_x)
    d. $x \rightarrow y : \alpha^{k_x}$

Phase–2.
Round–(h + 1) (1 = 1, ..., h).
a.   For all nodes x.i on level 1, $x \rightarrow x.i$: $m_{x,i}$

where:
$$m_{x,i} = <m_x, \alpha^{\varphi(K(x,j-1))}, \alpha^{k_{x,(i+1)}}, \alpha^{k_{x,(i+2)}}, ..., \alpha^{k_{x,c_x}} >$$
with m_ε being empty.
The resulting group key is $K(\varepsilon, c_\varepsilon) = k_\varepsilon$.

Discussion of the AT-GDH Initial Key Agreement Protocol

The AT-GDH protocol alleviates the dependence on network topology at group genesis. While this approach is feasible for IKA operations, AT-GDH cannot be extended to incorporate efficient AKA operations. Due to node mobility the network topology of MANETs is dynamic and therefore quickly amortizes the advantage of constructing the spanning tree according to the arbitrary network topology. The constructed spanning tree will only be relevant at the time

Figure 11. Phase 1, Round -1: For all nodes with $C_x = 0$ (i.e. has no children)

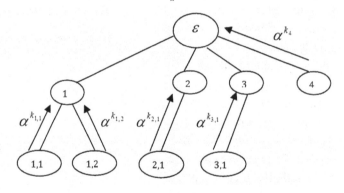

Figure 12. Phase 1, Round-i: Only nodes with children.

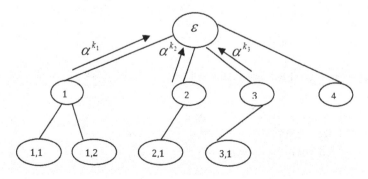

Figure 13. Phase 2, Round -1: For all nodes with $C_x = 0$ (i.e. has no children)

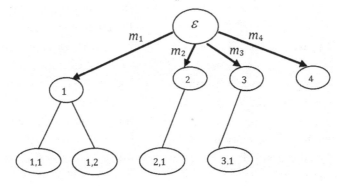

Figure 14. Phase 2, Round-i: Only nodes with children

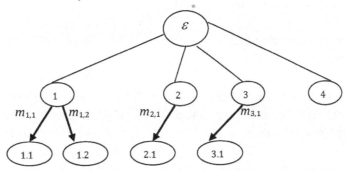

of IKA and will not reflect the network topology during the AKA operations at a later point in time. AT-GDH is thus not suitable for mobile ad hoc networks, but rather for ad hoc networks that become static after network deployment, for example in some applications of sensor networks (Akyildiz et al., 2002).

The second notion that supports AT-GDH's inefficiencies, when extended to incorporate AKA operations, is the fact that the key structure of AT-GDH protocol in its first phase is equivalent to the STR protocol proposed by (Steer et al., 1988):

$$K_n = \alpha^{k_n \alpha^{k_{n-1}\alpha \cdots k_3 \alpha^{k_1 k_2}}} \qquad (5)$$

The efficiency of AT-GDH's AKA operations will thus be comparable to STR. AT-GDH will be better suited for adding new members in a static network topology that is not known prior

to network formation. Membership exclusion will, on the other hand, be problematic especially if the leaving member's secret exponent is used in the innermost key computation (Steiner et al., 2000).

AT-GDH does not distribute the computational and communication overhead equally, although some attempt is made to perform most of the computations during the upflow stage in Phase 1 of the IKA protocol. AT-GDH fails to preserve the symmetric peer relationship between members, which is essential in MANETs. Successful execution of the protocol also depends heavily on the root node and its children, whose presence cannot be assumed in MANETs. Considering the nature and characteristics of MANETs in addition to the frequent AKA operations of DPGs, any dependence on the availability of any group member will not suffice.

CONTRIBUTORY KEY AGREEMENT: STAR TOPOLOGY

(Augot et al., 2007) present a contributory key agreements protocol where a group leader is responsible for collecting the key contributions from members. The Initial Key Agreement (IKA) protocol resolves some of the issues of the modified Centralized Key Distribution (CKD) protocol, for example, the group leader do not have to establish a secure channel with each of the group members and cannot control the group key. See Section *Decentralized Key Distribution* for an overview and discussion on the modified CKD protocol.

The IKA group key agreement (GKA) protocol takes 3 rounds to execute:

Round 1: The chosen group leader sends an initial request (INIT) along with his identity and a random nonce to all group members.

Round 2: Each group member responds to the leader with his identity, random nonce and a blinded secret. The blinded secret is calculated by raising the agreed generator (g) to the member's random secret.

Round 3: The group leader collects all the blinded secrets and raises each to its own secret. These calculated values are then broadcast along with the original contributions (blinded secrets) to all group members. The group members finally use these values to calculate the group key.

Before continuing it would be beneficial to take note of the following additional notation:

G — subgroup with prime order q and generator g.

U_i — protocol participant i among the n group participants.

U_l — current group leader.

r_i — the random secret of U_i chosen from (1, q-1).

g^{r_i} — blinder secret of U_i.

M — set of indices of participant (group M) in the current session.

J — set of indices of joining participant.

D — set of indices of leaving participant.

$x \longleftarrow y$ — x is assigned y.

$x \overset{r}{\longleftarrow} S$ — x is assigned a random draw from the uniform distribution S.

$U_i \longrightarrow U_j : \{msg\}$ —message msg sent unicast from participant i to j.

$U_i \overset{B}{\longrightarrow} M : \{msg\}$ — message msg broadcast from participant i to M.

msg_i^j — message j sent from participant i.

σ_i^j — signature on msg_i^j

GKA Initial Key Agreement Protocol

The GKA IKA protocol is a natural extension of the 2-party Diffie-Hellman (DH) protocol (Diffie and Hellman, 1976); the group leader is effectively executing a modified DH protocol with each of the other protocol participants. The group key is calculated in such as way that the contributions of all the participants are included.

The IKA protocol in (Augot et al., 2007), as illustrated in Figure 15, is as follows:

Round 1. Initial Request
$$l \overset{r}{\longleftarrow} M, N_l \overset{r}{\longleftarrow} \{0,1\}^k$$
$$U_l \overset{B}{\longrightarrow} M : \{msg_l^1 = \{INIT, U_l, N_l\}, \sigma_l^1\}$$

Round 2. Contribution Collection
$$\forall i \in M \setminus \{l\}, if(V_{PK_l}\{msg_l^1\}, \sigma_l^1\} == 1), r_i \overset{r}{\longleftarrow} [1, q-1], N_i \overset{r}{\longleftarrow} \{0,1\}^k,$$
$$U_l \longrightarrow U_l : \{msg_i^1 = \{IREPLY, U_l, N_l, U_i, N_i, g^{r_i}\}, \sigma_i^1\}$$

Round 3. Shares Distribution
$$r_l \overset{r}{\longleftarrow} [1, q-1], \forall i \in M \setminus \{l\}, if(V_{PK_i}\{msg_i^1, \sigma_i^1\} == 1),$$
$$U_l \overset{B}{\longrightarrow} M : \{msg_l^2 = \{IGROUP, U_l, N_l, \{U_i, N_i, g^{r_i}, g^{r_i r_l}\}_{\forall i \in M \setminus \{l\}}\}, \sigma_l^2\}$$

Key Computation.
$$if(V_{PK_l}\{msg_l^2, \sigma_l^2\} == 1) \text{ and } g^{r_i} \text{ is as contributed}$$

$$\text{Group Key} = g^{r_l} * \prod_{i \in M \setminus \{l\}} g^{r_l r_i} = g^{r_l(1 + \sum_{i \in M \setminus \{l\}} r_i)}$$

Figure 15. GKA IKA Key Agreement Protocol with n=7 and U_0 as group leader

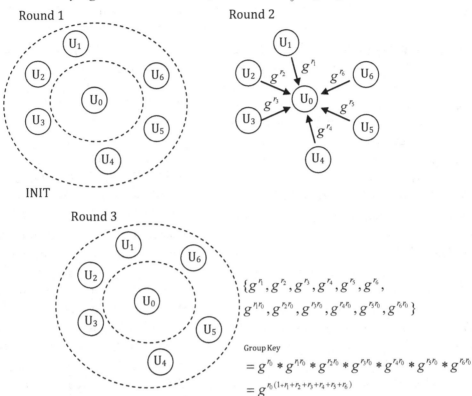

$\{g^{r_1}, g^{r_2}, g^{r_3}, g^{r_4}, g^{r_5}, g^{r_6},$

$g^{r_1 r_0}, g^{r_2 r_0}, g^{r_3 r_0}, g^{r_4 r_0}, g^{r_5 r_0}, g^{r_6 r_0}\}$

Group Key

$= g^{r_0} * g^{r_1 r_0} * g^{r_2 r_0} * g^{r_3 r_0} * g^{r_4 r_0} * g^{r_5 r_0} * g^{r_6 r_0}$

$= g^{r_0(1 + r_1 + r_2 + r_3 + r_4 + r_5 + r_6)}$

GKA Auxiliary Key Agreement Protocol: Join/Merge

The GKA join/merge protocol may execute under a different group leader due to the dynamic nature of ad hoc networks. If a new group leader is elected then the old group leader has to send all the participants' blinded secrets to the new group leader. The members joining the group broadcast their blinded secrets to the group along with a JOIN message. The new group leader raises all blinded secrets to its own, newly generated secret and broadcast the results to the group, which is then used to calculate the group key.

Round 1. Join Request

$\forall i \in J, r_i \xleftarrow{r} [1, q-1], N_i \xleftarrow{r} \{0,1\}^k,$

$U_l \xrightarrow{B} M : \{msg_i^1 = \{JOIN, U_i, N_i, g^{r_i}\}, \sigma_i^1\}$

Round 2. Contribution Transfer

$\forall i \in J, if(V_{PK_i}\{msg_i^1, \sigma_i^1\} == 1), r_l \xleftarrow{r} [1, q-1], l' \xleftarrow{r} M \cup J$

$U_l \longrightarrow U_{l'} : \{msg_l^1 = \{JREPLY, \{U_i, N_i, g^{r_i}\}_{\forall i \in M \cup J}\}, \sigma_l^1\}$

Round 3. Shares Distribution

$if(V_{PK_i}\{msg_l^1, \sigma_l^1\} == 1), l \xleftarrow{} l', r_l \xleftarrow{r} [1, q-1], M \xleftarrow{} M \cup J$

$U_l \xrightarrow{B} M : \{msg_i^2 = \{JGROUP, U_l, N_l, \{U_i, N_i, g^{r_i}, g^{r_l r_i}\}_{\forall i \in M \setminus \{l\}}\}, \sigma_i^2\}$

Key Computation.

$if(V_{PK_i}\{msg_i^2, \sigma_i^2\} == 1)$ and g^{r_i} is as contributed

Group Key $= g^{r_l} * \prod_{i \in M \setminus \{l\}} g^{r_l r_i} = g^{r_l(1 + \sum_{i \in M \setminus \{l\}} r_i)}$

The Delete/Partition Auxiliary Key Agreement (AKA) protocol is essentially an IKA round 3 broadcast message with the leaving members' contributions omitted. It is left to the reader to see (Augot et al., 2007) for details.

Discussion of the GKA Protocol Suite

The GKA IKA protocol uses broadcast messages for one-to-many communication from the group leader to group members. As the members are not dependent on the location of the other group members (excluding the leader) the protocol takes on a star topology.

The IKA protocol is contributory in the sense that the group leader and members cannot predict the group key and needs the contribution of all members, raised to the secret of the group leader, to calculate the key.

The GKA IKA protocol defend against passive adversaries by extending the 2-party DH protocol and ensures the integrity of messages by signing messages using a public key infrastructure.

There is however some problems with the GKA IKA protocol that makes it unfeasible for MANETs. Firstly the protocol requires the group leader to collect the contributions from all group members, which result in the group leader having to receive $n - 1$ messages within a narrow time-frame. It is clear that the route discovery from all group members to the group leader will result in a significant amount of traffic (broadcast storm) on the network as some route discovery attempt will fail due to the limited capacity of the shared wireless medium.

In (Augot et al., 2007) it is claimed that the protocol does not rely on a centralized authority. Although it is true that the group leader does not control the group key, the leader is in control of the group membership. For example, the corrupt leader can exclude a legitimate member from the group by not raising the blinder secret of the member to the secret of the leader. This allows an attacker to focus on the group leader election protocol in order to compromise the GKA protocol.

Mobile ad hoc networks are also dynamic in nature (van der Merwe et al., 2007), that is,

nodes cannot be assumed to be connected to the network at all times. The GKA AKA protocols rely on the old group leader to share the blinded secrets of the group with the new group leader during the AKA protocols. It is not clear how this will work, since the group leader will normally only be replaced if not available.

CONTRIBUTORY KEY AGREEMENT: TOPOLOGY INDEPENDENT SCHEMES

(Burmester & Desmedt, 1994a) propose a well-known group key agreement protocol family. In literature, the topology independent protocol that is based on a broadcast system is referred to as the BD protocol. The BD protocol supports a constant number of rounds and inexpensive computations (Steiner et al., 1996). While the BD protocol still requires no less than n+2 exponentiations per M_i, all of these but three are $\in (1, n - 1)$. This leads to significant computational savings. The BD protocol takes only two rounds to complete, but because each round requires n broadcast messages, this translates into high communication overhead. Each member (M_i) generates a random number as secret exponent and calculates a public value z_i that is broadcast to all other group members. The members compute and broadcast a key value X_i in the second round. X_i is the exponent of M_i's personal secret value N_i to the base (z_{i+1} divided by z_{i-1}). A group member who has received all n partial key values X_i can compute the conference key K_n using a cyclic function.

BD Initial Key Agreement

The BD IKA protocol executes in two synchronous broadcast rounds:

Round–1. Each member M_i generates a random secret N_i, computes and broadcasts $z_i = \alpha^{N_i}$.

Round–2. Each member M_i does the following.

a. Computes and broadcasts $X_i = \left\{ \dfrac{z_{i+1}}{z_{i-1}} \right\}^{N_i}$

b. Computes (modulo n) the conference

key:

$$K_n = z_{i-1}^{n.N_i}.X_i^{n-1}.X_{i+1}^{n-2} \ldots\ldots X_{i+2} \bmod p \qquad (6)$$

BD Auxiliary Key Agreement: Membership Addition

(Burmester & Desmedt, 1994a) does not specify any protocols to support AKA operations. Investigations have shown that such AKA operations based on the BD IKA protocol would all be very similar. To illustrate the basic concept of these AKA operations, the BD membership addition protocol is defined as follows.

For all BD AKA operations at least one of the existing group members M_k has to renew its share in the conference key K by generating a new exponent N'_i whenever a member is added. This is required in order to ensure key freshness (Steiner et al., 2000). Assume that the new member is added as M_{n+1}. Choosing M_k to neighbor the new member would be the most efficient choice, i.e. $M_k = M_n$ or $M_k = M_1$, since it would then affect only M_{n-1} or M_2 as members not neighboring the new member during the rekeying process.

The BD membership addition protocol requires two synchronous broadcast rounds:

Round–1. Current member M_n and joining member M_{n+1} each compute and distribute individual contributions $z'_n = \alpha^{N'_n}$ and $z_{n+1} = \alpha^{N_{n+1}}$.

Round–2.

a. $M_1, M_{n+1}, M_n, M_{n-1}$ generate and broadcast $X'_1, X'_{n+1}, X'_n, X'_{n-1}$ where:

$$X'_p = \left\{ \frac{z_{p+1}}{z_{p-1}} \right\}^{N_p} , p \in \{1, (n+1), n, (n-1)\}$$

b. Each member M_i computes (modulo n) the conference key:

$$K_n = z_{i-1}^{n.N_i}.X_i^{n-1}.X_{i+1}^{n-2} \ldots\ldots X_{i+2} \bmod p \qquad (7)$$

where X_1, X_{n+1}, X_n, X_{n-1} is equivalent to $X'_1, X'_{n+1}, X'_n, X'_{n-1}$ respectively.

Discussion of the BD Protocol Suite

In (Burmester & Desmedt, 1994a), an efficient conference key distribution system is proposed and proved to be secure (in the pre-proceeding version (Burmester & Desmedt, 1994b)) provided that the computational Diffie-Hellman problem is intractable. Burmester and Desmedt make important assumptions to support the feasibility of the BD protocol:

- Each member P_i has the ability to broadcast to the rest of the group.
- The system has the ability to support n simultaneous broadcast messages.
- Each member P_i has the ability to receive n - 1 messages in a single round.

The latter two assumptions are impractical since there are no means in existing networking protocols for MANETs to accommodate n simultaneous broadcasts, nor can devices receive n simultaneous messages without advanced hardware. This forces serialized broadcasting, which effectively eliminates the BD protocol's low round advantage. The Burmester and Desmedt protocol with serial broadcasting is referred to in literature as the BD* protocol. Rounds 1 and 2 in the BD protocol are thus replaced in the BD* protocol by n rounds respectively where each member M_i broadcasts its calculated z_i in round i and X_i in round i+n. The extra rounds in BD* are thus due to nodes waiting for a chance to broadcast their values (z_i, X_i).

(Steiner et al., 2000) point out that an extension of the BD protocol to incorporate AKA operations, may not be feasible for DPGs. Although AKA operations can be performed in only two rounds, four messages have to be received from four different sources. In comparison with the Cliques AKA operations this translates into high overhead (Steiner et al., 2000; Steiner et al., 2000) also claims that closer inspection reveals that all group members have to refresh their share of the group key to prevent leaking too much information or prevent members from serving as exponentiation oracles. The BD AKA operations therefore have similar computational and communication cost as the BD IKA operations making it impractical for DPGs. Also note that (Burmester & Desmedt, 1994a) does not specify any protocols to support AKA operations. The BD protocol is vulnerable to attacks from active adversaries since it provides no means of authenticating the protocol participants.

(Katz & Yung, 2007) presents a compiler that transform the unauthenticated BD protocol into a provably secure authenticated group key agreement protocol that will withstand active adversaries.

Despite its disadvantages the BD protocol's topology independence makes it a very attractive option for realizing group key agreement in MANETs. The topology independence aids in achieving robustness within a dynamic, fully distributed network setting. The BD protocol also preserves the symmetric relationship between protocol participants by distributing the burden of key management equally between all group members. With its low exponentiation cost it suits MANETs' limited computational resources.

KEY PRE-DISTRIBUTION SCHEMES

In (Chan, 2004), a Distributed Key Pre-distribution Scheme (DKPS) is proposed, which eliminates the dependence of the key agreement protocol on a TTP. The proposal stems from research (Chan et al., 2003; Eschenauer & Gligor, 2002) on sensor networks (Akyildiz et al., 2002) that suggests that key pre-distribution schemes (KPS) are the only practical solution in scenarios where the network topology is a priori unknown.

DKPS is a collection of distributed cryptographic protocols that enable a number of nodes, sharing no prior secret, to jointly realize the key pre-distribution function. Each node individually picks a set of keys from a large publicly-known key space such that at completion, the key patterns of all the nodes satisfy the following exclusion property with high probability: any subset of nodes can find from their key patterns (in a secure manner) at least one common key that is unobtainable by a limited number of colluding nodes not belonging to the subset (Chan, 2004). If a node finds that its key pattern cannot satisfy the exclusion property, after confirmation with other nodes, it will re-select another key subset. The key selection is memoryless, therefore it is assumed that the nodes will probably derive a proper key pattern on the retry. The probability of key patterns satisfying the exclusion property can be increased by feasible parameter selection. DKPS therefore has its roots in a combination of probabilistic method and privacy homomorphism (Rivest et al., 1978).

The proposed DKPS scheme contains three phases:

Phase–1. Distributed key selection (DKS).
Phase–2. Secure shared-key discovery (SSD).
Phase–3. Key exclusion property testing (KEPT).

Distributed Key Selection (DKS)

In the DKS phase each node generates or agrees on a publicly known universal key set P and randomly picks keys to form a key-ring ($P_i \subseteq P$). This selection process satisfies an exclusion property defined as a special case of the probabilistic cover-free family (CFF) (Chan 2004). Note that (Chan 2004) does not specify a procedure for generating P, but specify P to be simply Z_N.

The generalized definition of the CFF, as given in (Chan, 2004), is as follows:

Let P be an N-set of points $\{p_1, p_2, \ldots\ldots, p_N\}$ and β be a set of subsets X (also called blocks) of P. This can also be written as: $X \subseteq P, \forall X \in \beta$. Let N and T denote $|P|$ and $|\beta|$ respectively, then the set system (P, β) is called a (w, r; d) - CFF(N, T) (cover-free family) if, for any w subsets X_1, ..., $X_w \in \beta$ and any other r blocks Y_1, ..., $Y_r \in \beta$, satisfies

$$\left| (\bigcap_{i=1}^{w} X_i) \setminus (\bigcup_{j=1}^{r} Y_j) \right| \geq d,$$

with d as a positive integer.

CFF is a widely adopted benchmark for formulating the security property of KPS (Chan, 2004). The conventional construction methods of CFFs found in coding theory and design theory are centralized and therefore not suitable for MANETs (Chan, 2004). In (Chan, 2004), the reliance on a TTP is eliminated by constructing the CFF in a distributed manner using a probabilistic method. By constructing (w, r; 1) — CFF over a publicly known universal key set P, each node or user

picks a subset $X_i \subset P$ as key-ring. It follows that based on the properties of the constructed (w, r ; d) — CFF, any subset of nodes with size up to w can find at least one common key from their key patterns and any collusion of nodes outside this subset with size smaller than r cannot derive the common key. In Figure 16 (Chan, 2004), it is shown how two users in a probabilistic construction can individually pick keys to form their key rings, while satisfying the exclusion property of (w, r ; d) — CFF.

If the capacity of each node's key-ring is denoted by k_B the DKS construction of (w, r; d) — CFF is as follows:

Step–1. The nodes select $k \leq k_B$ such that d divides k.
Step–2. The universal key set P is formed with size N = k . u . r, where u = k/d .
Each node holds its own instance of P.
Step–3. Key set P is divided into k partitions P_1, P_2,……., P_k, each of size u . r.
Step–4. The nodes individually pick keys for their rings to form β = $\{p_1, p_2, ..., p_k\}$, with each p_i randomly selected from the partition P_i,$1 \leq i \leq k$.

Secure Shared-Key Discovery (SSD)

In the key discovery phase all nodes pairwise establish which keys in their key-rings they have in common, without revealing information about the keys not in common. The SSD protocol is based on private homomorphic encryption (PH encryption) (Ahituv et al., 1987; Brickell & Yacobi, 1988; Paillier, 1999). In (Chan, 2004), the author introduces a Modified Rivest's Scheme (MRS) based on the original algorithm by (Rivest et al., 1978) to eliminate problems identified in other PH encryption schemes.

In conventional KPS the TTP gives each node a corresponding key identifier for each key in the node's key-ring. The TTP also knows the mapping between all keys and identifiers. The TTP reveals to the nodes the mapping between the keys and

Figure 16. DKS based on probabilistic CFF construction

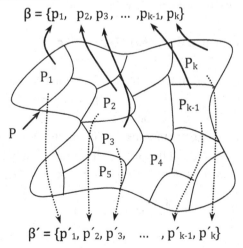

identifiers relevant only to the keys on the node's key-ring. In this case the nodes can easily initiate SSD by broadcasting their key identifiers to other protocol participants. Consequently only those nodes that have the same keys can gain knowledge of the keys they have in common.

For a system without a TTP, SSD is not so trivial. The DKPS proposed in (Chan, 2004) implements an SSD protocol using MRS. The SSD or secure set intersection problem is defined by (Chan, 2004) as follows:

Two parties, Alice and Bob, have two key sets A = $\{a_1, a_2,..., a_l\}$ and B = $\{b_1, b_2,..., b_m\}$ respectively. How can two parties obtain $A \cup B$ without allowing other parties to learn the elements outside the intersection? The exchange of $A \cup B$ must also be secure from passive adversaries, eavesdropping on the SSD procedure.

The SSD-MRS protocol (Chan 2004) attempts to solve the SSD problem in four steps:

Step–1. Alice forms a polynomial, $f_A(x) = x^l + A_{l-1}x^{l-1} + ... + A_1x + A_0$ and encrypts the coefficient using $E_{K_A}(.)$ where K_A is her keys in subset A. These are transferred to Bob.

Step–2. Bob sorts his key set B in descending order and chooses a random secret r_B. The homomorphic properties of $E_{K_A}(.)$ allows Bob to compute $z_i = E_{K_A}(r_B f_A(B))$ for $1 \le i \le m$.

Step–3. Alice receives all z_i's and decrypts them using K_A. Alice thus obtains $r_B f_A(B) \forall 1 \le i \le m$. Because B is blinded by r_B, Alice gains no knowledge of Bob's keys. What Alice knows is $B \in A$ that satisfy $r_B f_A(B) = 0$.

Step–4. Alice returns a m-bit bitmap with 1 at the bits where $r_B f_A(B) = 0$. All common keys in $A \cup B$ can be used to compute a session key only known by Alice and Bob.

Note that the SSD-MRS must be executed in parallel from both parties' perspective. The afore-mentioned description applies to Bob checking with Alice which keys they have in common.

Key Exclusion Property Testing (KEPT)

The third and final phase of the DKPS scheme ensures that the exclusion property holds. If not, the protocol has to be re-executed from phase 1 with DKS followed by SSD-MRS in phase 2.

Each node can represent the pattern of how its keys are shared with other nodes in a binary structure called an incidence matrix. Using an incidence matrix each node can verify whether all keys satisfy the exclusion property of (w, r; d) — CFF. The definition of an incidence matrix is given in (Chan 2004) as follows: if a node has k keys in its key-ring and there are m other nodes then its incidence matrix is a m x k binary matrix A = (a_{ij}) with:

a_{ij} = 1, if the jth key is shared with the ith node

and

a_{ij} = 0 , otherwise

If the exclusion property holds then a vector formed by the bitwise-AND operation of any w rows of A will have at least d bit positions of '1' different from the vector formed by taking the bitwise-OR of any other r rows.

Computing the Group Key

After completing the DKPS protocols, each node can find a block of keys in common with any group of other nodes. The subset of keys are used by all group members to compute the group key known to all by taking a hash function h(.) of the concatenation of all the common key's k_i.

$$K_{group} = h(k_1 \|......\|k_i \|.......\|k_x) \qquad (8)$$

Discussion of the Distributed Key Pre-Distribution Scheme

In (Chan, 2004), asymmetric/public key crypto-systems are deemed unsuitable for ad hoc networks due to their inefficiency. The author of (Chan, 2004) refers to (Carman et al., 2000), an investigation into key management schemes for sensor networks, to substantiate this statement. While this statement is accurate for sensor networks, this is not the case for MANETs. Although having similar constraints to MANETs, sensor networks have much tighter constraints on the nodes' energy, computational and memory resources. The nodes in sensor networks, as a result of their intended application, are very small with dimensions in the cubic millimeter range (Kahn et al., 1999). These 'stringent' constraints on energy, computational and memory resources makes asymmetric schemes (currently) impractical for use in sensor networks (Chan et al., 2003; Eschenauer & Gligor, 2002). Although nodes in MANETs have limited resources, these resources are sufficient to support asymmetric cryptosystems (Zhou & Haas, 1999; Capkun et al., 2003; Yi & Kravets, 2003). This is in particular true with recent advances in elliptic curve cryptography (Hankerson et al., 2004; Brown et al., 2000).

From the discussion on the distributed key selection (DKS) protocol, it should be clear that any node that has the universal publicly known key set P, can randomly pick keys to form an individual key-ring. By the properties of the cover-free family (CFF), (w, r; 1) — CFF, the adversary executing the DKS protocol shares at least one common key with all of the nodes in the network.

The SSD-MRS protocol given in sub-section *Secure Shared-key Discovery (SSD)* allows users to discover what keys they have in common with other nodes, while satisfying the exclusion property. The SSD-MRS protocol offers no mechanism to provide protocol participants with implicit key authentication, i.e., a member M_i of a group M has

no assurance that an adversary $M_q \notin M$ cannot impersonate a legitimate M_i and learn the common group keys and therefore compute K_{group}. DKPS is intended for nodes forming a group with no prior contact or pre-distributed shared secrets, except a publicly known pool of keys P (Chan, 2004). With no prior secret share between the group members as stated in (Chan, 2004), it is not clear how DKPS will achieve implicit key authentication. In a truly ad hoc setting, nodes may initially not be concerned with the identities of the other nodes since these nodes have no relationships prior to group formation. Nevertheless, a mechanism is required to uniquely bind a node to its identity in order to hold a node accountable for its actions. It should be clear that as these nodes build relationships after group genesis an authentication mechanism will become essential.

An authenticated group key agreement protocol (AGKAP) allows group members to establish a shared secret key in the presence of an active adversary (Menezes et al., 1996; Ateniese et al., 1998). Providing key authentication using DKPS as a stand alone symmetric group key management scheme, without a TTP, is not possible. It is well known that asymmetric key cryptosystems require computational and energy resources that are orders of magnitude more than symmetric key cryptosystems. Despite the inefficiency, asymmetric cryptosystems have properties making them superior for distributing keys, providing authentication, data integrity and non-repudiation (Menezes et al., 1996; Zhou & Haas, 1999). The latter three of these functionalities provided by asymmetric cryptosystems play an important role in group key management protocols. The most feasible security mechanisms will therefore incorporate a hybrid cryptoscheme drawing from the advantages of both symmetric and asymmetric based schemes.

The security of DKPS rests on the probability of the system satisfying the criteria of a cover-free family (CFF). As explained in (Chan, 2004), most of the nodes would successfully establish a good key set satisfying the exclusion property. Although there is a high probability of success, it is in fact only known if the exclusion property holds after execution of the key exclusion property testing (KEPT) protocol. If the exclusion property is violated then the two protocol participants need to re-execute the DKPS protocols until the KEPT protocol returns a positive result.

Suppose a node M_1 in the initialization phase of the network performs DKS and SSD with M_2 and SSD with each of the other $n - 2$ nodes in the network. After each execution of the DKS and SSD-MRS protocols, KEPT is used to test if the exclusion property holds. Assume that KEPT returns a positive result for the first $i - 2$ nodes, but returns a negative result for the common keys shared between M_1 and M_i. What this implies is that the whole process must start over as M_1 has to repeat the DKS protocol and consequently SSD-MRS with all the other nodes for which KEPT has already returned a positive result. It is thus not clear if the DKPS scheme will converge and yield good key sets that satisfy the exclusion property for all node combinations in the network. If convergence is possible, then DKPS requires all n group members to perform DKS once, twice or even more times, with SSD followed by the execution of KEPT with the remaining $n - 1$ members. Without optimization, this will result in a best case latency of $n(n - 1)$ DKPS executions before K_{group} can be calculated. Robust implementation and practicality of DKPS may therefore be problematic.

It is noted here that DKPS fails to provide members of dynamic peer groups with key freshness, perfect forward secrecy, key independence and resistance to known key attacks as defined in (van der Merwe et al., 2007). It can thus be concluded that DKPS is not suitable for DPGs found in MANETs.

DECENTRALIZED KEY DISTRIBUTION

The Centralized Key Distribution (CKD) protocol suite as given in (Amir, Kim, Nita-Rotaru, & Tsudik, 2004) is not suitable for DPGs. In order to satisfy the properties of general decentralized key distribution protocols, as defined in Section *Introduction*, only one modification was made to the CKD scheme. As illustrated in Figure 1, centralized key management is a subset of key transport that is normally used by large non-collaborative groups. The primary difference between centralized and decentralized key transport protocols is that centralized schemes have a designated TTP responsible for all initial key transport (IKT) operations and auxiliary key transport (AKT) operations, while these operations are performed by any randomly chosen group member in the decentralized schemes. In the case of the CKD scheme (Amir, Kim, Nita-Rotaru, & Tsudik, 2004), the TTP (group controller) is always the oldest group member. By allowing the role of group controller to be randomly assigned to any group member, the CKD scheme as presented in (Amir, Kim, Nita-Rotaru, & Tsudik, 2004) can be grouped with decentralized key agreement schemes as opposed to centralized schemes. The modified CKD scheme will thus randomly select any group member to take on the responsibility of group controller at the beginning of each AKT operation.

Regardless of the group event (IKT or AKT operations) the protocol executes in two phases:

Phase–1. Each group member and the randomly chosen group controller agree on a symmetric key using the authenticated II-party DH protocol (Diffie et al., 1992). On each AKT operation the new group controller has to repeat this operation with every member.

Phase–2. The group controller independently generates and distributes the group key. For this reason CKD can be seen as a key transport protocol.

CKD Auxiliary Key Transport: Mass Join

The CKD mass join protocol adds k members to a group of size n. Assume member M_1 to be the randomly chosen group controller.

The CKD mass join protocol executes in four steps:

Step–1. M_1 selects a random secret $r_1 \in Z_q$.
$$M_1 \to \{M_{n+j} \mid j \in [1,k]\} : \alpha^{r_1} \bmod p$$

Step–2. For each $j \in [1, k]$, M_{n+j} selects a random secret $r_{n+j} \in Z_q$.
$$M_1 \leftarrow M_{n+j} : \alpha^{r_{n+j}} \bmod p$$

Step–3. M_1 selects a random group secret r_{gs}.
$$M_1 \to M_i : r_{gs}^{\alpha^{r_1 r_i}} \bmod p \, \forall i \in [2, n+k]$$

Step–4. All group members n + k compute K' from the broadcast message.

CKD Auxiliary Key Transport: Mass Leave

The CKD mass leave protocol excludes l members from a group of size n. Assume members M_1 to be the randomly chosen group controller.

The CKD mass leave protocol executes in two steps:

Step–1. M_1 selects a new group random secret r'_{gs}
$$M_1 \to M_i : r_{gs}^{\alpha^{r_1 r_i}} \bmod p, M_i \notin l$$

Step–2. All group members n - l compute K' from the broadcast message.

Discussion of the CKD Protocol Suite

Some features of decentralized group key distribution protocols make them unsuitable for MANETs:

- The central entity (group controller) presents a single point of vulnerability although it is randomly chosen among the group members.
- On each AKT operation, the new randomly chosen group controller is required to perform an authenticated II-party DH key exchange with each group member, which results in significant additional communication and computational overhead.
- MANETs are highly dynamic in nature and no group member can be assumed to be present all the time. The central group controller may be unavailable due to any number of factors such as moving out of transmission range, error-prone wireless connectivity or depleted resources. In the event of the controller not being available a new controller must take over the responsibility, which results in additional overhead.
- Centralized key distribution cannot provide perfect forward secrecy (Steiner et al., 2000).
- Group members do not get assurance that the group key is random to satisfy key freshness (Steiner et al., 2000).

As pointed out in (Steiner et al., 2000), a central point is however needed for the administration of group membership operations. The functionality of group controller should be performable by any group member. The group controller serves only to synchronize the IKA and AKA operations to prevent confusion. It should thus be clear that the existence and assignment of the group controller should be orthogonal to the key agreement protocols and depend solely on group policy.

PERFORMANCE ANALYSIS

The computational and communication overhead of contributory key agreement protocols are important issues to consider when determining the protocols' suitability for MANETs. This is due to MANETs' limited computational and communication resources. Table I to Table V compare the worst case communication and computational cost of the most promising existing schemes (Cliques (Steiner et al., 2000), TGDH (Kim et al., 2004) and BD* (Burmester & Desmedt, 1994a)) that incorporate IKA and AKA operations.

Efficiency of IKA Operations

Table-I shows that in terms of communication cost, Cliques IKA.1 and IKA.2 protocols outperform the BD* protocol. Although the BD protocol executes in only two rounds, a synchronous broadcast system is impractical (see sub-section *Discussion of the BD Protocol Suite*). The BD* protocol's 2n broadcast messages would result in more network congestion than Cliques IKA.1 and IKA.2, which predominantly use unicast messages. In the BD* protocol's defense it should be realized that in order to place an equivalent amount of overhead on each group member in a fully distributed, contributory system, the scheme is bound to be based on a broadcast system. In such a scenario broadcast is not only the most efficient means of communication, but has been proven to be the most reliable in MANETs (Yi and Kravets, 2003). The reader is also referred to (Becker & Wille, 1998), which defines the lower bound on message exchange of a contributory, broadcast based key agreement scheme to be n broadcast messages. The BD* protocol thus requires its communication overhead to be halved in order to be optimal.

The BD and BD* protocols' key construction procedure allows for significant savings in computational cost. As illustrated in Table II, of the

n+2 exponentiations performed by each member, n-1 of these are 'low cost' (although the additional time complexity added by these smaller exponentiations may not be insignificant for larger group sizes). From the computational efficiency analysis results given in Table II through to Table V it is clear that Cliques fails to distribute the burden of key management fairly between all group members. (Steiner et al., 2000) improves on the computational overhead distribution of Cliques IKA.1 with IKA.2, reducing the exponentiations per protocol participant to only four. There may however be a few inherited problems with this enhancement if Cliques IKA.2 protocol were to be used in MANETs:

The highest indexed member (M_n) is still required to perform n exponentiations. The improvement thus will not aid in mitigating selfishness attacks (Buttyan & Hubaux, 2003).

The improvement from IKA.1 to IKA.2, in terms of computational overhead distribution, comes at the cost of significant communication overhead.

The highest indexed member's role in the initial key agreement protocol becomes centralized, giving adversaries a single point of attack.

The computational cost introduced by message authentication (which implicitly implies member authentication) is given in Table IV and Table V in terms of the number of signatures generated and signatures verified by each group member. The number of signatures generated by members during initial key agreement is very similar for all protocols. The major difference relates to the number of verifications per member. Here the Cliques IKA.1 and IKA.2 protocols (Steiner et al., 2000) prove to be superior to the BD* IKA protocol (Burmester & Desmedt, 1994a). One should however consider that signature schemes such as RSA, provides significantly faster signature verification than signature generation procedures (Menezes et al., 1996).

Efficiency of AKA operations

In DPGs, efficient AKA operations are more important than IKA operations, since the latter is performed only once (Steiner et al., 2000). It is therefore important for key management schemes, designed for MANETs, to minimize the communication and computational overhead associated with the AKA operations (see Figure 2).

As mentioned in sub-section *Discussion of the BD Protocol Suite*, (Steiner et al., 2000) claims that closer inspection reveals that all group members have to refresh their share of the group key on each group event in order to prevent leaking too much information or prevent serving as exponentiation oracles. Since this is not formally proved in literature, the efficiency analysis of the BD* protocols AKA operations is given for the optimal case where only one member is required to renew its share in the group key.

To make a feasible comparison between the AKA operations of the existing schemes (Steiner et al., 2000; Kim et al., 2004; Burmester & Desmedt, 1994a), communication and computational overhead have to be considered simultaneously. An overall assessment shows that tree-based protocols (TGDH) are superior to the serial topology protocols (Cliques) and topology independent protocols (BD*) with respect to changes in group membership. Tree-based protocols are thus more easily scalable and better suited for large groups (n > 100). In a dynamic peer group setting, group sizes will however be small, which limits the improved performance of tree-based schemes. In order to make an overall performance comparison between the existing schemes, the time complexity of the respective AKA operations might be a more feasible parameter to consider. Since the time complexity is dependent on numerous factors (such as node processing power, network environment, group size, and number of members leaving or joining) a more realistic study is required through simulation. It is however noted that since the existing schemes (Steiner et al.,

2000; Kim et al., 2004; Burmester & Desmedt, 1994a) are unsuitable for MANETs, the conclusions drawn from such simulations with respect to efficiency comparisons may be impractical or limited. Simulations and a performance comparison on the existing group key management schemes in a conventional network setting have been presented by Amir et al. and the reader is referred to (Amir, Kim, Nita-Rotaru, & Tsudik, 2004) for details.

CONCLUDING REMARKS

This chapter presents a survey on the published group key management schemes with respect to their suitability for mobile ad hoc networks (MANETs). Studies within the available literature have shown that group-oriented communication in MANETs will generally occur in the form of dynamic peer groups (DPGs). The protocols for DPG settings were categorized in terms of their underlying key establishment mechanisms. These categories included:

- Contributory key agreement and key pre-distribution as subsets of key agreement.
- Decentralized key distribution as a subset of key transport.

Contributory key agreement was further uniquely subdivided based on the topology enforced upon the group members as a derivative of the construction method used to obtain a desired group key form. Each of these subsets was discussed by introducing at least one prominent group key management scheme from within the grouping.

The analysis of each group key management scheme was followed by a discussion on the scheme's suitability for MANETs. The performance of the protocol suites that consider both initial key agreement (IKA) and auxiliary key agreement (AKA) operations was presented and analyzed.

The conclusion drawn from the survey is that distinct challenges arrive when adapting group key management protocols designed for conventional networks to suit MANETs:

- Protocols cannot be dependent on any specific order of nodes participation or hierarchical structure (topology) due to a MANETs' dynamic network topology.

- Integration of a robust authentication mechanism is required to mitigate attacks from stronger active adversaries. It is essential that these mechanism introduce minimal additional computational and communication overhead.

- The computational and communication overhead should be fairly or equally distributed to all members or participants. This is essential to mitigate selfishness attacks.

- The protocol should be deployable in a self-organized network and thus ideally eliminate any imbalance between the responsibilities of nodes. The protocol should therefore be fully distributed to avoid single points of vulnerability.

- If special responsibilities (such as group controller) are delegated to the group members, such roles should be randomly assigned to any group member based on group policy and therefore be orthogonal to the key establishment process. It should however be noted that the protocols managing these roles (e.g. group leader election protocol) may be subject to attack, which may in turn lead to compromised of the group key management protocol.

Adhering to the latter three of these conditions allows the group key management scheme to preserve the strong symmetric relationships between the members of the DPGs found in MANETs.

The final conclusion drawn from the discussions on the existing key agreement schemes for DPGs, is that the Burmester and Desmedt (BD) topology independent contributory key agreement protocol (Burmester & Desmedt, 1994a), which is based on a broadcasting system, seems to satisfy most of the fundamental properties of MANETs. According to (Steiner et al., 2000), the BD key agreement protocol however suffers from some disadvantages, for example, high communication overhead and susceptibility to active adversaries, which makes it impractical.

As concluded in (van der Merwe et al., 2007), this study confirms again that key management mechanisms proposed to support the security of conventional networks are not necessarily suitable or adaptable to MANETs. New techniques, designed specifically for MANETs, are necessary. Key management for DPGs in MANETs is still an interesting research area with room for innovation.

REFERENCES

Ahituv, N., Lapid, Y., & Neumann, S. (1987). Processing encrypted data. *Communications of the ACM, 20*(9), 777-780.

Akyildiz, I. F., Su, W., Sankarasubramaniam, Y., & Cayirci. (2002). A survey on sensor networks. *IEEE Communications Magazine, 40*(8), 102-114.

Amir, Y., Ateniese, G., Hasse, D., Kim, Y., Nita-Rotaru, C., Schlossnagle, T., Schultz, J., Stanton, J., & Tsudik, G. (2000). Secure group communication in asynchronous networks with failures: Integration and experiments. In *Proceedings of the 20th IEEE International Conference on Distributed Computing Systems.*

Amir, Y., Kim, Y., Nita-Rotaru, C., Schultz, J., Stanton, J., & Tsudik, G. (2004). Secure group communication using robust contributory key agreement. *IEEE Transactions on Parallel and Distributed Systems, 15*(5), 468-480.

Amir, Y., Kim, Y., Nita-Rotaru, C., Stanton, J., & Tsudik, G. (2005). Secure spread: An integrated architecture for secure group communication. *IEEE Transactions on Dependable and Secure Computing, 2*(3), 248-261.

Amir, Y., Kim, Y., Nita-Rotaru, C., & Tsudik, G. (2002). On the performance of group key agreement protocols. In *Proceedings of the ACM International Conference on Distributed Computing Systems (ICDCS).*

Amir, Y., Kim, Y., Nita-Rotaru, C., & Tsudik, G. (2004). On the performance of group key agreement protocols. *ACM Transactions on Information Systems Security, 7*(3), 457-488.

Asokan, N., & Ginzboorg, P. (2002). Key agreement in ad-hoc networks. In *Proceedings of the ACM Workshop on Wireless Security (WiSe).*

Ateniese, G., Steiner, M., & Tsudik, G. (1998). Authenticated group key agreement and friends. In *Proceedings of the ACM Conference on Computer and Communications Security.*

Augot, D., Bhaskar, R., Issarny, V., & Sacchetti, D. (2007). A three round authenticated group key agreement protocol for ad hoc networks. *Pervasive and Mobile Computing, 3*(1), 36-52.

Becker, K., & Wille, U. (1998). Communication complexity of group key distribution. In *Proceedings of the ACM Conference on Computer and Communications Security.*

Bellovin, S. M., & Merritt, M. (1992). Encrypted key exchange: Password-based protocols secure against dictionary attacks. In *Proceedings of the IEEE Symposium on Research in Security and Privacy.*

Bresson, E., & Manulis, M. (2008a). Securing group key exchange against strong corruptions. In *Proceedings of the ACM Symposium on Information, Computer and Communications Security.*

Bresson, E. & Manulis, M. (2008b). Securing group key exchange against strong corruptions and key registration attacks. *International Journal of Applied Cryptography, 1*(2), 91-107.

Brickell, E. F., & Yacobi, Y. (1988). On privacy homomorphism. In *Proceedings of Advances in Cryptology - EUROCRYPT'87*, (LNCS 304, pp. 117-125).

Brown, M., Cheung, D., Hankerson, D., Hernandez, J., Kirkup, M., & Menezes, A. (2000). PGP in constrained wireless devices. In *Proceedings of the 9th USENIX Security Symposium.*

Burmester, M., & Desmedt, Y. (2006). Efficient and secure conference key distribution system. In *Security Protocols*, (LNCS 1189/1997, pp. 119-129).

Burmester, M., & Desmedt, Y. (1994a). A secure and efficient conference key distribution system. In *Proceedings of Advances in Cryptology - EUROCRYPT'94*, (LNCS 950, pp. 275-286).

Burmester, M., & Desmedt, Y. (1994b). A secure and efficient conference key distribution system. *Pre-proceedings of Advances in Cryptology - EUROCRYPT'94.*

Buttyan, L., & Hubaux, J. P. (2003). Stimulating cooperation in self-organizing mobile ad hoc networks. In *ACM Mobile Networks and Applications, 8*(5), 579-592.

Capkun, S., Buttyan, L., & Hubaux, J.-P. (2003). Self-organized public-key management for mobile ad hoc networks. *IEEE Transactions on Mobile Computing, 2*(1), 52-64.

Carman, D. W., Kruus, P. S., & Matt, B. J. (2000). *Constraints and approaches for distributed sensor security* (Tech. Rep. 00-010). Cryptographic Technologies Group, Trusted Information Systems, NAI Labs.

Chan, A. C.-F. (2004). Distributed symmetric key management for mobile ad hoc networks. In *Proceedings of the IEEE International Conference on Computer and Communications.*

Chan, H., Perrig, A., & Song, D. (2003). Random key predistribution schemes for sensor networks. In *Proceedings of the IEEE Symposium of Privacy and Security*.

Desmedt, Y., Lange, T., & Burmester, M. (2006). Scalable authenticated tree based group key exchange for ad-hoc groups. *Financial Cryptography and Data Security*, (LNCS 4886, pp. 104-118).

Diffie, W., & Hellman, M. E. (1976). New directions in cryptography. *IEEE Transactions on Information Theory, 22*(6), 644-654.

Diffie, W., van Oorschot, P. C., & Wiener, M. J. (1992). Authentication and authenticated key exchanges. *Designs Codes and Cryptography, 2*(2), 107-125.

Dutta, R., & Barua, R. (2005). *Overview of key agreement protocols* (Rep. 2005/289). ePrint Archive, from http://eprint.iacr.org

Eschenauer, L., & Gligor, V. D. (2002). A key-management scheme for distributed sensor networks. In *Proceedings of the ACM Conference on Computer and Communication Security*.

Haas, Z. J., & Tabrizi, S. (1998). On some challenges and design choices in ad-hoc communications. In *Proceedings of the IEEE Military Communications Conference*.

Hankerson, D., Menezes, A. J., & Vanstone, S. A. (2004). *Guide to elliptic curve cryptography*. Springer Professional Computing.

Hietalahti, M. (2001). Efficient key agreement for ad hoc networks. Unpublished master's thesis, Department of Computer Science and Engineering, Laboratory for Theoretical Computer Science, Helsinki University of Technology, Finland.

Ingemarsson, I., Tang, D., & Wong, C. (1982). A conference key distribution system. *IEEE Transactions on Information Theory, 28*(5), 714-720.

Kahn, J. M., Katz, R. H., & Pister, K. S. J. (1999). Mobile networking for smart dust. In *Proceedings of the ACM/IEEE International Conference on Mobile Computing and Networking (Mobi-Com)*.

Katz, J., & Yung, M. (2007). Scalable protocols for authenticated group key exchange, J*ournal of Cryptology, 20*(1), 85-113.

Kim, Y., Perrig, A., & Tsudik, G. (2004). Tree-based group key agreement. *ACM Transactions on Information Systems Security, 7*(1), 60-96.

Menezes, A., van Oorschot, P., & Vanstone, S. (1996). *Handbook in applied cryptography*. CRC Press.

Paillier, P. (1999). Public-key cryptosystems based on composite degree residuosity classes. In *Proceedings of Advances in Cryptology - EUROCRYPT'99*, (LNCS, 2139, 223-238).

Pereira, O., & Quisquater, J.-J. (2004). Generic insecurity of cliques-type authenticated group key agreement protocols. In *Proceedings of the 17th IEEE Computer Security Foundations Workshop*.

Rivest, R. L., Adleman, L., & Dertouzos, M. L. (1978). On data banks and privacy homomorphisms. In *Foundations of secure computation*. New York: Academic Press.

Steer, D. G., Strawczynski, L., Diffie, W., & Wiener, M. (1988). A secure audio teleconference system. In *Proceedings of Advances in Cryptology - CRYPTO'88*, (LNCS 403, 520-528).

Steiner, M., Tsudik, G., & Waidner, M. (1996). Diffie-Hellman key distribution extended to groups. In *Proceedings of the ACM Conference on Computer and Communication Security*.

Steiner, M., Tsudik, G., & Waidner, M. (2000). Key agreement in dynamic peer groups. *IEEE Transactions on Parallel and Distributed Systems, 11*(8), 769-780.

van der Merwe, J., Dawoud, D.S., & McDonald, S. (2007). A survey on peer-to-peer key management for mobile ad hoc networks. *ACM Computing Surveys, 39*(1), 1-32.

Yi, S., & Kravets, R. (2003). MOCA: Mobile certificate authority for wireless ad hoc networks. In *Proceedings of the 2nd Annual PKI Research Workshop.*

Zhou, L., & Haas, Z. J. (1999). Securing ad hoc networks. *IEEE Network: Special Issue on Network Security, 13*(6), 24-30.

FURTHER READING

Dutta, R., & Barua, R. (2005a). Constant round dynamic group key agreement. *Information Security,* (LNCS 3650/2005, 74-88).

Dutta, R., & Barua, R. (2005b). Dynamic group key agreement in tree-based setting. In *Proceedings of the 10th Australasian Conference on Information Security and Privacy.*

Joseph Chee Ming, T., Chik How, T., & Jim Mee, N. (2006). Security analysis of provably secure constant round dynamic group key agreement. *IEICE Transactions on Fundamentals of Electronics, Communications and Computer Sciences, E89-A*(11), 3348-3350.

Lee, P. P. C., Lui, J. C. S., & Yau, D. K. Y. (2006). Distributed collaborative key agreement and authentication protocols for dynamic peer groups. *IEEE/ACM Transactions on Networking, 14*(2), 263-276.

Lee, P. P. C., Lui, J. C. S., & Yau, D. K. Y. (2006). SEAL: A secure communication library for building dynamic group key agreement applications. *Journal of Systems and Software, 80*(3), 356-370.

Lijun L., & Manulis, M. (2006). Tree-based group key agreement framework for mobile ad-hoc networks. In *Proceedings of the 20th IEEE International Conference on Advanced Information Networking and Applications.*

Lijun L., & Manulis, M. (2007). Tree-based group key agreement gramework for mobile ad-hoc networks. *Future Generation Computer Systems, 23*(6), 787-803.

Manulis, M. (2005). Contributory group key agreement protocols, revisited for mobile ad-hoc groups. In *Proceedings of the International Workshop on Wireless and Sensor Networks Security (WSNS).*

Stanisław, J., Kim. J., & Tsudik, G. (2007). Robust group key agreement using short broadcasts. In *Proceedings of the 14th ACM Conference on Computer and Communications Security.*

APPENDIX: TABLES

Table 1. Communication cost comparison between reviewed protocol suites

Initial Key Agreement Protocols		Rounds	Messages	Unicast	Broadcast
Cliques	IKA.1	n	n	$n-1$	n
	IKA.2	$n+1$	$2n-1$	$2n-3$	2
TGDH		n/a	n/a	n/a	n/a
BD		2	2n	0	2n
BD*		2n	2n	0	2n

Auxiliary Key Agreement Protocols		Rounds	Messages	Unicast	Broadcast
Cliques [a]	MA	2	2	1	1
	ME	1	1	0	1
	MJ	$u+1$	$u+1$	u	1
	ML	1	1	0	1
TGDH [b]	MA	2	3	0	3
	ME	1	1	0	1
	GM	$\lceil \log_2 k \rceil + 1$	2k	0	2k
	GP	$\min((\log_2 v + 1), h)$	$\min 2v, \frac{n}{2}$	0	$\min 2v, \frac{n}{2}$
(BD*) [a c]	MA	5	5	0	5
	ME	4	4	0	4
	MJ	$u+4$	$u+4$	0	$u+4$
	ML	$2(w+c+1)$	$2(w+c+1)$	0	$2(w+c+1)$

[a] u denotes the number of members joining the group.

[b] k denotes the number of subgroups, v the number of leaving members and h the height of the key tree.

[c] $w = \{M_i\}$, where each M_i represents an isolated leaving member. $c = \{c_j\}$ represents the set of leaving subgroups where $c_j = \{M_j, M_{j+1}, ..., M_{j+k}\}$, for $k \geq 1$ and , denotes a subgroup of indexed neighboring members leaving together. The total number of leaving members is thus v = w c. The total number of rounds is given for $i - j > 1$. For the sake of simplicity the case when $i - j = 1$ will not be considered in this table.

Table 2. Computational cost comparison between reviewed protocol suites with respect to exponentiations per group member

Initial Key Agreement Protocols		Exponentiations per M_i
Cliques	IKA.1	$(i + 1)$ for $i < n$, n for M_n
	IKA.2	4 for $i < (n - 1)$, $\{2, n\}$ for $\{M_{n-1}, M_n\}$
TGDH		n/a
BD		$n + 2$
BD*		$n + 2$

Auxiliary Key Agreement Protocols		Exponentiations per M_i
Cliques [a]	MA	$\{n + 1, n + 2\}$ for $\{M_c, M_{n+1}\}$, 1 for other M_i
	ME	$(n - 1)$ for Mc, 1 for other M_i
	MJ	$(i + n)$ for M_{i+n}, $0 \le i < u$, $(u + n)$ for M_{n+u}, 1 for other M_i
	ML	$(n - v)$ for M_c, 1 for other M_i
TGDH [b]	MA	$2(h - 1)$ for M_s, $(h - 1)$ for other M_i
	ME	$2(h - 1)$ for M_s, $(h - 1)$ for other M_i
	GM	$2(h - 1)$ for M_s, $(h - 1)$ for other M_i
	GP	$2(h - 1)$ for M_s, $(h - 1)$ for other M_i
(BD*) [a] [c]	MA	$(n + 1)$ [e] for M_i, $i \in \{(n - 1), n, (n + 1), 1\}$, n [e] for other M_i
	ME	$(n + 1)$ [e] for M_i, $i \in \{(j - 2), (j - 1), (j + 1)\}$, n [e] for other M_i
	MJ	$(n + 1)$ [e] for M_i, $i \in \{(n - 1), n, ..., (n + u), 1\}$, n for other M_i
	ML	$(n + 1)$ [e] for M_i, $i \in \sigma$ [d], n [e] for other M_i

[a] u denotes the number of members joining the group.

[b] k denotes the number of subgroups, v the number of leaving members and h the height of the key tree.

[c] $w = \{M_i\}$, where each M_i represents an isolated leaving member. $c = \{c_j\}$ represents the set of leaving subgroups where $c_j = \{M_j, M_{j+1}, ..., M_{j+k}\}$, for $k \ge 1$ and , denotes a subgroup of indexed neighboring members leaving together. The total number of leaving members is thus $v = w \cup c$. The total number of rounds is given for $i - j > 1$. For the sake of simplicity the case when $i - j = 1$ will not be considered in this table.

[d] Members neighboring w, c and M_k, form the set σ.

[e] n - 1 of these exponents are 'low' cost, i.e. $\in (1, n)$.

Table 3. Computational cost comparison between reviewed protocol suites with respect to total exponentiations

Initial Key Agreement Protocols		Total Exponentiations
Cliques	IKA.1	$\dfrac{n(n+3)}{2} - 1$
	IKA.2	$5n - 6$
TGDH		n/a
BD		$n(n + 2)$
BD*		$n(n + 2)$

Auxiliary Key Agreement Protocols		Total Exponentiations
Cliques [a]	MA	$3n + 2$
	ME	$2n - 3$
	MJ	$\dfrac{u}{2}(u + 1) + n(u + 2) - 1$
	ML	$2(n - v) - 1$
TGDH [b]	MA	$3h - 3$
	ME	$3h - 3$
	GM	$3h - 3$
	GP	$3h - 3$
(BD*) [a c]	MA	$n^2 - n + 4$
	ME	$n^2 - n + 3$
	MJ	$n^2 - u(n - 1) + 3$
	ML	$n^2 - vn + 2(w + c) + 1$

[a] u denotes the number of members joining the group.

[b] k denotes the number of subgroups, v the number of leaving members and h the height of the key tree.

[c] $w = \{M_i\}$, where each M_i represents an isolated leaving member. $c = \{c_j\}$ represents the set of leaving subgroups where $c_j = \{M_j, M_{j+1}, ..., M_{j+k}\}$, for $k \geq 1$ and $j \in \beta$, denotes a subgroup of indexed neighboring members leaving together. The total number of leaving members is thus $v = w \cup c$. The total number of rounds is given for $i - j > 1$. For the sake of simplicity the case when $i - j = 1$ will not be considered in this table.

Table 4. Computational cost comparison between reviewed protocol suites with respect to signatures per group member

Initial Key Agreement Protocols		Signatures per M_i
Cliques	IKA.1	1
	IKA.2	1 for M_n, 2 for other M_i
TGDH		n/a
BD		2
BD*		2

Auxiliary Key Agreement Protocols		Signatures per M_i
Cliques [a]	MA	1 for $\{M_c, M_{n+1}\}$
	ME	1 for M_c
	MJ	1 for M_i, $i \in \{n, (n+1), ..., (n+u)\}$
	ML	1 for M_c
TGDH [b]	MA	2
	ME	1
	GM	$\lceil \log_2 k \rceil + 1$
	GP	$\min((\log_2 v + 1), h)$
(BD*) [a][c]	MA	1 for M_i, $i \in \{(n-1), n, (n+1), 1\}$, 2 for M_n
	ME	1 for M_i, $i \in \{(j-2), (j-1), (j+1)\}$, 2 for M_{j-1}
	MJ	1 for M_i, $i \in \{(n-1), n, ..., (n+u), 1\}$, 2 for M_n
	ML	1 for M_i, $i \in \sigma$ [d], 2 for M_k

[a] u denotes the number of members joining the group.

[b] k denotes the number of subgroups, v the number of leaving members and h the height of the key tree.

[c] $w = \{M_i\}$, where each M_i represents an isolated leaving member. $c = \{c_j\}$ represents the set of leaving subgroups where $c_j = \{M_j, M_{j+1}, ..., M_{j+k}\}$, for $k \geq 1$ and $j \in \beta$, denotes a subgroup of indexed neighboring members leaving together. The total number of leaving members is thus $v = w \cup c$. The total number of rounds is given for $i - j > 1$. For the sake of simplicity the case when $i - j = 1$ will not be considered in this table.

[d] Members neighboring w, c and M_k, form the set σ.

Table 5. Computational cost comparison between reviewed protocol suites with respect to verifications per group member

Initial Key Agreement Protocols		Verifications per M_i
Cliques	IKA.1	1 for $\{M_1, M_n\}$, 2 for other M_i
	IKA.2	1 for $\{M_1, M_{n-1}\}$, $(n-1)$ for M_n, 3 for other M_i
TGDH		n/a
BD		$2n$
BD*		$2n$

Auxiliary Key Agreement Protocols		Verifications per M_i
Cliques [a]	MA	1
	ME	1 for M_i, $i \neq c$
	MJ	2 for M_i, $i \varepsilon \{(n+1), (n+u-1)\}$, 1 for other M_i
	ML	1 for M_c
TGDH [b]	MA	3
	ME	1
	GM	$\lceil \log_2 k \rceil$
	GP	$\min[(2v, \lceil \frac{n}{2} \rceil]$
(BD*) [a c]	MA	3 for M_n, 4 for other M_i
	ME	2 for M_{j-1}, 3 for other M_i
	MJ	$u+2$ for M_n, $u+3$ for other M_i
	ML	$2(w+c)$ for M_k, $2(w+c)+1$ for other M_i, $i \varepsilon \sigma$ [d]

[a] u denotes the number of members joining the group.

[b] k denotes the number of subgroups, v the number of leaving members and h the height of the key tree.

[c] $w = \{M_i\}$, where each M_i represents an isolated leaving member. $c = \{c_j\}$ represents the set of leaving subgroups where $c_j = \{M_j, M_{j+1}, ..., M_{j+k}\}$, for $k \geq 1$ and $j \in \beta$, denotes a subgroup of indexed neighboring members leaving together. The total number of leaving members is thus $v = w \cup c$. The total number of rounds is given for $i - j > 1$. For the sake of simplicity the case when $i - j = 1$ will not be considered in this table. [d] Members neighboring w, c and M_k, form the set σ.

Chapter XIII
A Tool Supported Methodology for Developing Secure Mobile P2P Systems

James Walkerdine
Lancaster University, UK

Peter Phillips
Lancaster University, UK

Simon Lock
Lancaster University, UK

ABSTRACT

The growth of mobile devices with near PC equivalent capabilities has brought with it the possibility of mobile Peer-to-Peer (P2P) systems. However, the unique nature of mobile devices introduces new challenges that need to be considered during the development process, especially when considering critical aspects such as system security. This chapter presents the PEPERS Development Methodology (PDM), a tool-supported methodology that aims to assist designers in developing secure mobile P2P systems, and encourages them to consider specific mobile P2P design issues from an early stage. The PDM is demonstrated within the context of a real-world case study of a system developed for a security company.

INTRODUCTION

The rapid growth in availability of mobile devices with ever increasing functionality has brought with it the possibility of mobile Peer-to-Peer (P2P) systems. More recently, advances in wireless networking and mobile computing technologies, such as wireless LANs, wireless mesh networks and 3G cellular networks have further facilitated the migration of the P2P paradigm into wireless mobile computing. The combination of mobile and P2P technologies could be ideal for organisations that possess characteristics such as, decentralised management styles, geographically dispersed or highly mobile workforces, a wide range of computing and communications devices, etc.

However in developing real-world mobile P2P systems, designers can face a new set of development challenges - particularly when it comes to providing security and privacy. Ensuring such characteristics exist within a system is of particular importance in an environment that, by its very nature, is ad-hoc and heterogeneous.

The issue is complicated, however, by the fact that the P2P approaches used and the underlying mobile technologies will also have an impact on a system's characteristics (Walkerdine, 2001). For example, the choice of P2P topology can significantly impact on how well a system can provide security. Decentralised P2P systems are likely to be better suited for handling denial of service attacks; the central authority provided by semi-centralised P2P systems would be better suited for handling authentication. Likewise the resource constraints (e.g. memory, battery life) of mobile devices can limit the amount of computation that can be performed or the level of communication between devices.

Such issues are important, and necessary to consider when developing a secure mobile P2P system. Having a development method to accommodate them is vital but, unfortunately, is something which is currently lacking within the domain. This chapter presents the PEPERS Development Methodology (PDM), a tool-supported methodology that provides such development assistance. The PDM encourages designers to consider the issues that are central to mobile P2P system development (for example, identifying security concerns, considering mobility and technical constraints, and making architectural design decisions) from an early stage. It supports the designer throughout the development cycle, from initial requirements elicitation through to the final implementation - ensuring that security and mobile concerns are properly addressed throughout. In particular, it assists developers in determining the most suitable P2P topologies and application reference architectures for their design, based on the system, security and mobility requirements that they have identified. The PDM comes with tool support and this is also illustrated within this chapter.

The PDM was developed as part of the EU funded PEPERS (PEPERS, 2006) project that has developed an infrastructure to support the design, development and operational deployment of secure mobile P2P applications. The outcomes of the project have been utilised and evaluated by industrial user partners within their own business domains, as well as a number of mobile software development companies. In order to help illustrate the use of the PDM and support tool, a real-life case study is provided that involves one of these industrial systems.

This chapter begins by discussing some of the key issues that need to be considered when developing a secure mobile P2P system. An overview of the PDM is then provided, along with a description of the case study and developed tool support. The PDM is then described in detail, referring to the case study to demonstrate each stage in use.

BACKGROUND

Although in general developers can draw upon existing software engineering techniques for developing secure mobile P2P systems, the distributed and unpredictable nature of P2P coupled with the technical challenges of mobile technology and security constraints, means that there are a number of specific issues that designers must consider.

Making Security Central to the Design

Successful security functionality is not something that can be bolted onto a system as an afterthought. The broad nature of security means that it is something that should be considered at all stages of a systems development. For example, technical and company policy issues can have an impact on proposed security requirements; the choice of P2P topology can impact on how these requirements are met; the 3rd party encryption component that is to be used can likewise have an impact, etc. It is therefore important to make security a central concern throughout the development lifecycle. Such activities can also be supported from an organisational perspective by adopting a rigid review process, and assigning members of the development team specific roles to ensure that security requirements are being properly considered.

Mobility Requirements and Constraints

Mobile applications and mobile technologies introduce new sets of requirements and constraints. For example, the degree of mobility that is expected within an application will impact on how it is designed (from a P2P perspective high mobility might suggest a more decentralised approach). In addition, the technology capabilities of a mobile device can restrict memory availability (and thus program size), or the amount of processing the device can perform. Likewise mobile technology will introduce its own requirements such as battery life or those derived from restrictions imposed by the devices OS. Given the influence mobility can have on a systems design, it is important for developers to consider it at all stages of the development lifecycle and, where practical, for mobile technology decisions to be finalised as early as possible.

Network and Communication Requirements and Constraints

The carrier or network type, and the expected network coverage level can all have implications on a developed system. Of particular importance is the communication mechanism that will be used, with various tradeoffs that exist between bandwidth capabilities, range capabilities and power consumption characteristics. During development designers will need to consider the characteristics/requirements of their system and how these relate to the functionality provided by the available technology. This will also influence other design decisions, for example the type of P2P topology that should be used.

P2P Technology Requirements and Constraints

An important part of P2P software development is the definition and analysis of the underlying topology that is to be used. Our previous work (Walkerdine, 2002) has shown that the choice of topology can have a significant impact on the properties (e.g. security) of a system, perhaps most clearly highlighted with the differences between decentralised and semi-centralised architectures. It is important for designers to realise and understand the effect that the choice of topology can have on a systems specification and design (and likewise how a system's requirements can influence the choice of topology). For context, Figure 1 presents a summary of the key classes of P2P topologies.

The choice of P2P technology (for example, the protocol and implementations used) can also have an influence, with each typically offering varying degrees of functionality to the developer. For example, JXTA provides considerably more P2P development support than .NET, and consequently less needs to be provided within any system design. Likewise, the distributed P2P security implementations that are provided

Figure 1. Key classes of P2P topologies

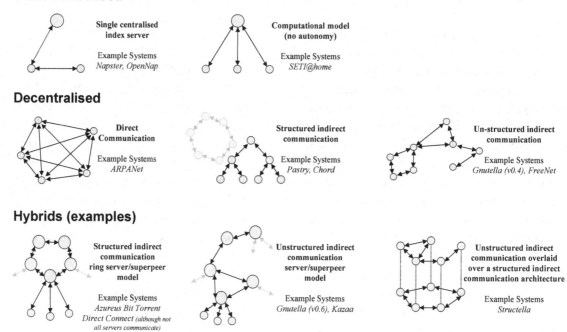

by (Berket et al., 2004) and (Agarwal et al., 2001), each offers differing levels of security support. Given this, it will be important for developers to commit to a technology at an early stage within the development lifecycle.

Adopting an Architectural Driven Design Approach

Due to the fact that architectures play a key role in P2P development, it is beneficial to use a design approach that places a greater emphasis on these issues. Architectural driven design approaches specifically encourage the development of the system architecture from early within the development lifecycle, and so represent an ideal option for supporting P2P system development. Such approaches also support the use of reference architectures that can act as inputs to the design process - helping developers determining the architectural building blocks they might need.

THE PEPERS DEVELOPMENT METHODOLOGY

The PEPERS Development Methodology (PDM) was originally conceived in the BANKSEC project (BANKSEC, 2000), in which a methodology was needed for specifying system and component security requirements. During P2P ARCHITECT (P2P ARCHITECT, 2001), this methodology was further developed and tailored for use in the specification and design of dependable P2P software systems. Within PEPERS it has been further refined to support the development of secure mobile P2P applications. Within each project the methodology has been used and evaluated by end user industrial partners. As a consequence, the PDM is a result of many years of practical industrial use and theoretical refinement (it has been successfully applied in the development of banking and P2P based online booking systems).

Existing methodologies already exist for more general mobile application development (for example the UML based development approach described in (B'Far, 2004) and the work on network-based software architectures in (Fielding, 2000)). Middleware solutions, such as PROEM (Kortuem, 2002) have also been developed to provide a foundation for the development of mobile P2P systems. In addition there has also been work in developing more innovative methods, such as ontology-based development methods, e.g. Tropos (Bertolini, 2002; Mouratidis, 2003), to aid P2P system design. However, no general software engineering methodology exists that particularly encourages developers to consider security and P2P issues, and thus in this regard, the PDM is novel.

The PDM is based on a 5-stage spiral model as illustrated in Figure 2. This spiral model is comprised of five segments:

- *Requirements Elicitation*
- *Propose P2P system architecture*
- *Propose sub-system design*
- *System Implementation*
- *Verification and Validation*

The spiral nature of the PDM provides the advantage of a flexible development process in which designers are not rigidly constrained by

fixed phases. An important characteristic of the method is that it is *iterative*, in that during the design of a P2P application the designers can revisit stages of the model as new requirements, architectural issues, etc, come to light. It is likely, for example, that early on in a P2P applications development, iterations of the model will largely focus on the gathering and defining of requirements, and later stages on sub-system design. This spiral and iterative nature of the process is important for accommodating the fact that a P2P system's design will often change during development. This may be as a result of a range of factors, including the resolution of requirement conflicts, the late identification of additional requirements, changes in the application domain or business context and so on.

The PDM is flexible enough to accommodate different types of software engineering techniques during development. For example, different requirement elicitation techniques, or design approaches.

A detailed breakdown of the PDM is provided later in this chapter. To help illustrate this and the use of the support tool a real-world case study is also presented. To provide some background, the chapter will first provide an overview of the case study and the supporting tool.

Case Study: Supporting a Security Firm

To help in the design and evaluation of the methods and tools developed within PEPERS, the project consortium includes industrial user partners who wish to use P2P technology to support their own business practices. One of these is a major international security firm who wishes to support their guards in communicating, collaborating and sharing information with each other whilst on patrol. Another is a media company who wishes to allow their journalists, photographers and editors to work together in the creation of magazines and newspaper articles. In both cases

Figure 2. The stages that comprise the PDM

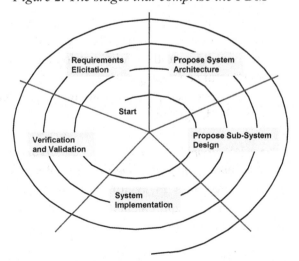

the companies wish to use P2P to support secure communication and data exchange between their personnel, who may be geographically dispersed or particularly mobile, and may only have access to mobile devices. Within the project each user partner has built a secure mobile P2P system that specifically supports elements of their business processes. The PDM was used as the underlying methodology for the development of the applications in both cases.

For this case study we will focus on the pilot that was developed with the security firm. Its aim was to allow its security guards and mobile patrols to receive and transmit sensitive customer information in a dynamic environment via their mobile devices. Such environments are typically ad-hoc exceptional situations which the guards/patrols have responded to and which involves them co-operating with one another. Guards are initially assigned tasks via the ARC, a central computer based in the company's headquarters.

The pilot was built for operation on a Sony Ericsson Symbian 9 OS phone, and has been successfully deployed and evaluated within the organisation for a period of 6 months. Figure 3 provides a screenshot of the developed security pilot application running on the phone.

Figure 3. The Security firm pilot

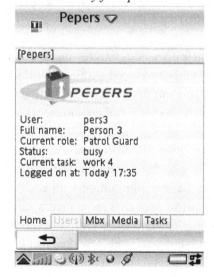

Using the application guards are able to receive tasks from the ARC, update it on their progress, as well as communicate messages and images directly with each other. All communication is encrypted, and repeated authentication is required to access the applications functionality. Dynamic verification techniques are also used to ensure that the user does not perform actions that are inappropriate for their role.

Tool Support for the PDM

In order to support designers in using the PDM, web based tool support was also built. Designed to be generic in nature, it is able to work alongside different system engineering paradigms (for example, architectural driven or component based design). Not only does the tool support the development of systems in accordance with the PDM, it also actively encourages the consideration of security issues by the developers.

The tool itself can play a part during the first three stages of the method. It provides support for requirement gathering and analysis, as well as assisting the designers in making informed decisions with regards to the architectural design. Designers are able to draw upon a knowledge base of topologies and P2P application reference architectures, and the characteristics (i.e. the effect on system properties, etc). They are also able to identify and provide initial descriptions for the sub-systems within their design. The intention is that designers use separate tools (for example, Rational Rose) to then fully develop the system architecture and design.

The tool itself provides a number of key features for designers:

- *Support for identifying, specifying and managing requirements.* The tool can assist developers in identifying and specifying system requirements during software development.

- *Support for topology selection.* The tool draws upon a knowledge base of P2P topologies and details about the impact they may have on a range of security and mobility properties. The tool is able to present this knowledge to the developers enabling them to make informed decisions, as well as being able to suggest suitable topologies.
- *Support for the identification of key secure mobile P2P application functionality.* The tool assists the designer in identifying key areas of desired application functionality (functional capabilities). This could be, for example, encryption or instant messenger capabilities.
- *Support for secure mobile P2P Application Reference Architecture selection.* The tool is able to draw upon a knowledge base of application reference architectures and the capabilities they typically support. The tool can present this knowledge to the designers and suggest application reference architectures that may be of relevance.
- *Support for Sub-system identification and initial description.* The tool provides facilities to allow designers to identify and provide initial descriptions for the sub-systems used within their design. These can be outputted and further developed within separate design packages.
- *Support for general managerial and trace ability activities.* The tool provides a number of managerial features including report generation and traceability support, allowing designers to trace their various decisions throughout the design process. For example, by linking the choice of topology to the set of requirements that motivated this design decision. The output of the tool can also be imported into UML tools (via XMI).

BREAKDOWN OF THE PDM

The chapter will now move on to describe the five stages of the PDM in detail. The case study will be visited at each stage to help illustrate the PDM in use. It should be noted that although the user partner performed many iterations of the PDM's spiral before the design was complete; for the sake of brevity these are not all fully documented here.

Requirements Elicitation

Before commencing this stage, a business decision to procure a P2P system to support some business activity must first have been made. From this decision, a number of business requirements will be generated. These business requirements set out the critical functionality that the P2P system is expected to provide and define the constraints on the operation of the system that is to be developed.

From these high level goals, more concrete system requirements are generated and specified. Part of this will involve the identification of security requirements many of which will be applicable to the P2P system as a whole rather than to the individual parts that comprise it. In summary, activities in this stage of development would include:

- *Elicitation of business goals and requirements from stakeholders.* The identification of mobile and security requirements should play a central role in the elicitation process. Part of this should involve a detailed security analysis, using techniques such as threat modelling to help identify the security risks and the (differing) levels of security that will exist within the system. Stakeholders should also be encouraged to identify the mobility attributes they desire for the system.
- *Elicitation system requirements from stakeholders and business requirements.* Again

mobile and security aspects should be an important focus.

- *Analysis and negotiation of agreed system requirements.* Negotiate any conflicts between stakeholder requirements.
- *Production of system requirements document.*

The properties of the various P2P topologies and the effect that these can have on system requirements will play a significant part at this stage of development. For example, identified requirements may restrict the choice of topology (for example, a system that is to be highly managed would benefit most from a semi-centralised topology). Conversely the selection of a topology may produce additional functional requirements for the system (for example, the need for super peers). In either case, there is likely to be conflicting issues between the requirements and the topologies that would need to be resolved.

Case Study

During the initial iterations of the model in this stage the user partner identified a number of business and security requirements for their P2P system (a small selection of which are as follows):

- Mechanisms should be in place to verify the identity of users when taking on specific roles within the system (e.g. ARC operator, Mobile Unit member, Team Leader etc)
- The system should manage data on a strict need-to-know basis
- It is essential that location, status, activity, assignment, incident and project data does not become available to unauthorised individuals
- The system should not require additional hardware expenditure of more than 5000 euros

The user partner then proceeded to identify a set of initial viewpoints and system requirements for their P2P system, using the tool support to help document them. As the designers gained a clearer understanding of the different stakeholders needs, the system requirements were revised and specified in more detail. Identified viewpoints and requirements included:

- **Shift Supervisor:** The person in change of assigning shifts, briefing and de-briefing guards
- **Shift Creation:** The system should allow the Shift Supervisor to create and describe shifts (including relevant security data)
- **Guard Monitoring:** The system should be able to log all the activities of a mobile unit (guard) including all communications, actions on data, changes in status and movements in the real world
- **Guard:** The person who takes part in security related activities
- **Information Request:** The guard should be able to request information from the system that is required in order to complete their task.

As the specification and design developed, the designers were able to use the support tool to begin identifying which security properties and system capabilities where relevant. In turn the tool was able to suggest topology and P2P application reference architectures that may be suitable for their design (as described below).

Propose System Architecture

The architecture of any system is the framework that defines how the entities within it (e.g. components, objects, etc) are organised and what relationships may exist between them.

Before developing the architecture it is usually necessary for at least some requirements to have been defined. However a complete set of requirements will usually not be available in the very early stages of the development. Initial requirements can be used to generate preliminary ideas of the architectural design, and by defining architectures early on it can provide the designers with ways of organising the process of specification and design. From a secure mobile P2P perspective, however, it is important that initial security and mobility requirements have been identified and considered, before this stage is begun.

Furthermore, when developing mobile P2P systems it is highly likely that the specification and the design will be interwoven, with each affecting the other as system development proceeds. The utilisation of an iterative approach allows these two to be developed in concert with each other.

The activities designers of mobile P2P systems would carry out in this development phase include:

- *Select topologies.* Based on the identified system requirements, and mobile and security properties for the P2P system, designers can filter and select the appropriate topologies. Knowledge of the different topologies and their influence on system properties (Walkerdine, 2002; Walkerdine, 2006) can be used as an input into this activity. For example, semi-centralised topologies can assist in the provision of authentication and authorisation functionality. However, the centralised points they possess also act as points of weakness in the architecture – making them susceptible to attacks.

- *Derive system functional capabilities.* Designers should derive from the identified requirements, system functional capabilities. These capabilities represent abstract system functionality that the system should possess. For example, it may be desired for the system to possess Instant Messaging capabilities, or encryption capabilities. The identification of these capabilities can help designers in selecting relevant secure mobile P2P application reference architectures.

- *Select mobile P2P application reference architectures.* Designers can use the capabilities that have been identified in the previous activity to help select secure mobile P2P application reference architectures that could be used as input into the design of their system. Within PEPERS a set of reference architectures have been developed that reflect key application domains within the field (e.g. shared workspace, distributed storage, etc) and the different types of P2P topology (Walkerdine, 2005).

- *Establish architectural model.* This is where an overall model of the system at a high level is developed; it shows the system entities and the relationships between them. Designers can draw upon the application reference architectures and their capabilities to help them gain an understanding of what may be required, and also to provide references to compare their own designs against. Furthermore, the choice of topology and identified requirements will also have an effect on the architectural model (for example, whether it is to be a decentralised or semi-centralised system). Identified security and mobility requirements will play a key role within this activity, impacting on the architectural model and vice versa - and so should be considered carefully.

- *Describe sub-systems.* Here the functionality of each sub-system is defined and attention is drawn to sub-system boundaries. Again the application reference architectures can be used to help the designers to initially think about the sub-systems, the services they provide and their boundaries. Likewise the identified requirements will be an important input to this activity.

- *Where possible, allocate requirements to sub-systems.* Requirements that have been identified and specified for the system should be mapped on to the architecture and its sub-systems. Ideally, each requirement will be assigned to a single sub-system. In practice, however, this is rarely possible as a requirement may encompass several sub-systems (particularly with mobility and security requirements).

- *Evaluate architecture*. This involves checking to ensure that all requirements have been assigned to sub-systems, looking for mismatches between the architecture and the requirements and assessing what problems may arise when implementing the architecture. Assessing how well the security and mobile technology requirements have been satisfied will be particularly important.

Case Study

Having performed initial requirements elicitation activities, the designers began to investigate the suitability of the different topologies and application reference architectures for use in their architectural design.

As shown in Figure 4, the designers used the supporting tool to assign ratings to a range of security properties (top diagram). For each property the developers indicated its importance to their design and to what requirements it related to. Based on this input the tool was able to suggest that a semi-centralised topology would be the most suit-

Figure 4. Rating the importance of security properties, and using these to suggest suitable topologies

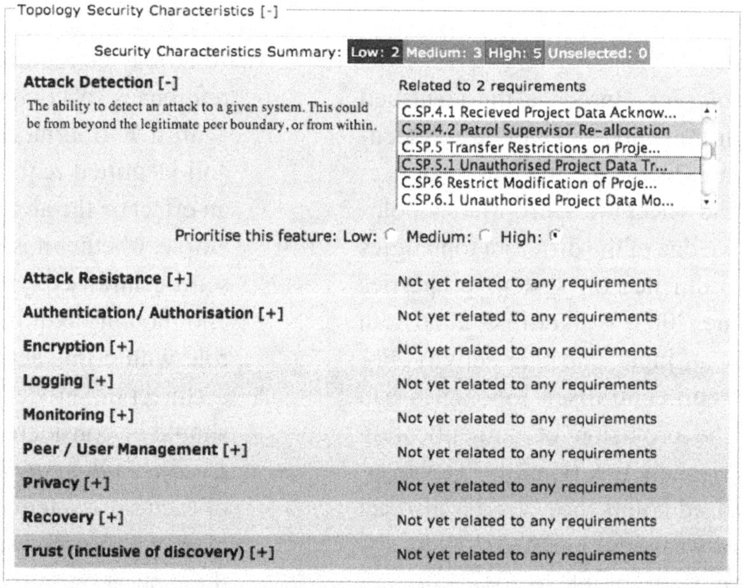

	Attack detection	Attack resistance	Authentication/ Authorisation	Encryption	Logging	Monitoring	Peer / User management	Privacy	Recovery	Trust (inclusive of discovery)
Semi-centralised Architectures	high	low	high	high	high	high	high	medium	medium	high
Decentralised Direct Communication Architectures	medium	high	high	high	medium	low	high	low	high	high
Decentralised Structured In-Direct Communication Architectures	medium	medium	low	medium	medium	medium	medium	high	high	medium
Decentralised Unstructured In-Direct Communication Architectures	low	high	low	medium	low	low	low	high	low	low

able for meeting their requirements. The bottom diagram shows the topology recommendations based on the desired security properties, with the most suitable at the top. In both diagrams, green represents high priority, orange for medium priority and red for low priority.

Upon further analysis of the system requirements (in particular the fact that the existing system possesses a single centralised server - the ARC), a design decision was made to use a semi-centralised topology as a basis for the system. Because the users existing system already possessed a central server, the choice of topology did not impose any additional requirements/constraints onto the design that had not already been considered. Figure 5 provides a general overview of the topology used within the system.

The designers also made use of the support tool in order to gain suggestions for secure mobile P2P application reference architectures that could provide an input to their design. Although none of the reference architectures known by the tool were directly relevant to the system being

developed, the Instant Messenger and Shared Workspace reference architectures were found to be the closest fit.

At this time the designers also began to develop the architectural model for their system. The topology was the foundation of the system design, and this was extended so that the structure of the different peer types (standard or super peers) that comprised it, were then specified. As part of this process, the designers drew upon the reference architectures, and the requirements document.

From studying the reference architectures the designers identified the key sub-systems they would require in their architectural design. Not all of the sub-systems described within the reference architectures were used, with the designers feeling that the functionality relating to real-time connection monitoring and logging was unnecessary in their pilot. Likewise the designers decided that limited awareness functionality would be incorporated within the P2P Communication sub-system, rather than as a standalone sub-system as proposed within the reference architectures. Using

Figure 5. General overview of the topology used within the developed system

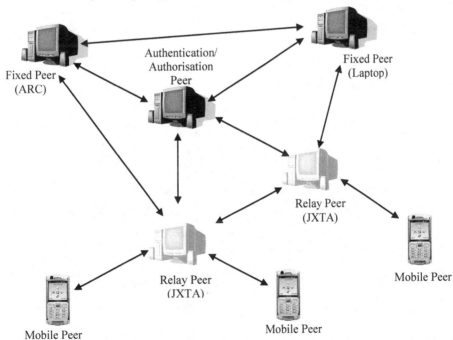

the support tool, the designers began to briefly describe the sub-systems they had identified for their system. Figure 6 provides a screenshot of the tool showing topology and reference architecture choices, and the sub-systems that have been identified. Using a separate design tool, these sub-systems were then organised into high-level

architectures for the peer (Figure 7), before being developed into a full design.

Propose Sub-System Design

This stage focuses on the actual design of the P2P system; taking the proposed system architecture

Figure 6. Reviewing choices and identifying sub-systems

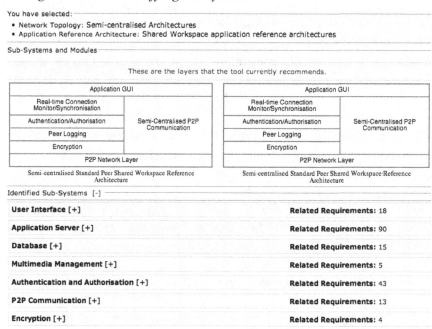

Figure 7. High level architecture for a standard peer

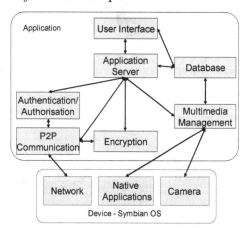

and requirements specification, and using these to create a detailed design for the system. To do this an initial architecture for the system must have been developed.

The activities the designers would carry out in this stage include:

- Specifying the entities that make up the system architecture and its subsystems (objects, components, etc)
- Specifying the relationships that may exist between these entities.
- Specifying the allocation of system requirements to these entities.
- Specify, if necessary, the non-functional attributes that an entity should have

As part of PEPERS a set of runtime modules have been developed that provide general functionality (for example, encryption, secure P2P communication, etc) intended for use by mobile P2P applications (Walkerdine, 2007). When designing the various application sub-systems, developers may wish to make use of these modules. The tool support has knowledge of such modules and can direct the developer towards using them during the design process.

Initial implementation choices will also impact on the design stage. Because a single development standard does not exist for P2P systems, a design can change significantly depending on the underlying technology that is to be used. Likewise the choice of mobile technology will also have repercussions on the system design. To support the design process, initial implementation choices should be made early, with the PDM's design and implementation stages re-visited as the development progresses.

Case Study

By the time the user partner focused their efforts on this stage, the requirements and application architecture had been through a number of itera-

tions of development and some initial decisions had been made with regards to implementation technology. The design progressed with reference to the Shared Workspace reference architecture suggested by the support tool. The designers proceeded to specify the design of the various sub-systems in detail, using a separate design tool (Rational Rose). For those they intended to develop themselves, this involved breaking them down into components, which were then further expanded with class definitions. The individual classes were then specified, with attributes and methods defined.

The designers decided that, where possible, the sub-systems would be based around those provided by the PEPERS runtime modules. In particular their design would draw upon P2P Communications, Authentication/Authorisation and Encryption modules. The designers integrated the interfaces for these modules into their design.

The design was also influenced by the implementation technology decisions that had been made. In particular it was decided that a Sony Ericsson phone would be used and the application would be developed in Java. This in turn introduced requirements that fed back into the requirements elicitation and placed limitations on the architecture/design stages.

System Implementation

This stage takes the requirements, high-level architecture and detailed design from the previous stages and uses them to guide the actual construction of the final system. Initial iterations of this stage will typically focus on determining the types of technology that would be used as part of the implementation. The PDM does not prescribe set implementation approaches and instead allows developers and organisations to use the processes they are already familiar with.

The activities developers would carry out in this stage include:

- *Decide on P2P technologies.* For example, the P2P protocol and API
- *Decide on mobile technologies.* For example, the mobile device and communication technologies.
- *Decide on security technologies.* For example, encryption algorithms and related API's.
- *Implement system entities.* Using PEPERS runtime module implementations if applicable.
- *Integrate system entities.*

Designers should carefully consider the impact technology choices will have on their development (in terms of requirements/constraints). In many cases legacy technologies will also play a role within the system, especially if the system is to integrate with a clients existing setup (which typically will be more centralised and less mobile). Certainly during early stages of the development it will be important to re-visit the previous stages of the PDM, until the technical impact on the design has been fully considered.

Case Study

During early iterations of the development model, the user partners began to make decisions on how their system was to be implemented. It was decided that, where possible, the PEPERS runtime modules would be utilised and that the rest of the system would be built using Java. As a result of this decision, the bulk of the security functionality would be provided by the PEPERS modules. Additionally it was decided that a Sony Ericsson/Symbian 9 OS phone would be used as the basis of the mobile system hardware. The overall system would also need to integrate with the existing centralised system that formed the basis of the ARC central computer.

In later iterations, the focus moved to prototyping and implementing the sub-system designs developed during the previous stages. A key part

of this was the integration of the PEPERS runtime modules with the rest of the components that had been developed in-house.

Verification and Validation

This stage focuses on the verification and validation of the system development and will occur at various points of the development lifecycle as the requirements, design and implementation are refined. Verification involves checking the system conforms to its specification. Validation involves checking the system as implemented meets the expectations of the client.

The activities carried out in this stage include:

- Validate the requirements against the stakeholders.
- *Validate the architecture against the requirements.* The architecture/requirements mapping performed in the Propose System Architecture stage will support this activity.
- *Validate the sub-system design against the architecture and requirements.* The requirement/ sub-system mapping performed as part of the Sub-system Design stage will support this activity.
- *Validate the implementation against the requirements/design.* Validating the implementation using testing techniques.
- *Verify the design models against the requirements.* Design models representing abstract system behaviour are verified against the requirements. Within PEPERS this activity is supported by the Static Verification Framework (SVF) (Siveroni, 2008).
- *Verify the implementation against the requirements.* The runtime execution of the system is verified against the requirements. Within PEPERS this activity is supported by the Dynamic Verification Framework (DVF) (Spanoudakis, 2008).

As a consequence of these activities, further iterations of the development model may be required so that additional requirements elicitation and negotiation, architecture and design refinement can be performed. As the PEPERS runtime platform modules have already been through a process of verification and validation, there use within a development can further help to support this process and help reduce the resources required for this stage.

Case Study

This stage was frequently visited during the development lifecycle. Initially the focus was on validating the identified business, security and system requirements with the clients. This was achieved through the use of sets of documented requirements (which were signed off by the user partners) as well as face to face requirement checking and negotiation workshops.

In later iterations of the methodology, validation moved on to focus on the architecture and sub-system design. During this phase of development, the user partners constructed semi-formal behavioural models of the system. These were then checked verified automatically using the SVF toolkit (Siveroni, 2008) to ensure the correct and expected operation of the system.

Finally the implementation was tested and debugged; drawing upon the DVF at runtime to make sure that incorrect usage behaviour was being blocked/reported.

EXPERIENCES IN USING THE PDM

As mentioned previously, industrial partners utilised the PDM to assist in the development of their pilot applications. This not only allowed the method and tool to be evaluated but also allowed refinements to be made based on feedback from industrial partner experiences. In addition, workshops were held with local mobile phone soft-

ware companies to obtain additional third-party feedback. These companies were typically small in size, and so provided a different perspective to the software development process.

Overall the developers found the PDM and supporting tool to offer significant help in guiding the development of their secure mobile P2P applications. The smaller industrial companies were less sure about its use to them, mainly because they do not have the resources to follow a traditional development process and time to market is critical to them. They tended to use 'extreme programming' approaches to mobile software development. The larger companies, on the other hand, used more comprehensive development approaches and found the PDM to be of more relevance. This also highlights how the use of software engineering techniques within the real world is very much dependent on an organisations situation and its available resources.

The current development approaches they used were particularly linear in fashion (modelled on the 'waterfall model') and although it took time to get used to, they found the iterative nature of the PDM to benefit their way of working. The developers also found that the methodology and tool support was flexible enough to allow them to use existing processes and tools (such as their current UML design tools).

The developers found that the method encouraged them to consider specific security, mobile technology and P2P issues early within their systems development - something which their existing approaches did not achieve. Designers found the recommended secure mobile application reference architectures useful and that they were able to contribute to the development of a suitable architecture for their application.

However, despite these positive outcomes, due in part to the lack of experience with the method and the criticality of the application development, a number of issues were identified where it was felt the PDM could be improved.

Understanding the PDM

Many of the developers found the PDM to be significantly different from their current approaches to software development. As a result it took them a while to learn and gain an understanding of the steps that are involved. In particular the spiral, iterative approach was novel to them and it meant that their management style had to adapt to accommodate it. Given their inexperience with the method, there were times when this caused problems, resulting in detailed design decisions being made too early. When this occurred it became necessary for the designers to step back and re-assess their development. As the developers became more familiar with the methodology, however, such issues occurred less often. Given that all software development approaches take time to learn and understand, such findings are not that surprising.

Difficulty in Selecting Suitable Mobile P2P Application Reference Architectures

The developers initially found it difficult to identify which mobile P2P application reference architectures would be able to assist them in their design. The reference architectures themselves tackle specific types of application functionality, when in reality an actual system development may involve a combination of these functionalities. Initially the industrial partners tried to identify a single reference architecture that would satisfy all their requirements. It was only when they realised that this could not be achieved that they started to understand the true utility of these architectures; as points of reference for their own design. Supporting documentation that clarifies the use and benefit of reference architectures would encourage designers to make more appropriate use of them.

The Concept of Capabilities within the Reference Architectures

The developers had some difficulty in initially understanding the notion of a "capability" as used within the methodology and supporting tool. In particular their lack of experience of the P2P domain meant that they found it difficult to identify which capabilities would be relevant to their design. Such difficulties diminished as their experience grew, however it highlights the importance of novice P2P developers gaining a good understanding of the domain prior to development.

Improved Recommendation Support

Developers felt that that security property analysis provided by the tool could be made finer grained. Some of the security properties could be further broken down into sub-characteristics, reflecting the fact that developers may desire for a property to be provided for in different ways. For example, a systems attack resistance can be represented in different ways (lack of central points of failure, ability to resist tampering, etc). In addition, developers commented that the tool should provide a more detailed rationale behind its recommendations, further helping them to make their final architectural choices.

The Consideration of Other Non-Functional Properties

Although PEPERS has predominantly focused on mobility, security and P2P, the developers pointed out that for the PDM to be accepted as a development methodology it would also need to consider other non-functional properties such as reliability, scalability, etc. Although beyond the scope of the PEPERS project, expanding the PDM to consider such properties (or at least allowing it to draw upon suitable related work from areas such as dependability) is an area of future work.

CONCLUSION

There is an increasing interest in building mobile P2P applications. However for mobile P2P to be utilised within such an environment it also needs to be secure and the nature of P2P can make this difficult. A key problem is that the choice of P2P technologies can influence the properties of a systems design, and so consequently existing methodologies need to be extended or new ones developed in order to take this into account.

This chapter has presented the PEPERS Development Methodology, a method designed to assist in the development of secure mobile P2P systems. It adopts an architectural driven development approach and encourages developers to consider issues related to security, mobility and P2P from early within the development cycle.

The PDM was developed as part of the PEPERS project, one aspect of which involved its use within the development of real industrial P2P systems. To help in describing the PDM we have used one of these as a case study.

Experiences with using the PDM have shown that it can be a valuable aid in developing secure mobile P2P systems. In particular developers found that it made them more aware of architectural design issues and it encouraged them to think and consider them early on within their developments. There are a few areas where it could still be further refined. In particular the developers found the approach to be quite different from the more linear methods that they currently used, and the provision of clearer steps and more detailed examples would have helped in the quicker understanding of the method. The PDM also needs to consider other non-functional properties to widen its applicability.

Because we believe that tool support can play a crucial role within the development process, a tool has also been built that assists the designers in using the PDM. This tool has also been discussed and demonstrated within the chapter.

ACKNOWLEDGMENT

This work has been funded by the European Commission within the PEPERS project (IST-2004-026901). More information and the PDM support tool can be found at http://www.pepers.org

REFERENCES

Agarwal, D. A., Chevassut, O., Thompson, M. R., & Tsudik, G. (2001). An integrates solution for secure group communication in wide-area networks. In *Proceedings of 6th IEEE Symposium on Computers and Communications*, Hammamet, Tunisisa.

B'Far, R. (2004). *Mobile computing principles*. Cambridge Press.

BANKSEC (2000). EC funded project (IST-1999-20711). Retrieved on October 2, 2008, from http://www.atc.gr/banksec/

Berket, K., Essiari, A., & Muratas, A. (2004). *PKI*-Based Security for Peer-to-Peer Information Sharing. In *Proceedings of P2P 2004*, Zurich, Switzerland.

Bertolini, D., Busetta, P., Molani, A., Nori, M., & Perini, A. (2002). Designing peer-to-peer applications: An agent-oriented approach, In *Proceedings of the International Workshop on Agent Technology and Software Engineering*, Erfurt, Germany.

Fielding, R. T. (2000). *Architectural styles and the design of network-based software architectures*. Unpublished doctoral dissertation, University of California at Irvine, USA.

Kortuem, G. (2002). Proem: A middleware platform for mobile peer-to-peer computing. *ACM SIGMOBILE Mobile Computing and Communications Review (MC2R), 6*(4), 62-64.

Mouratidis, H., Giorgini, P., & Manson, G. (2003). An ontology for modelling security: The tropos approach. In *Proceedings of the 7th International Conference on Knowledge-based Intelligent Information and Engineering Systems*, Oxford, UK.

P2P ARCHITECT (2001). EC funded project (IST-2001-32708). Retrieved on October 2, 2008, from http://www.atc.gr/p2p_architect/index.htm

PEPERS (2006). EC funded project (IST-2004-026901). Retrieved on October 2, 2008, from http://www.pepers.org

Siveroni, I., Zisman, A., & Spanoudakis, G. (2008). Property specification and static verification of UML models. *Proceedings of the International Conference on Availability, Reliability and Security*, Barcelona, Spain.

Spanoudakis, G., Kloukinas, C., & Androutsopoulos, K. (2008). Dynamic verification and control of mobile peer-to-peer systems. In *Proceedings*

of the 3rd International Conference on Internet Monitoring and Protection (ICIMP), Bucharest, Romania, to appear.

Walkerdine, J., Melville, L., & Sommerville, I. (2002). Dependability properties of P2P architectures. In *Proceedings of the IEEE P2P*, Sweden.

Walkerdine, J,. Melville, L., & Sommerville, I. (2005). *Reference Architectures for Peer-to-Peer Applications* (Tech. Rep. COMP-009-2005). UK: Lancaster University, Computing Department.

Walkerdine, J., Lock, R., & Lock, S. (2006). D2 - analysis of security characteristics of peer-to-peer architectures. EC Project Deliverable, PEPERS IST-2004-026901.

Walkerdine, J., & Lock. S. (2007). Towards secure mobile P2P systems. In *Proceedings of the P2P Systems and Applications (P2PSA)*, Mauritius.

Section VI
Standards and Protocols

Chapter XIV
Integration and Interworking of Fixed and Mobile P2P Systems

Spyridon L. Tompros
University of the Aegean, Greece

ABSTRACT

Enabled by the emergence of high-speed Internet access in last mile communications, P2P systems have witnessed significant growth in the recent years, mainly due to their intrinsic characteristic of being independent of the underlying network and the different services that operators offer in various subscription models. The advent of the Next Generation Networks (NGN) technology is expected to further strengthen the growth of P2P services as it will allow their deployment in any network and with any terminal type. In this chapter, the author first gives an overview of the NGN technology, and then presents its first real implementation called the IP Multimedia Sub-system (IMS), with a discussion of the issues on integrating and interworking P2P applications in converged communications networks.

INTRODUCTION

Achieving seamless interworking between fixed and mobile networks is one of the main goals of contemporary networks technologies. The main driver for achieving this goal is the requirement for establishing IP communications convergence over *heterogeneous networks*, where networks of different protocols and physical communica- tion technologies could come together under a common communications framework in order to offer *service uniformity* and *seamless continuity* through the establishment of *common user man- agement procedures* (e.g. authentication, mobility management, etc.).

To enable the roll out of integrated fixed- mobile network services on the market, several standardization bodies and industrial forums have been involved in definition of architectures that function as overlay communication frameworks for current technology networks. In this process, the ITU (International Telecommunications Union) paved the way with definition of Next Generation Networks (NGN) technology, in which it recommends a number of generic mechanisms for the following:

- Packet-based communications between different access technology networks
- The integration of signalling and data management procedures of different network technologies within the Internet Protocol (IP)
- Common services deployment in mobile, wireless and fixed networks
- Quality of Service (QoS) implementation in mixed communication scenarios over heterogeneous networks

Following ITU recommendations, two standardization organizations of the telecommunication industry: 3GPP (3G UMTS Partnership Project) and ETSI (European Telecommunications Standardization Institute) went further to define the first real implementation of NGN network, the IP Multimedia Sub-system (IMS).

The IMS is independent of the underlying protocols of the data plane (as long as they are implemented over IP) and handles only the signalling and traffic management operations using the Session Initiation Protocol (SIP; Rosenberg 2002) as a unification mechanism for all user procedures.

This chapter aims to explain how integration and interworking of fixed and mobile networks is achieved in the context of IMS technology. The description commences with the definitions for network convergence and main principles, which is then followed by an explanation of the IMS components and procedures, and finally a discussion of the issues concerning the binding of P2P services with NGN networks.

BACKGROUND: TOWARDS ACHIEVING FIXED AND MOBILE NETWORKS INTEROPERABILITY

Achieving interoperability between different technology networks has been a major goal of the telecommunications industry in order to achieve services uniformity and homogeneous user management mechanisms. The advent of IP and the widespread adoption of Internet communications have unveiled the potential of huge revenues out of the use of user-driven applications. The first effort for introducing IP communications in the context of subscriber networks has been made with the definition of NGN by ITU and latter with the definition of IMS by 3GPP and ETSI.

Today, IMS networks have been deployed experimentally by operators and research groups, with the objective of assessing the quality of high bandwidth communication services, such as multimedia streaming, IPTV and distributed P2P applications.

Although a high-level comparison of NGNs with P2P communication architectures reveals that the two systems are antagonistic, i.e. NGNs being centralized network architectures and P2P being highly distributed software entities that function autonomously, the two systems may in reality function complementarily, e.g. NGNs can provide a service environment that ensures portability of P2P applications in all-IP networks (Chen et al., 2006). On the other hand, by providing the network infrastructure with many degrees of freedom, P2P applications are emerging as an easy way of implementing 'pay-and-go' applications, without having to invest in expensive centralised service execution environments (Yao & Chen, 2007). Following this observation, recent research efforts have recognised the potential of NGN for accommodating P2P applications, and have focused on solving a number of integration issues.

Among them, the mobility that a user enjoys in NGN environments poses strict requirements for service continuity and seamless handover in 3G UMTS and wireless mesh networks. To solve the problem, recent studies strive to adapt the functionality of the Mobile IP (MIP) and IEEE 802.21 MIH (Media Independent Handover) to the operations of P2P applications (Chen et al, 2006). MIP supports transparency of protocols above IP layer and ensures service continuity in wireless networks, while MIH enables seamless handover between different networks.

Due to their intrinsic characteristic of building overlay networks that function independently of the underlying networks, serving P2P applications presents two major challenges.

One is the naming method utilised by P2P applications to identify each other. In pure P2P systems, naming is performed independently of the underlying network, which has no clue of the processes taking place in real time. To allow recognition of P2P applications, effort is recently placed on the definition of naming methods compatible with the operations of the NGN (Farha & Leon-Garcia, 2007).

Another challenge faced by telecommunication industry is related to the negative consequences of having P2P application running uncontrollably over operator networks. The huge amounts of uncontrollable traffic produced and the evaded costs of using network infrastructure free-of-charge have motivated the engineering of algorithms for distributed network management. These algorithms feature autonomy and capability for self-organisation and are useful for preventing network crashes under congestive conditions (Klenk et al., 2008).

Moreover, the definition of signalling procedures for integrating P2P signalling methods in NGN infrastructure is an ongoing process, which will enable network operators to monitor and charge the use of P2P applications over subscriber networks (Wa & Zhu, 2008).

NETWORK CONVERGENCE IN THE CONTEXT OF NGN

Network convergence is the concept of integrating the services provided by different network technologies into a common architecture so as to make them available over any network type, through generic user handling mechanisms.

In recommendation Y.2001 for NGN, ITU sets out a number of goals briefly summarized as follows: the promotion of fair competition between network operators and third party players wishing to build their own platforms over subscriber networks; the encouragement of private investment in telecommunication networks; the establishment of a framework for architecture and capabilities able to meet various regulatory requirements; and the provisioning of open access to IP networks.

Although these goals target mainly at the telecommunication market, they are aimed to create wider impacts on societal aspects with relation to:

- Ensuring universal provision of and access to services
- Promoting equality of opportunity to the citizen
- Promoting diversity of content, including cultural and linguistic diversity
- Recognising the necessity of worldwide cooperation with particular attention to less developed countries

In technological terms, the NGN can be defined by the following fundamental characteristics:

- Packet-based transfer (user traffic is transferred encapsulated in IP packets)
- Separation of control functions in bearer capabilities, call/session, and application/ service
- Decoupling of service provisioning from transport

- Support for any type of service and content compatible with the IP protocol
- Broadband communication capabilities with end-to-end QoS (Quality of Service) reservation mechanisms
- Interworking with legacy and circuit switched (non-IP) networks
- Generalized user and terminal mobility
- Unified service characteristics and provisioning
- Support for multiple last mile access network technologies and mixed communication scenarios (e.g. mobile-fixed and wireless-mobile)

NGN Capabilities

NGN provides the capabilities (infrastructure, protocols, etc.) to make creation, deployment and management of services possible. Services may employ any kind of media, i.e. audio, video and multiplexed audiovisual (e.g. MPEG), or they may be coded with any coding scheme and support any communication scheme, i.e. unicast, multicast, broadcast and messaging, under any bandwidth requirement, from few Kbit/s to hundreds Mbit/s.

To allow further diversity of services, NGN provides mechanisms for service customization, whereby users are given the possibility of creating and customizing their own services. NGN makes that possible by enabling implementation of APIs (Application Programming Interfaces) between the user applications and the service logic of the network.

Concerning service accommodation, NGN implements a flexible scheme that allows decoupling of service provisioning from the data transport. Under that scheme, the network takes care of the signalling procedures required for service set up, management and resources reservation, and leaves the choice of data protocols up to the user application.

Mechanisms such as user authentication, charging, session management and media resources management are bound to the user applications by means of using dedicated *Application Servers* (AS). The role of the AS is to allow the NGN core network logic to recognise the user service and perform the required call management scheme, e.g. perform point-to-point/ point-to-multipoint calls and reserve network resources.

Due to its intrinsic characteristic of being independent from the data transport, NGN is compatible with any user terminal type: fixed, mobile/wireless, and maintains the compatibility of signalling operations. Signalling procedures of applications hosted on different terminals become unified by means of using the SIP protocol, thus allowing the implementation of data calls over different technology networks, such as 3G UMTS to xDSL, and IEEE 802.11 to 3G UMTS.

In the same unification framework, NGN integrates mechanisms for the mobility management of mobile and wireless terminals. These mechanisms have the role of maintaining service continuity by implementing seamless service handover for mobile users. Along with these mobility management mechanisms, the network provides procedures for service roaming implementation. A popular example of such mechanism is the Unlicensed Mobile Access (UMA), a technology that allows mobile and wireless terminal users to get attached to wireless networks, poll the services they offer and become charged for making use of them without being registered users of the visited network (UMA Consortium, 2004).

NGN Functional Architecture

The separation between services and the data transport is achieved by the introduction of the *transport stratum* and the *service stratum*.

The horizontal relationship of these two strata is shown in Figure 1, and their vertical decoupling is shown in Figure 2.

The transport stratum is mainly concerned with issues pertaining to the exchange of digital information of any kind between any geographically separate points, such as:

- User-to-user connectivity
- User-to-services connectivity
- Services-to-services connectivity

The transport stratum may be implemented with any single network type or combinations of them, including connection-oriented circuit-switched (CO-CS), connection-oriented packet-switched (CO-PS) and connectionless packet-switched (CLPS) network technologies (ITU-T Recommendation G.805, 2000; ITU-T Recommendation G.809, 2003).

The services stratum provides the user services such as a telephone service, Web service, etc. The service stratum may involve a complex set of geographically distributed service platforms or in simple cases just the service functions in two end-user sites.

Each stratum is further divided into vertical layers (planes), with each being composed of a *data (or user)* plane, a *control* plane, and a *management* plane. The data plane provides functions that take care of data transfer, while the other two planes provide functions that control procedures involved in data transferring and functions that manage procedures of the stratum.

Based on the aforementioned clarifications, the following concepts are defined:

NGN service stratum: It provides the user functions that transfer service-related data and the functions that control and manage service resources and network services to enable user services and applications. The service stratum is concerned with the application and the corresponding services that operate between peer entities. For example, the services may be related to voice, data or video applications, which are either arranged separately or in some combination in the case of multimedia applications.

NGN transport stratum: It provides the user functions that transfer data and the functions that control and manage transport resources necessary to carry such data between terminating entities. The data carried conveys user, control and/or management information. Dynamic or static associations are established between peer entities to control and/or manage information transfer. From an architectural perspective, each layer in the transport stratum has its own user, control and management planes.

Figure 1. Conceptual model of separating services from transport in NGN (adapted from ITU-T Recommendation Y.2011, 2004)

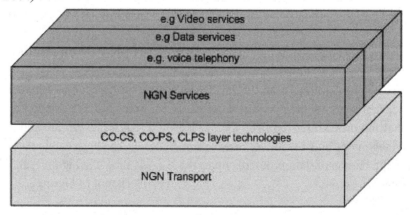

Figure 2. NGN Reference model (adapted from ITU-T Recommendation Y.2011, 2004)

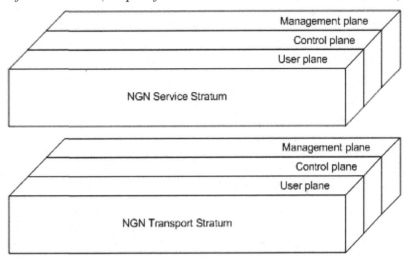

Figure 3 illustrates a de-composition of the NGN reference model into individual functions of the two strata.

Resources provide the physical and non-physical (logical) components (e.g. transmission links, processing resources and storage capacity) needed for the operation of services and networks. Resources are categorized in transport resources, offered by the network components (e.g. switches, routers and transmission links) and processing and storage resources such as service execution platforms or databases for user content storage.

Support of multimedia services requires dedicated control functions that perform accurate resource allocations through control or management plane functions. These functions are usually identified as the "invocation" process.

The control functions involved in the "invocation" process can be classified into two generic sets: the functions related to the control of services such as the user authentication, user identification and service admission control; and functions that relate to the control of the transport network, consisting of functions for network resources policy control and dynamic connectivity provision.

Customer operations are very much correlated to the "invocation" process as they interact with the network, either prior to or following a service invocation. These processes belong to what is usually called the "Management".

- Management functions usually include:
- Fault Management
- Configuration Management
- Accounting Management
- Performance Management
- Security Management

In the scope of NGN a set of additional management functions is foreseen. These are mainly related to the management of the two strata, providing functions for:

- Configuration of service resources vs. configuration of transport resources,
- Status retrieval

The transfer functions are a set of separate functions that serve for both the transfer of user information and transfer of control and management information. Conceptually, it is useful to represent the resources of the NGN as being separate from the transfer, control, management functions and services.

Figure 3. Internal functional model of NGN (adapted from ITU-T Recommendation Y.2011, 2004)

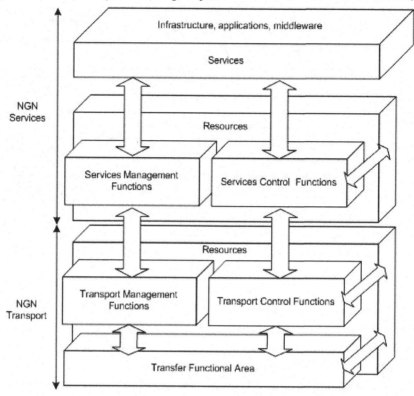

Following this approach, NGN takes a layered schema in the implementation of interoperability across heterogeneous networks.

In cooperating layered networks, there are controlling entities employed individually by each network. The ordering of networks within the

Figure 4. Illustration of cooperation between layered networks

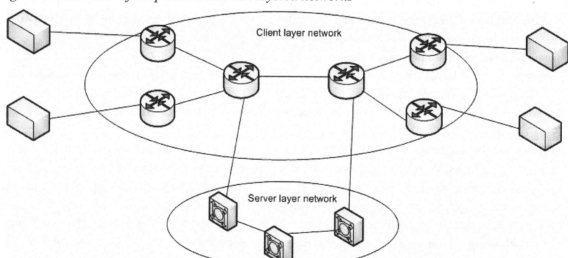

hierarchy is referred to as service requester/provider relationship, whereby the higher layer network requests services from the lower layer network. In addition, the exchange of control information is needed before the two networks are ready to collaborate. The information exchange may include both resource and topology details.

The graphical representation of layered networks is shown in Figure 4. Hops between nodes in the higher (client) layer network may span multiple hops within the lower (server) layer network. Interaction between the two networks at the borders (edges) allows resources and topology information to be exchanged in order to be used for coordinating activities.

Under this layered approach, the implementation of interoperability between access networks is performed via two interaction types. *Inter-layer interaction* occurs between two distinct client/server layers. Depending on the realization of the inter-layer interaction, internal and external interfaces have to be defined to exchange control information. Exchanged information may include details of the capabilities, topology, and resource information provided by the server layer network to the client layer network. *Intra-layer interaction* occurs between functional entities within the same layer to support co-existence of multiple networks at another layer. Examples of such interaction include address mapping functions when independent address spaces are used by the collaborating (layer) networks (Figure 5).

Figure 6 shows a typical multi-layer NGN network setup. The inter/intra-layer functional interactions are represented as distributed control plane entities.

Furthermore, by separating the address spaces of the client layer network and the server layer network, multiple distinct client layer networks can be easily accommodated. Inter-layer interaction occurs between functional entities belonging to control planes of different layers. Intra-layer interaction occurs between the functional entities of the control plane entities in the server layer in order to support the client-layer control planes.

As would be further elaborated in the next section, the concept of multi-layer networks is fundamental for the establishment of heterogeneous networks as it provides the architectural framework for the implementation of centralized logic (server networks) that controls several underlying networks (client networks).

Access to Networks Services

In PSTN networks, end-users invoke services by sending a signal to the network. Upon receiving this signal, the network reacts in two ways: firstly

Figure 5. Inter/intra-layer interaction

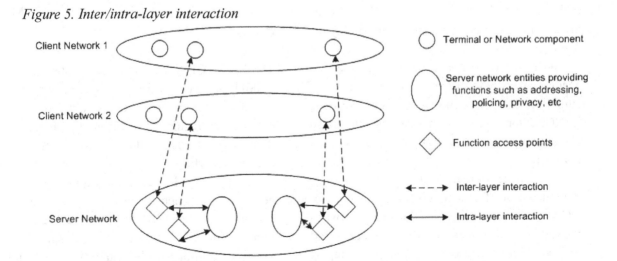

Figure 6. Multi-layer network scenario

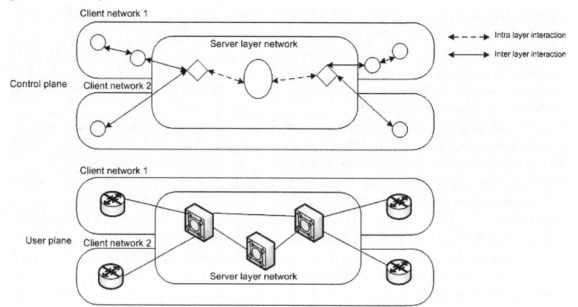

establishes the call, and secondly provides the necessary resources required for this call.

In contemporary networks, services are distinguished as *conversational* or *non-conversational* and follow the *call control* or *session control* principles in what concerns call establishment and maintenance. It is generally known that calls operated using signaling protocols compatible with the IP protocol are called sessions, while calls operated using legacy signaling protocols (e.g. PSTN, Q.931, etc) are simply referred as calls. By that distinction in NGN, all call types are considered sessions because they employ the SIP protocol.

Moreover, while conversational services are accompanied by resources set up as a result of signaling exchanged between user-terminals, in NGN, non-conversational services may also be set up with signaling initiated by the service platform.

The support of multimedia services is a key domain of study for the functional architecture of NGN. Very often, a strict relation exists between the service and the way this service is addressed and how network resources needed to support

that service are provided by the underlying network. Presently, most network architectures are still dedicated to voice services. Nevertheless, the NGN architecture permits resources to be requested either in a conversational or in a non-conversational manner.

In the next section, we present the first real implementation of the NGN, which is called the IP Multimedia Sub-system (IMS).

THE IP MULTIMEDIA SUB-SYSTEM (IMS)

The IMS (3GPP Technical Specification 23228, 2006) represents the first real implementation of the NGN network architecture, and it specifies all components required for the implementation of the NGN services and the NGN transport strata presented earlier.

Concerning the services stratum, the IMS networks implement services using the Session Initiation Protocol (SIP) for the signalling operations, while leaving up to the user application to make the choice of the data protocol. Despite such flexibility, IMS is only compatible with data protocols that operate over the IP, such as the Real Time Transport Protocol (RTP) and the Resource ReserVation Protocol (RSVP), so that the traffic produced is manageable by the IMS core network (IM CN).

Apart from the IM CN that provides centralised network management functions, IMS networks are distinguished from IP-Connectivity Access Networks, called IP-CANs, which can be of fixed (e.g. xDSL), wireless (e.g. WiFi) or mobile type (e.g. 3G UMTS). An IMS network is composed of a single IM CN and any combination of IP-CANs.

Architecture

Figure 7 depicts the reference architecture for IMS, including peer interfaces towards legacy networks and foreign IMS networks and logical components representing internal logic.

The logical components have specific roles and contributions to the operations of the overall IMS architecture. Their functions are analysed in detail in section *Building blocks*.

The lines connecting the logical components are logical interfaces implementing signalling and transport protocols. These interfaces are described in detail in section *Logical interfaces*.

The *Circuit Switched (CS) networks* are non-IP telecommunication platforms such as PSTN and ISDN networks, while *Legacy mobile signalling networks* are IP and non-IP mobile networks that do not support the SIP protocol and therefore are not compatible with the IMS operations.

Building Blocks

The CSCF (Call State Control Function) is the most important logical component of the IM CN as it takes on various roles depending on the way it is interconnected in the network.

The *Proxy CSCF (P-CSCF)* serves as the first contact point within the IMS CN. Its address is discovered by the User Equipments (UE or user

Figure 7. Reference Architecture of the IP Multimedia Core Network Subsystem (adapted from 3GPP Technical Specification 23228, 2006)

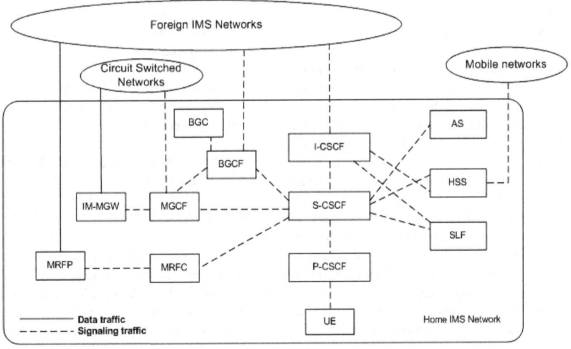

terminals) using SIP signalling. The P-CSCF behaves like a Proxy, routing signalling messages coming from the UE to the *Serving CSCF (S-CSCF)* and those coming from the S-CSCF to the appropriate recipient of the IP-CAN (Connectivity Access Network) UE or any IP-CAN component, i.e. resources controller.

The functions performed by P-CSCF include:

- Forwarding of signalling messages received from the UE to the S-CSCF
- Forwarding of signalling responses to the UE
- Generation of Charging Data Records (CDRs)
- Maintenance of security in the communication path between itself and the IP-CAN
- Authorisation of user requested resources and Quality of Service (QoS) management

The S-CSCF performs session control services for the UE. Upon user request the S-CSCF creates and maintains communication sessions separately for each requested service. Different S-CSCFs may have different roles within an IMS network, offering the following functions:

- Handling of registration requests and delivery of user information to the location server (e.g. HSS)
- Handling of service requests for local servicing or forwarding to external IMS networks
- Handling of signalling operations for connected users
- Provisioning of endpoints with service-related network components, such as media controllers, resources admission and enforcement control, gateways to foreign IMS networks, etc
- Address resolution mechanisms between user terminals and serving networks

- Message forwarding for roaming users wishing to get connected to visited IMS networks and make use of the services of the home IMS network
- Handling of signalling messages of users communicating with counterparts in circuit switched networks
- Handling of signalling messages exchanged between application servers and the users
- Arbitration of calls between IMS networks, and between IMS and circuit switched networks

The *Interrogating CSCF (I-CSCF)* is the contact point for all calls destined to a user, regardless of whether he belongs to the current network or is a roaming user. There may be multiple I-CSCFs within a single IM CN. The functions they perform include:

- Assignment of a S-CSCF to users requesting network registration
- Handling of user-generated signalling messages received from external networks towards the S-CSCF of the home network
- Routing of user-generated signalling messages coming from non-IMS networks to the appropriate BGF or return of failure responses

The *Breakout Gateway Control Function (BGCF)* serves as the contact point for message transit between:

- The IMS network and non-IMS SIP based networks
- The IMS network and non-IP networks, such as PSTN or ISDN

The transit functions involve translation of signalling messages and data traffic to match the protocol requirements of the transit network. The transit functions are put into operation by the network when an IMS UE connects to a non-IMS UE of IP type or PSTN/ISDN terminals.

Only the operations of the BGCF are adequate for supporting communication between IMS and non-IMS networks, whereas implementation of transit functions between IMS and non-IMS non-IP networks additionally requires the use of Media Gateway Control Function (MGCF). The MGCF performs the management functions that control media gateways dedicated to translating data traffic from one format into another, hence satisfying the protocol and timing requirements of the target data network.

For example, in the case of IMS users connecting to PSTN networks, the BGCF selects the network in which PSTN/CS Domain breakout is to occur. If the BGCF determines that the breakout is to occur in the same network in which the BGCF is located, then the BGCF selects the MGCF to perform data traffic (media) interworking with the PSTN. Otherwise, it called the CS domain. If the break out is in another network, then the BGCF forwards the user request to another BGCF in the selected network.

The *MRF* (Multimedia Resource Function) provides the control of resources of the connected networks and is functionally divided into *MRF Controller (MRFC) and MRF Processor (MRFP)*.

The MRFC performs the following tasks:

- Control of the media stream resources of the MRFP
- Parsing of signalling messages coming from the S-CSCF and implementation of control on the MRFP functions

Tasks performed by the MRFP include:

- Bearer control on the Mb reference point
- Provisioning to the MRFP a pool of media resources to be exploited in setting up the data bearer between the IP and the CS networks
- Multiplexing of media streams established between the IP and CS networks
- Re-formatting of media streams established between the IP and CS networks with func-

tions performing protocol re-formatting and media transcoding
- Implementation of flow control pertaining to the access of users to shared resources of IP network.

The *Application Server (AS)* implements logic for the realisation of services over the IMS network. Depending on the number and complexity of the supported services, each IM CN may encompass one or more ASs. An AS is always addressed via the S-CSCF following a user request.

It is important to note that an AS does not host the service logic itself, but a number of network parameters required for the establishment of the service. Such parameters may be the quality of service values, call types (e.g. multicast or unicast), call setup mechanism (e.g. call forwarding or bridging), etc.

The *Home Subscriber Server (HSS)* is a database that maintains user profiles and identities as well as service profiling information needed for the C-CSCF to discover the AS that corresponds to each supported service. A HSS is unique in each IM-CN and provides data that allow the S-CSCF to support functions for:

- User authentication
- Mobility management
- Service establishment
- Service charging
- Intelligent services (e.g. IN and CAMEL) support

The *Subscription Locator Function (SLF)* provides the S-CSCF and I-CSCF with HSS resolution functions. By polling the SLF, both components obtain information concerning to which HSS and AS they should route the service requests of the users.

Logical Interfaces

As explained earlier, the IMS networks are overlay architectures that make use of underlying real networks to route the data traffic. As such, IM CN handles only the control procedures that unify the functions of the underlying network.

Therefore, the logical interfaces depicted in Figure 7 are used for transporting signalling messages realised with the SIP protocol and can be categorized on the basis of the type of control/ management procedures that they implement. For example, the Gm interface implements session management procedures such as call setup and user registration. These procedures take place as a sequence of SIP messages exchanged between the UE and S-CSCF.

For a more detailed description on all logical interfaces of the IM CN, the reader may refer to (3GPP Technical Specification 23002, 2007).

Basic IMS Operations

End-to-End QoS Setup

End-to-end QoS reservation is done in IMS networks by means of using dedicated policy decision and enforcement functions at the borders of the IP-CAN with CN. Depending on the type of IP-CAN, a particular policy decision function is attached. For instance, in 3G UMTS IP-CANs, QoS reservation is performed by means of employing the Policy Decision Function (PDF), which is attached on the GGSN (Gateway GPRS Support Node), the gateway that connects a mobile network to the CN network. On the other hand, fixed networks, such as xDSL or optical networks implement QoS with the so-called Resource and Admission Control Subsystem (RACS), which is attached on the Border Gateway (BG).

To implement QoS mapping on the user traffic, 3GPP and ETSI's TISPAN have specified a number of extra control interfaces, exhibiting the layout illustrated in Figure 8. Due to the high heterogeneity displayed by IP-CANs in bandwidth capacity, user operations and charging schemes, a hot issue of the area remains to be the engineering of uniform QoS values for all network types and user operations (Tompros & Denazis, 2008).

The Gq, Go and Gq', Go' interfaces enforce the user-requested QoS parameters in the access network and in the backbone network that

Figure 8. Signalling interfaces and data paths for IMS data traffic routing across heterogeneous access networks

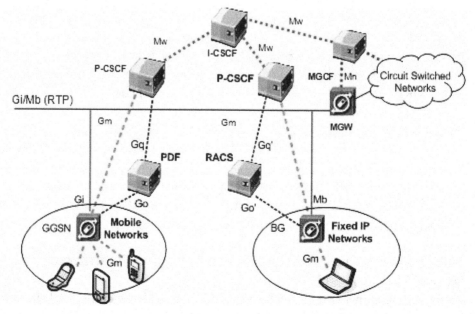

interconnects the access networks involved in the call. QoS enforcement is done through dedicated Connection Admission Control (CAC) mechanisms that perform:

- Translation of user-requested QoS parameters into a data path description, consisting of parameters such as delay variation, loss ratio and data rate.
- Data path allocation in the CN connecting the IP-CAN, taking into account of the QoS capabilities of the access networks and the available QoS allocation mechanisms of the CN, e.g. the DiffServ capability.

IP Version Interworking

The IMS supports interworking of IP users that use different versions of IP networks and UE. Two types of interworking are in general supported:

- *Application Level Interworking:* Users connected to an IMS network can communicate with users that are connected to SIP based networks and use different IP version.
- *Transport Level Interworking:* This type of interworking allows tunnelling of data traffic over IP networks of different IP version (3GPP Technical Specification 23221, 2008). Figure *9* shows an example scenario where two IPv6 IMS networks are connected via

an IPv4 network. The opposite is also possible.

The IP version interworking is performed transparently to the user and its implementation does not require any notion of the UE type or the capabilities of the IM CN.

Mobility Management

During mobility management, the IM CN performs a number of procedures, including:

- Maintenance of connectivity to IP-CAN through the acquisition of a new IP address every time the IP connectivity with the IM CN is re-established
- Re-registration of the user and terminal on the visited IM CN network
- Restoration of the data path that was established prior to session handover
- Management of handover procedure that takes place every time a user makes use of communication applications while moving

Roaming

The IMS architecture follows the mobility management principles of the mobile networks, where a roaming user is always serviced by the

Figure 9. Example of IPv6 traffic tunnelling over IPv4 networks

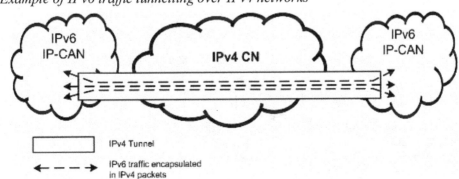

home network (Figure 10). The management of user communications, such as service selection and communication charging is done via the establishment of an interrogation process between the visited and home network.

Besides service control, which is always performed centrally by the home network, service provisioning may be performed in two ways:

- Through the service platform in the home network

- Through an external service platform connected to the home network (e.g. third party or visited network)

The candidate external service platform may be located on either the visited network or in the 3rd party platform.

During roaming, the CSCF performs two main functions:

Figure 10. Service platform of the Home IM CN network

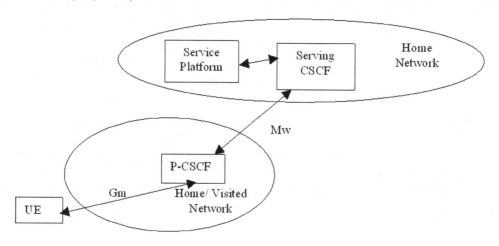

Figure 11. Communication of the Home IM CN network with external service platforms

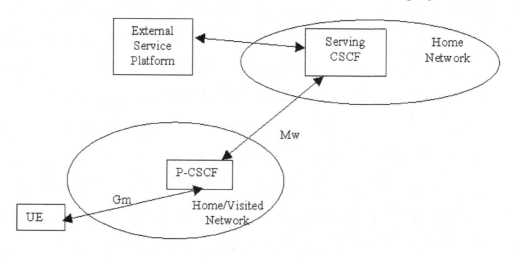

- The Proxy CSCF of the visited IM CN network enables session control to be passed to the Serving CSCF of the visited network
- The Serving CSCF of the visited network starts the interrogation procedure through the I-CSCF with external network in order to find the home IM CN to which the user belong
- After the home IM CN is found, the visited network passes control for service activation to the S-CSCF of the home network.

Interoperability Among Heterogeneous IP-CANs

Interoperability between heterogeneous IP-CANs is done by means of employing higher layer IP compatible data transfer protocols. The IMS architecture does not designate the use of any specific protocol but is up to the network operator to decide (depending on the capabilities of the UE and CN) which protocol is to be used for the realisation of user services.

Currently, RTP, RSVP and TCP/UDP are the most popular protocols used for the implementation of multimedia services. As depicted in Figure 12, the negotiation and selection of data protocols are performed during the session setup and involves the PDF (Policy Decision Function), RACS (Resource and Admission Control Subsystem) components and logic of the IM CN.

User Operations

The IMS architecture supports every foreseeable user related procedures for accomplishing traditional network operations:

User identification: An IM CN recognises the IMS user on the basis of his IMPI (IMS Personal Identity), which is submitted to the network during user registration

User authentication and authorisation for service use: Before a user is registered to the network, he is authenticated with regard to his capability to use the IMS network and each time he requests to make use of a service, the IMS

Figure 12. Deployment of the session control and QoS enforcement mechanisms in NGN networks

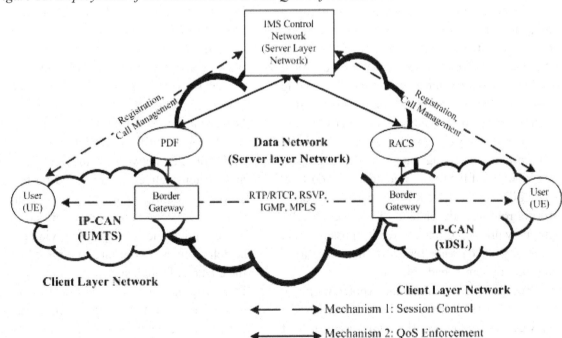

network authorises him if he is permitted to use the requested service.

Secured communications: The IMS network provides secure communications to both service and transport strata and their vertical layers. On the transport stratum, this is done via the implementation of appropriate encryption mechanisms, whereas on the services stratum, security is implemented with the ciphering of SIP messages.

Service operation charging: The IMS network charges the user for the utilisation of each service, via particular Charging Data Records (CDR) that are created and retained at the billing server for each user. Using the CDRs, the network may apply to service using different charging rates, depending on different user access privileges, billing rules and service capabilities.

BINDING P2P SERVICES WITH NGN NETWORKS

Lately, the interest of network operators in P2P applications and network services has grown considerably, mainly due to their high popularity among the network users.

P2P applications for data sharing, conferencing, streaming, etc, have started to gradually replace traditional communication applications. According to recent studies (Yao and Chen, 2007), this trend would continue to grow. Among the main reasons for this phenomenon are their independence from the underlying network and their efficient way of managing network resources, where users receiving data are also helping in distribution of the data (or content). In addition, the ability of P2P networks to perform overlay traffic routing independently from the underlying network makes path diversity possible, and thus they could greatly relieve the network traffic through dynamic load balancing.

Recognizing their huge market potential, many network operators have started integrating P2P services into their networks. NGN has the role of

the enabling technology in support of this effort. NGN networks allow homogeneous integration of different network types and give P2P systems an appealing outset by letting them to be also exploited by the mobile users. Furthermore, the possibility of the underlying network to 'understand' the users of P2P applications and consequently the amount of traffic they produce, will allow implementation of granular charging models beyond the existing traffic volume charging.

Integration Issues

However, deploying P2P applications in IMS networks is not straightforward. The business model of existing P2P systems contradicts to that of the network operator. The charging schemes conventionally used in telecommunication networks are based on static revenue-sharing models that are not applicable to P2P systems.

Also, the way resources of the IMS network are shared among applications using dedicated QoS reservation mechanisms, is not compatible with the highly autonomous nature of P2P applications considering resources utilisation.

Another problem of deploying P2P applications in IMS networks comes from their intrinsic characteristic of generating and broadcasting content. According to the service utilisation principles applied in past IP and CS networks, and also in the current IMS networks, the issue of generating and distributing content is a legal issue that needs to be taken into consideration in the implementation of P2P service utilisation charging.

Before P2P networks come into play, service and content delivery were based on the client/server paradigm (Figure 13a). For example, Internet based content utilisation services, such as video on demand, are operating via centralised search engines that point the targeted server to the client. Although such applications have been in widespread use, the traditional client/server approach has started to show its limitations with increasing demands for better scalability, availability, and efficient operations. Also, clients in the traditional approach normally have a single entry point to the server for registration, authentication and service access, and that could also constitute a computational and communication bottleneck.

The advent of converged network technology enabled servers to be integrated into a single network and maintain visibility of clients that are attached even to different technology networks. In this case, the server acts also as a proxy or a relay for information targeting other clients. In

the reference communication scenario depicted in Figure 13b), a user terminal may initiate, manage, and terminate sessions, but desired functionality can only be achieved via the server. A representative application of such communication type is the Voice over IP (VoIP) service. Today, VoIP applications are widely in use over the Internet and in the IMS networks.

The reference communication scenario, which is referred to in literature as *service-mediated P2P*, provides only basic P2P communication

Figure 13. Migration from the traditional server/client communication model to P2P overlay networks; a) Initial state: Traditional client/server model, b) 1ˢᵗ intermediate step: Client/server communication over converged networks, c)2ⁿᵈ intermediate step: servers organisation into peer entities, d) final form: deployment of peer servers in NGN networks.

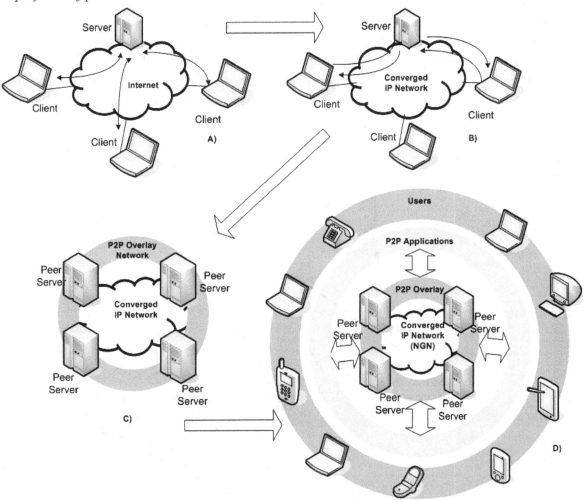

functionality and is not what we usually call a P2P service. This is because P2P applications rely on virtual networks containing many fragments of information, constituting small servers (Figure 13c). In such a case, a server can be a dedicated server, a user terminal or a network component such as a router. The various information servers, called peers, federate themselves using a common set of P2P services that are accessible by user applications at central points in each P2P network through: a) **publish protocols** that ensure that content is spread among peers; b) **redundancy management protocol** that ensures that the same data is replicated several times to increase service availability and resilience; and c) **search protocol** that enables user applications to retrieve the content of interest. In this way, the user terminals and the peers of other type, form a self-organized, application-level network, whereby any peer may act as a client (i.e. a service and/or content requestor), a server (i.e. a service and/or content provider), or a router (e.g. a proxy).

Despite their agility in content sharing, P2P applications still look for servers in the network to obtain the content in small pieces, and in order to do so, they submit requests massively, creating huge amounts of traffic.

Although the autonomous networking approach is very attractive, in principle the current solutions contradict the main reason of P2P existence, which is the unobstructed sharing of information/resources and communication between terminals of any type. Today, the most popular P2P systems are proprietary, non-interoperable solutions. For example, Skype (Baset & Schulzrinne, 2006), a popular IP telephony application, does not interoperate with other VoIP applications, whereas Kazaa (Liang, Kumar & Ross, 2005) has turned into a popular content sharing community not accessible by third party applications.

In the subsequent sections, we explain how interoperability problems of P2P systems could be avoided by integrating P2P operations in the standardised communications framework of IMS.

Figure 14. Unstructured communication across P2P systems

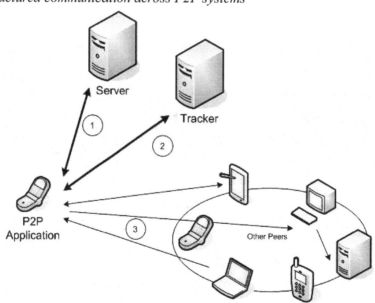

P2P Overlay Network Architecture

Principles

P2P services give rise to user applications that make unstructured use of the network in order to scan for, track down, and download user requested content.

Figure 14 illustrates the way P2P applications and supplementary components interact in order to discover the source of the requested content. Firstly, the P2P application running on the user terminal communicates with a *P2P server* in order to get content description, which usually consists of a file name, size, a hash table and the address of the *tracker* (flow 1). The tracker is a special server that contains descriptions of a list of peers that are downloading the same content or have pieces of the user-requested content (flow 2).

In addition to the aforementioned reference communication model, the following rules apply:

- The content is broken into files of 256Kbytes in size
- Peers that download content may also upload content
- Rarest pieces are uploaded first
- Uploading peers receive higher communication rates than downloading peers

Furthermore, the legitimacy of content distribution and security of content sharing must be guaranteed with the adoption of licensing schemes

Figure 15. Architecture for integrating P2P applications in IMS networks

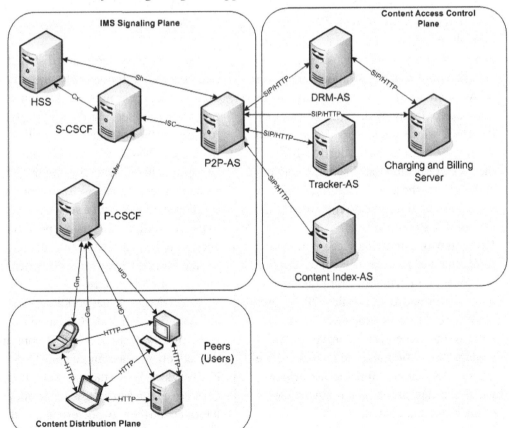

subject to the Digital Right Management (DRM) rules. Although this concept is not native to P2P networks, in the following section, it is shown that in the case of IMS networks, DRMs can be safeguarded with dedicated DRM servers.

Network Architecture

Figure 15 illustrates the network architecture for integrating P2P applications in subscriber networks.

As it is shown, the implementation of P2P applications in IMS networks becomes feasible with the introduction of Application Servers (P2P-AS) that provide the following call control operations:

- **User recognition and authentication:** Firstly, the user is recognised by the network on the basis of his IMPI, and he is then authenticated for a particular P2P service. Both operations are triggered by the user himself once he sends user registration and session setup messages. Successful completion of user registration in the IMS network allows the second message to be intercepted: firstly by the S-SCSF and then the HSS, which decides by judging from the service description header, to which AS the message is directed. Then, the network authenticates the user for the given service, using the charging scheme contained in the user profile stored in the HSS.

- **P2P gateway:** Following successful session setup, the user receives content description and location information from the content index server, addressed via the P2P-AS. According to the rules explained in previous section, the content index server provides content description and the address of the tracker AS that contains the list of peers, which are currently maintaining the pieces of the requested content.

- **Safeguarding of the digital rights of content producers:** Legitimate use of content may only be safeguarded by applying the digital rights of the content producer. In IMS networks, charging for content sharing may be applied as a premium to the charges incurred for accessing the network services. Following this concept, the digital rights for each particular content are placed in dedicated application servers (DRM-AS) in the form of charging values, in order to be manageable by the network. Each time the user requests particular content, the P2P-AS resolves the costs for sharing the content by polling the corresponding DRM-AS.

- **Service charging:** Is a function of the cost for accessing the network and the cost for content sharing. Network access costs are implemented by the IMS network with Radius servers, whereas content sharing costs may arise from DRM-AS, depending on the type of content being requested.

Since peer systems are distributed entities that function autonomously, the service charge of network access must be the sum of cost of all peers used for serving the *served peer*. In order to measure the cost of network utilisation by each peer, the radius server should employ a dynamic charging scheme, whereby unitary credits are assigned for service access. Each time a served peer establishes a link with a serving peer, it requests to pass a credit to the serving peer in order to get access on the path. In the end, all credits used are counted by the radius server in order to calculate the cost of service access.

In carrier grade networks, service charging is always a function of the QoS used for serving the user. To deal with this issue in P2P communications, the network may assign a default QoS value for all P2P services. When the user wants to have a better QoS, he sends a request to the network via the client interface and the network responds with a proposal. If the proposal is accepted, the network enforces

Figure 16. Message flow of P2P systems integrated in IMS networks

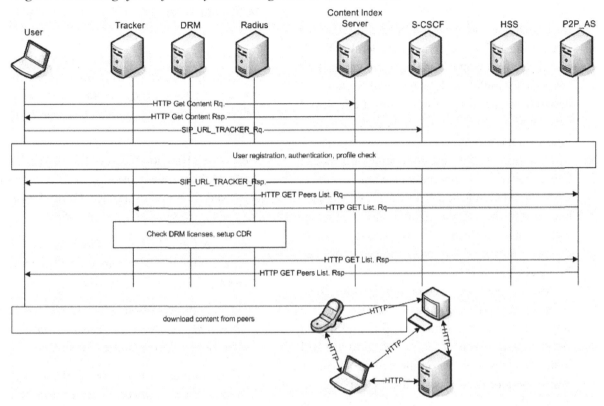

the QoS settings on the path between the serving and server peers, and the served peer informs the serving peer through in-band signaling.

Communication Scenarios

Figure 16 illustrates an exemplar message flow for P2P systems communicating over IMS networks. For simplicity, messages relating to operations of the IMS network are suppressed.

Initially, the user contacts the content index server to obtain the file that describes the content and the address (URL) of the tracker server (HTTP Get Content Rq/Rsp.). Using the returned tracker address, the user requests the IMS network to provide the list of peers having parts of the requested content (SIP_URL_TRACKER_Rq.).

The latter request triggers the process of user registration and authentication in the network to take place, whereby the user is authorized for accessing the requested P2P service. After the authorisation process is successfully accomplished (SIP_URL_TRACKER_Rsp.), the user may communicate with the tracker (HTTP GET Peers List Rq/Rsp.) and the rest of the P2P servers of the network (HTTP GET List. Rq./Rsp.).

Upon receiving the request for the peer list file, the tracker server asserts the DRM settings of the requested content and presets accordingly the Charging Data Records (CDR) contained in the radius server for the given user. Finally, by obtaining the peer list (HTTP GET Peers List Rsp.), the user is able to communicate with the peers to download the requested content.

CONCLUSION

In this chapter, we have outlined a method for integrating P2P systems in interoperable fixed-mobile environments. It has been shown that P2P systems are highly agile in terms of content and network usage and therefore can only be deployed according to the heterogeneous network communication concept.

Moving along this line, the chapter introduced to the reader, firstly the main principles of interworking in heterogeneous networks, which have been established very recently under the framework of NGN and IMS initiatives, and secondly an overlay architecture for integrating P2P services in the context of IMS networks.

Many aspects of P2P communications, such as the provisioning of quality of service, flexible implementation of service charging and digital rights management for content sharing are still under investigation for implementation across multi-operator networks, which are expected to attract the interest of the telecommunications industry in the near future.

The main driver for integrating P2P systems in IMS networks is the keen interest of the subscriber network operators to provide converged services in an all-IP network. In this emerging communications landscape, the users will replace the operators as producers of potential *killer applications*, giving the telecommunications market a new dynamicity and prospective for revenue generation by different actors, such as third party application developers and service providers.

REFERENCES

3GPP Technical Specification 23002. (2007). *Network architecture*. Third Partnership Project.

3GPP Technical Specification 23221. (2008). *Architectural requirements*. Third Partnership Project.

3GPP Technical Specification 23228. (2006). *IP multimedia subsystem (IMS)*. Third Partnership Project.

Baset, S. A., & Schulzrinne, H. (2006). An analysis of the Skype peer-to-peer Internet telephony protocol. In *Proceedings of the IEEE International Conference on Computer Communications (INFOCOM)*.

Chen, W.-P., Hamada, T., Yao, J. J., & Wei, H.-Y. (2006). QoS management and peer-to-peer mobility in fixed-mobile convergence. *Fujitsu Scientific and Technical Journal, 42*(4), 535-546.

Farha, R., & Leon-Garcia, A. (2007). A novel peer-to-peer naming infrastructure for next generation networks. (LNCS 4786, pp. 1-12).

ITU-T Recommendation G.805. (2000). *Generic functional architecture of transport networks*. International Telecommunications Union.

ITU-T Recommendation G.809. (2003). *Functional architecture of connectionless layer networks*. International Telecommunications Union.

ITU-T Recommendation Y.2001. (2004). Series Y: Global information infrastructure, Internet protocol aspects and next-generation networks. *General overview of NGN*. International Telecommunications Union.

ITU-T Recommendation Y.2011. (2004). Series Y: Global information infrastructure, Internet protocol aspects and next generation networks. *General principles and general reference model for next generation networks*. International Telecommunications Union.

Klenk, A., Kleis, M., Radier, B., Elmoumouhi, S., Carle, G., & Salaun, M. (2008). Towards autonomic service control in next generation networks. In *Proceedings of the Fourth International Conference on Autonomic and Autonomous Systems*.

Liang, J., Kumar, R., & Ross, K.W. (2004). The KaZaa overlay: A measurement study. In *Proceedings of the IEEE Annual Computer Communications*.

Rosenberg, J., Schulzrinne H., G. Camarillo, Johnston, A., Peterson, J., Sparks, R., Handley, M., & Schooler, E. (2002). SIP: The Session initiation protocol, *RFC 3261*.

Tompros, S., & Denazis S. (2008). Interworking of heterogeneous access networks and QoS provisioning via IP multimedia core networks. *Computer Networks, 52*(1), 215-227.

UMA Consortium. (2004). Unlicensed mobile access (UMA). Architecture (Stage 2), R1.0.0, Technical specification.

Wa, L., & Zhu, W. (2008). A carrier grade peer-to-peer network architecture. In *Proceedings of the First ITU-T Kaleidoscope Academic Conference on Innovations in NGN: Future Networks and Services*.

Yao, J. J., & Chen, H. H. (2007). Fixed-mobile convergence, streaming multimedia services, and peer-to-peer communication. (LNCS 4577, pp. 52-56).

Chapter XV
Peer–to–Peer SIP for Mobile Computing:
Challenges and Solutions

Erkki Harjula
MediaTeam Oulu Group, University of Oulu, Finland

Jani Hautakorpi
Ericsson Research Nomadiclab, Jorvas, Finland

Nicklas Beijar
Department of Communications and Networking, TKK, Helsinki University of Technology, Espoo, Finland

Mika Ylianttila
MediaTeam Oulu Group, University of Oulu, Finland

Due to the increasing popularity of Peer-to-Peer (P2P) computing, the information technology industry and standardization organizations have started to direct their efforts on standardizing P2P algorithms and protocols. The Internet Engineering Task Force (IETF) has recently formed the Peer-to-Peer SIP (P2PSIP) working group for enabling serverless operation of Session Initiation Protocol (SIP). This chapter introduces the P2PSIP by presenting its background and purpose, operational principles, current status, and application areas. The focus is on the challenges and problem areas from the viewpoint of standardization and related research. The mobile- and heterogeneous environments are considered with special care. The authors provide a glance to the existing and emerging solutions that may be used in tackling the mentioned challenges and thus paving the way for successful deployment of P2PSIP in mobile environments.

INTRODUCTION

Peer-to-Peer (P2P) networks have reached an important role in the communications between end users in Internet. Since the first file sharing applications, the P2P technology has gone through several evolutionary steps. The academic community has primarily focused on the development and optimization of the network algorithms, whereas the open-source community has been active in developing applications. Only recently, the information technology industry has become aware of the significance and business potential of P2P.

On the other hand, recent technological advances in mobile networking and mobile device capabilities have made it feasible to use mobile devices as fully functional Internet nodes. Due to this, the possibilities of using P2P networks have extended to the mobile domain as well. Extending IP-based communications to the mobile domain has highlighted the need for common standards for the purpose of interoperability. In the mobile domain, Session Initiation Protocol (SIP) plays an important role since it is the de-facto signaling protocol for session management, instant messaging, and presence information exchange in Third Generation (3G) mobile networks. SIP provides the potential of connecting a mobile device with any SIP-enabled node in Internet, removing the barriers between the mobile and fixed networking.

Due to the growing interest of the information technology industry and academia, the Internet Engineering Task Force (IETF) has established the Peer-to-Peer SIP (P2PSIP) working group (P2PSIP, 2008) for developing the standards for serverless use of SIP. P2PSIP aims to provide a decentralized, effortlessly administrated, scalable, and failure-tolerant platform for SIP communications in heterogeneous network environments, based on global standards. A principal aspect in the development of P2PSIP is that it is not meant to replace the traditional client/server SIP, but instead extend it to work in new environments. Fundamentally, P2PSIP builds upon a structured overlay, which is managed by the collaborative effort of participating P2PSIP nodes. This removes the need for extensive use of centralized server components and allows true P2P networking between the SIP nodes.

In this chapter, we provide an overview of the P2PSIP technology and standardization status, and present its fundamental operating principle and structure. The potential of P2PSIP is illustrated by presenting different applications in different environments. Then we point out the challenges regarding performance, restricted and heterogeneous networks, mobility, interoperability, security, as well as incentives. We elaborate from the viewpoint of mobile environments, and focus on the infrastructure-type mobile networking, such as wireless local area network (LAN) and mobile telephone networks. Solving the presented challenges is essential for enabling the secure, reliable, and efficient use of the protocol in mobile and other restricted network environments. The chapter strives to give the reader a glance to P2PSIP technology as an example of a lightweight peer-to-peer based protocol for communication, session management, and service provisioning purposes in mobile environment.

BACKGROUND: PEER-TO-PEER SIP

The scientific background of P2PSIP is built on the University of Columbia's P2PSIP (Singh & Schulzrinne, 2004) and the College of William & Mary's SOSIMPLE (Bryan et al., 2005) projects. Based on the results of these early projects and multiple ad-hoc meeting sessions between the interested parties during 2005-2007, IETF formed the P2PSIP working group in 2007 for developing standards for serverless use of SIP. The goal has later extended towards a more general P2P architecture, where the applications can also utilize P2PSIP overlay directly, instead of limiting the usage to only SIP-based communication. The focus of P2PSIP is in the general functions providing decentralized node- and resource location and communication, and the essential supportive functions that ensure the secure and unrestricted access to the mentioned services. As the focus is tightly in building a general-purpose enabling technology, the supplementary services are outside the scope of P2PSIP.

Reference Architecture

P2PSIP Reference Model (Bryan et al., 2008) defines the general framework for P2PSIP. It presents a high-level view of the P2PSIP concepts, terminology and operation principles, as well as points out the related open problems.

The *P2PSIP Network* builds upon *P2PSIP peers* (i.e. supernodes) and *P2PSIP clients* (i.e. ordinary nodes) and a *P2PSIP Overlay*, formed and managed by P2PSIP peers. The P2PSIP peers are higher in hierarchy, taking care of the overlay management, message transport and other services, and provide P2PSIP clients the access to the P2PSIP network. The functionality of the clients is under debate, but it has been agreed that they do have the ability to add, modify, inspect, and delete information in the overlay. In other words, they do not store or route third-party data and messages. Peers communicate with each other using the lightweight binary *Peer Protocol* and clients communicate with peers using the *Client Protocol*. The client protocol will most probably be a subset of the peer protocol. (Bryan et al., 2008)

Figure 1 illustrates the P2PSIP reference model and some possible node roles within it. A P2PSIP peer may have multiple roles. A *UA Peer* is a P2PSIP peer, which is co-located with a SIP User Agent (UA), whereas a *Gateway Peer* is co-located with a gateway, such as a Public Switched Telephone Network (PSTN) gateway. A *Redir Peer* is a P2PSIP peer, co-located with a SIP redirect server and a *Proxy Peer* with a SIP Proxy, through which basic SIP UAs are able to communicate with UA peers in P2PSIP network.

The P2PSIP overlay is basically a logical network of nodes built on top of a physical network of devices. Nodes in the overlay are connected by logical links that may be formed by physical connections between multiple physical devices in the underlying network. One or more peers form the overlay, which is collectively managed by these peers. Thus, the P2PSIP overlay is a *structured* P2P network, where the nodes in the overlay collaborate to provide a distributed mechanism for mapping names to overlay locations. This is realized by a distributed database, where the data is stored on peers. The data management, including the mechanisms for storing data reliably on the overlay and retrieving it from the overlay, is managed by the peer protocol based on a *Distributed Hash Table* (DHT) algorithm. The DHT-based database stores information in *(key, value)* pairs.

Figure 1. P2PSIP reference model

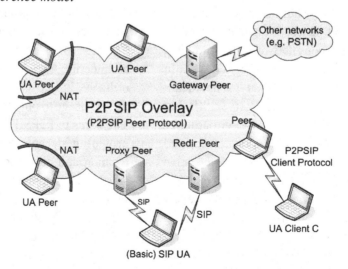

The fundamental functions provided by the database are *put(key, data)* to store an element, and *data = get(key)* to retrieve an element. The key uniquely identifies the element, and is usually in the form of an integer. Keys of other data types, such as strings (e.g. a SIP Uniform Resource Identifier (URI)), are converted to integers using a *hash* function, which maps the data element to a smaller data element that the overlay is able to store and locate.

Several DHT algorithms have been developed by the research community. P2PSIP does not commit oneself to any specific DHT algorithm, but it may later define a given algorithm to be used as the default one. The most well-known DHT algorithms are Chord (Stoica et al., 2003), Content Addressable Network (CAN) (Ratnasamy et al., 2001), Kademlia (Maymounkov et al., 2002), Tapestry (Zhao et al., 2004), and Pastry (Rowstron & Drusche, 2001). The fundamental ideas in all algorithms are similar. Information and nodes have keys identifying their location in an abstract key-space. Each node is assigned a partition of the key-space and is responsible for storing the keys within that partition. To store and retrieve information, the node responsible for the given key is located via several steps, where each step contacts a node logically closer to the node. The main differences between the algorithms are in the organization of the key-space and the definition of the distance between two keys.

In addition to storing, locating, and retrieving node addresses and data, P2PSIP peers also provide additional *services* to other P2PSIP nodes. (Bryan et al., 2008) defines service as a "capability contributed by a peer to an overlay or to the members of an overlay" (p.12). To allow service provision in P2PSIP, the distributed database also needs to store information about the services a certain peer offers. For enabling successful SIP signaling between the P2PSIP nodes, the P2PSIP peer and client protocols also need to provide a *transport function* for SIP messages to allow them to be transported between any nodes in the P2PSIP network.

The nodes in the P2PSIP overlay may leave the system at any moment, regardless of their responsibilities. The reliable storage of the data in the overlay needs a replication mechanism for ensuring the existence of the data stored on the overlay, also in networks with high *churn*. Churn means the turnover of existing nodes leaving and new nodes joining the overlay, i.e. the fluctuation of node population in the overlay. Thus, automatic data replication mechanism is an integral part of the P2PSIP peer protocol.

Network Address Translators (NATs) and *Firewalls* (FW) are major obstacles, especially for P2P networks, since they hinder direct communication between peers – and P2PSIP is no exception. Since the major part of Internet users are behind NATs and FWs, this problem has to be solved for enabling universal usability. Thus, P2PSIP messages must be able to traverse NATs and FWs, which is one of the most important supportive features the P2PSIP network has to provide.

High-Level Functionality

When started up, a P2PSIP peer needs to – depending on the situation – either join an existing overlay or create a new overlay. In order to join to an existing overlay, the peer must enroll and authenticate itself for obtaining a Peer-ID and possibly also a set of credentials. The enrollment will most probably be realized by centralized servers for trust and security reasons. Then, the peer needs to locate some P2PSIP peer that already participates in the overlay. This peer is referred to as the *Bootstrap Node*. There are many ways for finding a bootstrap node, including using a cached, a manually configured or the last known bootstrap peer address, broadcasting requests for bootstrap peers, using DNS-based service discovery, or using publicly known bootstrap servers. The bootstrap server may be co-located with the enrollment server. After bootstrapping, the peer must – in most cases – traverse NATs and firewalls between itself and the other nodes, and insert itself to the overlay. The NAT traversal may be done in several ways: utilizing Interactive Connectivity Establishment (ICE), Session Traversal Utilities for NAT (STUN)/Traversal Using Relays around NAT (TURN) or with some new lighter mechanism based on them. Clients do not in any situation directly participate in the overlay, even though they can utilize the overlay through their associated peers. They may not be given any Peer-ID, and thus the need for overlay-wide enrolling and authentication is unclear at the moment of writing this chapter.

After joining the P2PSIP overlay, either directly as a peer or indirectly as a client, the node is able to *publish, locate,* and *remove resource objects.* The resource object may contain information about, e.g. the address, location or presence state, device capabilities, service description, or shared files of the user. The peers of the overlay are collectively used to store and replicate these records, route queries, and manage the overlay population according to the DHT algorithm used. When publishing a resource, the publishing node first calculates the hash code for the resource and then this resource (or a pointer to it if the resource is, e.g. a large file) is stored in the overlay peer responsible of the generated hash. When querying the resource, the querying node calculates the hash for the resource and sends the query regarding this hash code to the overlay. The overlay routes the query via the overlay to the peer responsible of the queried hash. If the target overlay peer has the resource (or a pointer to it), the resource (or an address of the node containing the actual resource) is returned to the querying node. The requesting node can now, depending on its original intention, establish a SIP session, file transfer, or any other interaction with the peer containing the requested resource. This interaction after finding the requested resource or node is outside of the scope of P2PSIP.

P2PSIP peers are collectively responsible of the overlay management tasks when participating in overlay, including storing and transferring the resource objects, maintaining the *routing table* (a table that is used to store the addresses of known nodes), routing messages, etc. Thus, when leaving the overlay, a peer must unregister from the overlay. By unregistering from the overlay, a peer transfers resource records, routing table entries, and other similar information to other peers in the overlay. This is necessary for minimizing the negative effects of churn and for maintaining the overlay integrity. If a peer leaves the overlay without proper unregistration, data it stores is lost, which has negative effects on the overlay functionality, even though it is tolerated to some extent due to replication.

Applications

The primary purpose of P2PSIP is to provide a standardized platform for serverless operation of SIP. For this, it provides a distributed mechanism for mapping names to overlay locations and a distributed transport function for SIP message routing. Moreover, as P2PSIP is basically a peer-to-peer layer below SIP and provides a support for additional services and an Application Programming Interface (API), it can also be utilized directly by applications. Together, these features make it possible to use P2PSIP as a general-purpose communication technology enabler for a wide variety of SIP- and non-SIP applications.

Basic SIP applications should work on P2PSIP with only minor changes or no changes at all on the application level, depending on the SIP stack between the applications and P2PSIP. Changes are needed at the SIP stack for making it work properly on P2PSIP layer, but this is not necessarily affecting the applications at all. The traditional SIP appliances in mobile devices include simple applications, such as *Voice over IP* (VoIP) telephony, instant messaging and presence. The user may, for example, call to a friend using a SIP-based VoIP application in her mobile device without noticing any changes in the service quality, even though the actual technology (SIP+P2PSIP) behind the session establishment does not use any centralized components anymore. In the protocol layer, instead of utilizing centralized SIP proxies and location servers, the callee's address is mapped in a decentralized manner using the P2PSIP overlay.

P2PSIP is an enabling technology that can form a basis for many kinds of P2P services, not only for the higher-level protocols, such as SIP, but also directly for applications. It is noteworthy that the fundamental P2P concept is general and not limited to any specific application type. Contrary to the prevalent understanding, P2P as a technology can be used for far wider application areas than just file sharing, which has erroneously become synonymous for P2P technology. Examples of enabled application services are content delivery, media streaming, games, and many other types of inter-personal- and inter-service communication.

ISSUES, CONTROVERSIES AND PROBLEMS

Since P2PSIP is a novel, rapidly developing technology, it is difficult to forecast the future direction of any discipline. However, it is possible to highlight a number of challenges and developments of the immediate horizon that could affect the direction taken by the standardization over the coming years. This section will highlight those open research issues, controversies, and problems that affect the development of P2PSIP. We start by discussing the general performance- and overhead-related issues and network barriers hindering the operation of the protocol. Then, we move to elaborate the special requirements and challenges set by mobile environment. The interoperability with other systems is also considered one of the most essential issues for ensuring the general feasibility of the technology. Finally, we discuss the challenges related to security and incentives.

Performance and Overhead

P2PSIP network can be implemented using one of several DHT algorithms. The choice of a DHT algorithm and the parameters of the DHT largely influence the overhead and the perceived performance of the P2PSIP network. From the network perspective, it is important to minimize the message overhead of maintaining the structure, and the traffic resulting from lookups and refreshing stored information. The performance seen by the user is affected by the lookup latency, the success rate, the availability of information, the battery consumption, and the balancing of load. Even though the DHT algorithm development is out of the scope of P2PSIP working group, selecting a DHT algorithm with suitable features for a P2PSIP-based network plays an important role in optimizing the performance and overhead.

In contrast to centralized hash tables, DHTs maintain only a partial knowledge of other nodes in the network. This knowledge is stored in the routing table. When information is stored or retrieved, a query is routed to the node responsible for the given key. Since each node has limited knowledge about other nodes, several nodes must be queried for a lookup, each node being logically closer to the destination than the previous one. Figure 2 illustrates the operating principle of DHT by a simple 8-node circle-based DHT overlay with a hash space of 0000-1111. Each peer is responsible of the hash codes between it and its successor peer on the ring. In this case, each peer has a lookup table of two entries: the successor node on the ring and the node on the opposite side of the ring. After receiving a request ("Where is 1101?"), the peer 0000 inspects first its own hash cache and detects that it does not have the requested resource, and then routes the request to the peer in its routing table with the address closest to the requested resource (in this case, peer 1000 is closer than 0010). This is continued until the requested resource is found from the node 1100. The 1100 peer then returns the response directly to the requesting node.

Figure 2. DHT Lookup operation

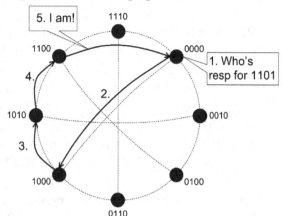

Hop count vs. routing table size

Table 1. Properties of common DHT algorithms

	Routing table size	Hop count
Chord	$\log N$	$O(\log N)$
Pastry	$B \log_B N + B \log_B N$	$O(\log_B N)$
Tapestry	$\log_B N$	$O(\log_B N)$
CAN	$2d$	$O(dN^{1/d})$
Kademlia	$B \log_B N + B$	$O(\log_B N) + c$ [*]

[*] c is a small constant

The number of required hops affects the lookup latency and the lookup traffic. Generally, there is a tradeoff between the size of the routing table and the number of hops. In the extreme case where all nodes are known, a single hop is required for a lookup. In the opposite extreme, each node only knows one neighbor and the lookup must traverse all nodes. The former case corresponds to an ordinary hash table, while the latter to a linked list (e.g. using only the successor in Chord). Practical algorithms, such as the one presented in Figure 2, are in between these extremes. Table 1 shows the order of the routing table size and the hop count in different DHTs in a network with N nodes (Lua et al., 2004). The parameters B (the base) and d (the dimension) are adjustable parameters of the respective algorithms. Most DHTs behave similarly, with the exception of CAN.

Hop count also depends on the used routing mode. In the *iterative* routing, the requesting node queries a node and obtains the address of the node closer to the destination. This node is contacted next. The sequence continues until the destination is reached. In the *recursive* routing, the receiving node passes the query directly to node closer to the destination until the destination is reached. The requesting node thus only receives the final response routed through the query path.

Semi-recursive (direct) routing (Jiang et al., 2008) works otherwise similarly to recursive routing mode, but the responses are routed directly from the destination to the source, leading to a lower hop count. Figure 2 illustrates the semi-recursive routing mode.

Performance vs. Overhead

The size of the routing table affects the maintenance traffic. Every routing table entry needs to be refreshed periodically. In Chord, refreshing an entry, called finger, requires performing a lookup, thus, the cost is $O(\log N)$. In a network with a high churn rate, the routing table entries must be refreshed frequently. Still, a few incorrect entries do not prevent the DHT from operating correctly. In Chord, only a single routing table entry, the successor, is needed for correct operation. Incorrect entries, however, slow down the routing process, as requests may be sent to unavailable nodes, and later resent to another node. The update rate therefore controls the compromise between overhead and lookup delay. The performance vs. cost framework (PVC) introduced in (Li et al., 2005) assumes that a protocol consumes a certain amount of network bandwidth to achieve a given lookup latency. Li et al. have shown that with optimal selection of parameters, the tradeoff between lookup latency and bandwidth is similar in all algorithms. By adjusting the routing table size, additional bandwidth can be used efficiently. Instead of actively maintaining a routing table, part of the routing table can be maintained opportunistically through existing lookup traffic. When a node performs a lookup, it learns the location of the destination node and, in case of iterative routing, also the locations of other nodes. This information can be used in addition to the actively maintained routing table entries to increase the lookup performance. The actively maintained routing table can be smaller, which reduces the maintenance traffic. Opportunistic learning is used in Kademlia, which relies on lookup traffic to learn about new neighbors. (Li et al., 2005) states that opportunistic learning is a more efficient way to maintain routing tables than explicit stabilization.

Most simulation studies of DHTs assume the use patterns of file-sharing or similar applications. Compared to these, the VoIP scenario is assumed to have a higher churn rate in comparison to the lookup frequency. Using P2PSIP in mobile scenarios requires low maintenance overhead, both to save bandwidth and battery consumption.

Load Balance vs. Overhead

For distributing the load equally between the nodes, most DHTs use a random hash function in generating the IDs for nodes. This leads to a characteristic $O(log N)$ imbalance of address space between the nodes (Rao et al., 2003), where N denotes the number of nodes in the system. During the past years, a great amount of research has been conducted to improve the *load balancing* in structured P2P networks. Load balancing in DHT-based networks can roughly be divided into two types: address space balancing and item balancing (Karger & Ruhl, 2004). Address space balancing focuses on partitioning the address space evenly, while item balancing is dealing with the imbalance of the actual data items between the hosting nodes. The latter mechanism is needed when the distribution of items in the address space cannot

be randomized. This kind of situations may occur in, e.g. range searches in database applications. Another load balancing problem is the imbalance of service popularity, where some services are more popular than others.

Virtual server model (Stoica et al., 2003) improved later by dynamic virtual server allocation (Dabek et al., 2001; Rao et al., 2003), is the most commonly used load balancing technology, as it has several benefits. Firstly, it can be used for addressing both address space balancing and item balancing problems. Secondly, it is independent of the underlying DHT algorithms and does not require any special features from them. In a nutshell, in the virtual server model, each physical node pretends to be several nodes, each participating independently in the DHT overlay. The device's load is the combined load of several virtual nodes. Load between the physical nodes is then balanced by controlling the number of virtual servers per physical node. Maintenance load, however, increases as more (virtual) nodes are participating in the network. Thus, there is a tradeoff between the quality of load balancing and overhead.

Network Barriers

Nowadays, only a minority of network nodes are freely accessible from Internet, due to the increasing use of private networks. The communication between the private and public networks is handled by Network Address Translator (NAT) devices that enable the communication between the networks having different namespaces. The routing from the private network to the public one is straightforward, since the private network routers are set up to route the traffic addressed to the public network through the NAT. The actual problem is the other direction: public networks are not inherently able to route the messages addressed to private network without exactly knowing the right NAT device behind which the target node is located, due to the different namespace. This means that the initiator of the traffic must always be the node in the private network and the corresponding node must be in the public network. In addition, *firewalls* (FW), that might be co-located with NAT, sometimes block certain types of traffic. The existence of NATs is a problem, especially for P2P-networking, including P2PSIP, where the called node is often located in the private network, in contrast to client/server architectures where the called nodes are usually server nodes located in the public network. Due to the P2P's bad reputation, in the sense of caused network load and legal issues, the firewalls are often set up to block P2P traffic. Thus, for ensuring the successful operation of P2PSIP, there is a need for mechanisms for traversing NATs and FWs.

Types of NATs

Various different types of NATs are deployed in the networks today. The NAT devices differ regarding their mapping and filtering behaviors. Mapping behavior means the way how a NAT maps ports to outbound connections, and filtering means the way how inbound connections are treated. (Audet & Jennings, 2007) have explained three different mapping and filtering behaviors. The mapping behaviors are *endpoint-independent, address-dependent*, and *address and port-dependent mapping*. Filtering behaviors have similar names:

endpoint-independent, address-dependent, and *address and port-dependent filtering*.

Some of the NATs are made easy to deal with from the viewpoint of NAT traversal. For example, it is not necessary to use a relay for media on a scenario where both endpoints are behind a NAT with an endpoint-independent mapping and filtering. However, some combinations always require a relay for media, if probabilistic NAT traversal methods, such as port prediction, are not used. An example of such a combination is a scenario where one NAT has an endpoint dependent mapping and another has an endpoint and port dependent filtering, see Figure 3. (Guha et al., 2006) have studied Skype, and they have found that relays are used for media in 9.6% of the connections.

Endpoints behind a NAT have to be able to determine the external transport layer address (IP and port) assigned to them by the NAT. Different mapping behaviors of NATs affect this assignment. For example, if an endpoint is behind a NAT with an endpoint-independent mapping, the assigned transport layer address does not change from one connection to another, as it does when an endpoint is behind a NAT with an endpoint-dependent mapping. The ability to determine the external transport layer address is especially important for P2PSIP endpoints, because they have to be able to signal to the parties they want to communicate with, what transport layer address they are using

Figure 3. Scenario where a media relay is needed

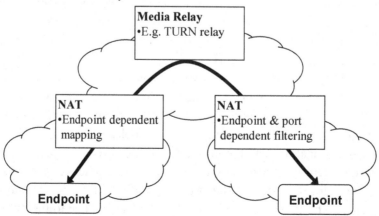

for receiving media. Endpoints should also be able to determine the optimal path between the two endpoints. There can be, for example, a case where two endpoints are behind the same NAT, but still they are using a media relay outside the NAT, because the endpoints are not aware of the network topology.

Refreshing NAT Bindings and Failure Detection

In P2PSIP network, each P2PSIP peer has multiple logical links (e.g. TCP connections) to other peers, and P2PSIP clients have at least one logical link to a peer. If these logical links go across NATs, periodic keep-alive messages need to be sent for each connection in order to keep the NAT bindings alive. Typically, NAT bindings for UDP timeout are in the order of tens of seconds or few minutes, and the NAT bindings for TCP timeout in the order of few hours. Thus, if UDP is used, there is a need to send keep-alive messages rather frequently. This is problematic for mobile nodes, and especially problematic for mobile P2PSIP peers, because the sending of frequent keep-alive messages increases the power consumption and decreases the battery duration. The use of TCP does not completely remove the need for sending messages rather frequently to the network. For example, if the failure detection feature is required, then the keep-alive messages – which can be also be used for failure detection – should be sent quite frequently, even if TCP is used. There can be, for example, a scenario where a P2PSIP client is behind a NAT that has rebooted itself and lost all the state information, and the P2PSIP client cannot be reached before it sends the next keep-alive message. In fact, in this scenario, the P2PSIP client does not even know that it cannot be reached, if it does not send keep-alive messages.

Firewalls

Firewall traversal for P2P traffic is especially problematic in networks that use highly restric-

tive rule sets in their firewalls. For example, some corporate FWs often drop almost all or all such inbound connections that do not have an associated state in the FW, and allow outbound connections only to selected transport layer ports. Ports that are commonly open are, for example, well-know ports 80 and 443. Those ports are meant to be used for Hypertext Transfer Protocol (HTTP) and HTTP Secure (HTTPS) traffic (IANA, 2008). Skype has such firewall traversal technique that it is listening ports 80 and 443 (Baset & Schulzrinne, 2006). The disadvantage of this kind of approach, in addition to breaking IANA guidelines, is that only one application per host at a time can use this kind of FW traversal technique. Only one application can use it, because the application has to listen to ports 80 and 443, and only one application at a time can listen to a given port. Some FWs also inspect that the protocol on top of open, well-know ports is the protocol that it should be. In that kind of scenario, the application data has to be carried on top of legitimate protocol, such as HTTP on port 80. It is noteworthy that most likely the protocol used for carrying the application data across firewalls is sub-optimal for the needs of the utilizing application, because it was not designed for that particular application in the first place.

Mobile Environment Special Requirements

Mobile environment sets challenging requirements for P2P networking, as compared with a fixed environment. As the P2PSIP is meant be utilized also in mobile environments, it has to meet these requirements. The additional requirements are partly consequences of the limited physical capabilities of the devices and networks, but also the result from the transient nature of device usage (Kellerer et al., 2005), and the networking costs (Verkasalo, 2007). Despite the rapid development of mobile devices, their performance is still behind desktop- and laptop computers. The main physical limitations of mobile devices have traditionally concerned the computational performance, access network restrictions, memory capacity, battery capacity, and screen- and keyboard size. Some of these limitations have been facilitated due to the technological development, but many of them seem to persist nevertheless. Mobile devices are mostly running on battery power. The increased performance of mobile devices demands more and more energy. Even though the power-saving functions have evolved, the battery duration seems to remain the same or even decrease slightly. Without proper battery duration, the benefits brought by mobility are mainly lost. This makes the battery consumption a very important factor for mobile networking. From the networking point of view, the power saving requirement means that the device cannot keep the data link open continuously, forcing the network usage to be very transient.

Transient Usage

Mobile devices are used in different environment and situations than fixed devices, e.g. when the user is on the move, or when fixed terminals are not available. In these situations, the users' needs may differ radically from the situations with the fixed devices. The situation- and context-awareness are emphasized. On the other hand, the technical constraints mentioned before affect the usage as well. Together, they make usage of mobile devices very transient in nature. Due to this, the mobile device's data connection is usually open only when it is needed by the user. This makes mobile devices transient in the sense of network presence, negatively affecting the operation of P2PSIP network if mobile devices are participating in the overlay, since the DHT-based overlay is maintained by a collaborative effort of participating nodes. The whole network has to frequently adapt to changed situation, i.e. churn is increased. The increased churn, for one, increases the needed network management signaling. Thus,

the importance of *failure tolerance* is emphasized in overlays with mobile nodes.

Mobile Node as P2PSIP Peer

Failing or overloaded nodes do not necessarily hinder the P2PSIP overlay from correct operation, but may significantly degrade the performance. A direct consequence of the collaborative network maintenance is that the performance of the whole network depends on the average performance and stability of the participating nodes. On the other hand, the mobile devices participating in the overlay may have as much responsibility as the more capable nodes in the network. This problem is principally managed by the hierarchical structure of the network, where only the most efficient and stable nodes (P2PSIP peers) participate in the overlay and the less efficient and less stable nodes (P2PSIP clients) have less common responsibilities.

However, the hierarchical structure does not bring any help in some special cases. For example in the networks where most of the nodes are mobile devices (e.g. closed mobile operator networks) and thus acting as clients, load of the few peers may become exhausting to them. In this situation, it would be beneficial that also the mobile devices become peers even though they are less stable and efficient as the fixed devices. Thus, distributing the overlay management load based on performance and stability of the contributing nodes would be beneficial.

Node Mobility

Today's mobile and portable terminals may have several physical connectivities available, meaning that the device may access the P2PSIP network from different networks, i.e. have different IP address. An example of a terminal with several physical connections is a mobile phone with 3G and Wireless Local Area Network (WLAN) interfaces. Depending on the policy of the home overlay, the node may not be able to join the overlay from outside the specified network domain. Thus, the node may be online in some other overlay and willing to be reached from its home overlay. For making P2PSIP feasible with this kind of setups, P2PSIP overlay should provide an inter-overlay redirection service, similar to the one used in ordinary SIP. Another option is to use lower-layer mobility solutions, such as *Mobile IP* (Perkins, 2002; Johnson et al., 2004) or *Host Identity Protocol* (HIP) (Moskowitz & Nikander, 2006; Moskowitz et al., 2008), to keep the node available from a single IP address regardless of node's location.

An increasing number of smartphones and PDAs are able to change the network connectivity (i.e. IP address) on fly, which brings another challenge. Inter-overlay redirection service can provide a continuous reachability, or even a mobility support for connectionless sessions, such as page-mode instant messaging, when a node changes its network connectivity. However, with real-time sessions, such as VoIP call, this is not enough and lower-layer mobility solutions are needed to ensure the session continuity.

NATs and Firewalls

The previously discussed challenges related to traversing NATs and/or firewalls are emphasized in mobile environments. Almost all of the terminals in cellular operator networks, and majority of the WLAN terminals are behind NATs. In addition, due to the operators' willingness to restrict the traffic for minimizing the load inflicted to their networks, the mobile networks are often behind firewalls with strict filtering functions.

Interoperability with Existing Systems

According to the Metcalfe's law (Kirsner, 1998), the value of a telecommunications network is pro-

portional to the square of the number of users in the system. Thus, there is an inherent motivation to interconnect a network with other networks. To enable large-scale use, a user of P2PSIP should be able to connect with destinations in the *Public Switched Telephone Network* (PSTN) and in cellular networks. For this interconnection, a media gateway is used to convert between packet and circuit switched transmission where needed. The P2PSIP network can also be connected to a conventional server-based SIP network, such as an *IP Multimedia Subsystem* (IMS). We concentrate on the issues of connecting P2PSIP to conventional SIP networks such as the IMS, as these can further provide connectivity to the PSTN.

SIP nodes are able to establish calls to P2PSIP nodes using normal SIP procedures. The challenge, however, is how to address a P2PSIP node from outside the overlay. The conventional SIP node cannot be assumed to be aware of the overlay or to support mechanisms specific to P2PSIP. The routing process of SIP requires an entry in the DNS, indicating a server able to resolve the location of the node in a given domain. In P2PSIP, the role of the server is distributed, and any peer can perform address resolution once it is contacted. The overlay must thus be bound to a domain name. Indicating a single peer as an entry point in DNS assumes that this peer is always available, which often cannot be guaranteed. This peer also receives excess load. This suggests that the entry is implemented as a fixed server, which can be seen as being against the serverless philosophy of P2PSIP. An alternative solution is inserting the addresses of all or a subset of the peers in DNS. This, however, clearly destroys the distributed nature of P2PSIP and makes the DHT lookup redundant.

Interconnection to an IMS network presents further challenges, as the IMS network is centrally managed with high requirements on authentication, authorization, and accounting. These functions practically require a fixed gateway connecting the networks. The gateway can be a separate entity connected to an *Application Server* (AS) or a *Call Session Control Function* (CSCF), or fully integrated into one of these. Separate gateways may be used for different directions of the call, and for different geographical locations. The implementation and usage of the gateway depend on the scenario where P2PSIP is used. An operator-specific P2PSIP network used as an extension to IMS may, in a highly managed fashion, be connected to the IMS with a few gateways available to subscribers only. On the other hand, a publicly open P2PSIP network may have a large number of gateways connected to different operators, where the availability may depend on subscription to a gateway service. Such an approach is similar to the one used in Skype (http://www.skype.com), where calls to and from external networks require a subscription. The caller must be able to locate the gateways connecting to a given operator's IMS network. These gateway addresses can be stored in the *Subscriber Identity Module* (SIM) or in the overlay.

Due to charging, calls to the IMS require the caller to be authorized by the IMS network and, in practice, a subscription. It is, however, not impossible to envision scenarios where the P2PSIP user does not need to be authenticated. In an IMS scenario, it may be feasible to equip the terminal with separate user agents for the P2PSIP network and for the IMS. In that case, both share a common user interface and the difference may be invisible to the user. The terminal contains a full IMS terminal implementation. Using separate clients avoids the use of a gateway for outbound calls. Determining whether a given destination is in the P2PSIP network is simple – if the lookup gives no results, the destination is assumed to be outside the P2PSIP network and the IMS client is used for establishing the call.

(Marocco, Manzalini, Sampo, & Canal, 2007) identify some open issues, threatening proper interoperability between P2PSIP and IMS networks: IMS networks use IPv6, while P2PSIP most likely is used with IPv4. IMS handsets do not by default support NAT traversal techniques required by the P2PSIP nodes. Conventional peering agreements are ill-suited to regulate peering with uncontrolled peer-to-peer networks, causing security threats, and open possibilities for spam and phishing.

The key feature of P2PSIP is the decentralized nature without centralized servers. This feature may easily be lost with bad design. Solutions for interconnecting P2PSIP networks with external networks may lead to centralized entities, where information about individual P2PSIP users is stored. Such a solution might store records of individual P2PSIP users in DNS or in an IMS server, making the information distributed in the overlay redundant.

Security

The security issues in traditional client/server SIP and in P2PSIP networks are quite different. The main difference is that, whereas in traditional client/server SIP messages are being forwarded by centralized SIP proxies, in P2PSIP messages are being forwarded by the endpoints themselves (Bryan et al., 2008). In traditional client/server SIP, the SIP UA trusts, at least to some extent, the SIP proxies that are typically operated by communication service providers or enterprises, while in P2PSIP an endpoint most probably does not have existing trust relationship with the possible intermediate nodes. Thus, in order to be able to have a certain level of trust to the intermediate nodes, each P2PSIP endpoint should have a set of credentials (e.g. certificates) that provide a verifiable identity to the other endpoints in the P2PSIP network.

The users of the P2PSIP systems could want the P2PSIP system to provide a reliable and secure communication service for them. From the perspective of P2PSIP system, this translates to requirements for providing the following functions: secure and reliable lookup of users and resources, strong user identity, confidentiality and integrity for end-to-end communication, easy enrollment method, and measures for ensuring privacy. (Matuszewski et al., 2007)

The P2P networks in general are vulnerable to *Peer-ID mapping attacks* (Cerri et al., 2005). The Peer-ID mapping attack means a situation where a malicious peer is able to choose its own Peer-ID, and therefore its location, in the keyspace of a P2P network. If a peer is able to choose its own location in the P2P network, it can gain control over a selected part of P2P network's keyspace. For P2P-SIP networks, the Peer-ID mapping attack could mean, for example, a situation where a malicious peer is able to block all or most communication attempts to a selected user (victim).

Incentives

Issues related to *incentives* are a difficult problem to solve in any P2P network. The fundamental assumption in decentralized P2P networks is that the peers constituting the overlay provide all, or at least most of, the services required by the overlay. These services range from simple, not very resource consuming services, such as message forwarding, to more complex, resource consuming services, like media relaying.

The incentive problems, in this context, mean the problems related to peers' motivation for providing services to other peers in a P2P network. Issues related to incentives are more difficult to solve on open, standardized systems than on closed, non-standardized systems. For example Skype, which is such an application, solves incentive problems in a way that the client application itself decides what kind of services it provides for other peers. In other words, the Skype client application can decide whether to act as an ordinary node or as a super node on its own, and the ordinary users do not have the possibility affect to this decision (Baset & Schulzrinne, 2006).

P2PSIP networks suffer, like other P2P networks, from incentive problems. P2PSIP networks have two types of nodes: peers and clients. One specific incentive problem in P2PSIP networks is the incentive for being a peer. Naturally, every node in a P2PSIP network would prefer being a client, because it consumes fewer resources than being a peer. The nodes behind certain types of NATs require media relays in order to reach, and be reached by, other nodes. The incentive problem here is *why a node would provide a relay service for some other node?* Given that the P2PSIP system is an open, standardized system, it is not feasible to use mechanisms analyzing the node status for solving the incentive problem. In other words, what would be the vendor's incentive to implement standardized behavior along the lines of "node must be a peer if its uptime is more than a day and its bandwidth is at least 1Mb/s?"

SOLUTIONS AND FUTURE TRENDS

This section presents some existing and emerging solutions to the issues and challenges pointed out in the previous section. As the P2PSIP is at the very beginning of its standardization, and at the same time, represents a new type of technology, there are few existing solutions that can be used as they are. However, with some modifications, many of these existing solutions may be used as the fundamental basis for tackling problems in P2PSIP.

Performance and Overhead Solutions

The performance and overhead of a structured, DHT based P2P network is mainly affected by two factors: the DHT algorithm and the used protocol which implements it. In this chapter, we do not go deeper in presenting the optimization of DHT algorithms, since it is out of the scope of P2PSIP. Instead, we analyze those measures that might be utilized in P2PSIP peer protocol.

The protocol can use the DHT either in iterative, recursive, or semi-recursive routing mode.

Generally, iterative routing provides robustness towards DoS (Denial of Service) attacks, while recursive routing is well-suited to NAT traversal, and semi-recursive lookup, in its turn, reduces signalling overhead (Hautakorpi & Camarillo, 2007).

Load balancing is a technique for improving the performance of a P2P network by balancing the load between nodes in P2P networks. The virtual server load balancing model (Dabek et al., 2001; Rao et al., 2003) provides the basic tools for DHT-independent load balancing in DHT-based P2P overlays. Many publications have later been proposed to improve the virtual server model, regarding general performance (Bianchi et al., 2006; Shen & Xu, 2005; Song & Yang, 2006; Zhu & Hu, 2004, 2005), network dynamicity and churn (Godfrey et al., 2004; Shen & Xu, 2005), and network heterogeneity (Godfrey & Stoica, 2005; Tsai & Chen, 2006; Zhu & Hu, 2004). Although, many of these proposals consider the features of mobile networks, such as high churn and heterogeneity, none of them provide any actual mechanisms for distributing the overlay load between the contributing nodes based on their hardware resources. Thus, it is an important research topic in the area of DHT optimization for better suitability with mobile environments.

Interestingly, hardware resource -aware load balancing has been studied in the area of client/server distributed computing. (Faik, 2005) has proposed a model for resource-aware load balancing on heterogeneous clusters. The model was specifically created for client/server type distributed computing and its communication model was thus based on client/server communication. However, its node capability assessment model is fundamentally suitable for P2P computing as well.

In order to detect failing or overloaded nodes, (Song et al., 2008) propose diagnosing mechanisms that allow examining routes and the status of a node. These can be used either automatically or manually to locate problems, and could also

be useful for providing status information to load balancing mechanisms.

Organizing the overlays hierarchically is another interesting measure for tackling the performance and overhead issues, especially in heterogeneous environments. (Peng et al., 2007) have proposed a hybrid hierarchical architecture with two sub-overlay levels. Moreover, (Le et al., 2007) presented a hierarchical P2PSIP system made up of more than two levels of sub-overlays.

Mobility Solutions

For ensuring the real-time session continuity in P2PSIP application scenarios where nodes move between different IP-domains and different networks, lower-layer mobility solutions are needed. One option is using IP-layer mobility solutions, such as *Mobile IPv4* (Perkins, 2002) or *Mobile IPv6* (Johnson et al., 2004). The basic idea of Mobile IP solutions is to allow mobile nodes to move from one network to another while maintaining a permanent IP address, allowing the uninterrupted session continuity with handovers. For P2PSIP, Mobile IP can provide a transparent mobility mechanism. In other words, P2PSIP applications (like most applications) do not need to be aware of the existence of Mobile IP in order to benefit from it.

Another alternative is to use the HIP (Moskowitz & Nikander, 2006; Moskowitz et al., 2008), which separates the end-point identifier and locator roles of IP addresses. The HIP is used to establish an authenticated connection between two hosts and to provide continuity of communications between those hosts, independent of the networking layer. In essence, connections between P2PSIP nodes are bound to identifiers, which make it possible to change the locators, IP addresses, without breaking upper-layer connections. In addition to mobility support, HIP also provides authentication capabilities and data encryption between nodes. These features provide solution components to some of the security threats P2PSIP networks face. Furthermore, there is currently an ongoing effort to enable NAT traversal on the HIP layer (Komu et al., 2008), so that the applications would not have to implement NAT traversal mechanisms by themselves. Contrary to Mobile IP, the P2PSIP nodes could be aware of the existence of HIP, and provide some services to the HIP layer, such as finding relays.

Alongside the benefits of the previously mentioned mobility solutions, they also bring challenges. Since P2PSIP is not necessarily aware of the changes in the lower layer during vertical handovers (e.g. if a mobile node moves from WLAN network to low-performance and unreliable GPRS network), the node's performance and reliability might suddenly drop dramatically. Thus, even though sessions can continue while node is moving between the network domains, the quality of the session still depends on the underlying network connectivity. Even a more important issue is that lower-layer mobility also affects the system-wide performance and reliability of the P2PSIP overlay. For example, a previously stable mobile peer may become unreliable after changing the underlying network connectivity. Thus, the load balancing mechanisms used should be capable of reacting quickly to changes in the node's behavior. Many existing load balancing mechanisms, such as virtual servers (Dabek et al., 2001; Rao et al., 2003) already provide protocol-level support for this kind of dynamic node behavior.

Another challenge is the interoperability between the regular nodes and nodes with HIP functionality. While Mobile IP nodes are fully interoperable with regular nodes, HIP nodes may require HIP on the opposite end of communication to be able to take advantage of the technology's features.

NAT Traversal Solutions

IETF has developed, and is developing, a number of specifications that facilitate the NAT traversal.

There are techniques, for example, for determining the external transport layer address (IP and port) that the NAT has assigned to an endpoint, for relaying packets, and for determining an optimal path between the endpoints.

The external transport layer address a NAT has assigned to an endpoint can be determined, for example, by using *Session Traversal Utilities for NAT* (STUN) protocol (Rosenberg et al., 2008a). STUN is a binary, client-server protocol that specifies two entities: *STUN server*, which is typically outside the NAT, and a *STUN client*, which is typically bundled with an endpoint. The basic operation of STUN is such that first the STUN client send a "what transport layer address NAT has assigned to me?" request to a STUN server, and the STUN server replies with a message carrying the external transport layer address of the STUN client. It is noteworthy that STUN can also be used for sending keep-alive messages.

The relaying of packets can be done, for example, by using *Traversal Using Relays around NAT* (TURN) (Rosenberg et al., 2008b) protocol. TURN is an extension to STUN and it specifies two entities: *TURN server*, which is typically outside the NAT, and a *TURN client*, which typically bundled with an endpoint. The basic operation of TURN is such that first the TURN client sends a "can you allocate a relayed transport layer address to me?" request to a TURN server, and the TURN server replies with a message carrying the allocated transport layer address. A relayed transport layer address is actually an IP and a port in a TURN relay which are logically reserved for a TURN client. Once a TURN client has obtained the relayed transport layer address, it can use the associated TURN server as its media relay from there on.

Selection of an optimal path between the endpoint can be done, for example, by using the *Interactive Connectivity Establishment* (ICE) protocol (Rosenberg, 2007). ICE protocol messages are exchanged between the endpoints by using some offer/answer protocol. Prerequisite for ICE usage is an existing signaling path between the endpoints, which are called *agents* in ICE. The basic operation of ICE is such that first the agents gather candidate transport layer addresses, for example by using STUN and TURN. Then the agents exchange those candidate addresses to with each other via the exiting signaling path. After that, the agents perform connectivity checks for all candidate addresses, and as an end result, both agents know the optimal transport layer address pair that they can use for further communication.

These aforementioned protocols – STUN, TURN, and ICE – can be utilized in P2PSIP networks. For example, REsource LOcation And Discovery (RELOAD) (Jennings et al., 2008), which is a peer protocol proposal, utilizes all of these protocols. It is noteworthy to mention that the RELOAD protocol itself provides a pre-established signaling path between all the P2PSIP peers in the network, which is very convenient for ICE. Another protocol proposal, the Service Extensible P2P Peer Protocol (SEP) (Jiang et al., 2008), defines a mechanism for locating relaying peers that operate as TURN servers. This relaying peer is also used to support direct responses between the destination peer and the source peer. SEP alternatively proposes to route the response using the overlay in a way similar to that for routing the request.

Interoperability Solutions

In order to allow calls from a conventional SIP network, the P2PSIP network can provide one or several entry points that can be located using standard SIP methods. (Marocco & Bryan, 2007) defines the operation of these entry points, called P2P proxy peers. The P2PSIP proxy peer is able to communicate with a SIP host that has a public Internet address, and it is also able to query the DNS. The proxy peer should not be behind a NAT. The P2PSIP network is recognized by an

overlay identifier that is a fully qualified domain name. The proxy peer maintains DNS records that bind the overlay identifier to the proxy peer, thus, a resolution for the overlay identifier returns a list of P2PSIP proxy peers. Registering proxy peers with the DNS requires special security considerations that are still unsolved. From the outside, the P2PSIP network therefore appears like a conventional SIP network. The proxy peer receives the INVITE request from the conventional SIP client, performs a lookup in the DHT for the destination, and routes the INVITE to the obtained destination. In many cases, the user may use URIs that are not in the domain of the overlay. For that purpose, a user can use the proxy peer as an outbound proxy for updating registrations on a public SIP network. This allows the user to register bindings for which the overlay is not authoritative.

The proxy peer in this solution is also used for calls from a P2PSIP user to a user in a conventional SIP network. The proxy peer must therefore be registered in the overlay, so that the caller can query the overlay for the location of a P2PSIP proxy peer. The proxy peer forwards the INVITE request and adds a Record-Route header field identifying the overlay to direct other requests to the proxy peer in the same overlay. Because the address of the proxy peer is often requested, the host responsible for storing the mapping of the proxy peer address receives an unproportional number of lookups, which may create a load balancing problem.

(Marocco, Manzalini, et al., 2007) also presents a model for interworking between P2PSIP and IMS depicted in Figure 4. Here, the P2PSIP user can register to the IMS network as a visiting subscriber. The proxy peer plays the role of a P-CSCF, allowing a user agent to be registered from an external network. The solution still does not solve the problems of link encryption, authentication without SIM, quality of service control, and stability.

Figure 4. Interoperability between P2PSIP and IMS

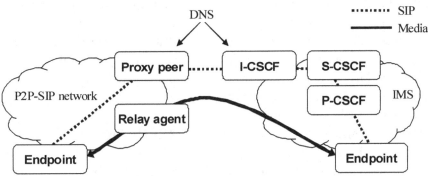

For compatibility with traditional PSTN terminals with only numerical keypads, an E.164 number (ITU-T, 1997) may be assigned to the terminal. This can be implemented with the Telephone Number Mapping (ENUM) (Faltstrom et al., 2004). As ENUM is an extension to DNS, the support for E.164 can easily be included in solutions based on DNS.

Security Solutions

There are solutions proposed to some security issues in P2PSIP networks. One of them is RELOAD's (Jennings et al., 2008) preferred security framework which is based on enrollment server distributing credentials in the form of certificates, with Peer-IDs, to all new peers who want to join a P2PSIP network. This security framework reduces the risk for Peer-ID mapping attacks by performing the Peer-ID selection in a centralized enrollment server instead of peers themselves. The RELOAD's preferred security framework also mitigates the problems related to an untrusted message forwarding path. The untrusted forwarding paths can be made more secure by signing the messages on the sender's peer in an end-to-end fashion before giving the messages to the P2PSIP network for forwarding.

CONCLUSION

P2PSIP is a novel decentralized platform for enabling serverless operation of SIP. It builds upon a structured overlay, which is managed by the collaborative effort of participating P2PSIP nodes, removing the need for extensive use of server components. Originally, P2PSIP aimed to allow true P2P networking between the SIP nodes, but the goal has later extended towards a more general P2P architecture, where the applications can also utilize P2PSIP overlay directly without SIP. In this chapter, we provided an overview of the P2PSIP technology and its current status, and discussed the challenges and possible solutions to them. We aimed to give the reader a glance to P2PSIP technology as an example of a lightweight peer-to-peer based protocol for communication, session management, and service provisioning purposes in mobile environment. The potential of P2PSIP was briefly illustrated by presenting different application types where the P2PSIP may be used.

The main contribution of this chapter was to point out and discuss the issues, controversies, and problems regarding performance, special requirements of mobile environment, node mobility, interoperability, security, and incentives. The performance and overhead of P2PSIP network is mainly affected by the DHT algorithm and the P2PSIP peer protocol implementing it. This chapter focused on analyzing those measures that might be utilized in the peer protocol, since the algorithm-level DHT optimization is outside of the scope of P2PSIP. Along with the optimized usage of DHT, such as routing mode selection, the resource-aware load balancing and hierarchically organized overlays are potential, yet relatively unexplored, solutions to improve the P2PSIP performance. On the other hand, mobility management and NAT traversal are crucial for enabling the seamless usage of P2PSIP in mobile environments. The existing mobility solutions, such as Mobile IPv4, Mobile IPv6, and HIP, are useful technologies for handling the mobility in P2PSIP networks, but they also generate additional challenges related to the dynamic behaviour of the underlying networks, due to vertical handovers. The existing NAT traversal solutions, STUN, TURN, and ICE, are feasible technologies to be used with P2PSIP, although they set some limitations to certain protocol-level solutions, such as the routing mode selection.

In order to enable widespread use, P2PSIP should be interoperable with at least conventional SIP networks, such as IMS, as well as PSTN and mobile telephone networks. Gateway solutions are needed for this purpose, but designing them is challenging. The key benefit of P2PSIP is the decentralization, which should not be compromised with wrong design decisions. Security, trust, and incentive issues are emphasized in P2P networks, and P2PSIP is no exception. Many existing proposals require centralized components that tend to move P2PSIP again towards higher centralization. However, completely decentralized and effective security framework would be impossible to implement based on the current knowledge. Instead, the goal should be to reduce the use and dependency of centralized components. Yet another unsolved problem is managing the incentives in relation to the node's role as a peer that provides additional services to the other peers.

Addressing these issues is essential to enabling secure, reliable, and efficient use of the P2PSIP

protocol in mobile and other networks. Both the academic community and industry are working together to address these challenges with the aim of achieving standardized solutions that pave the way for a successful deployment of P2PSIP in mobile environments.

REFERENCES

Audet, F., & Jennings, C. (2007). Network address translation (NAT) behavioral requirements for unicast UDP. *RFC4787*. IETF.

Baset, S., & Schulzrinne, H. (2006). An analysis of the Skype peer-to-peer Internet telephony protocol. In *Proceedings of the IEEE International Conference on Computer Communications*. Retrieved May 30, 2008, from IEEE database.

Bianchi, S., Serbu, S., Felber P., & Kropf P. (2006). Adaptive load balancing for DHT lookups. In *Proceedings of the International Conference on Computer Communications and Networks* (pp. 411-418).

Bryan, D., Lowekamp, B., & Jennings, C. (2005). SOSIMPLE: A serverless, standards-based, P2P SIP communication system. In *Proceedings of the International Workshop on Advanced Architectures and Algorithms for Internet Delivery and Applications* (pp. 42- 49).

Bryan, D., Matthews, P., Shim, E., Willis, D., & Dawkins, S. (2008). *Concepts and terminology for peer to peer SIP: draft-ietf-p2psip-concepts-02* (work in progress). Retrieved July 7, 2008, from IETF Internet Draft Database.

Cerri, D., Ghioni, A., Paraboschi, S., & Tiraboschi, S. (2005). ID mapping attacks in P2P networks. In *Proceedings of the IEEE Global Telecommunications Conference,* (Vol. 3, p. 6).

Dabek, F., Kaashoek, M.F., Karger, D., Morris, R., & Stoica, I. (2001). Wide-area cooperative storage with CFS. In *Proceedings of the ACM*

Symposium on Operating System Principles (pp. 202-215).

Faik, J. (2005). *A model for resource-aware load balancing on heterogeneous and non-dedicated clusters.* Unpublished doctoral dissertation, Department of Computer Science, Rensselaer Polytechnic Institute.

Faltstrom, P., & Mealling, M. (2004). The E.164 to uniform resource identifiers (URI) dynamic delegation discovery system (DDDS) application (ENUM). *RFC3761.* IETF.

Godfrey, B., Karp, R.M., Lakshminarayanan, K., Surana, S., & Stoica, I. (2004). Load balancing in dynamic structured P2P systems. In *Proceedings of the Annual Joint Conference of the IEEE Computer and Communications Societies,* (Vol. 4, pp. 2253-2262).

Godfrey, P.B., & Stoica, I. (2005). Heterogeneity and load balance in distributed hash tables. In *Proceedings of the Annual Joint Conference of the IEEE Computer and Communications Societies,* (Vol. 1, pp. 596-606).

Guha, S., Daswani, N., & Jain, R. (2006). An experimental study of the Skype peer-to-peer VoIP system. In *Proceedings of the International Workshop on Peer-to-Peer Systems.* Retrieved May 30, 2008, from IPTPS database.

Hautakorpi, J., & Camarillo, G. (2007). Evaluation of DHTs from the viewpoint of interpersonal communications. In *Proceedings of the International Conference on Mobile and Ubiquitous Multimedia* (pp. 74-83).

Internet Assigned Numbers Authority (IANA). (2008). Port numbers. Retrieved May 14, 2008, from http://www.iana.org/assignments/port-numbers

ITU-T. (1997). The International public telecommunication number plan, *ITU-T recommendation E.164.* ITU.

Jennings, C., Lowekamp, B., Rescorla, E., Rosenberg, J., Baset, S., & Schulzrinne, H. (2008). *Resource location and discovery (RELOAD): draft-bryan-p2psip-reload-03* (work in progress). Retrieved May 14, 2008, from IETF Internet Draft Database.

Jiang, X., Zheng, H., Macian, C., & Pascual, V. (2008). *Service extensible P2P peer protocol: draft-jiang-p2psip-sep-01.* IETF. Retrieved September 10, 2008, from IETF Internet Draft Database.

Johnson, D., Perkins, C., & Arkko, J. (2004). IP mobility support for IPv6. *RFC3775.* IETF.

Karger, D.R., & Ruhl, M. (2004). Simple efficient load balancing algorithms for peer-to-peer systems, In *Proceedings of the International Conference on Peer-to-Peer Systems* (pp. 131-140).

Kellerer, W., Kunzmann, G., Schollmeier, R., & Zölsb, S. (2005). Structured peer-to-peer systems for telecommunications and mobile environments. *AEU - International Journal of Electronics and Communications, 60*(1), 25-29.

Kirsner, S. (1998). The legend of Bob Metcalfe. *Wired, 11*(6).

Komu, M., Henderson, T., Matthews, P., Tschofenig, H., & Keränen, A. (2008). *Basic HIP extensions for traversal of network address translators: draft-ietf-hip-nat-traversal-04* (work in progress). Retrieved Sep 10, 2008, from IETF Internet Draft Database.

Le, L., & Kuo, G.S. (2007). Hierarchical and breathing peer-to-peer SIP system. In *Proceedings of the IEEE International Conference on Communications* (pp. 1887-1892).

Li J., Stribling J., Morris R., Kaashoek M.F., & Gil M.T. (2005). A performance vs. cost framework for evaluating DHT design tradeoffs under churn. In *Proceedings of the Annual Joint Conference of the IEEE Computer and Communications Societies.* (Vol. 1, pp. 225-236).

Lua, E.K., Crowcroft, J., Pias, M., Sharma, R., & Lim, S. (2004). A survey and comparison of peer-to-peer overlay network schemes. *IEEE Communications Survey and Tutorial*, 72-93.

Marocco, E., & Bryan, D. (2007). *Interworking between P2PSIP overlays and conventional SIP network: draft-marocco-p2psip-interwork-01* (work in progress). Retrieved May 22, 2008, from IETF Internet Draft Database.

Marocco, E., Manzalini, A., Sampo, M., & Canal, G. (2007). Interworking between P2PSIP overlays and IMS networks – scenarios and technical solutions. In *Proceedings of the International Conference on Intelligence in Service Delivery Networks*. Retrieved May 30, 2008, from ICIN database.

Matuszewski, M., Ekberg, J.E., & Laitinen, P. (2007). *Security requirements in P2PSIP: draft-matuszewski-p2psip-security-requirements* (work in progress). Retrieved May 14, 2008, from IETF Internet Draft Database.

Maymounkov, P., & Mazieres, D. (2002). Kademlia: A peer-to-peer information system based on the XOR metric. In *Proceedings of the International Workshop on Peer-to-Peer Systems* (pp. 53-61).

Moskowitz, R., & Nikander, P. (2006). Host identity protocol (HIP) architecture. *RFC4423.* IETF.

Moskowitz, R., Nikander, P., Jokela, P., & Henderson, T. (2008). Host identity protocol. *RFC5201.* IETF.

Peer-to-Peer SIP (P2PSIP). (2008). Peer-to-peer SIP charter. Retrieved May 30, 2008, from http://www.ietf.org/html.charters/p2psip-charter.html

Peng, Z., Duan, Z.H., Qi, J.J., Cao, Y., & Lv, E.T. (2007). HP2P: A hybrid hierarchical P2P network. In *Proceedings of the International Conference on the Digital Society* (pp. 18-22).

Perkins, C. (2002). IP mobility support for IPv4. *RFC3344.* IETF.

Rao, A., Laksminarayanan, K., Surana, S., Karp, R., & Stoica, I. (2003). Load balancing in structured P2P systems. In *Proceedings of the International Workshop on Peer-to-Peer Systems* (pp. 68-79).

Ratnasamy, S., Francis, P., Handley, M., Karp, R., & Shenker S. (2001). A scalable content addressable network. *ACM Special Interest Group on Data Communication, 31*(4), 161-172.

Rosenberg, J. (2007). *Interactive connectivity establishment (ICE): A protocol for network address translator (NAT) traversal for offer/answer protocols: draft-ietf-mmusic-ice-19* (work in progress). Retrieved May 14, 2008, from IETF Internet Draft Database.

Rosenberg, J., Mahy, R., Matthews, P., & Wing, D. (2008a). Session traversal utilities for NAT (STUN): *draft-ietf-behave-rfc3489bis-15* (work in progress). Retrieved May 14, 2008, from IETF Internet Draft Database.

Rosenberg, J., Mahy, R., & Matthews, P. (2008b). *Traversal using relays around NAT (TURN): Relay extensions to session traversal utilities for NAT (STUN): draft-ietf-behave-turn-07* (work in progress). Retrieved May 14, 2008, from IETF Internet Draft Database.

Rowstron, A., & Drusche, P. (2001). Pastry: Scalable, distributed object location and routing for large scale peer-to-peer systems. In *Proceedings of the IFIP/ACM International Conference on Distributed Systems Platforms* (pp. 329-350).

Shen, H., & Xu, C-Z. (2005). Locality-aware randomized load balancing algorithms for DHT networks. In *Proceedings of the International Conference on Parallel Processing* (pp. 529-536).

Singh, K., & Schulzrinne, H. (2004). *Peer-to-peer internet telephony using SIP* (Tech. Rep.

CUCS-044-04, pp. 63-68). NY, USA: Columbia University.

Song, J.W., & Yang, S.B. (2006). Improved load balancing algorithms in DHT-based dynamic P2P systems. In *Proceedings of the IASTED International Conference on Communications, Internet, and Information Technology* (pp. 218-224).

Song, H., Zheng, H., & Jiang, X. (2008). *Diagnose P2PSIP overlay network failures; draft-zheng-p2psip-diagnose-02* (work in progress). Retrieved September 10, 2008, from IETF Internet Draft Database.

Stoica, I., Morris, R., Liben-Nowell, D., Karger, D.R., Kaashoek, M.F., Dabek, F., & Balakrishnan, H. (2003). Chord: A scalable peer-to-peer lookup protocol for internet applications. *IEEE/ACM Transactions on Networking, 11*(1), 17-32.

Tsai, K.C., & Chen, C. (2006). A server reassignment algorithm for DHT load balance and the effect of heterogeneity. In *Proceedings of the IEEE Global Telecommunications Conference*. Retrieved May 30, 2008, from IEEE database.

Verkasalo, H.T. (2007). Handset-based measurement of smartphone service evolution in Finland. *Journal of Targeting, Measurement and Analysis for Marketing. 16*(1), 7-25.

Zhao, B.Y., Huang L., Stribling, J., Rhea, S. C., Joseph, A. D., & Kubiatowicz, J. (2004). Tapestry: A global-scale overlay for rapid service deployment. *IEEE Journal on Selected Areas in Communications, 22*(1), 41-53.

Zhu, Y., & Hu, Y. (2005). Efficient, proximity-aware load balancing for DHT-based P2P systems. *IEEE Transactions on Parallel and Distributed Systems, 16*(4), 349-361.

Zhu, Y., & Hu, Y. (2004). Towards efficient load balancing in structured P2P systems. In *Proceedings of the International Parallel and Distributed Processing Symposium*. Retrieved May 30, 2008, from DBLP database.

Section VII
Architectures and Platforms

Chapter XVI
Mobile P2P in Cellular Networks:
Architecture and Performance

Kurt Tutschku
University of Vienna, Austria

Andreas Berl
University of Passau, Germany

Tobias Hossfeld
University of Würzburg, Germany

Hermann de Meer
University of Passau, Germany

ABSTRACT

The telecommunication industry has recently seen two areas with very high growth rates: cellular networks, for example, GSM (Global System for Mobile Communications) or UMTS (Universal Mobile Telecommunications System), and P2P (Peer-to-Peer) file-sharing applications. A combination of both might be highly attractive: a) for attracting new users; and b) for exploiting the potential of cellular broadband technologies. From a system's perspective, architectures and performance figures of cellular mobile network applications and services that have edge-based intelligence (e.g,. P2P applications) are, to the best of the authors' knowledge, less researched and many questions remain open. This chapter presents the design of MP2P (Mobile P2P) applications for cellular mobile networks by using the example of a MP2P content-distribution application. First, the incompatibilities between the P2P paradigm and properties of cellular mobile networks are identified. Then, a design methodology for MP2P applications for cellular mobile networks is proposed. The proposed method is based on a functional analysis of the two basic P2P functions, resource mediation and resource access control. The result is a hybrid P2P content-distribution architecture, which is enhanced by different operator-controlled infrastructure elements. The suggested architecture does not only overcome incompatibilities between P2P and cellular mobile communication systems, it also meets the functional needs and performance requirements of future P2P applications in cellular environments, while still largely preserves the user characteristics and efficiency of P2P systems. Finally, the performance enhancements by the architecture for the two basic P2P functions are investigated by comprehensive simulative and analytical performance evaluations.

INTRODUCTION

The telecommunication industry has recently seen two major areas with very high growth rates. First, the GSM (Global System for Mobile Communications) system has reached two billion users in 2006 and still shows an annual growth rate of more than 10%. Second, P2P (Peer-to-Peer) file-sharing applications have surpassed Web surfing by up to one order of magnitude in terms of data volume. Thus, a combination of cellular mobile networks and controllable P2P content distribution would be highly attractive for the attraction of new users and for exploiting the potential of broadband wireless technologies like UMTS (Universal Mobile Telecommunications System).

A first experience of cellular mobile networks and of P2P systems might imply that the concepts fit well. Both systems have features like point-to-point or group-oriented communication and permit the roaming of users. At closer look, however, the architectures of both systems differ tremendously. Thus, their architectures and requirements make a combination of both systems difficult.

In this chapter, we first identify the incompatibilities between cellular mobile systems and P2P systems. Then, we propose a new design methodology for MP2P (Mobile P2P) applications for cellular mobile networks. The suggested method is based on a functional analysis of the two basic P2P functions, *resource mediation* and *resource access control*. The result is a *controllable,* hybrid P2P content-distribution architecture. The controllability feature is obtained by applying three different operator-controlled P2P infrastructure

elements. The suggested architecture does not only overcome incompatibilities between P2P and cellular mobile communication systems, it also largely preserves the usability characteristics and efficiency of P2P systems. Finally, the performance enhancements for the two basic P2P functions by the infrastructure elements are investigated by comprehensive simulative and analytical performance evaluations.

Since P2P overlays mainly operate on application layer, cross-layer design and radio resource management mechanisms are not the focus of this chapter.

INCOMPATIBILITIES BETWEEN CELLULAR MOBILE NETWORKS AND P2P NETWORKS

In general, cellular mobile networks and P2P networks are both communication systems which enable users to directly exchange information. However, incompatibilities arise between the concepts since they implement their capabilities on different layers. To identify the design challenges of MP2P applications, the key characteristics of cellular mobile networks and P2P systems need to be compared. First, a brief review of the features of cellular networks is given, then an example of a P2P application is described, and afterwards incompatibilities are discussed.

Cellular Mobile Networks

In cellular mobile networks, the wireless nodes communicate via dedicated elements such as base stations or switches. Hence, such networks

Figure 1. Intra-cell data path in an UMTS architecture

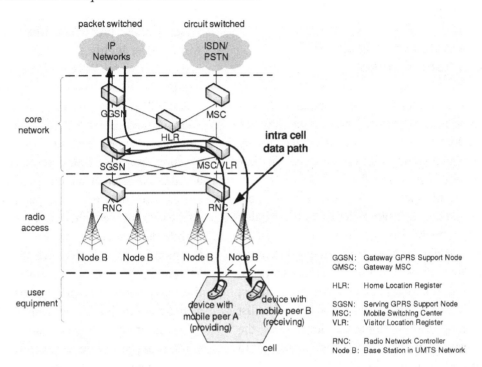

can be divided into a *radio network* part, which implements the wireless transmission, and a *core network* part, which transports the information and which offers additional functions such as mobility management. In this chapter, we use the UMTS system as an exemplification for cellular networks.

The UMTS architecture is derived from the GSM architecture (Eberspächer et al, 2001) and is hierarchically organized, cf. Figure 1. The UMTS system extends the capabilities of its predecessor to high speed data communication. The Node Bs are senders and maintain broadband radio links to the mobile devices with asymmetrical capacity, starting at speeds of 64kbps (uplink) and 386kbps (downlink). The RNCs (Radio Network Controller) coordinate the Node Bs and facilitate the radio resource management. Mobility for data communication is supported in the UMTS core network by using GSNs (General packet radio

service Support Nodes). When a new data communication session is requested, the GGSN (Gateway GSN) establishes a tunnel to the SGSN (Serving GSN), denoted as the PDP (Packet Data Protocol) context, cf. Figure 1. The SGSN coordinates the connection of a mobile device served by a Node B that is controlled by a specific RNC. When a mobile device moves from one cell to another, a packet is forwarded to the new SGSN by relocating the PDP tunnel. In cellular networks, the applications and services are typically provisioned out of the core to mobile stations located at the network edge. This provisioning principle saves radio resources since it requires only a single wireless hop to reach a mobile device. A cellular system can be viewed as a *centralized* system since the core network part is providing the services to the devices. This characteristic is also reflected by the PDPs since they start at distinct central locations, i.e. at the GGSN. Finally, cellular networks have a fixed infrastructure. Hence, their topologies are assumed to be static.

An Example of a Popular P2P Application: eDonkey

eDonkey is one of the most popular P2P file-sharing applications[i] (note that in this chapter, the term "eDonkey" subsumes the original eDonkey 2000 application and its derivatives). The eDonkey architecture is shown in Figure 2. *Index servers* are storing the location of files. eDonkey peers publish and look up shared files using these index servers (cf. "publish edges" and "query edges" in Figure 2). Before an eDonkey peer can download a file, it first gathers a list of all file providers. To accomplish this, the peer connects to an index server and sends a query to it, which returns a list of matching files and their locations. Thus, the index servers handle all of the queries in order to relieve peers from this kind of traffic.

eDonkey uses the MSD (Multiple Source Download) concept. It permits a requesting peer to download different parts of a file from multiple providing peers in parallel (cf. "MSD edges" in Figure 2). The MSD concept also allows peers to share fragments of a file before having completed a download.

General Incompatibilities

First, wireless broadband links in cellular networks differ highly from high-bandwidth links in fixed networks. Wireless links have still orders of magnitude less capacity, compared to wireline links. P2P systems, however, assume that bandwidth is inexpensive and always available. Radio capacity is expensive and restricted in wireless systems. Wireless links are of variable quality and there is often an asymmetrical split between uplink and downlink. Their quality depends, e.g., on the users movement, the number of concurrent mobile devices connected to a base station, and the mobile device's distance to a base station. Moreover, there are dead spots where wireless links break down completely, possibly leading to a change of mobile devices' IP addresses.

A feature of public cellular mobile networks is the provision of general connectivity and the convergence between mobile and wireline networks. They connect mobile entities with mobile devices as well as with wireline entities. As a result, the heterogeneity of the connected entities with respect to access capabilities is increased. Mobile devices have strongly different properties, compared to wireline computers. They have much

Figure 2. eDonkey file-sharing application

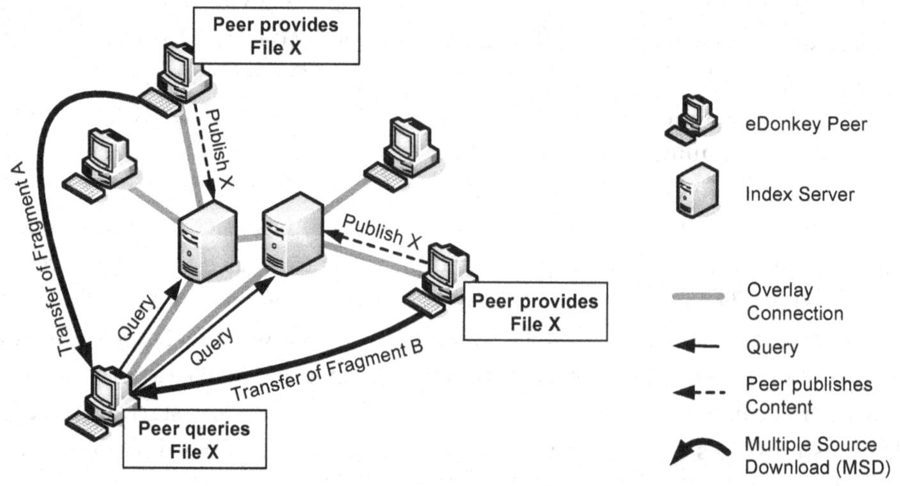

less CPU power, memory, and storage space and can manage significantly less simultaneous TCP connections[1] than wireline computers. Mobile devices depend on short battery life times, limiting time and intensity of their usage. Additionally, periodic keep-alive messages of a single open connection can drain the battery's energy within a few hours[2]. Hence, mobile devices switch into dormant mode, if there is no communication required for a longer time, e.g. for more then 30-60 seconds. In this mode, network resources are released and power is saved (Kempf, 2001). Additionally, billing in cellular mobile networks is based on resource consumption. Hence, mobile devices prefer to remain off-line when not used. In contrast, the end systems and users in wireline networks prefer to stay "always on" in order to be able to communicate at any time. This behavior is reinforced by commonly having Internet flat rates for billing in these networks. As a result, mobile peers might have higher *churn* rates with short on-line times than wireline peers[3].

Cellular public mobile networks derive their advantages largely from a fixed and hierarchical structured architecture. P2P systems, however, avoid hierarchies and form dynamic overlays. As a result a mismatch might occur between the information flow in the overlay and the physical transmission paths in the infrastructure. For example, two peers, that are located in the same UMTS cell, are not able to directly share resources via the air interface. In fact, the data flows through the hierarchy of the UMTS architecture, cf. "intra cell data path" in Figure 1. As a result, the exchange of data consumes a high amount of resources in the core network, experiences additional delays, and has to bridge two air interfaces. P2P systems are based on application layer overlays and are therefore decoupled from the radio resource management.

In infrastructure-based networks, operators have to invest into assets. Hence, they need control mechanisms to manage and coordinate the resources. P2P services, however, are edge-based, self-organizing, and assume often that network resources, such as transmission capacity, are free and available without any restriction due to altruistic user behavior.

Incompatibilities Concerning Popular P2P Networks

A highly interesting MP2P research area is the integration of mobile devices in already existing popular P2P applications, e.g. file-sharing applications, which already have a large user community. Although most mobile devices have enough performance to directly join such P2P networks with ordinary P2P clients, this straightforward approach has severe disadvantages. The convergence of wireless mobile devices and wireline computers in P2P networks introduces *heterogeneity*. This heterogeneity is in contradiction to the rather homogeneous perspective of P2P networks. It affects both, wireline peers in and mobile devices. Wireline peers are affected by increased churn rates and delayed downloads, as described in the following section. However, mobile devices experience particular disadvantages in heterogeneous P2P networks. They find themselves in severe competitive situations with wireline computers. Often hundreds of peers are requesting popular downloads concurrently. A peer, that is providing such a download, distributes its upload bandwidth among the requesting peers. A certain number of peers are served instantly, other peers have to wait in queues to be served later. Peers in queues are in competition with each other, wanting to be served as soon as possible. Mobile devices however, do not perform well in these competitions:

- In queues often those peers are preferred that provide content in return, e.g. based on the "tit-for-tat" principle. It is not possible for mobile devices to provide equal amounts of content as wireline computers do, due to their hardware limitations, restrictions of the wireless link, and short on-line times.

- Mobile devices are not able to enqueue themselves in many queues simultaneously, due to their limited ability of managing concurrent TCP connections and limited memory. Wireline computers are often waiting in up to hundreds of queues to increase the probability of being served.

- Mobile devices are often hidden behind NAT boxes or firewalls, depending on their mobile operator. Thus, other peers can't establish direct communication with this mobile device, which is complicating P2P communication and often leads to penalties within P2P networks.

- If mobile devices go voluntarily or involuntarily off-line, e.g. because of dead spots or low battery power, they are likely to be deleted from queues and have to restart waiting periods again.

According to these discriminations, mobile devices have to wait much longer time periods for downloads in P2P content-distribution networks, than wireline computers. During these increased download times the frequent P2P communication prevents mobile devices from changing into dormant mode, which affects heavily their battery lifetime.

Measurements of Incompatibilities for P2P-File Sharing

According to the aforedescribed theoretical problems, in this section a concrete problem of MP2P in cellular networks is investigated, which is how the download performance of peers in the eDonkey network is affected, if the network consists of mobile and wired peers.

The expected download performance of mobile file sharing in an eDonkey network for GSM networks using GPRS and UMTS networks has been investigated by various measurement studies (Hoßfeld, Tutschku & Andersen, 2005a; Hoßfeld,

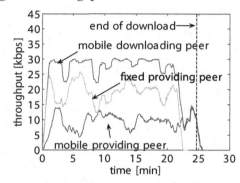

Figure 3. Throughput in GPRS

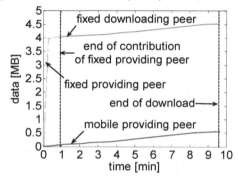

Figure 4. Download delayed by GPRS mobile

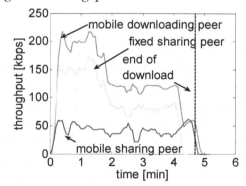

Figure 5. Throughput in UMTS

Tutschku & Andersen, 2005b). The case studies consider a simplified eDonkey MSD scenario: an eDonkey peer downloads a MP3 file of 4.8 MB in multiple blocks of 540 KB from two providing peers. A heterogeneous, wireless and wireline, scenario without physical mobility is considered for the peers. Their access schemes are either *fixed*, i.e. the peer is located in the wired Internet and connected by Ethernet (10 Mbps), or *mobile*. i.e. the peer is located in a GPRS network or an UMTS network. The gross transmission rates of a peer with GPRS connectivity is 13.4 kbps (uplink) and 53.6 kbps (downlink); in the UMTS network these values are 64 kbps (uplink) and 384 kbps (downlink).

Different effects of a MSD download in a heterogeneous environment with GPRS and UMTS connectivity are illustrated in Figures 3 – 5. Figure 3 depicts the throughput in the GPRS system with a moving average of 60 sec. The ramp-up at the beginning of the curves is a result of the moving window. The providing mobile peer exploits its uplink while the providing fixed peer fills up the downlink of the downloading entity. This indicates a fair split of the downlink bandwidth. The downlink of the mobile peer determines the throughput in the wireless system which is in contrast to wireline networks where the uplink is often the bottleneck. This effect is caused by the convergence requirement of public mobile networks where wireline peers can overload their mobile counterparts. Figure 4 shows a related challenge. Here, the transmission of a single block by a mobile peer delays the MSD file download at a fixed peers significantly, cf. "end of download" label. Finally, Figure 5 depicts the throughput (with a moving average of 60 sec) when the mobile peers are located in an UMTS network. The throughput of the downloading peer reaches up to 200 kbps and the download is completed in approx. 5.5 min. This value appears suitable for the exchange of a music file.

The measurements show that the important P2P resource access control function MSD can be applied in UMTS and in GPRS networks. While it works well for UMTS networks, the performance of GPRS networks is poor and incurs large delays in downloading files. These real world results underline that MP2P file-sharing applications have to deal with the different network capabilities. The

heterogeneity of peers is imposed that has to be considered to enable efficient file sharing.

MOBILE P2P PROJECTS FOR CELLULAR MOBILE NETWORKS

There are several MP2P approaches which focus on cellular radio networks. The approaches can be partitioned in three different classes. First, there are solutions that connect mobile devices to P2P networks without providing them any additional support. Second, there are solutions in which support for mobile devices is provided by the P2P protocol itself and third, there are solutions where support for mobile devices is provided, but it is not part of the P2P protocol.

No Support

Solutions of this class are reshaping P2P client software to the requirements of mobile devices, considering the mobile devices limitations, whereas the P2P protocol remains unchanged. Mobile devices join P2P networks like ordinary peers without getting further support. Symella[4], e.g., is a P2P client for the Gnutella[5] P2P file-sharing network. The mobile device is able to download files, but upload of files is not supported. Another example of this class is Mopiphant[6], a P2P client for the eDonkey[7] file-sharing network.

Support from P2P Protocols

In this class of MP2P approaches support for mobile devices is provided by the P2P protocol itself. To achieve this kind of support, either all peers or some specialized peers of a P2P network have to assist mobile devices. Peers are often determined to support mobile devices, because of having certain properties (e.g. high-bandwidth links). An example for this solution class is the *hybrid chord protocol* (Zoels, Schollmeier, Kellerer & Tarlano, 2005). It modifies the well known *chord*

(Stoica, Morris, Karger, Kaashoek & Balakrishnan, 2001) protocol to cope more efficiently with effects of mobility. Peers are divided into *static* nodes and *temporary* nodes. Temporary nodes (nodes with short on-line times) are relieved from storing object references, improving the overall network performance. (Park, Kwon, and Choi, 2006) propose a distributed mobility management mechanism that is based on hierarchical DHTs. The mechanism differentiates between stable and unstable peers in order to handle peer mobility. Information about resource locations is stored on stable peers only. The optimal split between stable and unstable peers has been investigated in further work (Zoels, Despotovic & Kellerer, 2006; Zoels, Schubert, Kellerer & Despotovic, 2006).

Other approaches suggest P2P networks, in which specialized peers are determined to support mobile devices by aggregating or filtering data for them. In these solutions, mobile devices are partly or entirely relieved from network maintenance and routing tasks. (Sumino, Ishikawa, and Kato, 2006) uses *proxy servers* to integrate mobile devices into a P2P architecture. They suggest a MP2P group communication application which uses a hierarchical architecture and mobile proxy nodes. The proxies facilitate resource exchange by multicast on behalf of the mobiles, thus, releasing them from being continuously on-line and from unnecessary data transmission on the uplink. The architecture and efficiency of a Gnutella-based P2P application on smart phones in cellular environment was investigated in (Bakos, Farks, and Nurminen, 2006). The Gnutella protocol has been modified, e.g. to get a topology which provides so called *hubs* which are required to support MP2P clients. (Horozov, Grama, Vasudevan, and Landis, 2002) uses *surrogate peers* support mobile devices and the JXME[8] project defines *relay peers* to connect mobile peers to the JXTA[9] P2P environment (nowadays mobile devices are also able to participate *proxyless* in JXTA).

Other Support

Solutions of this class support mobile devices without modifying P2P protocols of large user communities. Instead, either "voluntary" peers within the network are changing or extending their protocols to provide support for mobile devices, or support is provided from outside the P2P network. An example for this solution class is *MobileMule*[10]. This is a project in which users support their own mobile device by a second, fully featured computer which has access to the P2P network. However, in this approach mobile devices do not really profit from the P2P network. Mobile devices (MDs) just remotely control the second computer, being not able to download or share any content at their current location. Another approach is a MP2P file sharing application which uses the IMS (IP Multimedia Subsystem) and the SIP (Session Initiation Protocol) for resource mediation (Matuszewski, Beijar, Lehtinen & Hyyrylainen, 2006). The proposed system has a rather centralized P2P-over-SIP architecture. It uses a P2P application server (P2P-AS) for indexing the location of files. The resource control and exchange function is not addressed.

A CONTROLLABLE AND EFFICIENT MOBILE P2P CONTENT DISTRIBUTION ARCHITECTURE

An architecture of MP2P applications in cellular networks has to bridge the incompatibilities between the systems. Next, the design of a controllable MP2P content distribution architecture is discussed in detail.

Designing an Architecture

The proposed design of a MP2P content distribution architecture is independent of the applied specific transmission technology, e.g. GPRS or UMTS, since P2P overlays operate on application level. The design addresses mainly the functional requirements, the usability characteristics, and the performance of MP2P applications. In particular, it concentrates on: *a)* the usability and the controllability of the system; and *b)* the mobility and the heterogeneity of the peers.

Requirements of MP2P Content Distribution

P2P content distribution applications profit from contributions of a huge number of entities. The *usability* of a MP2P content distribution application is indicated by its popularity. A MP2P application should foster the popularity by using an already existing and well accepted P2P application with a large user base.

The *controllability* of a MP2P content distribution application is about the operator's need for functions to control the way how content is exchanged. Operators require mechanisms for determining how often a file traverses the air interface and for keeping file swapping traffic in the domain of the operator to minimize inter-domain traffic. In addition, they are responsible for the use of the system. Hence, operators need possibilities for monitoring and controlling which files are offered by the system in order to avoid copyright infringements.

The *mobility* of a peer can impact the time it is connected to the overlay. Thus, the mobility might decrease the performance of the P2P system. A mobile peer might not be long enough on-line to locate all peers it can download data from. In addition, it might not sufficiently long be part of the overlay for providing or downloading all data. The *peer heterogeneity* might easily overload the downlink of a mobile downloading entity or an uplink might delay as a bottleneck the transmission to a high-capacity peer.

Design Space and Design Method

P2P systems provide two *basic P2P functions* (Tutschku, 2007): *resource mediation,* which is

the capability to locate resources, and *resource access control,* which specifies how resources are exchanged. These functions define the general design space for P2P applications. They provide mechanisms for influencing the way how P2P applications behave. The design range of the basic P2P functions is constituted by the locations where the functions are implemented and where control on them is placed.

Hence, the tasks of the *design method for a MP2P file-sharing application* are to select the initial architecture of the MP2P application based on the functional requirements and to define the characteristics of the P2P functions, i.e. centralized vs. decentralized implementation. Finally, a fine tuning of the system is carried out based on performance evaluation, e.g. for choosing an efficient resource mediation strategy.

Choosing an Architecture and Defining its Characteristics

Selecting the appropriate architecture for a MP2P files-sharing application is complex since the basic P2P functions can be implemented using a wide range of mechanisms. Hence, *cartography of P2P applications* simplifies the decision process. Figure 6 provides a two-dimensional cartography of the control characteristics of P2P architectures and compares them with well-established information dissemination mechanisms.

The need of maintaining control by an operator requires a hybrid P2P architecture as a basis for a MP2P file-sharing architecture. The cartography of Figure 6 indicates that the hybrid eDonkey application constitutes a good starting point for a solution. If located on the premise of the operator, the index server of eDonkey permits easy controllability to operators for resource mediation. The choice of eDonkey satisfies also the usefulness and popularity requirement since this application has a very large user base.

In general, static architecture elements such as proxies can level the effects of mobility. Hence, the original eDonkey architecture should be en-

Figure 6. Cartography of P2P applications and content distribution architectures

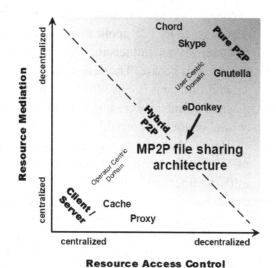

should be applied only if necessary, i.e. only for highly popular files. For resource mediation, active proxies (denoted here as *crawlers*) can be used to locate peers and pass this information to requesting entities. The detailed implementation of the entities is described further as follows.

The effect of enhancing the original eDonkey architecture by centralized entities is depicted in the cartography of Figure 6. The MP2P file-sharing architecture becomes more hybrid than the original one has been before. The nature of the architecture is moved towards the domain of the operator-centric systems, as indicated by the arrow in Figure 6.

A Mobile P2P Architecture

The details of the derived MP2P file-sharing architecture are depicted in Figure 7. The eDonkey system is enhanced by three additional entities which are placed in the operator domain (Oberender et. al, 2005): *a)* the MIS (Mobile Index Server); *b)* the CA (Caching Peer); and *c)* the CP (Crawling Peer).

hanced by central, operator-run entities which process information on behalf of mobile peers. For resource access, this aim can be facilitated by using *caches*. However, the P2P characteristic must not be compromised. Therefore, caches

Figure 7. Mobile P2P file-sharing architecture concept for cellular mobile networks

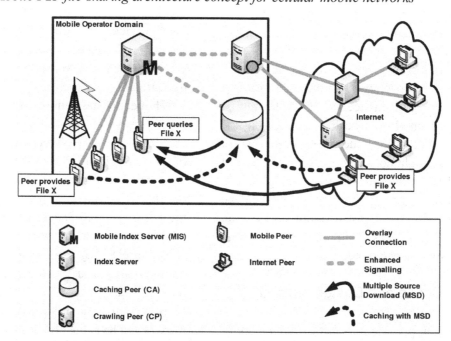

The MIS is an enhanced eDonkey index server. It tracks frequently requested content, triggers the CA to fetch it, and may force the mobile peers to download files from the CA by returning it as the major source. The MIS can apply three different source returning policies: *a)* it does not return the CA a source, i.e. the CA is switched off; *b)* it returns the CA as a random source among all sources; and *c)* it returns the CA as the only source. The returning policy, however, influences significantly the performance of the content distribution. Therefore, the selection of the policy is discussed in performance evaluation of the resources access control. In addition, the MIS is determining how often a file is transmitted over the air interface. Its decision on which files to store on the CA imposes adaptivity and self-organization in the MP2P architecture. The content is automatically placed on the CA if a certain download performance is needed. Content for which efficiency is not needed as well as downloaded files remain on the peer. Hence, the MP2P application can still be denoted as a P2P application. Last but not least, the MIS can enforce copyright control by deregistering inappropriate contents.

The CA is a modified eDonkey peer. It appears to be an ordinary peer to other peers, but distributes popular content only. Since the CA is located in the wireline part of the network it replaces mobile-to-mobile file exchange by wireline-to-mobile communication, thus reducing the uplink data volume of mobile peers. Furthermore, the CA levels the heterogeneity of peers by serving wireline peers with high capacity and mobile peers with reduced capacity. The CA permits downloads even then when original providing peers are off-line. Thus, it supports the mobility of users. In addition, the CA avoids the multiple exchange of the files across operator domains, thus reducing interdomain traffic.

The CP supports resource mediation, i.e. the locating of files. It searches for sources of files on behalf of mobile peers. In this way, it reduces the mediation traffic on the air interface. In addition,

it can perform the task even if the requesting peer goes off-line, thus reinforcing the support of peer mobility in terms of churn.

PERFORMANCE EVALUATION

The performance and the fine tuning of the suggested MP2P content distribution system are investigated by simulation and analytical studies. First, we consider the performance of resource access control by the CA and then we investigate the capabilities of the proposed resource mediation mechanisms for the CP.

Resource Access Control in MP2P

The performance of the CA is investigated by discrete-event, stochastic simulations (Banks, Carson, Nelson, and Nicol, 2004). The major component of the simulation is the *simulation model*. The aim of the model is to describe the actual behavior the considered system in an abstract way such that it can easily be transferred into simulation rules. Thus, the model describes the semantics and parameters of the simulated entities and the relationship and interactions among them.

Simulation Model

The simulation model for investigating the performance of the resource access control of the MP2P content distribution architecture is depicted in Figure 8. It consists of a resource model, a peer model, and an architecture model. The dashed lines indicate the interaction between the different components of the model.

Resource Model

The resource model describes the characteristics of the content which is distributed by the suggested MP2P architecture. It describes for a content

Figure 8. Components of the mobile P2P simulation model

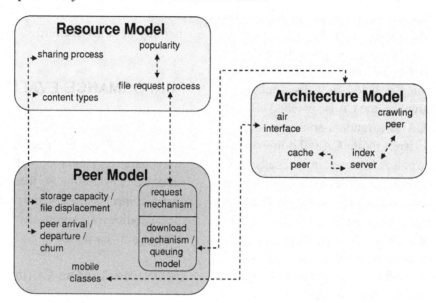

the features type, size, popularity, sharing, and request process. In detail, the considered model assumes four types of mobile specific contents: ring tones, games for mobile hand-sets, digital images or audio files. The file sizes for the different content types were obtained by measurements in the public eDonkey network and fitted by a lognormal distribution. The parameters for size distributions are given in Table 1.

The occurrence probabilities, i.e. the frequencies how often a content type occurs in the collection of all files, are depicted in Table 2.

The simulation model assumes that a total number of N_{files} will be shared within the network. The files are classified into two popularity categories: popular files, i.e. which are more frequently requested for download, and unpopular files, i.e. which are less often requested. The total number of popular files is denoted by N_{pop} and the number of unpopular files is N_{files}.- $N_{pop.}$ For each popular-

ity category, the file request process is assumed to follow a Poisson process with rate $\lambda_{popular}$ and $\lambda_{unpopular}$, respectively. The model supposes for the resource sharing process that a file is shared with probability p_{new} when a peers goes on-line. A downloaded file is provided for redistribution as long as the peer is online.

Peer Model

The peer model characterizes the peer's behavior, its technical capabilities and the mechanisms implemented on it. In particular, it describes the type of the peer, the churn characteristic, the storage capability, the file displacement policy, the file mix, and the detailed file request and download mechanism of the applied P2P protocol.

For the simulation of the heterogeneous scenario of the considered MP2P content distribution

Table 1. File sizes of mobile P2P contents

	ring tone	game	image	mp3-audio
mean [kB]	8.576	37.93	420.2	4829
std. dev.[kB]	9.348	26.58	21.40	2305

Table 2. Occurrence probabilities for the different file types

	ring tone	game	image	mp3-audio
probability	33.0%	33.0%	27.7%	6.8%

architecture, two types of peers are assumed: a) mobile peers, which are connected by GPRS or by UMTS, and b) Internet peers, which are connected by a generic wireline technology.

For mobile peers using GPRS, the mobile class of a peer is characterized by the number of available uplink and downlink slots, cf. Table 3. A mobile class is assigned to a GPRS peer with equal probability. For mobile peers using UMTS, an uplink capacity of 64 kbps and a downlink capacity of 384 kbps are assumed.

Each peer is initialized with a random contingent N_{pop}^{init} of popular files according to a binomial distribution which is described by the maximal and the average number of popular files. Hereby, the average number of popular files is determined by the fraction of popular content in the collection of shared files. The remaining memory capacity on a mobile peer is filled with unpopular files, i.e. the peer utilizes completely its capacity. The considered simulation model assumes that the storage capacity of a mobile peer is either: 4 MB, 8 MB, 64 MB, or 128 MB and is selected with equal probability for a peer. If a newly requested file exceeds this capacity then a first-in/first-out file displacement policy is applied until sufficient memory is available.

The Internet peers are placed in the wired part of the system. They differ from their mobile counterparts in their transmission capacity, the maximum number of upload connections, cf. Table 3, and that they never leave the overlay. The model assumes that there is no congestion present in the Internet. In the performed simulations, the ratio of mobile to internet peers is 2:1. In order to reflect the highly fluctuating connection status of mobile peers, their participation in the overlay is characterized by an ON/OFF-process. The ON period and OFF period are determined by exponential distributions with means L_{ON} and L_{OFF}. Therefore, the transition rates between these two states are $1/L_{ON}$ and $1/L_{OFF}$. During the ON period, mobile peers participate in the P2P network by providing their own files and requesting other files. The mean on/off durations L_{ON} and L_{OFF} have been chosen equal. L_{OFF} is denoted as the churn time. The values for these parameters are summarized in Table 4.

The eDonkey application maintains an upload list, reflecting the simultaneously served peers, and a waiting list containing all downloading requests. The simulation model assumes that a peer always utilizes its full capacity in uplink and downlink direction. Hereby, the uplink bandwidth of a providing peer is equally split among the served peers in the upload list. If an uploading peer cannot utilize the offered bandwidth by the downloading peer then the downloading peer will fairly share the remaining bandwidth among all other uploading peers. The upload list at a providing peer is limited to a maximum number n in order to assure a minimal download bandwidth at served peers. The waiting list is unlimited. A newly arriving file request joins the end of the waiting list. It has to be noted that in eDonkey, a file is structured into chunks and pieces. For the

Table 3. Access types of the peers in the P2P network

access type of peer	upload bandwidth	download bandwidth	max. upload connections
GPRS class n; $n \in \{1, 2, 3, 4\}$ 1	2 kbps	$n \cdot 12$ kbps	4
UMTS 6	4 kbps 3	84 kbps	4
Internet 1	28 kbps	768 kbps 1	0
cache	4 Gbps 4	Gbps	400

simulations, a chunk size of 9.5MB is assumed. The chunks are downloaded in smaller pieces of 560 kB each. These parts are denoted as download units. After receiving a download unit, a requesting peer is enqueued at the end of the waiting list. Immediately after downloading a whole chunk, the peer is registered as a source at the index server and can act as a provider of the chunk.

Architecture Model

The architecture model describes the mechanisms of the original and the additional infrastructure elements and of the transmission technology of the underlying physical networks. Hereby, the transmission technology has to match the one used by the peers. In particular, it corresponds to chosen parameters of the air interface of the mobile units. For the investigation of the resource access control of the MP2P architecture the model assumes that every mobile peer connects to the MIS. Thus, the MIS is always aware about the location of all files in the network and immediately notices when a peer goes online. In addition, it is assumed that the MIS discovers instantaneously, i.e. with no delay, when a peer goes offline. The

MIS returns at most 200 sources to the requesting peer. This value is in accordance to the original eDonkey behavior. The returned sources are selected randomly from all known sources at the MIS. Without the loss of generality for the performance of the access control, the model assumes that there is only MIS present in the network. If the CA shares a requested file then it will always returned by the MIS a source for the file. In addition, it can be selected in the model that the CA is returned as the only source and all other sources are hidden.

The CA is assumed to be attached to the network with a 4 Gbps link and the number of parallel upload connections is limited to 400. These values have been selected such that any bottleneck effect at the CA can be neglected. The CA uses the IMU (Intelligent Memory Usage) caching strategy (Oberender et. al., 2005), which considers the request frequency for files as well as their size. The original eDonkey protocol permits peers to retrieve sources of files from the index server as well as directly from other peers. The behavior has to be approximated since the number of sources influences significantly the download performance (Hoßfeld, Leibnitz, Pries,

Table 4. Simulation scenario parameters

parameter	Description	standard value
$\frac{N_{pop}}{N_{files}}$	ratio of popular files	$\frac{20}{50000} = 0.04\%$
N_{pop}^{init}	initial number of popular files	$binom(10,2)$
λ_{pop}	request rate for each popular file	$4.50\ h^{-1}$
λ_{unpop}	request rate for all unpopular files	$7.13\ h^{-1}$
$\frac{N_{mobile}}{N_{internet}}$	ratio between mobile and internet peers	$\frac{666}{333} = 2:1$
p_{new}	probability to share a new file	0.10%
L_{ON}, L_{OFF}	churn time	30 min
$N_{sources}$	maximal number of returned sources by the index server	200

Tutschku, Tran-Gia & Pawlikowski, 2004). Thus, the simulation model models this behavior by updating every 10 min the available sources for a peer with information from the index server and from on-going downloads.

Performance Values

The performance of the resource access control of the proposed MP2P content distribution architecture will be investigated with regard to three main factors: a) the effect of infrastructure elements, in particular the impact of the CA; b) the influence of user behavior and mobility; and c) the impact of the transmission technology. Complementing the factorial split, the performance will be characterized by metrics from the view point of the involved parties, i.e. by values which describe the operator's view on the system performance and user's perspective on the efficiency of the content distribution.

Operator Metrics. An operator is mainly interested in the utilization and the effectiveness of his infrastructure and the provided resources. The data volume transferred by the infrastructure elements describes the utilization of the elements during the content distribution. The effectiveness of the CA in supporting the download process is expressed by the "byte-hit-ratio". The ratio

compares the transmitted download volume of the CA with the totally transmitted download volume within the entire P2P network. The effectiveness of the infrastructure elements for controlling the content exchange between networks domains is described by the "kion-ratio" (keep in own network-ratio). The ratio compares the file-swapping traffic volume in the operator's network with the one of the entire P2P network. Hereby, the mobile network is considered as the operator's domain.

User Metrics. The main user metric for describing the performance of the MP2P distribution architecture is the time to download content. Here, this time is defined as the duration from the first file request by a peer arriving at an index server until the successful completion of the content retrieval.

Impact of the CA

The CA interacts directly with the MIS. Therefore its influence is considered in conjunction with the different source returning policies of the MIS. First, the operator metrics for the CA are investigated.

Figure 9 shows the observed download volume in a scenario when only one file of 3MB size is shared among 10.000 peers which are participating in the distribution (6.667 mobile peers and 3.333

Figure 9. Download volume for a 3 MB file

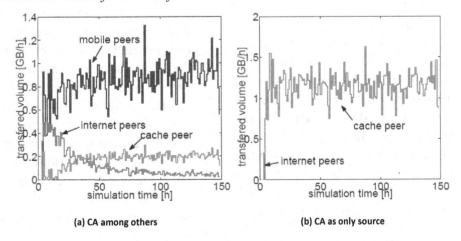

(a) CA among others   (b) CA as only source

internet peers). The file has an initial diffusion of 0.1% among the 10.000 peers.

Figure 9(a) depicts the performance for the policy when the MIS returns the CA as a random source among all sources. The upload volume per hour of the mobile peers reaches immediately very high values and stays on this level even after the CA serves requests. With each mobile peer having successfully finished a download, the number of sharing entities increases and thus does the probability of a mobile peer being returned as a source. As result, the data volume per hour transmitted from the internet peers decreases since it is less likely to choose such a peer, cf. internet peers in Figure 9(a). The transfer volume of the CA increases as soon as it has completed the download, but stays at a low level. The low volume is rooted in the fact that downlink of mobile peers form bottlenecks. The downlink bandwidth at mobile peers is equally shared as long as the uploading peers can provide sufficient data. With many active downlink connections at a specific peer, the CA receives only the equal share as uploading mobile peers. Hence, the CA is not able to play out its high bandwidth upload capacity and is detained from improving the service performance.

Figure 9(b) depicts the results for the policy when the CA is returned as the only source. Now, the internet peers provide the file only at the very beginning of the considered scenario. Mobile peers are not involved since they are not returned by the MIS. As soon as the CA has downloaded the file, it serves all further requests. This result demonstrates the real capability of the CA. It efficiently serves the download request and controls in cooperation with the MIS for popular content, i.e. for a large amount of the distribution volume, when and how content is distributed. The combination of MIS and CA facilitates adaptive resource management on applications layer.

Table 5 shows the effectiveness of the CA from the provider's point of view. Without the involvement of the CA, the kion-ratio reaches a high level of 89.0% due the larger number of mobile

Table 5. Effectiveness values of the CA for the download 3MB file

CA policy	kion-ratio [%]	byte-hit-ratio [%]
without CA	89.0	n.a.
as random source among other sources	89.1	15.3
as only source	99.7	99.2

peers than internet peers. A further increase to almost 99.7% is achieved if the CA is returned as the only source by the MIS. The CA serves all requests after it has downloaded the file. The missing 0.3% is the result from the start phase of system when the caching is not yet able to answer requests. In contrast, the byte-hit-ratio is poor when the CA is returned as a random source among other sources.

The mobile peers still serve requests for popular files. If the CA is returned as the only source then the byte-hit-ratio improves to 99.2%. The user perspective on the CA performance is depicted in Figure 10. It shows the complementary cumulative distribution function (CCDF) of the download time for the three scenarios: a) without using the CA (the "without CA" curve, used as reference scenario); b) the CA is returned among other sources (the "CA and others" curve); and c) the CA is returned as the only source (the "only CA" curve). Figure 10 shows that the policy to return the CA as a random source leads to no improvement, cf. label "CA and other". The average download time does even increase when compared with the reference scenario. That means that just adding a CA without interaction with the MIS is even of disadvantage of the overall performance. This characteristic is rooted in the fact that the waiting lists for download requests at mobile sources are nearly empty when the CA is used. Thus, requests at mobile peers are immediately served. However, the serving of the requests delays the overall download time due to the fact that uploading mobile peers are being bottlenecks. This bottleneck is identified by the rough decay in the CCDF in Figure 10 at about 34 minutes. In this case, the complete file is downloaded from mobile sources. In contrast, returning of the CA as the only source leads to the desired effect of smaller download times, cf. the "only CA" in Figure 10.

Impact of User Behavior and Mobility

Mobile users show a highly spontaneous usage pattern to the ubiquitous nature of the service and their physical mobility. These effects are combined into the peer's temporal behavior and are characterized by the churn time. The effect of three different and complementing values of churn times on the download performance is considered: 30 min, 2 h and 12 h. While the first two values fit well to mobile subscribers, the latter one describes a wireline-like behavior. Figure 11 depicts the dependence of download time CCDF on the peer's temporal behavior in combination of the application of the CA. The simulation considers a download of a file of 5 MB size using GPRS in order to make the effects more visible. The MIS returns the CA as the only source. Figure 11 (a) depicts the CCDF of the download time for popular files.

Figure 10. Download time of a 3MB file for different applications of the CA

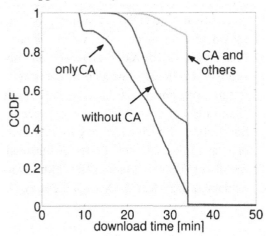

As expected, the peers with the longest churn time of 12h in Figure 11(a) reveal the smallest download times. The more the average churn time decreases in Figure 11(a), i.e. 2h and 30min, the more the download time increases. A similar behavior is observed when the CA is not used, i.e. the exchange of an unpopular file is considered, cf. Figure 11(b). The exponential decay of the CCDFs is caused by the exponentially distributed OFF periods of the peers. Furthermore, Figure 11 shows that the download time decreases faster when the CA is in operation. Moreover, the caching leads to a lower probability of long download times. This effect is strong for a long churn times of 12h and still significant for short churn times of 30min. The comparison shows that the CA reduces also the effects of dynamical user behavior and mobility.

Impact of Wireless Transmission

The access type of the mobile peers is assumed to have a considerable impact on the system performance. In particular, the asymmetric and limited transmission capacities on the air interface in cellular wireless networks constitute different bottlenecks. The downlink of mobile peers is a bottleneck when the uploading entity has significant higher capacity, e.g. in the case of the CA. In turn, the uplink bandwidth of mobile sharing peers restricts the downlink bandwidth of other peers.

Requirement for Supporting Resource Access Control

The previously presented results show that the performance of the MP2P resource access control depends strongly on: a) the features of the additional infrastructure elements in involved in the content exchange; b) the churn characteristic of the peers; and c) the applied transmission technology. In particular, GPRS should not be used for large files in the context of MP2P content distribution. UMTS, however, seems to be a good candidate

Figure 11. Download time for different churn times

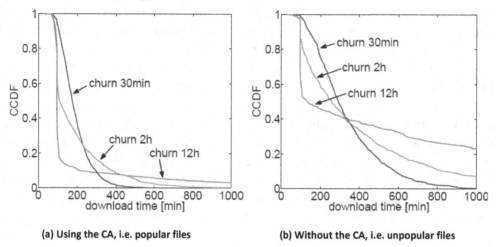

(a) Using the CA, i.e. popular files   (b) Without the CA, i.e. unpopular files

for enabling MP2P file swapping even for larger size contents.

In addition, the design of P2P resource access control mechanisms assumes that all peers are equal. However, the peers in a MP2P system differ significantly in their behavior and throughput values. Neglecting this characteristic may lead to a decreased performance. A performance reduction can be overcome in different ways. The suggested MP2P architecture proposes the application of a CA together with an appropriate MIS policy for the returning of sources. The additional infrastructure elements, i.e. the CA and the MIS, provide for stability is the MP2P system while being adaptive in the selection of files which are stored in the cache. An alternative approach is to modify the MIS to provide a list with the upload speeds of providing peers. In this way, the downloading peer can choose a source which seems to provide the resource most rapidly. However, this would require a modification of the eDonkey protocol and might limit the compatibility of the solution since eDonkey peer without this extension can take advantage are handicapped in their download performance.

Resource Mediation in MP2P

Resource mediation is the second basic P2P function which impacts the performance of P2P systems. Due to controllability and mobility requirements, the proposed MP2P architecture applies a centralized approach for this function and uses the two distinct entities for implementing this work: the MIS and the CP. While the MIS interacts mainly with requesting peers in a simple client/server like request and response pattern, the CP reveals a higher complexity. It queries other index servers on behalf of a large community of mobile peers. A high request rate of the CP, however, might overload a certain resource mediation mechanism. The eDonkey system, for example, uses a scoring mechanism which blocks peers that issue too many requests. Hence, an improved strategy for the CP is needed which provides for fast answers and avoids blocking (also known as "banning") of the CP. The performance and the fine-tuning of such a strategy by mainly means of an analytical Markov model are outlined next, see also (Hoßfeld, Mäder, Tutschku, Tran-Gia, Andersen, De Meer & Dedinski, 2005).

CP Model and Request Strategies

The performance model for the CP focuses on the case that a community of mobile peers delegates identically and independently their requests to the CP. Hence, this community generates a Poisson stream for file requests with rate λ. The CP asks for the requested files by a specific request strategy at index servers. The servers are drawn from known set of a known index servers I. In order to increase the efficiency of the search, the CP may ask a number of k servers simultaneously. The search stops when the first request was successful. The file request success probability for a certain file on a specific index server $i \in I$ is modeled by the probability f_i. The values for f_i have been obtained by measurements. Without loss of generality, the performance model assumes that only one file is requested. The blocking of peers at eDonkey index servers has been introduced by the developers of the so-called "Lugdunum" index server, which is the major server implementation in the public eDonkey network. The blocking mechanism is modeled as following. The index server assigns each requesting peer p a credit point counter c_p that is set initially to c_{init}. With each file request, the credit counter of a peer is decreased by c_r while in turn in each second one credit is added. Typical values for c_{init} and c_r are 1000 and 16 respectively[11]. A peer is blocked by the index server when its credit counter c_p reaches the level of zero. Once a peer, in particular the CP, is blocked by the index server then it is assumed that the peer is blocked forever. This is a worst case assumption since there is no common blocking time implemented in the public eDonkey network. In the model, the return time for a single request from the CP to a specific eDonkey index server is modeled by measurements of actual round trip times and can be approximated by a *shifted log-normal distribution*. The time that an index server needs to access the file location database is neglected. The aim is to design a request strategy for the CP that has a high file success probability and thus a small search time. The file success probability $p_{s,i}$ is defined as the probability that a file is located by the CP after asking i index servers. Next, three request strategies are described and their success probabilities are outlined.

Randomly Requesting Servers - RaRe Strategy: In the random request (RaRe) strategy, the CP chooses the index servers randomly from the set of all servers and sends a file request to each of them. The requests can be sent sequentially or in parallel. The search stops when a file is located and has been reported back to the CP. Hence, assuming that no blocking occurs, the success probability $p_{s,i}$ for the RaRe strategy is a one-shifted geometric distribution:

$$p_{s,i} - GEO_1(i) - (1-p)^{i-1} p,$$

with $\mu = \dfrac{1}{p}$ and $\mu = \dfrac{\sum_{i' \in I} f_{i'}}{|I|}$. The value μ describes the average file request success probability for all servers. In addition, it has to be noted that this success probability is only valid when blocking is neglected.

Optimizing Success Probability - Psi Strategy: The Psi strategy optimizes the success probability $p_{s,i}$ by ordering the list of index servers by their individual file request success probability f_i. Thus, the CP asks at first the index server with the highest f_i, then the one with second highest probability number and so on. The file success probability $p_{s,i}$, when blocking is neglected, is given by:

$$p_{s,i} = f_i \prod_{j=1}^{i-1}(1-f_j)$$

The Psi strategy outperforms the RaRe strategy since the servers with the highest success probabilities are asked first. However, this strategy has also a disadvantage. It queries at first servers which have high a success probability, thus increasing the probability for a requesting entity to be blocked at them.

Smart Requesting without Banning - NoBan Strategy: The NoBan strategy avoids a blocking of the CP. The strategy assumes that the CP knows its own credit points and therefore asks only servers where it has sufficient credit. The request order is analogous to the Psi strategy such that index server with high success probability are asked first.

Numerical Results

Next, the proposed request strategies are investigated with respect to response time and success probability.

Comparison of the Strategies for Sequential Requests

At first, the blocking of the CP is neglected and a sequential order of requests are assumed. This intermediate step permits an analytical formulation of the probability density functions for the response times of unsuccessful, successful, and all requests. In a second step, the performance is assessed by simulations for the more complex case of the CP being blocked.

Analytical investigation: An unsuccessfully answered search requests means that each of the N index servers have been contacted and none has reported a hit. Hence, the response time for unsuccessful requests $Tunsuc$ is a sum of N shifted log-normal distributed random variables which is again log-normal distribution with parameters (Fenton, 1960):

$$Tunsuc = \sum_{i=1}^{N} \min(R_i) + LOGN(\mu_{unsuc}, \sigma_{unsuc})$$

with $\mu_{unsuc} = \sum_{i=1}^{N}(\mu(R_i) - \min(R_i))$,

$\sigma unsuc = \sqrt{\sum_{i=1}^{N}\sigma(R_i)^2}$, R_i as the shifted lognormal response time distribution for server i, $\mu(R_i)$ as the mean response time of server i, and $\sigma(R_i)$ as the standard deviation of the response time for

server i. Now, the density function $r_{suc}(t)$ for the response time T_{suc} of successful requests will be calculated for the Psi strategy since this strategy outperforms the RaRe strategy. It can be calculated by using the theorem of total probabilities:

$$r_{suc}(t) = (\sum_{i=1}^{N-1} p_{s,i} \cdot r(t \mid i)) + r(t \mid N)$$

with $p_{s,i} = f_i \prod_{j=1}^{i-1}(1 - f_i)$ and $r(t \mid i) = *_{j=1}^{i} rj(t)$. Hereby, $rj = \dfrac{d}{dt} P\{R_i \leq t\}$ describes the probability density function of the response time of server i and the sign * denotes the convolution operator.

At last, the density function $r_{all}(t)$ for the response time of all requests can be computed:

$$r_{au}(t) = p_{s,N} \cdot r_{suc}(t) + (1 - p_{s,N}) \cdot \frac{d}{dt} P\{T_{unsuc} \leq t\}$$

The derived equations for the response times are only valid as long as requests are not blocked, i.e. that the CP imposes a small load on index servers.

Figure 12 depicts the cumulative distribution functions of the response times of the CP to search requests. It shows that the request response time for all request (label "not blocked requests") is dominated by the response time for successful requests as long as the off-set for contacting all servers is not reached. After that, it is dominated by the response of unsuccessful requests (more detailed information on the parametric values can be found in Hoßfeld et al., 2005).

Simulations: Now, the blocking of the CP is considered. That means that the crawling imposes significant load on the index servers. Due to the increased complexity, the performance of the strategies has been investigated by simulations (Hoßfeld et al., 2005).

The mean response times for successful requests and the success probabilities for the three strategies are depicted in Figure 13. As expected, the success probabilities for the RaRe and Psi strategies decrease with increasing load due to blocking, cf. Figure 13(b). The response time of the Psi and RaRe strategy stays on the same level or decreases strongly, cf. Figure 13(a). The significant decay in the response time of the RaRe strategy is a result of the high blocking probability. A different behavior can be observed for the NoBan strategy. Its success probability stays on a high level and its mean response time increases only slightly for high load. This results show the superiority of this strategy in term of response time and success probability.

The Impact of Parallel Requests
The aim of issuing parallel requests to index servers is to decrease the response time. However,

Figure 12. Influence of simultaneous requests in the NoBan strategy

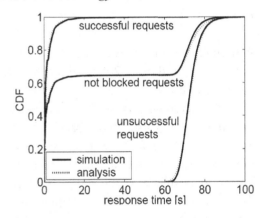

parallel requests might also impose higher load the index server and thus, can possibly increase the probability of the CP being blocked. Next, only the NoBan strategy is considered since it outperforms the other strategies in terms of response times. The blocking probability is defined here as the probability that a request cannot be answered successfully since the CP is blocked. The blocking of the CP can still occur in the NoBan strategy when previous requests have consumed all credits and new requests are issued.

Figure 14(a) shows the mean response time for successful searches for different numbers k of parallel requests. The mean response time is nearly halved if an additional parallel request process is added, such that with eight parallel search processes the mean response time does not exceed the one-second mark, even in high-load situations.

The price for this gain is paid by an increasing blocking probability. The probability grows as soon as the load exceeds the threshold of 225 requests per hour, cf. Figure 14(b). This corresponds to a mean interarrival time of 16s which is also the penalty in credits a request on an index server costs. The blocking probabilities also correlate to the number of parallel requests since a higher degree of parallelism also increases the load. So for k=8, the users experience a block-

Figure 13. Influence of the request strategy on the performance of the CP

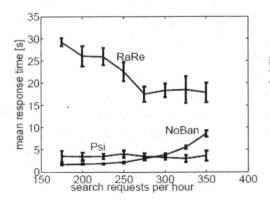

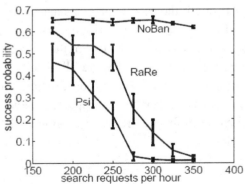

(a) Mean response time of successful requests   (b) Success probability of search requests

Figure 14. Influence of simultaneous requests in the NoBan strategy

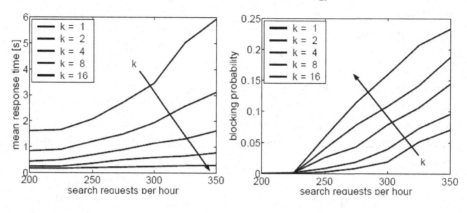

(a) Mean response time of successful requests   (b) Blocking probability of search requests

ing probability of approx. 20% in the case of 350 file requests per hour. This result suggests that a proper selection of the number parallel request is necessary for a given number of index servers and request rate.

While the RaRe and the Psi strategies reveal a negative correlation between increasing load and low success probabilities, the NoBan strategy maintains high performance value over a wide range of load values. With a proper selection of the number of parallel request, an even better performance for the NoBan strategy can be achieved. The advantage of the NoBan strategy is achieved by a higher complexity of the CP. The significance of the performance advantage of the NoBan strategy for high load values, however, easily justifies the higher complexity.

All in all, the performance enhancement by the CP is not simply constituted by its simple application. The request strategy of the CP and its parameters have also to be carefully selected for a sensitive use. Once this is done, the crawling becomes a key factor for the support of efficiency and mobility for resource mediation in a MP2P architecture.

CONCLUSIONS: OPPORTUNITIES FOR THE EMERGING FUTURE INTERNET

Although the suggested MP2P architecture is based on today's P2P concepts, it already addresses future network challenges such as overlays, heterogeneity, mobility support, self-organization and user participation (Tutschku, Tran-Gia and Andersen, 2008). Furthermore, the suggested architecture may give guidelines for the mechanisms in the future Internet. The future network should directly support the easy set-up of the additional infrastructure elements. The future core elements, i.e. the future access points or routers, should assign the infrastructure elements and the peers to a specific instance of an *overlay for participation* (Anderson, 2006). Thus, they achieve a closed but well-controllable virtual community. In an overlay, the peers (i.e. user peers and infrastructure elements) should be able to set-up virtual links, to configure the resource management of the access link, and to set the routing tables on the core elements for efficient content distribution. The technologies for providing these features are already under development (Bavier, Feamster, Huang, Peterson & Rexford, 2006). Hereby, the infrastructure elements should have the right of performing the final decision. Thus, the overlay architecture can address the needs of the user and their applications as well as of the future operators.

The selection of the future mechanisms and the fine tuning of their parameters have to be carried out based on performance analysis which considers the: *a)* entity's behavior, e.g. the peer's churn characteristic; *b)* resource model, e.g. the size and popularity of content; and *c)* architectural model, e.g. the type of the overlay, infrastructure elements and their strategies. Such an approach will ensure future high performance MP2P applications.

REFERENCES

Anderson, C. (2006). People power. *Wired Magazine*. Retrieved September 28, 2008, from http://www.wired.com/wired/archive/14.07/people.html

Bakos, B., Farks, L., & Nurminen, J. (2006). P2P applications on smart phones using cellular communications. In *Proceedings of the IEEE Wireless Communications and Networking Conference (WCNC 2006),* (Vol. 4, pp. 2222-2228).

Banks, J., Carson, J., Nelson, B., & Nicol, D. (2004). *Discrete-event system simulation* (4th ed.). Jersey City, NJ: Prentice-Hall.

Bavier, A., Feamster, N., Huang, M., Peterson, L., & Rexford, J. (2006). In VINI veritas: Realistic and controlled network experimentation. *SIGCOMM Computer Communiation. Review, 36*(4), 3-14.

Eberspächer, J., Vogel, H.-J., & Bettstetter, C. (2001). *GSM switching, services and protocols* (2nd ed.). New York: John Wiley & Sons, Inc.

Fenton, L. (1960). The sum of lognormal probability distributions in scatter transmission systems. *IRE Trans. Commun. Syst., 8*(3), 57–67.

Horozov, T., Grama, A., Vasudevan, V., & Landis S. (2002). Moby - a mobile peer-to-peer service and data network. In *Proceedings of the 2002 International Conference on Parallel Processing (ICPP'02)* (p. 437). Washington: IEEE Computer Society.

Hoßfeld, T., Leibnitz, K., Pries, R., Tutschku, K., Tran-Gia, P., & Pawlikowski, K. (2004). Information diffusion in edonkey filesharing networks. In *Proceedings of Australian Telecommunication Networks and Applications Conference (ATNAC 2004)*.

Hoßfeld, T., Mäder, A., Tutschku, K., Tran-Gia, P., Andersen, F.-U., de Meer, H., & Dedinski, I. (2005). Comparison of crawling strategies for an optimized mobile p2p architecture. In *Proceedings of the 19th International Teletraffic Congress (ITC19)*.

Hoßfeld, T., Oechsner, S., Tutschku, K., Andersen, F.-U., & Caviglione, L. (2006). Supporting vertical handover by using a pastry peer-to-peer overlay network. In *Proceedings of the 3rd IEEE International Workshop on Mobile Peer-to-Peer Computing (MP2P'06)*.

Hoßfeld, T., Tutschku, K., & Andersen, F.-U. (2005a). Mapping of file-sharing onto mobile environments: Enhancement by UMTS. *Proceedings of the 2nd IEEE International Workshop on Mobile Peer-to-Peer Computing (MP2P'05)*.

Hoßfeld, T., Tutschku, K., & Andersen, F.-U. (2005b). Mapping of file-sharing onto mobile environments: Feasibility and performance of edonkey with GPRS. In *Proceedings of 2005 IEEE Wireless Communciations and Networking Conference (WCNC 2005)*.

Kamienski, C., Sadok, D., J. Fidalgo, D., Lima, J., & Ohlman, B. (2006). On the use of peer-to-peer architectures for the management of highly dynamic environments. In *Proceedings of the 2ⁿᵈ IEEE International Workshop on Mobile Peer-to-Peer Computing (MP2P'06).*

Kempf, J. (June, 2001). Dormant mode host alerting ('IP paging') problem statement. IETF, *RFC3132.*

Matuszewski, M., Beijar, N., Lehtinen, J., & Hyyrylainen T. (2006). Content sharing in mobile P2P networks: Myth or reality? *International Journal of Mobile Network Design and Innovation, 1*(3/4), 197-207.

Oberender, J., Andersen, F.-U., de Meer, H., Dedinski, I., Hoßfeld, T., Kappler, C., Mäder, A., & Tutschku, K. (2005). Enabling mobile peer-to-peer networking. *Wireless Systems and Mobiliy in Next Generation Internet* (p. 26). Berlin / Heidelberg: Springer.

Pack, S., Park, K., Kwon, T., & Choi, Y. (2006). SAMP: Scalable application-layer mobility protocol. *IEEE Communications Magazine, 44*(6), 86-92.

Stoica, I., Morris, R., Karger, D., Kaashoek, F., & Balakrishnan H. (2001). Chord: A scalable peer-to-peer lookup service for internet applications. In *Proceedings of ACM SIGCOMM 2001.*

Sumino, H., Ishikawa, N., & Kato, T. (2006). Design and implementation of P2P protcol for mobile phones. In *Proceedings of the 3ʳᵈ IEEE International Workshop on Mobile Peer-to-Peer Computing (MP2P'06).*

Tutschku, K. (2007). *P2P-based network and service operation for the emerging future internet* (Tech. Rep. No. 397). Würzburg, Germany: University of Würzburg, Lehrstuhl für Informatik III.

Tutschku, K., Tran-Gia, P., & Andersen, F.-U. (2007). *Trends in network and service operation for the emerging future internet* (Tech. Rep. No.

431). Würzburg, Germany: University of Würzburg, Lehrstuhl für Informatik III.

Zoels, S., Despotovic, Z., & Kellerer, W. (2006). Cost-based analysis of hierarchical DHT design. In *Proceedings of the 6ᵗʰ IEEE International Conference Peer-to-Peer Computing (P2P2006).*

Zoels, S., Schollmeier, R., Kellerer, W., & Tarlano, A. (2005). The hybrid chord protocol: A peer-to-peer lookup service for context-aware mobile applications. In *Proceedings of the 4ᵗʰ International Conference on Networking (ICN 2005).*

Zoels, S., Schubert, S., Kellerer, W., & Despotovic, Z. (2006). Hybrid DHT design for mobile environments. In *Proceedings of the International Workshop on Agents and Peer-to-Peer Computing (AP2PC 2006).*

ENDNOTES

[1] Current mobile phones and features - https://developer.sprint.com/show_devices.do

[2] Forum NOKIA, S60 Platform: IP Bearer Management - http://sw.nokia.com/id/190358c8-7cb1-4be3-9321-f9d6788ecae5/S60_Platform_IP_Bearer_Management_v1_0_en.pdf

[3] In P2P notion, the term "churn" denotes the stochastic process of peers joining or leaving the system.

[4] Homepage of the symella project - http://symella.aut.bme.hu

[5] The Gnutella protocol specification v0.4 - http://www.clip2.com

[6] Homepage of the mopiphant project - http://www3.informatik.uni-wuerzburg.de/staff/mopi/mopiphant.shtml

[7] Homepage of the edonkey project - http://www.overnet.org

[8] Homepage of the jxme project - http://jxme.jxta.org

9   Homepage of the jxta project - http://www.
     jxta.org

10   Homepage of the mobilemule project - http://
     mobil.emule-project.net

11   Explanation on blacklisting by servers.
     in Newsgroup: alt.pl.edonkey2000, Aug.
     2003 - http://groups.google.de/group/alt.
     pl.edonkey2000

Chapter XVII
Peer–to–Peer Networking Platform and Its Applications for Mobile Phones

Norihiro Ishikawa
NTT DOCOMO, Japan

Hiromitsu Sumino
NTT DOCOMO, Japan

Takeshi Kato
NTT DOCOMO, Japan

Johan Hjelm
Ericsson Research, Japan

Shingo Murakami
Ericsson Research, Japan

Kazuhiro Kitagawa
Keio University, Japan

Nobuo Saito
Komazawa University, Japan

ABSTRACT

Compared with traditional Internet technologies, peer-to-peer technologies has functions to realize resource discovery, resource sharing, and load balancing in a highly distributed manner. In addition to the Internet, new networks such as home network, ad-hoc network and sensor network are emerging. An easy prediction is the emergence of a new environment in which many sensors, people, and many different kinds of devices coexist, move, and communicate with one another over such heterogeneous networks. Peer-to-peer technology is one of the most important and suitable technologies for such ubiquitous networking since it supports discovery mechanisms, simple one-to-one communication, free and extensible distribution of resources, and distributed search to handle the enormous number of resources. The authors have designed and implemented a peer-to-peer networking platform for realizing applications, which include various applications for mobile phones. This chapter presents their peer-to-peer networking architecture, protocols, and applications for mobile phones.

INTRODUCTION

Peer-to-peer (P2P) technology has become popular and has been extensively used in overlay networks that handle vast amounts of data daily, and balancing loads over a large number of servers. It has been used for applications such as distributed search (Gnutella, 2001), file sharing (KaZaa, 2002), distributed storage (Clarke et al., 2000) and groupware (Microsoft Corporation, 2000). Additionally, a generalized platform for peer-to-peer applications has been proposed and developed (JXTA, 2001).

At the same time, various devices have recently been enhanced through the addition of communication abilities. In the near future, an environment where many sensors, persons and different kinds of objects exist, move, and communicate with one another will appear. In fact, peer-to-peer communication is one of the most important and suitable networking technologies for such communications since it effectively supports one-to-one communication, the free and extensible distribution of resources, and the distributed search mechanisms needed to handle the enormous resources on the Internet. As mentioned before, peer-to-peer communication has the ability to link heterogeneous network environments in a cross-sectional manner such as the Internet, ad-hoc networks, and home networks. It can realize seamless connection between various devices via various networks and handle the enormous resources as an overlay network.

We have designed a peer-to-peer architecture and protocols (Ishikawa et al., 2007), and developed a general peer-to-peer networking platform that enhances the communication capabilities of various devices via various networks for realizing applications in ubiquitous networking environment, which include applications for mobile phones

ARCHITECTURE

In the proposed architecture, bidirectional communication entities, called peer-to-peer nodes, construct a peer-to-peer network by establishing peer-to-peer connection between them. The peer-to-peer nodes communicate one another using the peer-to-peer connections. Each peer-to-peer node has a unique ID. The key elements of our architecture are defined as follows.

Peer-to-peer node: Peer-to-peer node is an independent, bidirectional communication entity. In our architecture, it can be a mobile device, a PDA, a personal computer, a server, a workstation, or any of a variety of devices. Each node has a unique ID and communicates using the ID independent from physical networks.

Peer-to-peer network: The term "peer-to-peer network" means a logical collection of peer-to-peer nodes that have a common interest and obey a common set of policies. The connection between peer-to-peer nodes is established on mutual trust. Each peer-to-peer node can enter or depart the peer-to-peer network at its convenience. Messages are sent from one peer-to-peer node to another directly or via some intermediary peer-to-peer nodes. Routing information is discovered by broadcasting an inquiry message to the network.

Peer-to-peer message: This is data object which is sent and received between peer-to-peer nodes. The peer-to-peer message is a basic unit of exchanging data and has a unique ID.

Peer-to-peer connection: This is a communication channel established between peer-to-peer nodes. The peer-to-peer messages are transmitted across the peer-to-peer connections.

The proposed Peer-to-Peer architecture is shown in Figure. 1.

Figure 1. Peer-to-Peer Architecture

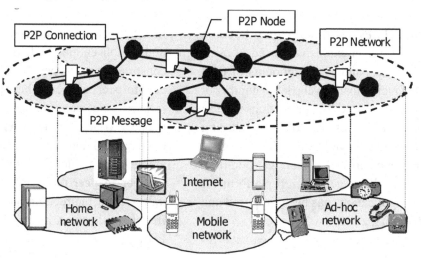

PEER-TO-PEER COMMUNICATION MODEL

In the peer-to-peer communication model, the role of each communicating entity is not always clearly distinguishable. In order to design an effective peer-to-peer communication protocol, the "role" concept is introduced. We have established the peer-to-peer communication model by looking into existing peer-to-peer applications. For example, we found three kinds of nodes in peer-to-peer distributed search applications (Gnutella, 2001; KaZza, 2002; Clarke et al., 2000). The first provides content information (e.g. its location) in response to search requests, the second requests the content search and the third relays the search request and their replies. This suggests that peer-to-peer nodes can have three roles.

Producer role: A node acts as a Producer when it provides application data or services.

Consumer role: A node acts as a Consumer when it asks for a service or consumes application data without any request or in response to its request.

Relay role: A node acts as a Relay when its current communication task is just to forward application data, service requests and their replies.

In peer-to-peer applications, a node may play any of these three defined roles and the peer-to-peer application dynamically determines which one is to be used. Based on the roles described before, we define two peer-to-peer communication modes. (See Figure 2)

- Proactive communication mode: This mode represents the unsolicited transmission of information that does not require any specific response. It is generally used by a node to notify the others of its own existence or resources it holds.
- Reactive communication mode: This mode represents the transmission of information that requires a response. It is generally used by a node that requests certain services or resources provided by other nodes.

As shown in Figure 3, our architecture also supports basic communication types such as unicast (includes multi-hop unicast), broadcast, and multicast.

Figure 2. Roles and communication modes

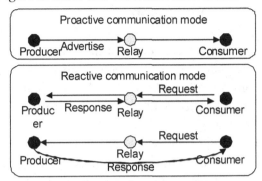

Node Naming

In peer-to-peer networks, each node should have a unique name. This name will be extensively used for various purposes such as node search, routing information to a node and cache table management. A naming system should satisfy the following requirements.

Uniqueness: Peer-to-peer node names should be unique within the scope of a community.

Manageability, Simplicity: Peer-to-peer names should be able to be autonomously generated in particular for pure peer-to-peer networks. Its naming structure should use simple for manageability and generality.

Scalability: The peer-to-peer naming system has to support extremely large number of nodes.

Anonymity, Privacy and security: Nobody should be able to infer any type of private information from node names.

Security: Node names should not be arrogated.

Independency: Node names should be independent of location, user, transport protocol, and application, etc.

Considering the aforementioned requirements, we have defined a naming system that is based on UUID (Paul et al., 1998) where a node name is assigned by the node itself. UUID is, however, not human-readable. User-ID, which ambiguously identifies a user over a peer-to-peer node may be defined for human-readability and user authentication.

Peer-to-Peer Message Routing

Message routing is one of the key mechanisms for realizing efficient and reliable peer-to-peer communication. In the traditional Internet, routing is performed by a router according to a routing table it holds. However, since a peer-to-peer node freely enters and leaves a peer-to-peer network, the topology of a peer-to-peer network changes very frequently. Routing based on a stable routing table is hence inadequate and inefficient for a peer-to-peer network. Since peer-to-peer nodes communicate with each other across heterogeneous network environments, a transport layer independent routing mechanism is required. In this architecture, *name-based routing* mechanism is proposed. This is a mechanism that finds a source route towards a destination node using a heuristic

Figure 3. Peer-to-Peer Communication Types

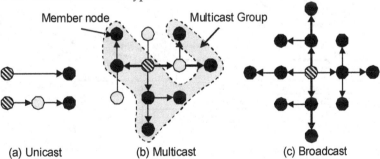

procedure. The peer-to-peer routing mechanism is shown in Figure 4. Here, the peer-to-peer routing mechanism is based on an application layer overlay routing and each peer-to-peer node has a routing table that manages the Node ID and transport address of adjacent nodes. This mechanism does not depend on a specific transport layer protocol such as TCP.

We have also designed a node naming scheme that is independent of the specific naming system of a transport network such as DNS. As a result, the name of a peer-to-peer node is assigned independently of the transport network. The mapping between the name of a peer-to-peer node and its network address is dynamically resolved, when a peer-to-peer node joins the peer-to-peer network over a new transport network. Good examples of this type of routing mechanism are ad-hoc network routing mechanisms such as Dynamic Source Routing (DSR) (Johnson et al., 2000). One advantage of this method is its simplicity because it does not need complicated routing protocols and a particular server. Obviously, it consumes a lot of network resources and incurs long delay. Hence, performance and efficiency could not be sufficiently ensured in large peer-to-peer network environments.

Peer-to-Peer Multicast Communication

In peer-to-peer networks, multicast communication can be used by various applications, such as groupware applications. The requirements on peer-to-peer multicast communications are as follows.

- **Optimization of multicast distribution tree:** Peer-to-peer multicast should be able to optimize the distribution tree even in dynamic network environments where nodes frequently join and leave.
- **Dynamic management of members in a multicast group:** Peer-to-peer multicast should efficiently manage members of a multicast group, because such members may change very frequently.
- **Efficient support for multiple multicast senders:** For Internet, the research and IETF communities have been focusing on single-source multicast, where it is assumed that there exists a single multicast sender. However, in the peer-to-peer network, a node can be both a multicast sender and receiver simultaneously due to its inherent symmetric nature of the peer-to-peer communication. Peer-to-peer multicast should efficiently

Figure 4. Peer-to-peer routing mechanism

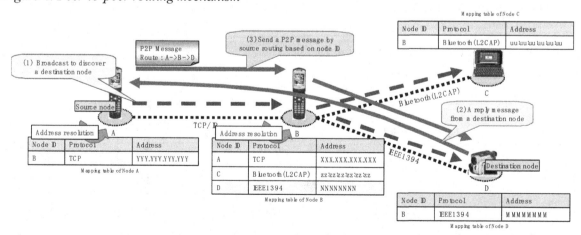

support the case where each member in the multicast group sends and receives multicast messages simultaneously.

- **Fault tolerance:** Peer-to-peer multicast should have recovery mechanisms to recover from the failure of the peer-to-peer network (e.g. node failure).

As mentioned in the foregoing section, the peer-to-peer network supports basic communication methods between the peer-to-peer nodes such as unicast, multi-hop unicast and broadcast. By using those methods, the proposed peer-to-peer multicast architecture is realized by constructing a multicast distribution tree over the peer-to-peer network as shown Figure 5. In the proposed architecture, only the functions to manage the overlaying multicast distribution tree are required. In the following, we discuss the mechanisms for the peer-to-peer multicast in more detail:

1. Optimization of Multicast Distribution Tree

Multicast distribution methods can be classified as shown in Fig 6 (Kousiur, 1999). We discuss advantages and problems of these methods in the case that they are applied to the peer-to-peer multicast. Flooding method is not optimum because it broadcasts messages. The spanning tree

Figure 5. Multicast distribution tree over the peer-to-peer network

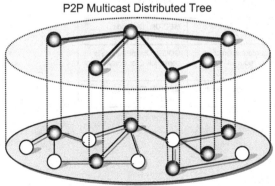

P2P Multicast Distributed Tree

P2P Network Layer

method is not optimum because it constructs an overall network-wide distribution tree. Its main advantage is that it constructs a simple and loop-free tree. With the shared tree method, it is difficult to determine a RP (Rendezvous Point), but it can effectively manage multicast groups because routing information on each node is relatively small. The source-based tree method has a problem in that the routing table tends to be large because routing information is needed for each source node. Another problem is that it reconstructs distribution trees by using message flooding.

2. Dynamic Management of Members in a Multicast Group

We compared these multicast distribution methods from the perspective of managing a multicast distribution tree. The proposed peer-to-peer multicast requires dynamic management of members because member nodes will join and leave frequently. Figure 7 shows the impact of each distribution method when member nodes leave the multicast group and when tree reconstruction is triggered. As shown in Figure 7, the reconstruction cost is relatively small with flooding and spanning tree methods.

3. Efficient Support of Multiple Multicast Senders

We also compared these multicast distribution methods assuming that all group members act as senders. Table IV shows the problems of each distribution method. As shown in Figure 8, the flooding method and source-based tree method are suitable for multiple multicast senders.

4. Fault Tolerance

Finally, we compared these multicast distribution methods with regard to member node failure. Figure 9 shows the fault tolerance of each multicast

Figure 6. Comparing in distribution method

Method	Application for peer-to-peer			Suitability
	Policy	**Advantage**	**Problem**	
Flooding	Eliminate duplicate message and forward other messages to adjacent member nodes except for transfer source node	Routing information of each node is only adjacent member node information	Traffic congestion happens as well as broadcast	**BAD** (non optimum just like broadcast)
Spanning Tree	Forward messages to adjacent member nodes according to spanning tree	Simple and loop-free structure	Load of routing is centralized in branch node	**MIDIUM** (spanning tree is constructed in entire network)
Source Based Tree	Forward message to adjacent member nodes according to source base tree for each source member node	Every member node can have routing information optimized for each source member node	Routing information is required for each source member node	**GOOD** (tree is constructed and optimized for each sender)
Shared Tree	Each sender sends a message to RP. Forward messages to adjacent member node according to shared routing information among all member nodes	Routing information is small because all member nodes share the tree	Distribution tree is not optimum, RP is required, and load on RP is high	**MEDIUM** (It is difficult to determine RP in the peer-to-peer network)

Figure 7. Comparing in cost of management of tree

Method	Extent of the impact	Remarks	Suitability
Flooding	The node whose adjacent relationship is changed by reconstruction	update routing information according to adjacent member nodes	**GOOD** (low impact)
Spanning Tree	The node whose adjacent relationship is changed by reconstruction	update routing information according to adjacent member nodes in new spanning tree	**GOOD** (low impact)
Source Based Tree	All nodes belong to a distribution tree that is changed by reconstruction	update routing information according to adjacent member nodes for each new source based tree	**BAD** (Flooding needed for tree reconstruction)
Shared Tree	The node whose adjacent relationship is changed by reconstruction	update routing information according to adjacent member nodes in new shared tree	**BAD** (If RP leaves, overall reconstruction of tree is required.)

Figure 8. Comparing in adaptation for multiple senders

Method	Impact with Multi Sender	Remarks	Suitability
Flooding	Sender independent because a distribution tree is not constructed.	Multicast message is flooded over entire network.	**GOOD** (Sender independent)
Spanning Tree	Depends on shape of distribution tree	MST (Minimum Spanning Tree) is optimum	**MEDIUM** (Depend on shape of tree)
Source Based Tree	Optimized tree is constructed for every member node.	Routing information of each sender is required	**GOOD** (Optimized tree is constructed for every node)
Shared Tree	Depends on shape of distribution tree	All messages go through RP.	**MEDIUM** (Depend on shape of tree)

distribution method. The flooding and source-based tree methods are nearly unaffected by the failure of a member node, while the other two methods are affected. The shared tree method suffers the worst from the failure of a RP.

We also compared these methods in terms of support for peer-to-peer communication. The flooding method is not suitable because its multicast distribution tree is not optimized. A tree constructed by the source-based tree method is optimized but the flooding used to construct the trees causes a problem. The shared tree method has a problem determining an optimal RP. The spanning tree method is very suitable for peer-to-peer networks, but has a disadvantage that its multicast distribution tree covers the entire network. Consequently, we adopted the Spanning Tree method for peer-to-peer multicast. In the proposed method, all member nodes share one

spanning tree and new participating node connects to appropriate member nodes. A multicast sender must belong to a multicast group.

The proposed peer-to-peer multicast architecture is presented in Figure 10; the multicast network overlays the peer-to-peer network. Multicast forwarding is carried out by multi-hop or multi-destination unicast, so it is not necessary for all nodes to support multicast forwarding. Figure 9 shows the peer-to-peer multicast path construction procedure. When a peer-to-peer node tries to join a certain multicast group: (1) it sends a join message to the nearest member node; (2) The nearest member node sends a join response message to it; and (3) the two nodes establish a relationship regarding the multicast group; (4) Next, the multicast message propagates along the multicast paths. In the pure peer-to-peer architecture, the node floods a request message

Figure 9. Comparing in fault tolerance

Method	Impact	Remarks	Suitability
Flooding	None	Update routing information at next distribution.	**GOOD** (Low impact)
Spanning Tree	Splitting	Need to find new adjacent member nodes.	**MEDIUM** (need a function to find adjacent member nodes)
Source Based Tree	None	Update routing information at next reconstruction	**GOOD** (Low impact)
Shared Tree	Splitting	Failure of RP has strong impact	**BAD** (High impact)

Figure 10. Peer-to-peer multicast

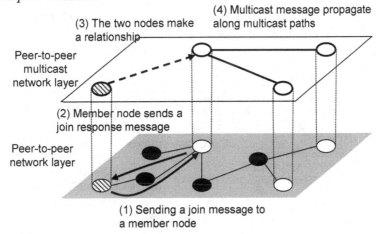

(3) The two nodes make a relationship

(4) Multicast message propagate along multicast paths

Peer-to-peer multicast network layer

(2) Member node sends a join response message

Peer-to-peer network layer

(1) Sending a join message to a member node

over the peer-to-peer network when it wants to join a multicast group. In the hybrid peer-to-peer architecture, the control node informs the node of the nearest member node in response to the node's request.

Several key peer-to-peer multicast functions are described as follows.

1. Construction of Distribution Tree

The bi-directional shared minimum spanning tree (MST) is well suitable for peer-to-peer multicast where each member in the group is destined to be a multicast sender and receiver simultaneously. The characteristic of MST is to minimize the total distances between all nodes. Therefore, the distances between nodes are well optimized. It is relatively easy to construct a distribution tree using a control node, but difficult to construct it in a pure peer-to-peer network. We will consider a tree construction algorithm in a distributed autonomous manner.

2. Reconstruction of Distribution Tree

In peer-to-peer networks, each node basically knows only its adjacent nodes. Therefore, when a node leaves a multicast group, the node has to notify its adjacent nodes of which node they should reconnect to. In the simplest algorithm, a node notifies its adjacent downstream node of its adjacent upstream nodes so the downstream nodes can reconnect to the upstream nodes. As a result, connectivity of the entire tree is assured.

Other algorithms for reconstruction of distribution tree seem possible.

3. Recovery from Splitting of Distribution Tree

There is a well-known method to notify adjacent nodes about the node to which they should reconnect in advance. Other algorithms for recovery seem possible.

4. Improvement of Distribution Tree

In peer-to-peer multicast, a node frequently leaves or fails. Therefore, a multicast distribution tree shape gradually becomes non-optimum. We will also consider a tree improvement algorithm in a distributed autonomous manner. Additionally, Peer-to-peer multicast is similar to application layer multicast (Jannotti, 2000; Chawathe, 2000; Chu, 2000). Application layer multicast mechanisms might be applicable to peer-to-peer multicast with some modifications.

Protocol Design

The Proposed protocols are designed to realize the proposed peer-to-peer architecture. The protocols described herein are designed with consideration of the following requirements.

Extensibility: Peer-to-peer protocols should be layered, generic, and have extensibility so that they can support various peer-to-peer applications.

Figure 11. Peer-to-peer communication types

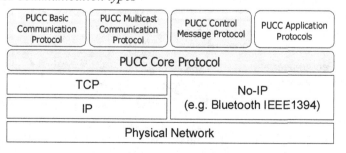

Utilization of existing technology: Peer-to-peer protocols should leverage existing technologies such as XML, and support existing network infrastructures such as the Internet to simplify implementation and deployment.

Independence of transport protocols: Peer-to-peer protocols should be independent of transport protocols for realizing peer-to-peer applications over heterogeneous network environments (e.g. the Internet, home networks and ad-hoc networks).

As shown in Figure 11, the proposed protocols are currently defined over TCP/IP and Bluetooth (Bluetooth, 1999) and also defined over IEEE 1394 (IEEE 1394, 1994). The proposed protocols consist of the following protocols.

P2P Core Protocol

This Protocol processes peer-to-peer messages according to the peer-to-peer communication model. Three message types are defined in the previous section. Request and response messages are defined for the reactive communication mode while an advertise message is defined for the proactive communication mode. A message is sent to the destination node either directly or using multi-hop unicast. A node sends a broadcast message to all adjacent nodes. The message routing mechanisms of the P2P Core Protocol are independent of transport protocols. Other P2P protocols are defined over this protocol.

P2P Basic Communication Protocol

This Protocol establishes and releases peer-to-peer sessions. In our architecture, all communications are based on a peer-to-peer session between pair adjacent peer-to-peer nodes. This protocol also has the function of exchanging node resource information such as names of its adjacent nodes, and supported applications.

P2P Multicast Communication Protocol

This Protocol constructs a multicast distribution tree for multicast member nodes and forwards multicast messages along it. A node finds a member node of a multicast group, and sends a Join message to it, and a multicast routing table is generated at each node along the path toward it at the same time. When a node wants to send a multicast message, it sends the message towards the adjacent member nodes based on the multicast routing table. The multicast messages are forwarded along the multicast distribution tree using the bi-directional shared tree mechanism. When the node leaves the multicast group, it sends a Leave message to the adjacent member nodes.

P2P Control Message Protocol

This Protocol provides ancillary functions such as notification of message forwarding error, keep-alive for peer-to-peer sessions, and first peer-to-peer node discovery in pure peer-to-peer network environments. For example, an ErrorReport message is used to notify the source node of the forwarding error of a message. A Diagnose message is used to measure RTT (Round Trip Time) between peer-to-peer nodes. A Lookfor message is used to find the first peer node to which a node should connect in pure peer-to-peer network environments.

P2P Application Protocols

P2P application protocols may be defined over P2P Core Protocol, to realize various P2P applications. Such protocols include P2P Service Discovery and Service Invocation Protocol and P2P Streaming Protocol.

Example of Protocol Sequence

Figure 12 shows a basic sequence when a peer-to-peer node participates in a peer-to-peer network. At first, Node A sends a Lookfor message using network specific broadcast or multicast mechanisms (e.g. IP multicast) and receives the corresponding LookforResponse messages from certain nodes. Then, Node A sends a Hello message to one of discovered nodes (Node B) to participate in a peer-to-peer network. When a HelloResponse Message from Node B is received, a peer-to-peer session is established between Node A and Node

B. Resource information will be exchanged using Resource Information Advertisement messages in the next step.

Prototype Implementation

We have currently implemented a prototype, which is developed in Java (J2SE 1.4.2, 2003) on Microsoft Windows XP and Linux (Fedora Core 3). This prototype provides the basic functions of the peer-to-peer protocols and some utility tools. The protocol APIs have been provided for application developers.

Figure 12. An Example of Sequence

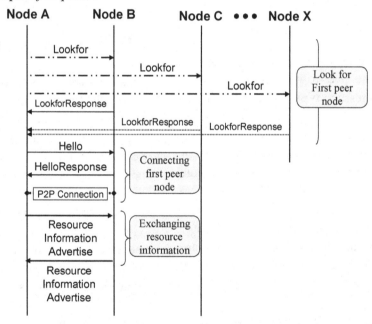

Figure 13. Peer-to-peer networking platform software architecture

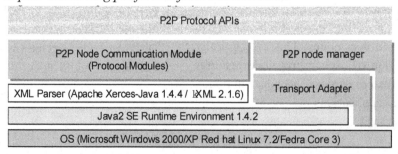

Applications for Mobile Phones

To demonstrate the effectiveness of our platform, we developed various applications over it, toward creating a ubiquitous communication environment in which heterogeneous networks and heterogeneous devices coexist. Applications for mobile phones among them include multimedia content search for mobile phones (Sumino et al., 2003), instant messaging over Bluetooth between mobile phones (Sumino et al., 2004), and home appliance applications from mobile phones (Tsutsui et al., 2007; Sumino et al., 2007). Some of these applications are described briefly in this section.

Multimedia Content Search for Mobile Phones

In recent years, mobile phones that handle multimedia content such as music, picture, and JAVA content have been widely developed and deployed. As the number of multimedia contents is increasing, the demand for search engines that can effectively find multimedia content is becoming greater among mobile phone users. However, most of the current search engines extract text information from Web pages to make search index, and do not work effectively for multimedia content search.

The use of metadata is one of the approaches to realize multimedia content search and there have been some standardization efforts such as MPEG-7 (MPEG-7, 2002) or Dublin Core (Dublin Core, 1995). Since it is possible to describe the semantics of the content by using metadata, the use of metadata makes the search result more precise. W3C has been standardizing RDF (Lassila et al., 1999) as a framework and a language for describing metadata. Such metadata may be exchanged among distributed search engines over a peer-to-peer network.

Using our networking platform, we have implemented prototype software. Our system is designed based on RDF to make multimedia content search more effective and precise. Then, the prototype system consists of distributed search nodes and the proxy node for mobile phones over the peer-to-peer network. Since current mobile phones use HTTP to access the Internet, we cannot directly implement P2P protocols on mobile phones. Therefore, our architecture defines a proxy node for mobile phones as shown in Figure 14. The proxy node provides HTML/HTTP interface for mobile phones when a mobile phone user accesses to it. The proxy node is also connected to the peer-to-peer network, and communicates with peer-to-peer nodes using the P2P protocols. The Proxy node can also act as

Figure 14. System architecture

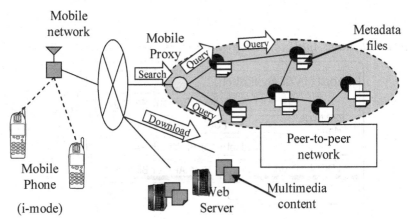

385

peer-to-peer nodes on behalf of multiple mobile phones simultaneously.

In the concept of Semantic Web, metadata that correspond to the indexes of Web contents are distributed on Web servers. In the same way, a peer-to-peer node in our system stores the metadata of content, but does not always store the content itself in the same system. The metadata of content is uploaded to the database of a search engine on a peer-to-peer node. The search engine searches its database and the location of the content is indicated by the search result. When a mobile phone user requests a multimedia content search, the proxy node extracts the search information from it and translates it into a RDF query message and forwards it to peer-to-peer nodes. When receiving the query message, the peer-to-peer node retrieves its database, to find metadata that satisfies the search condition. At the same time, the peer-to-peer node propagates the query message to the adjacent peer-to-peer nodes. We use the RSSDB (Alexaki et al., 2001) developed by ICS-FORTH as the metadata database.

From our experience with this system, there is a possibility that peer-to-peer metadata search systems could provide more flexible and powerful search functionalities with lower maintenance cost and are more suitable for multimedia content search, as compared to existing server-based keyword search systems.

Instant Messaging over Bluetooth among mobile phones

Many people are using Instant Messaging (IM) services throughout the Internet. Existing IM services are provided by IM servers that manage IM users on the Internet. Those services require IM users to be connected to the Internet and registered with the servers. However, since a user is not always able to access the Internet, there has been demand for IM systems that support ad-hoc network environments where IM servers do not exist. As one approach to realizing an IM service for ad-hoc network environments, the peer-to-peer approach appears to be attractive, because IM users exchange instant messages directly each other, and there is no need to prepare a server in advance.

Using our peer-to-peer networking platform, we have implemented the multicast IM system over Bluetooth for mobile phones. The basic operations of the proposed IM system are as follows. When an IM user participates in a peer-to-peer network and starts the IM service, or when an IM user updates its presence information, the presence information is notified to other IM users over the peer-to-peer network. In most peer-to-peer applications, proxy servers are used to support mobile phones since capabilities of mobile phones are limited. However, peer-to-peer communication via proxy is not effective and not suitable for communication on ad-hoc networking environments. Therefore, we

Figure 15. Instant Message Application software architecture

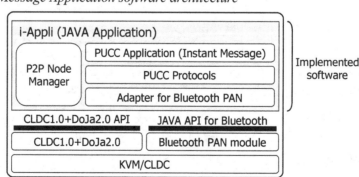

have designed and implemented the P2P protocol for mobile phones, in order to directly realize peer-to-peer communications between mobile phones without having a proxy server.

Software architecture of the prototype system is shown in Figure 15. The mobile phone supports JAVA API for bluetooth communication. The Bluetooth Personal Area Network (PAN) profile, which supports TCP or UDP, is used for underlying networks. In this study, we use 4 mobile phones and each is connected as shown in Figure 16. PAN User (PANU) and Group ad-hoc Network (GN) are roles defined in the Bluetooth PAN profile. A GN can only connect with a PANU, and likewise a PANU can only connect with a GN. Therefore, 3 PANU nodes are connected with one GN node in this case. Since a peer-to-peer network is constructed over a Bluetooth network, the connections between peer-to-peer nodes are independent of the underlying Bluetooth connections.

The proposed IM application is very attractive since it realizes communication over ad-hoc networks without using an IM server.

Home Appliance Application from mobile phones

Since the proposal of home networks in the 1990s, there have been various attempts at standardization and product development. With the advanced functions that information appliances have begun to offer in recent years, however, we can expect that home networks will finally come into wide use. A very important factor in encouraging the widespread use of home networks is inter-connectivity of devices, and there has been progress in standardization for audio-visual (AV) home electronics, home appliances and other such individual devices. Now, the evolution of mobile phones has focused attention on using mobile phones to control home appliances. This situation motivated our research and development of technology for unified control various home appliances over home networks from a mobile phone, which may range from AV home electronics and home devices such as door phones and electronic keys, etc. This technology enables the use of a mobile phone for remote operation, such as turning on air conditioners and other devices before returning home, and checking to make sure that the front door is locked, thus increasing even further the usability of a mobile phone as a device for creating new Life-Style.

Various standards have been established for different classes of home appliances over home networks, e.g. DLNA/UPnP (DLNA, 2003), ECHONET (ECHONET, 2000), Open Service Gateway Initiative (OSGi, 1999) and High-Definition Multimedia Interface (HDMI, 2002).

Universal Plug and Play (UPnP) is a technology that allows the use of standard Internet technology for connections between networked devices. The Digital Living Network Alliance (DLNA) has been established to develop guidelines for the sharing of video and other digital content by home appliances, personal computers, and mobile devices through the use of UPnP and other standard Internet technology. Digital media players (DMP), which present content for display devices, use a protocol such as Simple Service Discovery Protocol (SSDP) to discover digital media servers (DMS) or other such servers that have content, and retrieve a list from a Content Directory Service (CDS). Then the request for desired content is sent and the

Figure 16. Communication among mobile phones

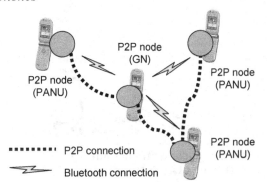

content is streamed from the server via the LAN to the display device for viewing it.

Energy Conservation and Homecare Network (ECHONET) is a standard for controlling air conditioners, lighting, and other home appliances and facility devices such as power consumption monitors and other sensors.

Open Services Gateway Initiative (OSGi) was founded in March 1999 and has since been working on developing standards for controlling home gateway functions from remote servers. OSGi middleware, which is installed on a home gateway, is running over Java VM, and enables the home gateway to extend its functions by dynamically downloading Java components called bundles from the servers of bundle providers.

High-Definition Multimedia Interface (HDMI) is a high-speed interface specification for AV devices that can transmit HiVision video streams, allowing the sharing of high-quality content between devices. It is equipped with High-bandwidth Digital Content Protection system (HDCP) copyright protection technology for preventing the unauthorized copying of content. HDMI can also be used as interface technology for Blu-ray or other next-generation DVD devices.

As a single HDMI cable can transmit video, audio and control information at the same time, coordinated control of products connected by HDMI interface is possible. For example, by using the remote controller of a Blu-ray player, a user can simultaneously turn on both the TV and the Blu-ray player at the same time. However, two serious issues regarding current standards for home appliances are described as followed (Figure 17).

Issue 1: Incompatibility among standards for different classes of home appliances

The current situation is that there exists no compatibility among the various specifications for home appliances. To control home appliances that comply with different specifications of a mobile phone, a mobile phone must also support multiple specifications for home appliances. However, current mobile phones cannot support multiple standards for home appliances due to their limited processing capability and memory capacity.

Issue 2: No means of remote access to home networks from a mobile phone

Figure 17. Issues regarding remote access to home networks from a mobile phone

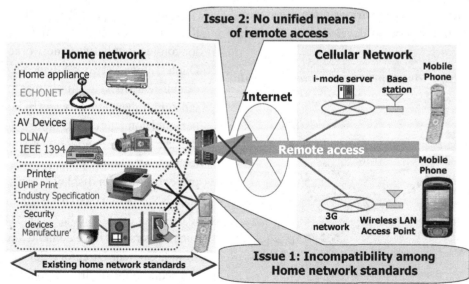

From the mobile phone point of view, it is very important for a mobile phone to be able to remotely control home appliances over a home network via a cellular network. Current standards for home appliance do not however provide such functions.

To solve these issues, we have applied peer-to-peer/overlay networking technologies to unify the control of various classes of home appliances from a mobile phone via a cellular network.

As shown in Fig 18, we developed peer-to-peer application protocols (i.e. Device Discovery and Service Invocation Protocol) to control various home appliances over various underlying transport networks such as cellular network, Bluetooth, Institute of Electrical and Electronics Engineers

Figure 18. Protocol stack for the home appliance applications

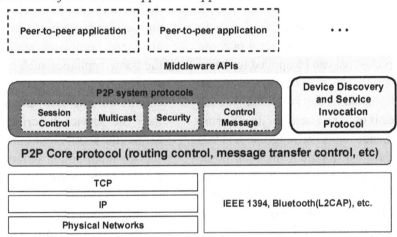

Figure 19. Device Discovery and Service Invocation Protocol

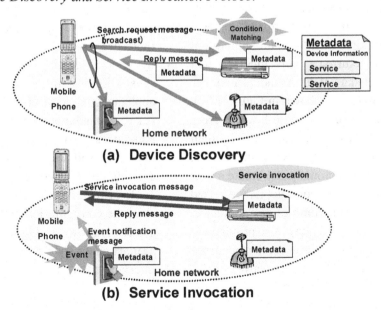

(a) **Device Discovery**

(b) **Service Invocation**

1394 (IEEE 1394, 1999), OBEX/IrDA and TCP/IP.

To control home appliances that are connected to a home network, it is first necessary to discover a home appliance that is connected to the network, the characteristics of the home appliance and the services that it offers.

Protocols for executing the various services offered by the home appliance are also required. We have therefore defined a device discovery and service invocation protocol as a P2P application protocol for controlling home appliances from a mobile phone.

An overview of this protocol is shown in Figure 19. This protocol uses general-purpose metadata templates that can be applied to define characteristics and services of various home appliances. The metadata that is defined for each home appliance is used as a basis for discovering the home appliance and executing the services it offers. As shown in Figure 17(a), each home appliance on a home network has metadata that describes its characteristics and the services it offers. A user searches for home appliances by broadcasting a search request message over the home network. This search request message contains search condition parameters such as characteristics of home appliances and key words (e.g. TV). Each home appliance that receives the search request message compares its own metadata description with the search condition parameters and returns a reply message that contains the metadata if its metadata matches the search condition. As shown in Figure 17(b), the user selects the service to be invoked from the services described in the metadata and then request the home appliance to execute the service. A mobile phone may automatically create a user interface for controlling a home appliance, based on the metadata received from the home appliance. An event notification function is also provided to inform a mobile phone of the event that occurred to a home appliance (e.g. security alarm).

The metadata describes the home appliance name, type, attributes and the services the home appliance offers in Extensible Markup Language (XML) format. The various functions provided by the home appliance are defined as service lists included in the metadata. When defining a service, it is possible to define it as a series of operations. For example, a "view video" service could be defined as a series of three operations (i.e. "the TV be turned on", "the input set to video" and "the video player be turned on"). Each service has a unique URI (Uniform Resource Identifier), and that URI is used as an ID for service discovery and service invocation. The metadata of a home appliance comprises static information about the home appliance such as the name and type, state variables that may be related with event conditions, a service list and a primitive device list. The service description of a service list defines the service name and the data types of the service input-output parameters. The primitive devices are used to define individual components in multi-function devices, such HDD recorders. Multi-function device metadata is defined as a combination of primitive device metadata.

The proposed metadata is compatible with UPnP and ECHONET metadata to ensure interconnectivity with UPnP/ECHONET-compliant devices, and has been extensible for other home appliances as well. It can be therefore used to express functions defined by various existing home network standards, thus allowing interconnectivity with home appliances that conform to different existing home network standards. When controlling such home appliances, a home gateway converts our device discovery and service invocation protocol into existing home appliance control protocols.

To provide an example of the protocol conversion, the configuration of an AV device control system is shown in Figure 20. In this example, a smart phone (hTc Z, etc.) with a wireless LAN interface connects to the home gateway via the

Figure 20. Configuration of the AV device control system

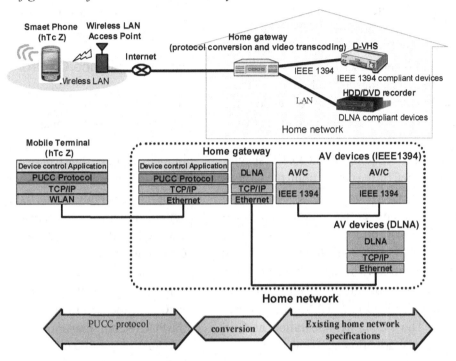

wireless LAN to view a video stored on a DLNA-compliant HDD/DVD recorder or an IEEE1394-compliant Data Video Home System (D-VHS) player that reside on the home network. In this configuration, our device discovery and service invocation protocol is used between the mobile terminal and the home gateway, and the home gateway converts from our protocol to the existing protocols such as IEEE 1394 Audio Video/Control (AV/C) commands or UPnP protocols.

PUCC Activities

PUCC (Peer-to-peer Universal Computing consortium) (Saito et al., 2007) was established in December 2004, to deploy our P2P protocols and its networking platform, and encourage PUCC members to develop applications over it. PUCC has 17 industry members (e.g. NTT DoCoMo, Ericsson, Hitachi, Toshiba, EPSON) and 9 university members (e.g. Keio University, Kyoto University) as of March 2008. PUCC did several demonstra-

tions at CES 2008 and other exhibitions, which include viewing DLNA contents from a mobile phone, controlling security camera from a mobile phone and controlling a projector from a mobile phone, with the support of Japan External Trade Organization (JETRO).

Overview of PUCC

PUCC is a consortium that was established for the development of peer-to-peer overlay networking technology for the interconnection and operation of various devices through cooperation with the various vendors of home appliances, printers, home gateways, mobile phone middleware etc, with network operators and others in the communication industry, and with universities that conduct basic technological research.

The PUCC consortium has multiple working groups for cooperating with relevant organizations to study specifications and conduct verification experiments concerning specific topics. The 13 specifications were developed as the first version of the PUCC Architecture and PUCC Protocol Specifications in September 2007. The home appliances controlling technology developed by DoCoMo and others described in previous section was adopted for the base technology of those specifications, and the comments of vendors and other relevant parties were reflected in the PUCC specifications.

To verify the technology of the PUCC specifications developed by the consortium, the various vendors and network operators cooperated to conduct verification experiments with implementations of the PUCC protocols for mobile phones and home gateways and so on. The prototypes used in the experiments have been exhibited annually at prominent home appliance exhibitions in Japan and abroad (CEATEC in JAPAN, International CES, etc.). The PUCC demonstration at CES 2008 drew great attention as a new technology developed in Japan from major media around the world, including the media in Europe and the US, and the PUCC booth attracted over 1500 visitors during the exhibition.

PUCC Verification Experiments

Some of the verification experiments related to applications for mobile phones developed by

PUCC are described later. These demonstration systems were also exhibited at prominent exhibitions such as CES 2008.

Home Appliance Control

An overview of the prototype system for home appliances control from a mobile phone is shown in Figure 21. The prototype system involves i-mode phones, smart phones (e.g. M1000), or other such mobile phones to control ECHONET-compliant air conditioners, lights, and other home appliances via a home gateway. An i-mode phone connects to the home gateway remotely via the cellular network and M1000 directly connects to the home gateway via a wireless LAN. The home gateway implements functions for converting the PUCC protocol to the ECHONET protocol, and the PUCC-compliant mobile phone could control ECHONET-compliant home appliances via the PUCC/ECHONET gateway.

AV Streaming

An overview of the prototype system for AV equipment control from a mobile phone is shown in Figure22. This prototype system involves the functions for the transfer of video content that is stored in a DLNA-compliant HDD/DVD recorder or an IEEE1394-compliant D-VHS video

Figure 21.Prototype system (Home appliance Control)

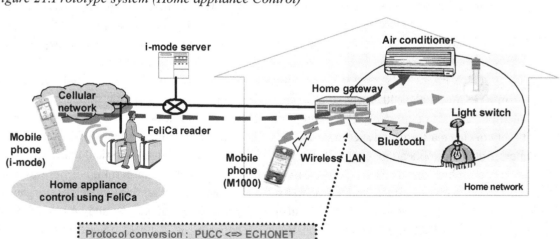

player on a home network via the home gateway to a mobile phone for viewing the content. The PUCC protocol is implemented on an hTc Z smart phone, which retrieves the content list and controls content play, fast-forward, and rewind. Its Control is performed by the PUCC protocol between the smart phone and the home gateway, and the home gateway converts the PUCC protocol to the IEEE 1394-compliant protocol for the D-VHS video player and to the DLNA-compliant protocol for the HDD/DVD recorder. The PUCC protocol establishes the PUCC session between the mobile phone and the home gateway, and controls the AV devices via the home gateway. The video streaming is done between the home gateway and the smart phone with an existing Real-time Transport Protocol (RTP, etc.). The home gateway transcodes the MPEG-2 encoded content in the AV devices to MPEG-4 encoded content for the transmission to the smart phone.

Home Security

An overview of the prototype system for controlling security cameras from a mobile phone is shown in Figure 23. This prototype system involves reception of video streaming from a home security camera for monitoring it on a mo-

bile phone. The operations for a security camera such as orientation zoom level and other settings can be controlled from the mobile phone. This technology allows real-time video monitoring of situations in the home through the remote control of security cameras from a mobile terminal when triggered by an intrusion sensor.

Related Works

Peer-to-Peer Networking Platform

JXTA (JXTA, 2001) is probably the most well-known general-propose peer-to-peer networking platform; our design goals are similar to those of JXTA. Both are aimed at a general peer-to-peer networking platform for developing peer-to-peer applications, providing a set of functionalities needed by the applications, and being independent of particular peer-to-peer applications, programming languages, operating systems and network devices (PC or PDA etc.). JXTA has a service-oriented architecture that uses the concept of metadata advertisement from peer nodes. Similarly, the PUCC platform also uses device metadata for device discovery and service execution. However, the PUCC platform is closer to Jini than JXTA because the main use cases of PUCC

Figure 22. Prototype system (AV Device Control and Video Streaming)

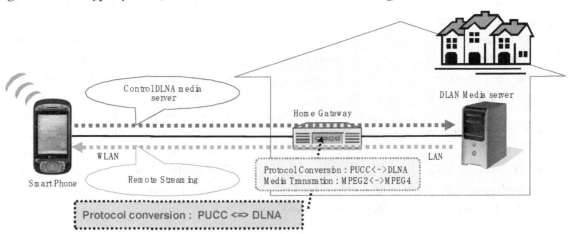

Figure 23. Prototype system (Security Camera Control)

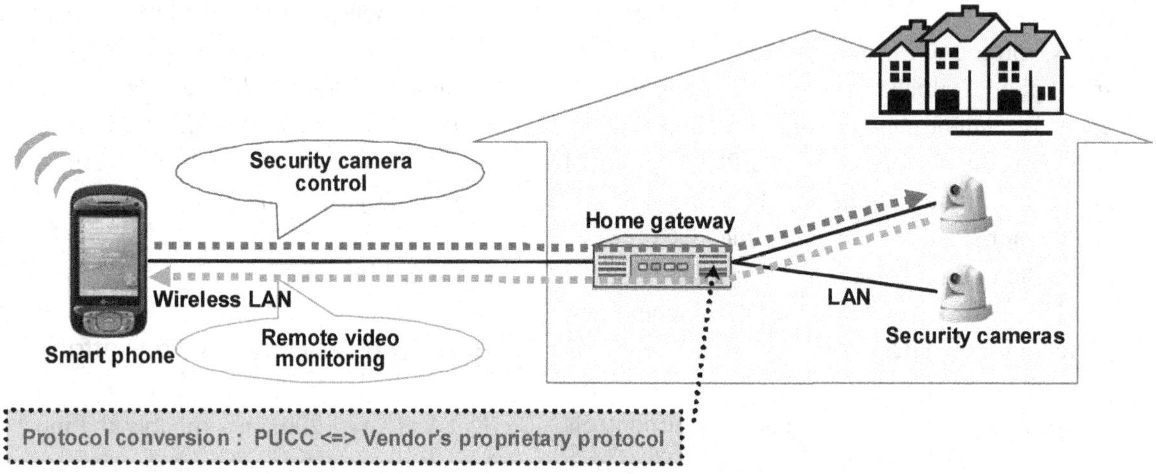

platform are home appliance control applications as described in the previous sections. Unlike Jini, PUCC platform is compatible with existing home network standards (e.g. DLNA, ECHONET). We implemented a gateway function for them. By introducing the PUCC platform, we can resolve incompatibility issues among standards for different classes of home appliances.

MyNet (Kalofonos, 2008) is a data sharing platform among personal devices such as mobile phones. Data sharing application is also a use case of PUCC platform. In addition, MyNet may be built on PUCC platform as an application. Windows P2P infrastructure (Mueller, 2007) is a P2P networking platform and API for windows OS. Different from the PUCC networking platform is that the windows P2P infrastructure is based on windows OS and Internet infrastructure such as TCP/IP. PUCC platform is independent of transport layer protocol and work on both internet and non-IP network such as Bluetooth and IrDA.

DHT Routing in Peer-to-Peer Network

The Distributed Hash Table (DHT) has been proposed as an efficient routing mechanism for structured peer-to-peer networks. Pastry (Row-stron, 2001) and Tapestry (Zhao, 2001) use the Plaxton algorithm (Plaxton, 1997) and a prefix-based lookup protocol. They design the network topology to reduce the routing latency. CAN and Chord use a modified Plaxton algorithm. CAN (Ratnasamy, 2001) uses an n-dimensional torus model to implement a distributed hash table that associates keys with values. In CAN, a node occupies a zone which is part of a Cartesian coordinate space. A node forwards a query message to a node that occupies an adjoining zone. Chord (Stoica, 2001) uses a one-dimensional cyclic identifier space. Each node has node list which contains adjacent nodes and nodes which are several hops away. The deficiency of structured peer-to-peer network is that a network is reconstructed when a node joins or leaves and its const if not negligible. These DHT routing methods are applicable to our peer-to-peer networking platform for resource discovery, including efficient node discovery, service discovery and so on. We plan to apply DHT to not only content search, but also to other applications such as collaboration among mobile phones. We will investigate and determine which DHT algorithm is the most suitable for our peer-to-peer architecture.

REFERENCES

Alexaki, S., & Tolle, K. (2001) The ICS-FORTH RDF suite: Managing voluminous RDF description bases. In *Proceedings of the 2nd International Workshop on Semantic Web.*

Bluetooth. (1999). *Bluetooth.com: The official Bluetooth technology website.* Retrieved May 30, 2008, from http://www.bluetooth.com/

Chawathe, Y., McCanne, S., & Brewer,E. A. (2000). *An architecture for internet content distribution as an infrastructure service.* Retrieved May 30, 2008, from http://citeseerx.ist.psu.edu/viewdoc/summary?doi=10.1.1.35.1680

Chu, Y., Rao, S.G., & Zhang H. (2000). A case for end system multicast. In *Proceedings of the ACM SIGMETRICS International Conference on Measurement and Modeling of Computer Systems.*

Clarke I., Sandberg O., Wiley B., & Hong T. W. (2000). Freenet: A distributed anonymous information storage and retrieval system. In *Proceedings of the ICSI Workshop on Design Issues in Anonymity and Unobservability.*

DLNA. (2003). *DLNA home networked device interoperability guidelines.* Retrieved May 30, 2008, from http://www.dlna.org

Dublin Core Metadata Initiative. (1995). *Dublin Core Metadata Initiative (DCMI).* Retrieved May 30, 2008, from http://dublincore.org/

ECHONET Consortium. (2000). Retrieved May 30, 2008, from http://www.echonet.gr.jp/english/

Gnutella. (2001). *The Gnutella protocol specification v0.4.* Retrieved May 30 2008, from http://www9.limewire.com/developer/gnutella_protocol_0.4.pdf

HDMI. (2002). Retrieved May 30, 2008, from http://www.hdmi.org/

IEEE 1394. (1994). *1394 Trade Association.* Retrieved May 30, 2008, from http://www.1394ta.org/

Ishikawa, N., et al. (2007). PUCC architecture, protocols and applications. In *Proceedings of the 4th IEEE Consumer Communications and Networking Conference.*

Jannotti, J., Gifford, D. K., Johnson, K. L., Kaashoek, M. F., & O'Toole, J. W., Jr. (2000). Overcast: Reliable multicasting with an overlay network. In *Proceedings of the 4th Symposium on Operating System Design and Implementation.*

Johnson, D. B., Maltz, D. A., & Hu. Y. C. (2006). The dynamic source routing protocol for mobile ad hoc networks (DSR). *IETF MANET Working Group: draft-ietf-manet-dsr-10.txt.*

Java J2SE 1.4.2. (2003). Sun *Microsystems Java2 standard edition version 1.4.2.* Retrieved May 30, 2008, from http://java.sun.com/j2se/1.4/

JXTA. (2001). *Sun Microsystems project JXTA.* Retrieved May 30, 2008, from http://wwwjxta.org/

Kalofonos, D. N., Antoniou, Z., Reynolds, F. D., Van-Kleek, M., Strauss, J., & Wisner, P. (2008). MyNet: A platform for secure P2P personal and social networking services. In *Proceedings of the 6th Annual IEEE International Conference on Pervasive Computing and Communications (PerCom).*

KaZaa. (2002). Retrieved September 29, 2008, from http://www.kazaa.com/us/index.htm

Kousiur, D. (1999). *IP multicasting: The complete guide to interactive corporate networks.* New York: John Wiley & Sons, Inc.

Lassila, O., Swick, R. (1999). Resource Description Framework (RDF) Model and Syntax Specification. *W3C Recommendation, http://www.w3.org/TR/1999/REC-rdf-syntax-19990222.*

Leach, P.J., & Salz, R.. (1998). *UUIDs and GUIDs; draft-leach-uuids-guids-01.txt* (Expired). Retrieved March 9, 2009, from http://www.open-group.org/dce/info/draft-leach-uuids-guids-01.txt

Microsoft Corporation. (2000). *Microsoft Office Groove.* Retrieved May 30, 2008, from http://office.microsoft.com/ja-jp/groove/default.aspx

MPEG-7. (2002). *The MPEG-7 standard ISO/IEC 15938.*

Mueller, U., Young, M., & Gefflaut, A. (2007). Running the Windows P2P infrastructure on mobile phones. In *Proceedings of the 7ᵗʰ IEEE International Conference on Peer-to-Peer Computing.*

Open Service Gateway Initiative. (2003). *The OSGi service platform specification, release 3.*

OSGi Alliance. (1999). Retrieved May 30, 2008, from http://www.osgi.org/Main/HomePage

Peer-to-peer Universal Computing Consortium (PUCC). (2004). Retrieved May 30, 2008, from http://www.pucc.jp

Plaxton, C., Rajaram, R., & Richa, A.W. (1997). Accessing nearby copies of replicated objects in a distributed environment. In *Proceedings of the 9ᵗʰ Annual ACM Symposium on Parallel Algorithms and Architectures.*

Ratnasamy, S., Francis, P., Handley, M., Karp, R., & Shenker, S. (2001). A scalable content-addressable network. In *Proceedings of ACM SIGCOMM Conference on Applications, Technologies, Architectures, and Protocols for Computer Communications.*

Rowstron A., & Druschel P. (2001). Pastry: Scalable distributed object location and routing for large-scale peer-to-peer systems. In *Proceedings*

of the 18ᵗʰ IFIP/ACM International Conference on Distributed System Platforms.*

Saito, N., & Kitagawa, K. (2007). Overview of Peer-to-Peer Universal Computing Consortium (PUCC): Background, current status and future plan. In *Proceedings of 4ᵗʰ IEEE Consumer Communications and Networking Conference.*

Stoica, I., Morris, R., Karger, D., Kaashoek, M.F., & Balakrishnan, H. (2001). Chord: A scalable peer-to-peer lookup service for Internet applications. In *Proceedings of ACM SIGCOMM Conference on Applications, Technologies, Architectures, and Protocols for Computer Communications.*

Sumino, H., et al. (2003). A mobile multimedia content search using RDF. In *Proceedings of the 4ᵗʰ International Conference on Mobile Data Management.*

Sumino, H., et al. (2004). Design and implementation of a multicast instant messaging system on the mobile P2P network. In *Proceedings of the 1ˢᵗ International Conference on Mobile Computing and Ubiquitous Networking (ICMU).*

Sumino, H., et al. (2007). Home appliance control from mobile phones. In *Proceedings of the 4ᵗʰ IEEE Consumer Communications and Networking Conference (CCNC).*

Tsutsui, H., et al. (2007). Implementation of AV streaming system using peer-to-peer communication. In *Proceedings of 4ᵗʰ IEEE Consumer Communications and Networking Conference.*

UPnP Forum. (1999). Retrieved May 30, 2008, from http://www.upnp.org

Zhao, B. Y., Kubiatowicz, J., & Joseph, A. D. (2001). *Tapestry: An infrastructure for fault-tolerant wide-area location and routing.* Retrieved May 30, 2008, from http://cs-www.cs.yale.edu/homes/arvind/cs425/doc/tapestry.pdf

Chapter XVIII
Evaluation Platform for Large–Scale P2P Mobile Ad–hoc Networks

Raphaël Kummer
University of Neuchâtel, Switzerland

Peter Kropf
University of Neuchâtel, Switzerland

Jean-Frédéric Wagen
TIC Institute, University of Applied Sciences of Fribourg, Switzerland

Timothée Maret
TIC Institute, University of Applied Sciences of Fribourg, Switzerland

ABSTRACT

Many innovative P2P algorithms designed for mobile ad-hoc networks (MANETs) have been designed to scale smoothly when handling a very large number of nodes and transmissions. To cope with the complexity of software development for large-scale MANETs, simulations are widely used instead because hardware implementations are too costly. Simulations are very well suited to testing and evaluating concepts, but when implementing algorithms for testing on target systems, unexpected problems can often surface. Thus, once simulations have provided satisfactory results, emulation is a more desirable approach for detecting and handling unexpected behavior before committing to large-scale deployment. In particular, given that large P2P testbeds require a large number of devices spread over a prohibitive space and are limited by complex programming models, the authors are featuring a Java-based emulator called Freemote. To demonstrate some of the practical advantages of combining simulation and emulation, Freemote makes it possible to integrate real and emulated nodes, and the real nodes (JMotes) run exactly the same Java programs as emulated nodes. Since the JMotes are still not very widely used, the

Freemote emulator and JMotes have been designed to be compatible with the more popular Berkeley's motes. Furthermore, remarkable visualization and development tools have been implemented to undertake large-scale emulation of ad-hoc algorithms, featuring a high level of realism. Freemote has been tested in emulations for up to 10,000 nodes, distributed over ten computers (refer to a preceding chapter of this book "P2P Information Lookup, Collection and Distribution in Mobile Ad-Hoc Network" for a test application running DHT algorithms). In this chapter, the authors present the Freemote platform along with the results of a brief comparison of emulation and simulation experiments.

INTRODUCTION

P2P systems first emerged as overlays stacked on top of the Internet for many useful applications including file sharing, VoIP, distributed data storage (Freenet), collaborative tools, etc. (Khan & Wierzbicki, 2008). Their success is usually based on the peer-to-peer property intrinsic to the Internet, providing transmission routes between end-nodes. In MANETs, the situation is different because end-nodes can also act as routers; or more precisely wireless routers. This means that each end-node/router has at least one wireless link to all physical neighbors defined by its radio coverage area. MANETs also differ from the classical Internet because their wireless links are usually much less reliable than fixed links, and are often impaired by congestion. Also, assumptions generally made regarding bidirectional links may not be true, given differences between nodes caused by implementations, remaining battery power levels, time variances, physical environments, etc. Finally each end-node/router's participation also varies in time in certain cases, due to its joining or leaving the MANET for a variety of reasons: changes in geographical position, turning itself off for some period of time to reduce power consumption, etc. The MANET node's wireless router role can however be seen as an advantage, and for this reason many innovative algorithms have been designed for them. One possible goal for these algorithms is to ensure smooth scaling when applied to very large number of nodes and transmissions. Simulations must often be used however to evaluate P2P/MANETs applications, given the difficulty and expense involved

in deploying a real, large-scale testing network. Also, monitoring of nodes in a real network is a time-consuming and complex task, given that nodes are usually distributed geographically, communicate over changing routes and might only provide few output modalities (often limited to a few LEDs) used to track execution, even during testing phases. Moreover, the deployment an ad-hoc network in real size for testing purposes requires extensive resources: equipment, space, time and manpower. Thus, since this phase cannot usually be actually conducted it may in some cases be replaced by specially designed software tools and frameworks able to run repeatable experiments in controlled environments or provide meaningful numerical values based on averages and statistical analyses. Due to time and resource constraints however, even experiments such as these cannot be always conducted.

Once a P2P algorithm has been designed and its performance demonstrated analytically or through simulation, it would be ideal to take the proposed algorithm's source code and simply port it and run in an environment closer to reality, but without the irreproducible effects encountered in real environments. The same source code would have to be used to avoid any potential differences between the specifications and implementation.

With the afore-mentioned facts in mind, we developed the Freemote emulator in order to provide a suitable platform on which to test P2P applications and algorithms designed for MANETs of any size (a few or several thousands nodes). To ensure their practical suitability and behavior credibility in the simulated environment, we decided to link the emulated nodes with real nodes, thus forming an integrated ad-hoc network environment. These capabilities were thought to be the most important ones compared to other last-step performance evaluations preceding full-scale deployment in a real environment. Thus, to facilitate many aspects related to software development we chose the Java language. This choice is also justified given the availability of Java programmable *JMote* prototypes developed at the University of Applied Sciences in Fribourg (http://www.eia-fr.ch). This Freemote emulator is able to run the same Java source code on the real and emulated nodes, thus bringing experimental results closer to reality.

Given that Java programmed nodes are not widely used, we chose a transmission format compatible with the popular Berkeley motes programmed using the nesC programming language (nesC, 2008). This internodes communication is in fact based on the TinyOS (TinyOS, 2008) message format, allowing the well-known MICAZ and TelosB Berkeley type nodes to be used as real nodes.

This mixing of emulated and real nodes was carried out via a "bridge" node attached to the workstation running the emulation. The emulated and real nodes communicate over this dedicated bridge, which operates as a normal node during the experiment. The real nodes could be any nodes compatible with the bridge node. At the physical level, the current Freemote system uses hardware based on any IEEE 802.15.4 compliant radio chip, and can thus handle both our Java nodes (*JMote*) and the well-known Berkeley motes.

To ensure Freemote emulation system's scalability, emulated nodes can be distributed on many workstations connected in a LAN in a classic configuration (i.e. TCP/IP). Experiments have shown that the Freemote system is able to support emulated systems having up to 10,000 nodes, distributed over a number of networked computers. The maximum number of nodes is currently defined by the addressing scheme chosen, set at 65,536 addresses. The Freemote software also includes a Graphical User Interface (GUI), thus making it possible to set up the desired experiment in an intuitive manner and easily follow the emulation using the information provided.

To learn more about an application using the Freemote emulator, see the companion chapter entitled: "P2P Information Lookup, Collection and Distribution in Mobile Ad-Hoc Networks." The Freemote system is also readily available on the Internet (Freemote, 2008) and can be tuned or modified to allow experiment with any P2P algorithms or applications designed for networks having "small" nodes or motes.

This chapter on our Freemote testbed is organized as follows. The *P2P mobile ad-hoc system testbeds* section reviews background information about MANET simulators and emulators, as well as their suitability for P2P applications. The *Wireless ad-hoc network emulation environment* section gives a detailed description of the Freemote emulator system. Sample results comparing the Freemote emulator with a dedicated simulator are presented in the *FreeMote emulator validation* section. Finally, the chapter is summarized in the *Conclusion* section.

P2P MOBILE AD-HOC SYSTEM TESTBEDS

This section presents an overview of the various approaches related to MANET simulations and emulations, and also discusses their suitability for P2P applications.

Although numerous tools are available for analyzing P2P and MANET applications, none of them is suitable for all the experiments being carried out by researchers. We thus have to select the tool that will provide the most realistic results for a specific setup. As pointed out in (Göktürk, 2007), these tools can be classified into three categories, according to their level of realism, which varies from less accurate simulators to emulators and finally to highly accurate testbeds.

Current tools available for evaluating MANET algorithms include real Berkeley mote networks such as Emulab (Johnson et al., 2006) and Motelab (Werner-Allen, Swieskowski, & Welsh, 2005). One instance of these networks can be shared between many research teams, with each one remotely controlling and using the network during a given number of hours or days. These tools provide useful features that help reduce the time needed for experimental setups and allow scenarios to be reproduced during experiments, given that a node's motion and initial position can be configured. P2P experiments carried out with the help of these tools resemble real situations quite closely but only involve a relatively small number of nodes.

ATEMU (Polley, Blazakis, McGee, Rusk, & Baras, 2004), Avrora (Titzer, Lee, & Palsberg, 2005) and MSPsim (Eriksson, Dunkels, Finne, Osterlind, & Voigt, 2007) are "fine-grain simulators" which operate at the instruction level through simulating Berkeley mote processor instruction sets such as the MSP430 or AVR chip family. Experiments with these simulators can handle several hardware setup variations, including aspects related to timing or power consumption, and can also provide highly accurate evaluation results. However, they require high computational power and provide only basic visualization tools. Thus "fine-grain simulators" are usually too detailed to investigate P2P applications over a large MANET. TOSSIM (Levis, Lee, Welsh, & Culler, 2003) is a step-by-step discrete event simulator for TinyOS applications which when coupled with TinyViz makes for an extensible visualization tool. It runs an unmodified NesC code application and simulates the TinyOS behavior of those components tied to hardware. Although TOSSIM has some of the same drawbacks mentioned before, it is useful for testing the basic functionalities of node software for a given P2P application, but not for investigating overall behavior across a complete network.

The EMStar (Girod et al., 2007), SENS (Sundresh, Wooyoung, & Agha, 2004) and COOJA (Osterlind, Dunkels, Eriksson, Finne, & Voigt, 2006) more closely resemble the Freemote emulator environment previous ones, as they provide a less accurate simulation model for the low level and radio parts. Moreover, they focus more on network behavior analyses than on time-based performance evaluations. SENS is similar to the Freemote emulator, providing a layered and modular environment able to run applications (composed of interchangeable modules) written in C++. Also, the code written for the emulated nodes is not directly executable on real nodes but must be ported to Berkeley motes. Not only does SENS use a different programming language (C++ instead of Java), it differs from the Freemote emulator in that it does not support any bridges to real nodes.

COOJA (Osterlind et al., 2006) is a Java-based simulator for the popular Contiki OS (Dunkels, 2008) and is able to mix simulated nodes at varying levels of detail within the same experiment. For prototyping it is able to simulate Java code, yet it is not executable on real nodes and thus must be adapted or ported. Furthermore, this simulator does not provide any bridges to real nodes, and thus the testing of P2P applications across MANETs is limited to simulated environments.

Finally the EMStar (Girod et al., 2007) runs on Linux microservers, providing an environment in which wireless network applications can be tested. EMStar provides the EmTOS facility enabling the execution of TinyOS applications written in NesC. The EMStar environment is highly versatile as it can mix microservers and emulated motes in the same experiment and can provide either simulated or real radio channels for connecting emulated nodes based on Berkeley mote arrays.

WIRELESS AD-HOC NETWORK EMULATION ENVIRONMENT

To simulate or emulate their P2P application developments using MANETs, researchers often run a set of experiments, each associated with a predefined scenario and a specific environment configuration. The scenario defines the role of each network node as well as the application being tested. The environment configuration defines the network topology and node motion. Ideally scenarios and environments are identical and reproducible from one experiment, thus allowing testing and solution comparisons against the same conditions. The type of information gathered during an experiment depends on the application being tested. Generally speaking the information required includes: (1) number of messages exchanged; (2) length of routes linking distant nodes; (3) network mean throughput and delay; (4) node power consumption; and (5) code execution time.

"Fine-grain simulators" are not suitable for assessing applications on large MANETs. They need large amounts of computational power to maintain precise execution times and to provide non-relevant details such as power and memory consumption. For large network experiments high-level simulators should be considered instead. They limit the computational power required and still provide accurate information. Simulations may however have limited credibility if the effects of implementation cannot be taken into account. Emulations on the other hand offer greater control over implementation issues but are usually limited to one or a few nodes. The Freemote emulator was thus developed to combine the advantages of simulation and emulation, mixing not only these two aspects but also allowing real nodes to participate in the simulated network of emulated nodes.

In experimental and industrial MANET deployments, while the C language or nesC may have become popular due to its hardware constraints, virtual machines (VMs) have emerged as new software environments for running applications on sensors (Barr, 2004) (Levis & Culler, 2002). While VMs are less optimized to fit the limited hardware constraints of low-cost nodes than highly optimized operating systems (e.g. TinyOS) and languages (e.g. nesC), for developers they offer numerous advantages. In fact, VMs such as Maté (Levis & Culler, 2002) or SwissQM (Müller, Alonso, & Kossmann, 2007) provide a simpler programming model, a smaller program footprint and well-defined programming interfaces, making development much simpler. These virtual machines run on top of optimized operating systems, provide extensible machine code and can support different programming languages. Although extensible, VMs have the disadvantage of providing a relatively small initial set of specialized programming functionalities. To make them more useful, programmers thus have to code special extensions for each specific application in the operating system's machine language. Highly optimized VMs have however been developed for well-known, portable and general-purpose programming languages such as Java (VM* framework (Koshy & Pandey, 2005), Squawk (Shaylor, Simon, & Bush, 2003), Sentilla Point (Sentilla Corporation, 2008)). The Freemote emulator is thus a suitable emulation tool for the emerging Java-based motes, while also running the same Java byte code on both emulated nodes and Sun's CLDC 1.0 compliant Java motes. Currently the code runs on *JMotes*, a CLDC prototype based on Java motes developed at the University of Applied Sciences in Fribourg (http://www.eia-fr.ch). Although the Java code does not run on widely popular Berkeley's motes (e.g. TelosB, MICAz), the latter can also be used as real nodes or even to bridge nodes since the message transmission format chosen is based on TinyOS messages. Thus the experiments are able to run in a highly heterogeneous set of real nodes.

Freemote Emulator

Figure 1 shows the typical deployment of an experiment conducted with the Freemote emulator. Many nodes are emulated across various Java processes distributed over different computers and linked together on a standard LAN. In each process the number of nodes emulated is only limited by the computer's available memory and addressing space, currently set to handle up to 65,536 nodes. The emulated node topology is computed by the Topology Manager server and spread to all Topology Manager clients. This client-server approach ensures experimental scalability since it allows an unlimited number of clients. These clients can be run on very powerful workstations, thus guaranteeing simulation results within a reasonable time. Each workstation contains at least a Topology Manager client but only one machine will run the GUI and the Topology Manager server.

The Freemote emulator simulates the MAC and physical radio layers in a lightweight manner, ensuring reasonable running times. The focus on behavior credibility is achieved by mixing emulated and real nodes by means of a dedicated

bridge. At the physical level, compatibility is ensured using the IEEE 802.15.4 radio standard, as in several Berkeley mote implementations.

Many P2P applications take it for granted that a physical node is accessible from any other node, as in an IP based network. With MANETs, however, routing remains a challenging research topic. The NST-AODV (Gomez, Salvatella, Alonso, & Paradells, 2006) mote implementation was used for testing purposes. A Java implementation of NST-AODV developed for the Freemote system was "optimized" for the IEEE 802.15.4 standard, because it uses MAC-level acknowledgements to detect broken routes. Our NST-AODV also implements an enhancement, enabling it to handle asymmetric radio links between nodes, as mentioned in the next section.

The Freemote emulator provides a powerful Graphical User Interface (GUI). As shown in Figure 2, it displays the emulated network during

Figure 1. Typical deployment during an experiment

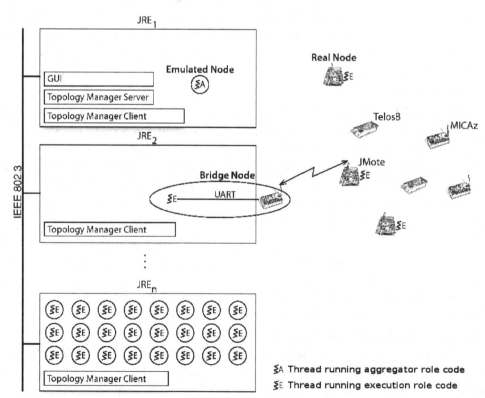

runtime and the emulated nodes are shown in a square map, showing not only the node positions and their motions but also the physical links between nodes (delimited by simple circles) and the content of the messages sent (lower part of Figure 2). The GUI also displays and records all network operations. They are output in log format and thus are useful during the development for debugging complex network issues. Execution can also be slowed down, thus making it easier to visualize network behavior (the exchange of messages for example).

As an example, Figure 2 shows the information displayed during an experiment. The bridge node is represented in the right part and the emulated nodes are shown on the left part. The gray circle represents the radio range of the node with the address 2, which is sending a DATA message. The 8 LEDs of the real *JMotes* are also displayed for each emulated node in the Freemote GUI. It is thus possible to track behavior for both the real and emulated nodes.

Software Implementation

The Freemote emulator software was designed for easy adaptation to P2P application investigations on MANETs and sensors networks. Figure 3 shows the layered architecture design along with 3 layers representing the three node types (emulated, bridge and real nodes) that might take part in an experiment. These three layers are:

1. Usual physical and data link layers merged into the lowest layer. The IEEE 802.15.4 is used for real nodes and bridge nodes on the real network side. The UDP/IP/802.3 (Ethernet) is used on the LAN side to link the emulated nodes. TCP/IP is used to control the simulation parameters (e.g., position, radio coverage, transmission error rate) of the emulated nodes.
2. Routing layer, which currently implements the afore-mentioned NST-AODV.

Figure 2. GUI with emulated node visualization tool

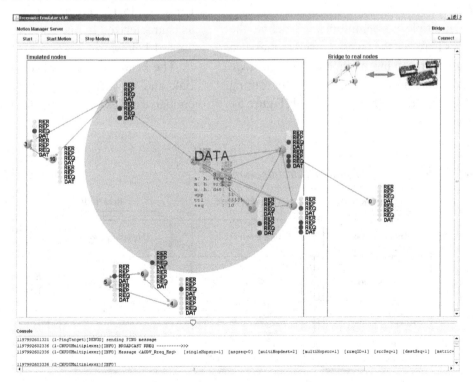

3. Classical transport and upper layers that are merged into the Freemote application layer. P2P research or MANET applications usually do not focus on end-to-end transport layers.

As usual the layered approach allows new sets of experiments to be built by mostly reusing code already developed. A cross-layer design is still possible since the developer retains full control of the interface between layers (Mux/Demux in Figure 3). The implementations selected for each layer along with experimental parameters are defined in a single XML file. This file also contains sections on each node type (emulated, bridge and real) and defines a custom role for each network node. Typical experiments consist of two roles: aggregation and execution. Usually only one node carries out the aggregation role, intended to gather all experimental results. Many nodes are involved in the execution role, intended to run a specific P2P application and generate experimental results. The configuration file is easily created, stored and edited thanks to a GUI that maps all XML tags for graphic objects.

The multiplexers/demultiplexers define the interfaces between the layers as well as message sending and receiving methods. Each message sent on the data link and physical layer or routing layer is associated with an 8-bit label (Figure 5).

Typically used upon reception, this label differentiates one type of message from another one. On the lowest layer this information is directly mapped to the TinyOS active message type field, while a new field is added for the routing layer. Any application receiving messages must be programmed to register as a listener for the corresponding label on the multiplexer/demultiplexer. The lowest layer must then implement a promiscuous mode, allowing it to receive every message sent by physical neighbors, even if the message's destination is not the current node.

The current Freemote software[1] provides some sample applications such as the Ping-like test illustrated in Figure 4, Figure 5 and Figure 6. These figures are not further detailed here but are shown to trigger the interest of P2P developers to implement their algorithms in their own Freemote testbed.

MANET SIMULATIONS

The emulated nodes and bridge node simulate IEEE 802.15.4 behavior in a lightweight manner, as characterized by the features summarized in Table 1 below.

The bridge node interconnects the two data link and physical layers: one identical to the emulated nodes on the emulated network side and

Figure 3. Layered view of software architecture

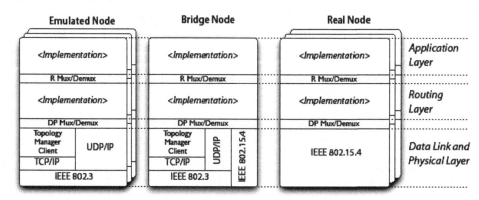

Figure 4. Layered view of software architecture for "ping" application illustrated in Figure 6

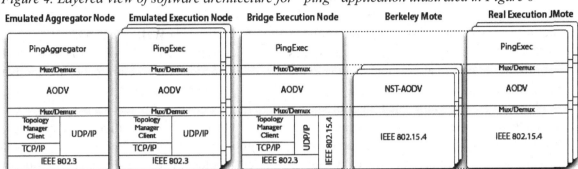

Figure 5. Code templates used to facilitate implementation of each layer

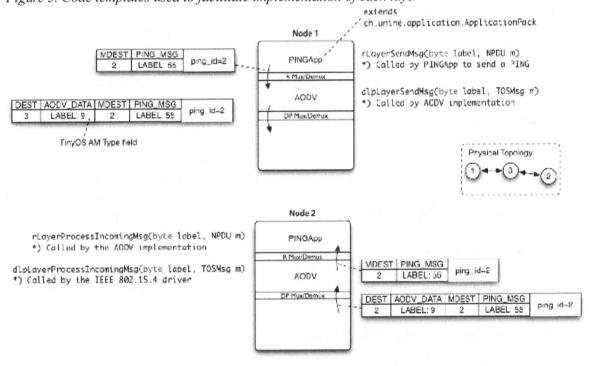

Figure 6. Freemote experimental "ping" configuration mixing real and emulated nodes

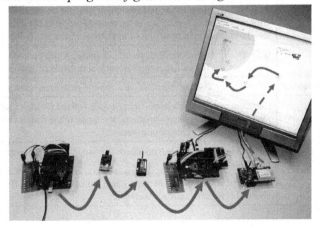

another one identical to the real nodes with which it must interface. On the emulated network side, the software interface uses the existing TinyOS Java API for sending and receiving messages over the serial port to a real mote mounted on a programmer board.

To simulate the radio medium's broadcast characteristic within its radio coverage, a node must know its physical neighborhood before sending a message, i.e., other nodes within its radio coverage. This list is provided to each node by the Freemote Topology Manager set up in a client/server manner. Each Topology Manager client (Figure 1) stores topological information on the emulated nodes in the associated process. A single Topology Manager server maintains a Cartesian map containing all emulated nodes and periodically updates node positions according to the mobility scheme chosen. Currently, the following three mobility schemes are provided:

1. **Fixed Model:** Useful for repeatable experiments, able to define each node's specific angle, speed, initial position and radio range.

2. **Random Uniform:** Each node chooses a random speed within the [MINSPEED, MAXSPEED] range, along with an angle and initial position. All nodes have the same radio range.

3. **Random Walk:** Each node chooses a random speed and angle and then runs for a random time before choosing another set of parameters.

Once the node positions are computed, the Topology Manager server computes the new physical topology. The Topology Manager's algorithm first sorts the nodes along the X-axis and then in a single run through the list of nodes, creates all the physical bindings. It operates within O [N (logN + C)] time complexity, where C is the network's average connectivity and N is the number of emulated nodes. The bindings are unidirectional, as each emulated node can have its own circular radio range. The asymmetry in the radio links is used to simulate the acknowledgements (ACK) as explained below.

The Topology Manager server proactively pushes the topological modifications to the Topology Manager clients using TCP sockets to add or remove neighbors. This process guarantees that the Topology Manager clients always contain up-to-date topological information. Each node fetches a list of its physical neighbors from the Topology Manager client and then sends a copy of the mes-

Table 1. Data link and physical layer features

Feature	Definition
Transmissions errors	A random error rate is applied to each message sent, i.e., for each message generated by an emulated node. The node computes a random number to decide whether or not the message is effectively sent to all the neighbors. Future releases might improve this feature in order to compute a transmission error per neighbor, depending on the node-to-neighbor environment. An indoor coverage prediction tool developed might be used for this purpose (Echenard & Wagen, 2006).
ACK or Acknowledgments	IEEE 802.15.4 acknowledgments are not implemented but their effects are taken into account since a node verifies the radio coverage of each of its listed neighbors.
Promiscuous mode and broadcast	A sending node's neighbors receive a copy of each message sent (if no transmission error).
Radio range	Currently circular radio range for each node is fixed for the experiment's duration. Future releases might include radio range variations, according to the node's remaining power, other power limitations or geographical positions.
Unidirectional links	Physical links between two nodes could be unidirectional if one of the nodes has a radio range greater than the other.
Output power	The output power affects the radio range radius and can be different at each node. As discussed above, this feature is already included.

sage to each of its neighbors using UDP sockets. The sending node also checks to see if the message destination is within its neighborhood and if an acknowledgement is requested. It then verifies that the destination node is able to send it back (i.e., if there is a sending node in its neighborhood). This simulates the IEEE 802.15.4 standard efficiently by avoiding the sending of acknowledgement messages during the simulations.

The current IEEE 802.15.4 simulation comprises several limitations which might need to be improved if the following effects prove important: a) it does not simulate channel collision detection and thus the transmission error rate must account for those cases where two physical neighbors send messages simultaneously; b) it does not account for radio propagation delays, and considers neither the throughput nor path loss and fading in order to automatically adjust the transmission error rate.

FREEMOTE EMULATOR VALIDATION

The Freemote emulator was first developed in order to validate the performance of certain improvements in the DHT (Distributed Hash Table) algorithms used in P2P applications over ad-hoc networks. The DHT algorithms and early performance results are given in (Kummer, Kropf, & Felber, 2006) (Maret, Kropf, & Hirsbrunner, 2007). For a more detailed description of DHT algorithms, refer to our companion chapter entitled: *"P2P Information Lookup, Collection and Distribution in Mobile Ad-Hoc Networks."* In this section, the early simulation results presented in (Kummer et al., 2006) can serve as a reference when evaluating Freemote emulator results when mixing real and emulated Java nodes. The two main metrics used in comparing results are:

- Average percentage of logical shortcuts to determine their use frequency
- Average number of physical steps per request to compare performance in terms of physical complexity

Figure 7 illustrates a request path in an ad-hoc network during the lookup process. The request may take various shortcuts within the logical space in order to shorten the overall physical steps required to reach the node responsible for the key being sought.

These metrics are measured in 3 different configurations:

Figure 7. Path of request routed by DHT with two extensions

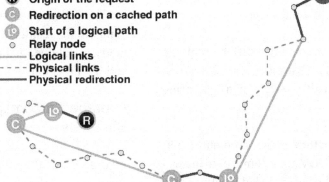

1. **Basic:** Basic DHT lookup
2. **Neighbors-of-Neighbors (NoN):** Basic algorithm that evaluates physical neighbors and their neighbors in order to choose the next step.
3. **Cache (C):** NoN algorithm uses a cache to memorize a finite history of previous forwarding choices. The Cache (*C*) configuration includes the neighbors-of-neighbors (*NoN*) extension.

Extended simulations conducted in the companion chapter demonstrate that the Cache version always performs best. Although not as efficient as the DHT with Cache, in all cases the NoN version outperforms the Basic algorithm.

For these tests the Freemote emulator environment was deployed on 6 *JMotes* and up to 10,000 emulated motes. Ten 2.7 GHz CPU/2GB RAM standard machines running Windows XP SP2 were used over a 100 Mb/s switched Ethernet LAN. One computer was dedicated to the (emulated) aggregator node, the bridge node and the Topology Manager server. All other emulated nodes were equally distributed across the nine other machines. Each computer was also running a Topology Manager client. The emulated nodes were randomly distributed in the simulation space: a simple square. The average connectivity was 14 and the DHT based overlay network was implicitly constructed: each node computed its key in the logical space based on its routing address. Hence, the logical space a node was responsible for, as well as its logical neighborhood, were provided by the node's position on the ring.

The following parameters differ from the reference simulations (Kummer et al., 2006) and thus explain certain differences when comparing results.

- **Routing algorithm:** In the Freemote emulator the NST-AODV algorithm is used instead of the LAR (Location Aided Routing) (Ko

& Vaidya, 2000) applied in the reference simulations. The simplified LAR algorithm used takes advantage knowledge assumed about the node's geographical position to send messages to the physical neighbor closest to the destination node, and LAR is able to obtain shorter routes. Our NST-AODV implementation was tested with real and emulated nodes in different scenarios including mobile configurations. These preliminary experiments showed that the AODV algorithm performed poorly over asymmetric links, because it assumed symmetric links when building the routing paths. This issue is discussed in the AODV literature and so we decided to implement the black list solution in our handling of asymmetric links.

- **DHT key management:** The DHT algorithms implemented use a non-standard scheme to manage keys: nodes are placed at the beginning of their key spaces rather than the middle. A node is thus responsible for a key that is not necessarily the closest one. This scheme is used to solve the problem of keys being exactly at the same logical distance from two consecutive nodes (i.e., the same logical distance with the previous and the next node on the logical ring). Thus, a node is always responsible of all the IDs included in the logical subspace, starting at its own node ID and on to the node ID preceding its direct successor.

The following two paragraphs describe and compare the results of the two above-mentioned metrics, obtained using the dedicated simulator and the Freemote emulator.

Average Percentage of Logical Shortcuts

Figure 8 shows the percentage of logical shortcuts found during the routing of a request. It can be seen that the DHT algorithm's Freemote emulation shows behavior similar to that of the simulated one. In both systems, more logical shortcuts were found when extensions were applied, the number of logical shortcuts found increased in proportion to network size, except for the emulated cache version. This was expected because for a greater number of nodes, longer physical routes are required and thus more shortcuts are found.

The smaller percentage of logical shortcuts found by the DHT simulated cache version of the algorithm was due to the underlying routing methodology, which may route a request to a node where no further neighbors can be found in the following step. Thus, to avoid a costly backtracking process, the request was directly sent to the destination node, costing an average logical step, and consequently for this process no

logical shortcut could be found. This simulation choice also explains the smaller percentage of logical shortcuts found by simulated algorithm in the 10,000 node network.

Since the results for the Freemote emulators are in line with those found in the reference simulations, they tend to validate the emulations with numerical differences (Δ) shown in Table 2, ranging from a few percent for 1,000 nodes to a maximum of 15% for the 10,000 node networks.

Average Number of Physical Steps per Request

As illustrated previously by comparing the percentage of logical shortcuts found in the emulated and simulated DHTs, Figure 9 shows that

Figure 8. Average use of logical shortcuts during a request's logical path

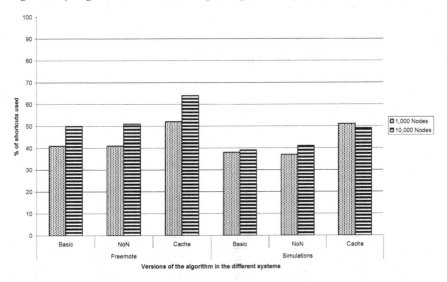

Table 2. Average percentage of logical shortcuts – N/A = not available

Nb of Nodes	Basic			NoN			Cache		
	Freemote	ref.	Δ	Freemote	ref.	Δ	Freemote	ref.	Δ
100	30%	N/A	*N/A*	19%	N/A	*N/A*	26%	N/A	*N/A*
1'000	41%	38%	*3%*	41%	37%	*4%*	52%	51%	*1%*
10'000	50%	39%	*11%*	51%	41%	*10%*	64%	49%	*15%*

algorithm's implementation results in the same behavior for all network sizes. When applying extensions, the number of physical steps needed to achieve a lookup decreases. This is not surprising, given that the purpose of these extensions is to provide more logical shortcut opportunities. Thus, by providing more shortcuts, the algorithm reduces the number of logical hops per lookup and reduces the average number of physical steps.

As shown in emulation environment, the number of physical steps is greater, which can be explained in two ways: 1) Different key maintenance schemes are used. The nodes are not placed in the middle but at the beginning of the key space, and on average at least one more logical link is required to reach the node responsible for a DHT key. 2) Different routing schemes. As detailed above, when blocked at an intermediate node a request may be directly delivered to its next destination. When this rescue routing process is applied, the average physical cost of a logical hop is counted, thus perhaps slightly reducing the overall average physical cost of requests.

Table 3 again shows that the results obtained using the Freemote emulator are in line with the

simulations. In fact, the numerical differences (Δ) are all below 21%, meaning satisfactory results given the differences between the implementations and the underlying routing methodology.

Finally, Table 4 shows the average reduction in the number of physical steps for the *NoN* and *Cache* DHT implementations, compared to the Basic DHT version. As expected, the DHT algorithm extensions make it possible to reduce request routing costs. Again the results of both implementations are close, with the Freemote emulator and the reference results being within a 10% margin.

The above comparisons show that the Freemote emulator's results fall within a few percentage points of those for simulation, usually less than 15%. A worst-case discrepancy of 21% can be explained by the differences between the routing algorithms. The variations in results are due to differences between the two setups, but overall results show that the Freemote environment provides realistic outcomes.

Figure 9. Average # of physical steps to achieve a request

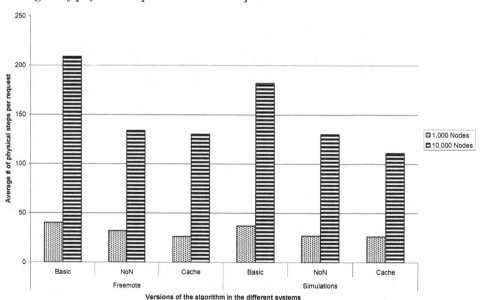

Table 3. Average number of physical steps per request

Nb of Nodes	Basic			NoN			Cache		
	Freemote	Ref.	Δ	Freemote	Ref.	Δ	Freemote	Ref.	Δ
100	7.33	N/A	*N/A*	6.89	N/A	*N/A*	6.50	N/A	*N/A*
1'000	40	37	*8.2%*	32	27	*19.1%*	26	22	*21%*
10'000	209	182	*14.9%*	134	130	*3.1%*	115	111	*4.1%*

Table 4. Average gain in physical steps compared to "basic" DHT, for NoN and Cache DHT

Nb of Nodes	NoN			Cache		
	Freemote	Ref.	Δ	Freemote	Ref.	Δ
100	6.0%	N/A	*N/A*	11.3%	N/A	*N/A*
1'000	19.7%	27%	*-7.3%*	33.6%	40.5%	*-6,9%*
10'000	36.1%	28.8%	*7.3%*	45%	39.3%	*5.7%*

CONCLUSION

The research on P2P and MANET include the use of simulations and also analytical studies. These two methods confirm expected performances and to reveal the benefits and limitations of the various innovative approaches. To ensure that any benefits are not lost during practical implementation, real and usually large testbeds have to be used, even though their cost and complexity are often prohibitive. Furthermore, due to the lack of repeatability, certain experimental results can be difficult to investigate. Emulation is therefore a more convenient way of assessing the behavior of innovative algorithms in real P2P application implementations on MANETs. The Freemote emulator was used to investigate improvements in P2P algorithms in realistic scenarios.

The Freemote emulator was designed to run the same code on emulated and real nodes, and to mix both nodes in the same experiment. It is thus hoped that the Freemote emulator could on the one hand provide an interesting solution for students and newcomers discovering MANETs and sensor network domains, allowing them to begin developing programs in the well know Java language. On the other hand, for researchers and developers, Freemote should prove to be an interesting tool because it allows the running of large-scale experiments. They might be distributed over a network of computers and as such provide remarkable execution performances. Furthermore, the possibility of mixing emulated nodes with real Java nodes and real Berkeley motes is expected to attract a certain amount of attention.

The Freemote emulator results were compared with certain reference simulations. In this case, there were three versions of a DHT algorithm especially tuned to run P2P applications on MANETs. Despite certain differences, it was shown that similar trends and numerical values could be obtained. Typical differences between these two results were only within a few percentage points, explained by different routing algorithm and methods: NST-AODV for the Freemote emulator and a simplified LAR (Location Aided Routing) for simulation. The documentation and source codes for the Freemote emulator are freely available on (Freemote, 2008).

REFERENCES

Barr, R. (2004). *An efficient, unifying approach to simulation using virtual machines.* Unpublished docotoral thesis, Cornell University.

Dunkels, A. (2008). *Contiki: A dynamic operating system for memory-constrained networked embedded systems.* Retrieved September 10, 2008, from http://www.sics.se/contiki/

Echenard, N., & Wagen, J.-F. (2006). WLAN service coverage based on PixelFlow predictions. In *Proceedings of the 4th International Conference, WWIC.*

Eriksson, J., Dunkels, A., Finne, N., Osterlind, F., & Voigt, T. (2007). Mspsim - an extensible simulator for msp430-equipped sensor boards. In *Proceedings of the European Conference on Wireless Sensor Networks.*

Freemote. (2008). Retrieved September 30, 2008, from http://mote.tic.eia-fr.ch/freemote/

Girod, L., Ramanathan, N., Elson, J., Stathopoulos, T., Lukac, M., & Estrin, D. (2007). Emstar: A software environment for developing and deploying heterogeneous sensor-actuator networks. *Transactions on Sensor Networks, 3*(3).

Göktürk, E. (2007). A stance on emulation and testbeds, and a survey of network emulators and testbeds. In *Proceedings of the European Conference on Modeling and Simulation.*

Gomez, C., Salvatella, P., Alonso, O., & Paradells, J. (2006). Adapting AODV for IEEE 802.15.4 mesh sensor networks: Theoretical discussion and performance evaluation in a real environment. In *Proceedings of the IEEE International Symposium on a World of Wireless Mobile and Multimedia Networks.*

Johnson, D., Stack, T., Fish, R., Flickinger, D. M., Ricci, L. S. R., & Lepreau, J. (2006). Mobile Emulab: A robotic wireless and sensor network testbed. In *Proceedings of the Conference on Computer Communications (INFOCOM).*

Khan, I. J., & Wierzbicki, A. (2008). Foundation of peer-to-peer computing. *Elsevier Journal of Computer Communication, 31*(Special Issue 2).

Ko, Y.-B., & Vaidya, N. H. (2000). Location-aided routing (LAR) in mobile ad hoc networks. *Wireless Networks, 6*(4), 307-321.

Koshy, J., & Pandey, R. (2005). Vm*: Synthesizing scalable runtime environments for sensor networks. In *Proceedings of the Conference on Embedded Networked Sensor Systems.*

Kummer, R., Kropf, P., & Felber, P. (2006). Distributed lookup in structured peer-to-peer ad-hoc networks. In *Proceedings of the On the Move to Meaningful Internet Systems: CoopIS, DOA, GADA, and ODBASE.*

Levis, P., & Culler, D. (2002). Mate: A tiny virtual machine for sensor networks. In *Proceedings of the International Conference on Architectural Support for Programming Languages and Operating Systems.*

Levis, P., Lee, N., Welsh, M., & Culler, D. (2003). TOSSIM: Accurate and scalable simulation of entire TinyOS applications. In *Proceedings of the Sensys: The ACM Conference on Embedded Networked Sensor Systems.*

Maret, T., Kropf, P., & Hirsbrunner, B. (2007). *Un environnement d'émulation hybride pour un algorithme de DHT adapte au contexte des réseaux ad-hoc.* Universities of Fribourg and Neuchâtel.

Müller, R., Alonso, G., & Kossmann, D. (2007). A virtual machine for sensor networks. In *Proceedings of the EuroSys.*

nesC. (2008). Retrieved October 24, 2008, from http://nescc.sourceforge.net/

Osterlind, F., Dunkels, A., Eriksson, J., Finne, N., & Voigt, T. (2006). Cross-level sensor network simulation with COOJA. In *Proceedings of the IEEE International Workshop on Practical Issues in Building Sensor Network Applications.*

Polley, J., Blazakis, D., McGee, J., Rusk, D., & Baras, J. S. (2004). ATEMU: A fine-grained sensor network simulator. In *Proceedings of the First IEEE Communications Society Conference on Sensor and Ad Hoc Communications and Networks.*

Sentilla Corporation, S. (2008). *Software architecture.* Retrieved September 10, 2008, from http://www.sentilla.com/software.html

Shaylor, N., Simon, D. N., & Bush, W. R. (2003). A Java virtual machine architecture for very small devices. In *Proceedings of the Special Interest Group on Programming Languages.*

Sundresh, S., Wooyoung, K., & Agha, G. (2004). SENS: A sensor, environment and network simulator. In *Proceedings of the Simulation Symposium.*

TinyOS. (2008). Retrieved October 27, 2008, from http://www.tinyos.net/

Titzer, B. L., Lee, D. K., & Palsberg, J. (2005). Avrora: Scalable sensor network simulation with precise timing. In *Proceedings of the International conference on Information processing in sensor networks.*

Werner-Allen, G., Swieskowski, P., & Welsh, M. (2005). MoteLab: A wireless sensor network testbed. In *Proceedings of the IEEE International Conference on Information Processing in Sensor Networks.*

ENDNOTE

[1] The Freemote Software can be freely downloaded from http://mote.tic.eia-fr.ch/freemote

Section VIII
Applications and Services

Chapter XIX
Mobile Peer–to–Peer Collaborative Framework and Applications

Alf Inge Wang
Norwegian University of Science and Technology, Norway

ABSTRACT

This chapter presents the Peer2Me mobile peer-to-peer framework, Peer2Me applications, and discusses the experiences from using the Peer2Me framework. Peer2Me supports mobile collaboration utilizing Bluetooth and Java ME. The framework runs on standard Java ME-enabled mobile phones, thus enabling rapid development of various kinds of collaborative peer-to-peer applications. In this chapter, the author describes some of the developed applications and his experiences from implementing these applications, which include: a file-sharing application, a chat application, a quiz game, a face-to-face meeting scheduler, a real-time game, an automatic business exchange application, and a find the right person application. All of these applications were analyzed for their potential usefulness, and investigated to discover the limitations of the framework, and the underlying technologies. Finally, the author summarizes his analysis to provide a complete picture of the potential and limitations of Bluetooth and Java ME for implementing mobile peer-to-peer applications.

INTRODUCTION

Most peer-to-peer applications and architectures today are designed to work in a fixed and wired infrastructure like the Internet. The development of wireless network technologies, mobile devices and programming environment for mobile devices have made it possible to migrate the peer-to-peer computing to a wireless environment (Kortuem et al., 2001; Maibaum & Mundt, 2002). The downside of bringing peer-to-peer computing to the mobile and wireless platform is that we have to face the classical challenges of mobile computing related to how to handle wireless communication, how to solve issues related to mobility of the user, and how to overcome the limitations introduced by the portability of the mobile device (Satyanarayanan, 1996). Mobile peer-to-peer computing also offers new opportunities that can be utilized like providing location-based services (Davies et al., 2001; Long et al., 1996) and social computing (Eagle & Pentland, 2005; Holmquist et al., 1998) using short-range networks.

Most wireless devices support some kind of personal area network (PAN) technologies like irDA and/or Bluetooth (Miller & Bisdikian, 2004). PANs are commonly used for transferring data between two mobile devices. A PAN can be seen as a digital sphere around the mobile device enabling a collaborative network for users within range. The digital sphere opens for mobile computer supported cooperative work (mobile CSCW) (Wiberg & Grönlund, 2000; Papadopoulos, 2006). In such environments, the support for mobile peer-to-peer is essential, and the support and establishment of mobile ad hoc networks (MANETs) are necessary. A MANET is a self-configuring network where peers can join and leave the network dynamically making the wireless network topology unstable and unpredictable (Mohapatra, 2004). MANETs can be utilised in situations where persons with mobile devices meet and there is a need for exchange of data.

MANETs opens for new kinds of user-interaction. The interaction between users can either be explicitly initiated by the users; it can be automatically initiated by the mobile devices, or a hybrid of the two (Wang et al., 2006). Such applications can be used for initiating collaboration between users of same interests, e.g., an application for finding people with same research interest at a conference (Wang et al., 2005). Furthermore, MANETs can be used to create application for proximity chats and file exchanges, or simply for leisure like games.

This chapter describes a framework for implementing mobile peer-to-peer applications, explores and evaluates several mobile peer-to-peer applications, and investigates the limitations of Java ME and Bluetooth in this context.

BACKGROUND

This section gives an introduction to the background and important terms used in our framework, and describes related work.

Mobile Computer Supported Cooperative Work

Research within Computer Supported Cooperative Work (CSCW) has grown to be a mature research area. However, there are still problems concerning the use of computers for cooperation that remain unsolved. (Olson et al., 2002) list several advantages of collocating a work force to improve cooperation such as efficient communication paths, less ambiguity in communication, more efficient synchronization of work, and better knowledge management. The advantages from being collocated stem from the fact that collaboration is probably the most complex, advanced, and unstructured form of human-to-human interaction. Current technology is too limited to cope with such complexity and is therefore not sufficient to solve all the problems in the CSCW domain.

(Clarence et al, 1991) describe the different types of CSCW systems/applications in the two dimensions time and place. The *time dimension* divide CSCW applications either into real time or asynchronous applications, while the *place dimension* divide such applications into same place or different place. An email-application would according to this model typically be characterised as asynchronous and different place, while a chat-application would be characterised as real time and different place. Most CSCW research has focused on applications that fall into the "Different Place" category where the CSCW application will be the only communication channel used for collaboration. The users' abilities to communicate and cooperate are limited by the insufficiencies in the technologies and applications used. In the "Same Place" category, especially coupled with "Real Time", CSCW becomes more of a support for the collaborative effort to enrich or strengthen the processes and communication paths.

The Peer2Me framework and applications described in this chapter covers both real time and asynchronous applications in the "Same Place" category in a mobile environment. The targeted platform for our framework is mobile phones or similar mobile devices as the computer devices must be where the user is (not the opposite). Any mobile device like a PDA or an ultra mobile PC can be used as a target platform for such applications. The main benefit of using a mobile phone as a mobile platform instead of PDAs or ultra mobile PCs is the user base (number of users) for mobile phones is much larger. Further, to use mobile phones as the execution platform for CSCW applications has several advantages over traditional CSCW. *Firstly*, the mobile phones are personal devices meaning that can be used to identify a user. *Secondly*, a user can store his profile on the mobile phone because it is a personal device, enabling the mobile phone to function according to the user's specific needs when interacting with other users. *Thirdly*, mobile phones can be considered to be always on, always present. Due to this, someone using his mobile phone for CSCW purposes will achieve a high degree of user availability compare to traditional CSCW systems where the user is not always with his computer.

Current mobile phones support more than one communication network/technology. Still the most important, and the one with the longest range, is the cellular network provided by the telecom operators. In addition, most mobile phones support low-range personal area networks (PANs). Such networks have a typically range from a few meters up to 50 meters depending on the blocking of signals in the environment. Examples of such PAN technologies provided in many mobile phones are infrared (requires line of sight), Bluetooth and WiFi. Such ad hoc network technologies enable devices to detect and connect to devices that are in sufficient proximity in a decentralized manner. The characteristics of such networks resemblance strongly to the nature of human spontaneity, which make PANs suitable for making spontaneous collaborative applications. A PAN creates a *digital sphere* around a person. The communication range of the PAN limits the digital sphere.

From the perspective of mobile CSCW, people are physically collocated when the digital spheres of two or more persons overlaps (see Figure 1). When digital spheres overlap, the mobile devices can start to interact and form a *mobile ad hoc network (MANET)*. The topology of such networks can often be characterised as peer-to-peer. A distributed network architecture may be called a peer-to-peer network, if the participants share a part of their own hardware resources (processing power, storage capacity, network link capacity, printers, etc). These shared resources are necessary to provide the *service* and *content* offered by the network (e.g. file sharing or shared workspaces for collaboration). They are accessible by other peers directly, without passing intermediary entities. The participants of such a network are thus resource providers as well as resource requestors

Figure 1. Illustration of digital sphere

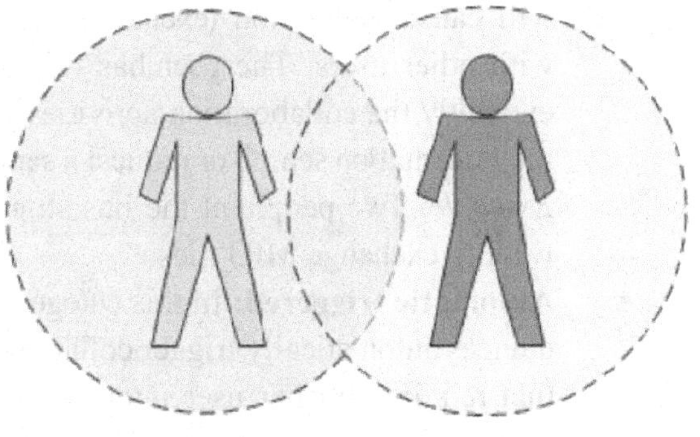

(Schollmeier, 2001). The peer-to-peer topology is better suited to cope with dynamic changes compared to the classical client-server topology. This is mainly because client-server has a single point of failure, while in a peer-to-peer network any node can communicate with any other node. Also the peer-to-peer topology better describes and models collaborative patterns between users, as there are direct communication paths between the users. Together, PANs and the P2P topology provide the most suitable basis for building collaborative applications that can be characterised as same place applications.

By using low-range PANs for mobile CSCW applications, the collaborative efforts will have to be either based on chance encounters between peers (impromptu collaboration) or a planned meeting or gathering of peers (formal collaboration). Impromptu collaboration can involve different degrees of user interaction (Wang et al., 2006):

- **Controlled:** In this category the application controls how the users interact through a well-defined protocol where typically one of the peers in the network must be a master controlling the user interaction. This user interaction pattern is typically used for applications that are turn-based or applications that require that the users exchange data according to a predefined pattern. *Example:* A turn-based game like the strategy game Risk.
- **User interaction:** In this category, the users have explicitly to trigger actions that will cause interaction (exchange of data) with other users. The user has to trigger explicitly the collaboration activities, start the information search or request a service. *Example*: Two people at the bus stop that want to exchange MP3 files.
- **Automatic triggered:** In this category the devices automatically trigger collaboration that requires further user interaction. Ex-

ample: The mobile devices carried by two different people automatically communicate without user interaction and discover that the two persons are sharing the same taste in music. The two people are alerted and are given the possibility to share some MP3 files.

- **Automatic:** In this category the application is responsible for automatically initiating communication between his device and other devices on behalf of the user. The user stores a profile that defines how the application should act with respect to other devices/users and available services. *Example*: A person automatically exchanges MP3 recommendations with other people he or she meets when walking around at the campus.

Formal collaboration can be characterized as being proximity-based, but due to its organized nature it is not opportunistic and spontaneous. This more formal form of using CSCW on mobile phones is more suitable in situations where a collection of users automate parts of their collaborative work process - typically a workflow system (Jing et al., 1999). Our framework focuses mainly on support for impromptu collaborative applications, but can also support formal collaboration like planning the next meeting.

The research within the area of mobile peer-to-peer collaboration has focused on three main areas: Development of frameworks, architectures or technologies to support mobile peer-to-peer applications, development of new innovative applications to support mobile collaborative work, and evaluation of mobile peer-to-peer frameworks, architectures, technologies and applications. The next sections review some of the work in this area.

Mobile Technologies

Mobile technologies have developed rapidly in the last couple of years, resulting in many different types of mobile devices, a wide spectrum of mobile execution and development platforms, and many types of wireless network technologies.

It is a critical decision for the mobile application developer to choose the appropriate mobile platform for the target audience. The following gives an overview of existing mobile technologies.

The types of mobile devices can be categorised in many ways, but it is hard to find one taxonomy that covers everything as the functionality and abilities of the mobile devices tend to overlap. The most popular mobile device is the mobile phone, which has by far the largest number of users. Previously, personal digital assistants (PDAs) (Davids, 1996a; Davids, 1996b) were popular, but their popularity has fallen mainly because most mobile phones now include PDA functionality. Smart phones (Zheng & Ni, 2006) are hybrid devices that combine the functionality of a mobile phone and a PDA, but the functionality gap between mobile phones and smart phones are decreasing day by day. Another category of mobile devices is mobile computers, also known as ultra mobile PCs (UMPCs) (Broll et al., 2008). The main difference between mobile computers, mobile phones, and smart phones is that mobile computers are bigger in size and usually runs the same operating system as larger computers. Most mobile phones and mobile computers can install and run mobile applications made for the appropriate mobile platform (elaborated in the next paragraph). In addition to these multipurpose mobile devices, there are several types of specialized mobile devices such as handheld game consoles, mobile media players or recorders, personal navigation devices (like GPS) and others. Some of these mobile devices built for specific purposes are programmable and thus opens for new use of specific-purpose mobile devices. In the recent years, the trend has been to develop one mobile device that can do everything. One example of such a device is the iPhone from Apple. The iPhone (Macedonia, 2007) is a mobile phone, a smart phone, a GPS, a handheld game console,

and a media player. Mobile devices can vary in many respects: size, capacity (CPU, memory, hard drive), screen size, input devices, operating system, support for wireless networks, sensors, special purpose electronics for RFID (Michahelles et al., 2007), GPS (Schreiner, 2007), and smart cards (Husemann, 1999).

Most existing mobile devices allow development of applications that runs on different execution/development platforms (Vaughan-Nichols, 2003). The pioneers of popular mobile operating systems were the Palm OS, originally developed for PDAs (later also for smart phones) and Symbian OS for mobile phones. Later, the Windows mobile platform and Linux were launched for development on PDAs, smart phones and mobile phones. The programming languages used for these platforms are C, C++, and C#. The most popular development platform for mobile devices today is the Java Micro Edition (Java ME) (Helal, 2002), which runs on top of a mobile operating system. The main reason for its popularity is that Java ME applications are device independent and can run on most kind of devices and operating systems. This is only partly true, as the implementation of Java ME virtual machines are slightly different on different operating systems and devices, and that usually the user interface must be tailored to the various screen sizes and input devices. There have also been some attempts on developing pure Java-based operating systems for mobile devices, but this platform has not become very popular. Lately, two new platforms have received a lot of attention. One is the Apple's iPhone SDK (Apple, 2008) that allows developers to develop applications for iPod Touch and iPhone running a minimized version of Mac OS X. iPhone or iPod Touch applications are written in the programming language objective-C, C or C++. The other platform is Google's open source Android platform (Google, 2008), which runs the Dalvik virtual machine on top of a Linux mobile operating system. The applications in Android are written in the Java language, but compiled into Dalvik Bytecode.

Most mobile devices have built-in support for at least one wireless network technology. Since this chapter is about peer-to-peer applications for users being co-located, telecommunication wireless networks such GSM will not be described here. Most of the network technologies for close-range communication are based on radio, but there are also alternatives using infrared or ultrasound. The most common alternative to radio-based networks today is infrared data association standard (IrDA) (Ashok & Agrawal, 2003). IrDA can provide data transmission speed from 2.4Kbit/s up to 16Mbit/s, and the range can be up to 5 meters. IrDA transmitters and receivers are cheap to implement and does not consume much battery. The main disadvantage is that IrDA transmissions require line of sight to work. The most common radio-based wireless network technologies used today is Bluetooth (Reynolds, 2008) and WiFi (Kapp, 2002). Bluetooth was design for smaller devices, requires less battery, but suffers from lower transmission speeds (max 3Mbit/s for version 2.0) and a max range of up to 100 meters. The IEEE 802.11 standards (a, b, g, n and y) for WiFi comes in various configurations with different speeds and range from 2Mbit/s and range of 100 meters outdoors and up to 248Mbit/s and range of 250m outdoors. An alternative is ZigBee (Geer, 2005), which is a radio-based wireless network technology intended for simple lightweight devices and provides data transmission speeds from 20Kbit/s to 250Kbit/s with range from 10 to 75 meters. In 2008, two new wireless network standards mainly to be used instead of cables between devices have been defined. The Wireless USB (WUSB) (Leavitt, 2007) standard is a short-range, high-bandwidth radio communication standard with data transmission speeds up to 480Mbit/s at 3 meters and 110Mbit/s at 10 meters. The competing standard is the Wireless firewire (Zhang et al., 2001) standard that should give data transmission speeds up to 480Mbit/s at the range up to 9 meters.

To be able to develop mobile peer-to-peer applications that are highly available and usable, the underlying mobile technology needs to be:

- **Widely available and supported by most mobile devices:** This would ensure a huge number of potential users.
- **The mobile device must be highly portable:** Users must be able to utilise the peer-to-peer services wherever they are. In practise, this means that the mobile device must be small and lightweight.
- **The range and the speed of the mobile network technology must be sufficient to establish networks:** The digital spheres must have some radius to ensure that people in the same area can connect, and the data transmission speed is sufficient for normal data exchanging data.

The underlying mobile technology for Peer2Me was chosen based on the requirements described before. When we considered the target mobile device for the Peer2Me framework, it was obvious that the mobile phone would give the highest potential number of users. In Norway where the Peer2Me framework was developed, nearly 100% of the population has a mobile phone. In addition, we chose to implement Peer2Me in Java ME. The Java ME platform makes it possible to run Peer2Me application on most mobile phones as well as many PDAs and smart phones that have a Java ME virtual machine installed. In addition, the choice of Java ME also enables Peer2Me applications to run on mobile computers. Since the mobile phone and Java ME was chosen as the device and software platform, Bluetooth was the only viable choice for a wireless network technology as Bluetooth is the network technology supported by most mobile phones, PDAs and smart phones. Bluetooth has sufficient range (about 50 meters in open air for mobile phones) and sufficient transfer speed (about 320Kbit/s for average mobile phones). Another reason for choosing Bluetooth was that it requires less battery than e.g. WiFi. In practice this means that the Peer2Me applications can be used for longer period of time before a recharge of the battery is required.

Other Peer-to-Peer Platforms

There are several projects that have developed frameworks for developing peer-to-peer application in MANETs. We will in this section present the most prominent projects.

JXTA (Maibaum & Mundt, 2002) is an open-source framework for developing P2P applications. JXTA provides a set of protocols and APIs for general-purpose, computer-to-computer communication and is platform and network independent. JXME (Kawulok et al., 2005) is JXTA for Java 2 Micro Edition (J2ME) and is a lightweight implementation of JXTA for mobile devices. It is specifically aimed at devices without sufficient computation and/or communication resources to participate in the network on their own. The JXME implementation provides full JXTA functionality through the use of a relay host. There is also a JXME proxiless initiative, but there is currently no stable implementation. As JXTA does not have a pure peer-to-peer version working for J2ME, it cannot be compared to Peer2Me.

Mobile Chedar (Auvinen et al., 2006) is a middleware being an extension to the Chedar peer-to-peer network allowing mobile devices to access the Chedar network and communicate to other Mobile Chedars. The goal of the Chedar software is similar to Peer2Me: To provide a convenient API for peer-to-peer application developers. The Mobile Chedar is implemented in J2ME and Bluetooth are used for communication. In contrast to Peer2Me, the Mobile Chedar is based on a hybrid peer-to-peer model that uses a Mobile Chedar gateway node as the master in the network. The Mobile Chedar gateway node is run on a PC that also provides an Internet gateway for the mobile nodes. However, this approach

suffers from having a single point of failure like client-server solutions.

MOBY (Horozov, 2002) provides a network for mobile peer-to-peer exchange of services and data. MOBY offer a dynamic service location and client mapping to achieve an adaptive network optimising performance and reliability. MOBY uses heavily JINI functionality and can there for not be run in a J2ME environment.

Proem (Kortuem, 2002) is a framework for developing and deploying P2P collaborative applications in a mobile ad-hoc networking environment. The main objective of Proem is to provide a common framework for rapid development of applications for ad-hoc network environments. The framework is implemented in Java, and can be run on various wireless mobile devices. Proem is designed to be independent of underlying network transport protocols, and can be implemented on top of TCP/IP, HTTP, Bluetooth and others. The original Proem was based on a Java Standard Edition, limiting the devices to run Proem to powerful PDAs. There have been attempts to create a J2ME version of Proem that have not succeeded.

PnPAP (Harjula et al., 2004) is a middleware developed at the University of Oulu in Finland. PnPAP is a plug-and-play application platform that enables dynamic selection between diverse peer-to-peer networks and session management protocols while preserving the best available network connectivity. The architecture of PnPAP consists of an API-layer, a PnPAP engine layer and a layer for handling the actual connection. The PnPAP platform has been developed for Symbian S60 platform and can support the UMTS, Bluetooth, GPRS and WLAN networks.

The JMobiPeer (Bisignano et al., 2005) framework is very similar to Peer2Me in many respects. It provides support for discovery, group management and peer management. In addition JMobiPeer offers interoperability with JXTA. The implementation of JMobiPeer is based on J2ME. However, the actual execution of JMobiPeer has only been tested on emulators on standard PCs.

This is probably because the framework has high requirements on CPU and memory. In addition, the framework does not reveal any details on the API or if they provide a pure or hybrid peer-to-peer solution.

PEER2ME: A PEER-TO-PEER FRAMEWORK

The Peer2Me project was initiated to enable rapid development of proximity-based peer-to-peer applications for mobile devices built on top of the Java Micro Edition (Java ME) platform (Helal, 2002). Our main goal was to develop a high-level programming framework enabling developers to use simple primitives and methods to manage the complexity of peer-to-peer mobile ad hoc networks. It was also essential that the Peer2Me framework should be transparent and hide the network technology used for communication.

Our current implementation of the framework is based on the CLDC 1.1 and MIDP 2.0. In addition, the Peer2Me framework uses two optional packages (Java ME APIs):

- **JSR82** to access and manage Bluetooth networks
- **JSR75** to access Personal Information Management (PIM).

The current Peer2Me implementation only supports Bluetooth networks, but the architecture is made modular to also support other types of networks such as WiFi when they are supported in the Java ME environment and/or by the devices.

The Peer2Me architecture is based on a layered architectural pattern where each layer is assigned with its own responsibility, and one layer is based on the layer below. By using the layered approach, the architecture would gain positive characteristics like modularity and transparency. The negative effect by using this approach could be slower execution if the applications often have to go up and down several layers to carry out the operations. As the Peer2Me framework should be used on resource constrained execution platform, we decided to use few layers in the architecture. Figure 2 shows the high-level architecture and the main parts of Peer2Me framework (note that the MIDlet is not a part of the Peer2Me framework).

Figure 2. The Peer2Me High-level architecture

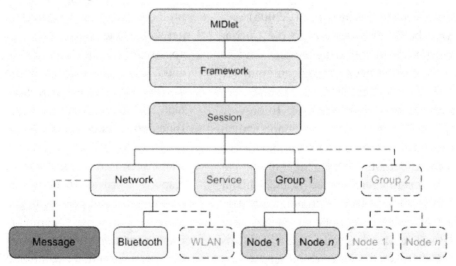

The Peer2Me high-level architecture consists of the following parts:

- **Node:** A node is a logical representation of a peer, i.e., a mobile phone running the framework. Nodes can form a mobile ad hoc network.
- **Group:** A group is a collection of nodes that know of each other's existence. All the nodes in a group can communicate with each other.
- **Service:** A service is a description and acts as a unique ID for an application running the framework. Only Peer2Me applications *sharing the same service* can interact.
- **Network:** A network is an abstraction of the network layer representing the communication medium accessed by the framework instance. The network layer can consists of several network implementations that also can be run simultaneously. Note that if some functionality is specific to the network technology used, it must be accessed directly in the specific network implementation (e.g., Bluetooth).
- **Message:** A message is an entity that can be exchanged between the nodes. A message can be sent to single nodes or to groups and can contain text, serialised objects, and any data type or binary data such as pictures, video, documents etc.
- **Session:** A session represents the lifetime of all the communication between the nodes in a group. A session keeps track of known nodes, groups and available network mediums.
- **Framework:** A framework represents the core entity between the application and the rest of the system. The framework hides all the complexity for the application developer and provides the interface to Peer2Me.
- **Application:** A Peer2Me application will be implemented as a MIDlet running on top of the Peer2Me framework.

To implement a Peer2Me application, the developer needs to import several parts of the framework: The *framework interface* itself, a *subscriber interface* acting as a listener for nearby peers, a *message interface* handling message exchange between peers, the *network interface* for setting the network, and the *node interface* giving a local representation of the nodes in the network. After the Peer2Me framework has been initiated, the Peer2Me application will automatically set a peer-to-peer mobile ad hoc network and search for other nearby devices running the same Peer2Me service. The Peer2Me framework will dynamically detect coming and going peers, which is handled through events. It is up to the developer of the Peer2Me application to define how to react to events in the peer-to-peer network. Through the subscriber interface, the developer must implement four methods that defines how the application should react to events:

- **searchCompleted:** This method is called when the Peer2Me framework has completed a search for nearby Peer2Me peers running the same service.
- **nodeDiscovered:** This method is called when a new node has been detected in the network.
- **nodeLost:** This method is called when a node can now longer be detected. The node detection mechanism is running in a separate thread and it sends out a ping to all nearby peers and waits for an echo from all of them.
- **messageReceived:** This method is called when a message has been sent from another peer.

The source code for the initialisation of a Peer2Me application is shown in Listing 1.

In line 1, the MIDlet Chat2Me must implement the FrameworkSubscriber interface from the Peer2Me framework. The CommandListener is a Java ME interface to catch events from the

Listing 1. Initialisation of Peer2Me

```
public class Chat2Me extends MIDlet implements FrameworkSubscriber, Commandlistener {    1
private Frameworkframework ;                                                             2
framework = Framework.getInstance("MyGroup", "Chat2Me", new Bluetooth(), this) ;        3
framework.initialize() ;                                                                 4
framework.search() ;                                                                     5
```

user interface. Then a framework variable must be created (line 2). The lines 3 and 4 initiate the framework with the parameters for the name of group, name of service, the network used and a reference to the MIDlet itself. The device running the application is now available for service discovery from other devices running Peer2Me. Line 5 searches for nearby devices running the same Peer2Me service.

The Peer2Me framework has been downloaded and used at institutions other than Norwegian University of Science and Technology (NTNU), but we do not have a complete overview of the usage and application developed in Peer2Me by external institutions. For more details on the Peer2Me framework, see (Wang et al., 2007).

FRAMEWORK TO CHARACTERIZE AND EVALUATE MOBILE PEER-TO-PEER APPLICATIONS

The motivation behind the evaluation of the Peer2Me applications was to discover the usefulness and the usability of the applications, to assess how well the Peer2Me supported the implementation of the applications, and if there were any limitations of the application due to the

Table 1. Framework for characterising mobile peer-to-peer applications

ID	Evaluation criteria/Characteristics	Measure
1	Number of users typically involved	(1-100 users)
2	Classification according to the place	(Same place, Different place, Both)
3	Classification according to time	(Asynchronous, Real time, Both)
4	Classification according to planning	(Impromptu collaboration, Formal collaboration)
5	Classification according to user interaction	(Controlled, User interaction, Automatic triggered, Automatic)
6	Classification according to collaboration pattern	(Master controlled, True peer-to-peer)
7	Classification according to how collaboration is improved	(Initiate collaboration, Improve coordination, Improve negotiation, Improve exchange, Improve communication)
8	The degree of usefulness of application	(Very low, Low, Medium, High, Very high)
9	The degree of replacing manual collaboration	(Very low, Low, Medium, High, Very high)
10	The degree of replacing existing collaboration support	(Very low, Low, Medium, High, Very high)
11	Limitations in the application due to wireless technology (Bluetooth)	(None, Some limitations, Severe limitations)
12	Limitations in the application due to development platform (Java ME)	(None, Some limitations, Severe limitations)
13	Limitations in the application due to the device (mobile phone)	(None, Some limitations, Severe limitations)
14	Limitations in the application due to framework (Peer2ME)	(None, Some limitations, Severe limitations)

underlying technology used (Java ME, mobile phone and Bluetooth). The framework consists of 14 characteristics, which are measured either as a number or in selection of a few specified textual short descriptions. Table 1 shows the framework composed of 14 characteristics and how each characteristic is measured. The characterisation is based on what has been described in the previous section Mobile Computer Supported Cooperative Work. The framework can be used to compare various mobile peer-to-peer applications, but also as a checklist of issues the developer should consider when developing a mobile peer-to-peer application.

EVALUATION AND DESCRIPTION OF MOBILE PEER-TO-PEER COLLABORATIVE APPLICATIONS

This section describes various peer-to-peer applications that have been developed using the Peer2Me framework. The different applications have been developed to explore the possibilities of mobile face-to-face collaborative applications, and to discover the usefulness and limitations of such applications. This section also describes an evaluation and characterisation of the applications in terms of usefulness, usability, how difficult it was to realise the applications in Peer2Me, and how well the underlying technology can support the applications using the Peer2Me framework.

The Peer2Me developers performed the evaluation of the framework and applications themselves. The results of the following evaluation are based on more than four years of experimentation with development and usage of peer-to-peer applications. The subjects used in the usability tests were students at NTNU who volunteered to test Peer2Me applications, and we collected the usability data through a combination of observation, interviews and evaluation forms.

Peer2Share – A File Sharing Application

Peer2Share is a simple application for easily exchanging files between mobile devices using Bluetooth. Any kind of files like mp3-files, ringtones, pictures, and movie clips can be exchanged. The application searches for all nearby devices running Peer2Share. The user must initiate the file exchange himself, and choose who to share files with and what files to share. The main difference with this application compared to the native file exchange support in most mobile phones is that the network connections and discovery of users are set up automatically and a user-interface specific for file exchange is provided. Figure 3 shows two screenshots from setting up the Peer2Share application.

The characterisation of Peer2Share is shown in Table 2. The characterisation shows that this application is master-controlled meaning that one mobile device is in charge for managing the communication. Two users typically use the Peer2Share application, although more users are supported. The application does not suffer from limitations in Bluetooth, Java ME, the mobile

Figure 3. Screenshots from the Peer2Share application

Table 2. Characterisation of Peer2Share

ID	Evaluation criteria/Characteristics	Result
1	Number of users typically involved	2 users
2	Classification according to the place	Same place
3	Classification according to time	Asynchronous
4	Classification according to planning	Impromptu collaboration
5	Classification according to user interaction	User interaction
6	Classification according to collaboration pattern	Master controlled
7	Classification according to how collaboration is improved	Improve exchange
8	The degree of usefulness of application	Medium
9	The degree of replacing manual collaboration	High
10	The degree of replacing existing collaboration support	Low
11	Limitations in the application due to Bluetooth	None
12	Limitations in the application due to Java ME	None
13	Limitations in the application due to the mobile phone	None
14	Limitations in the application due to Peer2ME	None

phone or Peer2Me. The Peer2Share application does not bring any new functionality compare to existing functionality on mobile phones, and the main contribution is an easier set-up and a more convenient user interface.

Peer2Chat – A Chat Application

Peer2Chat is a simple chat application for people being co-located. The application works like any other chat application and can be used to communicate with people in areas where you are not allow to talk like at a library or in a class room. In addition, the chat application can be used to start communicating with people you do not know at waiting areas like bus-stops, train stations and airports or at public transportation like in busses, trains etc. You can also use the chat application to play text-based games, like guessing riddles, quiz, etc.

The characterisation of Peer2Chat is given in Table 3. The characterisation that follows shows that from two to seven users are typically involved. The Peer2ME framework and how Bluetooth connections are established limits the maximum

number of users. More than seven users can be supported if dynamic establishment of Bluetooth connections is added to the Peer2ME framework. Although this application is regarded as real time, it is not critical that the messages between the users are exchanged with less delay than 1 second. This application is regarded as a true peer-to-peer application as there is no central node managing the network traffic.

Compared to traditional chat applications, Peer2Chat is a bit limited as you can only chat with people within your digital sphere (up to 50 meters). However, this application was developed just for this purpose. This limitation can be removed if a scatternet (a network consisting of several linked PANs) is established. The most useful usage of Peer2Chat is for communicating in areas where you are not allowed to talk.

PeerQuiz – A Quiz Game

PeerQuiz is a quiz-game for mobile phones for co-located players. PeerQuiz is initiated by one user sending a set of questions to all surrounding users. All users that accept the challenge will

Table 3. Characterisation of Peer2Chat

ID	Evaluation criteria/Characteristics	Result
1	Number of users typically involved	2-7 users
2	Classification according to the place	Same place
3	Classification according to time	Real time
4	Classification according to planning	Impromptu collaboration
5	Classification according to user interaction	User interaction
6	Classification according to collaboration pattern	True peer-to-peer
7	Classification according to how collaboration is improved	Improve communication
8	The degree of usefulness of application	Medium
9	The degree of replacing manual collaboration	Medium
10	The degree of replacing existing collaboration support	Medium
11	Limitations in the application due to Bluetooth	Some limitation (no scatternet support)
12	Limitations in the application due to Java ME	None
13	Limitations in the application due to the mobile phone	None
14	Limitations in the application due to Peer2ME	Some limitations (maximum 7 users)

have to choose between the given alternatives, and a winner will be declared based on most correct answers. This application requires that one user acts as a master and sets up the game before other players can join in. The master will decide the number of questions to be played and all communication in the game goes through the

Figure 4. Screenshots from the PeerQuiz application

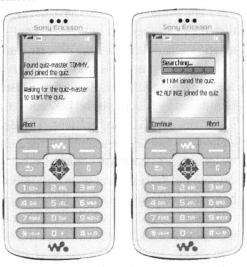

master device. Figure 4 shows screenshots from setting up a PeerQuiz game.

A characterisation of PeerQuiz is given in Table 4. The PeerQuiz application is master-based, where the device of the initiator of the game will be the coordinator of the communication and control flow. The communication between the devices must be carried out in real time, to give the fast user response required for games. As this is a quiz game, the real time requirements are not so high that the lag and limited bandwidth in Bluetooth introduce any problem.

Peer2Schedule – A Face-to-Face Meeting Scheduler

Peer2Schedule is an application made for making planning of meeting easier. The person that initiates the meeting planning will input a time frame for when the meeting should be. This mobile device will connect to all nearby mobile devices and check their calendar entries for availability. The initiator can then choose an open time spot for next meeting and the calendar of all the mobile devices involved will be updated with a new cal-

Table 4. Characterisation of PeerQuiz

ID	Evaluation criteria/Characteristics	Result
1	Number of users typically involved	2-7 users
2	Classification according to the place	Same place
3	Classification according to time	Real time
4	Classification according to planning	Impromptu collaboration
5	Classification according to user interaction	Controlled
6	Classification according to collaboration pattern	Master controlled
7	Classification according to how collaboration is improved	Improve communication
8	The degree of usefulness of application	Low
9	The degree of replacing manual collaboration	Low
10	The degree of replacing existing collaboration support	Low
11	Limitations in the application due to Bluetooth	None
12	Limitations in the application due to Java ME	None
13	Limitations in the application due to the mobile phone	None
14	Limitations in the application due to Peer2ME	None

endar entry with all necessary meeting information. This application is very useful at meetings to find the time for next meeting. To make this meeting planning work, all mobile devices must run the Peer2Schedule application. The main goal of this application is to provide workflow automa-

Figure 5. Screenshots from the Peer2Schedule application

tion. Figure 5 shows the process of scheduling a meeting using Peer2Schedule.

The characterisation of Peer2Schedule is given in Table 5. The Peer2Schedule application is a good example of an application where the user interaction is controlled by the application through one master. The device of the initiator will be the master, and the workflow is controlled through the master peer. Peer2Schedule can also be classified as an application to support formal collaboration, as it is a mobile workflow application. The initiator will also have a different role than the other users, as he needs to configure the meeting schedule before the process can start.

Although this application is a very useful collaborative tool, it is limited by restrictions introduced by Bluetooth and how current mobile phone run Java ME applications. The Bluetooth technology reduces the usability of the application by long time to establish connection between all devices and the search for open times slots cannot be performed automatically without user intervention, as all users involved must accept a security prompt before the search can be performed.

Table 5. Characterisation of Peer2Schedule

ID	Evaluation criteria/Characteristics	Result
1	Number of users typically involved	2-7 users
2	Classification according to the place	Same place
3	Classification according to time	Asynchronous
4	Classification according to planning	Formal collaboration
5	Classification according to user interaction	Controlled
6	Classification according to collaboration pattern	Master controlled
7	Classification according to how collaboration is improved	Improve coordination
8	The degree of usefulness of application	High
9	The degree of replacing manual collaboration	High
10	The degree of replacing existing collaboration support	High
11	Limitations in the application due to Bluetooth	Severe limitations
12	Limitations in the application due to Java ME	Some limitations
13	Limitations in the application due to the mobile phone	Some limitations
14	Limitations in the application due to Peer2ME	None

Peer2BrickBlock – A Peer-to-Peer Real-time Game

The Peer2BrickBlock game is a mobile real-time peer-to-peer game where to goal is for the player to push other player into traps. Every player controls a brick, which can be moved around in a 2D playfield. The playfield is an open area where you have a trap and several power-ups to increase the size of your brick, make your brick move faster and make your brick stronger (easier to push other bricks around). The trap and the power-ups are randomly placed on the screen. When a player has been pushed into a trap, he will loose one life and the brick will re-spawn after some seconds on the playfield. All the user's screens should reflect all players movements in real-time.

Table 6 shows the characterisation of Peer-2BrickBlock. Due to the small screen on mobile phones, this game is best suited for few players (four or less). This is a real time game where it is important that the game events are distributed without any long delays to all players. The user interaction is user-driven, meaning that the network traffic between the devices depends on how the users interact. This is also a pure peer-to-peer application where no player is the master, e.g. any player can change the game preferences and the game starts when one of the players pushes the start button.

The Peer2BrickBlock application caused us some major headache, and we discovered major limitations in our Peer2ME framework and in Bluetooth. The main problem was that in Peer2ME Bluetooth connections are established when needed between the devices. For a real time game this takes too much time, making the network lag ruining the game play. Also we found that the performance of the OBEX protocol in Bluetooth that Peer2ME uses is not sufficient for real time updates with minimum lag.

PeerCardExchange – An Automatic Business Card Exchange Application

The PeerCardExchange is an application used to automatically exchange digital business card stored on a mobile device with people with the same interests. The user must first enter informa-

Table 6. Characterisation of the Peer2BrickBlock applications

ID	Evaluation criteria/Characteristics	Result
1	Number of users typically involved	2-4
2	Classification according to the place	Same place
3	Classification according to time	Real time
4	Classification according to planning	Impromptu collaboration
5	Classification according to user interaction	User interaction
6	Classification according to collaboration pattern	True peer-to-peer
7	Classification according to how collaboration is improved	Initiate collaboration
8	The degree of usefulness of application	Low
9	The degree of replacing manual collaboration	Low
10	The degree of replacing existing collaboration support	Low
11	Limitations in the application due to Bluetooth	Severe limitations (slow discovery)
12	Limitations in the application due to Java ME	None
13	Limitations in the application due to the mobile phone	Some limitations (screen)
14	Limitations in the application due to Peer2ME	Severe limitations (slow connection)

tion like name, contact information, company, position, picture, URLs, etc to complete his own digital business card. The next step is to enter the domains his is working in using a pre-defined ontology mapping the existing domains, e.g. computer graphics, mobile computing, software engineering, etc. The ontology is hierarchically defining high-level domains at the top and more specific domains further down in the tree structure. The final step is to enter the domains of the persons he wants to receive business cards from. After this initialisation process has been completed, the users can let the mobile device search for other mobile devices running the same service. If a match of domain is found, digital business cards are exchanged between the mobile devices. This application is useful for instance at conferences with many people where the mobile device will collect business cards from people with the same interests automatically on behalf of the users. After the user has initiated the application, he can just walk around to automatically collect business cards without any user intervention. However, this application requires that most people in the same area run the same application to be useful

(must have a critical mass). The application can also be used for non-professional services like dating by using other domain models.

Table 7 shows the characterisation of Peer-CardExchange. This is an application where a lot of users can be involved in a big area. However, the user interaction is mostly sequential in that two mobile devices check for matching domains and then continues for a new search for another device. This application is after initialisation automatic and requires no user interaction. The user can simply look at the result (collected business cards) after walking around in an area with other users for a time. The usefulness of this application is limited both by the slow discovery time in Bluetooth (20+ seconds for Bluetooth 1.x and 10+ seconds for Bluetooth 2.x) and that few mobile phones allow Java ME applications run as background process.

Peer2FindPerson – A Find-the-Right-Person Application

This application is very similar to PeerCardExchange, but it will initiate direct contact between

Table 7. Characterisation of the PeerCardExchange application

ID	Evaluation criteria/Characteristics	Result
1	Number of users typically involved	2-100
2	Classification according to the place	Same place
3	Classification according to time	Asynchronous
4	Classification according to planning	Impromptu collaboration
5	Classification according to user interaction	Automatic
6	Classification according to collaboration pattern	True peer-to-peer
7	Classification according to how collaboration is improved	Improve exchange
8	The degree of usefulness of application	High
9	The degree of replacing manual collaboration	High
10	The degree of replacing existing collaboration support	High
11	Limitations in the application due to Bluetooth	Severe limitations
12	Limitations in the application due to Java ME	Some limitations
13	Limitations in the application due to the mobile phone	None
14	Limitations in the application due to Peer2ME	None

two users. The initialisation process is the same as for PeerCardExchange, where the user must enter his own domain and enter the domain of the person he is interested in meeting. After the initialisation process has been completed, the mobile device will search all nearby mobile devices for a match in domains. If a match is found, the mobile device will notify both users by vibrating or making a sound and showing the picture of the matching person found. Both persons can then find each other and start talking. As with the PeerCardExchange, this application is useful where many people that do not know each other are meeting e.g. at a conference. The application makes it easier to find people interested in the same topics and that would have mutual benefits of collaborating. This application can also be used for searching for persons with specific skills to solve a problem. A picture of the Peer2FindPerson in use is shown in Figure 6.

Table 8 shows the characterisation of Peer2FindPerson. Although this application resembles PeerCardExchange it has some noticeable differences. Peer2FindPerson is intended to initialise collaboration between two persons and the in-

volved users are notified in real time if a match is found. Also the user interaction in Peer2Find-Person must be regarded as automatic triggered as the application searches for a match and notifies the users if a match is found.

As with the PeerCardExchange application, Peer2FindPerson suffers from the same problems

Figure 6. A picture of two users that have found that they have matching interests

Table 8. Characterisation of the Peer2FindPerson application

ID	Evaluation criteria/Characteristics	Result
1	Number of users typically involved	2
2	Classification according to the place	Same place
3	Classification according to time	Real time
4	Classification according to planning	Impromptu collaboration
5	Classification according to user interaction	Automatic triggered
6	Classification according to collaboration pattern	True peer-to-peer
7	Classification according to how collaboration is improved	Initiate collaboration
8	The degree of usefulness of application	High
9	The degree of replacing manual collaboration	High
10	The degree of replacing existing collaboration support	High
11	Limitations in the application due to Bluetooth	Severe limitations
12	Limitations in the application due to Java ME	Some limitations
13	Limitations in the application due to the mobile phone	None
14	Limitations in the application due to Peer2ME	None

with long discovery time in Bluetooth and that JaveME applications normally cannot be run in background.

Evaluation Summary

In the previous sections we have presented seven different mobile collaborative applications with different characteristics. The most noticeable differences is in how collaboration is improved through applications covering functionality to initiate collaboration, improve coordination, improve exchange and improve communication. The only area missing identified in evaluation framework is improvement of negotiation that could typically be an application to negotiate about desired resources on behalf of the users. The described Peer2Me applications had variations in being asynchronous or real time, impromptu collaboration or formal, and the full range of variation in how user interaction was managed by the application. Most applications typically involved between 2 and 7 users, but some involved fewer due to the limited screens on mobile phones and some more due to the fact that interaction between lots of devices

are handled sequentially. None of the applications supported collaboration at different place although this could be provided if e.g. Peer2Chat supported scatternet (not currently supported in Bluetooth). Some applications were limited by the underlying technology and suffered from the slow device discovery process in Bluetooth, the low bandwidth of Bluetooth, the lack of support for running Java ME applications in background, the usage of the OBEX protocol in Peer2ME, and how security is handled in Bluetooth.

The choice of using Java ME and Bluetooth to implement Peer2Me was both a blessing and a curse. The main benefit is that the Peer2Me framework can run on most mobile phones, PDAs and mobile computers as Java ME and Bluetooth are supported on most mobile devices. For peer2peer applications that do not require short discovery and connection time between the devices, the Peer2Me works fine. This problem has been minimised with the Bluetooth 2.x standard where the discovery time has been reduced from about 20 seconds to 10 seconds. The problems of running Java ME applications in background and the security prompt issues in Bluetooth are device-dependent and are solved for most new mobile devices. These issues would not have been any problems if Peer2Me has been implemented as native code. However, this would have limited the usefulness of the framework. To use WiFi instead of Bluetooth as a wireless network technology will solve problems related to slow discovery and low bandwidth, but this will also limit the framework to be supported by fewer devices.

The roster of Peer2Me applications presented in this chapter consists of rather simple applications. More complicated applications can be implemented by combining the functionality of two or more existing Peer2Me applications. One example would be to combine the Peer2Schedule and Peer2Share applications to implement a more complete meeting application that supports both planning of meetings and events as well as sharing of documents. Another example would be to combine the Peer2Chat and Peer2Quiz applications to implement a more versatile application to kill time in waiting areas. The final example is to combine the Peer2Share, PeerCardExchange and Peer2FindPerson applications into one, leaving it up to the user if he just wants to exchange business cards, to get a notification when a matching person is close by and give the opportunity to exchange documents with this person. The main challenge in implementing more advanced peer-to-peer applications is that some mobile devices have problems with large Java ME applications in terms of footprint or memory usage.

FUTURE TRENDS

As seen from the conclusion of this chapter, mobile network technologies like Bluetooth and Java ME still have some shortcomings to prevent a real break-through for mobile peer-to-peer applications. However, as the network technologies improve, new opportunities arise and new applications appear. Today, there are PAN-technologies

that do not suffer from the same problems you have to deal with in Bluetooth. The main problem is that most mobile devices do not support these technologies. There is a need to define standard technologies and frameworks for mobile peer-to-peer enabling all kinds of applications and devices to collaborate using pre-defined well-proven protocols and architectures.

The mobile technology changes rapidly and it is hard to predict the future. The two most interesting recent mobile implementation platforms are iPhone SDK from Apple and Android from Google. None of these platforms have built-in support for peer-to-peer applications, but there are some on-going projects to develop peer-to-peer frameworks for these platforms. However, none of the currently on-going projects provide support for co-located peer-to-peer (directly between the devices). The introduction of sensors and activators brings new opportunities for mobile peer-to-peer applications. Up till now, the introduction of sensors in mobile environment has not been utilized due to the size and power consumption of existing sensors. However, the sensors in the future can be seen as smart dust or brilliant rocks where the sensors are so small that they can be integrated into any material and any device (Satyanarayanan, 2003). This makes it possible for mobile applications to sense location, proximity, temperature, pressure, etc., which can be used to give the application the required input to give only the most relevant services to the users. To make such context-aware systems, it is required to have an architecture that can handle sensor networks, and retrieve and manage the sensor information in a sufficient manner (Anagnostopoulos, 2007). A combination of sensor technology, a strong integration with web-services such as that provided in the iPhone SDK and Android, and support for co-located peer-to-peer data transfers will open to a new range of applications that can enrich, support, simplify and automate human-to-human collaboration.

CONCLUSION

In this chapter we have presented the Peer2ME framework for developing mobile peer-to-peer application to support collaboration. Further, we have presented several Peer2ME applications and classified them according to an evaluation framework for such applications. The evaluation framework presented is useful for characterising and evaluating mobile peer-to-peer applications as well as it can be used as a checklist when developing new mobile peer-to-peer applications. We have also discovered some limitations in Bluetooth, Java ME and Peer2ME that will limit the usability of such applications.

ACKNOWLEDGMENT

We would like to thank Thomas Fossum, Lars Kirkhus, Anders R. Sveen, Michael Sars Norum, Carl-Henrik Wolf Lund, Steinar Hestnes, Torbjørn Vatn, Tommy Bjørnsgård, Kim Saxlund, Martin Jarrett, Eivind Sorteberg, and Hassan Syed Shah for their invaluable effort in the Peer2Me project.

REFERENCES

Anagnostopoulos, C. B., Tsounis, A., & Hadjiefthymiades, S. (2007). Context awareness in mobile computing environments. *Wireless Personal Communications, 42*(3), 445-464.

Apple Computer. (2008). *iPhone dev center.* Retrieved September 9, 2008, from http://developer.apple.com/iphone/

Ashok, R. L., & Agrawal, D. P. (2003). Next-generation wearable networks. *Computer 36*(11), 31-39.

Auvinen, A., Vapa, M., Weber, M., Kotilainen, N., & Vuori, J. (2006). Chedar:Peer-to-peer middleware. In *Proceedings of the Parallel and Distributed Processing Symposium*, Rhodes Island, Greece.

Bisignano, M., Di Modica, G., & Tomarchio, O. (2005). *JMobiPeer: A middleware for mobile peer-to-peer computing in MANETs.* In *Proceedings of the First international Workshop on Mobility in Peer-To-Peer Systems (MPPS)*, Columbus, Ohio, USA.

Broll, W., Lindt, I., Herbst, I., Ohlenburg, J., Braun, A-K., & Wetzel, R.(2008). Toward next-gen mobile AR games. *IEEE Computer Graphics and Applications, 28*(4), 40-48.

Ellis, C. A., Gibbs, S. J., & Rein, G. (1991). *Groupware: Some issues and experiences.* Communications of the ACM, 34(1), 39-58.

Davids, N. (1996a). Personal digital assistants: Part 1. *IEEE Computer 29*(9), 96-99.

Davids, N. (1996b). Personal digital assistants: Part 2. *IEEE Computer 29*(11), 100-104.

Davies, N., Cheverst, K., Mitchell, K., & Efrat, A. (2001). Using and determining location in a context-sensitive tour guide. *IEEE Computer, 34*(8), 35-41.

Eagle, N. & Pentland, A. (2005). Social serendipity: Mobilizing social software. *IEEE Pervasive Computing, 04*(2), 28-34.

Geer, D. (2005). Users make a beeline for ZigBee technology. *Computer, 38*(12), 16-19.

Google. (2008). *Android – an open handset alliance project.* Retrieved September 18, 2008, from http://code.google.com/android/

Harjula, E., Ylianttila, M., Ala-Kurikka, J., Riekki, J., & Sauvola, J. (2004). Plug-and-play application platform: Towards mobile peer-to-peer. In *Proceedings of the 3rd International Conference on Mobile and Ubiquitous Multimedia*, College Park, Maryland, USA.

Helal, S. (2002). Pervasive Java. *IEEE Pervasive Computing 1*(1), 82-85.

Holmquist, L. E., Wigstrom, J., & Falk, J. (1998) The Hummingbird: Mobile support for group awareness. Demonstrated at the *ACM Conference on Computer Supported Cooperative Work*, Seattle, Washington, USA.

Horozov, T., Grama, A., Vasudevan, V., & Landis, S. (2002). MOBY-a mobile peer-to-peer service and data network. In *Proceedings of the International Conference on Parallel Processing*, Vancouver, British Columbia, Canada.

Husemann, D. (1999). The smart card: Don't leave home without it. *IEEE Concurrency, 7*(2), 24-27.

Jing, J., Huff, K., Sinha, H., Hurwitz, B., & Robinson, B. (1999). Workflow and application adaptations in mobile environments. In *Proceedings of 2nd IEEE Workshop on Mobile Computer Systems and Applications*, New Orleans, Louisiana, USA.

Kapp, S. (2002). 802.11: Leaving the wire behind. *IEEE Internet Computing, 6*(1), 82-85.

Kawulok, L., Zielinski, K., & Jaeschke, M. (2005). Trusted group membership service for JXME (JXTA4J2ME). In *Proceedings of the Wireless And Mobile Computing, Networking And Communications (WiMob)*, Montreal, Canada.

Kortuem, G. (2002). Proem: A middleware platform for mobile peer-to-peer computing. *ACM SIGMOBILE Mobile Computing and Communications Review, 6*(4), 62-64.

Kortuem, G., Schneider, J., Thaddeus, D. P., Thompson, G. C., Fickas, S., & Segall Z. (2001). When peer-to-peer comes face-to-face: Collaborative peer-to-peer computing in mobile ad hoc networks. In *Proceedings of the 1st International Conference on Peer-to-Peer Computing*, Linköping, Sweden.

Leavitt, N. (2007). For wireless USB, the future starts now. *Computer, 40*(7), 14-16.

Long, S., Kooper, R., Abowd, G. D., & Atkeson, C. G. (1996). Rapid prototyping of mobile context-aware applications: The cyberguide case study. In *Proceedings of the ACM International Conference on Mobile Computing and Networking*, Rye, New York, USA.

Macedonia, M. (2007). iPhones target the tech elite. *Computer, 40*(6), 94-95.

Maibaum, N., & Mundt, T. (2002). JXTA: A technology facilitating mobile peer-to-peer networks. In *Proceedings of the International Mobility and Wireless Access Workshop (MobiWac)*, Fort Worth, Texas, USA.

Michahelles, F., Thiesse, F., Schmidt, A., & Williams, J. R. (2007). Pervasive RFID and near field communication technology. *IEEE Pervasive Computing, 6*(3), 94-96.

Miller, B. A., & Bisdikian, C. (2004). *Bluetooth revealed* (2nd ed.). Addison-Wesley.

Mohapatra, P., Gui, C., & Li, J. (2004). Group communications in mobile ad hoc networks. *IEEE Computer, 37*(2), 52-59.

Olson, J.S., Teasley, S., Covi, L., & Olson, G. (2002). The (currently) unique advantages of collocated work. MIT Press.

Papadopoulos, C. (2006). Improving awareness in mobile CSCW. IEEE Transactions on Mobile Computing, 5(10), 1331-1346.

Reynolds, F. (2008). Whither Bluetooth? IEEE Pervasive Computing, 7(3), 6-8.

Satyanarayanan, M. (1996). Fundamental challenges in mobile computing. In Proceedings of the 15th ACM Symposium on Principles of Distributed Computing, Philadelphia, PA, USA.

Satyanarayanan, M. (2003). From the editor in chief: Of smart dust and brilliant rocks. *IEEE Pervasive Computing, 2*(4), 2-4.

Schollmeier, R. (2001). A definition of peer-to-peer networking for the classification of peer-to-peer architectures and applications. In *Proceedings of the 1ˢᵗ International Conference on Peer-To-Peer Computing (P2P)*, Washington, DC, USA.

Schreiner, K. (2007). Where we at? Mobile phones bring GPS to the masses. *IEEE Computer Graphics and Applications, 27*(3), 6-11.

Vaughan-Nichols, S. J. (2003). OSs battle in the smart-phone market. *Computer, 36*(6), 10-12.

Wang, A. I., Bjørnsgård, T., & Saxlund, K. (2007). Peer2Me - rapid application framework for mobile peer-to-peer applications. In *Proceedings of International Symposium on Collaborative Technologies and Systems (CTS)*, Orlando, Florida, USA.

Wang, A. I., Norum, M. S., & Lund, C.-H. W. (2006). Issues related to development of wireless peer-to-peer games in J2ME. In *Proceedings of the 1ˢᵗ Conference on Entertainment Systems (ENSYS)*, Guadeloupe, French Caribbean.

Wang, A. I., Sørensen, C.-F., & Fossum, T. (2005). Mobile peer-to-peer technology used to promote spontaneous collaboration. In *Proceedings of International Symposium on Collaborative Technologies and Systems (CTS)*, Saint Louis, Missouri, USA.

Wiberg, M., & Grönlund, Ä. (2000). Exploring mobile CSCW: Five areas of questions for further research. In *Proceedings of IRIS23 (Information Research in Scandinavia)*, Trollhättan, Sweden.

Zhang, H., Udagawa, T., Arita, T., Tsuji, J., Okada, K., Sasase, I., & Nakagawa, M. (2001). Wireless 1394: A new standard for integrated wireless broadband home networking. In *Proceedings of IEEE Vehicular Technology Conference (VTC)*, Rhodes Island, Greece.

Zheng, P., & Ni, L. M. (2006). Spotlight: The rise of the smart phone. *IEEE Distributed Systems Online, 7*(3), 1-14.

Chapter XX
Service Discovery Approaches to Mobile Peer–to–Peer Computing

Antônio Tadeu A. Gomes
National Laboratory for Scientific Computing (LNCC), Brazil

Artur Ziviani
National Laboratory for Scientific Computing (LNCC), Brazil

Luciana S. Lima
National Laboratory for Scientific Computing (LNCC), Brazil

Markus Endler
Pontifical Catholic University of Rio de Janeiro (PUC-Rio), Brazil

ABSTRACT

This chapter surveys the approaches to service discovery that are relevant to mobile peer-to-peer systems in a variety of scenarios. More specifically, the authors consider approaches that may be employed in infrastructure wireless networks, single-hop and multi-hop ad hoc wireless networks. They analyze each approach based on design and functional aspects that have implications for its flexibility, scalability, and discovery efficiency. The authors also point out some promising research and development directions in the area of service discovery, with a special focus on ad hoc wireless networks. They comment on specific variants of such networks that are emerging in practice, and their reflections on the design of effective service discovery solutions.

INTRODUCTION

A service in a distributed system is any remote software or hardware entity that a user[1] of such a system wishes to use. Service discovery mechanisms allow the user to locate these entities in the system. Designing such mechanisms is particularly challenging for mobile distributed systems. Typically, mobile systems are built of portable devices, which are scarcer of hardware resources (*e.g.* slower CPU, less memory, limited I/O capabilities and energy) than stationary systems. Besides, mobile systems are more prone to intermittent connectivity. Therefore, these systems call for mechanisms that allow devices to interoperate casually or opportunistically, *i.e.* without prior assumptions regarding the surrounding environment. *Casual interoperability* may lead to administrative overhead, since services may become unavailable (or new ones may appear) in the system anywhere, anytime. Service discovery mechanisms must therefore function as seamlessly as possible, automating the delivery of service information, as well as the selection and configuration of such services within the system, thereby enhancing its usability.

Classical scenarios of service discovery for mobile systems include PDAs and laptops detecting nearby printers and/or high-definition displays for opportunistically improving their I/O capabilities. Such examples illustrate the typical case of a master-slave relationship between devices. Nevertheless, there are mobile systems in which devices may exhibit a P2P (peer-to-peer) servicing pattern—we refer to such systems as *mobile P2P systems*. Examples of scenarios in which such systems would be useful include:

- **E-learning**. Consider the scenario presented in (König-Ries & Klein, 2002), in which a student connects her PDA to a wireless network in the university campus to download a certain article. Another device in the network provides the article in PostScript format. Nevertheless, the student's PDA cannot display such a format. She then searches the network for a "PostScript2PDF" converter service. A third device in the network may provide this service to the student.
- **Emergency response**. Consider a large rescue and medical team working in a natural disaster scenario, such as the one caused by the Indian Ocean tsunami in December 2004 or the earthquake in the Sichuan province of China in May 2008. In such scenarios, the seamless integration of services from on-site mobile devices may be crucial for rapidly achieving advanced forms of collaborative work, as for example to collect and automatically process information about groups of injured people (*e.g.* for triage) and thus better allocate rescue teams and medical resources.
- **Field research**. Consider a team of hydrogeologists throughout a large semi-arid region, such as the Northeastern Brazil. Such a team can exchange data about underground water resources (*e.g.* hydraulic head) being collected by their mobile devices, and can use the computational resources of such devices for *in-loco*, preliminary numerical analysis on the collected data, so as to simulate and predict some aquifer condition of interest (*e.g.* the effect of irrigation developments). This application is an instance of a novel type of mobile P2P systems that has gathered momentum in the past few years—the *mobile grids* (Hwang & Aravamudham, 2004).

The aforementioned e-learning scenario illustrates a case in which traditional service discovery approaches would provide efficient solutions if there were an underlying network infrastructure. Nonetheless, the other two scenarios may happen at places or conditions where such an infrastructure may be—or may suddenly become—unavailable. In such scenarios, alternative service discovery approaches are clearly indispensable, since these scenarios demand the self-organization of nearby devices in such a way these devices can cooperatively forward packets from/to other devices.

This chapter surveys some representative approaches to service discovery that are relevant to mobile P2P systems in a variety of scenarios. More specifically, we consider approaches that may be employed in infrastructure wireless networks, single-hop and multi-hop ad hoc wireless networks. The focus of this chapter is on the analysis of each approach based on a set of design and functional aspects. The chosen aspects are similar to the ones used in a few previous surveys on service discovery (Ahmed, Limam, Xiao, Iraqi, & Boutaba, 2007; Richard, 2000; Zhu, Mutka, & Ni, 2005; Seno, Budiarto, & Wan, 2007), being adapted to reflect the particularities of mobile P2P systems.

The remainder of this chapter is organized as follows. The *Background* section introduces the seven aspects used for comparing the approaches presented in the following two sections— *Approaches to Infrastructure and Single-hop Ad hoc Wireless Networks* and *Approaches to Multi-hop Ad hoc Wireless Networks*. The *Summary of the Approaches* section summarizes the characteristics of the presented approaches in terms of these seven aspects. The *Future Trends* section gives a flavor of some promising research and development directions in the area of service discovery, with a special focus on ad hoc wireless networks. Finally, the *Concluding Remarks* section comments on specific variants of such networks that are emerging in practice, and their reflections on the design of effective service discovery solutions.

BACKGROUND: SERVICE DISCOVERY ASPECTS

We have chosen seven key aspects to compare the approaches presented in this chapter: *service information exchange, discovery architecture, service information maintenance, discovery scope, service description and matching, service selection and invocation,* and *discovery security*. All of these aspects have implications for the flexibility, the scalability, and the discovery efficiency of each of the presented approaches.

Service Information Exchange

There are two ways for devices in a mobile P2P system to exchange service information: *service queries* and *service announcements*. Service queries involve some form of devices sending requests throughout the network and making the devices providing the required services—or a central server on their behalf (see the Discovery Architecture subsection)—reply to these requests. Service announcements permit that devices (or, again, a central server on their behalf) advertise their provided services in the network to interested devices. Most mobile P2P systems employ a combination of the two techniques. The scope of diffusion of queries and announcements (see the Discovery Scope subsection), and the periodicity and caching policies of announcements are important parameters that determine the efficiency and accuracy of service discovery in such systems.

Discovery Architecture

The architecture of a service discovery mechanism is mainly defined by the presence (or absence) of a *centralized service directory*. In a centralized service directory, a global lookup server facilitates the interaction between devices in the P2P system. This server may be known *a priori* or learned automatically during system startup. For mobile P2P systems, we can further characterize a service directory as *purely decentralized* or *partially centralized*. In a purely decentralized directory, all devices in the network may perform queries and announcements, without any central coordination. This is particularly suitable for systems deployed over ad hoc wireless networks. In a partially centralized directory, some devices play the role of localized lookup servers. Some approaches call these devices *super-nodes, super-peers,* or *ultra-nodes*. Depending on the way super-nodes exchange service information, they may build a *flat* directory (*i.e.* information is simply replicated or randomly distributed among super-nodes) or a *hierarchical* directory (*i.e.* information is distributed across super-nodes in a structured way, such as a tree or a distributed hash table – DHT). Moreover, in partially centralized approaches, the super-node role may be dynamically assigned to devices in the network. This way, a device's outage (*e.g.* due to a network disconnection) may trigger its replacement by another device, whereas a performance degradation may trigger the assignment of the super-node role to additional devices. This provides additional robustness to the system, at the cost of much higher complexity.

Service Information Maintenance

In purely decentralized and partially centralized directories, a device may keep information about services that both it and other devices may provide. In *cooperative* approaches, each device may keep (partial) information about services being provided by other devices in the network, and may disclose such information to other devices. In *uncooperative* approaches, all service information gathered by a device is used only for its own benefit. To balance the usage of a device's local resources, cooperative approaches usually employ *in-network filtering* policies, which limit the amount of information such a device may keep or disclose to other devices. Such policies aim at reducing the amount of network traffic related to discovery messages while maintaining the efficiency of discovery, but usually incur additional security breaches due to stronger involvement of intermediate devices.

A service directory may keep information about services as *soft state* or *hard state*. Soft state information requires periodic service announcements to keep service information up to date. While keeping soft state information makes it easier for a mobile P2P system to adapt to changing network conditions, it raises concerns regarding the scalability of the announcement protocol. Hard state information implies that providers must explicitly inform the system about service withdrawals, which compromises the system adaptability to changing network conditions.

Discovery Scope

The discovery scope corresponds to the set of services that a certain device can get information about. Defining a discovery scope may be important for a number of reasons, including security, scalability, and discovery efficiency. We can identify three different criteria that define the discovery scope in a mobile P2P system: the *network topology*, the *user role*, and the *user contextual information*. Purely decentralized directories usually employ network topology-scoped approaches. In such approaches, service queries and announcements may reach neighboring devices only, or may be flooded to devices farther away, as for instance in multi-hop ad hoc wireless networks. The forwarding of such messages may be accomplished by broadcast, multicast, or unicast, and may be limited to a certain range (*e.g.* to a maximum number of hops) or message characteristic (*e.g.* only some neighbors receive a specific query because they are known to reach the desired service). The approaches that employ network topology scopes usually focus on increasing their scalability by reducing the amount of network traffic related to the discovery phase, at the cost of lower discovery efficiency. In fully and partially centralized directories, where authentication and authorization is easier to manage, users of the mobile P2P system may define trust relationships between them. Therefore, users may play previously authenticated roles that constrain their queries (*e.g.* an employee cannot discover a color laser printer located in the chief executive office). Such directories also facilitate the implementation of context-aware services. For instance, the geographical location of a user may be used as an attribute to its query (*e.g.* the same employee may ask for the nearest color laser printer to which he or she has access right).

Service Description and Matching

Service description allows a device to specify the services it is willing to use or provide in the network. The process of service discovery involves the matching of such descriptions to queries and announcements. In *homogeneous* P2P systems (*e.g.* file-sharing systems), simpler approaches to service description may be employed. For instance, file-sharing systems typically use information such as file names and file metadata. In *heterogeneous* P2P systems, the service discovery approaches need to consider a broader range of services, such as processing capacity, printing and display services, and sensor readings, among others. For such approaches, there are two main techniques for service description: *attributes* and *description languages*. In the first technique, a unique identification and a set of well-known key-value pairs describe a service. Some approaches build on this basic technique by defining *templates*, which allow a standardized set of attributes to describe a group of similar services, thus facilitating the matching process. Description languages allow the use of syntactic conventions, such as XML schemas, as a means of describing services semantically. One particular set of such languages has gained widespread consideration in the area of service discovery: ontology languages (DARPA, 2006; W3C Consortium, 2004). Such languages support queries with more expressiveness and inference power, thereby allowing richer matching options (*e.g.* partial matchings). It is worth noting, however, that such expressiveness incurs some additional computational cost in terms of both processing time and memory footprint, which may be unacceptable in scenarios involving resource-poor devices.

Service Selection and Invocation

Despite the techniques used for discovery scoping and service matching, the candidate service descriptions a user may receive—whether they are announcements or results of a service query the user has issued before—may outnumber the real user needs. When this happens, either the user *manually* selects the desired services from the set of candidate services, or the system *automatically* selects them on behalf of the user. Automatic selection usually requires the combination of a good service matching technique and some selection criteria that together are able to deliver the 'best' service offerings to the user. For instance, in ad hoc wireless networks a selection algorithm might take into account some metrics such as connectivity quality, number of hops between the user and the provider, and the provider's current service load.

When selecting a service, the user should also know how the service is to be invoked. Both service announcements and replies to service queries must convey such information, which may encompass the *service location* (network address), the supported *communication protocols* (*e.g.* RPC, XML document exchanging), and the *service access rights* (*e.g.* the service operations the user is allowed to invoke according to its role and/or contextual information—see the Discovery Scope section).

Discovery Security

Security is a major challenge for any service discovery approach, especially in mobile P2P systems (Ahamed, Buford, Sharmin, Haque, & Talukder, 2008). Among the issues related to discovery security we can mention the trade-off between security and enhanced usability by automatic service discovery, selection and configuration, and the additional computing and communication overhead incurred by security techniques such as cryptography and spot checking (Monrose, Wyckoff, & Rubin, 1999).

In the context of ad hoc wireless networks, additional security issues arise. One of them is the difficulty in dynamically assigning certification authority entities upon which strong authentication mechanisms can be built. This issue usually leads to the adoption in these networks of security mechanisms that are established at deployment time—*e.g.* user authentication (identification and password) and access control lists—, thus being limited to centralized administrative domains, such as in military or emergency response scenarios. The Future Trends section further comments on the research challenges related to security in service discovery approaches to mobile P2P systems.

APPROACHES TO INFRASTRUCTURE AND SINGLE-HOP AD HOC WIRELESS NETWORKS

Until recently, most of the approaches to service discovery were based on variations of the classical client-server paradigm. Examples include Jini, Salutation and SLP. Such systems usually employ centralized service directories, thus being, at first glance, more adequate for wired and infrastructure wireless networks. It is worth mentioning, however, that all of these approaches allow some sort of decentralization of their service directories. Other approaches, such as UPnP and JXTA, follow the P2P paradigm and employ decentralized directories. Besides, all the aforementioned approaches implement flexible bootstrapping procedures that make it unnecessary the previous knowledge of lookup servers' addresses during system startup. Therefore, in principle all these approaches might be also deployed in ad hoc wireless networks. [2] Nevertheless, most of these approaches are either uncooperative, or have cooperative strategies that do not consider the utilization of resource-poor devices—*e.g.* in general these approaches lack in-network filtering policies. Thus, they offer inefficient solutions in the case of multi-hop ad hoc wireless networks (see the Approaches to Multi-hop Ad hoc Wireless Networks section).

The following subsections comment on the aforementioned service discovery systems, and also present two other solutions specifically designed for single-hop ad hoc wireless networks: the Bluetooth SDP and the DEAPSpace architecture.

Jini

Jini (Arnold, Scheifler, Waldo, O'Sullivan, & Wollrath, 1999) is a service discovery system implemented on—and designed for—the Java platform. A device running Jini must run a version of the JVM (Java Virtual Machine), or must have a surrogate running the JVM on its behalf. The limited applicability of Jini is also one of its strengths, as a client can download a service fully implemented as software from the provider and run it locally.

Jini is based on centralized directory servers called LUSes (LookUp Servers). Many LUSes may be present in the same network at the same time, but without any coordination between them, in an uncooperative way. A Jini client discovers LUSes by issuing multicast or broadcast 'pre-discovery' queries throughout the network. Alternatively, LUSes may 'pre-announce' themselves to Jini clients (again, through multicast or broadcast). After learning about LUSes, a Jini client issues discovery queries directly to them through unicast. (If no LUS can be found, a Jini client may play the role of a LUS by announcing itself to providers.) Providers employ the very same process when they announce their services. LUSes keep announcements as soft state, and thus need to be periodically refreshed by providers. In principle, Jini clients issue queries on demand to a LUS, but they can also enroll in a 'notification service' provided by a LUS to receive service announcements from it.

In the Jini system, services are described as attributes implemented as Java objects. Service providers register such attributes at LUSes together with other Java objects called *remote controls*.

A remote control either completely implements a service (*e.g.* a rendering algorithm), or plays the role of a *proxy* to the real service (*e.g.* a printing service). A LUS employs simple attribute matching in response to a service query. The matching may result in one or more remote controls being sent to the Jini client, which delegates to the user the selection of the desired service. After a Jini client selects a service, it may be invoked either locally (when the remote control completely implements the service) or through Java RMI (Remote Method Invocation), which allows both remote invocation and migration of remote services to Jini clients.

The Jini system depends on the security model embedded in the JVM, which includes cryptography (RMI over SSL – Secure Socket Layer) and authorization policies (through access control lists) that limit the activities performed by remote controls and migrated services.

Salutation

Salutation (Salutation Consortium, 2005) is an open, royalty-free service discovery architecture developed by a consortium dissolved in 2005. The Salutation architecture is independent of particular operating systems, network protocols or hardware platforms.

Salutation is based on directory servers called SLMs (Salutation Managers). Unlike Jini LUSes, this architecture allows the coordination of multiple SLMs in a single directory structure, which may be either flat or hierarchical. Such a structure is defined during the startup of SLMs; for flat structures, an SLM tries to locate other SLMs through multicast; for hierarchical structures, each SLM is statically configured with the network address of a central SLM. The Salutation architecture also allows of purely decentralized and partially centralized directories by setting up local SLMs within client and provider devices. Irrespective of the directory structure, each client and provider is typically set up to query/announce

services through a single SLM throughout its lifecycle.

The Salutation architecture employs attributes for service description and matching. Such attributes are grouped together in *functional units*, which describe common services such as "Print" and "Scan". A set of functional units defines a *description record*. For instance, a record describing a fax service may encompass the "Print", "Scan", and "Fax" functional units, each with specific attribute values. Any description record must follow the ASN.1 standard (ISO/IEC, 1990).

Salutation defines an API with operations that users and SLMs may invoke—through an RPC protocol (Sun Microsystems, Inc., 1988)—for exchanging service information. A client uses one of these operations for getting a list of SLMs keeping description records that match its query, and another one for getting further details about a certain service of interest (manually selected by the user) from a specific SLM. Providers use two other operations for registering and deregistering such records, which are kept at SLMs as hard state. As an alternative to service queries, a client may ask its SLM to check periodically whether a service is still available.

An SLM usually needs to exchange information with other SLMs to answer client queries, since each provider registers its services in a single SLM. The Salutation architecture, however, allows the implementation of reply caches in the SLMs to reduce the communication overhead caused by such information exchange.

The Salutation architecture offers a complete solution for service invocation. SLMs may play different roles—called *personalities* in Salutation—during this phase, depending on whether they take part in the discovery phase only (native personality) or they act as bridges between clients and providers that do not share a common native transport protocol to communicate (emulated and salutation personalities).

The Salutation architecture offers some simple security mechanisms, such as user authentication based on identification and password.

SLP

SLP (Service Location Protocol) (Guttman, Perkins, Veizades, & Day, 1999) is a service discovery protocol defined by the IETF (Internet Engineering Task Force). Unlike Jini and Salutation, which are (in different ways) independent of any transport protocols, SLP was designed for IP networks.

SLP can configure any directory structure. For purely decentralized directories, SLP defines two main entities: UAs (User Agents) and SAs (Service Agents). UAs multicast queries to SAs, which answer by unicast. SAs may also multicast announcements directly to UAs. For partially centralized directories, SLP defines a new entity—the DA (Directory Agent)—that is responsible for caching SA announcements and answering to UAs queries. Service announcements are soft state, thus being periodically refreshed by SAs.

One or more DAs may be available in the network, and may be reached by either unicast or multicast. For unicast communications with DAs, UAs and SAs can learn the DAs' addresses by static configuration or by DHCP. Like SAs, DAs may also announce themselves periodically. It is worth noting that in SLP, unlike the Salutation architecture, SA multicast announcements implicitly build a flat, replicated directory structure, without any need for DA coordination.

In SLP, services are described as URLs and standardized sets of attributes (templates). Unlike Salutation, however, SLP allows richer matching rules based on the LDAP predicate language (Legg, 2006). Like in Jini and Salutation, when an SLP query returns multiple services, the user is in charge of selecting the desired services. Unlike Jini and Salutation, however, SLP does not offer any particular service invocation mechanisms.

SLP employs a security model that focuses on avoiding erroneous propagation of service locations. SAs and DAs may associate digital signatures to their announcements so that UAs can verify their authenticity.

UPnP

UPnP (Universal Plug and Play) (UPnP Forum, 2007) is a service discovery model that is currently maintained by a forum involving several companies. The main idea behind UPnP is to extend the original PnP model for discovering, announcing and controlling networked devices. Like SLP, UPnP is based on the TCP/IP stack.

UPnP defines the following main entities: UPnP *devices*, UPnP *services*, *control servers*, *event servers*, *control points*, and *bridges*. A UPnP device is a container for services and other (nested) devices. For instance, a multifunction printer in UPnP may consist of a printing service and a nested scanning device, which hosts a photocopying service. A UPnP service implements actions that a control server (hosted in the same device as the service) may invoke. Such a service also keeps variables describing the current state of the service, which an event server (also co-located within the same device) may monitor. Such a server may announce changes on these state variables to subscribed entities. A control point plays the role of a client, discovering and controlling UPnP devices—PDAs and remote controls are typical examples of devices that can host control points. Finally, a UPnP bridge is used for mapping the UPnP protocols onto native transport protocols a non-compliant device may offer. As can be seen, the UPnP model gives a strong emphasis on the service invocation phase.

The UPnP model is based on a fully decentralized directory structure. During the discovery process, all communication between UPnP entities is via a protocol called SSDP (Simple Service Discovery Protocol). SSDP query and announcement messages are encapsulated in either HTTPU (HTTP over unicast UDP) or HTTPMU (HTTP over multicast UDP).

The UPnP model employs a service description format based on XML schemas. Despite that, a control point can only refine its search criteria by identifying particular device types, service types, or a particular device. The fact that the UPnP model emphasizes the use of service announcements instead of service queries may explain the absence of richer matching rules. As to service selection, UPnP is similar to the other, aforementioned approaches.

A service announcement in UPnP conveys a URL that points to an XML document describing the service. UPnP devices and control points keep information about announced services as soft state. An XML description document includes such information as manufacturer name, version of device, and serial numbers, as well as URLs that point to the device's control and event servers. Such servers implement SOAP (Simple Object Access Protocol) objects offering methods that control points can invoke. Some UPnP devices may also issue an additional URL pointing to an optional *presentation server* (again, usually co-located within the same device). Such a URL points to a webpage from which a user of a control point can manage or monitor the corresponding device.

Regarding security, the UPnP model implements user authentication mechanisms, as well as support for cryptography during service invocation (SOAP over SSL).

JXTA

JXTA (short for "Juxtapose") (JXTA Project, 2007) is an open standard for P2P communications based on the establishment of overlays on top of a network infrastructure. It defines a general framework comprising a rich set of services and protocols, which range from group membership and discovery to overlay routing and peer interaction.

JXTA allows partially centralized and fully decentralized service directories based on the organization of *peer groups*. A peer group is a set of peers providing a common set of services. The scope of service discovery in JXTA is always associated with a peer group. Typically, on startup,

a peer automatically belongs to a generic peer group that provides group discovery services. After discovering the specific group of interest and before searching services in this group, such a peer must subscribe to the group through an authentication credential provided by a peer already belonging to the group.

JXTA employs service queries and—when super-nodes are used—announcements. JXTA uses XML as its service description language. The JXTA framework does not attempt to address how users can invoke discovered services. JXTA provides standardized service invocation interfaces only for core services, *e.g.* group discovery services.

Peers may cache service announcements and replies to queries locally as soft state. In JXTA, if a peer cannot resolve a service query locally in its cache, it sends the query over the peer group. When the query reaches a peer that owns the service, this peer will answer directly to the inquiring peer. The JXTA framework does not specify matching rules between queries and services. Likewise, there is no mention as to how a peer selects among a set of discovered services.

Peers in JXTA are of three types: *edge peers*, *relay peers*, and *rendezvous peers*. The edge peers use and provide services. They may have transient, low bandwidth network connectivity. Relay peers and rendezvous peers act as super-nodes in a partially centralized service directory. They are also responsible for propagating service queries and announcements from edge peers. Relay peers enable peers interaction over heterogeneous scenarios (*e.g.* firewalls, sensor networks). Rendezvous peers configure an additional overlay on top of a JXTA-based system. In such a configuration, an edge peer sends a query to a specific rendezvous peer (learned during system configuration), which then conducts a search between the other rendezvous peers. The employed search mechanism depends on the volatility of rendezvous peers. If the rendezvous overlay is stable, the system may employ a hierarchical directory structure based on a DHT; otherwise, it may use a combination of DHT and random walk among the rendezvous peers. The JXTA framework also allows edge peers to subscribe to a special announcement service that rendezvous peers provide.

JXTA provides security mechanisms based on digital certificates. The structure of JXTA messages also allows applications to add arbitrary security metadata information to such messages, such as digests.

In spite of its generality, The JXTA framework introduces high communication overhead because its architecture does not take into account the locality of devices. The work by (Bisignano, Di Modica, & Tomarchio, 2005) introduces new features to the JXTA framework to adapt it to ad hoc wireless networks. Among such features, this work introduces an additional routing layer that implements multicast functionality on top of the ad hoc wireless network, so that queries can be propagated between edge peers directly, without the help of super-nodes.

Bluetooth SDP

The Bluetooth standard for PANs (Personal Area Networks) (Bluetooth Consortium, 2007) comprises a protocol called SDP (Service Discovery Protocol), which implements a fully decentralized service directory. Due to the characteristics of the Bluetooth standard, its scope is limited to nearby devices. Nordbotten et al (2004) proposed extensions to the Bluetooth SDP that allow using such protocol in *scatternets* (groups of independent PANs whose coverage areas overlap).

Each Bluetooth device may implement two entities: *SDP clients* and *SDP servers*. An SDP server has a registry for each service its device provides (without cooperation with other SDP servers), which is kept as hard state. Such a registry comprises a UUID (Universally Unique Identifier) identifying the service, a list of attributes describing the service, and information describing the network address and the transport protocol to be used during service invocation.

The Bluetooth SDP is totally query-based. SDP clients send queries to an SDP server to get information about a specific service or about all available services at the corresponding device. The Bluetooth SDP defines two different discovery phases. In the *device discovery* phase, SDP clients broadcast queries to learn about available SDP servers—such a server may be unavailable because of configuration or because of the device entering a standby or suspended mode. Available SDP servers answer to such queries by providing the device's hardware address. After that, a SDP client enters the *service discovery* phase, in which it establishes point-to-point communication channels to SDP servers to find out about service functionalities within their devices. In both phases, service selection is the responsibility of users.

The Bluetooth standard implements confidentiality and authentication with custom algorithms. Key generation is based on a Bluetooth PIN, which must be configured into both devices taking part in the conversation.

DEAPSpace

DEAPSpace (Herman, Husemann, Moser, Nidd, Rohner, & Schade, 2001) is a service discovery architecture for ubiquitous and context-aware computing. The DEAPSpace architecture implements a fully decentralized service directory. The scope of service discovery is constrained by the network topology—DEAPSpace employs broadcast for all its communication.

Contrary to the Bluetooth SDP, the DEAPSpace architecture is completely announcement-based. Each device keeps a complete view of all services other devices currently provide in the network (its *worldview*), and periodically broadcasts such a view to its neighbors, in an uncooperative way. A device may suppress a scheduled announcement if its worldview is exactly the same as that of a previously received announcement, thus alleviating the overhead of announcement messages in the network. If a device has just received an announcement with a world view that does not include a service it is currently providing, the device may anticipate its announcement to reduce the convergence time.

A worldview describes services in terms of attributes that follow the ASN.1 notation. A DEAPSpace-based system keeps information about services a device provides as soft state. For each service described in a worldview, there is an associated validity time. Before broadcasting its worldview, a device may renew the validity time associated with its own services; besides, it may update the validity time associated with services other devices provide, so that newcomers may receive a correct worldview.

Service selection in the DEAPSpace architecture is manual. Both service invocation and security mechanisms are not supported.

APPROACHES TO MULTI-HOP AD HOC WIRELESS NETWORKS

Multi-hop ad hoc wireless networks (hereafter, MANETs) allow mobile devices to self-organize into arbitrary and temporary topologies that expand the basic communication coverage of these devices through cooperative packet forwarding. The mechanisms for service discovery in MANETs must be fundamentally different from those used in other networks, as the former are much more sensitive to network behavior. This is due to the very dynamic nature of MANETs—for instance, devices may move, or the QoS (Quality of Service) properties of the wireless medium may vary over short periods. Network awareness is therefore central in the design of such mechanisms in the case of MANETs.

Lately, service discovery has been a hot topic in the area of MANET research. In spite of the many differences among existing approaches, we can point out two common characteristics.

First, approaches to service discovery in MANETs usually employ constrained forms of service querying and announcement that try to limit the amount of packet transmissions in the network. Unconstrained queries and announcements—such as those implemented by the aforementioned approaches—impose prohibitive communication overhead on devices in charge of forwarding such messages between clients and providers. Such overhead implies higher energy consumption in the mobile devices, which may limit the operational lifetime of the whole network. Moreover, such overhead may not substantially enhance the discovery efficiency—a service announcement, for instance, is usually associated with a validity time defined by the provider; this validity time may be, however, further limited in practice by the connectivity instability of the network.

Second, some approaches to service discovery in MANETs employ some kind of semantic matching algorithm. The purposes are twofold: (i) to allow results that are more precise and, consequently, that reduce transmissions related to unwanted services; and (ii) to provide intermediate devices with enough information that allows queries and announcements to be selectively forwarded to their destinations.

The following subsections comment on some of the main approaches to service discovery in MANETs: GSD, Konark SGP, Allia, the work by Varshavsky et al., FTA, ORION, MOBI-DIC, and DICHOTOMY.

GSD

GSD (Group-based Service Discovery) (Chakraborty, Joshi, Yesha, & Finin, 2006) is a service discovery architecture for pervasive environments. Discovery actions in GSD are constrained by the network topology; intermediate devices in the MANET forward service queries and announcements to a maximum number of hops. For service queries, a selective forwarding mechanism defines such a hop limit, which is based on information about service *groups*. In GSD, services are described in terms of such groups, which are part of an ontology built on the DReggie framework (Chakraborty, Perich, Avancha, & Joshi, 2001). Conceptually, all services take part in the general group "Service", which is divided into two subgroups "Hardware" and "Software", which are further divided according to the different types of services and resources that can be made available through the GSD architecture (*e.g.* a group "Printer" with subgroups "InkJet" and "LaserJet", and so forth).

In the GSD architecture, a device periodically announces its services to neighboring devices through broadcast, in a cooperative way. Such neighbors may forward such announcements to devices farther away, until these announcements reach a predefined hop limit. Whenever a device receives an announcement, it caches the conveyed information about the service, including the identification of the neighboring device from which it received the announcement. Before forwarding the announcement to devices farther away, the device also piggybacks on this announcement information about the service groups it has previously learned from other announcements. The announcement cache at each device keeps all such information as soft state.

A device interested in a specific service firstly queries its local announcement cache about such a service. If the device has local information about this service, it may access the service straightaway. If the device has no local information about this service but it has local information about the group the service belongs to, the device sends queries only to those neighboring devices from which it received the announcements related to such group information. If the device has no local information about this service or its service group, the device simply broadcasts a query to its neighbors in the network. Each neighboring device repeats this process until the queries find devices that provide the desired service, or reach a predefined hop limit. Devices providing the desired service reply to these queries and the replies are forwarded to the inquiring device through

the same (reverse) routes the queries used. Each device must therefore keep a reverse routing table that is filled in for each query forwarded in the network. Each entry in such a table is also kept as soft state. If the reverse route is not available (*e.g.* a device in the route moved away), the GSD architecture automatically resorts to using traditional ad hoc routing protocols to forward the reply to the inquiring device.

In the GSD architecture, each device proactively manages the service group information in its own announcement cache. When the device or its neighborhood starts to move faster, the announcement rate, its hop limit, and its validity time all decrease accordingly. The GSD architecture, as expressed in (Chakraborty, Joshi, Yesha, & Finin, 2006), does not focus on service selection or security mechanisms.

Konark SGP

Konark (Helal, Desai, Verma, & Lee, 2003; Lee, Helal, Desai, Verma, & Arslan, 2003) is a service discovery architecture for m-commerce applications—although the main mechanisms employed by the architecture could certainly be useful for other mobile P2P applications. It is based on the TCP/IP stack and, like GSD, its discovery actions are constrained by the network topology—which, in the case of Konark, is based on multicast group membership. In the Konark architecture, a device keeps service information as soft state in a *service information tree*, which hierarchically represents the ontology of possible *service types* that the device currently knows. Any service registration and discovery action is based on the service information tree. For instance, when a device receives a new service announcement, it is entered in the service information tree of the device. Service information trees make it possible the application of semantic matching algorithms in a Konark-based system.

Each leaf in the service information tree of a device keeps the description of an actual service such a device knows. The Konark architecture employs an XML-based service description language. Each service is represented in such a language by two components: (i) a set of *keywords* (key-value pairs) characterizing the service and a URL that locates the service; and (ii) a service description file, from which an inquiring device may build a proxy object (similar to Jini remote controls) for SOAP-based service invocations. Similar to UPnP, service discovery is accomplished in two phases: the first one obtains the URL from the service type and keywords, and the second one downloads the service description file.

The basic Konark architecture (Helal, Desai, Verma, & Lee, 2003) has been extended in (Lee, Helal, Desai, Verma, & Arslan, 2003) with a protocol called SGP (Service Gossip Protocol), which aims at reducing message overhead in MANETs. With SGP, providers multicast service announcements—called *delta messages*—that convey information about services the device knows (irrespective of their being locally provided by the device or not) but other, neighboring devices have not announced recently. The rationale behind such strategy is similar to the 'world views' in the DEAPSpace architecture: to avoid the propagation of duplicate service information, while allowing devices to share a global view of all available services in the network.

In the Konark architecture, when a client does not have information about a service in its local service information tree, it may issue a service query (containing information such as the path in the tree to such service and keywords that further describe the service) to the network by multicast. In this case, the providers matching the query issue replies to the query by unicast, using the same message format as that of delta messages. Users must manually select the desired service.

The Konark architecture has been implemented in the JME (Java Micro Edition) platform (Sun Microsystems, Inc., 1994). Each provider hosts a micro SOAP server that allows clients to directly invoke its services after the discovery

phase. The Konark architecture does not deal with any security issues.

Allia

Allia (Ratsimor O. , Chakraborty, Joshi, & Finin, 2002; Ratsimor O. , Chakraborty, Joshi, & Finin, 2004) is a highly configurable service discovery framework for MANETs. Its main difference to other approaches is the definition of local discovery policies. Each device taking part in an Allia-based system hosts a set of discovery agents that enforce such policies. One example is when a device receives a service announcement; in this case, an agent hosted by the device decides whether it should keep the announcement (as soft state) or discard it, based on the associated policy. Similar policies—and associated agents—can be defined for selectively forwarding queries, caching announcements from neighbors, and so forth. The Allia framework employs the FIPA (Foundation for Intelligent Physical Agents) platform (Poslad, Buckle, & Hadingham, 2000) to manage such agents.

One particular feature of Allia-based systems is the establishment of group policies through device *alliances*. The alliance of a device comprises a set of other devices from which it may cache service announcements. The number of members in a device alliance, its diameter (*i.e.* the maximum hop distance between the device and the farthest device in its alliance), and the periodicity of announcements in it are all defined as part of the device's local policies. To determine such characteristics of its alliance, a device may take into account its current resource availability. Similar to GSD, each device proactively manages such characteristics. The Allia framework also permits that the devices employ local policies to define security restrictions (*e.g.* user credentials) on their alliances.

The Allia framework is independent of any service description and invocation techniques. For instance, devices in an Allia-based system may employ an ontology language for service descriptions and Jini remote controls for invocations.

A Cross-Layer Approach

Varshavsky et al. (2005) propose the integration of application-level service discovery functionality over network-level ad hoc routing protocols. In principle, this *cross-layer* approach can be implemented over any routing protocol, whether it be reactive (*i.e.* devices build routes on demand) or proactive (*i.e.* devices keep fresh lists of destinations and their routes by periodically distributing their routing tables).

The service discovery architecture proposed by Varshavsky et al. provides applications with enough information that allows them to select the best provider among those the protocol finds out. Moreover, the architecture can monitor the ongoing QoS that the services provide to applications by tracking changes in the network topology. QoS degradation can trigger a reassessment of possible providers, which may lead to the selection of a new provider. Therefore, the architecture takes into account the inherent dynamism of MANETs even after service selection.

The cross-layer architecture comprises two main components, which are deployed together in each device in the MANET: an SDL (Service Discovery Library) and an RLD (Routing Layer Driver). The SDL aims at keeping information about services in the network and making it transparent to clients and providers the use of a specific routing protocol. The RLD interacts directly with the routing protocol to propagate service queries and announcements piggybacked on its messages. It is also responsible for detecting changes in the network topology and triggering the reassessment of providers, if needed.

The basic *modus operandi* of the architecture proposed by Varshavsky et al. is as follows. The RLD intercepts routing messages conveying service information and directs them to the SDL. The SDL updates its local service information table—kept as soft state—with the service description and location, and additional information extracted from the routing protocol (*e.g.* number of hops from the device to the service provider). The SDL may notify interested applications about changes in its service information table through a callback interface. When the underlying protocol is reactive, the SDL may encapsulate service queries in modified route request messages; similarly, replies to such queries are encapsulated in modified route reply messages. When the underlying protocol is proactive, the SDL asks the RLD to make periodic route distribution messages; such routes are extended with the desired service information.

The architecture proposed by Varshavsky et al. is independent of any service description technique, and the user defines the matching algorithm to be employed. Service selection may be automatic, based on the additional information extracted from the routing protocol. Varshavsky et al. do not discuss security issues in their paper.

FTA

Lenders et al. (2005) describe an approach to service discovery in MANETs that is based on the theory of electric fields. In the FTA (Field Theoretic Approach) approach, a service of a certain type is regarded as a positive charge with a surrounding field in the network, and queries to the same service type are regarded as negative test charges that the service attracts, based on its field gradient. The intermediate devices selectively forward such queries to the providers that have the stronger gradients matching the same service type. When there is more than one provider for the same service type, the forwarding mechanism selects the 'best' service (*i.e.* the one with strongest gradient) automatically. Besides, the forwarding mechanism ensures the use of the shortest path from the client to the selected provider. Lenders et al. do not detail how clients and providers could describe services (the authors mention the use of an ontology language as a possibility), nor how clients could invoke such services.

In the FTA approach, a device participating in the process of service discovery calculates the gradient of a service based on its hop distance to the provider and the service's CoS (Capacity of Service)—*e.g.* the CoS of an Internet gateway service could indicate the provider's output bandwidth, and the CoS of a printer could indicate its speed in pages per minute. A provider starts the process of service announcement by broadcasting the CoS of its service to its neighboring devices. Each of its neighbors caches such an announcement (as soft state) and repeats the broadcast process until the announcement reaches a predefined hop limit. Before forwarding an announcement it received from a neighbor, a device recalculates the gradient value of the type of the newly learned service as the sum of all received CoS values related to such service type divided by their corresponding hop distance to their providers. Different from the aforementioned approaches, the FTA approach defines a third type of discovery message that devices can use to periodically exchange information with their immediate neighbors about their local gradient values for the different service types they know of. These messages are used both as a way for neighbors to know the gradient values of each other (which is necessary during the selective forwarding of queries) and as 'hello' messages that help neighbors with monitoring changes in the network topology.

To reduce the total amount of information exchanged in the MANET, an approach similar to Konark's delta messages is employed on service announcements. When a device receives an announcement with a service type it already knows of, it may postpone the broadcasting of the announcement since a gradient is already defined on the network for this service type. If, during this time, the device collects additional announcements from other services, it may forward the announcements together in one single message.

Lenders et al. do not consider security aspects in their FTA approach.

ORION

Unlike the other approaches presented so far, ORION (Optimized Routing-Independent Overlay Network) (Klemn, Lindemann, & Waldhorst, 2003) is a homogeneous system in the sense that it only concentrates on a single type of service: file sharing. Crucially, the ORION system allows the definition of file distribution overlays on top of MANETs.

The ORION system implements a query-based discovery protocol whose discovery scope is based on the overlay topology. Each device maintains this topology locally through two tables: a *local file table* and a *file routing table*. Service queries contain keywords (key-value pairs) describing one or more files of interest. Inquiring devices send such queries through flooding. When a neighboring device receives a query, it checks its local file table. If it finds any files matching the keywords in the query, it returns to the inquiring device the file identifier corresponding to each of these files in a reply message, and adds to its file routing table an entry that relates the query to the matched file identifiers. The neighboring device also rebroadcasts the query to devices farther away from the inquiring device. Such devices may try to return further file identifiers to the inquiring device by using the same path traversed by the queries. When such replies reach a device that has previously replied to the same query, this device examines the reply contents and suppresses those file identifiers that are identical to the ones it has sent before, as defined in its file routing table. As a consequence, the ORION system allows reducing the amount of information the devices exchange in the MANET.

The same routes used for file discovery are also employed during file transfer. Details about the file transfer mechanism can be found in (Klemn, Lindemann, & Waldhorst, 2003). It is worth noting that, even though replicated information about a file identifier that a reply conveys is usually suppressed, the ORION system does not guarantee that a single copy of such identifier will reach the inquiring device. Typically, ORION automatically selects the nearest copy. As regards security, there is no mention of it in the ORION system.

MOBI-DIC

MOBI-DIC (MOBIle Discovery of loCal resources) (Cao, Wolfson, Xu, & Yin, 2005) is a resource discovery engine that devices in a MANET may use for querying and announcing resource information. MOBI-DIC employs a fully decentralized service directory; however, when an infrastructure is available, the directory structure may be augmented (as a partially centralized structure) to make the search more efficient. In MOBI-DIC, the discovery scope is based on the network topology, although providers may employ policies that further limit the availability of their resources to certain periods.

In MOBI-DIC, a resource description is based on attributes. Two attributes are particularly important for MOBI-DIC: *resource-time* and *resource-location*. Resource-time is the time when the resource description is generated. Resource-location is a (possibly uncertain) trajectory that gives the current location of the resource provider as a function of time. Each announcement or reply to a query (*reports* in MOBI-DIC parlance) is associated with a *relevance degree* at location *l* and at time *t* that is determined by a *relevance function*. The relevance degree is used for prioritizing reports and, indirectly, defines an automatic service selection approach. When a device receives new reports, it incorporates them into its *local reports database*, as soft state, and broadcasts the new reports database to its neighbors, which repeat the process, thus spreading the reports across the network, in a cooperative way. In order to limit the broadcast volume, each device only broadcasts the *k* most relevant reports

to its neighbors, as defined by its own relevance function. This paradigm is called *rank-based broadcast* (RBB) in MOBI-DIC.

MOBI-DIC does not provide service invocation and security mechanisms.

DICHOTOMY

DICHOTOMY (DIscovery and sCHeduling prOTOcol for MobilitY) (Gomes, Ziviani, Lima, & Endler, 2007) is a protocol aimed at tackling resource discovery in ad hoc mobile grids. Although initially conceived for remote job execution services, the protocol may be certainly employed for other mobile P2P applications.

DICHOTOMY is a purely query-based protocol. As stated in (Gomes, Ziviani, Lima, & Endler, 2007), announcements are inadequate for offering job execution services, since their suitability depends on the availability of resources such as CPU load and available memory, which may vary considerably in very short periods. Furthermore, for these resources it may be advisable to associate their discovery with some form of advance reservation (which can only be triggered in response to a query), to ensure that they are available at the provider when the user submits the intended job.

Each device in a DICHOTOMY-based system keeps information about its availability as a resource provider as hard state. Contrary to the aforementioned approaches, the protocol allows the automatic selection of *multiple* providers in a single query. This feature is based on a distributed mechanism that combines two algorithms: DR (Delayed Replies) and SbV (Suppression by Vicinity).

In the DICHOTOMY protocol, an inquiring device floods a resource query (constrained by a configurable hop limit) into the MANET. The DR algorithm delays the transmission of replies from providers according to a timer set to be inversely proportional to the availability of the required resources at such providers. This way, providers that are more resourceful reply earlier. Such replies are sent towards the inquiring device through hop-by-hop broadcast. The SbV algorithm constrains such broadcast so that the more suitable replies (as selected by the DR algorithm) suppress unnecessary replies from other devices alongside the paths used for forwarding the more suitable replies. Each reply uses the already known path traversed by the corresponding query. Each device has a list of pending queries that keeps information, for each query, about this query's return path, the maximum number of replies this query is asking for, and the number of replies associated with this query that the device has already overheard. When a device receives a reply addressed to another device, it first checks whether there is an entry for the corresponding query in its list of pending queries. If so, the device increments the number of replies already overheard in the corresponding entry of its list of pending queries, regardless of the device being on the return path of the reply. If the maximum number of replies has been reached for the corresponding query, the device suppresses the reply. It is worth noting that, due to the hop-by-hop broadcasting mechanism, each intermediate device in the return path implicitly informs its own vicinity about queries that have already been replied, thus allowing for further suppressions at devices nearby the reply's return path.

The DICHOTOMY protocol is currently implemented in the JME platform. This protocol adopts a similar approach to Jini in regard to resource description, matching, and job submission—*i.e.* by using Java objects. Like most of the other approaches, the DICHOTOMY protocol does not focus on security mechanisms.

SUMMARY OF THE APPROACHES

Table 1 presents an overview of the service discovery approaches introduced in this chapter, showing the characteristics of each approach in terms of the seven key aspects presented in the *Background* section.

FUTURE TRENDS

Most of the challenges of service discovery reside in its application to MANETs. In this section, we give a flavor of some promising research and development directions in this area.

Service discovery in MANETs using *anycasting* is a promising approach to integrating routing and discovery (Frank & Karl, 2004; Wu & Zitterbart, 2001). Some researchers propose to use application-layer anycasting to enable transparent selection of the best providers for a given type of service. The service providers are grouped as an anycast group identified by an ADN (Anycast Domain Name). Within the network, a hierarchy of ADN resolvers performs the ADN-to-IP translation. There are also proposals for network-layer anycasting, which extend either proactive or reactive ad hoc routing protocols to provide anycast routing. However, such proposals inherit the same problems as those of routing ad hoc routing protocols, such as high maintenance overhead, or high discovery overhead and delay. Although anycasting may seem a useful approach, it must still be further investigated to ensure its feasibility, perhaps for certain types of MANETs only (*e.g.* with restricted mobility), and for some types of services.

Another open topic of research in MANETs is how to define and guarantee some QoS parameters such as reliability, response time, or high availability. In particular, one challenge is how to achieve *service continuity* (Jørstad, Thanh, & Dustdar, 2004; Handorean, Sen, Hackmann, & Roman, 2005) in spite of the high vulnerability of provider's connectivity, which is intrinsic to dynamic network topologies. Several research groups are working on mechanisms and protocols—usually based on group communication technology—that enable the seamless and application-transparent

Table 1. Overview of service discovery approaches.

Aspects and Convention	Approaches to Infrastructure and Single-hop Ad hoc Wireless Networks							Approaches to Multi-hop Ad hoc Wireless Networks							
	Jini	Salutation	SLP	UPnP	JXTA	Bluetooth SDP	DEAPspace	GSD	Konark SGP	Allia	Cross-Layer Approach	FTA	Orion	MOBI-DIC	Dichotomy
Information Exchange **B**: broadcast **M**: multicast **U**: unicast **A**: announcements **Q**: queries **N**: notifications	MA, BA, UQ (Lookup Server), MQ, BQ, N	BA, UQ (Salutation Manager), BQ (distributed directory)	MA, UQ (Directory Agent), MQ (Server Agent)	MA, UQ, MQ	UA (super-nodes), UQ (peer groups), N	BQ	BA (world views)	BA (limited by # of hops), BQ (selective forwarding)	BA (deltas), MQ	BA (limited by # of hops), BQ, MQ (subject to agents' policies)	BA or MA (depending on proto used), BQ (e.g. DSR and AODV), UQ (e.g. CBRP)	BA (limited by # of hops), UQ	MQ, BQ	BA (rank-based), BQ	BQ (limited by # of hops, replies forwarded selectively)
Discovery Architecture **C**: centralized **D**: decentralized **F**: flat **H**: hierarchical **S**: single directory **M**: many directories	C, F, S (Lookup Server)	C, D, F, H, M (Salutation Manager)	C, D, F, M	D, S	C, D, M	D, S	D, S	D, S	D, S (service info. tree)	D, S	D, S	D, S	D, S	D, S	D, S
Information Maintenance **C**: cooperative **U**: uncooperative **H**: hard state **S**: soft state	U, S (*leasing*)	U, H	U, S	U, S	C, S	U, H	U, S	C, S	U, S	C, S	C, S	C, S	C, H (LRU policy)	C, S (relevance function)	C, H
Discovery Scope **T**: net topology **U**: user role **C**: contextual info.	T, U, C (location)	T (PANs to WANs)	T (LANs), U (scopes)	T (PANs to WANs)	T (peer groups)	T (PANs)	T	T	T (multicast group)	T	T	T	T (overlay)	T (LAN)	T, C

continued on following page

Table 1. continued

Description/Matching A: attributes, T: templates, E: predef. elements, L: desc. language, N/A: not available	Selection M: manual, A: automatic, N/A: not available	Invocation L: location, M: comm. mech., O: operations, N/A: not available	Discovery Security N/A: not available
A (prog.-lang.-based)	M	L (net address), M (RMI), O (interfaces)	Cryptography and authorization policies (prog.-lang.-based)
A, T, E (functional units)	M	L (net address), M (personalities)	User authentication (RPC)
A, T (matching using logic predicates)	M	L (URLs)	Authentication and digital certificates (SPI)
A, L (XML-based) (matching of one attr only)	M	L (net address), M, O	Framework for access control and device authentication (SOAP over SSL)
L (XML-based)	N/A	O (interfaces, only for standardized services, e.g. group discov. services)	Authentication credentials, digital certificates and messages digests
A, T, E (matching of multiple attributes)	M	L (net address)	Confidentiality and authentication with custom algorithms
A (ASN.1 notation)	M	N/A	N/A
L (ontology)	M	N/A	N/A
L (XML-based), T	M	L (URL), M (SOAP), O	N/A
N/A	M	N/A	Local policies defining security restrictions (access rights and credential validations)
N/A	A	N/A	N/A
N/A (the authors mention the use of ontologies as a possibility)	A	N/A	N/A
A	A	L (net address), M (file transfer mechanisms)	N/A
A (prog.-lang.-based)	A	L (net. address), M (sockets), O (interfaces)	N/A

hot swapping of providers during an ongoing service access session. As with anycasting, service continuity will most probably only be achievable in a reliable form for certain classes of MANETs and services.

The unique characteristics of MANETs also pose several challenges to the design of security mechanisms for such systems, such as open P2P architectures, shared wireless communication medium, devices with stringent resource limitations, and highly dynamic network topologies where centralized approaches are not feasible. Moreover, in most research related to MANETs, it is commonly assumed that all devices cooperate towards a common goal. This assumption, however, is not valid in an open P2P environment, where there is no effective means of enforcing cooperation among the devices. Hence, malicious attackers can disrupt network operation, including routing and discovery, by violating established protocol specifications. In the particular case of the network-layer, the vulnerabilities are of two types: routing or packet forwarding attacks. At the application-layer, some possible attacks include malicious service announcements, DoS (Denial-of-Service) attacks, and identity theft, among others.

Some approaches to discovery security in MANETs may be found in the literature; most of it, however, rely on subjective concepts such as trustworthiness (Almenarez, Marin, Diaz, & Sanchez, 2006) and reputation (Wishart, Robinson, Indulska, & Jøsang, 2005), which are less robust than traditional security mechanisms, such as public key infrastructures. Another issue is the exposure of a user's desire to consume a specific service when he or she is querying the system, since the aforementioned security mechanisms usually focus on service selection and invocation. In this sense, (Zhu et al., 2005) proposes an approach in which users and service providers expose minimal sensitive information at first place, and identify necessary exposure during the service discovery process. Of course, any

security measure has its cost, *e.g.* as more security features are introduced into the network, also the computation, communication and management overhead is increased, which affects the overall network performance.

CONCLUDING REMARKS

So far, at least three different mobile P2P systems based on specific variants of MANETs are emerging in practice, which reflect on the design of effective service discovery solutions.

In wireless *mesh* networks, some devices are fixed, and function either as routers or as Internet access providers. By removing the assumption that all service providers are mobile, the reliability and robustness of the network is greatly improved. In these systems, the main service made available is probably Internet access.

Pure MANETs are being applied also for opportunistic networking. In these networks, the assumption is that many devices are equipped with interfaces for different wireless technologies (*e.g.* 3G and WiFi), and hence disconnections or network partitions of one wireless network can be overcome by using the other wireless interface to communicate with nearby devices, opportunistically using them as routers. When routing is provided in a non-continuous way, the networks are also called *delay-tolerant* networks, and their main application is for asynchronous communication and data sharing. More recently, however, opportunistic networking is being applied also to synchronous communication, but only for urban environments and situations that are characterized by high device density. In these networks, any device may provide any sort of service, such as data streaming, VoIP, messaging, file sharing, sensor data collection, or resource sharing in general.

Finally, pure MANETs have also been successfully designed and deployed according to well-defined requirements of specific sets of applications, *e.g.* in military or emergency-response scenarios. The fact that in these scenarios the networks belong to the same authority simplifies some management and security issues. In such scenarios, the main provisioned services are communication and data sharing.

One can notice that in all these current uses of MANETs, service discovery, service description, service selection, and service access are central issues that must be designed taking into account the variant state and limited availability of bandwidth and device's resources, the inherent mobility of devices, as well as possible security threats.

REFERENCES

Ahamed, S. I., Buford, J., Sharmin, M., Haque, M. M., & Talukder, N. (2008). Secure service discovery. In Y. Zhang, J. Zeng, & M. Ma (Eds.), *Handbook of research on wireless security.* Hershey, PA: Information Science Reference.

Ahmed, R., Limam, N., Xiao, J., Iraqi, Y., & Boutaba, R. (2007). Resource and service discovery in large-scale multi-domain networks. *IEEE Communications Surveys & Tutorials, 9*(4), 2-30.

Almenarez, F., Marin, A., Diaz, D., & Sanchez, J. (2006). Developing a model for trust management in pervasive devices. In *Proceedings of the Fourth Annual IEEE Conference on Pervasive Computing and Communications Workshops*, (pp. 1-5).

Arnold, K., Scheifler, R., Waldo, J., O'Sullivan, B., & Wollrath, A. (1999). *Jini specification* (1st ed.). Boston, MA, USA: Addison-Wesley Longman Publishing Co, Inc.

Bisignano, M., Di Modica, G., & Tomarchio, O. (2005). JMobiPeer: A middleware for mobile peer-to-peer computing in MANETs. In *Proceedings of the 25th IEEE International Conference on Distributed Computing Systems Workshops* (pp. 785-791). Columbus, OH, USA: IEEE Computer Society.

Bluetooth Consortium. (2007, Jul 26). *Bluetooth core specifications.* Retrieved May 27, 2008, from http://www.bluetooth.com/NR/rdonlyres/F8E8276A-3898-4EC6-B7DA-E5535258B056/6545/Core_V21__EDR.zip

Cao, H., Wolfson, O., Xu, B., & Yin, H. (2005). MOBI-DIC: Mobile discovery of local resources in peer-to-peer wireless networks. *IEEE Data Engineering Bulletin, 28*(3), 11-18.

Chakraborty, D., Joshi, A., Yesha, Y., & Finin, T. (2006). Toward distributed service discovery in pervasive computing environments. *IEEE Transactions on Mobile Computing , 5*(2), 97-112.

Chakraborty, D., Perich, F., Avancha, S., & Joshi, A. (2001). DReggie: A smart service discovery technique for e-Commerce applications. In *Proceedings of the 20th International Symposium on Reliable Distributed Systems.* New Orleans, LA, USA: IEEE Computer Society.

DARPA. (2006, Jan 13). *DAML services.* Retrieved May 22, 2008, from http://www.daml.org

Frank, C., & Karl, H. (2004). Consistency challenges of service discovery in mobile ad hoc networks. In *Proceedings of the 7th ACM International Symposium on Modeling, Analysis and Simulation of Wireless and Mobile Systems,* Venice, Italy (pp. 105-114).

Gomes, A. T., Ziviani, A., Lima, L. S., & Endler, M. (2007). DICHOTOMY: A resource discovery and scheduling protocol for multihop ad hoc mobile grids. In *Proceedings of the 1st International Workshop on Context-Awareness and Mobility in Grid Computing* (pp. 719-724). Rio de Janeiro, RJ, Brazil: IEEE Computer Society.

Guttman, E., Perkins, C., Veizades, J., & Day, M. (1999). *Service location protocol, version 2.* RFC 2608.

Handorean, R., Sen, R., Hackmann, G., & Roman, G. (2005). Context-aware session management for services in ad hoc networks. In *Proceedings of the 2005 IEEE International Conference on Services Computing*, (pp. 113-120).

Helal, S., Desai, N., Verma, V., & Lee, C. (2003). Konark -- a service discovery and delivery protocol for ad hoc networks. In *Proceedings of the 3ʳᵈ IEEE Conference on Wireless Communication Networks.* New Orleans, LA, USA: IEEE Computer Society.

Herman, R., Husemann, D., Moser, M., Nidd, M., Rohner, C., & Schade, A. (2001). DEAPspace: Transient ad hoc networking of prevasive devices. *Computer Networks, 35*(4), 411-428.

Hwang, J., & Aravamudham, P. (2004). Middleware services for P2P computing in wireless grid networks. *IEEE Internet Computing, 8*(4), 40-46.

ISO/IEC. (1990). *Information technology -- open systems interconnection -- specification of abstract syntax notation one (ASN.1).* ISO/IEC 8824.

Jørstad, I., Thanh, D., & Dustdar, S. (2004). An analysis of service continuity in mobile services. In *Proceedings of the 13ᵗʰ IEEE International Workshops on Enabling Technologies: Infrastructure for Collaborative Enterprises* (pp. 121-126). IEEE Computer Society.

JXTA Project. (2007, Oct 16). *JXTA v2.0 protocols specification: Revision 2.5.3.* Retrieved Jun 6, 2008, from https://jxta-spec.dev.java.net/

Klemn, A., Lindemann, C., & Waldhorst, O. P. (2003). A special-purpose peer-to-peer file sharing system for mobile ad hoc networks. In *Proceedings of the Semiannual Vehicular Technology Conference.* Orlando, FL, USA: IEEE Press.

König-Ries, B., & Klein, M. (2002). Information services to support e-learning in ad-hoc networks. In *Proceedings of 1ˢᵗ International Workshop on Wireless Information Systems (WIS)*, Ciudad Real, Spain (pp. 13-24).

Lee, C., Helal, A., Desai, N., Verma, V., & Arslan, B. (2003). Konark: A system and protocols for

device independent, peer-to-peer discovery and delivery of mobile services. *IEEE Transactions on Systems, Man and Cybernetics, 33*(6), 682-696.

Legg, S. (2006). *Lightweight directory access protocol (LDAP): Syntaxes and matching rules.* RFC 4517.

Lenders, V., May, M., & Plattner, B. (2005). Survey and new Approach in service discovery and advertisement for mobile ad hoc networks. *Pervasive and Mobile Computing, 1*(3), 343-370.

Monrose, F., Wyckoff, P., & Rubin, A. (1999). Distributed execution with remote audit. In *Proceedings of the 1999 ISOC Network and Distributed System Security Symposium*, (pp. 103-113).

Nordbotten, N. A., Skeie, T., & Aakvaag, N. D. (2004). Methods for service discovery in Bluetooth scatternets. *Computer Communications, 27*(11), 1087-1096.

Poslad, S., Buckle, P., & Hadingham, R. (2000). The Fipa-OS agent platform: Open source for open standards. In *Proceedings of the 5ᵗʰ International Conference and Exhibition on the Pratical Application of Intelligent Agents and Multi-Agents*, Manchester, UK.

Ratsimor, O., Chakraborty, D., Joshi, A., & Finin, T. (2002). Allia: Alliance-based service discovery for ad-hoc environments. In *Proceedings of the 2ⁿᵈ International Workshop on Mobile Commerce.* Atlanta, GA, USA: ACM Press.

Ratsimor, O., Chakraborty, D., Joshi, A., & Finin, T. (2004). Service discovery in agent-based pervasive computing environments. *Mobile Networks and Applications, 9*(6), 679-692.

Richard, G. G. (2000). Service advertisement and discovery: Enabling universal device cooperation. *IEEE Internet Computing, 4*(5), 18-26.

Salutation Consortium. (2005, Jun 30). *Salutation architecture specification.* Retrieved May 27, 2008, from http://web.archive.org/

web/20050627074915/http://www.salutation.org/

Seno, S., Budiarto, R., & Wan, T.-C. (2007). Survey and new approach in service discovery and advertisement for mobile ad hoc networks. *International Journal of Computer Science and Network Security, 7*(2), 275-284.

Sun Microsystems, Inc. (1994). *Java 2 micro edition technology for creating mobile devices.* Retrieved May 27, 2008, from http://java.sun.com/j2me

Sun Microsystems, Inc. (1988). *RPC: Remote procedure call protocol specification version 2.* RFC 1057.

UPnP Forum. (2007, Sep 7). *UPnP device architecture.* Retrieved May 27, 2008, from http://www.upnp.org/resources/upnpresources.zip

Varshavsky, A., Reid, B., & de Lara, E. (2005). A cross-layer approach to service discovery and selection in MANETs. In *Proceedings of the 2nd International Conference on Mobile Ad hoc and Sensor Systems*, Washington, DC, USA (pp. 1-8).

W3C Consortium. (2004, Feb 14). *Ontology web language reference.* Retrieved May 22, 2008, from http://www.w3.org/TR/owl-ref/

Wishart, R., Robinson, R., Indulska, J., & Jøsang, A. (2005). SuperstringRep: Reputation-enhanced service discovery. In *Proceedings of the 28th Australasian Conference on Computer Science*

(pp. 49-57). Newcastle, Australia: Australian Computer Society, Inc.

Wu, J., & Zitterbart, M. (2001). Service awareness and its challenges in mobile ad hoc networks. In *Proceedings of the Tagungsband der GI/OCG-Jahrestagung*, Vienna, Austria (pp. 551-557).

Zhu, F., Mutka, M. W., & Ni, L. M. (2005). Service discovery in pervasive computing environments. *Pervasive Computing, 4*(4), 81-90.

Zhu, F., Zhu, W., Mutka, M., & Lionel, N. (2005). Expose or not? A progressive exposure approach for service discovery in pervasive computing environments. In *Proceedings of the 3rd IEEE International Conference on Pervasive Computing and Communications*, (pp. 225-234).

ENDNOTES

[1] The term 'user' is employed throughout this chapter to refer to any type of service consumer, whether it be a person, an application on his/her behalf, or any other component in the system.

[2] Other important approaches to service discovery, such as INS (Intentional Naming System), INS/Twine, and SDS (Secure Service Discovery Service), depend heavily on a central server that clients must know *a priori*. Thus, they were not included in this survey.

Chapter XXI
Context–Aware P2P Over Opportunistic Networks

Marco Conti
IIT Institute – CNR, Pisa, Italy

Franca Delmastro
IIT Institute – CNR, Pisa, Italy

Andrea Passarella
IIT Institute – CNR, Pisa, Italy

ABSTRACT

Recently, the popularity of p2p computing paradigm has been increasing, especially in the mobile environments, due to the large use of mobile devices as tools to generate and share content among users. Several works have been proposed in ad hoc networks literature to optimize legacy p2p systems over a mobile environment, mainly relying on the necessity of a stable path between pairs of nodes wishing to communicate. However, in the last few years, resources limitations and high mobility of users have introduced a new networking paradigm characterized by intermittent connectivity and frequent partitioning: the opportunistic networks. In such a dynamic environment, where systems must exploit all communication opportunities to enable the users to get in touch and exchange data, the authors propose a novel definition of mobile p2p, which exploits context information to enhance distributed services. In addition, they present a Context-aware opportunistic File Sharing application as a practical example of an optimized p2p service over opportunistic networks.

INTRODUCTION

In the last few years mobile p2p computing is increasingly emerging as an important paradigm for building next generation distributed mobile applications. The main motivation is the increasing use of mobile devices as tools to *generate* and *share* content among users according to the

Web 2.0 model. Until now, this paradigm has been supported by the legacy client/server model (e.g., through web sites such as YouTube). In a pervasive mobile environment, the p2p paradigm is conceptually closer (with respect to the client/server paradigm) to Web 2.0 content generation and sharing models. In p2p systems users directly communicate with each other without any intermediate entity such as a server. They can join and leave dynamically equally sharing the load of communication and data management. Unfortunately, p2p systems in mobile environments are not (yet) as successful as the legacy p2p systems for the wired Internet are. This is essentially due to the difficulties of running efficient p2p systems in resource-scarce and possibly challenged networking environments, which is the typical case of mobile pervasive environments. However, there is no reason not to foresee that p2p system will play a fundamental role to support data sharing in mobile environments as well, as – in principle – they represent a very efficient and natural solution.

Recently a lot of studies on p2p over self-organizing ad hoc networks have been conducted providing optimized solutions for mobile users (see (Conti, Delmastro, & Turi, 2007) as an example) but they are essentially based on the assumption that there always exists a stable path between pairs of nodes wishing to communicate. Actually, while it's foreseeable that users' devices be able to communicate wirelessly with each other, it's not realistic to envision a single, well-connected, ad hoc network including all devices. A pervasive network made up of a large number of mobile devices is *intrinsically* disconnected. Due to nodes' mobility, clouds of connected devices appear, disappear, and re-configure dynamically. Some of these clouds can include devices connected to the legacy Internet (e.g., Wi-Fi Access Points), while some others can be (temporarily) disconnected from the rest of the network. This scenario can be supported by the new communication paradigm called *opportunistic networking*

(Pelusi, Passarella, & Conti, 2006). It fits well the behavior of mobile users who need to exchange data while they are moving even in areas without the Internet coverage. In this case nodes must be enabled to communicate even if a route connecting them never exists. Mobile nodes are not supposed to possess or acquire any knowledge about the network topology, which instead is necessary in traditional routing protocols for mobile ad hoc networks (MANETs).

In opportunistic networks routes are built dynamically, hop by hop, while data flows towards the destination(s). In this way any possible node can opportunistically be used as next hop, provided its probability to bring the message closer to the final destination is sufficiently high. In this scenario nodes must exploit all the available opportunities to get in touch and communicate. In this type of networks the topological information about the network states is often unreliable and not precise. Therefore, *data*-centric communication paradigms should be preferred with respect to conventional *topology*-based paradigms. Furthermore, as the network is very dynamic and possibly unstable, *context* information should be exploited to complement the inaccurate knowledge provided by topological information alone. This makes an outstanding case for the use of *context-aware p2p systems in opportunistic networks*, as p2p systems are one of the most natural ways of supporting data-centric communication. Available systems designed for ad hoc networks are not directly applicable in such an environment, and network protocols and services must be enhanced to exploit all possible opportunities to deliver messages on the network. However, characteristics of p2p systems for MANETs must be considered as a basis for designing data-centric services for opportunistic networks.

For this reason in this chapter, before analyzing current solutions for p2p over opportunistic networks, we review the most popular p2p systems for mobile ad hoc networks in the background section. Then, we investigate how it is possible to improve data sharing and dissemination over opportunistic networks by exploiting context information. To this aim we present in detail two examples of context-aware architectural frameworks for pervasive environments. We also describe other solutions that do not propose complete architecture, but address specific issues related to context management. Finally we present a Context-aware File Sharing application for opportunistic networks as a real example of data- and user-centric service.

BACKGROUND

Since designing p2p systems for opportunistic networks is a research area still in its early stages, it is highly important to look at the most closely related body of work, i.e. p2p systems for mobile ad hoc networks.

Actually, p2p systems and ad hoc networks share a number of similar features. P2p systems provide a decentralised, self-organising and self-healing environment, along with features like subject-based routing, distributed data storage/retrieval, and load balancing. Such features, originally devised for p2p overlay networks in the legacy Internet, are also well suited for a decentralized and dynamic environment like a multi-hop ad hoc network. It is thus extremely important to understand how p2p systems designed for the Internet can be integrated into ad hoc networks.

p2p Overlays for Ad Hoc Networks

The key challenge to the usability of data-sharing p2p systems consists in implementing efficient techniques for search and retrieval of shared data. To this aim virtual ad hoc topologies (i.e., *overlays*) are defined on top of real network infrastructures to provide inexpensive, but at the same time scalable, fault tolerant and robust platforms. Such as in the traditional Internet, proposals for

p2p overlays in ad hoc networks are categorised in *structured* and *unstructured* overlays, implementing *subject-based* or *content-based* lookup procedures respectively. As main representatives of structured solutions we consider Ekta (Pucha, Das, & Hu, 2006), (Pucha, Das, & Hu, 2004), MADPastry (Zhan & Schiller, 2005), Virtual Ring Routing (Caesar, Castro, Nightingale, O'Shea, & Rowstron, 2006), and CrossROAD (Delmastro, 2005), while we present XL-Gnutella (Conti, Gregori, & Turi, 2005) as the main representative of unstructured approaches.

We recall that structured overlays (also known as Distributed Hash Tables), organise nodes in a logical infrastructure (e.g., in the form of a logical ring) through a logical address, e.g. the result of a known hash function applied to the node's IP address. Once the infrastructure is established, nodes become "responsible" for a portion of the logical address space close to their logical address. This is exploited in several ways, for example for implementing distributed and decentralised storage systems.

Each data object is tagged with a key, which is a value in the same logical address space of nodes' addresses. The object is stored on the node responsible for the portion of the logical space in which the key value falls. DHT nodes maintain some state about the overlay structure, such as a list of logical and physical neighbours. This state is necessary to guarantee routing convergence on the overlay.

The main idea of structured overlays for MANETs is to integrate discovery and maintenance mechanisms of the L3 routing protocol with the overlay routing layer to reduce the network overhead. The bottom-line idea is that, since the L3 routing already achieves knowledge about the topology of the network, this knowledge should be exploited to build and maintain the overlay structures, as well. Both Ekta and CrossROAD provide a Pastry-like DHT by optimising its operations thanks to cross-layer interactions between the overlay and L3 routing protocols.

Pastry implements a DHT along the lines described before (more information about the Pastry algorithms can be found in (Rowstron & Druschel, 2001)). The main costs of Pastry in terms of networking overhead are due to *i)* the overlay creation and management that require periodic communications between nodes, and *ii)* the multi-hop middleware routing caused by the incomplete knowledge of the overlay at each node, which possibly results in significant path stretches. These costs are well justified in large-scale wired networks, where the ability to scale to large number of nodes (possibly thousands) is correctly traded for additional bandwidth consumption (brought by points *i)* and *ii)*). However, the cost of this trade-off is turned upside-down in multi-hop ad hoc networks, where the number of nodes is limited, bandwidth is scarce, and paths should be kept as short as possible since nodes communications can be severely affected by unstable links.

CrossROAD has been designed to overcome Pastry's inefficiencies on multi-hop ad hoc networks. It provides the same DHT features, but implements them via a cross-layer optimised approach. Specifically, CrossROAD interacts with a proactive routing protocol (such as Optimized Link State Routing (OLSR)) via the cross-layer architecture proposed in (Conti, Maselli, Turi, & Giordano, 2004).These interactions are mediated by a cross-layer module (called NeSt), which provides standard interfaces for cross-layering, thus granting both performance optimisations and stacks manageability. A node wishing to join a CrossROAD overlay embeds few bytes into periodic routing advertisements, announcing its participation to a specific service. This information eventually reaches all the other nodes in the network through the proactive flooding of the routing protocol. Therefore, every node in the overlay knows the IP address of all the other nodes currently running the same service, and it is able to autonomously build the overlay by simply hashing their IP addresses. In this way,

CrossROAD drastically reduces the bandwidth overhead with respect to Pastry (Borgia, Conti, & Delmastro, 2006), (Conti, Delmastro, & Turi, 2007)), because building the overlay does not require any connection between nodes to exchange overlay information. Furthermore, p2p messages always travel just one-hop on the overlay because every node knows all the others (assuming that the routing protocol provides a consistent view at all nodes).

Even though using a proactive routing protocol over ad hoc networks might sound costly, experimental results (Borgia, Conti, & Delmastro, 2006) show that the overhead of the proactive routing protocol (OLSR in the particular case) is completely affordable. More details on CrossROAD operations can be found in (Delmastro, 2005) and (Borgia, Conti, & Delmastro, 2006)

Ekta (Pucha, Das, & Hu, 2006), (Pucha, Das, & Hu, 2004) and MADPastry (Zhan & Schiller, 2005) also provide a Pastry-like DHT exploiting the general concept of integrating L3 routing with overlay routing through a cross-layer approach. In contrast to CrossROAD, they exploit reactive routing protocols such as DSR (Johnson & Maltz, 1996) in the case of Ekta, and AODV (Perkins & Royer, 1999) in the case of MADPastry.

The main idea of Ekta is keeping source routes of nodes stored in the Pastry *leaf-set* (which, for each node, is the set of closest logical neighbors in the Pastry overlay network) and routing tables just on an on-demand basis, when forwarding operations are required, without generating additional overhead with respect to the traffic required by DSR to compute these source routes.

MADPastry enhances the standard Pastry system by storing fewer entries in the routing and leaf-set tables, so as to reduce the network overhead. Furthermore, overlay and L3 forwarding are closely interacting together. When an intermediate hop in an overlay path discovers to be a better match, in the overlay, with respect to the intended destination, the overlay multi-hop forwarding is stopped, and the intermediate node initiates a new multi-hop path on the overlay towards the final destination.

In Virtual Ring Routing (VRR (Caesar, Castro, Nightingale, O'Shea, & Rowstron, 2006)) overlay and L3 routing procedures are provided at once by the same protocol, i.e. there is no distinction between L3 and the overlay layer anymore, even providing a Pastry-like DHT. In VRR each node maintains a *vset* and a *pset*. The *vset* is a set of *r* paths to the *r* closest neighbors in the logical ring (actually, paths to the closest *r/2* clockwise and counter-clockwise neighbors are maintained). Paths to the *vset* members are proactively maintained in the routing table, together with paths towards end points whose path happens to go through the node. The *pset* of a node is the set of physical neighbors, reachable through direct communication at the link layer. The members of the *pset* are also kept in the routing table, and are used as next hops to route messages along *vset*-paths. VRR completely avoids flooding, as *vset*-paths are built by exploiting current information on the routing table. Performance results presented in (Caesar, Castro, Nightingale, O'Shea, & Rowstron, 2006) show the advantage of VRR with respect to standard MANET routing in terms of delivery delay, packet loss and overhead.

As far as unstructured overlays, they organize nodes according to loose rules in contrast with well-defined overlay infrastructures seen previously. This results in a random graph possibly with some level of hierarchy (e.g., the SuperPeers in the Gnutella protocol), and lookup procedures are implemented through flooding or random walks on this graph, until the sought object is found. They are usually more efficient than structured overlays to locate popular, wide spread contents, but they tend to be inefficient for rare content, as the search has to involve a large number of peers.

Looking at unstructured overlays for MANET, the work in (Conti, Gregori, & Turi, 2005) proposes XL-Gnutella, which is an optimization of the standard Gnutella protocol for mobile ad hoc networks. Even in this case, the bottom-line idea is to exploit routing traffic to spread information related to the overlay management over the physical network. Specifically, in XL-Gnutella, Gnutella agents exploit OLSR proactive routing messages to spread their availability in the network. The standard routing protocol is modified so as to provide overlay peers with information about the set of peers seen in received L3 advertisements. Therefore, peers in the overlay know about each other without requiring any additional traffic generated at the overlay level. Performance results presented in (Conti, Gregori, & Turi, 2005) show that such a system is extremely more stable and requires significantly less overhead traffic with respect to a standard Gnutella implementation run on top of conventional MANET stacks.

MOVING TOWARDS OPPORTUNISTIC NETWORKS

The main obstacle to directly import the approaches seen previously in opportunistic networks resides in the original purpose of MANET routing protocols, especially proactive ones. In fact they are originally designed to build a complete view of the network topology at any point in time, updating routing tables whenever mobility occurs. In an opportunistic environment this approach is totally unsuitable since numerous and rapid topology changes not only result in a relevant quantity of control traffic, but they also generate unreliable routing structures, useless to deliver messages to more than few hops distance. For this reason, solutions such as CrossROAD or XL-Gnutella cannot be straightforwardly ported to opportunistic networks.

Nevertheless, these systems share their main purpose of data distribution and recovery over the wireless medium with potential users of opportunistic networks, who essentially need to exchange and share information even in high mobility and intermittent connectivity conditions. In opportunistic networks *data*-centric approaches are very promising indeed and p2p systems are the most natural way of supporting them. Users interested in data objects (files, clips, advertisements, news) might be completely unaware of other users that generate the content they wish to get, and, vice versa, users generating content might ignore who is interested in their data. The network might be so unstable that content producers and consumers might never be connected together. Therefore, it is important to disseminate content in the network so as to reach possibly interested users. Working on possible customizations and optimizations of legacy p2p systems for ad hoc networks, we can introduce a novel definition of p2p for opportunistic networks. Actually, p2p systems for MANETs are mainly designed to distribute and recover data independently of possible devices' heterogeneities, specific users' requirements, or application content, simply following specific algorithms (e.g. DHTs) that optimize system's performance. Instead, thinking at opportunistic networks as networks of *people* carrying mobile devices, we can exploit additional personal and/or environmental information to define resilient data dissemination techniques. In this view, exploiting *context* information about the environment users are roaming in, and about the personal behavior of users themselves, is a very promising direction.

In addition, the bottom-line concept of blending together routing and overlay management procedures in mobile p2p systems can be extended in opportunistic networks to all layers of a legacy node architecture, obtaining thus a layer-less architecture in which all functions (from routing and forwarding up to applications) cooperate to improve the entire system. Note that this is one of the core ideas of the Haggle project (Haggle Project website) in which context- and content-aware routing schemes already implement some form of local advertisement upon pair-wise contacts between nodes, which replaces the legacy L3 advertisement traffic of MANET routing schemes.

These mechanisms, enriched by context information, e.g. users' behavior, interactions and interests, allow nodes to achieve a *people-centric* knowledge of the network. In this way they are not only able to perform informed forwarding decisions, coping with problems related to disconnections and network partitions (see HiBOp (Boldrini, Conti, & Passarella, 2008a) and Bubble Rap (Hui & Crowcroft, 2007) protocols as an example), but also to optimize overlay services considering specific applications requirements and resources availability.

At this point, before defining possible opportunistic p2p architectures and applications, it is worth giving a general definition of context, explaining what kind of information could be considered and how it could be managed to design feasible applications and communications algorithms.

CONTEXT MANAGEMENT IN OPPORTUNISTIC NETWORKS

The most general definition of context and context-awareness has been originally given by Anind K. Dey in 2001 in (Dey, 2001) with the following terms:

- *"Context is any information that can be used to characterize the situation of an entity. An entity is a **person**, **place**, or **object** that is considered relevant to the interaction between a user and an application, including the user and applications themselves."*
- *"A system is context-aware if it uses context to provide relevant information and/or services to the user, where relevancy depends on the user's task."*

In opportunistic networks and more in general in pervasive and ubiquitous computing, environment is continuously changing, and using context makes applications able to react accordingly, improving the overall system performance. As described by the previous definition, context information can include environmental characteristics revealed by sensors, personal information related to mobile users, and physical characteristics of devices, involving all layers of the legacy node architecture and requiring a close collaboration among them.

In the last ten years several works on context-awareness have been conducted, encouraged by the emergence of even more pervasive devices and new networking paradigms to establish communications. Some of them (e.g. Henricksen, Indulska, & Rakotonirainy, 2002; Henriksen & Indulska, 2004; Schmidt, 2006) tried to give models and software architectures to manage context information in order to make applications more flexible and autonomous. A good survey on these studies can be found in (Strang, 2004). However, to investigate how these models could be applied in opportunistic networks, it is really useful to highlight the main characteristics of context in such environment starting from the general view presented in (Henricksen, Indulska, & Rakotonirainy, 2002):

- **Context information is characterized by temporal constraints.** It can be divided in *static* and *dynamic* information. Static context describes invariant aspects like, e.g., user's date of birth and hardware characteristics of the mobile device. However, the majority of information is dynamic and characterized by different time constraints, e.g. users' location can vary with a granularity of minutes, while job's information can be valid for months or years. In addition, to make services able to correctly react to a highly dynamic environment, probabilistic predictions for the next future are required. To this aim, context history should be maintained as part of the context description.
- **Context information is imperfect.** This essentially depends on the accuracy of the captured information and possible delays in distributing and recovering it. Specifically, context can be *incomplete* if some aspects are missing, *inconsistent* in case of contradictions, and *incorrect* if it does not reflect the true state of the world it models. Giving a different weight to each level of accuracy prevents the system from taking wrong decisions.
- **Context can be represented in several alternative ways.** It can be represented in different forms and with different levels of abstractions depending on the application purpose, e.g. location information can be represented by GPS coordinates or simply by the number of the room a user is in. To manage all the possible abstractions, the system should be able to capture also possible relationships among them.
- **Context information is highly interrelated.** Generally, relationships among context information are mainly characterized by derivation rules which describe how information is obtained from one or more pieces of information. Rules definition represents one of the main steps of the development of a modeling system.

These general characteristics fit well the continuously changing environment of opportunistic networks, especially looking at users' context information. In fact, users' context information is characterized by a high-level of abstraction, imperfection and strong time-dependency and it could be efficiently modeled following the approach presented in (Henricksen, Indulska, & Rakotonirainy, 2002; Henriksen & Indulska, 2004). This model provides a formal basis for representing and managing all of these properties following an object-oriented approach that can result in an entity-relationship (ER) model for distributed environments. This model provides a graphical notation for describing types of information (denoted as *fact types*) that are classified, according to their persistence, either as *static* (i.e., facts that remain unchanged as long as the entities they describe persist) or *dynamic*. The latter category is then further classified depending on the entity's originator either as *profiled* (i.e., information supplied by users), *sensed* (i.e., information derived from sensors) or *derived* (obtained from one or more associations using a derivation function such as a mathematical computation or a complex algorithm). Each of these categories identifies a different level of reliability of the specific fact type that is further characterized by quality metadata, (e.g. accuracy, freshness). Finally, the model includes also dependencies between fact types, and a history fact type to support probabilistic predictions on future events.

The strength of this model is the structure of the contextual knowledge for real applicability purposes, as the definition of an ER model, including also a qualitative evaluation of used information. For this reason we can assume that this model, compared with several others presented in literature based on ontology or markup schemes (a survey can be found in (Strang, 2004)), is really suitable for defining a general Context Manager module in a context-aware node architecture for pervasive environments.

To better understand how this general view of context can be applied in realistic scenarios, we present in the next subsections two examples of context-aware architectural frameworks developed under the AURA project at Carnegie Mellon University (Judd & Steenkiste, 2003; Garlan et al., 2002; Sousa & Garlan, 2002; Aura Project, 2002), and the FET-SAC Haggle project funded by the European Community (Haggle Project, 2004) respectively. Both projects are specifically intended for highly pervasive computing environments involving wireless communication, wearable or handheld devices, smart spaces, and high mobility conditions. These two examples propose an environment-independent framework, supporting several categories of context-aware services. This is a major improvement with re-

spect to traditional context-management systems that are typically focused on specific issues (we present a few examples after describing AURA and Haggle).

AURA's Architecture

The AURA project aims to maximize the use of available resources in a pervasive environment and minimize users' distractions due to the explicit management of their computing resources. To this aim the project introduces the concept of *personal aura,* which allows users to move their computational tasks easily from one environment to another, automatically reconfiguring services to continue running and using the new available resources. In practice, when a user enters a new environment, his or her aura selects the appropriate resources to support the current task (e.g., writing a paper, sending an email or attending a conference call). Thus, the aura essentially deals with *physical context* surrounding the user by capturing constraints imposed on tasks (e.g., supported operating system on the final device, connectivity conditions, and available displays), and information related to the user's intent in terms of tasks priority, scheduled operations for the next future, and other.

Figure 1 shows a schematic view of the architectural framework composed of four main components:

- **Task Manager** (called **Prism**) embodies the concept of personal aura;
- **Environment manager** provides resource monitoring and tasks adaptation;
- **Context Observer** manages information on the physical context;
- **Service Suppliers** provide services abstractions needed to support a user's task.

Prism represents the core component of the entire system. It is mainly designed to represent user intent and provides to the system all the necessary information to correctly adapt or anticipate user needs. To do this, Prism directly interacts with the Context Observer, from which it obtains information and event notifications about changes in the physical context. Then it starts a negotiation with the Environment manager that is aware of which Suppliers are available to supply a specific service.

In order to better understand how Aura manages context information and provides it to applications, we must focus on the Context Observer module. Specifically, the Context Observer is designed to efficiently manage information avoiding customizations depending on each specific service, with particular attention to dynamic information. To this aim, the Context Observer is represented by several "Contextual Information Providers" (Judd & Steenkiste, 2003) that are organized in a virtual database. Each provider is associated to a specific entity in the model (e.g., people, devices, physical spaces) and it is in charge of collecting information related to it *on demand*. Thus, instead of maintaining all the information with the same accuracy and granularity, each provider manages its information depending on the service requirements. This mechanism to support on demand retrieval of contextual information allows the system to store updates at different granularity levels, and to distribute computational efforts of complex queries. The system also stores quality indexes of dynamic attributes as metadata (e.g. accuracy, confidence and freshness), maintaining a simple SQL-like query interface towards applications.

Therefore, the Context Observer manages information following a modeling approach similar to that presented in the previous section, taking into consideration all inaccuracies of context information. In addition, it improves the overall system performance making use of information providers that allow applications to easily synthesize required context information, with a minimal effort from individual services.

In terms of context-aware applications, tasks migration represents the basic functionality of Aura, however several other services have been developed on top of this architecture. Portable Help Desk (PHD) and Idealink are two examples presented in (Garlan, Siewiorek, Smailagic, & Steenkiste, 2002) focused on exploiting Aura's capabilities to support collaborations among campus students. Specifically, PHD deals with spatial awareness in terms of user's relative and absolute position and orientation, and temporal awareness in terms of scheduled time of public and private events. It allows users to determine the position of other students in the campus, general and personal information about them, and notifies the local user of campus events that fit her interests. Idealink instead represents a virtual collaboration environment that facilitates planned and ad hoc collaborations among mobile users through a shared distributed whiteboard.

Haggle's Architecture

While AURA mainly targets conventional pervasive networking environments, the Haggle project aims to define a new autonomic architecture for *opportunistic* networks able to allow devices communications even in high mobility and intermittent connectivity conditions. Thus, the architectural framework is mainly designed to

Figure 1. Aura's architecture (adapted from Sousa & Garlan, 2002)

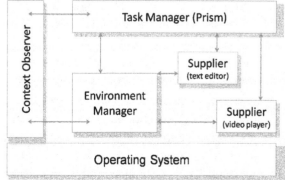

establish communications between users for delivering messages even when a stable path between them never exists. To this end, instead of leaving all the responsibility of nodes communications to the network layer, as it happens in legacy TCP/IP architecture, Haggle defines new paradigms of application-driven message forwarding, exploiting context information related to users' behavior and social interactions. Therefore, Haggle tries to reflect the human way of communicating, pushing all the technical aspects of nodes communication into the background. Thus, we can define Haggle both as a *data-centric* and a *people-centric* system. The former because the main purpose of the system is to deliver and exchange messages, which contain data to be shared among users, and its entire decisions are based on context information. The latter because people are the main actors of the network while their devices represent only the communication medium.

Figure 2 shows Haggle node architecture. It is completely layer-less above the data-link, and a set of managers is defined to implement all the features needed to communicate and deliver

messages (e.g., security, protocols definition, forwarding algorithms, connectivity, resource, and context management). Then, managers can make use of modules to implement specific functionality related to particular algorithms. All the managers interact with a central entity: the Haggle Kernel, a minimal event queue that coordinates actions and communications between managers, and waits for incoming data. All data is then stored in the DataStore and managed by the DataObject Manager.

The Haggle node architecture natively supports context awareness of all networking tasks. The core concept of Haggle's architecture is Data Object (DO) as a general representation of all information generated inside Haggle or coming from the network. Specifically, both application and control messages generated or received by Haggle are represented as DOs. They consist of a descriptive header in XML format (i.e. the metadata part of a DO) and the optional application data (e.g., a binary stream or a text string). Metadata includes a list of attributes, as name-value pairs, aimed at describing context information in control messages or application data (content and format). All this information is organized in the DataStore specifying four main entities strictly connected among them:

- **Interfaces:** Physical communication interfaces of the local device.
- **Attributes:** Set of name-value pairs describing data, users and devices.
- **Data:** Virtual representation of persistent DOs such as application data; associated metadata is stored in the Attributes set.
- **Node:** Virtual representation of a device or a user; this entity is directly connected with Interfaces entity to retrieve information about devices' physical interfaces, while it is connected with Attributes for descriptive information about devices and users.

Figure 2. Haggle node architecture (adapted from Haggle Project, 2007)

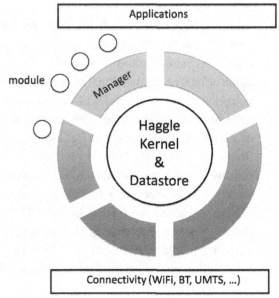

All these entities and their relationships represent a general context model in Haggle. Haggle is able to collect all context information about both encountered users and devices through periodical beaconing. Probabilistic and qualitative analysis of content is then left to single managers in charge of taking specific decisions to interact with other managers or with the network. Note that individual managers and modules can define and exchange context information by generating custom DOs.

In the framework of this project we analyzed issues related to context-aware forwarding algorithms (Boldrini, Conti, & Passarella, 2008a), context- and resource-aware data dissemination (Boldrini, Conti, & Passarella, 2008b), by particularly focusing on the impact of social mobility and relationships on these topics. Actually, Haggle considers social relationships and users behavior as one of the most interesting pieces of context information to be exploited in the design of opportunistic networks. As nodes in opportunistic networks are primarily devices carried with by people, users' mobility patterns and their social relationships provide information about future contact opportunities and other users likely to be met in the future. Therefore, understanding and exploiting information about social network structures (e.g., how communities of users are formed, behave, and evolve over time) is also an active and promising track in the Project activities. Therefore, work on networking support is complemented by additional studies on social networks (Daly & Haahr, 2007; Yoneki, Hui, Chan, & Crowcroft, 2007) that highlight how much the human behavior can be correctly predicted following its habits and contacts. In this way a people-centric view of the network is given, and simulation studies proved that exploiting this type of context information highly improves the overall system performance in such a dynamic environment. The combination of all these studies represents the basis for the definition of real attractive services for opportunistic users. To support this assumption, after giving a brief overview of other context management solutions, we present a *Context-aware Opportunistic File Sharing* application as a practical example of context-aware p2p service over opportunistic networks based on the Haggle architecture. Through this novel service we are able to show how using context enriches the classical p2p paradigm overcoming the view of peers only as physical devices, and highlighting individual users' requirements.

Traditional Context Management Systems Overview

The examples presented before represents two system architectures aimed to provide several context-aware services supported by general mechanisms to manage context information. In literature, many context management systems have been presented, but only few of them propose general frameworks independent of the surrounding environment or the specific category of provided services. In addition some of them limit their features to single aspects of context management such as gathering and exchanging context information relevant for a specific set of services, without considering how to process this information to enhance upper-layer services. For example (Ye, Li, Zhu, Gu, & Shi, 2007) proposes a context management system based on registration-query mechanism mainly designed for "sentient" applications (i.e. applications that can change their behavior based on a model of the environment derived from sensor data). This system aims at establishing communication channels among ubiquitous terminals to collect context information by using broadcast messages for available terminals discovery and unicast messages for remote registration of local Context Database Agents. These agents provide an access interface to the local database, so that by distributing this information on the network each node is able to identify which agent can access the information it is interested in. In this way context information is maintained locally by each node, and only context agents are remotely registered, reducing the cost for context distribution and maintenance. Another approach to collect context information in a ubiquitous environment is presented in (Strohbach, Bauer, Kovacs, Villalonga, & Richter, 2007). In this case the authors introduce the notion of "Context Session" as a communication relationship between a source and a sink over which notifications about requested context information is exchanged. Thus, the system implements two distinct protocols: a signaling protocol to set up and control a session, and a protocol to exchange requested context information. This separation allows for a flexible and adaptive management of context information, e.g. according to load and availability of context sources.

The main problem of these systems is that context-aware applications that rely on a specific context management system are not able to exploit context information of users residing in an environment served by another system. In this way operations of context-aware applications are strictly limited to the local environment they are running within, and to the information managed by the specific context manager. In order to solve this problem (Hesselman, et al., 2008) propose a system in which bridges are placed between different context management systems to enable applications to obtain context information generated by other systems, not directly interacting with them. The bridges facilitate the interaction of different systems and related environments, which is essential for the deployment of large scale ubiquitous computing systems. However, the limitation of bridges is that each of them is specific for a pair of context management systems and most likely a large number of instances is needed. Even in this case there is no attention to context analysis and elaboration.

CONTEXT-AWARE OPPORTUNISTIC FILE SHARING

In order to highlight the efficiency of a context-aware architecture for pervasive environments, such as that proposed in the Haggle Project, to support context-aware services, we present a File Sharing (FS) application enhanced by context information in opportunistic networks. FS belongs to the set of content sharing applications that are extremely appreciated both in wired and wireless networks. Nowadays this paradigm is evolved into a new model called User-Generated Content in which users are not only passive content consumers, but also active content producers (blogs, YouTube, Flickr are some examples of this kind of services on Internet). Mobile devices further encourage this paradigm, since users are able to generate and share content anytime and anywhere. Thus, considering FS as an example, we can show how using context information enhances features of this kind of application guaranteeing an efficient service for opportunistic networks in terms of minimum messages dissemination and service reliability.

Social Context Information for Opportunistic File Sharing

In this scenario, we mainly refer to context information in terms of users' interests, habits, social contacts and mobility patterns. In fact, since users are mobile and carry devices with them, users' social behavior is a valid signal of users' mobility patterns, and it may be really useful to predict future contacts among users, improving forwarding decisions on the network. In addition, people's social relationships generally vary much more slowly than the network topology, thus exchanging information about social behavior requires less control traffic than topology control messages typical of MANET routing protocols.

In literature several solutions have been proposed to model human social behavior (e.g.

(Wasserman & Faust, 1994)). Specifically, following social network models and small-world theories (Watts, 1999), we can assume that users are grouped in communities, and users of the same community have strong social links between each other, usually related to common interests. A user is generally represented as belonging to a *"home"* community in which she spends more time, and characterized by a *centrality* parameter as the popularity degree within the community in terms of number of interactions with the other members. Some nodes can also have social links outside their *"home"* community, modeling social relationships with users of different groups. Small-world theories have shown that these *"external"* links act as shortcuts and enable communications across the network with a small average number of hops (6 hops in the "classical" small-world models derived from the work by Stanley Milgram (Milgram, 1967), less than O(log n), where n is the size of the network, in several types of real networks (Newmann, 2003)). Thus, these users can work, for instance, as bridges between disconnected communities and can be exploited to move data objects from one community to the others they are in contact with, following communities interests. In this way, making the system able to identify users' behavior and their role in the network highly enhances services efficiency and reliability. To this aim, several communities' detection algorithms have been presented in literature (Newmann, 2004; Danon & Duch, 2005; Hui & Crowcroft, 2007; Yoneki, Hui, Chan, & Crowcroft, 2007). They are mainly based on the analysis of contact duration and number of contacts between pairs of users assuming that individuals meet at high rate if they have one or more mutual friends. Therefore, a user belongs to a community if she has a high number of contacts and long contact duration with the other members; she is a *familiar stranger* if she has a high number of contacts but short contact duration (probably someone periodically visiting that community); she is a *stranger* if characterized by low number of contacts and short duration (occasional visits), and she is a *friend* if she has a low number of contacts but longer duration. Continuously monitoring users' behavior and defining a threshold on the number of contacts and their duration it is possible to dynamically identify the social role of a specific user.

Opportunistic File Sharing: Application Design

The social role of users, as detected, for instance, by the mechanisms summarized before, can be exploited to optimize the opportunistic file sharing design. For example, by exchanging information about users' interests the service running on a user device can select interesting data for specific sets of users and replicate it only on nodes that are probably in contact with them. This is one of the main innovations of our Context-aware Opportunistic FS application: when a user gets in touch with new neighbors, she is able to identify data on these nodes that could be requested in the next future by its previous neighbors. She can thus dedicate part of her resources to pre-fetch this data for the benefit of the other members of her community.

To better understand all improvements obtained by using social context in opportunistic FS, we give a detailed description of the service's features in the following.

First of all we must specify that Context-aware Opportunistic FS has been designed to allow distributed sharing of content even in case the content producers and consumers might never be connected together. To this aim, users getting in touch with each other are in charge of downloading both data in which they are directly interested, and those files probably interesting for their friends. To do this, two different notions of context related to a single user are introduced following the model presented in (Boldrini, Conti, & Passarella, 2008a) for a forwarding algorithm: the *current context* and the *context evolution* over time. The current context maintains information about the user itself and its current physical neighbors. Generally, each user is identified by a set of personal information (e.g. name, address, city, job, hobbies) enriched with additional information depending on the specific service. In case of opportunistic FS, this information is represented by preferred file categories, genres, and topics, and the file list the user wants to share.

Each node running Context-aware Opportunistic FS maintains context information in a local data structure called Identity Table (IT). By exchanging ITs during the neighbor discovery procedure, each node knows the interests of all its neighbors and the related file lists, and it adds them to its current context. However, since ITs can contain a huge quantity of data, it is not efficient to periodically broadcast them on the network. Thus, each node periodically announces its presence in the network broadcasting a unique identifier that can be represented by the hash of its IT. Then, when it receives an unknown identifier from one or more neighbors, it broadcasts its IT. Once a user has collected neighbors' context information, she can directly download an interesting file from one of them through a direct p2p connection.

However, the current context gives only an instant picture of the network and the social interactions of the local user. Since these conditions can change over time due to users' movements, it is necessary to maintain also information about past experiences and encounters of each user as the evolution over time of her general context. In this way, when a user moves to a new community, the application can exploit the interests of past encountered nodes to identify additional files in which previous neighbors could be interested, and pre-fetch them to satisfy possible future requests. Let us consider a practical example just to better understand the service's functionality.

In Figure 3 two social communities of users are presented. We assume that users of the same community share some common interests. In fact, we can note that, on the left-hand side, users A

and C are interested in mp3 and jpeg files, while B is interested in jpeg and avi files and, on the right-hand side, both users D and E are interested in mp3 and avi files. Assuming that all nodes in each community are able to communicate to each other, after the neighbor discovery phase each of them knows the interests and the file list of the others, updating thus their current context. In addition, supposing that user C originally belongs to both communities or has several friends in the second community, it is highly probable that she moves towards the other community and can thus share additional files. When she reaches the other community, she broadcasts her IT and collects information from the new neighbors. In this way, she becomes aware of the files shared by the new neighbors and she is able to select and download those she is interested in (see Figure 4).

In this practical example, since user C is directly interested in mp3 and jpeg files, she decides to download first of all F1.jpg from D and F5.jpg from E. Then, she decides to dedicate part of the remaining memory to download avi files that are probably interesting for the users belonging to the other community. In this way, coming back to the original community, C is able to serve requests for those specific files, avoiding requests' dissemination over the network and reducing the delay to satisfy them.

Generalizing this social cooperative behavior, the application is able not only to allow users to directly download files available on their current neighbors, but also to dedicate part of their local resources to pre-fetch the more likely interesting files for the users of previous encountered contexts. The selection of these additional files mainly depends on two factors: local resource availability (e.g. memory and battery capacity) and the *utility* of those data both for the local user and the social contexts she is in touch with. This cooperative downloading scheme is thus designed to maximize the utility of a data object for the social contexts the local user is in touch with.

Figure 3. Context-aware Opportunistic FS: scenario 1

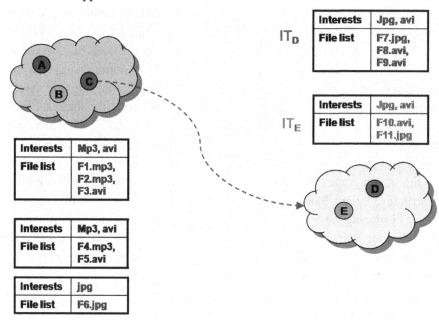

Interests	Jpg, avi
File list	F7.jpg, F8.avi, F9.avi

IT_D

Interests	Jpg, avi
File list	F10.avi, F11.jpg

IT_E

Interests	Mp3, avi
File list	F1.mp3, F2.mp3, F3.avi

Interests	Mp3, avi
File list	F4.mp3, F5.avi

Interests	jpg
File list	F6.jpg

Before analyzing in detail the definition of our utility-based mechanism it is important to give some other general consideration on the use of context in the specific case of file sharing services. In general, managing possibly sensible information about users requires addressing privacy issues. For what specifically concerns file sharing, several cases have to be distinguished. First of all, the nodes need to advertise the following information: *i)* the local id, *ii)* the types of files the node's user is interested into, and *iii)* the list of files currently stored by the node. Different privacy requirements can be appropriate. On the one hand, none of this information might actually be considered as sensitive data from a privacy standpoint. Note that the same kind of information is already published by users of traditional p2p systems without any significant privacy protection mechanism. On the other hand, all this information might be considered sensitive from a privacy standpoint, meaning that users are willing to disclose it only to a subset of trusted users on the network, which can be identified by the community the user belongs to.

We assume that an encryption system is in place, allowing members of communities to securely encode information that has to remain private within the community. In this case, the id of the nodes, the users' interests, and the names of files to be shared (as well as the files themselves) can be encrypted. Nodes belonging to the same community can clearly decrypt the information, if needed. At the same time, nodes belonging to different communities can collaboratively participate to the file sharing system despite the data being encrypted. As will be clear from the following, everything a node has to know is the fact that a given file of a given type is required by one node it has encountered, and available on another node it is encountering. Such "match" between interests of users and availability of files can be detected also by looking at encrypted strings representing interests and file types, as long as the encryption function is not ambiguous (i.e., it produces the same encrypted string starting from the same unencrypted string). This is possible only in case matched data reside on users of the same community using the same encryption key. Thus, a *stranger* node can help a pair of community members currently not connected to share their information and exploit cooperative downloading mechanisms even though context information is encrypted. Instead, applying this privacy policy, there is no way to identify the interests or file types on nodes belonging to different communities without decrypting data. In this case, only commuting nodes that originally belong to more than one community have the possibility to implement cooperative mechanisms knowing the key of each community. Finally, in such (rare) cases in which even the match of encrypted strings might be regarded as a privacy threat (e.g. in case encrypted data are used by malicious nodes to define possible interests' profiles of users running the service), only nodes belonging to the same community will participate to the file sharing function for that community, of course with reduced performance. More details about the related issues of key distribution and matching encrypted strings in opportunistic networks are provided in (Boldrini, Conti, & Passarella, 2008a). As supporting the aforementioned privacy

requirements is clearly orthogonal with respect to the file sharing mechanisms, in the following we continue the description of utility-based mechanisms without including privacy policies.

Utility-Based Opportunistic File Sharing

Each node should be able to compute the utility of data objects stored by the other encountered peers, and that one of the data objects it currently stores, in terms of utility for the local user (e.g. data belonging to the same category she is interested in) and utility for the users belonging to the different contexts the user is in touch with. The main idea is to select those files that maximize the utility function, without violating device's constraints in terms of resource usage (e.g., buffer occupation, bandwidth or energy usage). A study on the utility function for data dissemination in opportunistic environment has been recently presented in (Boldrini, Conti, & Passarella, 2008b), and here we propose a summary of the most important characteristics. For further details on the probabilistic analysis you can refer

Figure 4. Context-aware Opportunistic FS: scenario 2

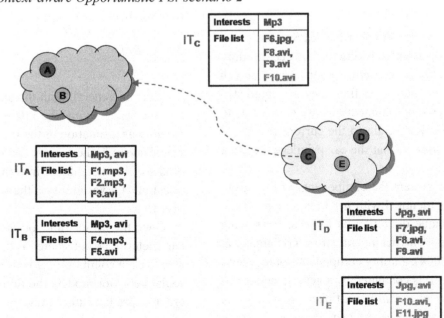

to (Boldrini, Conti, & Passarella, 2008b) and the associated report available at (http://bruno1.iit.cnr. it/~chiara/dataDisseminationTR.pdf).

According to previous assumptions, a generic node computes the utility value of a data object k with the equation (1) in which $u_k^{(l)}$ represents the utility for the local user, $u_{k,i}^{(c)}$ represents the utility for the i-th context the user is in contact with, and ω_i is a cooperation index that defines the willingness of the user to cooperate with the i-th context (i.e., to spend own resources to increase data availability for that context).

$$U_k = u_k^{(l)} + \sum_i \omega_i u_{k,i}^{(c)} \qquad (1)$$

Note that, by using cooperation indexes greater than 0, we can avoid the selfish users behavior in which they tend to maximize their own utility. In addition, defining the utility functions $u_k^{(l)}$ and $u_{k,i}^{(c)}$ as homogeneous functions of context parameters, we can summarize the utility value of the data object as the sum of the utilities related to the contexts the user is in touch with, considering also the local user as one of these contexts. Therefore the same equation can be expressed as:

$$U_k = \sum_i \omega_i u_{k,i} \qquad (2)$$

Then, in case of opportunistic FS, since generally users currently visiting the same community are probably in communication range, or can directly download the files they are interested in with few-hops connections, we can decide to assign a lower weight to the current context of the local user, so that she can privilege the other contexts.

In our system the components of the utility functions (denoted with $u_{k,i}$ in equation (2) follow a unique definition as follows. Borrowing from the Web-caching literature (Balamash & Krunz, 2004), a utility component (for a generic data object) is computed by a generic node A as its *access probability* multiplied by a measure of its *value*. The *access probability* is the prob-

ability of the data object being requested in the context specified in the utility component (denoted as p_{ac}), and it depends on the popularity of the object in that context. The *value* of a data object for a specific context is defined as a measure of the advantage the users of that context can take from the fact that node A cooperative downloads the object. The value of a data object depends on several parameters, which can be combined as shown in (Boldrini, Conti, & Passarella, 2008b). Here it is denoted as p_{av}. In the simplest case, the value is a decreasing function of the availability of the object, i.e. the probability for node A of encountering the object on the context specified in the utility component. The rationale is the fact that, the more the data object is available in the context, the less it is useful to store it also on node A, as it is already wide spread in the context. Furthermore, even in a simple case, the value should also reflect the *local resources availability* for each possible download or, on the contrary, the actual *resource consumption* related to downloading the investigated object. In the simplest case, the memory occupation is the only resource to be considered, and the value is thus a decreasing function also of the object size. Therefore, the form of the utility component function becomes as follows:

$$U = \frac{p_{ac} e^{-\lambda p_{av}}}{s} \qquad (3)$$

More in general, both the access probability and the value should be related to the *context stability* as a function of the time the local node would spend in the current context, the mobility model of her neighbors (in terms also of churn rates), and the variability of the access probability over time.

Once the utility function is defined, the last parameter to be considered is the weight associated to each community. To correctly evaluate it, social behavior models should be considered in order to predict future movements and contacts of the local user. In this way, the system is able to favor users belonging to a selected community by downloading files in which most of them are interested. For example, the system could decide to favor the community she is more likely in contact with, e.g. in terms of contact duration, or the community that is more likely she will visit in the next future.

The utility values of data objects computed in this way allow each node to rank objects it can possibly download when meeting other nodes. To this end, each node constantly tries to maximize the utility of the data objects it currently carries, without violating constraints on the available resources (e.g., in terms of memory occupation or battery consumption). This can be achieved by solving a simple multi-constrained Knapsack problem, as discussed in detail in (Boldrini, Conti, & Passarella, 2008b).

Results presented in that work show that such a social-aware file sharing system performs better than other reference solutions, in terms of accessibility of data objects, fairness, and resource consumption. Nevertheless, in order to further improve the overall service performance, the system should be able to identify the changing context around the local user. In fact, to avoid redundant pre-fetching of the same files from different users originally belonging to the same community, or from users currently inside the same community, cooperative download mechanisms should run only on nodes that actually bridge together disconnected communities, exploiting at most the possibility of disseminating information between interested users that might never be connected. To this aim, each node should become aware of the community change and only in that moment begin the cooperative downloading technique. How social behavior models and communities detection algorithms can support this feature is currently a work in progress.

In the meanwhile, a preliminary version of the Context-aware Opportunistic FS running on top of Linux laptops has been presented in (Conti, Delmastro, & Passarella, 2007) in the framework of Haggle project. In that demonstration we deployed the mobility scenario shown in Figure 3 and 4 as a possible use case. Currently, we are adapting the service implementation to run on top of Windows Mobile smartphones, exploiting the main features of Haggle's architecture. In this way, we will be able to set up a realistic testbed environment for opportunistic networks, thus enabling performance evaluations of this kind of services depending on resource limitations and intermittent connectivity issues.

CONCLUSION AND FUTURE WORK

In this chapter we investigated main issues related to designing and developing p2p systems over opportunistic networks as an evolution of mobile ad hoc networking paradigm characterized by frequent disconnections and partitioning. Starting from the solutions proposed in literature for ad hoc networks, we highlighted the main obstacles to directly import these approaches in opportunistic networks. The main issues include the assumption of the presence of a stable path between each pair of nodes wishing to communicate, and the continuous and dynamic update of the network topology resulting in a relevant quantity of control traffic from the routing standpoint and the generation of usually unreliable data structures, especially in case of intermittent connectivity. However, mobile p2p systems share their main objectives of data distribution and recovery with potential users of opportunistic networks, even though they are mainly based on data-centric approaches, not involving possible devices' heterogeneities and users' requirements. Thus, we introduced a novel definition of p2p for opportunistic networks both as data- and people-centric systems. In this view, referring to opportunistic networks as networks of people carrying mobile devices, we can exploit context information, in terms of information describing users, devices, and the surrounding environments, to define efficient and resilient data dissemination techniques.

To this aim we introduced a general definition of context and context-aware services in order to give a general view of these abstract concepts. We also analyzed a general modeling approach for context management that fits well opportunistic environment characteristics. As far as context management issues, we presented in detail two important projects aimed at exploiting context information to improve distributed service features on top of pervasive and opportunistic environments respectively. On the one hand, AURA project aims to minimize users' distraction due to explicit management of their computing resources, allowing the system to automatically reconfigure after an environment change or provide tasks migration on different platforms while the user is moving. On the other hand, Haggle project aims to define a new autonomic architecture for opportunistic networks able to allow devices communications even in high mobility and intermittent connectivity conditions.

We presented thus a Context-aware Opportunistic File Sharing application, developed in the framework of Haggle, as a practical example of context-aware p2p service for opportunistic networks. In this case we mainly refer to context information as data related to users' interests and shared data. To optimize the service features this information must be publicly exchanged among nodes and users are completely aware of it, thus the absence of a privacy policy to protect context information not represents a great issue in this particular case. However, due to the importance of privacy working with personal information about users, we briefly discuss a possible solution in the proposed application. In Context-aware Opportunistic FS, the service is designed to exploit information about past, present and probable future contacts of a user, mainly related to their interests and shared files, to implement cooperative downloading and data dissemination mechanisms. In this way, a user usually in contact with different communities is able not only to download files she is directly interested in, but also to pre-fetch files that are available in the current context, and that

can be really useful for neighbors belonging to a different context she is in touch with. The system is thus able to exploit social context information to improve users cooperation aimed at making resource available among users that could probably never meet.

To analytically support these assumptions, we defined a probabilistic analysis of the utility function associated with data belonging to a specific context. However, this functionality should be reserved to users that actually commutes between different social groups, bridging together disconnected communities, in order to avoid redundant pre-fetching of the same files. To this aim, we are currently investigating how social behavior models and communities detection algorithms can support users' awareness of changing context. At the same time we are refining the Context-aware Opportunistic FS implementation to set up a realistic testbed for opportunistic networks, thus enabling experimental evaluation of this kind of distributed services.

As a general conclusion, we can assert that context management in opportunistic p2p systems and context-awareness in related services represent a real enhancement in pervasive and ubiquitous environments by increasing the autonomous behaviors of the systems and even exploiting users' and nodes' cooperation.

ACKNOWLEDGMENT

This work was partially funded by the European Commission under the HAGGLE (027918) and SOCIALNETS (217141) FET Projects.

REFERENCES

Aura Project (2002). Retrieved September 30, 2008, from http://www.cs.cmu.edu/~aura/

Balamash, A., & Krunz, M. (2004). An overview of web caching replacement algorithms. *IEEE Communications Surveys, 6*(2), 44-56.

Boldrini, C., Conti, M., & Passarella, A. (2008a). Exploiting users' social relations to forward data in opportunistic networks: The HiBOp solution. *Pervasive and Mobile Computing (PMC).*

Boldrini, C., Conti, M., & Passarella, A. (2008b). Context and resource awareness in opportunistic network data dissemination. In *Proceedings of the AOC 2008 - colocated with IEEE WoWMoM 2008.*

Borgia, E., Conti, M., & Delmastro, F. (2006). MobileMAN: Design, integration and experimentation of cross-layer mobile multi-hop ad hoc networks. *IEEE Communication Magazine, Ad Hoc & Sensor Network Series, 44*(7).

Caesar, M., Castro, M., Nightingale, E., O'Shea, G., & Rowstron, A. (2006). Virtual ring routing: Network routing inspired by DHTs. In *Proceedings of the ACM SIGCOMM,* Pisa, Italy.

Conti, M., Delmastro, F., & Passarella, A. (2007). Context-aware file sharing for opportunistic networks. In *Proceedings of the IEEE MASS 2007,* Pisa, Italy.

Conti, M., Delmastro, F., & Turi, G. (2007). Peer-to-peer computing in mobile ad hoc networks. In P. Bellavista, & A. Corradi (Eds.), *The handbook of mobile middleware.* Auerbach Publications.

Conti, M., Gregori, E., & Turi, G. (2005). A cross-layer optimization of Gnutella for mobile ad hoc networks. In *Proceedings of the ACM MobiHoc 2005.*

Conti, M., Maselli, G., Turi, G., & Giordano, S. (2004). Cross layering in mobile ad hoc network design. *IEEE Computer.*

Daly, E., & Haahr, M. (2007). Social network analysis for routing in disconnected delay-tolerant MANETs. *MobiHoc.*

Danon, L., & Duch, J. (2005). Comparing community structure identification. *Journal of Statistical Mechanics.*

Delmastro, F. (2005). From Pastry to CrossROAD: Cross-layer ring overlay for ad hoc networks. In *Proceedings of the IEEE PerCom MP2P Workshop,* Kauai Island, Hawaii.

Dey, A. (2001). Understanding and using context. *Personal and Ubiquitous Computing, 5*(1), 4-7.

Garlan, D., Siewiorek, D. P., Smailagic, A., & Steenkiste, P. (2002). Project aura: Toward distraction-free pervasive computing. *Pervasive Computing, 2*(1), 22-31.

Haggle Project (2004). Retrieved September 30, 2008, from http://www.haggleproject.org

Haggle Project (2007). *Specification of the CHILD-Haggle , deliverable D1.2.* Retrieved from http://www.haggleproject.org/index.php/Deliverables

Henricksen, K., Indulska, J., & Rakotonirainy, A. (2002). Modeling context information in pervasive computing systems. In Proceedings of the *1st International Conference on Pervasive Computing,* Zurich, Switzerland.

Henriksen, H., & Indulska, J. (2004). A software engineering framework for context-aware pervasive computing. In *Proceedings of the 2nd IEEE Conference on Pervasive Computing and Communications (PerCom),* Orlando, USA.

Hesselman, C., Benz, H., Pawar, P., Liu, F., Wedgam, M., Wibbels, M., et al. (2008). Bridging Context Management Systems for Different Types of Pervasive Computing Environments. In *Proceedings of the Mobilware '08.* Innsbruck, Austria.

Hui, P., & Crowcroft, J. (2007). *Bubble rap: Forwarding in small world dtns in every decreasing circles.* UCAM-CL-TR684, University of Cambridge.

Johnson, D. B., & Maltz, D. A. (1996). Dynamic source routing in ad hoc wireless networks. In T.

Imielinski, & H. Korth (Eds.), *Mobile computing.* Kluwer Academic Publisher.

Judd, G., & Steenkiste, P. (2003). Providing Contextual information to pervasive computing applications. In *Proceedings of the IEEE International Conference on Pervasive Computing (PerCom)*, Dallas, USA.

Milgram, S. (1967). The small world problem. *Psychology today*, 60-67.

Newmann, M. E. (2004). Detecting community structure in networks. *European Physical Journal B, 38*, 321-330.

Newmann, M. E. (2003). The structure and function of complex networks. *SIAM Review, 45*(2), 167-256.

Pelusi, L., Passarella, A., & Conti, M. (2006). Opportunistic networking: Data forwarding in disconnected mobile ad hoc networks. *IEEE Communication Magazine, 44*(11), 134-141.

Perkins, C. E., & Royer, E. M. (1999). Ad hoc on-demand distance vector routing. In *Proceedings of the IEEE Workshop on Mobile Computing Systems and Applications.*

Pucha, H., Das, S. M., & Hu, Y. C. (2004). Ekta: An efficient dht substrate for distributed applications in mobile ad hoc networks. *IEEE WMCSA.*

Pucha, H., Das, S. M., & Hu, Y. C. (2006). Ekta+: Opportunistic multiplexing in a wireless DHT. In *Proceedings of the ACM Mobishare*, Los Angeles, USA.

Rowstron, A., & Druschel, P. (2001). Pastry: Scalable, decentralized object location and routing for large scale peer-to-peer systems (LNCS 2218, 329-350).

Schmidt, A. (2006). Ontology-based user context management: The challenges of dynamics and imperfection. In *Proceedings of the ODBASE 2006, On the Move Federated Conferences (OTM)*, Montpellier, France.

Sousa, J. P., & Garlan, D. (2002). Aura: An architectural framework for user mobility in ubiquitous computing environments. In *Proceedings of the 3rd Working IEEE/IFIP Conference on Software Architecture*, (pp. 29-43).

Strang, T. L.-P. (2004). A context modeling survey. In Proceedings of the *UbiComp 1st International Workshop on Advanced Context Modelling, Reasoning and Management*, Nottingham (pp. 34--41).

Strohbach, M., Bauer, M., Kovacs, E., Villalonga, C., & Richter, N. (2007). Context Sessions - A Novel Approach for Scalable Context Management in NGN Networks. In *Proceedings of the MNCNA '07.* Port Beach, CA, USA.

Wasserman, S., & Faust, K. (1994). *Social network analysis: Method and applications.* Cambridge University Press.

Watts, D. (1999). *Small worlds: The dynamics of networks between order and randomness.* Princeton Univeristy Press.

Ye, J., Li, J., Zhu, Z., Gu, X., & Shi, H. (2007). PCSM: A Context Sharing Model in Peer-to-Peer Ubiquitous Computing Environment. In *Proceedings of the IEEE International Conference on Convergence Information Technology.* DOI 10.1109/ICCIT.2007.257.

Yoneki, E., Hui, P., Chan, S. Y., & Crowcroft, J. (2007). A socio-aware overlay for publish/subscribe communication in delay tolerant networks. In *Proceedings of the 10th ACM/IEEE International Symposium on Modeling, Analysis and Simulation of Wireless and Mobile Systems (MSWiM)*, Crete, Greece.

Zhan, T., & Schiller, J. (2005). MadPastry: A dht substrate for practicably sized MANETs. In *Proceedings of the 5th Workshop on Applications and Services in Wireless Networks (ASWN).*

Compilation of References

3GPP Technical Specification 23002. (2007). *Network architecture*. Third Partnership Project.

3GPP Technical Specification 23221. (2008). *Architectural requirements*. Third Partnership Project.

3GPP Technical Specification 23228. (2006). *IP multimedia subsystem (IMS)*. Third Partnership Project.

Acharya, S., Alonso, R., et al. (1995). Broadcast disks: Data management for asymmetric communication environments. In *Proceedings of the ACM SIGMOD International Conference on Management of Data*.

Acharya, S., & Muthukrishnan, S. (1998). Scheduling on-demand broadcasts: New metrics and algorithms. In *Proceedings of the International Conference on Mobile Computing and Networking*, Dallas, Texas, USA.

Acharya, S., Franklin, M. J., et al. (1995). Dissemination-based data delivery using broadcast disks. IEEE *Personal Communications, 2*(6), 50-60.

Acharya, S., Franklin, M. J., et al. (1996). Prefetching from broadcast disks. In *Proceedings of the International Conference on Data Engineering*.

Acharya, S., Franklin, M. J., et al. (1997). Balancing push and pull for data broadcast. In *Proceedings of the ACM SIGMOD International Conference on Management of Data*.

Agarwal, D. A., Chevassut, O., Thompson, M. R., & Tsudik, G. (2001). An integrates solution for secure group communication in wide-area networks. In *Proceedings of 6th IEEE Symposium on Computers and Communications*, Hammamet, Tunisisa.

Ahamed, S. I., Buford, J., Sharmin, M., Haque, M. M., & Talukder, N. (2008). Secure service discovery. In Y. Zhang, J. Zeng, & M. Ma (Eds.), *Handbook of research on wireless security*. Hershey, PA: Information Science Reference.

Ahituv, N., Lapid, Y., & Neumann, S. (1987). Processing encrypted data. *Communications of the ACM, 20*(9), 777-780.

Ahmed, R., Limam, N., Xiao, J., Iraqi, Y., & Boutaba, R. (2007). Resource and service discovery in large-scale multi-domain networks. *IEEE Communications Surveys & Tutorials, 9*(4), 2-30.

Ahuja, R. K., Magnanti, T. L., & Orlin, J. B. (1993). *Network flows: Theory, algorithms, and applications*. Englewood Cliffs, N.J., Prentice Hall.

Aksoy, D., & Franklin, M. J. (1998). Scheduling for large-scale on-demand data broadcasting. In *Proceedings of the IEEE Conference on Computer Communications*.

Akyildiz, I. F., Su, W., Sankarasubramaniam, Y., & Cayirci. (2002). A survey on sensor networks. *IEEE Communications Magazine, 40*(8), 102-114.

Alexaki, S., & Tolle, K. (2001) The ICS-FORTH RDF suite: Managing voluminous RDF description bases. In *Proceedings of the 2nd International Workshop on Semantic Web*.

Almenarez, F., Marin, A., Diaz, D., & Sanchez, J. (2006). Developing a model for trust management in pervasive devices. In *Proceedings of the Fourth Annual IEEE Conference on Pervasive Computing and Communications Workshops*, (pp. 1-5).

Alpean, T., Basar, T., Srikant, R., & Altman, E. (2001). CDMA uplink power control as a noncooperative game. In *Proceedings of the 40th IEEE Conference on Decision Control*.

Altinel, M., Aksoy, D., et al. (1999). DBIS-toolkit: Adaptable middleware for large scale data delivery. In *Proceedings of the ACM SIGMOD International Conference on Management of Data*, Philadelphia, Pennsylvania, USA.

Amir, A., Efrat, A., Myllymaki, J., Palaniappan, L., & Wampler, K. (2004). Buddy tracking – efficient proximity detection among mobile friends. In *Proceedings of IEEE Conference on Computer Communications (INFOCOM)*.

Amir, Y., Ateniese, G., Hasse, D., Kim, Y., Nita-Rotaru, C., Schlossnagle, T., Schultz, J., Stanton, J., & Tsudik, G. (2000). Secure group communication in asynchronous networks with failures: Integration and experiments. In *Proceedings of the 20th IEEE International Conference on Distributed Computing Systems*.

Amir, Y., Kim, Y., Nita-Rotaru, C., & Tsudik, G. (2004). On the performance of group key agreement protocols. *ACM Transactions on Information Systems Security, 7*(3), 457-488.

Amir, Y., Kim, Y., Nita-Rotaru, C., Schultz, J., Stanton, J., & Tsudik, G. (2004). Secure group communication using robust contributory key agreement. *IEEE Transactions on Parallel and Distributed Systems, 15*(5), 468-480.

Amir, Y., Kim, Y., Nita-Rotaru, C., Stanton, J., & Tsudik, G. (2005). Secure spread: An integrated architecture for secure group communication. *IEEE Transactions on Dependable and Secure Computing, 2*(3), 248-261.

Anagnostakis, K. G., & Greenwald, M. B. (2004). Exchange-based incentive mechanisms for peer-to-peer file sharing. In *Proceedings of the 24th International Conference on Distributed Computing Systems*, Tokyo, Japan.

Anagnostopoulos, C. B., Tsounis, A., & Hadjiefthymiades, S. (2007). Context awareness in mobile computing environments. *Wireless Personal Communications, 42*(3), 445-464.

Anderegg, L., & Eidenbenz, S. (2003). Ad hoc VCG: A truthful and cost-efficient routing protocol for mobile ad hoc networks with selfish agents. In *Proceedings of the 9th Annual International Conference on Mobile Computing and Networking (MOBICOM)*.

Anderson, C. (2006). People power. *Wired Magazine*. Retrieved September 28, 2008, from http://www.wired.com/wired/archive/14.07/people.html

Andronache, A., Brust, M. R., & Rothkugel, S. (2006). Multimedia content distribution in hybrid wireless networks using weighted clustering. In *Proceedings of the 2nd ACM International Workshop on Wireless Multimedia Networking and Performance Modeling*.

Androutsellis-Theotokis, S., & Spinellis, D. (2004). A survey of peer-to-peer content distribution technologies. *ACM Computing Surveys, 36*(4), 335-371.

Antoniadis, P. (2006). Economic modelling and incentive mechanisms for efficient resource provision in peer-to-peer systems. Unpublished doctoral dissertation, Athens University of Economics and Business.

Antoniadis, P., & Courcoubetis, C. (2006). The case of multi-hop peer-to-peer implementation of mobile social applications. In *Proceedings of the International Conference on Systems and Networks Communication (ICSNC'06)*.

Antoniadis, P., Le Grand, B., & Amorim, M. D. (2008). Socially-motivated wireless neighborhood communities. In *Proceedings of the 3rd International Workshop on Wireless Community Networks*.

Apple Computer. (2008). *iPhone dev center*. Retrieved September 9, 2008, from http://developer.apple.com/iphone/

Araujo, F., Rodrigues, L., Kaiser, J., Liu, C., & Mitidieri, C. (2005). CHR: A distributed hash table for wireless ad hoc networks. In *Proceedings of the International Conference on Distributed Computing Systems Workshops*.

Arnold, K., Scheifler, R., Waldo, J., O'Sullivan, B., & Wollrath, A. (1999). *Jini specification* (1st ed.). Boston, MA, USA: Addison-Wesley Longman Publishing Co, Inc.

Ashok, R. L., & Agrawal, D. P. (2003). Next-generation wearable networks. *Computer 36*(11), 31-39.

Asokan, N., & Ginzboorg, P. (2002). Key agreement in ad-hoc networks. In *Proceedings of the ACM Workshop on Wireless Security (WiSe)*.

Ateniese, G., Steiner, M., & Tsudik, G. (1998). Authenticated group key agreement and friends. In *Proceedings of the ACM Conference on Computer and Communications Security*.

Audet, F., & Jennings, C. (2007). Network address translation (NAT) behavioral requirements for unicast UDP. *RFC4787*. IETF.

Augot, D., Bhaskar, R., Issarny, V., & Sacchetti, D. (2007). A three round authenticated group key agreement protocol for ad hoc networks. *Pervasive and Mobile Computing, 3*(1), 36-52.

Ausubel, L. M., & Milgrom, P. R. (2005). *The Lovely but lonely vickrey auction*. MIT Press.

Auvinen, A., Vapa, M., Weber, M., Kotilainen, N., & Vuori, J. (2006). Chedar:Peer-to-peer middleware. In *Proceedings of the Parallel and Distributed Processing Symposium*, Rhodes Island, Greece.

Axelrod, J. 1984. *The evolution of cooperation*. New York: Basic Books.

B'Far, R. (2004). *Mobile computing principles*. Cambridge Press.

Bächer, P., Holz, T., Kötter, M., & Wicherski, G. (2005). Know your enemy: Tracking botnets. *The Honeynet Project & Research Alliance*.

Bakos, B., Farks, L., & Nurminen, J. (2006). P2P applications on smart phones using cellular communications. In *Proceedings of the 2006 IEEE Wireless Communications and Networking Conference (WCNC 2006)*, Las Vegas, USA.

Bakos, B., Farks, L., & Nurminen, J. (2006). P2P applications on smart phones using cellular communications. In *Proceedings of the IEEE Wireless Communications and Networking Conference (WCNC 2006)*, (Vol. 4, pp. 2222-2228).

Balamash, A., & Krunz, M. (2004). An overview of web caching replacement algorithms. *IEEE Communications Surveys, 6*(2), 44-56.

Banks, J., Carson, J., Nelson, B., & Nicol, D. (2004). *Discrete-event system simulation* (4th ed.). Jersey City, NJ: Prentice-Hall.

BANKSEC (2000). EC funded project (IST-1999-20711). Retrieved on October 2, 2008, from http://www.atc.gr/banksec/

Bansal, S., & Baker, M. (2003). Observation based cooperation enforcement in ad hoc networks. *Stanford University Technical Report*.

Barbara, D., & Imielinski, T. (1994). Sleepers and workaholics: Caching strategies in mobile environments. In *Proceedings of the SIGMOD International Conference on Management of Data*.

Barr, R. (2004). *An efficient, unifying approach to simulation using virtual machines*. Unpublished docotoral thesis, Cornell University.

Barr, R., Bicket, J., Dantas, D., Du, B., Kim, T., Zhou, B., & Sirer, E. (2004), On the need for system-level support for ad hoc and sensor networks. *ACM SIGOPS Operating Systems Review, 36*(2), 1–5.

Barrett, C. L., Eidenbenz, S. J., Kroc, L., Marathe, M., & Smith, J. P. (2003). Parametric probabilistic sensor network routing. In *Proceedings of the 2nd ACM international conference on Wireless sensor networks and applications*.

Baset, S. A., & Schulzrinne, H. (2006). An analysis of the Skype peer-to-peer Internet telephony protocol. In *Proceedings of the IEEE International Conference on Computer Communications (INFOCOM)*.

Bavier, A., Feamster, N., Huang, M., Peterson, L., & Rexford, J. (2006). In VINI veritas: Realistic and controlled network experimentation. *SIGCOMM Computer Communiation. Review, 36*(4), 3-14.

Becker, K., & Wille, U. (1998). Communication complexity of group key distribution. In *Proceedings of the ACM Conference on Computer and Communications Security*.

Beenen, G., Ling, K., Wang, X., Chang, K., Frankowski, D., Resnick, P., & Kraut, R. (2004). Using social psychology to motivate contributions to online communities. In *Proceedings of the ACM conference on Computer supported cooperative work*.

Bellovin, S. M., & Merritt, M. (1992). Encrypted key exchange: Password-based protocols secure against dictionary attacks. In *Proceedings of the IEEE Symposium on Research in Security and Privacy*.

Bender, M., Michel, S., Parkitny, S., & Weikum, G. (2007). A comparative study of pub/sub methods in structured P2P networks. *Databases, Information Systems, and Peer-to-Peer Computing, Springer Lecture Notes in Computer Science, 4125*, 385-396.

Berket, K., Essiari, A., & Muratas, A. (2004). *PKI-Based Security for Peer-to-Peer Information Sharing*. In *Proceedings of P2P 2004*, Zurich, Switzerland.

Bertolini, D., Busetta, P., Molani, A., Nori, M., & Perini, A. (2002). Designing peer-to-peer applications: An agent-oriented approach, In *Proceedings of the International Workshop on Agent Technology and Software Engineering*, Erfurt, Germany.

Bertsekas, D., & Gallager, R. (1992). *Data networks*. Englewood Cliffs, New Jersey: Prentice-Hall.

Bettstetter, C., Resta, G., & Santi, P. (2003). The node distribution of the random waypoint mobility model for wireless ad hoc networks. *IEEE Transactions on Mobile Computing, 2*(3), 257-269.

Bianchi, S., Serbu, S., Felber P., & Kropf P. (2006). Adaptive load balancing for DHT lookups. In *Proceedings of the International Conference on Computer Communications and Networks* (pp. 411-418).

Bisignano, M., Di Modica, G., & Tomarchio, O. (2005). *JMobiPeer: A middleware for mobile peer-to-peer computing in MANETs*. In *Proceedings of the First international Workshop on Mobility in Peer-To-Peer Systems (MPPS)*, Columbus, Ohio, USA.

Biström, J., & Partanen, V. (2004). *Mobile P2P – creating a mobile file-sharing environment* (Tech, Rep. HUT T-111.590). Helsinki, Finland: Research Seminar on Digital Media, Telecommunications Software and Multimedia Laboratory, Helsinki University of Technology.

BitTorrent, (2001). BitTorrent. Retrieved September 9, 2008, from http://www.bittorrent.com/

Bloom, B. H. (1970). Space/time trade-offs in hash coding with allowable errors. *Communications of the ACM, 13*(7), 422–426.

Bluetooth Consortium. (2007, Jul 26). *Bluetooth core specifications*. Retrieved May 27, 2008, from http://www.bluetooth.com/NR/rdonlyres/F8E8276A-3898-4EC6-B7DA-E5535258B056/6545/Core_V21__EDR.zip

Bluetooth. (1999). *Bluetooth.com: The official Bluetooth technology website*. Retrieved May 30, 2008, from http://www.bluetooth.com/

Boldrini, C., Conti, M., & Passarella, A. (2008). Exploiting users' social relations to forward data in opportunistic networks: The HiBOp solution. *Pervasive and Mobile Computing (PMC)*.

Boldrini, C., Conti, M., & Passarella, A. (2008). Context and resource awareness in opportunistic network data dissemination. In *Proceedings of the AOC 2008 - colocated with IEEE WoWMoM 2008*.

Borg, J. (2003). A comparative study of ad hoc & peer to peer networks. Unpublished master's thesis, University College London, UK.

Borgia, E., Conti, M., & Delmastro, F. (2006). Mobile-MAN: Design, integration and experimentation of cross-layer mobile multi-hop ad hoc networks. *IEEE Communication Magazine, Ad Hoc & Sensor Network Series, 44*(7).

Bosneag, A. M., & Brockmeyer, M. (2005). GRACE: Enabling collaborations in wide-area distributed systems. In *Proceedings of the International Workshops on Enabling Technologies: Infrastructure for Collaborative Enterprises*.

Boukerche, A., Zarrad, A., & Araújo, R. (2006). Smart gnutella overlay formation for collaborative virtual environments over mobile ad-hoc networks. In *Proceedings of the IEEE International Symposium on Distributed Simulation and Real-Time Applications (DS-RT).*

Bresson, E. & Manulis, M. (2008). Securing group key exchange against strong corruptions and key registration attacks. *International Journal of Applied Cryptography, 1*(2), 91-107.

Brickell, E. F., & Yacobi, Y. (1988). On privacy homomorphism. In *Proceedings of Advances in Cryptology - EUROCRYPT'87*, (LNCS 304, pp. 117-125).

Broch, J., Maltz, D. A., Johnson, D. B., Hu, Y.-C., & Jetcheva, J. (1998). A performance comparison of multi-hop wireless ad hoc network routing protocols. In *Proceedings of the 4th Annual ACM/IEEE International Conference on Mobile Computing and Networking.*

Broll, W., Lindt, I., Herbst, I., Ohlenburg, J., Braun, A-K., & Wetzel, R.(2008). Toward next-gen mobile AR games. *IEEE Computer Graphics and Applications, 28*(4), 40-48.

Broustis, I., Jakllari, G., Repantis, T., & Molle, M. (2006). A comprehensive comparison of routing protocols for large-scale wireless MANETs. In *Proceedings of the 3rd International Workshop on Wireless Ad Hoc and Sensor Networks.*

Brown, A., Buford, J., & Kolberg, M. (2007). Tork: A variable-hop overlay for heterogeneous networks. In *Proceedings of the 4th IEEE International Workshop on Mobile Peer-to-Peer Computing (MP2P).*

Brown, M., Cheung, D., Hankerson, D., Hernandez, J., Kirkup, M., & Menezes, A. (2000). PGP in constrained wireless devices. In *Proceedings of the 9th USENIX Security Symposium.*

Bryan, D., Lowekamp, B., & Jennings, C. (2005). SO-SIMPLE: A serverless, standards-based, P2P SIP communication system. In *Proceedings of the International Workshop on Advanced Architectures and Algorithms for Internet Delivery and Applications* (pp. 42- 49).

Bryan, D., Matthews, P., Shim, E., Willis, D., & Dawkins, S. (2008). *Concepts and terminology for peer to peer SIP: draft-ietf-p2psip-concepts-02* (work in progress).

Retrieved July 7, 2008, from IETF Internet Draft Database.

Buchegger, S., & LeBoudec, J.-Y. (2002). Performance analysis of the CONFIDANT protocol: cooperation of nodes — fairness in dynamic ad hoc networks. In *Proceedings of the IEEE/ACM Symposium on Mobile Ad Hoc Networking and Computing (MobiHOC).*

Budiarto, Nishio, S., & Tsukamoto, M. (2002). Data management issues in mobile and peer-to-peer environments. *Elsevier Data and Knowledge Engineering, 41*(2-3), 183–204.

Burcea, I., Jacobsen, H. -A., Lara, E. D., Muthusamy, V., & Petrovic, M. (2004). Disconnected operation in publish/subscribe middleware. In *Proceedings of the IEEE International Conference on Mobile Data Management (MDM'04)*, Berkeley, CA, USA.

Burcea, I., Jacobsen, H., Lara, E., Muthusamy, V., & Petrovic, M. (2004). Disconnected operation in publish/subscribe middleware. In *Proceedings of the IEEE International Conference on Mobile Data Management.*

Burmester, M., & Desmedt, Y. (1994). A secure and efficient conference key distribution system. In *Proceedings of Advances in Cryptology - EUROCRYPT'94*, (LNCS 950, pp. 275-286).

Burmester, M., & Desmedt, Y. (2006). Efficient and secure conference key distribution system. In *Security Protocols*, (LNCS 1189/1997, pp. 119-129).

Buttyan, L., & Hubaux, J. P. (2003). Stimulating cooperation in self-organizing mobile ad hoc networks. In *ACM Mobile Networks and Applications, 8*(5), 579-592.

Buttyan, L., Dora, L., Felegyhazi, M., & Vajda, I. (2007). Barter-based cooperation in delay-tolerant personal wireless networks. In *Proceedings of the IEEE International Symposium on World of Wireless, Mobile and Multimedia Networks (WoWMoM).*

Caesar, M., Castro, M., Nightingale, E., O'Shea, G., & Rowstron, A. (2006). Virtual ring routing: Network routing inspired by DHTs. In *Proceedings of the ACM SIGCOMM Conference on Applications, Technologies,*

Architectures, and Protocols for Computer Communications.

Caesar, M., Castro, M., Nightingale, E., O'Shea, G., & Rowstron, A. (2006). Virtual ring routing: Network routing inspired by DHTs. In *Proceedings of the ACM SIGCOMM,* Pisa, Italy.

Cagalj, M., Ganeriwal, S., Aad I., & Hubaux, J-P. (2005). On selfish behavior in CSMA/CA networks. In *Proceedings of the IEEE INFOCOM.*

Cano, J.-C., & Manzoni, P. (2000). A performance comparison of energy consumption for mobile ad hoc network routing protocols. In *Proceedings of the 8th International Symposium on Modeling, Analysis and Simulation of Computer and Telecommunication Systems (MASCOTS).*

Cao, G. (2002). Proactive power-aware cache management for mobile computing systems. *IEEE Transactions on Computers, 51*(6), 608-621.

Cao, G. (2003). A scalable low-latency cache invalidation strategy for mobile environments. *IEEE Transactions on Knowledge and Data Engineering, 15*(5), 1251-1265.

Cao, H., Wolfson, O., Xu, B., & Yin, H. (2005). MOBI-DIC: MOBIle DIscovery of loCal resources in peer-to-peer wireless network. *Bulletin of the IEEE Computer Society Technical Committee on Data Engineering, 28*(3), 11–18.

Capkun, S., Buttyan, L., & Hubaux, J.-P. (2003). Self-organized public-key management for mobile ad hoc networks. *IEEE Transactions on Mobile Computing, 2*(1), 52-64.

Caporuscio, M., Carzaniga, A., & Wolf, A. L. (2003). Design and evaluation of a support service for mobile, wireless publish/subscribe applications. *IEEE Transactions on Software Engineering,* 29(12), 1059-1071.

Carlos, K., Djamel, S., Joseane Farias, F., Jennifer, L., & Borje, O. (2006). On the use of peer-to-peer architectures for the management of highly dynamic environments. In *Proceedings of the 4th annual IEEE international conference on Pervasive Computing and Communications Workshops,* Pisa, Italy.

Carman, D. W., Kruus, P. S., & Matt, B. J. (2000). *Constraints and approaches for distributed sensor security* (Tech. Rep. 00-010). Cryptographic Technologies Group, Trusted Information Systems, NAI Labs.

Carvalho, N., Araujo, F., & Rodrigues, L. (2006). Reducing latency in rendezvous-based publish-subscribe systems for wireless ad hoc networks. In *Proceedings of the International Conference on Distributed Computing Systems Workshops.*

Carzaniga, A., Rosenblum, A. D., & Wolf, A. L. (2001). Design and evaluation of a wide-area event notification service. *ACM Transactions on Computer Systems,* 19(3), 332–383.

Castro, M., Druschel, P., Kermarrec, A-M., Nandi, A., Rowstron A., & Singh, A. (2003). Split-stream: High-bandwidth multicast in a cooperative environment. In *Proceedings of the ACM Symposium on Operating Systems Principles.*

Cerri, D., Ghioni, A., Paraboschi, S., & Tiraboschi, S. (2005). ID mapping attacks in P2P networks. In *Proceedings of the IEEE Global Telecommunications Conference,* (Vol. 3, p. 6).

Chakrabarti, S., Vuong, S. T., Sinha, A. & Paul, R. (2005). BlueMobile-a mobile IP based handoff system for blue tooth, 802.11 and GPRS links. In *Proceedings of the IEEE Consumer Communications and Networking Conference.*

Chakraborty, D., Joshi, A., Yesha, Y., & Finin, T. (2006). Toward distributed service discovery in pervasive computing environments. *IEEE Transactions on Mobile Computing, 5*(2), 97-112.

Chakraborty, D., Perich, F., Avancha, S., & Joshi, A. (2001). DReggie: A smart service discovery technique for e-Commerce applications. In *Proceedings of the 20th International Symposium on Reliable Distributed Systems.* New Orleans, LA, USA: IEEE Computer Society.

Chan, A. C.-F. (2004). Distributed symmetric key management for mobile ad hoc networks. In *Proceedings of the IEEE International Conference on Computer and Communications.*

Chan, H., Perrig, A., & Song, D. (2003). Random key predistribution schemes for sensor networks. In *Proceedings of the IEEE Symposium of Privacy and Security.*

Chand, R., & Felber, P. (2005). A semantic peer-to-peer overlays for publish/subscribe networks. In *Proceedings of Euro-Par 2005*, Lisbon, Portugal.

Chawathe, Y., McCanne, S., & Brewer, E. A. (2000). *An architecture for internet content distribution as an infrastructure service.* Retrieved May 30, 2008, from http://citeseerx.ist.psu.edu/viewdoc/summary?doi=10.1.1.35.1680

Chen, Q., & Niu, Z. (2005). A game-theoretical power and rate control for wireless ad hoc networks with step-up price. *IEEE Transactions on Communications, E-88B*(9).

Chen, W.-P., Hamada, T., Yao, J. J., & Wei, H.-Y. (2006). QoS management and peer-to-peer mobility in fixed-mobile convergence. *Fujitsu Scientific and Technical Journal, 42*(4), 535-546.

Chen, X., & Wu, J. (2003). *Multicasting techniques in mobile ad hoc networks.* Boca Raton, FL, USA: CRC Press, Inc.

Chiang, K., & Lloyd, L. (2007). *A case study of the rustock rootkit and spam bot.* Paper presented at the First Workshop on Hot Topics in Understanding Botnets.

Choi, Y., & Park, D. (2006). Mirinae: A peer-to-peer overlay network for large-scale content-based publish/subscribe systems. *IEICE Transactions on Communications*, E89-B(6), 1755-1765.

Chow, C., Leong, H., & Chan, A. (2004). Peer-to-peer cooperative caching in mobile environments. In *Proceedings of the 24th International Conference on Distributed Computing Systems Workshops (ICDCSW).*

Chow, C.-Y., Leong, H. V., et al. (2004). Group-based cooperative cache management for mobile clients in a mobile environment. In *Proceedings of the International Conference on Parallel Processing (ICPP).*

Chow, C.-Y., Leong, H. V., et al. (2005). Distributed group-based cooperative caching in a mobile broadcast environment. In *Proceedings of the International Conference on Mobile Data Management.*

Chu, Y., Rao S., Seshan, S. & Zhang, H. (2002). A case for end system multicast. *IEEE Journal on Selected Areas in Communications, 20*(8), 1456-1471.

Chu, Y., Rao, S.G., & Zhang H. (2000). A case for end system multicast. In *Proceedings of the ACM SIGMETRICS International Conference on Measurement and Modeling of Computer Systems.*

Chu, Y.-H., Chuang J., & Zhang, H. (2004). Considering altruism in peer-to-peer Internet streaming broadcast. In *Proceedings of the 14th International Workshop on Network and Operating Systems Support for Digital Audio and Video.*

Cisco (2007). Cisco AIR-CB21AG technical specifications, from http://www.cisco.com

Clarke I., Sandberg O., Wiley B., & Hong T. W. (2000). Freenet: A distributed anonymous information storage and retrieval system. In *Proceedings of the ICSI Workshop on Design Issues in Anonymity and Unobservability.*

Clarke, E. (1971). Multipart pricing of public goods. *Public Choice, 1*, 17-33.

Clip2. (2000). The Gnutella protocol specification v0.4. Retrieved May 13, 2008, from http://www9.limewire.com/developer/gnutella_protocol_0.4.pdf

CMU Project (2004). *The CMU Monarch projects on wireless and mobility extension to ns.*

Cohen, B. (2003). Incentives build robustness in BitTorrent. In *Proceedings of the Workshop on Economics of Peer-to-Peer Systems.*

Conti, M., Delmastro, F., & Passarella, A. (2007). Context-aware file sharing for opportunistic networks. In *Proceedings of the IEEE MASS 2007,* Pisa, Italy.

Conti, M., Delmastro, F., & Turi, G. (2007). Peer-to-peer computing in mobile ad hoc networks. In P. Bellavista, & A. Corradi (Eds.), *The handbook of mobile middleware.* Auerbach Publications.

Conti, M., Gregori, E., & Turi, G. (2005). A cross-layer optimization of Gnutella for mobile ad hoc networks. In *Proceedings of the ACM MobiHoc 2005.*

Conti, M., Maselli, G., Turi, G., & Giordano, S. (2004). Cross layering in mobile ad hoc network design. *IEEE Computer.*

Corbo, J., & Parkes, D. (2005). The price of selfish behavior in bilateral network formation. In *Proceedings of the ACM PODC.*

Courcoubetis, C., & Weber, R. R. (2003). *Pricing communication networks: Economics, technology and modelling.* Wiley Europe.

Cramer, C., & Fuhrmann, T. (2005). ISPRP: A message-efficient protocol for initializing structured P2P networks. In *Proceedings of the 24th IEEE International Performance, Computing, and Communications Conference (IPCCC).*

Cramer, C., & Fuhrmann, T. (2005). Proximity neighbor selection for a DHT in wireless multi-hop networks. In *Proceedings of the 5th IEEE International Conference on Peer-to-Peer Computing.*

Crowcroft, J., Gibbens, R., Kelly, F., & Ostring, S. (2003). Modelling incentives for collaboration in mobile ad hoc networks. In *Proceedings of WiOpt'03: Modeling and Optimization in Mobile, Ad Hoc and Wireless Networks.*

Cugola, G., Di Nitto, E., & Fuggetta, A. (2001). The JEDI event-based infrastructure and its application to the development of the OPSS WFMS. *IEEE Transactions on Software Engineering, 27*(9), 827–850.

da Hora, D. N., Macedo, D. F., Nogueira, J. M. S., & Pujolle, G. (2007). Optimizing peer-to-peer content discovery over wireless mobile ad hoc networks. In *Proceedings of the 9th IFIP/IEEE International Conference on Mobile and Wireless Communications Networks (MWCN).*

Dabek, F., Kaashoek, M.F., Karger, D., Morris, R., & Stoica, I. (2001). Wide-area cooperative storage with CFS. In *Proceedings of the ACM Symposium on Operating System Principles* (pp. 202-215).

Daly, E., & Haahr, M. (2007). Social network analysis for routing in disconnected delay-tolerant MANETs. *MobiHoc.*

Danon, L., & Duch, J. (2005). Comparing community structure identification. *Journal of Statistical Mechanics.*

DARPA. (2006, Jan 13). *DAML services.* Retrieved May 22, 2008, from http://www.daml.org

Davids, N. (1996a). Personal digital assistants: Part 1. *IEEE Computer 29*(9), 96-99.

Davids, N. (1996b). Personal digital assistants: Part 2. *IEEE Computer 29*(11), 100-104.

Davies, N., Cheverst, K., Mitchell, K., & Efrat, A. (2001). Using and determining location in a context-sensitive tour guide. *IEEE Computer, 34*(8), 35-41.

De Couto, D. S. J., Aguayo, D., Bicket, J., & Morris, R. (2003). A high-throughput path metric for multi-hop wireless routing. In *Proceedings of the 9th Annual International Conference on Mobile Computing and Networking (MOBICOM).*

de Veciana, G., & Yang, X. (2003). Fairness, incentives and performance in peer-to-peer networks. In *Proceedings of the Forty-first Annual Allerton Conference on Communication, Control and Computing,* Monticello, IL, USA.

Debnath, T., Cranley, N., & Davis, M. (2006). Experimental comparison of wired versus wireless video streaming over IEEE 802.11b WLANs. In *Proceedings of the Irish Signals and Systems Conference.*

Deci, E., Koestner, R., & Ryan, R. (1999). A meta-analytic review of experiments examining the effects of extrinsic rewards on intrinsic motivation. *Psychological Bulletin, 125*(6), 627-668.

Delmastro, F. (2005). From pastry to CrossROAD: CROSS-layer ring overlay for ad hoc networks. In *Proceedings of the IEEE International Conference on Pervasive Computing and Communications Workshops.*

Delmastro, F. (2005). From Pastry to CrossROAD: Cross-layer ring overlay for ad hoc networks. In *Proceedings of the IEEE PerCom MP2P Workshop,* Kauai Island, Hawaii.

Desmedt, Y., Lange, T., & Burmester, M. (2006). Scalable authenticated tree based group key exchange for ad-hoc groups. *Financial Cryptography and Data Security,* (LNCS 4886, pp. 104-118).

Devarapalli, V., & Sidhu, D. (2001). MZR: A multicast protocol for mobile ad hoc networks. In *Proceedings of the IEEE International Conference on Communications.*

Dey, A. (2001). Understanding and using context. *Personal and Ubiquitous Computing, 5*(1), 4-7.

Diffie, W., & Hellman, M. E. (1976). New directions in cryptography. *IEEE Transactions on Information Theory, 22*(6), 644-654.

Diffie, W., van Oorschot, P. C., & Wiener, M. J. (1992). Authentication and authenticated key exchanges. *Designs Codes and Cryptography, 2*(2), 107-125.

Ding, G., & Bhargava, B. (2004). Peer-to-peer file-sharing over mobile ad hoc networks. In *Proceedings of the 2nd IEEE Annual Conference on Pervasive Computing and Communications Workshops.*

Ding, G., & Bhargava, B. (2004). Peer-to-peer file-sharing over mobile ad hoc networks. In *Proceedings of the Second IEEE Annual Conference on Pervasive Computing and Communications Workshops (PERCOMW).*

DLNA. (2003). *DLNA home networked device interoperability guidelines.* Retrieved May 30, 2008, from http://www.dlna.org

Douceur, J. 2002. The sybil attack. In *Proceedings of the 1st International Workshop on Peer-to-Peer Systems.*

Dublin Core Metadata Initiative. (1995). *Dublin Core Metadata Initiative (DCMI).* Retrieved May 30, 2008, from http://dublincore.org/

Duelli, M., Hoßfeld, T., & Staehle, D. (2007a). Impact of vertical handovers on cooperative content distribution systems. In *Proceedings of the Seventh IEEE International Conference on Peer-to-Peer Computing (P2P2007),* Galway, Ireland.

Duelli, M., Hoßfeld, T., & Staehle, D. (2007). Impact of vertical handovers on cooperative content distribution systems. In *Proceedings of the Seventh IEEE International Conference on Peer-to-Peer Computing (P2P2007),* Galway, Ireland.

Duelli, M., Hoßfeld, T., & Staehle, D. (2007b). *Impact of Vertical Handovers on Cooperative Content Distribution Systems* (Tech. Rep. No. 428). Würzburg, Germany: University of Würzburg.

Dunkels, A. (2008). *Contiki: A dynamic operating system for memory-constrained networked embedded systems.* Retrieved September 10, 2008, from http://www.sics.se/contiki/

Dutta, R., & Barua, R. (2005). *Overview of key agreement protocols* (Rep. 2005/289). ePrint Archive, from http://eprint.iacr.org

Eagle, N. & Pentland, A. (2005). Social serendipity: Mobilizing social software. *IEEE Pervasive Computing, 04*(2), 28-34.

Eberspächer, J., Vogel, H.-J., & Bettstetter, C. (2001). *GSM switching, services and protocols* (2nd ed.). New York: John Wiley & Sons, Inc.

Eberspaecher, J., Vogel, H.-J., & Bettstetter, C., B. (Eds.). (2001). *GSM switching, services, and protocols* (2nd ed.). Manchester: Wiley.

Echenard, N., & Wagen, J.-F. (2006). WLAN service coverage based on PixelFlow predictions. In *Proceedings of the 4th International Conference, WWIC.*

ECHONET Consortium. (2000). Retrieved May 30, 2008, from http://www.echonet.gr.jp/english/

Eidenbenz, S., Resta G., & Santi, P. (2008). The COMMIT protocol for truthful and cost-efficient routing in ad hoc networks with selfish nodes. *IEEE Transaction on Mobile Computing,* 2008.

El-Ansary, S. & Haridi, S. (2005). An overview of structured overlay networks. In J. Wu (Ed.), *Theoretical and algorithmic aspects of sensor, ad hoc wireless and peer-to-peer networks.* USA: CRC Press.

Ellis, C. A., Gibbs, S. J., & Rein, G. (1991). *Groupware: Some issues and experiences. Communications of the ACM, 34*(1), 39-58.

Erickson, T. (2005). Sustaining community: Incentive mechanisms in online systems. In *Final Report of the Group 2005 Workshop.*

Eriksson, J., Dunkels, A., Finne, N., Osterlind, F., & Voigt, T. (2007). Mspsim - an extensible simulator for msp430-equipped sensor boards. In *Proceedings of the European Conference on Wireless Sensor Networks.*

Erman, J., Mahanti, A., Arlitt, M., & Williamson, C. (2007). Identifying and discriminating between web and peer-to-peer traffic in the network core. In *Proceedings of the 16th International Conference on World Wide Web.*

Eschenauer, L., & Gligor, V. D. (2002). A key-management scheme for distributed sensor networks. In *Proceedings of the ACM Conference on Computer and Communication Security.*

Eshghi, K. (2002). *Intrinsic references in distributed systems* (Tech. Rep. HPL-2002-32). HP Labs.

Eugster, P. T., Felber, P., Guerraoui, R., & Kermarrec, A. M. (2001). *The many faces of publish/subscribe* (Tech. Rep.DSC ID: 2000104). Lausanne, Switzerland: Swiss Federal Institute of Technology (EPFL).

Fabrikant, A., Luthra, A., Maneva, E., Papadimitriou, C., & Shenker, S. (2003). On a network creation game. In *Proceedings of the ACM PODC.*

Faik, J. (2005). *A model for resource-aware load balancing on heterogeneous and non-dedicated clusters.* Unpublished doctoral dissertation, Department of Computer Science, Rensselaer Polytechnic Institute.

Fall, K., & Varadhan, K. (2001). *Network Simulator Notes and Documentation.* The VINT Project.

Faltstrom, P., & Mealling, M. (2004). The E.164 to uniform resource identifiers (URI) dynamic delegation discovery system (DDDS) application (ENUM). *RFC3761.* IETF.

Fan, L., Cao, P., Almeida, J., & Broder, A. (2000). Summary cache: A scalable wide-area web cache sharing protocol. *IEEE/ACM Transactions on Networking, 8*(3), 281-293.

Farha, R., & Leon-Garcia, A. (2007). A novel peer-to-peer naming infrastructure for next generation networks. (LNCS 4786, pp. 1-12).

Farooq, U., Majumdar, S., & Parsons, E. (2004). Engineering mobile wireless publish/subscribe systems for high performance. In *Proceedings of 12th IEEE International Symposium on Modeling, Analysis, and Simulation of Computer and Telecommunications Systems,* Volendam, Netherlands.

Farooq, U., Parsons, E., & Majumdar, S. (2004). Performance of publish/subscribe middleware in mobile wireless networks. In *Proceedings of 4th International Workshop on Software and Performance,* Redwood City, CA, USA.

Feeney, L. M., & Nilsson, M. (2001). Investigating the energy consumption of a wireless network interface in an ad hoc networking environment. In *Proceedings of the 20th Annual Joint Conference of the IEEE Computer and Communications Societies.*

Feigenbaum, J., Papadimitriou, C., Sami, R., & Shenker, S. (2002). A BGP-based mechanism for lowest-cost routing. In *Proceedings of the ACM PODC.*

Felber, P., & Biersack, E. W. (2004). Self-scaling networks for content distribution. In *Proceedings of the International Workshop on Self-* Properties in Complex Information Systems,* Berinoro, Italy.

Feldman, M., & Chuang, J. (2005). Overcoming free-riding behavior in peer-to-peer systems. *SIGecom Exch., 5*(4), 41-50.

Feldman, M., Chuang, J., Stoica, I., & Shenker, S. (2005). Hidden-action in multihop routing. In *Proceedings of the ACM Conference on Electronic Commerce.*

Feldman, M., Lai, K., Stoica, I., & Chuang, J. (2004). Robust incentive techniques for peer-to-peer networks. In *Proceedings of the 5th ACM conference on Electronic commerce,* New York, NY, USA.

Feldman, M., Papadimitriou, C., & Chuang, J. (2004). Free-riding and whitewashing in peer-to-peer systems. In *Proceedings of the ACM PINS.*

Feldman, M., Papadimitriou, C., Chuang, J., & Stoica, I. (2004). Free-riding and whitewashing in peer-to-peer systems. In *Proceedings of the ACM SIGCOMM Workshop on Practice and Theory of Incentives in Networked Systems.*

Félegyházi, M., Hubaux, J.-P., & Buttyán, L. (2004). Equilibrium analysis of packet forwarding strategies in wireless ad hoc networks – the dynamic case. In *Proceedings of the WiOpt'04: Modeling and Optimization in Mobile, Ad Hoc and Wireless Networks.*

Félegyházi, M., Hubaux, J.-P., & Buttyán, L. (2006). Nash equilibria of packet forwarding strategies in wireless ad hoc networks. *IEEE Transactions on Mobile Computing, 5*(5), 463-476.

Fenton, F. (1960). The sum of lognormal probability distributions in scatter transmission systems. *IRE Trans. Commun. Syst., CS-8*(3), 57–67.

Fenton, L. (1960). The sum of lognormal probability distributions in scatter transmission systems. *IRE Trans. Commun. Syst., 8*(3), 57–67.

Fiege, L., Gartner, F. C., Kasten, O., & Zeidler, A. (2003). Supporting mobility in content-based publish/subscribe middleware. In *Proceedings of ACM/IFIP/USENIX International Middleware Conference (Middleware'03),* Rio de Janeiro, Brazil.

Fielding, R. T. (2000). *Architectural styles and the design of network-based software architectures.* Unpublished doctoral dissertation, University of California at Irvine, USA.

Figueiredo, D. R., Garetto, M., & Towsley, D. (2004). *Exploiting mobility in ad hoc networks with incentives* (Computer Science Tech. Rep. 04-66).

Flick, H., Helpworth, E., Eisel, J. & Uno, S. (2004). Issues of advanced mobility management in ambient network. In *Proceedings of the 12th Wireless World Research Forum (WWRF).*

Fox, A., Gribble, S. D., Chawathe, Y., & Breuer, E. (1998). Adapting to network and client variation using infrastructure proxies: Lessons and perspectives. *IEEE Personal Communications, 5*(4), 10-19.

Franciscani, F. P., Vasconcelos, M. A., Couto, R. P., & Loureiro, A. A. F. (2005). (Re)configuration algorithms for peer-to-peer over ad hoc networks. *Journal of Parallel and Distributed Computing, 65*(2), 234–245.

Frank, C., & Karl, H. (2004). Consistency challenges of service discovery in mobile ad hoc networks. In *Proceedings of the 7th ACM International Symposium on Modeling, Analysis and Simulation of Wireless and Mobile Systems,* Venice, Italy (pp. 105-114).

Franklin, M., & Zdonik, S. (1996). Dissemination-based information systems. *IEEE Data Engineering Bulletin, 19*(3), 20-30.

Freemote. (2008). Retrieved September 30, 2008, from http://mote.tic.eia-fr.ch/freemote/

Fundenberg, D., & Tirole, J. (1992). *Game theory.* Cambridge: The MIT Press.

Gaertner, G., & Cahill, V. (2004). Understanding link quality in 802.11 mobile ad hoc networks. *IEEE Internet Computing, 8*(1), 55–60.

Garbacki, P., Iosup, A., Epema, D. H. J., & van Steen, M. (2006). 2Fast: Collaborative downloads in P2P networks. In *Proceedings of the Sixth IEEE International Conference on Peer-to-Peer Computing (P2P2006),* Cambridge, UK.

Garces-Erice, L., Biersack, E. W., Felber, P. A., Ross, K. W., & Urvoy-Keller, G. (2003). Hierarchical peer-to-peer systems. *Parallel Processing Letters, 13*(4), 643-657.

Garlan, D., Siewiorek, D. P., Smailagic, A., & Steenkiste, P. (2002). Project aura: Toward distraction-free pervasive computing. *Pervasive Computing, 2*(1), 22-31.

Geer, D. (2005). Users make a beeline for ZigBee technology. *Computer, 38*(12), 16-19.

Gerla, M., Lindemann, C., & Rowstron, A. (2005). P2P MANETs - new research issues. In *Proceedings of the*

Perspectives Workshop: Peer-to-Peer Mobile Ad Hoc Networks - New Research Issues.

Gifford, D. K. (1990). Polychannel systems for mass digital communications. *Communications of ACM, 33*(2), 141-151.

Girod, L., Ramanathan, N., Elson, J., Stathopoulos, T., Lukac, M., & Estrin, D. (2007). Emstar: A software environment for developing and deploying heterogeneous sensor-actuator networks. *Transactions on Sensor Networks, 3*(3).

Gkantsidis, C., Mihail, M., & Saberi, A. (2004). Random walks in peer-to-peer networks. In *Proceedings of the IEEE International Conference on Computer Communications (INFOCOM).*

Gnutella. (2001). *The Gnutella protocol specification v0.4.* Retrieved May 30 2008, from http://www9.limewire.com/developer/gnutella_protocol_0.4.pdf

Godfrey, B., Karp, R.M., Lakshminarayanan, K., Surana, S., & Stoica, I. (2004). Load balancing in dynamic structured P2P systems. In *Proceedings of the Annual Joint Conference of the IEEE Computer and Communications Societies*, (Vol. 4, pp. 2253-2262).

Godfrey, P.B., & Stoica, I. (2005). Heterogeneity and load balance in distributed hash tables. In *Proceedings of the Annual Joint Conference of the IEEE Computer and Communications Societies*, (Vol. 1, pp. 596-606).

Goel, S., Singh,M., Xu, D., & Li, B. (2002). Efficient peer-to-peer data dissemination in mobile ad-hoc networks. In *Proceedings of the International Conference on Parallel Processing Workshops.*

Goemans, M. X., Li, L., Mirrokni, V. S., & Thottan, M. (2006). Market sharing games applied to content distribution in ad hoc networks. *IEEE Journal on Selected areas in Communications, 24*(5).

Göktürk, E. (2007). A stance on emulation and testbeds, and a survey of network emulators and testbeds. In *Proceedings of the European Conference on Modeling and Simulation.*

Gold, R., & Mascolo, C. (2001). Use of context-awareness in mobile peer-to-peer networks. In *Proceedings of the Eighth IEEE Workshop on Future Trends of Distributed Computing Systems (FTDCS).*

Gomes, A. T., Ziviani, A., Lima, L. S., & Endler, M. (2007). DICHOTOMY: A resource discovery and scheduling protocol for multihop ad hoc mobile grids. In *Proceedings of the 1st International Workshop on Context-Awareness and Mobility in Grid Computing* (pp. 719-724). Rio de Janeiro, RJ, Brazil: IEEE Computer Society.

Gomez, C., Salvatella, P., Alonso, O., & Paradells, J. (2006). Adapting AODV for IEEE 802.15.4 mesh sensor networks: Theoretical discussion and performance evaluation in a real environment. In *Proceedings of the IEEE International Symposium on a World of Wireless Mobile and Multimedia Networks.*

Google. (2008). *Android – an open handset alliance project.* Retrieved September 18, 2008, from http://code.google.com/android/

Grassi, V. (2000). Prefetching policies for energy saving and latency reduction in a wireless broadcast data delivery system. In *Proceedings of the International Workshop on Modeling Analysis and Simulation of Wireless and Mobile Systems.*

Grizzard, J. B., Sharma, V., Nunnery, C., & Kang, B. (2007). *Peer-to-peer botnets: Overview and case study.* Paper presented at the First Workshop on Hot Topics in Understanding Botnets.

Groves, T. (1973). Incentives in teams. *Econometrica, 41*, 617-663.

Gruber, I., Schollmeier, R., & Kellerer, W. (2004). Performance evaluation of the mobile peer-to-peer service. In *Proceedings of the IEEE International Symposium on Cluster Computing and the Grid.*

GTRAN (2007). GTRAN DotSurfer 6210 technical specifications, from http://www.gtran.com

Guha, S., Daswani, N., & Jain, R. (2006). An experimental study of the Skype peer-to-peer VoIP system.

In *Proceedings of the Fifth International Workshop on Peer-to-Peer Systems*.

Guha, S., Daswani, N., & Jain, R. (2006). An experimental study of the Skype peer-to-peer VoIP system. In *Proceedings of the International Workshop on Peer-to-Peer Systems*. Retrieved May 30, 2008, from IPTPS database.

Guo, Y., Pinotti, M. C., et al. (2001). A new hybrid broadcast scheduling algorithm for asymmetric communication systems. *SIGMOBILE Mobile Computing and Communications Review, 5*(3), 39-54.

Gupta, N., & Kumar, P. R. (2003). A performance analysis of the IEEE 802.11 wireless LAN medium access control. *Communications in Information and Systems, 3*(4), 279-304.

Gupta, V., & Williams, M. G. (2007). IEEE 802.21, from http://www.ieee802.org/21

Gurun, S., Nagpurkar, P., & Zhao, B. Y. (2006). Energy consumption and conservation in mobile peer-to-peer systems. In *Proceedings of the 1st International Workshop on Decentralized Resource Sharing in Mobile Computing and Networking*.

Guttman, E., Perkins, C., Veizades, J., & Day, M. (1999). *Service location protocol, version 2*. RFC 2608.

Haas, J. (1997). A new routing protocol for the reconfigurable wireless networks. In *Proceedings of the 6th IEEE International Conference on Universal Personal Communications*.

Haas, Z. (1997). A new routing protocol for the reconfigurable wireless networks. In *Proceedings of the IEEE 6th International Conference on Universal Personal Communications Record*.

Haas, Z. J., & Tabrizi, S. (1998). On some challenges and design choices in ad-hoc communications. In *Proceedings of the IEEE Military Communications Conference*.

Habib, A., & Chuang, J. (2004). Incentive mechanism for peer-to-peer media streaming. In *Proceedings of the 12th IEEE International Workshop on Quality of Service*.

Habib, A., & Chuang, J. (2006). Service differentiated peer selection: an incentive mechanism for peer-to-peer media streaming. *IEEE Transactions on Multimedia, 8*(3), 610-621.

Haggle Project. (2004). Retrieved September 30, 2008, from http://www.haggleproject.org

Haggle Project. (2007). *Specification of the CHILD-Haggle, deliverable D1.2*. Retrieved from http://www.haggleproject.org/index.php/Deliverables

Hales, D. (2006). Emergent group level selection in a peer-to-peer network. *ComPlexUs, 3*, 108-118.

Hameed, S. & Vaidya, N. H. (1997). Log-time algorithms for scheduling single and multiple channel data broadcast. In *Proceedings of the International Conference on Mobile Computing and Networking*.

Handorean, R., Sen, R., Hackmann, G., & Roman, G. (2005). Context-aware session management for services in ad hoc networks. In *Proceedings of the 2005 IEEE International Conference on Services Computing*, (pp. 113-120).

Hankerson, D., Menezes, A. J., & Vanstone, S. A. (2004). *Guide to elliptic curve cryptography*. Springer Professional Computing.

Hara, K., Mitchell, A. S, & Vorbau, A. (2007). Consuming video on mobile devices. In *Proceedings of the SIGCHI Conference on Human Factors in Computing Systems*.

Hara, T. (2002). Cooperative caching by mobile clients in push-based information systems. In *Proceedings of the 11th International Conference on Information and Knowledge Management*.

Hara, T. (2002). Cooperative caching by mobile clients in push-based information systems. In *Proceedings of the* Conference on Information and Knowledge Management.

Harjula, E., Ylianttila, M., Ala-Kurikka, J., Riekki, J., & Sauvola, J. (2004). Plug-and-play application platform: Towards mobile peer-to-peer. In *Proceedings of the 3rd International Conference on Mobile and Ubiquitous Multimedia*, College Park, Maryland, USA.

Hautakorpi, J., & Camarillo, G. (2007). Evaluation of DHTs from the viewpoint of interpersonal communications. In *Proceedings of the International Conference on Mobile and Ubiquitous Multimedia* (pp. 74-83).

HDMI. (2002). Retrieved May 30, 2008, from http://www.hdmi.org/

He, Q., Wu, D., & Khosla, P. (2004). SORI: A secure and objective reputation-based incentive scheme for ad hoc networks. In *Proceedings of the IEEE Wireless Communications and Networking Conference*.

He, Y., Lee, I., Gu, X., & Guan, L. (2005). Centralized peer-to-peer video streaming over hybrid wireless network. In *Proceedings of the IEEE International Conference on Multimedia and Expo*.

He, Z., & Zeng, W. (2006). Rate-distortion optimized transmission power adaptation for video streaming over wireless channels. In *Proceedings of the IEEE International Conference on Image Processing*.

Hefeeda, M., Habib, A., Botev, B., Xu, D., & Bhargava, B. (2003). PROMISE: Peer-to-peer media streaming using CollectCast. In *Proceedings of the 11th ACM International Conference on Multimedia*.

Helal, S. (2002). Pervasive Java. *IEEE Pervasive Computing 1*(1), 82-85.

Helal, S., Desai, N., Verma, V., & Lee, C. (2003). Konark -- a service discovery and delivery protocol for ad hoc networks. In *Proceedings of the 3rd IEEE Conference on Wireless Communication Networks*. New Orleans, LA, USA: IEEE Computer Society.

Henderson, T., Kotz, D., & Abyzov, I. (2004). The changing usage of a mature campus-wide wireless network. In *Proceedings of the 10th Annual International Conference on Mobile Computing and Networking*.

Henricksen, K., Indulska, J., & Rakotonirainy, A. (2002). Modeling context information in pervasive computing systems. In Proceedings of the *1st International Conference on Pervasive Computing*, Zurich, Switzerland.

Henriksen, H., & Indulska, J. (2004). A software engineering framework for context-aware pervasive com-

puting. In *Proceedings of the 2nd IEEE Conference on Pervasive Computing and Communications (PerCom)*, Orlando, USA.

Herman, R., Husemann, D., Moser, M., Nidd, M., Rohner, C., & Schade, A. (2001). DEAPspace: Transient ad hoc networking of prevasive devices. *Computer Networks, 35*(4), 411-428.

Hietalahti, M. (2001). Efficient key agreement for ad hoc networks. Unpublished master's thesis, Department of Computer Science and Engineering, Laboratory for Theoretical Computer Science, Helsinki University of Technology, Finland.

Holmquist, L. E., Wigstrom, J., & Falk, J. (1998) The Hummingbird: Mobile support for group awareness. Demonstrated at the *ACM Conference on Computer Supported Cooperative Work*, Seattle, Washington, USA.

Horozov, T., Grama, A., Vasudevan, V., & Landis S. (2002). Moby - a mobile peer-to-peer service and data network. In *Proceedings of the 2002 International Conference on Parallel Processing (ICPP '02)* (p. 437). Washington: IEEE Computer Society.

Horozov, T., Grama, A., Vasudevan, V., & Landis, S. (2002). MOBY - A mobile peer-to-peer service and data network. In *Proceedings of the International Conference on Parallel Processing (ICPP '02)*, Vancouver, British Columbia, Canada.

Hoßfeld, T., Leibnitz, K., Pries, R., Tutschku, K., Tran-Gia, P., & Pawlikowski, K. (2004). Information diffusion in edonkey filesharing network. In *Proceedings of the Australian Telecommunication Networks and Applications Conference (ATNAC 2004)*, Sydney, Australia.

Hoßfeld, T., Leibnitz, K., Pries, R., Tutschku, K., Tran-Gia, P., & Pawlikowski, K. (2004). Information diffusion in edonkey filesharing networks. In *Proceedings of Australian Telecommunication Networks and Applications Conference (ATNAC 2004)*.

Hoßfeld, T., Mäder, A., Tutschku, K., Tran-Gia, P., Andersen, F. U., de Meer, H., & Dedinksi, I. (2005). Comparison of crawling strategies for an optimized mobile P2P architecture. In *Proceedings of the 19th International Teletraffic Congress (ITC19)*, Beijing, China.

Hoßfeld, T., Mäder, A., Tutschku, K., Tran-Gia, P., Andersen, F.-U., de Meer, H., & Dedinski, I. (2005). Comparison of crawling strategies for an optimized mobile p2p architecture. In *Proceedings of the 19th International Teletraffic Congress (ITC19)*.

Hoßfeld, T., Oechsner, S., Tutschku, K., Andersen, F. U., & Caviglione, L. (2006). Supporting vertical handover by using a pastry peer-to-peer overlay network. In *Proceedings of the 3rd IEEE International Workshop on Mobile Peer-to-Peer Computing (MP2P'06)*, Pisa, Italy.

Hoßfeld, T., Oechsner, S., Tutschku, K., Andersen, F.-U., & Caviglione, L. (2006). Supporting vertical handover by using a pastry peer-to-peer overlay network. In *Proceedings of the 3rd IEEE International Workshop on Mobile Peer-to-Peer Computing (MP2P'06)*.

Hoßfeld, T., Tutschku, K. & Andersen, F. U. (2005b). Mapping of file-sharing onto mobile environments: enhancement by UMTS. In *Proceedings of the Mobile Peer-to-Peer Computing MP2P, in conjunction with the 3rd IEEE International Conference on Pervasive Computing and Communications (PerCom'05)*. Kauai Island, Hawaii.

Hoßfeld, T., Tutschku, K., & Andersen, F. U. (2005a). Mapping of file-sharing onto mobile environments: feasibility and performance of eDonkey with GPRS. In *Proceedings of the Wireless Communications and Networking Conference, 2005 IEEE*. New Orleans, LA USA.

Hoßfeld, T., Tutschku, K., & Andersen, F.-U. (2005a). Mapping of file-sharing onto mobile environments: Enhancement by UMTS. *Proceedings of the 2nd IEEE International Workshop on Mobile Peer-to-Peer Computing (MP2P'05)*.

Hoßfeld, T., Tutschku, K., & Andersen, F.-U. (2005b). Mapping of file-sharing onto mobile environments: Feasibility and performance of edonkey with GPRS. In *Proceedings of 2005 IEEE Wireless Communciations and Networking Conference (WCNC 2005)*.

Hoßfeld, T., Tutschku. K., & Schlosser, D. (2005) Influence of the size of swapping entities in mobile P2P file-Sharing networks. In *Proceedings of the Peer-to-Peer-Systeme und -Anwendungen, GI/ITG-Workshop in conjunction with KiVS 2005*, Kaiserslautern, Germany.

Hsieh, R. Zhou, Z.G., & Seneviratne, A. (2003). S-MIP: A seamless handoff architecture for mobile IP. In *Proceedings of the IEEE International Conference on Computer Communications (INFOCOM)*.

Hu Y. C., Das S. M., & Pucha H. (2003). Exploiting the synergy between peer-to-peer and mobile ad hoc networks. In *Proceedings of the 9th Workshop on Hot Topics in Operating Systems*.

Hu, H., Xu, J., et al. (2003). Adaptive power-aware prefetching schemes for mobile broadcast environments. In *Proceedings of the International Conference on Mobile Data Management*.

Hu, Q., Lee, W. C., et al. (1999). Indexing techniques for wireless data broadcast under data clustering and scheduling. In *Proceedings of the Eighth International Conference on Information and Knowledge Management*, Kansas City, Missouri, USA.

Hu, Y. C., Das, S. M., & Pucha, H. (2003). Exploiting the synergy between peer-to-peer and mobile ad hoc networks. In *Proceedings of the 9th Workshop on Hot Topics in Operating Systems*.

Hu, Y., Das, S., & Pucha, H. (2004). Peer-to-peer overlay abstractions in MANETs. In J. Wu (Ed.), *Theoretical and algorithmic aspects of sensor, ad hoc wireless and peer-to-peer networks*. CRC Press.

Huang, C.-M., Hsu, T.-H., & Hsu, M.-F. (2007). Network-aware P2P file sharing over the wireless mobile networks. *IEEE Journal on Selected Areas in Communications, 25*(1), 204-210.

Huang, E., Crowcroft, J., & Wassell, I. (2004). Rethinking Incentives for Mobile Ad Hoc Networks. In *Proceedings of the ACM SIGCOMM workshop on Practice and theory of incentives in networked systems*.

Huang, Y., & Garcia-Molina, H. (2004). Publish/subscribe in a mobile environment. *Wireless Networks Journal, Special Issue on Pervasive Computing and Communications, 10*(6), 643-652.

Hubaux, J., Buttyan, L., & Capkun, S. (2001). The quest for security in mobile ad hoc networks. In *Proceeding of the ACM Symposium on Mobile Ad Hoc Networking and Computing.*

Hughes Network Systems, LLC. (2008). DIRECWAY. Retrieved May 25, 2008, from http://www.direcway.com/

Hui, P., & Crowcroft, J. (2007). *Bubble rap: Forwarding in small world dtns in every decreasing circles.* UCAM-CL-TR684, University of Cambridge.

Husemann, D. (1999). The smart card: Don't leave home without it. *IEEE Concurrency, 7*(2), 24-27.

Hwang, J., & Aravamudham, P. (2004). Middleware services for P2P computing in wireless grid networks. *IEEE Internet Computing, 8*(4), 40-46.

IEEE 1394. (1994). *1394 Trade Association.* Retrieved May 30, 2008, from http://www.1394ta.org/

Imielinski, T., Viswanathan, S., et al. (1994). Energy efficient indexing on air. In *Proceedings of the ACM SIGMOD International Conference on Management of Data.*

Imielinski, T., Viswanathan, S., et al. (1997). Data on air: Organization and access. *IEEE Transactions on Knowledge and Data Engineering, 9*(3), 353-372.

Ingemarsson, I., Tang, D., & Wong, C. (1982). A conference key distribution system. *IEEE Transactions on Information Theory, 28*(5), 714-720.

Internet Assigned Numbers Authority (IANA). (2008). Port numbers. Retrieved May 14, 2008, from http://www.iana.org/assignments/port-numbers

Ishikawa, N., et al. (2007). PUCC architecture, protocols and applications. In *Proceedings of the 4th IEEE Consumer Communications and Networking Conference.*

ISO/IEC. (1990). *Information technology -- open systems interconnection -- specification of abstract syntax notation one (ASN.1).* ISO/IEC 8824.

ITU-T Recommendation G.805. (2000). *Generic functional architecture of transport networks.* International Telecommunications Union.

ITU-T Recommendation G.809. (2003). *Functional architecture of connectionless layer networks.* International Telecommunications Union.

ITU-T Recommendation Y.2001. (2004). Series Y: Global information infrastructure, Internet protocol aspects and next-generation networks. *General overview of NGN.* International Telecommunications Union.

ITU-T Recommendation Y.2011. (2004). Series Y: Global information infrastructure, Internet protocol aspects and next generation networks. *General principles and general reference model for next generation networks.* International Telecommunications Union.

ITU-T. (1997). The International public telecommunication number plan, *ITU-T recommendation E.164.* ITU.

Jacquet, P., & Rodolakis, G. (2005). Multicast scaling properties in massively dense ad hoc networks. In *Proceedings of the 11th International Conference on Parallel and Distributed Systems.*

Jain, R.K., Chiu, D.M.W., & Hawe, W.R. (1984). *A quantitative measure of fairness and discrimination for resource allocation in shared computer system* (Tech. Rep. DEC-TR-301). Hudson, MA: Eastern Research Lab, Digital Equipment Corporation.

Jakobsson, M., Hubaux, J.-P., & Buttyan, L. (2003). A micro-payment scheme encouraging collaboration in multi-hop cellular networks. *Financial Cryptography.*

Jannotti, J., Gifford, D. K., Johnson, K. L., Kaashoek, M. F., & O'Toole, J. W., Jr. (2000). Overcast: Reliable multicasting with an overlay network. In *Proceedings of the 4th Symposium on Operating System Design and Implementation.*

Jaramillo, J. J., & Srikant, R. (2007). DARWIN: Distributed and adaptive reputation mechanism for wireless ad hoc networks. In *Proceedings of the 13th Annual ACM International Conference on Mobile Computing and Networking.*

Java J2SE 1.4.2. (2003). Sun *Microsystems Java2 standard edition version 1.4.2.* Retrieved May 30, 2008, from http://java.sun.com/j2se/1.4/

Jazayeri, M. (2007). Some trends in web application development. In *Proceedings of the International Conference on Software Engineering.*

Jennings, C., Lowekamp, B., Rescorla, E., Rosenberg, J., Baset, S., & Schulzrinne, H. (2008). *Resource location and discovery (RELOAD): draft-bryan-p2psip-reload-03* (work in progress). Retrieved May 14, 2008, from IETF Internet Draft Database.

Ji, X., Pollin, S., Lafruit, G., Moccagatta, I., Dejonghe, A., & Catthoor F. (2007). Energy-efficient bandwidth allocation for multi-user video streaming over WLAN. In *Proceedings of the IEEE International Conference on Acoustics Speech and Signal Processing.*

Ji, Z. J., Yu, W. A., & Liu, K. J. R. (2006). An optimal dynamic pricing framework for autonomous mobile ad hoc networks. In *Proceedings of the IEEE INFOCOM.*

Jiang, X., Zheng, H., Macian, C., & Pascual, V. (2008). *Service extensible P2P peer protocol: draft-jiang-p2psip-sep-01.* IETF. Retrieved September 10, 2008, from IETF Internet Draft Database.

Jing, J., Huff, K., Sinha, H., Hurwitz, B., & Robinson, B. (1999). Workflow and application adaptations in mobile environments. In *Proceedings of 2nd IEEE Workshop on Mobile Computer Systems and Applications*, New Orleans, Louisiana, USA.

Johnson, D. B., & Maltz, D. A. (1996). Dynamic source routing in ad hoc wireless networks. In T. Imielinski & H. Korth (Eds.), *Mobile Computing* (pp. 153-181). Kluwer Academic Publishers.

Johnson, D. B., & Maltz, D. A. (1996). Dynamic source routing in ad hoc wireless networks. In T. Imielinski, & H. Korth (Eds.), *Mobile computing.* Kluwer Academic Publisher.

Johnson, D. B., Maltz, D. A., & Hu. Y. C. (2006). The dynamic source routing protocol for mobile ad hoc networks (DSR). *IETF MANET Working Group: draft-ietf-manet-dsr-10.txt.*

Johnson, D., Maltz, D., & Broch, J. (2001). DSR: The dynamic source routing protocol for multi-hop wireless ad hoc networks. In C. E. Perkins (Ed.), *Ad hoc networking.* Addison-Wesley.

Johnson, D., Perkins, C., & Arkko, J.(2004). *IP mobility support for IPv6* (RFC 3775).

Johnson, D., Stack, T., Fish, R., Flickinger, D. M., Ricci, L. S. R., & Lepreau, J. (2006). Mobile Emulab: A robotic wireless and sensor network testbed. In *Proceedings of the Conference on Computer Communications (IN-FOCOM).*

Jørstad, I., Thanh, D., & Dustdar, S. (2004). An analysis of service continuity in mobile services. In *Proceedings of the 13th IEEE International Workshops on Enabling Technologies: Infrastructure for Collaborative Enterprises* (pp. 121-126). IEEE Computer Society.

Joseph, S. (2003). An extendible open source P2P simulator. *P2P Journal*, 1–15.

Judd, G., & Steenkiste, P. (2003). Providing Contextual information to pervasive computing applications. In *Proceedings of the IEEE International Conference on Pervasive Computing (PerCom),* Dallas, USA.

JXTA Project. (2007, Oct 16). *JXTA v2.0 protocols specification: Revision 2.5.3.* Retrieved Jun 6, 2008, from https://jxta-spec.dev.java.net/

JXTA. (2001). *Sun Microsystems project JXTA.* Retrieved May 30, 2008, from http://wwwjxta.org/

Kahn, J. M., Katz, R. H., & Pister, K. S. J. (1999). Mobile networking for smart dust. In *Proceedings of the ACM/IEEE International Conference on Mobile Computing and Networking (MobiCom).*

Kalofonos, D. N., Antoniou, Z., Reynolds, F. D., Van-Kleek, M., Strauss, J., & Wisner, P. (2008). MyNet: A platform for secure P2P personal and social networking services. In *Proceedings of the 6th Annual IEEE International Conference on Pervasive Computing and Communications (PerCom).*

Kamienski, C., Sadok, D., J. Fidalgo, D., Lima, J., & Ohlman, B. (2006). On the use of peer-to-peer architectures for the management of highly dynamic environments. In *Proceedings of the 2nd IEEE International Workshop on Mobile Peer-to-Peer Computing (MP2P '06).*

Kang, S.-S., & Mutka, M. W. (2005). A mobile peer-to-peer approach for multimedia content sharing using 3G/WLAN dual mode channels. *Wireless Communications and Mobile Computing Journal, Special Issue on WLAN/3G Integration for Next-Generation Heterogeneous Mobile Data Networks, 5*(6), 633-645.

Kangasharju, J. (2005). Peer-to-peer and ubiquitous computing. In R. Steinmetz & K. Wehrle (Eds.), *Peer-to-Peer Systems and Applications*. Springer Berlin / Heidelberg.

Kapp, S. (2002). 802.11: Leaving the wire behind. *IEEE Internet Computing, 6*(1), 82-85.

Karger, D.R., & Ruhl, M. (2004). Simple efficient load balancing algorithms for peer-to-peer systems, In *Proceedings of the International Conference on Peer-to-Peer Systems* (pp. 131-140).

Karp, B. & Kung, H. (2000). Greedy perimeter stateless routing for wireless networks. In *Proceedings of the 6th ACM/IEEE International Conference on Mobile Computing and Networking (MobiCom)*.

Karp, B., & Kung, H. T. (2000). GPSR: Greedy perimeter stateless routing for wireless networks. In *Proceedings of the 6th Annual International Conference on Mobile Computing and Networking*.

Katz, J., & Yung, M. (2007). Scalable protocols for authenticated group key exchange, J*ournal of Cryptology, 20*(1), 85-113.

Kawulok, L., Zielinski, K., & Jaeschke, M. (2005). Trusted group membership service for JXME (JXTA-4J2ME). In *Proceedings of the Wireless And Mobile Computing, Networking And Communications (WiMob)*, Montreal, Canada.

KaZaa. (2002). Retrieved September 29, 2008, from http://www.kazaa.com/us/index.htm

KaZaA. (2008). Music downloads now Kazaa.com: Music and ringtone downloads. Retrieved September 10, 2008, from http://www.kazaa.com

Keidar, I., Melamed, R., & Orda, A. (2006). EquiCast: Scalable multicast with selfish users. In *Proceedings of the 25th Annual ACM SIGACT-SIGOPS Symposium on Principles of Distributed Computing*.

Kellerer, W., Kunzmann, G., Schollmeier, R., & Zölsb, S. (2005). Structured peer-to-peer systems for telecommunications and mobile environments. *AEU - International Journal of Electronics and Communications, 60*(1), 25-29.

Kellerer, W., Schollmeier, R., & Wehrle, K. (2005). Peer-to-peer in mobile environments. In K. Wehrle & R. Steinmetz (Eds.), *Peer-to-Peer Systems and Applications, Springer Lecture Notes in Computer Science 3485*.

Kelly, F., Maulloo, A., & Tan, D. (1998). Rate control for communication networks: Shadow prices, proportional fairness and stability. *Journal of Operational Research Society, 49*(3), 237-252.

Kempf, J. (June, 2001). Dormant mode host alerting ('IP paging') problem statement. IETF, *RFC3132*.

Khan, I. J., & Wierzbicki, A. (2008). Foundation of peer-to-peer computing. *Elsevier Journal of Computer Communication, 31*(Special Issue 2).

Khan, S. U., & Ahmad, I. (2006). A pure Nash equilibrium guaranteeing game theoretical replica allocation method for reducing web access time. In *Proceedings of the 12th International Conference on Parallel and Distributed Systems*.

Kim, Y., Perrig, A., & Tsudik, G. (2004). Tree-based group key agreement. *ACM Transactions on Information Systems Security, 7*(1), 60-96.

Kirk, P. (2003) Gnutella – stable – 0.4. Retrieved September 9, 2008, from http://rfc-gnutella.sourceforge.net/developer/stable/index.html

Kirk, P. (2003). Gnutella - A protocol for a revolution. Retrieved September 10, 2008, from http://rfc-gnutella.sourceforge.net/

Kirk, P. (2003). Gnutella - A protocol for a revolution. Retrieved October 7, 2008, from http://rfc-gnutella.sourceforge.net/

Kirsner, S. (1998). The legend of Bob Metcalfe. *Wired, 11*(6).

Klemm, A., Lindemann, C., & Waldhorst, O. (2003). A special-purpose peer-to-peer file sharing system for mobile ad hoc networks. In *Proceedings of the Workshop on Mobile Ad Hoc Networking and Computing*.

Klemm, A., Lindemann, C., & Waldhorst, O. P. (2003). A special-purpose peer-to-peer file sharing system for mobile ad hoc networks. In *Proceedings of the IEEE Semi-Annual Vehicular Technology Conference*.

Klemn, A., Lindemann, C., & Waldhorst, O. P. (2003). A special-purpose peer-to-peer file sharing system for mobile ad hoc networks. In *Proceedings of the Semiannual Vehicular Technology Conference*. Orlando, FL, USA: IEEE Press.

Klenk, A., Kleis, M., Radier, B., Elmoumouhi, S., Carle, G., & Salaun, M. (2008). Towards autonomic service control in next generation networks. In *Proceedings of the Fourth International Conference on Autonomic and Autonomous Systems*.

Klingberg, T. & Manfredi, R. (2002). Gnutella Protocol Development. http://rfc-gnutella.sourceforge.net/src/rfc-0_6-draft.html

Ko, Y.-B., & Vaidya, N. H. (2000). Location-aided routing (LAR) in mobile ad hoc networks. *Wireless Networks, 6*(4), 307-321.

Komu, M., Henderson, T., Matthews, P., Tschofenig, H., & Keränen, A. (2008). *Basic HIP extensions for traversal of network address translators: draft-ietf-hip-nat-traversal-04* (work in progress). Retrieved Sep 10, 2008, from IETF Internet Draft Database.

König-Ries, B., & Klein, M. (2002). Information services to support e-learning in ad-hoc networks. In *Proceedings of 1ˢᵗ International Workshop on Wireless Information Systems (WIS)*, Ciudad Real, Spain (pp. 13-24).

Korhonen, J., & Wang, Y. (2005). Power-efficient streaming for mobile terminals. In *Proceedings of the 15ᵗʰ International Workshop on Network and Operating Systems Support for Digital Audio and Video*.

Kortuem, G. (2002). Proem: A middleware platform for mobile peer-to-peer computing. *SIGMOBILE Mobile Computing and Communication Review, Special Feature on Middleware for Mobile Computing, 6*(4), 62–64.

Kortuem, G. (2002). Proem: A middleware platform for mobile peer-to-peer computing. *ACM SIGMOBILE Mobile Computing and Communications Review (MC2R), 6*(4), 62-64.

Kortuem, G. (2002). Proem: A middleware platform

Kortuem, G., Schneider, J., Preuitt, D., Thompson, T. G. C., Fickas, S., & Segall, Z. (2001). When peer-to-peer comes face-to-face: Collaborative peer-to-peer computing in mobile ad hoc networks. In *Proceedings of the First International Conference on Peer-to-Peer Computing*.

Kortuem, G., Schneider, J., Preuitt, D., Thompson, T. G. C., Fickas, S., & Segall, Z. (2001). When peer-to-peer comes face-to-face: Collaborative peer-to-peer computing in mobile ad hoc networks. In *Proceedings of the IEEE 1ˢᵗ International Conference on Peer-to-Peer Computing (P2P)*.

Kortuem, G., Schneider, J., Thaddeus, D. P., Thompson, G. C., Fickas, S., & Segall Z. (2001). When peer-to-peer comes face-to-face: Collaborative peer-to-peer computing in mobile ad hoc networks. In *Proceedings of the 1ˢᵗ International Conference on Peer-to-Peer Computing*, Linköping, Sweden.

Koshy, J., & Pandey, R. (2005). Vm*: Synthesizing scalable runtime environments for sensor networks. In *Proceedings of the Conference on Embedded Networked Sensor Systems*.

Kothari, R., & Ganz, A. (2005). Archies: An end-to-end architecture for adaptive live MPEG-4 video streaming over wireless networks. In *Proceedings of the IEEE International Conference on Wireless and Mobile Computing, Networking and Communications*.

Kousiur, D. (1999). *IP multicasting: The complete guide to interactive corporate networks*. New York: John Wiley & Sons, Inc.

Kruglanski, A. (1978). Issues in cognitive social psychology. *The hidden cost of reward: New perspectives on the psychology of human motivation.* New York: John Wiley.

Kummer, R., Kropf, P., & Felber, P. (2006). Distributed lookup in structured peer-to-peer ad-hoc networks. In *Proceedings of the On the Move to Meaningful Internet Systems: CoopIS, DOA, GADA, and ODBASE.*

Kunz, T., & Omar, S. (2002). An adaptive MP3 player: Reducing power consumption and increasing application performance. In *Proceedings of the 35ʰ Hawaii International Conference on System Sciences (HICSS-35),* Hawaii, USA.

Lai, K., Feldman, M., Stoica, I., & Chuang, J. (2003). Incentives for cooperation in peer-to-peer networks. In *Proceedings of the Workshop on Economics of Peer-to-Peer Systems,* Berkeley, CA, USA.

Lassila, O., Swick, R. (1999). Resource Description Framework (RDF) Model and Syntax Specification. *W3C Recommendation, http://www.w3.org/TR/1999/REC-rdf-syntax-19990222.*

Lau, W. H. O., Kumar, M., et al. (2002). A cooperative cache architecture in support of caching multimedia objects in MANETs. In *Proceedings of the International Symposium on a World of Wireless, Mobile and Multimedia Networks.*

Le Fessant, F., Handurukande, S., Kermarrec, A. M., & Massoulie, L. (2004). Clustering in peer-to-peer file sharing workloads. In *Proceedings of the 3rd International Workshop on Peer-to-Peer Systems (IPTPS),* San Diego, CA, USA.

Le, L., & Kuo, G.S. (2007). Hierarchical and breathing peer-to-peer SIP system. In *Proceedings of the IEEE International Conference on Communications* (pp. 1887-1892).

Leach, P.J., & Salz, R.. (1998). *UUIDs and GUIDs; draft-leach-uuids-guids-01.txt* (Expired). Retrieved March 9, 2009, from http://www.opengroup.org/dce/info/draft-leach-uuids-guids-01.txt

Leavitt, N. (2007). For wireless USB, the future starts now. *Computer, 40*(7), 14-16.

Lee, C., Helal, A., Desai, N., Verma, V., & Arslan, B. (2003). Konark: A system and protocols for device independent, peer-to-peer discovery and delivery of mobile services. *IEEE Transactions on Systems, Man and Cybernetics, 33*(6), 682-696.

Lee, J. K., & Hou, J.C. (2006). Modeling steady-state and transient behaviors of user mobility: Formulation, analysis, and application. In *Proceedings of the seventh ACM international symposium on Mobile ad hoc networking and computing (MobiHoc06),* New York, NY, USA.

Lee, J.K. & Hou, J.C. (2006). Modeling steady-state and transient behaviors of user mobility: Formulation, analysis, and application. In *Proceedings of the seventh ACM international symposium on Mobile ad hoc networking and computing (MobiHoc06),* New York, NY, USA.

Lee, S., Carney, D., et al. (2003). Index hint for on-demand broadcasting. In *Proceedings of the International Conference on Data Engineering.*

Lee, S., Levin, D., Gopalakrishnan, V., & Bhattacharjee, B. (2007). Backbone construction in selfish wireless networks. In *Proceedings of the ACM Sigmetrics.*

Lee, U., Park, J.-S., Yeh, J., Pau, G., & Gerla, M. (2006). Code torrent: Content distribution using network coding in VANET. In *Proceedings of the 1ˢᵗ International Workshop on Decentralized resource sharing in mobile computing and networking (MobiShare).*

Legg, S. (2006). *Lightweight directory access protocol (LDAP): Syntaxes and matching rules.* RFC 4517.

Legout, A., Urvoy-Keller, G., & Michiardi, P. (2006). Rarest first and choke algorithms are enough. In *Proceedings of the 6ʰ ACM SIGCOMM on Internet measurement,* Rio de Janeiro, Brazil.

Lenders, V., May, M., & Plattner, B. (2005). Survey and new Approach in service discovery and advertisement for mobile ad hoc networks. *Pervasive and Mobile Computing, 1*(3), 343-370.

Leung, M.-F., & Chan, S.-H. (2007). Broadcast-based peer-to-peer collaborative video streaming among mobiles. *IEEE Transactions on Broadcasting Special Issue on Mobile Multimedia Broadcasting, 53*(1), 350-361.

Levin, D. (2006). Punishment in selfish wireless networks: A game theoretic analysis. In *Proceedings of the Workshop on Network Economics (NetEcon)*.

Levis, P., & Culler, D. (2002). Mate: A tiny virtual machine for sensor networks. In *Proceedings of the International Conference on Architectural Support for Programming Languages and Operating Systems*.

Levis, P., Lee, N., Welsh, M., & Culler, D. (2003). TOSSIM: Accurate and scalable simulation of entire TinyOS applications. In *Proceedings of the Sensys: The ACM Conference on Embedded Networked Sensor Systems*.

Li J., Stribling J., Morris R., Kaashoek M.F., & Gil M.T. (2005). A performance vs. cost framework for evaluating DHT design tradeoffs under churn. In *Proceedings of the Annual Joint Conference of the IEEE Computer and Communications Societies*. (Vol. 1, pp. 225-236).

Li, J. (2006). Peer-to-peer multimedia applications. In *Proceedings of the 14th Annual ACM International Conference on Multimedia*.

Li, X., and Wu, J. (2005). Searching techniques in peer-to-peer networks. In J. Wu (Ed.), Handbook on theoretical and algorithmic aspects of sensor, ad hoc wireless, and peer-to-peer networks. Boca Raton, FL, USA: CRC Press,.

Liang, J., Kumar, R., & Ross, K.W. (2004). The KaZaa overlay: A measurement study. In *Proceedings of the IEEE Annual Computer Communications*.

Liao, W.-C., Papadopoulos, F., & Psounis, K. (2006). A peer-to-peer cooperation enhancement scheme and its performance analysis. *Journal of Communications (JCM), 1*(7), 24-35.

Lim, S., Lee, W., Cao, G., & Das, C. (2004). Performance comparison of cache invalidation strategies for Internet-based mobile ad hoc networks. In *Proceedings of the 1st IEEE International Conference on Mobile Ad-hoc and Sensor Systems (MASS)*.

Lindemann, C. & Waldhorst, O. P. (2004). Exploiting epidemic data dissemination for consistent lookup operations in mobile applications. *ACM Mobile Computing and Communications Review, 8*(2), 44–56.

Liu, Y., & Knightly, E. (2003). Opportunistic fair scheduling over multiple wireless channels. In *Proceedings of the IEEE Conference on Computer Communications*.

Liu, Y., Li, X., Liu, X., Ni, L. M., & Zhang, X. (2005). Location awareness in unstructured peer-to-peer systems. *IEEE Transactions on Parallel and Distributed Systems, 16*(2): 163-174.

Liu, Y., Xiao, L. & Ni, L. M. (2007). Building a Scalable Bipartite P2P Overlay Network, *IEEE Transactions on Parallel and Distributed Systems (TPDS), 18*(9), 46-56.

Lo, S.-C., & Chen, A. L. P. (2000). Optimal index and data allocation in multiple broadcast channels. In *Proceedings of the 16th International Conference on Data Engineering*.

Long, S., Kooper, R., Abowd, G. D., & Atkeson, C. G. (1996). Rapid prototyping of mobile context-aware applications: The cyberguide case study. In *Proceedings of the ACM International Conference on Mobile Computing and Networking*, Rye, New York, USA.

Lua, E. K., Crowcroft, J., Pias, M., Sharma, R., & Lim, S. (2004). A survey and comparison of peer-to-peer overlay network schemes. *IEEE Communications Survey & Tutorials, 7*(2), 72-93.

Lua, E.K., Crowcroft, J., Pias, M., Sharma, R., & Lim, S. (2004). A survey and comparison of peer-to-peer overlay network schemes. *IEEE Communications Survey and Tutorial*, 72-93.

Lundquist, D. & Ouksel, A. (2007). An efficient demand-driven and density-controlled publish/subscribe protocol for mobile environments. In *Proceedings of the International Conference on Distributed Event-Based Systems*.

Luo, H., Ramjee, R., Sinha, P., Li, L., & Lu, S. (2003). UCAN: A unified cellular and ad-hoc network architecture. In *Proceedings of the 9th Annual International Conference on Mobile Computing and Networking*.

Lv, Q., Cao, P., Cohen, E., Li, K., and Shenker, S. (2002). Search and replication in unstructured peer-to-peer networks. In *Proceedings of the 16ᵗʰ International Conference on Supercomputing*.

Ma, R. T.B., Chiu, D.-M. Lui, J. C.S, Misra, V., & Rubenstein, D. (2006). A budget-balanced and price-adaptive credit protocol for MANETs. *Electrical Engineering*.

Macedonia, M. (2007). iPhones target the tech elite. *Computer, 40*(6), 94-95.

MacKenzie, A.B., & Wicker, S. B. (2003). Stability of multipacket slotted aloha with selfish users and perfect information. In *Proceedings of the IEEE INFOCOM*.

Magharei, N., Rejaie, R., & Y. Guo. (2007). Mesh or multiple-tree: A comparative study of P2P live streaming services. In *Proceedings of the IEEE International Conference on Computer Communications*.

Mahajan, R., Rodrig, M., Wetherall, D., & Zahorjan. J. (2005). Sustaining cooperation in multi-hop wireless networks. In *Proceedings of the Second Symposium on Networked Systems Design and Implementation (NSDI '05)*.

Maibaum, N., & Mundt, T. (2002). JXTA: A technology facilitating mobile peer-to-peer networks. In *Proceedings of the International Mobility and Wireless Access Workshop (MobiWac)*, Fort Worth, Texas, USA.

Maille P., & Tuffin, B. (2007). Why VCG auctions can hardly be applied to the pricing of inter-domain and ad hoc networks. In *Proceedings of the 3rd EuroNGI Conference on Next Generation Internet Networks*.

Malan, D. J., & Smith, M. D. (2005). Host-based detection of worms through peer-to-peer cooperation. In *Proceedings of the ACM Workshop on Rapid Malcode*.

Marbach, P., & Qiu, Y. (2005). Cooperation in wireless ad hoc networks: A market-based approach. *IEEE/ACM Transactions on Networking, 13*(6), 1325-1338.

Maret, T., Kropf, P., & Hirsbrunner, B. (2007). *Un environnement d'émulation hybride pour un algorithme de DHT adapte au contexte des réseaux ad-hoc*. Universities of Fribourg and Neuchâtel.

Marias, G. F., Georgiadis, P., Flitzanis, D., & Mandalas, K. (2006). Cooperation enforcement schemes for MANETs: A survey. *Wireless Communications and Mobile Computing, 6*, 319-332.

Marocco, E., & Bryan, D. (2007). *Interworking between P2PSIP overlays and conventional SIP network: draft-marocco-p2psip-interwork-01* (work in progress). Retrieved May 22, 2008, from IETF Internet Draft Database.

Marocco, E., Manzalini, A., Sampo, M., & Canal, G. (2007). Interworking between P2PSIP overlays and IMS networks – scenarios and technical solutions. In *Proceedings of the International Conference on Intelligence in Service Delivery Networks*. Retrieved May 30, 2008, from ICIN database.

Marti, S., Giuli, T.J., Lai, K., & Baker, M. (2000). Mitigating routing misbehaviour in mobile ad hoc networks. In *Proceedings of the ACM MOBICOM*.

Matuszewski, M., Beijar, N., Lehtinen, J., & Hyyrylainen T. (2006). Content sharing in mobile P2P networks: Myth or reality? *International Journal of Mobile Network Design and Innovation, 1*(3/4), 197-207.

Matuszewski, M., Beijar, N., Lehtinen, J., & Hyyrylainen, T. (2006). Content sharing in mobile P2P networks: Myth or reality? *International Journal of Mobile Network Design and Innovation, 1*(3/4), 10.

Matuszewski, M., Ekberg, J.E., & Laitinen, P. (2007). *Security requirements in P2PSIP: draft-matuszewski-p2psip-security-requirements* (work in progress). Retrieved May 14, 2008, from IETF Internet Draft Database.

Mavromoustakis, C. X., & Karatza H. D. (2006). Epidemic collaborative replication for maintaining file sharing reliability in mobile peer-to-peer devices. In *Proceedings of the International Symposium on Performance Evaluation of Computer and Telecommunication Systems (SPECTS)*.

Maymounkov, P., & Mazieres, D. (2002). Kademlia: A peer-to-peer information system based on the XOR metric. In *Proceedings of the International Workshop on Peer-to-Peer Systems* (pp. 53-61).

McMillian, D.W., & Chavis, D.M. (1986). Sense of community: A definition and theory. *Journal of Community Psychology, 14*(1), 6-23.

Mecella, M., Angelaccio, M., Krek, A., Catarci, T., Buttarazzi, B., and Dustdar, S. (2006). Workpad: An adaptive peer-to-peer software infrastructure for supporting collaborative work of human operators in emergency/disaster scenarios. In *Proceedings of the International Symposium on Collaborative Technologies and Systems*.

Menezes, A., van Oorschot, P., & Vanstone, S. (1996). *Handbook in applied cryptography*. CRC Press.

Michahelles, F., Thiesse, F., Schmidt, A., & Williams, J. R. (2007). Pervasive RFID and near field communication technology. *IEEE Pervasive Computing, 6*(3), 94-96.

Michal, F., Kevin, L., Ion, S., & John, C. (2004). Robust incentive techniques for peer-to-peer networks. In *Proceedings of the 5th ACM conference on Electronic commerce*, New York, NY, USA.

Michiardi, P., & Molva, R. (2002). CORE: A collaborative repudiation mechanism to enforce node cooperation in mobile ad hoc networks. In *Proceedings of the Sixth IFIP Conference on Security Communications, and Multimedia*.

Michiardi, P., & Urovoy-Keller, G. (2007). Performance analysis of cooperative content distribution in wireless ad hoc networks. In *Proceedings of the fourth annual conference on Wireless on Demand Network Systems and Services*, Obergurgl, Austria.

Microsoft Corporation. (2000). *Microsoft Office Groove*. Retrieved May 30, 2008, from http://office.microsoft.com/ja-jp/groove/default.aspx

Microsoft. (2008). MSN Direct. Retrieved May 25, 2008, from http://www.msndirect.com/

Milgram, S. (1967). The small-world problem. *Psychology Today, 1*(1), 60–67.

Miller, B. A., & Bisdikian, C. (2004). *Bluetooth revealed* (2nd ed.). Addison-Wesley.

Mohapatra, P., Gui, C., & Li, J. (2004). Group communications in mobile ad hoc networks. *IEEE Computer, 37*(2), 52-59.

Mondal, A., Madria, S. K., & Kitsuregawa, M. (2007). Research issues and overview of economic models in mobile-P2P networks. In *Proceedings of the 18th International Conference on Database and Expert Systems Applications*.

Monrose, F., Wyckoff, P., & Rubin, A. (1999). Distributed execution with remote audit. In *Proceedings of the 1999 ISOC Network and Distributed System Security Symposium*, (pp. 103-113).

Moscibroda, T., Schmid, S., & Wattenhofer, R. (2006). On the topologies formed by selfish peers. In *Proceedings of the Twenty-fifth annual ACM symposium on Principles of distributed computing*, Denver, Colorado, USA.

Moskowitz, R., & Nikander, P. (2006). Host identity protocol (HIP) architecture. *RFC4423*. IETF.

Moskowitz, R., Nikander, P., Jokela, P., & Henderson, T. (2008). Host identity protocol. *RFC5201*. IETF.

Motani, M., Srinivasan, V., & Nuggehalli, P. (2005). PeopleNet: Engineering a wireless virtual social network. In *Proceedings of the ACM International Conference on Mobile Computing and Networking (MobiCom)*.

Mouratidis, H., Giorgini, P., & Manson, G. (2003). An ontology for modelling security: The tropos approach. In *Proceedings of the 7th International Conference on Knowledge-based Intelligent Information and Engineering Systems*, Oxford, UK.

MPEG-7. (2002). *The MPEG-7 standard ISO/IEC 15938*.

Mueller, U., Young, M., & Gefflaut, A. (2007). Running the Windows P2P infrastructure on mobile phones. In *Proceedings of the 7th IEEE International Conference on Peer-to-Peer Computing*.

Müller, R., Alonso, G., & Kossmann, D. (2007). A virtual machine for sensor networks. In *Proceedings of the EuroSys*.

Mundinger, J., & Le Boudec, J.-Y. (2006). Reputation in self-organized communication systems and beyond. In *Proceedings of the Interperf '06: Proceedings from the 2006 workshop on Interdisciplinary systems approach in performance evaluation and design of computer & communications systems.* ACM Press.

Muthusamy, V., Petrovic, M., & Jacobsen, H.-A. (2005). Effects of routing computations in content-based routing networks with mobile data sources. In *Proceedings of 11th International Conference on Mobile Computing and Networking*, Cologne, Germany.

Myerson, R. B. (1997). *Game theory: Analysis of conflict.* Harvard University Press.

National Institute of Standards and Technology (2005). NIST Net Home Page. Retrieved September 30, 2008, from http://snad.ncsl.nist.gov/itg/nistnet/index.html

Neely, M.J. (2007). Optimal pricing in a free market wireless network. In *Proceedings of the IEEE INFOCOM.*

nesC. (2008). Retrieved October 24, 2008, from http://nescc.sourceforge.net/

Newmann, M. E. (2003). The structure and function of complex networks. *SIAM Review, 45*(2), 167-256.

Newmann, M. E. (2004). Detecting community structure in networks. *European Physical Journal B, 38,* 321-330.

Newsome, J., Shi, E., Song, D., & Perrig, A. (2004). The sybil attack in sensor networks: Analysis & defenses. In *Proceedings of the 3rd International Conference on Information Processing in Sensor Networks.*

Ng, S.K., & Seah, W.K.G. (2008). Game-theoretic model for collaborative protocols in selfish, tariff-free, multihop wireless networks. In *Proceedings of the IEEE INFOCOM.*

Ng, T., Chu, Y., Rao, S., Sripanidkulchai, K., & Zhang, H. (2003). Measurement-based optimization techniques for bandwidth-demanding peer-to-peer systems. In *Proceedings of the 22nd Annual Joint Conference of the IEEE Computer and Communications Societies INFOCOM*, San Francisco, CA, USA.

Ngan, T.-W., Wallach, D. S, & Druschel, P. (2004). Incentives-compatible peer-to-peer multicast. In *Proceedings of the 2nd Workshop on the Economics of Peer-to-Peer Systems.*

Nordbotten, N. A., Skeie, T., & Aakvaag, N. D. (2004). Methods for service discovery in Bluetooth scatternets. *Computer Communications, 27*(11), 1087-1096.

Norros, I., Prabhu, B., & Reittu, H. (2006). Flash crowd in a file sharing system based on random encounters. In *Proceedings of the Workshop on Interdisciplinary systems approach in performance evaluation and design of computer & communications systems*, Pisa, Italy.

Oberender, J., Andersen, F. -U., Meer, H. d., Dedinski, I., Hoßfeld, T., Kappler, C., Mäder, A., & Tutschku, K. (2005). Enabling mobile peer-to-peer networking. In *Mobile and Wireless Systems, (*LNCS, 3427*).*

Oberender, J., Andersen, F.-U., de Meer, H., Dedinski, I., Hoßfeld, T., Kappler, C., Mäder, A., & Tutschku, K. (2005). Enabling mobile peer-to-peer networking. *Wireless Systems and Mobiliy in Next Generation Internet* (p. 26). Berlin / Heidelberg: Springer.

Oberender, J., Andersen, F.-U., Meer, H. d., Dedinski, I., Hoßfeld, T., Kappler, C., Mäder, A., & Tutschku, K. (2005). Enabling mobile peer-to-peer networking. In *Mobile and Wireless System, (*LNCS, 3427*).*

Odlyzko, A. (2001). Internet pricing and the history of communications. *Computer Networks, 36,* 5-6, 493-517.

Oliveira, L. B., Siqueira, I. G., & Loureiro, A. A. F. (2003). Evaluation of ad hoc routing protocols under a peer-to-peer application. In *Proceedings of the IEEE Wireless Communications and Networking Conference (WCNC).*

Oliveira, L. B., Siqueira, I. G., & Loureiro, A. A. F. (2005). On the performance of ad hoc routing protocols under a peer-to-peer application. *Journal of Parallel and Distributed Computing (JPDC): Special issue on the design and performance of networks for super-, cluster-, and grid-computing, 65*(11): 1337–1347.

Oliveira, L. B., Siqueira, I. G., Macedo, D. F., Loureiro, A. A. F., Wong, H. C., & Nogueira, J. M. (2005). Evaluation of peer-to-peer network content discovery techniques over mobile ad hoc networks. In *Proceedings of the IEEE International Symposium on a World of Wireless, Mobile and Multimedia Networks.*

Oliveira, L. B., Siqueria, I. G., Macedo, D. F., Loureiro, A. A. F., Wong, H. C., & Nogueira, J. M. (2005). Evaluation of peer-to-peer network content discovery techniques over mobile ad hoc networks. In *Proceedings of the Sixth IEEE International Symposium on a World of Wireless Mobile and Multimedia Networks.*

Oliveira, L., Siqueira, I., & Loureiro, A. (2003). Evaluation of ad-hoc routing protocols under a peer-to-peer application. In *Proceedings of the IEEE Wireless Communications and Networking Conference (WCNC).*

Olson, J.S., Teasley, S., Covi, L., & Olson, G. (2002). The (currently) unique advantages of collocated work. MIT Press.

Ooi, W. T. (2005). Dagster: Contributor-aware end-host multicast for media streaming in heterogeneous environment. In *Proceedings of the 12th Annual Multimedia Computing and Networking.*

Open Service Gateway Initiative. (2003). *The OSGi service platform specification, release 3.*

Oram, A. (2001). *Peer-to-peer: Harnessing the power of disruptive technologies* (first ed.). O'Reilly.

Osborne, M. J. (2003). *An introduction to game theory.* Oxford University Press.

Osborne, M. J., & Rubinstein, A. (1994). *A course in game theory.* MIT Press.

OSGi Alliance. (1999). Retrieved May 30, 2008, from http://www.osgi.org/Main/HomePage

Osterlind, F., Dunkels, A., Eriksson, J., Finne, N., & Voigt, T. (2006). Cross-level sensor network simulation with COOJA. In *Proceedings of the IEEE International Workshop on Practical Issues in Building Sensor Network Applications.*

Ouksel, A. (2006). Self-balancing selective information dissemination and discovery in mobile environments. In *Proceedings of the 22nd IEEE International Conference on Data Engineering (ICDE).*

P2P ARCHITECT (2001). EC funded project (IST-2001-32708). Retrieved on October 2, 2008, from http://www.atc.gr/p2p_architect/index.htm

Pack, S., Park, K., Kwon, T., & Choi, Y. (2006). SAMP: Scalable application-layer mobility protocol. *IEEE COMMUNICATIONS MAGAZINE, 44,* 8.

Pack, S., Park, K., Kwon, T., & Choi, Y. (2006). SAMP: Scalable application-layer mobility protocol. *IEEE Communications Magazine, 44*(6), 86-92.

Padmanabhan, V. N., Wang, H. J., & Chou, P. A. (2003). Resilient peer-to-peer streaming. In *Proceedings of the 11th IEEE International Conference on Network Protocols.*

Paillier, P. (1999). Public-key cryptosystems based on composite degree residuosity classes. In *Proceedings of Advances in Cryptology - EUROCRYPT'99,* (LNCS, 2139, 223-238).

Papadopouli, M. & Schulzrinne, H. (2001). Effects of power conservation, wireless coverage and cooperation on data dissemination among mobile devices. In *Proceedings of the 2nd ACM International Symposium on Mobile Ad Hoc Networking and Computing (MobiHoc).*

Papadopouli, M., & Schulzrinne, H. (2001). Effects of power conservation, wireless coverage and cooperation on data dissemination among mobile devices. In *Proceedings of the International Symposium on Mobile Ad Hoc Networking and Computing.*

Papadopouli, M., & Schulzrinne, H. (2001b). A performance analysis of 7ds a peer-to-peer data dissemination and prefetching tool for mobile users. In *Proceedings of the Advances in wired and wireless communications, IEEE Sarnoff Symposium.*

Papadopoulos, C. (2006). Improving awareness in mobile CSCW. IEEE Transactions on Mobile Computing, 5(10), 1331-1346.

Park, H. -H., Kim W., & Woo M. (2007). A Gnutella-based P2P system using cross-layer design for MANET. *International Journal of Electronics, Circuits and Systems, 1*(3), 139-144.

Passarella, A., Delmastro, F., & Conti, M. (2006). XScribe: A stateless, cross-layer approach to P2P multicast in multi-hop ad hoc networks. In *Proceedings of the International Workshop on Decentralized Resource Sharing in Mobile Computing and Networking.*

Patil, A., Liu, Y., Xiao, L., Esfahanian, A., & Ni, L. (2004). SOLONet: Sub-optimal location-aided overlay network for MANETs. In *Proceedings of the 1st IEEE International Conference on Mobile Ad-hoc and Sensor Systems (MASS).*

Peer-to-Peer SIP (P2PSIP). (2008). Peer-to-peer SIP charter. Retrieved May 30, 2008, from http://www.ietf.org/html.charters/p2psip-charter.html

Peer-to-peer Universal Computing Consortium (PUCC). (2004). Retrieved May 30, 2008, from http://www.pucc.jp

Pelusi, L., Passarella, A., & Conti, M. (2006). Opportunistic networking: Data forwarding in disconnected mobile ad hoc networks. *IEEE Communication Magazine, 44*(11), 134-141.

Peng, Z., Duan, Z.H., Qi, J.J., Cao, Y., & Lv, E.T. (2007). HP2P: A hybrid hierarchical P2P network. In *Proceedings of the International Conference on the Digital Society* (pp. 18-22).

Penserini, L., Liu, L., Mylopoulos, J., Panti, M., & Spalazzi, L. (2003). Cooperation strategies for agent-based P2P systems. *Web Intelli. and Agent Sys., 1*(1), 3-21.

PEPERS (2006). EC funded project (IST-2004-026901). Retrieved on October 2, 2008, from http://www.pepers.org

Pereira, O., & Quisquater, J.-J. (2004). Generic insecurity of cliques-type authenticated group key agreement protocols. In *Proceedings of the 17th IEEE Computer Security Foundations Workshop.*

Pering, T., Agarwal, Y., Gupta, R., & Want, R. (2006). CoolSpots: Reducing the power consumption of wireless mobile devices with multiple radio interfaces. In *Proceedings of the 4th International Conference on Mobile Systems, Applications and Services.*

Perkins, C. & Bhagwat, B. (1994). Highly dynamic destination-sequenced distance-vector routing (DSDV) for mobile computers. *ACM SIGCOMM Computer Communication Review, 24*(4), 234-244.

Perkins, C. (1999). Ad hoc on-demand distance vector routing. In *Proceedings of the 2nd IEEE Workshop on Mobile Computing Systems and Applications.*

Perkins, C. (2002). IP mobility support for IPv4. *RFC3344.* IETF.

Perkins, C. E., & Belding-Royer, E. M. (1999). Ad-hoc on-demand distance vector routing. In *Proceedings of the IEEE Workshop on Mobile Computing Systems and Applications.*

Perkins, C. E., & Bhagwat, P. (1994). Highly dynamic destination-sequenced distance-vector routing (DSDV) for mobile computers. In *Proceedings of the ACM Conference on Communications Architectures, Protocols and Applications*, London, UK.

Perkins, C. E., & Royer, E. M. (1999). Ad hoc on-demand distance vector routing. In *Proceedings of the IEEE Workshop on Mobile Computing Systems and Applications.*

Perkins, C. (2002). *IP Mobility Support for IPv4* (RFC 3344).

Piccolo, F.L., Neglia, G., & Bianchi, G. (2004). The effect of heterogeneous link capacities in BitTorrent-like file sharing systems. In *Proceedings of the 2004 International Workshop on Hot Topics in Peer-to-Peer Systems (HOT-P2P04)*, Volendarn, The Netherlands.

Pitoura, E. & Samaras, G. (2001). Locating objects in mobile computing. *IEEE Transactions on Knowledge and Data Engineering, 13*(4):571–592.

Plaxton, C., Rajaram, R., & Richa, A.W. (1997). Accessing nearby copies of replicated objects in a distributed environment. In *Proceedings of the 9th Annual ACM Symposium on Parallel Algorithms and Architectures.*

Podnar, I., & Lovrek, I. (2004). Supporting mobility with persistent notifications in publish/subscribe systems. In *Proceedings of 3rd International Workshop on Distributed Event-based Systems (DEBS 2004)* Edinburgh, Scotland, UK.

Polley, J., Blazakis, D., McGee, J., Rusk, D., & Baras, J. S. (2004). ATEMU: A fine-grained sensor network simulator. In *Proceedings of the First IEEE Communications Society Conference on Sensor and Ad Hoc Communications and Networks.*

Poslad, S., Buckle, P., & Hadingham, R. (2000). The Fipa-OS agent platform: Open source for open standards. In *Proceedings of the 5th International Conference and Exhibition on the Pratical Application of Intelligent Agents and Multi-Agents*, Manchester, UK.

PPLive Inc. (2007). PPLive. Retrieved September 9, 2008, from http://pplive.com/

PPStream. (2005). Retrieved September 9, 2008, from http://ppstream.com/

Preece, J. (2000). *Online communities: Designing usability supporting sociability.* John Wiley & Sons Ltd.

Project Aura. (2002). Retrieved September 30, 2008, from http://www.cs.cmu.edu/~aura/

Pucha, H., Das, S. M., & Y. C. Hu, (2004). Ekta: An efficient DHT substrate for distributed applications in mobile ad hoc networks. In *Proceedings of the 6th IEEE Workshop on Mobile Computing Systems and Applications (WMCSA).*

Pucha, H., Das, S. M., & Hu, Y. C. (2004). Ekta: An efficient dht substrate for distributed applications in mobile ad hoc networks. *IEEE WMCSA.*

Pucha, H., Das, S. M., & Hu, Y. C. (2004). EKTA: An efficient DHT substrate for distributed applications in mobile ad hoc networks. In *Proceedings of the IEEE Workshop on Mobile Computing Systems and Applications.*

Pucha, H., Das, S. M., & Hu, Y. C. (2004). How to Implement DHTs in Mobile Ad Hoc Networks?. In *Proceedings of the 10th ACM International Conference on Mobile Computing and Networking.*

Pucha, H., Das, S. M., & Hu, Y. C. (2006). Ekta+: Opportunistic multiplexing in a wireless DHT. In *Proceedings of the ACM Mobishare,* Los Angeles, USA.

Raghavan, B. & Snoeren, A. C. (2003). Priority forwarding in ad hoc networks with self-interested parties. In *Proceedings of the Workshop on Economics of Peer-to-Peer Systems.*

Raivio, Y. (2005). A peer-to-peer overlay architecture for mobile networks. *T110.7190 Research Seminar on Telecom Software.*

Rao, A., Laksminarayanan, K., Surana, S., Karp, R., & Stoica, I. (2003). Load balancing in structured P2P systems. In *Proceedings of the International Workshop on Peer-to-Peer Systems* (pp. 68-79).

Ratnasamy, S., Francis, P., Handley, M., Karp, R. M., & Shenker, S. (2001). A scalable content-addressable network. In *Proceedings of the ACM SIGCOMM Conference on Applications, Technologies, Architectures, and Protocols for Computer Communications.*

Ratnasamy, S., Francis, P., Handley, M., Karp, R., & Shenker S. (2001). A scalable content addressable network. *ACM Special Interest Group on Data Communication, 31*(4), 161-172.

Ratnasamy, S., Francis, P., Handley, M., Karp, R., & Shenker, S. (2001). A scalable content-addressable network. In *Proceedings of ACM SIGCOMM Conference on Applications, Technologies, Architectures, and Protocols for Computer Communications.*

Ratnasamy, S., Karp, B., Yin, L., Yu, F., Estrin, D., Govindan, R., & Shenker, S. (2002). GHT: A geographic hash table for data-centric storage. In *Proceedings of the 1st ACM International Workshop on Wireless Sensor Networks and Applications (WSNA).*

Ratsimor, O., Chakraborty, D., Joshi, A., & Finin, T. (2002). Allia: Alliance-based service discovery for ad-hoc environments. In *Proceedings of the 2nd International Workshop on Mobile Commerce*. Atlanta, GA, USA: ACM Press.

Ratsimor, O., Chakraborty, D., Joshi, A., & Finin, T. (2004). Service discovery in agent-based pervasive computing environments. *Mobile Networks and Applications, 9*(6), 679-692.

Repantis, T. & Kalogeraki, V. (2005). Data dissemination in mobile peer-to-peer networks. In *Proceedings of the 6th IEEE International Conference on Mobile Data Management (MDM)*.

Repantis, T. (2005). *Adaptive data dissemination and content-driven routing in peer-to-peer systems.* Unpublished master's thesis, University of California, Riverside, USA.

Resnick, P., Zeckhauser, R., Friedman, E., & Kuwabara, K. (2000). Reputation systems. *Communications of the ACM, 43*,12.

Reynolds, F. (2008). Whither Bluetooth? IEEE Pervasive Computing, 7(3), 6-8.

Richard, G. G. (2000). Service advertisement and discovery: Enabling universal device cooperation. *IEEE Internet Computing, 4*(5), 18-26.

Risson, J., & Moors, T. (2006). Survey of research towards robust peer-to-peer networks: Search methods. *Computer Networks, 50*(17), 3485-3521.

Rivest, R. L., Adleman, L., & Dertouzos, M. L. (1978). On data banks and privacy homomorphisms. In *Foundations of secure computation*. New York: Academic Press.

Rogers, M. & Bhatti, S. (2007). A lightweight mechanism for dependable communication in untrusted networks. In *Proceedings of the 37th Annual IEEE/IFIP International Conference on Dependable Systems and Networks*.

Rong, Y., Lee, S-K., & Choi, H-A. (2006). Detecting stations cheating on backoff rules in 802.11 networks using sequential analysis. In *Proceedings of the IEEE INFOCOM*.

Rosenberg, J. (2007). *Interactive connectivity establishment (ICE): A protocol for network address translator (NAT) traversal for offer/answer protocols: draft-ietf-mmusic-ice-19* (work in progress). Retrieved May 14, 2008, from IETF Internet Draft Database.

Rosenberg, J., Mahy, R., & Matthews, P. (2008b). *Traversal using relays around NAT (TURN): Relay extensions to session traversal utilities for NAT (STUN): draft-ietf-behave-turn-07* (work in progress). Retrieved May 14, 2008, from IETF Internet Draft Database.

Rosenberg, J., Mahy, R., Matthews, P., & Wing, D. (2008a). Session traversal utilities for NAT (STUN): *draft-ietf-behave-rfc3489bis-15* (work in progress). Retrieved May 14, 2008, from IETF Internet Draft Database.

Rosenberg, J., Schulzrinne H., G. Camarillo, Johnston, A., Peterson, J., Sparks, R., Handley, M., & Schooler, E. (2002). SIP: The Session initiation protocol, *RFC 3261*.

Rowstron A., & Druschel P. (2001). Pastry: Scalable distributed object location and routing for large-scale peer-to-peer systems. In *Proceedings of the 18th IFIP/ACM International Conference on Distributed System Platforms*.

Rowstron, A. I. T., & Druschel, P. (2001). Pastry: Scalable, decentralized object location, and routing for large-scale peer-to-peer systems. In *Proceedings of the IFIP/ACM International Conference on Distributed Systems Platforms*.

Rowstron, A., & Drusche, P. (2001). Pastry: Scalable, distributed object location and routing for large scale peer-to-peer systems. In *Proceedings of the IFIP/ACM International Conference on Distributed Systems Platforms* (pp. 329-350).

Rowstron, A., & Druschel, P. (2001). *Pastry: Scalable, decentralized object location, and routing for large-scale peer-to-peer systems.* Paper presented at the Middleware 2001.

Rowstron, A., & Druschel, P. (2001). Pastry: Scalable, decentralized object location and routing for large scale peer-to-peer systems (LNCS 2218, 329-350).

Rowstron, A., & Druschel, P. (2001). Pastry: Scalable, distributed object location and routing for large-scale peer-to-peer systems. In *Proceedings of the IFIP/ACM International Conference on Distributed Systems Platforms (Middleware).*

Rowstron, A., & Druschel, P. (2001). Pastry: Scalable, distributed object location and routing for large-scale peer-to-peer systems. In *Proceedings of IFIP/ACM International Conference on Distributed Systems Platforms (MIDDLEWARE).*

Rowstron, A., Kermarrec, A.-M., Castro, M., & Druschel, P. (2001). *SCRIBE: The design of a large-scale event notification infrastructure.* Paper presented at the Networked Group Communication.

Royer, E. M., & Perkins, C. E. (1999). Multicast operation of the ad-hoc on-demand distance vector routing protocol. In *Proceedings of the International Conference on Mobile Computing and Networking.*

Ryan, R. M., & Deci, E. L. (2000). Intrinsic and extrinsic motivations: Classic definitions and new directions. *Contemporary educational psychology, 25*, 54-67.

Sailhan, F. & Issarny, V. (2003). Cooperative caching in ad hoc networks. In *Proceedings of the 4th International Conference on Mobile Data Management (MDM).*

Saito, N., & Kitagawa, K. (2007). Overview of Peer-to-Peer Universal Computing Consortium (PUCC): Background, current status and future plan. In *Proceedings of 4th IEEE Consumer Communications and Networking Conference.*

Salem, N. B., Buttyán, L., Hubaux, J.-P., & Jakobsson, M. (2003). A charging and rewarding scheme for packet forwarding in multi-hop cellular networks. In *Proceedings of the IEEE/ACM Symposium on Mobile Ad Hoc Networking and Computing (MobiHOC).*

Salutation Consortium. (2005, Jun 30). *Salutation architecture specification.* Retrieved May 27, 2008, from http://web.archive.org/web/20050627074915/http://www.salutation.org/

Saraydar, C. U., Mandayam, N. B., & Goodman., D. J. (2002). Efficient power control via pricing in wireless data networks. *IEEE Transactions on Communications, 50*(2).

Sato, K., Katsumoto, M., & Miki, T. (2006). P2MVOD: Peer-to-peer mobile video on-demand. In *Proceedings of the 8th International Conference on Advanced Communication Technology.*

Satyanarayanan, M. (1996). Fundamental challenges in mobile computing. In Proceedings of the 15th ACM Symposium on Principles of Distributed Computing, Philadelphia, PA, USA.

Satyanarayanan, M. (2003). From the editor in chief: Of smart dust and brilliant rocks. *IEEE Pervasive Computing, 2*(4), 2-4.

Schlosser, D., Hoßfeld, T., & Tutschku, K. (2006). Comparison of robust cooperation strategies for P2P content distribution networks with multiple source download. In *Proceedings of the Sixth IEEE International Conference on Peer-to-Peer Computing (P2P2006)*, Cambridge, UK.

Schmidt, A. (2006). Ontology-based user context management: The challenges of dynamics and imperfection. In *Proceedings of the ODBASE 2006, On the Move Federated Conferences (OTM)*, Montpellier, France.

Schoder, D., Fischbach, K., & Schmitt, C. (2005). Core concepts in peer-to-peer networking. R. Subramanian & B. D. Goodman (Eds.), *Peer-to-Peer Computing: The Evolution of a Disruptive Technology.* Hershey, PA: Idea Group Publishing.

Schollmeier, R. (2001). A definition of peer-to-peer networking for the classification of peer-to-peer architectures and applications. In *Proceedings of the 1st International Conference on Peer-To-Peer Computing (P2P)*, Washington, DC, USA.

Schollmeier, R., Gruber, I., & Finkenzeller, M. (2002). Routing in peer-to-peer and mobile ad hoc networks: A comparison. In *Proceedings of International Workshop on Peer-to-Peer Computing.*

Schollmeier, R., Gruber, I., & Finkenzeller, M. (2002). Routing in mobile ad hoc and peer-to-peer networks. A comparison. In *Proceedings of the International Workshop on Peer-to-Peer Computing.*

Schollmeier, R., Gruber, I., & Niethammer, F. (2003). Protocol for peer-to-peer networking in mobile environments. In *Proceedings of 12th IEEE International Conference on Computer Communications and Networks.*

Schreiner, K. (2007). Where we at? Mobile phones bring GPS to the masses. *IEEE Computer Graphics and Applications, 27*(3), 6-11.

Schuler, C., Weber, R., Schuldt, H., & Schek, H. (2003). Peer-to-peer process execution with OSIRIS. In *Proceedings of the First International Conference on Service-Oriented Computing (ICSOC).*

Schwotzer, T., & Geihs, K. (2002). Shark - a system for management, synchronization and exchange of knowledge in mobile user groups. *Journal of Universal Computer Science, 8*(6), 644-651.

Seet, B., Lau, C., & Hsu, W. (2007). P2P models and complexity in MANETs. In D. Taniar (Ed.), *Encyclopedia of mobile computing and commerce.* Hershey, PA: Information Science Reference.

Seet, B.-C., Lau, C.-T., Hsu, W.-J., & Lee, B.-S. (2005). A mobile system of super-peers using city buses. In *Proceedings of the PerCom Workshops.*

Sen, S., & Wang, J. (2004). Analyzing peer-to-peer traffic across large networks. *IEEE/ACM Transactions on Networking, 12*(2), 219-232.

Seno, S., Budiarto, R., & Wan, T.-C. (2007). Survey and new approach in service discovery and advertisement for mobile ad hoc networks. *International Journal of Computer Science and Network Security, 7*(2), 275-284.

Sentilla Corporation, S. (2008). *Software architecture.* Retrieved September 10, 2008, from http://www.sentilla.com/software.html

Servetto, S. D., & Barrenechea, G. (2002). Constrained random walks on random graphs: Routing algorithms for large scale wireless sensor networks. In *Proceedings of 1st ACM international workshop on Wireless sensor networks and applications.*

Shaylor, N., Simon, D. N., & Bush, W. R. (2003). A Java virtual machine architecture for very small devices. In *Proceedings of the Special Interest Group on Programming Languages.*

Shen, H., & Xu, C-Z. (2005). Locality-aware randomized load balancing algorithms for DHT networks. In *Proceedings of the International Conference on Parallel Processing* (pp. 529-536).

Shen, H., Joseph, M. S., et al. (2005). PReCinCt: A scheme for cooperative caching in mobile peer-to-peer systems. In *Proceedings of the International Parallel and Distributed Processing Symposium.*

Shen, H., Joseph, M., Kumar, M., & Das, S. (2005). PReCinCt: A scheme for cooperative caching in mobile peer-to-peer systems. In *Proceedings of the 19th International Parallel and Distributed Computing Symposium (IPDPS).*

Shida, T., Sato, T., Nakayama, H., Kosaka, H., & Sugiyama, K. (2007). Robust HD video stream transmission for wireless DTV. *IEEE Transactions on Consumer Electronics, 53*(1), 96-99.

Shirky, C. (2008). *Here comes everybody: The power of organizing without organizations.* Penguin Press.

Shivakumar, N., & Venkatasubramanian, S. (1996). Efficient indexing for broadcast based wireless systems. Mobile *Networks and Applications, 1*(4), 433-446.

Singh, K., & Schulzrinne, H. (2004). *Peer-to-peer internet telephony using SIP* (Tech. Rep. CUCS-044-04, pp. 63-68). NY, USA: Columbia University.

Siveroni, I., Zisman, A., & Spanoudakis, G. (2008). Property specification and static verification of UML models. *Proceedings of the International Conference on Availability, Reliability and Security,* Barcelona, Spain.

Song, H., Zheng, H., & Jiang, X. (2008). *Diagnose P2PSIP overlay network failures; draft-zheng-p2psip-diagnose-02* (work in progress). Retrieved September 10, 2008, from IETF Internet Draft Database.

Song, J.W., & Yang, S.B. (2006). Improved load balancing algorithms in DHT-based dynamic P2P systems. In *Proceedings of the IASTED International Conference on Communications, Internet, and Information Technology* (pp. 218-224).

Sousa, J. P., & Garlan, D. (2002). Aura: An architectural framework for user mobility in ubiquitous computing environments. In *Proceedings of the 3rd Working IEEE/IFIP Conference on Software Architecture*, (pp. 29-43).

Spanoudakis, G., Kloukinas, C., & Androutsopoulos, K. (2008). Dynamic verification and control of mobile peer-to-peer systems. In *Proceedings of the 3rd International Conference on Internet Monitoring and Protection (ICIMP)*, Bucharest, Romania, to appear.

Srinivasan, V., Nuggehalli, P., Chiasserini, C., & Rao, R. (2003). Cooperation in wireless ad hoc networks. In *Proceedings of the IEEE INFOCOM.*

Srivastava, V., Neel, J., MacKenzie, A. B., Menon, R., DaSilva, L. A., Hicks, J. E., Reed, J. H., & Gilles, R. P. (2005). Using game theory to analyze wireless ad hoc networks. In *Proceedings of the IEEE Communications Surveys and Tutorials, 7*(2005), 46-56.

Steer, D. G., Strawczynski, L., Diffie, W., & Wiener, M. (1988). A secure audio teleconference system. In *Proceedings of Advances in Cryptology - CRYPTO'88*, (LNCS 403, 520-528).

Steiner, M., Tsudik, G., & Waidner, M. (1996). Diffie-Hellman key distribution extended to groups. In *Proceedings of the ACM Conference on Computer and Communication Security.*

Steiner, M., Tsudik, G., & Waidner, M. (2000). Key agreement in dynamic peer groups. *IEEE Transactions on Parallel and Distributed Systems, 11*(8), 769-780.

Stoica, I., Morris, R., Karger, D., Kaashoek, M., & Balakrishnan. H. (2001). Chord: A scalable peer-to-peer lookup service for internet applications. In *Proceedings of the ACM SIGCOMM Conference on Applications, Technologies, Architectures, and Protocols for Computer Communications.*

Stoica, I., Morris, R., Karger, D., Kaashoek, M.F., & Balakrishnan, H. (2001). Chord: A scalable peer-to-peer lookup service for Internet applications. In *Proceedings of ACM SIGCOMM Conference on Applications, Technologies, Architectures, and Protocols for Computer Communications.*

Stoica, I., Morris, R., Liben-Nowell, D., Karger, D. R., Kaashoek, M. F., Dabek, F., & Balakrishnan, H. (2003). Chord: A scalable peer-to-peer lookup protocol for internet applications. *IEEE/ACM Transactions on Networking, 11*(1), 17–32.

Strang, T. L.-P. (2004). A context modeling survey. In Proceedings of the *UbiComp 1st International Workshop on Advanced Context Modelling, Reasoning and Management*, Nottingham (pp. 34--41).

Stutzbach, D., & Rejaie, R. (2006). Understanding churn in peer-to-peer networks. In *Proceedings of the Internet Measurement Conference.*

Su, C.-J., & Tassiulas, L. (1998). Joint broadcast scheduling and user's cache management for efficient information delivery. In *Proceedings of the International Conference on Mobile Computing and Networking.*

Sumino, H., et al. (2003). A mobile multimedia content search using RDF. In *Proceedings of the 4th International Conference on Mobile Data Management.*

Sumino, H., et al. (2004). Design and implementation of a multicast instant messaging system on the mobile P2P network. In *Proceedings of the 1st International Conference on Mobile Computing and Ubiquitous Networking (ICMU).*

Sumino, H., et al. (2007). Home appliance control from mobile phones. In *Proceedings of the 4th IEEE Consumer Communications and Networking Conference (CCNC).*

Sumino, H., Ishikawa, N., & Kato, T. (2006). Design and implementation of P2P protocol for mobile phones. In *Proceedings of the 4th annual IEEE international conference on Pervasive Computing and Communications Workshops*, Pisa, Italy.

Sumino, H., Ishikawa, N., & Kato, T. (2006). Design and implementation of P2P protcol for mobile phones. In *Proceedings of the 3ʳᵈ IEEE International Workshop on Mobile Peer-to-Peer Computing (MP2P'06)*.

Sun Microsystems (2008). Java message service (JMS) API specification. Retrieved September 30, 2008, from http://java.sun.com/products/jms

Sun Microsystems, Inc. (1988). *RPC: Remote procedure call protocol specification version 2*. RFC 1057.

Sun Microsystems, Inc. (1994). *Java 2 micro edition technology for creating mobile devices*. Retrieved May 27, 2008, from http://java.sun.com/j2me

Sundresh, S., Wooyoung, K., & Agha, G. (2004). SENS: A sensor, environment and network simulator. In *Proceedings of the Simulation Symposium*.

Sung, Y.-W., Bishop, M., & Rao, S. (2006). Enabling contribution awareness in an overlay broadcasting system. *ACM SIGCOMM Computer Communication Review, 36*(4), 411-422.

Sutton, P., Arkins, R., & Segall, B. (2001). Supporting disconnectedness-transparent information delivery for mobile and invisible computing. In *Proceedings of 1ˢᵗ International Symposium on Cluster Computing and the Grid*, Washington, DC, USA.

Talia, D., & Trunfio, P. (2003). Toward a synergy between P2P and grids. *IEEE Internet Computing, 7*(4), 94–95.

Tan, K.-L., & Ooi, B. C. (2000). D*ata dissemination in wireless computing environments*. Norwell, MA. USA: Kluwer Academic Publishers.

Tedjamulia, S. J. J., Dean, D. L., Olsen, D. R., & Albrecht, C. C. (2005). Motivating content contributions to online communities: Toward a more comprehensive theory. In *Proceedings of the 38ᵗʰ Hawaii International Conference on System Sciences*.

Terry, M., Mynatt, E. D., Ryall, K., & Leigh, D. (2002). Social net: Using patterns of physical proximity over time to infer shared interests. *CHI extended abstracts on Human Factors in Computing Systems*.

The Napster Protocol (2001). Retrieved May 13, 2008, from http://opennap.sourceforge.net/napster.txt.

The XLattice Project (2005). *XLattice*. Retrieved October 7, 2008, from http://xlattice.sourceforge.net/.

TinyOS. (2008). Retrieved October 27, 2008, from http://www.tinyos.net/

Titzer, B. L., Lee, D. K., & Palsberg, J. (2005). Avrora: Scalable sensor network simulation with precise timing. In *Proceedings of the International conference on Information processing in sensor networks*.

Tompros, S., & Denazis S. (2008). Interworking of heterogeneous access networks and QoS provisioning via IP multimedia core networks. *Computer Networks, 52*(1), 215-227.

Triantafillou, P., Xiruhaki, C., Koubarakis, M., & Ntarmos, N. (2003). Towards high performance peer-to-peer content and resource sharing systems. In *Proceedings of the Conference on Innovative Data Systems Research (CIDR)*, Asilomar, CA, USA.

Tsai, K.C., & Chen, C. (2006). A server reassignment algorithm for DHT load balance and the effect of heterogeneity. In *Proceedings of the IEEE Global Telecommunications Conference*. Retrieved May 30, 2008, from IEEE database.

Tsutsui, H., et al. (2007). Implementation of AV streaming system using peer-to-peer communication. In *Proceedings of 4ᵗʰ IEEE Consumer Communications and Networking Conference*.

Tutschku, K. (2004). A measurement-based traffic profile of the eDonkey filesharing service. In *Proceedings of the 5ᵗʰ Passive and Active Measurement Workshop (PAM2004)*, Antibes Juan-les-Pins, France.

Tutschku, K. (2007). *P2P-based network and service operation for the emerging future internet* (Tech. Rep. No. 397). Würzburg, Germany: University of Würzburg, Lehrstuhl für Informatik III.

Tutschku, K., Tran-Gia, P., & Andersen, F.-U. (2007). *Trends in network and service operation for the emerging future internet* (Tech. Rep. No. 431). Würzburg, Germany: University of Würzburg, Lehrstuhl für Informatik III.

UMA Consortium. (2004). Unlicensed mobile access (UMA). Architecture (Stage 2), R1.0.0, Technical specification.

UPnP Forum. (1999). Retrieved May 30, 2008, from http://www.upnp.org

UPnP Forum. (2007, Sep 7). *UPnP device architecture.* Retrieved May 27, 2008, from http://www.upnp.org/resources/upnpresources.zip

Urpi, A., Bonuccelli, M., & Giordano, S. (2003). Modeling cooperation in mobile ad hoc networks: A formal description of selfishness. In *Proceedings of the 1st Workshop on Modeling and Optimization in Mobile, Ad Hoc and Wireless Networks.*

van der Merwe, J., Dawoud, D.S., & McDonald, S. (2007). A survey on peer-to-peer key management for mobile ad hoc networks. *ACM Computing Surveys, 39*(1), 1-32.

Varian, H. (1992). *Microeconomic analysis.* Norton.

Varshavsky, A., Reid, B., & de Lara, E. (2005). A cross-layer approach to service discovery and selection in MANETs. In *Proceedings of the 2nd International Conference on Mobile Ad hoc and Sensor Systems,* Washington, DC, USA (pp. 1-8).

Vaughan-Nichols, S. J. (2003). OSs battle in the smartphone market. *Computer, 36*(6), 10-12.

Verkasalo, H.T. (2007). Handset-based measurement of smartphone service evolution in Finland. *Journal of Targeting, Measurement and Analysis for Marketing. 16*(1), 7-25.

Vickrey, W. (1961). Counterspeculation, auctions, and competitive sealed tenders. *Journal of Finance, 16*(1), 8-37.

Vroom, V. (1964). *Work and motivation.* John Wiley and Sons.

W3C Consortium. (2004, Feb 14). *Ontology web language reference.* Retrieved May 22, 2008, from http://www.w3.org/TR/owl-ref/

Wa, L., & Zhu, W. (2008). A carrier grade peer-to-peer network architecture. In *Proceedings of the First ITU-T Kaleidoscope Academic Conference on Innovations in NGN: Future Networks and Services.*

Walkerdine, J,. Melville, L., & Sommerville, I. (2005). *Reference Architectures for Peer-to-Peer Applications* (Tech. Rep. COMP-009-2005). UK: Lancaster University, Computing Department.

Walkerdine, J., & Lock. S. (2007). Towards secure mobile P2P systems. In *Proceedings of the P2P Systems and Applications (P2PSA),* Mauritius.

Walkerdine, J., Lock, R., & Lock, S. (2006). D2 - analysis of security characteristics of peer-to-peer architectures. EC Project Deliverable, PEPERS IST-2004-026901.

Walkerdine, J., Melville, L., & Sommerville, I. (2002). Dependability properties of P2P architectures. In *Proceedings of the IEEE P2P,* Sweden.

Wang, A. I., Bjørnsgård, T., & Saxlund, K. (2007). Peer2Me - rapid application framework for mobile peer-to-peer applications. In *Proceedings of International Symposium on Collaborative Technologies and Systems (CTS),* Orlando, Florida, USA.

Wang, A. I., Norum, M. S., & Lund, C.-H. W. (2006). Issues related to development of wireless peer-to-peer games in J2ME. In *Proceedings of the 1st Conference on Entertainment Systems (ENSYS),* Guadeloupe, French Caribbean.

Wang, A. I., Sørensen, C.-F., & Fossum, T. (2005). Mobile peer-to-peer technology used to promote spontaneous collaboration. In *Proceedings of International Symposium on Collaborative Technologies and Systems (CTS),* Saint Louis, Missouri, USA.

Wang, F., & Krunz, M. (2006). GMAC: A game-theoretic MAC protocol for mobile ad hoc networks. In *Proceedings of the WiOpt'06: Modeling and Optimization in Mobile, Ad Hoc and Wireless Networks.*

Wang, F., Xiong, Y., & Liu, J. (2007). mTreebone: A hybrid tree/mesh overlay for application-layer live video multicast. In *Proceedings of the International Conference on Distributed Computing Systems (ICDCS).*

Wasserman, S., & Faust, K. (1994). *Social network analysis: Method and applications.* Cambridge University Press.

Watts, D. (1999). *Small worlds: The dynamics of networks between order and randomness.* Princeton Univeristy Press.

Watts, D., & Strogatz, S. (1998). Collective dynamics of small-world' networks. *Nature, 393*(6), 440–442.

Wehrle, K., Gotz, S., & Rieche, S. (2005). Distributed hash tables. In R. Steinmetz & K. Wehrle (Eds.), *Peer-to-Peer Systems and Applications.* Springer Berlin / Heidelberg.

Wen, G., Longshe, H., & Qiang, F. (2006). Recent advances in peer-to-peer media streaming systems. *China Communications, 4*(5), 52-57.

Werner-Allen, G., Swieskowski, P., & Welsh, M. (2005). MoteLab: A wireless sensor network testbed. In *Proceedings of the IEEE International Conference on Information Processing in Sensor Networks.*

Wiberg, M., & Grönlund, Ä. (2000). Exploring mobile CSCW: Five areas of questions for further research. In *Proceedings of IRIS23 (Information Research in Scandinavia),* Trollhättan, Sweden.

Wishart, R., Robinson, R., Indulska, J., & Jøsang, A. (2005). SuperstringRep: Reputation-enhanced service discovery. In *Proceedings of the 28th Australasian Conference on Computer Science* (pp. 49-57). Newcastle, Australia: Australian Computer Society, Inc.

Wolfson, O., Xu, B., Yin, H., & Cao, H. (2006). Search-and-discover in mobile p2p network databases. In *Proceedings of the 26th IEEE International Conference on Distributed Computing Systems (ICDCS).*

World Wide Web Consortium. (2001). *Web services description language 1.1.* Retrieved May 13, 2008, from http://www.w3.org/TR/wsdl

World Wide Web Consortium. (2002). *SOAP version 1.2.* Retrieved May 13, 2008, from http://www.w3.org/TR/soap

World Wide Web Consortium. (2006). *Extensible markup language (XML) 1.0 (fourth edition).* Retrieved May 13, 2008, from http://www.w3.org/TR/xml

Wu, C., & Li, B. (2007). Strategies of conflict in co-existing streaming overlays. In *Proceedings of IEEE International Conference on Computer Communications (INFOCOM).*

Wu, J. (2005). *Handbook on theoretical and algorithmic aspects of sensor, ad hoc wireless, and peer-to-peer networks.* Boston, MA, USA: AUERBACH.

Wu, J., & Axelrod R. (1995). How to cope with noise in the iterated prisoner's dilemma. *Journal of Conflict Resolution, 39*(1), 183-189.

Wu, J., & Zitterbart, M. (2001). Service awareness and its challenges in mobile ad hoc networks. In *Proceedings of the Tagungsband der GI/OCG-Jahrestagung,* Vienna, Austria (pp. 551-557).

Wu, W., & Tan, K.-L. (2005). Cooperative prefetching strategies for mobile peers in a broadcast wnvironment. In *Proceedings of the International Workshop on Databases, Information Systems and Peer-to-Peer Computing.*

Wu, W., & Tan, K.-L. (2006). Global cache management in non-uniform mobile broadcast. In *Proceedings of the International Conference on Mobile Data Management,* Nara, Japan.

Xu, B., & Wolfson, O. (2004). Data management in mobile peer-to-peer networks. In *Proceedings of the International Workshop on Databases, Information Systems and Peer-to-Peer Computing.*

Xu, B., Ouksel, A., & Wolfson, O. (2004). Opportunistic resource exchange in inter-vehicle ad hoc networks. In *Proceedings of the IEEE International Conference on Mobile Data Management (MDM).*

Xu, J., Hu, Q., et al. (2000). SAIU: An efficient cache replacement policy for wireless on-demand broadcasts. In *Proceedings of the Conference on Information and Knowledge Management.*

Xu, J., Hu, Q., et al. (2004). Performance evaluation of an optimal cache replacement policy for wireless data dissemination. IEEE *Transactions on Knowledge and Data Engineering, 16*(1), 125-139.

Xue, G., Li, M., Deng, Q., & You, J. (2004). Stable group model in mobile peer-to-peer media streaming system. In *Proceedings of the 1ˢᵗ IEEE International Conference on Mobile Ad-hoc and Sensor Systems (MASS)*.

Xue, Y., Li, B., & Nahrstedt, K. (2003). Price based resource allocation in wireless ad hoc networks. In *Proceedings of the 11ᵗʰ International Workshop on Quality of Service*.

Yao, J. J., & Chen, H. H. (2007). Fixed-mobile convergence, streaming multimedia services, and peer-to-peer communication. (LNCS 4577, pp. 52-56).

Yeung, M. K. H., & Kwok, Y.-K. (2005a). Wireless cache invalidation schemes with link adaptation and downlink traffic. *IEEE Transactions on Mobile Computing, 4*(1), 68-83.

Yeung, M. K. H., & Kwok, Y.-K. (2005b). A game theoretic approach to energy efficient cooperative cache maintenance in MANETs. In *Proceedings of the 16ᵗʰ IEEE International Symposium on Personal, Indoor and Mobile Radio Communications*.

Yeung, M. K. H., & Kwok, Y.-K. (2006a). A game theoretic approach to power aware wireless data access. *IEEE Transactions on Mobile Computing, 5*(8), 1057-1073.

Yeung, M. K. H., & Kwok, Y.-K. (2006b). On maximizing revenue for client-server based wireless data access in the presence of peer-to-peer sharing. In *Proceedings of the 17ᵗʰ IEEE International Symposium on Personal, Indoor and Mobile Radio Communications*.

Yi, S., & Kravets, R. (2003). MOCA: Mobile certificate authority for wireless ad hoc networks. In *Proceedings of the 2ⁿᵈ Annual PKI Research Workshop*.

Yin, J., Wang, X., & Agrawal, D. P. (2005). Modeling and optimization for wireless local area network (WLAN). *Computer Communications Journal, Special Issue on Performance Issues of Wireless LANs, PANs, and Ad Hoc Networks, 28*, 1204 -1213.

Yin, L., & Cao, G. (2004). Adaptive power-aware prefetch in wireless networks. *IEEE Transactions on Wireless Communications, 3*(5), 1648-1658.

Yin, L. & Cao, G. (2004). Supporting cooperative caching in ad hoc networks. In *Proceedings of IEEE International Conference on Computer Communications (INFOCOM)*.

Yin, L., & Cao, G. (2006). Supporting cooperative caching in ad hoc networks. *IEEE Transactions on Mobile Computing, 5*(1), 77-89.

Yoneki, E., Hui, P., Chan, S. Y., & Crowcroft, J. (2007). A socio-aware overlay for publish/subscribe communication in delay tolerant networks. In *Proceedings of the 10ᵗʰ ACM/IEEE International Symposium on Modeling, Analysis and Simulation of Wireless and Mobile Systems (MSWiM)*, Crete, Greece.

Yoon, J., Liu, M., & Noble, B. (2003). Random waypoint considered harmful. In *Proceedings of the 22ⁿᵈ Annual Joint Conference of the IEEE Computer and Communications Societies*.

Zahn, T. C. (2006). *Structured peer-to-peer services for mobile ad hoc networks*. Unpublished doctoral dissertation, Fachbereich Mathematik u. Informatik, Freie Universitat, Berlin, Germany.

Zahn, T., & Schiller, J. H. (2005). MADPastry: A DHT substrate for practicably sized MANETs. In *Proceedings of the Workshop on Applications Services in Wireless Networks*.

Zeidler, A., & Fiege, L. (2003). Mobility support with REBECA. In *Proceedings of 23rd International Conference on Distributed Computing Systems Workshops*. Providence, Rhode Island, USA.

Zeinalipour-Yazti, D., Kalogeraki, V., & Gunopulos, D. (2004). Information retrieval in peer-to-peer systems. *IEEE CiSE Magazine, Special Issue on Web Engineering*, 12–20.

Zenel, B., & Duchamp, D. (1997). A general proxy filtering mechanism applied to the mobile environment, In *Proceedings of the Third Annual ACM/IEEE Confer-*

ence on Mobile Computing and Networking, Budapest, Hungary.

Zhan, T., & Schiller, J. (2005). MadPastry: A dht substrate for practicably sized MANETs. In *Proceedings of the 5ᵗʰ Workshop on Applications and Services in Wireless Networks (ASWN)*.

Zhang, H., Udagawa, T., Arita, T., Tsuji, J., Okada, K., Sasase, I., & Nakagawa, M. (2001). Wireless 1394: A new standard for integrated wireless broadband home networking. In *Proceedings of IEEE Vehicular Technology Conference (VTC)*, Rhodes Island, Greece.

Zhang, J., Niu, J., He, R., Hu, J., & Sun, L. (2007). P2P-leveraged mobile live streaming. In *Proceedings of the 21ˢᵗ International Conference on Advanced Information Networking and Applications Workshops*.

Zhang, X., Liu, J., Li, B., & Yum, T.-S. P. (2005). DONet/CoolStreaming: A data-driven overlay network for live media streaming. In *Proceedings of IEEE International Conference on Computer Communications (INFOCOM)*.

Zhao, B. Y., Kubiatowicz, J., & Joseph, A. D. (2001). *Tapestry: An infrastructure for fault-tolerant wide-area location and routing*. Retrieved May 30, 2008, from http://cs-www.cs.yale.edu/homes/arvind/cs425/doc/tapestry.pdf

Zhao, B.Y., Huang L., Stribling, J., Rhea, S. C., Joseph, A. D., & Kubiatowicz, J. (2004). Tapestry: A global-scale overlay for rapid service deployment. *IEEE Journal on Selected Areas in Communications, 22*(1), 41-53.

Zheng, B., & Lee, D. L. (2005). Information dissemination via wireless broadcast. *Communications of ACM, 48*(5), 105-110.

Zheng, B., Wu, X., et al. (2005). TOSA: A near-optimal scheduling algorithm for multi-channel data broadcast. In *Proceedings of the 6th International Conference on Mobile Data Management*, Ayia Napa, Cyprus.

Zheng, P., & Ni, L. M. (2006). Spotlight: The rise of the smart phone. *IEEE Distributed Systems Online, 7*(3), 1-14.

Zhong, S., Chen, J., & Yang, Y.-R. (2003). Sprite: A simple, cheat-proof, credit based system for mobile ad hoc networks. In *Proceedings of the IEEE INFOCOM*.

Zhong, S., Li, L. E., Liu, Y. G., & Yang, Y. R. (2005). On designing incentive-compatible routing and forwarding protocols in wireless ad hoc networks: an integrated approach using game theoretical and cryptographic techniques. In *Proceedings of the ACM MOBICOM*.

Zhou, L., & Haas, Z. J. (1999). Securing ad hoc networks. *IEEE Network, Special Issue on Network Security, 13*(6), 24–30.

Zhu, F., Mutka, M. W., & Ni, L. M. (2005). Service discovery in pervasive computing environments. *Pervasive Computing, 4*(4), 81-90.

Zhu, F., Zhu, W., Mutka, M., & Lionel, N. (2005). Expose or not? A progressive exposure approach for service discovery in pervasive computing environments. In *Proceedings of the 3ʳᵈ IEEE International Conference on Pervasive Computing and Communications*, (pp. 225-234).

Zhu, Y., & Hu, Y. (2004). Towards efficient load balancing in structured P2P systems. In *Proceedings of the International Parallel and Distributed Processing Symposium*. Retrieved May 30, 2008, from DBLP database.

Zhu, Y., & Hu, Y. (2005). Efficient, proximity-aware load balancing for DHT-based P2P systems. *IEEE Transactions on Parallel and Distributed Systems, 16*(4), 349-361.

Zoels, S., Despotovic, Z., & Kellerer, W. (2006). Cost-based analysis of hierarchical DHT design. In *Proceedings of the 6ᵗʰ IEEE International Conference Peer-to-Peer Computing (P2P2006)*.

Zoels, S., Schollmeier, R., Kellerer, W., & Tarlano, A. (2005). The hybrid chord protocol: A peer-to-peer lookup service for context-aware mobile applications. In *Proceedings of the Networking-ICN 2005, 4ᵗʰ International Conference on Networking*, Reunion Island, France.

Zoels, S., Schollmeier, R., Kellerer, W., & Tarlano, A. (2005). The hybrid chord protocol: A peer-to-peer lookup service for context-aware mobile applications. In *Proceedings of the 4th International Conference on Networking (ICN 2005)*.

Zoels, S., Schubert, S., Kellerer, W., & Despotovic, Z. (2006). Hybrid DHT design for mobile environments. In *Proceedings of the International Workshop on Agents and Peer-to-Peer Computing (AP2PC 2006)*, Hakodate, Japan.

About the Contributors

Boon-Chong Seet obtained his PhD in computer engineering from Nanyang Technological University, Singapore, in 2005. Upon graduation, he was employed as a research fellow under the Singapore-MIT (Boston) Alliance (SMA) program at the National University of Singapore. In March 2007, he was awarded a visiting scholarship to the Technical University of Madrid, Spain, to pursue research under an EU-funded project on multi-disciplinary advanced research in user-centric wireless network enabling technologies (MADRINET). Since December 2007, he is with Auckland University of Technology, New Zealand, as a faculty member in its Department of Electrical and Electronic Engineering. His research activities are mainly in the areas of mobile computing, mobile networking, and mobile communications.

* * *

Panayotis Antoniadis is a postdoctoral fellow at University Pierre & Marie Curie (Paris 6). His main research contributions are in the economic modelling and incentive mechanisms for peer-to-peer systems (2002-2006) and in distributed scheduling algorithms for high-speed switches (2000). He is currently working on the design of incentive mechanisms for shared network testbed infrastructures and social software and community building for neighborhood wireless mesh networks. He received his B.Sc. and MSc degree from the Computer Science Department of University of Crete in 1998 and 2000 respectively and his Ph.D degree from the Department of Informatics at Athens University of Economics and Business in 2006 under the supervision of Prof. Costas Courcoubetis.

Nicklas Beijar is working as a research scientist in the Department of Communications and Networking of Helsinki University of Technology. He received his MSc and LicSc degrees in telecommunications engineering from Helsinki University of Technology in 2002 and 2004, respectively. He is currently working towards a PhD degree in Helsinki University of Technology. His research interests include search and service discovery algorithms for mobile peer-to-peer networks and ad-hoc networks, especially focusing on performance evaluation. He is also studying specific application scenarios and architectures for mobile peer-to-peer systems, including P2PSIP.

Andreas Berl received his diploma degree (equiv. to Master of Science) from the University of Passau in Germany, in 2005. Since then he has been pursuing his PhD at the research group for computer networks and computer communications at the University of Passau, chaired by professor De Meer. His main research interests include the field of Mobile P2P (a combination of mobile communication and peer-to-peer mechanisms) and the field of virtualization technologies and their management in the context of next generation networks and home networks. He is involved in the Mobile P2P research project "Design and Performance Evaluation of Protocols for Peer-to-Peer Services in Mobile Networks". This project is done in cooperation with the research group "Informatik III" of the University of Würzburg, and is funded by the German research association (DFG - Deutsche Forschungsgemeinschaft). Additionally he is involved in the EU funded FP7 project AutoI (Autonomic Internet). He is member of the Networks of Excellence EuroNGI/EuroFGI/EuroNF (Design and Engineering of the Next Generation Internet), which is funded by the EU.

Marco Conti is a research director at IIT, an institute of the Italian National Research Council (CNR). He co-authored the book "Metropolitan Area Networks" (1997) and is co-editor of the books "Mobile Ad Hoc Networking" (2004) and "Mobile Ad Hoc Networks: From Theory to Reality" (2007). He published in journals and conference proceedings more than 200 research papers related to design, modeling, and performance evaluation of computer-network architectures and protocols. He served as TPC chair of *IEEE PerCom 2006,* IFIP-TC6 Conferences *Networking* 2002 and *PWC* 2003, and as TPC co-chair of *ACM WoWMoM 2002, WiOpt '04, IEEE WoWMoM* 2005, and *ACM MobiHoc* 2006. He served as general chair of *ACM REALMAN* 2006 and *IEEE MASS* 2007, and as general co-chair of *IEEE WoWMoM* 2006, and *ACM MobiOpp* 2007. He is the Associate Editor in Chief of *Pervasive and Mobile Computing* Journal, and he is on the editorial board of *IEEE Transactions on Mobile Computing*, and *Ad Hoc Networks*.

D.S. Dawoud received his BSc and MSc degrees from Cairo University in 1965 and 1969 respectively all in telecommunication. He received his PhD in 1973 from Russia in the field of computer engineering. Since 2002, he is a professor of computer engineering at the University of Kwa-Zulu Natal (former University of Natal), where he teaches and conducts researches in the fields of embedded systems, network security and computer architectures. Prior to 2002 he was Professor of Computer Engineering at the University of Botswana (from 1993 to 2001), an expert with United Nation at Nairobi- Kenya where he established a microprocessor department at Civil Aviation. From 1984 to 1993, he was a professor at the National Research Institute – Academy of Science and Technology – Egypt. He has published over 120 papers in international conferences and journals, holding three patents in the field of memory design, supervised more than 15 PhD and 30 MSc degrees.

Hermann de Meer has been an assistant professor at Hamburg University, Germany, a visiting professor at Columbia University in New York, USA, a research fellow of the German research association (DFG - Deutsche Forschungsgemeinschaft) and a reader at University College London. He is currently appointed as a professor at the Chair of Computer Networks and Computer Communications of the University of Passau. Since August 2006, he has been appointed as Director of the unique and interdisciplinary Institute of IT-Security and Security Law (ISL). Professor De Meer is co-authoring a highly cited book on Queuing Networks and Markov Chains - Modelling and Performance Evaluation with Computer Science Applications, published by John Wiley in its second edition in 2006. In 2005 he chaired one of the prime events in the area of quality of service in the Internet, the 13th International Workshop on Quality of Service (IWQoS'05 Passau). He has also chaired the first International Workshop on Self-Organizing Systems IWSOS 2006 in Passau. His research interests include performance modelling and simulation of computer and communication systems, quality of service, internet protocols, self-organization, peer-to-peer networks, home networking, security and mobile computing.

Franca Delmastro is a research associate at the IIT Institute of the National Research Council (CNR), Italy. She received the MS Degree in computer engineering and the PhD in information engineering, both from the University of Pisa, in 2002 and 2006 respectively. She joint IIT in 2003. Her research interests include ad hoc, mesh and opportunistic networks, with particular attention to routing and forwarding protocols, mobile p2p systems, multicasting for ad hoc networks, and distributed applications. She is currently working in the framework of EU Haggle project. She has been serving as the TPC member of the Annual IEEE Workshop on Mobile Peer-to-Peer computing since 2007.

Michael Duelli studied Computer Science and mathematics at the University of Würzburg, Germany. He received his university diploma degree in Computer Science in 2007. Since then, he is a researcher at the Department of Distributed Systems at the University of Würzburg and pursuing his PhD. His current research focuses on multi-layer network design and optimization of optical transport networks—especially Carrier Ethernet—in combination with performance evaluation and resilience analysis.

Markus Endler obtained his Dr. rer. nat. in Computer Science from the Technical University in Berlin in 1992, and the title of Professor Livre-docente from the University of São Paulo in 2001. From 1989 to 1993 he worked as a researcher at the GMD Forschungsstelle Karlsruhe (Germany), and from 1994 to 2000 as an Assistant Professor at the Institute of Mathematics and Statistics of the University of São Paulo. Since 2001, he is with the Department of Informatics of the Pontifícia Universidade Católica in Rio de Janeiro, where he is an Associate Professor. His main research interests include mobile and ubiquitous computing, and middleware for context- and location-aware mobile applications. He is member of the ACM, the Brazilian Computer Society (SBC) and of the IFIP Working Group 6.1.

Pascal Felber is a professor of Computer Science at the University of Neuchâtel, Switzerland, working in the field of dependable and distributed systems. Previously, he worked at Oracle Corporation and Bell-Labs (Lucent Technologies) in the USA, and at Institut EURECOM in France. He received his MSc and PhD degrees in Computer Science from the Swiss Federal Institute of Technology. He has published over 80 research papers in various journals and conferences.

Jie Feng is currently a PhD Candidate with professor Lisong Xu in the Department of Computer Science and Engineering at the University of Nebraska-Lincoln (UNL). Her research interests are design and analysis of network protocols and architectures. She is currently working as a Research Assistant on "Stochastic TCP Friendliness - Exploring the Design Space of TCP Friendly Traffic Control in the Best-Effort Internet", which is a research project funded by the University of Nebraska-Lincoln and by U.S National Science Foundation (NSF).

Abdulbaset Gaddah received his BS degree in 1993 from the Higher Institute of Science and Technology, Libya and MCS degree in 2000 from Carleton University, Canada. He is currently pursuing a PhD degree in systems and computer engineering at Carleton University. His primary research interests include middleware technologies (such as pub/sub, CORBA, Java RMI, JMS, and J2ME), techniques for multimedia transcoding and filtrations, and adaptive mobile applications.

Antônio Tadeu A. Gomes is a researcher at the National Laboratory for Scientific Computing (LNCC), Brazil. He received his PhD in Computer Science from the Pontifical Catholic University of

Rio de Janeiro (PUC-Rio), Brazil, in 2005. His research interests include quality of service, mobile computing, grid computing, and software architecture and modeling. He is a member of the ACM and the Brazilian Computer Society (SBC).

Erkki Harjula is working as a research scientist and a project manager in MediaTeam Oulu research group at University of Oulu, Finland. He received his MSc degree in Electrical and Information engineering from University of Oulu, Finland, in 2007. He is currently working towards a PhD degree in the same university. His interests lie on mobile computing and communication research. More specifically, he is focusing on the performance of heterogeneous structured P2P networks from the viewpoint of mobile devices and networks, including topics such as load balancing and protocol-level DHT optimization.

Jani Hautakorpi is working as a research scientist in Nomadiclab, which is part of Ericsson Research. He has a BSc degree from Satakunta University of Applied Sciences (SAMK) and an MSc degree from Tampere University of Technology (TUT). Currently he is working towards a PhD degree in Helsinki University of Technology (HUT), Finland. His research interests lie on decentralized interpersonal communication mechanisms, especially on the aspects related to security, interworking, service replication, and incentives. More concretely, a considerable amount of his work is related to P2PSIP (Peer-to-peer Session Initiation Protocol) technology. In addition, he also contributes to standardization work, mainly in the IETF.

Johan Hjelm is a senior research engineer in Ericsson Research Japan. He has been a project manager for various research projects in Ericsson, including EU FP5 and FP6 projects. A journalist of some 12 years, he was an editor in chief for the Swedish magazine Nätvärlden before switching to engineering. He has been a visiting engineer at MIT, and is the author of numerous research papers, including the first paper on how to use the web on mobile devices, and 12 books, the latest of which, "Why IPTV: Interactivity, Technologies, Services" has been published by John Wiley and Sons in October 2008.

Tobias Hoßfeld is a research assistant at the Chair of Distributed Systems, University of Würzburg, Germany, since 2003. His main research interests cover self-organization mechanisms in overlay networks and P2P systems, with a special focus on mobile environments like 3G and 4G, as well as investigations on quality of experience. In this context, the design and evaluation of ISP-friendly IPTV and P2P-TV systems applying QoE control are currently under investigation. Tobias Hoßfeld is involved in several industrial projects (Bosch, Datev, Siemens AG, Bertelsmann Arvato, TMobile, France Telecom) and national (MobileP2P funded by DFG) and international research projects (SmoothIt, EuroNF funded by European Commission). His recent publications cover the application, the modeling, and the performance evaluation of overlay techniques in complex, heterogeneous networks, as well as measurements and traffic characterization of popular Internet applications, like Skype, Joost or YouTube. Analytical queuing models of the user behavior in client/server and P2P-based content distribution networks were derived.

Norihiro Ishikawa received the BE, ME and PhD degrees in Information Engineering from Kyoto University, Japan, in 1978, 1980 and 2003, respectively. From 1980 to 1999, he was with NTT. Since 1999, he has been with NTT DoCoMo Inc., working on ATM, Internet protocols, multimedia communication, mobile Internet technologies, and ubiquitous computing. He is a member of IEEE.

Vana Kalogeraki is an associate professor at the University of California, Riverside. Her research interests include distributed and real-time systems, peer-to-peer systems and distributed sensor systems. She received her PhD from the University of California, Santa Barbara in 2000. In 2001-2002, she held a Research Scientist position at Hewlett-Packard Labs in Palo Alto, CA. She has published numerous technical papers, including co-authoring the Object Management Group (OMG) CORBA Dynamic Scheduling Standard. She has delivered tutorials and seminars on peer-to-peer computing. She has organized and served on program committees for several technical conferences. She has served as the General Chair of the "14th International Workshop on Parallel and Distributed Real-Time Systems (WPDRTS 2006)", Program co-Chair of the "10th IEEE International Symposium on Object/component/service-oriented Real-time distributed Computing (ISORC 2007)", the "IEEE International Conference on Pervasive Services (ICPS 2005)", the "13th International Workshop on Parallel and Distributed Real-Time Systems (WPDRTS 2005) and the "International Workshop on Databases, Information Systems and Peer-to-Peer Computing" at VLDB 2003. She is currently an associate editor for the *Ad hoc Networks Journal* and the *Computer Standards & Interfaces Journal*. Her research is supported by NSF.

Helen D. Karatza is an associate professor in the Department of Informatics at the Aristotle University of Thessaloniki, Greece. Her research interests include performance evaluation of parallel and distributed systems, scheduling, resource allocation in the grid and modeling and simulation.

Takeshi Kato received the BE degree in electrical engineering and ME degree in material science from Keio University, Japan in 1999 and 2001. Since 2001, he has been an engineer at NTT DoCoMo Inc., and involved in researches of mobile Internet.

Kazuhiro Kitagawa is associate professor at the Graduate School of Media and Governance, Keio University, Japan. He is also the vice-chair of PUCC (P2P Universal Computing Consortium). He was the Activity lead for the W3C World Wide Web Consortium's Device Independence and is responsible for the architectural and technical leadership in the area of universal Web access from various kinds of devices including cell-phones, PDAs and appliances. His research interests are markup language in general, computer networking, machine-to-machine communication and the Web for small devices. He holds a BA and a MS in mathematics from Keio University.

Peter Kropf has received his diploma (lic. phil. nat) in mathematics and his PhD degrees in Computer Science from the University of Bern, Switzerland. From 1994 to 1999, he was an assistant and associate professor at Laval University, Quebec, Canada. Thereafter, he was appointed as an associate professor at the Department of Computer Science and operations research (DIRO) at University of Montreal, Canada. Since October 2003, he is a full Professor and head of Department at the Computer Science Department of the University of Neuchâtel, Switzerland. Furthermore, he is a member and researcher at the Center of Research for Transportation (CRT), Montreal. He has published over 90 research papers in the field of parallel and distributed systems, simulation and e-commerce technologies.

Yu-Kwong (Ricky) Kwok is an associate professor in the Electrical and Computer Engineering Department at the Colorado State University. Prior to joining CSU, he was an associate professor at the University of Hong Kong. He received his PhD degree in Computer Science from the Hong Kong University of Science and Technology in 1997. In the areas of distributed systems and wireless networking, he has co-authored over 180 technical papers and two textbooks. Ricky currently serves on the editorial board of the *Journal of Parallel and Distributed Computing* for the subject area Peer-to-Peer (P2P) Computing, and the International Journal of Sensor Networks. His current research endeavors are mainly related to game theoretic security and incentive issues for wireless systems, and resource management for dynamically reconfigurable chip multiprocessor systems. Ricky received the Outstanding Young Researcher Award from the University of Hong Kong in November 2004.

Raphaël Kummer is a research assistant and PhD candidate at the University of Neuchâtel, Switzerland. He started his PhD studies in 2004 after receiving his MSc in Computer Science from the same university. He is currently working in the field of Mobile ad-hoc Networks (MANET), with focus on information lookup and distribution infrastructure in MANETs.

Thomas Kunz received a double honors degree in Computer Science and business administration in 1990 and Dr. Ing. degree in Computer Science in 1994, both from the Technical University of Darmstadt, Federal Republic of Germany. He is currently a professor in systems and computer engineering at Carleton University, Canada. His research interests are primarily in the area of wireless and mobile computing. The main thrust is to facilitate the development of innovative next-generation mobile applications on resource-constraint, hand-held devices, exploring the required network architectures (MANETs, wireless mesh networks, wireless sensor networks), network protocols (routing, Mobile IP, QoS support), and middleware layers. He has authored or co-authored over 130 technical papers, received a number of awards, and is involved in national and international conferences and workshops.

Li Li is a senior research scientist at the Communications Research Centre of the Government of Canada. Before joining CRC, she had worked in the telecommunications industry for 10 years, as an engineer, system architect, product manager and chief system architect. At CRC, Li Li works in the area of tactical radio networks, responsible for projects supporting Canadian national defence and NATO collaborations. Her current research interest includes routing in tactical mobile radio network, network enabled services, P2P in mobile ad hoc networks, localization in wireless sensor networks, and performance studies of mobile ad hoc and sensor networks.

Luciana S. Lima is a systems analyst at the Tecgraf Laboratory (PUC-Rio), Brazil. From 2005 to 2007 she worked as a researcher at the National Laboratory for Scientific Computing (LNCC), Brazil. She received her PhD in Computer Science from the Pontifical Catholic University of Rio de Janeiro (PUC-Rio), Brazil, in 2007. Her main research interests include quality of service, mobile computing, grid computing, and software architecture.

Simon Lock received his PhD in Computer Science from Lancaster University in 2000. His PhD work focused on the development of an approach to and support tool to aid in the analysis of change impact on the requirements of computer based systems. Since completing his PhD, Simon has worked on a number of different projects including the modeling and dependability analysis of socio-technical systems and the integration of federations of devices to support distributed user interaction. He has most recently been involved in an EU funded project focusing on providing analysis and design support for developers engineering secure, mobile, P2P systems

Fotis Loukos received his BS degree in applied mathematics from the Aristotle University of Thessaloniki, Greece in 2004 and MS degree in computer and communication engineering from the Polytechnic School of University of Thessaly in 2006. He is currently working towards his PhD degree in Computer Science at the Aristotle University of Thessaloniki. His research interests include ubiquitous computing and peer-to-peer networks.

Antonio A.F. Loureiro holds a BSc and a MSc in Computer Science, both from the Federal University of Minas Gerais (UFMG), and a PhD in Computer Science from the University of British Columbia, Canada. Currently, he is an associate professor of Computer Science at UFMG. He was the general chair of the Brazilian Symposium on Computer Networks in 2000, Technical Program Chair of LANOMS 2001 (Latin American NOMS), Brazilian Workshop on Wireless Communication 2002, and ACM Workshop on Wireless Multimedia Networking and Performance Modeling. His main research areas are mobile Computing, distributed algorithms, and network management.

Daniel F. Macedo holds a MSc and a BSc in Computer Science from Federal University of Minas Gerais (UFMG), and is currently pursuing a PhD on Université Pierre et Marie Curie-ParisVI. He is a member of the SensorNet project at Federal University of Minas Gerais. He participated in the program committee of IEEE ISCC 2006-2008 and ICWMC 2006, 2007. He received the "Best Simulation Article" award at IEEE ISCC'05 for the paper "A Pro-Active Routing Protocol for Continuous Data Dissemination Wireless Sensor Networks." His main research interests are wireless networks, distributed algorithms, network management, and peer-to-peer computing.

Timothée Maret received his BSc in communications engineering from the University of Applied Science of Fribourg and MSc in Computer Science from the University of Fribourg in 2007. During his studies, he developed the Freemote Emulator and was the main contributor for the development of the JMote embedded platform. His research focuses on peer-to-peer systems, wireless sensors networks and middleware systems. He is currently working as a research engineer for the Global Sensor Networks (GSN) project in the Distributed Information Systems Lab at the Swiss Federal Institute of Technology (EPFL).

Shingo Murakami received his MSc in Mobile-IP technology from University of Tsukuba, Japan, and joined Nippon Ericsson K.K in 2001. Since then, he has been working as a research engineer of the Japanese branch of Ericsson Research and has been involved into various research projects, including for peer-to-peer applications, sensor network applications, and IMS application. His current research focus is on multimedia service delivery technologies for enabling IMS based services to be reachable from residential networks.

José Marcos Nogueira is an associate professor of Computer Science at the Federal University of Minas Gerais (UFMG), Brazil. He received BS and MS degrees from UFMG and PhD degree in electrical engineering from University of Campinas, Brazil (1985). He held a post-doctoral position at the University of British Columbia, Canada (1988/1989) and passed a sabbatical year at Univ. Paris 6 and U. Evry, France (2004/2005). He headed the Department of Computer Science at the UFMG (1998/2000). He has served in various roles, including general chair (1985) of SBRC and LANOMS, TPC chair or co-chair of SBRC, WCS/Globecom 2006, ICC 2006. He has been TPC Member in IEEE/IFIP NOMS,

IEEE/IFIP IM, IEEE/IFIP MMNS, IPOM, SBRC IEEE/IFIP DSOM 2003/2005. His areas of interest and research include computer networks, telecommunications and computer networks management, and wireless sensor networks.

Leonardo Barbosa Oliveira received both MSc and BSc in Computer Science from Federal University of Minas Gerais (UFMG) in Brazil. He is currently pursuing a PhD at University of Campinas (UNICAMP), Brazil. He is also a Microsoft Research Fellow. His primary research interests include peer-to-peer computing over MANETs, sensor networks, and security.

Andrea Passarella is with IIT-CNR, Italy. Previously, he was a researcher at the Computer Laboratory, Cambridge, UK. He holds a PhD in Computer Engineering (Pisa University, Italy). He is working in the framework of the EU Haggle and SOCIALNETS projects, on opportunistic and self-organising networks, with special emphasis on data-management issues, routing and networking protocols, mobility models, and energy management. He was TPC member of IEEE PerCom and serves in the IEEE WoWMoM and IEEE MASS Program Committees. He was the TPC Co-Chair of ACM/SIGMOBILE MobiOpp 2007, and Vice-Chair for ACM REALMAN (2005/06), and IEEE MDC (2006). He is an associate technical editor for *IEEE Communications Magazine*.

Peter Phillips has a degree in computing and information systems from Manchester University and nearly ten years experience in creating services for mobile handsets in industry and academia. They have ranged from novel visualisations of search results to music recommendations and downloads. More recently, he has been investigating human visual perception and digital radiology, using eye tracking devices to analyse the visual attention of radiologists as they make diagnostic decisions using the latest medical imaging techniques. Peter is also a director of BigDog Interactive Ltd., a company of programmers and artists who create bespoke code for interactive installations and live performance events for artists, industry, advertising and academia.

Byrav Ramamurthy is currently an associate professor in the Department of Computer Science and Engineering at the University of Nebraska-Lincoln (UNL). He is the author of the book "Design of Optical WDM Networks - LAN, MAN and WAN Architectures" and a co-author of the book "Secure Group Communications over Data Networks" published by Kluwer Academic Publishers/Springer in 2000 and 2004 respectively. He serves as the IEEE INFOCOM 2008 Mini conference TPC Co-chair and as the INFOCOM 2008 TPC Vice Chair for Informational Systems (EDAS). He serves as the General Co-chair for the Broadnets 2008 conference and the TPC Chair of the ICCCN 2008 conference. His research areas include optical and wireless networks, distributed systems, computer security and telecommunications.

Thomas Repantis is a PhD candidate at the Computer Science and Engineering Department of the University of California, Riverside. His research interests lie in the area of distributed systems, distributed stream processing systems, middleware, peer-to-peer systems, pervasive and cluster computing. He holds an MSc from the University of California, Riverside and a Diploma from the University of Patras, Greece, and he has interned with IBM Research, Intel Research and Hewlett-Packard.

Nobuo Saito is associate chair of W3C in Asia, and dean and professor at the Faculty of Global Media Studies, Komazawa University, Japan. He is also the chair of PUCC (P2P Universal Computing Consortium), a Home and Sensor Network Standard Organization originated from Japan. Nobuo received his PhD in engineering from the Graduate School of Engineering at the University of Tokyo. He was the vice president of Keio University, and now Emeritus Professor of Keio University. Nobuo's areas of expertise are in Operating Systems, Parallel and Distributed Processing, Software Engineering, Digital Media Technology and Web Technology. He was engaged in several global standard activities such as JTC1/SC22/WG15(POSIX), AOW(Asia Oceania Workshop) for OSI and so on.

Daniel Schlosser received his diploma in Computer Science from University of Würzburg, Germany, in 2005, after which he joined the Chair of Distributed Systems, University of Würzburg, as a research assistant. His main research interests cover investigation on quality of experience (QoE) of network based application as well as traffic identification and traffic engineering. Daniel Schlosser is involved in several industrial projects (Bosch, Datev) as well as an international research project, namely EuroNF funded by the European Commision. His recent publications cover the modelling and evaluation of the QoE of terminal service applications with focus on Citrix based solutions.

Isabela G. Siqueira holds a MSc and a BSc in Computer Science from Federal University of Minas Gerais (UFMG), Brazil, and is currently working at Itaipu Binacional as a System Analyst. She was a member of the SensorNet project at Federal University of Minas Gerais and was involved in many other projects at UFMG related to peer-to-peer computing. Her main research interests are wireless sensor and mobile networks, distributed algorithms, network management, and peer-to-peer computing.

Dirk Staehle is an assistant professor at the Chair of Distributed Systems at the University of Würzburg, Germany. He received his diploma degree in Computer Science from the University of Würzburg in 1999 and his doctoral degree (PhD) from the same university in 2004. His research interests include radio network planning and radio resource management of mobile and wireless networks. He has published numerous papers on the analysis of coverage and capacity of UMTS networks. His current research focus is on adaptive resource allocation in cellular and mesh OFDMA networks. Additionally, he is interested in the problems of transmitting specific applications like P2P over wireless and mobile networks.

Hiromitsu Sumino received his BSc and MSc degree in information science from University of Nagoya, Japan in 1995 and 1997, respectively. Since 1997, he has been an engineer at NTT DoCoMo Inc., and involved in the researches of mobile Internet.

Kian-Lee Tan is a professor of Computer Science at the School of Computing, National University of Singapore (NUS). He received his PhD in Computer Science in 1994 from NUS. His current research interests include multimedia information retrieval, query processing and optimization in multiprocessor and distributed systems, database performance, and database security. He has published numerous papers in conferences such as SIGMOD, VLDB, ICDE and EDBT, and journals such as TODS, TKDE, and VLDBJ. Kian-Lee is a member of ACM.

Spyridon L. Tompros received his master degree in electrical engineering from the University of Patras and his PhD in telecommunications from the Department of Electrical Engineering and Computer Science of the National Technical University of Athens, in 1992 and 1997 respectively. In 1997, he joined 4Plus SA, Greece, as Senior Engineer and later as Managing Director, with a leading role in the design of ATM and UMTS traffic simulator and analysis systems. Since 1992, he has participated in and coordinated many private, EC funded and ESA projects on protocols design for broadband, mobile and satellite networks, systems and terminals and is a specialist in traffic engineering and quality of service issues. His scientific work includes over of 30 publications in conferences and scientific journals. Today, he is a project manager at APEX AG, Switzerland and research associate at the University of Aegean.

Phuoc Tran-Gia is professor and director of the Institute of Computer Science at the University of Würzburg, Germany. He is also chairman of the Advisory Board of Infosim. Previously, he was at academia in Stuttgart, Siegen (Germany) as well as industries at Alcatel (software development System 12), IBM Zurich Research Laboratory (Zurich, Switzerland, architecture and performance evaluation of communication networks). Professor Tran-Gia was chairperson of the management committee of the COST 257 action of the European Union entitled "Impact of new services on the performance and architecture of broadband networks". He is also founding director of the multi-university Nortel's "Center of Network Optimization." He is consultant and cooperation project leader with Siemens (ICN Board, Munich, ICM Berlin), Nortel (Texas), T-Mobile International (Bonn), France Telecom (Belfort), European Union (European Science Foundation, Brussels). Phuoc Tran-Gia is also founder of Infosim (Würzburg, Germany) and Codirector of Infosim Asia Pacific (Singapore), which specializes in IP network management products and services.

Kurt Tutschku holds the chair of "Future Communication" (endowed by Telekom Austria) at the University of Vienna. Prior to that, he was an assistant professor at the Department of Distributed Systems, University of Würzburg, Germany, where he led the department's group on Future Network Architectures and Network Management until December 2007. From Feb. 2008 to July 2008, he worked as an Expert Researcher at the NICT (National Institute for Information and Communication Technology, Japan). Kurt Tutschku received a doctoral degree in Computer Science from University of Würzburg in 1999 and completed his Habilitation ("State Doctoral Degree") at the University of Würzburg in 2008. His main research interests include future generation communication networks, quality-of-experience, and the modeling and performance evaluation of future network control mechanisms and P2P overlay networks.

Johann van der Merwe received his BSc degree in electronic engineering from the University of Natal and MSc degree in engineering from the University of KwaZulu-Natal. He is currently pursuing a part-time PhD degree on the security of distributed communication systems. His research and development works have been accepted by some of the most prominent local and international journals and conferences. Johann is currently being employed by the Enterprise Risk Services of Deloitte where he works as a manager in the Security & Privacy Services team. He specialises in infrastructure and network security, identity & access management and information security management. Johann is also the service line leader for infrastructure & operations security.

Jean Frederic Wagen is heading the mobile systems-competence group and is in charge of the Mobile Internet Platform of the Telecom Laboratory at the University of Applied Sciences in Fribourg. He is the leader and collaborator of several projects on mobile and multi-modal internet technologies involving applications, services and wireless networks. As a professor, he teaches computer communication, telecommunications, and graduate short courses on VoIP, wireless and mobile communications, and mobile Internet. Dr. Wagen serves as senior consultant to Wavecall SA, a unique provider of advanced radio coverage prediction tools. Dr. Wagen also serves as an expert to the Swiss delegate for the Joint Communication Board of the ESA. Since 1988, he has accumulated research experiences in the areas of mobile radio communications, radio propagation, radio network planning, mobile systems, service deployment and, while at the EIA-FR, applied research and prototype developments.

James Walkerdine is a research fellow at Lancaster University (UK) Computing Department with interests in the areas of Peer-to-Peer, Web services, software engineering and HCI. He has worked within the field of P2P for over 7 years, and has extensive expertise in developing P2P applications and experience of a wide range of P2P protocols and architectures. He worked on the EU project P2P ARCHITECT that developed methods for building dependable P2P systems, and the EU project PEP-ERS that developed methods to support the building of secure mobile P2P systems. He has performed pioneering work on the monitoring of P2P systems and the empirical analysis of P2P user behaviour. In 2006, he was involved in the first study to quantify the scale and characteristics of illegal pornographic distribution on P2P file-sharing systems. James is also the managing director of Isis Forensics - a consultancy that offers P2P monitoring solutions to organizations.

Lisong Xu received his BE and ME degrees in Computer Science from the University of Science and Technology Beijing in 1994 and 1997, respectively. He completed his thesis "Performance Analysis Of Optical Burst Switched Networks" under the direction of Dr. Harry Perros and Dr. George Rouskas, and received his PhD degree in Computer Science from North Carolina State University in 2002. From 2002 to 2004, he was a post-doctoral research fellow at North Carolina State University, working on Congestion Control for High-Speed Long-Distance Networks with Dr. Injong Rhee, and on PhysViz Project with Dr. James Lester. He is currently an assistant professor in Computer Science and engineering at the University of Nebraska-Lincoln. He is a recipient of NSF CAREER Award (2007), and UNL CSE Students' Choice Outstanding Teaching Award (2006, 2007).

Mark Kai-Ho Yeung received his PhD, M Phil, and BSc degrees in electrical and electronic engineering from University of Hong Kong in 2007, 2004, and 2002, respectively. His research interests are game theoretic algorithms, media streaming protocols, and wireless networking.

Mika Ylianttila is a professor and adjunct professor in Computer Science and information networks, respectively in the Information Processing laboratory at University of Oulu, Finland. He is also the Research Manager of MediaTeam Oulu research group at the same university. He received his MSc degree in Electrical and Information engineering from University of Oulu, Finland, in 1998; Licentiate of Technology degree in 2001, and Doctor of Technology (PhD) degree in 2005. He is focusing on mobile computing and communication research, especially in areas related to mobile peer-to-peer technologies, including protocol and middleware performance and design for mobile applications and services. He is a Senior Member of IEEE and the Chairman of the IEEE Finland Section.

Alf Inge Wang is currently working as an associate professor at the department of computer and information science at the Norwegian University of Science and Technology (NTNU) where he teaches courses on programming, software architecture, mobile application development and game development. He received his PhD in software engineering in 2001. His research interests are game development, game concept development, computer support for mobile collaborative work, peer-to-peer computing, software architecture, and software engineering education. He has published 60 scientific international papers including journal papers, book chapters and being editor for a book.

Wei Wu received his bachelor's and master's degrees from Nanjing University in 2002 and 2005, respectively. He is currently a PhD candidate in Computer Science at Singapore-MIT Alliance (SMA), National University of Singapore (NUS). He is the recipient of the SMA Graduate Fellowship for 2004-2008, and the NUS President Graduate Fellowship for 2006-2007 and 2007-2008. His research interests include database technologies and mobile computing. He is a student member of ACM.

Artur Ziviani received a BSc in Electronics Engineering in 1998 and a MSc in Electrical Engineering (emphasis in Computer Networking) in 1999, both from the Federal University of Rio de Janeiro (UFRJ), Brazil. In 2003, he received a PhD in Computer Science from the University of Paris 6, France, where he has also been a lecturer during 2003-2004. Since 2004, he is with the National Laboratory for Scientific Computing (LNCC), Brazil. His research interests include QoS provisioning, wireless computing, Internet measurements, and the application of networking technologies in computer-aided medicine.

Index

W